6/14
8

Grumman
Aircraft

since 1929

Avenging the 'Day of Infamy', an Eastern Aircraft built Grumman TBM-3 from Marine Torpedo Bomber Squadron 242 (VMTB-242) flies over Mt Suribachi in March 1945. This volcanic peak on Iwo Jima was the scene of heavy fighting between United States Marines and Japanese troops after Marines had landed on beaches located near the southeastern tip of the island (on the right edge of this photograph, below the tail of the *Avenger* in the morning of 19 February, 1945. (*USMC/National Archives*)

Grumman
Aircraft

since 1929

René J Francillon

NAVAL
INSTITUTE
PRESS

BY THE SAME AUTHOR

Japanese Aircraft of the Pacific War
Lockheed Aircraft since 1913
McDonnell Douglas Aircraft since 1920
Tonkin Gulf Yacht Club

First published in Great Britain 1989 by
Putnam Aeronautical Books,
an imprint of Conway Maritime Press
24 Bride Lane, Fleet Street
London EC4Y 8DR

Published and distributed in the United States of America
and Canada by the Naval Institute Press, Annapolis,
Maryland 21402

Library of Congress Catalog Card No. 88-63415

ISBN 0-87021-246-X

Manufactured in Great Britain.

CONTENTS

Preface and Acknowledgments	vii
History of the Corporation	1
Leroy Randle Grumman	2
The Grumman Aircraft Engineering Corporation, 1929-1969	5
The Grumman Corporation since 1969	33
Annual Employment, Gross Sales, and Net Income, 1930-1988	47
Aircraft designed and built by Grumman Aircraft Engineering Corporation and Grumman Corporation	
Grumman FF and SF	50
Grumman JF and J2F Duck	64
Grumman F2F	77
Grumman F3F	83
Grumman XSBF-1	92
Grumman G-21 Goose	95
Grumman F4F Wildcat	113
Grumman XF5F-1 Skyrocket	142
Grumman G-44 Widgeon	148
Grumman XP-50 and XP-65	157
Grumman TBF Avenger	161
Grumman F6F Hellcat	194
Grumman F7F Tigercat	222
Grumman G-63 Kitten I	237
Grumman F8F Bearcat	240
Grumman G-65 Tadpole	260
Grumman G-72 Kitten II	263
Grumman G-73 Mallard	267
Columbia XJL-1	272
Grumman XTB3F-1 and AF Guardian	274
Grumman UF and SA-16 (HU-16) Albatross	286
Grumman F9F (F-9) Panther	314
Grumman F9F (F-9) Cougar	331
Grumman XF10F-1 Jaguar	345
Grumman S2F (S-2) Tracker	350
Grumman F11F (F-11) Tiger	377
Grumman TF (C-1) Trader	387
Grumman G-164 Ag-Cat	394
Grumman WF (E-1) Tracer	401
Grumman G-159 Gulfstream I	406
Grumman OV-1 (AO-1) Mohawk	414

Grumman A-6 (A2F) Intruder 429
Grumman E-2 (W2F) Hawkeye 450
Grumman EA-6 Prowler 465
Grumman American AA-1, T-Cat and Lynx 478
Grumman C-2 Greyhound 481
Grumman/General Dynamics F-111B and EF-111A Raven 486
Grumman G-1159 Gulfstream II 495
Grumman American AA-5 Cheetah and Tiger 504
Grumman F-14 Tomcat 507
Grumman American GA-7 Cougar 524
Grumman X-29 526
Grumman E-8 530

Appendix A - Production Summary 533

Appendix B - Design Numbers and Representative Projects 540
Design 4 (Air Corps Observation Amphibian) 545
Design 16 (XF4F-1) 546
Design 55 (XTB2F-1) 547
Design 66 (XTSF-1) 549
Design 75 (XF9F-1) 550
Design 77 551
Design 91 553
Design 95 (XWF-1) 554
Design 97 555
Design 118 (XF12F-1) 557
Design 128G-12 558
Design 134E 560
Design 143 562
Designs 165 and 215 563
Design 235-4 Gadfly 565
Design 305 566
Design 607A 567
Design 698 569

Appendix C - The Lunar Module 570

Preface and Acknowledgments

The inclusion of a history of Grumman and its aircraft in the Putnam Aeronautical Series was inevitable. However, after Robert Gardiner, the Conway director then responsible for the series, John Stroud, its formidable and hard working editor, and I had agreed to proceed with this long-planned project I began having doubts about our timing. Numerous books and articles on Grumman and its aircraft were already available and I felt that writing this book would be 'comme enfoncer une porte ouverte' (like breaking down an open door). Nevertheless, the more I worked, the more it became obvious that much remained to be researched. Soon, as I sifted through an abundance of documents provided by Grumman and its customers and by fellow historians, my enthusiam for the project began to increase steadily. I hope some of that enthusiam has survived my numerous draft revisions and that readers will enjoy finding new tales and new details about old friends from the 'Bethpage Iron Works.'

I must admit deriving some malicious pleasure from including the Lunar Module in Appendix C. In reviewing the first edition of *McDonnell Douglas Aircraft since 1920* for the oldest aviation publication, a well-known author had deplored a '"deliberate omission... That omission, partly due to policy and partly due to space, is the lack of reference to any guided missile or space activities – no Genie, no Skybolt, no Quail, no LEM.' Covering the story of the Lunar Module – not an aircraft as normally included in the Putnam Aeronautical Series but definitely a piloted flying machine – in a book on McDonnell Douglas might have pleased my fellow author but would certainly have displeased my Grumman friends! Likewise, it is with pleasure that, again, I follow the practice of sequencing the aircraft described in the main part in strict chronological order based on the first flight date of their prototype, not 'in roughly chronological order' as another noted colleague wrote in a distinguished naval aviation magazine when reviewing the second edition of *Lockheed Aircraft since 1913.*

I am most grateful to Lois Lovisolo and Schoney Schonenberg who not only were cordial hosts during my visit to Bethpage and provided an abundance of help while I was researching archives at the Grumman History Center but who also indefatigably searched for obscure details to provide answers to my steady stream of queries. Quite frankly, this book is theirs as much as it is mine. Other Grumman employees, past and present, to whom I am indebted for suggesting corrections and additions to the original typescript are Bill Barto, Lonny Borts, Joel DiMaggio, Leonard Drace, Bill Ennis, Clif Fenwick, Doug Fredericks, Ed Kavanaugh, Bud Gillies, Bill Hughes, Ed Kavanaugh, Peter Kirkup, Joseph Lippert, John Lovisolo, Paul McDermott, Joe Rivera, Ray Ryan, Dave Seeman, William Tagliarini, Jim Wallis, and Bob Wolk. I am also grateful to Jean Stewart for her help and hospitality during my visit to the X-29A team at Edwards Air Force Base.

As had been the case with previous undertakings, I was most fortunate in obtaining the co-operation of numerous individuals and of private and public entities in the United States and abroad. Jointly they provided a wealth of historical documents, operational data, and photographs. In this regard, I wish to express my thanks to the following: *Private Individuals* – Harold Andrews, William J Balogh, Warren M Bodie, Christian Boisselon, Humbert Charvé, Alain Crosnier, Fred C Dickey, Jim Dunn, John M Elliott, Jean-Michel Guhl, G Warren Hall, Harold L James, Clay Jansson, Bud Joyce, Robert E Kling, Robert L Lawson, Peter B Lewis, Peter J Mancus, David W Menard, Peter B Mersky, Jay Miller, Rick Morgan, John Motum, Stéphane Nicolaou, Alain Pelletier, W E Scarborough, Dr Richard K Smith, R C Sturtivant, Gordon Swanborough, Norman E Taylor, and the late Gordon S Williams; *Aerospace Companies* – Edo Corporation (with special thanks to Mr Martin H Friedman for his very detailed answer to my query regarding Edo's work on the Goose), and Schweizer Aircraft Corporation; *US Government Agencies* – Department of Defense (Still Media Record Center), Department of the Army (Media Inquiry Branch/OCPA; 641st Military Intelligence Battalion, Oregon ArNG), Department of the Air Force (Air Force Museum; Strategic Air Command/ PAM; Tactical Air Command/PAM; and Public Affairs Officers at Mountain Home AFB and Nellis AFB), Department of the Navy (Media Services Division/CHINFO; Naval Air Systems Command; Naval Aviation History and Archives; Public Affairs Officers aboard the USS *Coral Sea* and USS *Kitty Hawk*, and at COMNAVAIRPAC, MCAS El Toro, MCAS Yuma, NAS Fallon, NAS Key West, NAS Miramar, NAS Whidbey Island, and the Naval Air Test Center), Department of Transportation (Federal Aviation Administration and US Coast Guard/Office of Public Affairs), National Aeronautics and Space Administration (Public Affairs Officers at Headquarters, the Ames Research Center, the Dryden Flight Research Facility, the Lyndon B Johnson Space Center, and the Langley Research Center), and National Archives; *Foreign Government Agencies* – Canada (Public Archives); Israel (Air Force Attaché in Washington, DC); Italy (Office of the Defence and Air Attachés in Washington, DC; and Ufficio Documentazione e A P, Stato Maggiore Aeronautica, in Rome); Japan (Defence and Naval Attaché in Washington, DC); and Sweden (Office of the Armed Forces Attachés in Washington, DC; and Försvarsstaben/Bildarkivet in Stockholm); *Magazines* – Air Classics, Air Fan, Air Force Magazine, Air Forces Monthly, AIR International, Air Pictorial, Airpower, Aviation News, Aviation Week & Space Technology, Flight International, FlyPast, Le Fanatique de l'Aviation, Naval Aviation News, The Hook, Warplane, and Wings.

Those who know us will appreciate my wife's contribution to this work. Not only was she by my side to smooth my feathers when I was losing patience with this project, but above all she undertook the daunting task of smoothing my syntax when my gallic enthusiasm threatened to overtake Anglo-Saxon precision.

Vallejo, California
March 1989

Grumman F2F-1s from the Second Section of Fighting Two (VF-2) in 'razzle-dazzle' formation near NAS San Diego, California, in July 1939. (*USN/Grumman*)

History of the Corporation

When the *Red Rippers* of Fighting Five took delivery of their FF-1 biplanes during the spring and summer of 1933, some thirty months after Leroy Grumman and five associates had organized the Grumman Aircraft Engineering Corporation, no one, not even the company's sanguine founders, would have dared to predict that Grumman aircraft would continuously serve aboard United States Navy carriers until the twenty-first century and that 77 per cent of the nearly 33,000 aircraft built by the company until 1988 would be carrier aircraft. Yet, this amazing degree of dependency on a single customer, the Department of the Navy, came about even though the company sought right from the beginning to diversify its activities into non-aviation related fields, repeatedly tried to win aircraft production contracts from the Army Air Corps and later from the Air Force and the Army, and made several forays into the private aircraft market.

The world's leading manufacturer of carrier-based aircraft had come into being as the result of the desire of three senior employees of the Loening Aeronautical Engineering Company not to remain with that company when it moved to Pennsylvania and to go into business for themselves. They organized Grumman Aircraft Engineering Corporation on 5 December, 1929, less than two months after the October 1929 stock market crash which triggered the Great Depression. Notwithstanding this less than propitious timing, the fledgeling company quickly obtained a Navy contract for amphibious floats, managed to end its first year of operations with a small profit by relying on aircraft repairs and the manufacture of aluminium truck

1

The Gulfhawk III, a two-seat derivative of the F3F naval fighter, was built for Al Williams, the demonstration pilot of the Gulf Oil Company. When first flown on 6 May, 1938, it was registered NR1051; later, as illustrated, it was re-registered NC1051. During the war, it was impressed into Air Force service and, designated UC-103, was given the military serial 42-97044. *(Grumman)*

bodies, and was awarded its first aircraft contract within fifteen months of its incorporation. Thereafter, employment, sales, and net profit grew steadily up to the Second World War. During that war, Grumman Aircraft Engineering Corporation and its employees distinguished themselves by delivering the greatest number of aircraft from a single factory during one month (605 Hellcats and 59 aircraft of four other types coming off the lines in March 1945) and by producing more pounds of airframes per employee than any other US manufacturer. Much of this success was due to Roy Grumman's business acumen, his commendable concern for the welfare of his employees, and his understanding of US Navy requirements.

Leroy Randle Grumman

Son of George Tyson Grumman, a carriage shop owner, and Grace Ethel (née Conklin), Leroy Randle 'Roy' Grumman was born in Huntington, New York, on 4 January, 1895. Raised on Long Island, an area often called the 'cradle of aviation', young Roy took an early interest in aviation and, when graduating from high school in June 1912, he chose to discuss the infant industry in his salutorian address. Retaining his interest in aircraft engineering, he then worked his way through Cornell University from which he received a Bachelor of Science degree in Mechanical Engineering in 1916.

2

After graduation, Roy Grumman worked briefly for the Engineering Department of the New York Telephone Company, before enlisting in the US Navy Reserve in June 1917, two months after the United States' entry into the Great War. Following a few months as machinist's mate, 2nd class, he was sent by the Navy first to Columbia University for a six-week course in the operation of petrol engines powering submarine chasers, and, after he had applied for aviation duty, to the Massachusetts Institute of Technology (MIT) for ground training. Learning to fly at Miami and Pensacola, Grumman graduated in September 1918, was designated Naval Aviator No1216, and was commissioned an ensign prior to being assigned as a pilot instructor to the Naval Air Training School at Pensacola. In 1919, after completing the four-month Naval Course in Aeronautical Engineering at MIT, he was transferred to the League Island Naval Yard on the Delaware River just south of Philadelphia as an acceptance test pilot for Curtiss and Navy-built biplane flying-boats and as Project Engineer for the Loening M-8 observation monoplanes about to be built in the Navy Yard.

While working at the Navy Yard, Grumman got to know the designer of the M-8, Grover Loening, and his brother Albert, and impressed them so much with his talent as an engineer and his skill as a test pilot that they offered him a job. Resigning his Naval commission in October 1920, Grumman accepted this offer and joined the Loening Aeronautical Engineering Corporation in New York where he began by test flying various types of Loening amphibians and doing some design and development on these aircraft. He quickly moved up in the Loening organization, with which he became Factory Manager and then General Manager at a time when the firm was busy with the production of amphibians, including the OL series for the Navy, the OA series for the Army Air Service, and the Air Yacht series for private owners.

During the last years of the 1920s, after Charles Lindbergh's New York – Paris flight in May 1927 led many to expect a rapid expansion in air travel and aircraft manufacturing, financiers were showing a sudden interest in the then primarily small-scale United States aircraft industry and, seeking to gain dominance in this emerging market, started acquiring small manufacturers and merging them into larger and, it was hoped, more efficient organizations. Among the companies which fell by the wayside as a result of this new trend was Loening which, in 1928, was bought by the banking firm of Hayden, Stone and Company, which intended to merge it with the Keystone Aircraft Corporation. In turn, control of Keystone was acquired in 1929 by a holding company, North American Aviation Inc, which went on with the merging plans and prepared to move Loening's assets to the Keystone plant in Bristol, Pennsylvania, before the end of that year. For Loening's employees, this meant either unemployment or a move to Pennsylvania. Rather than face either, Grumman and two of his colleagues – Leon A 'Jake' Swirbul, the factory manager, and William T Schwendler, a talented engineer and assistant plant manager – resolved to establish their own firm.

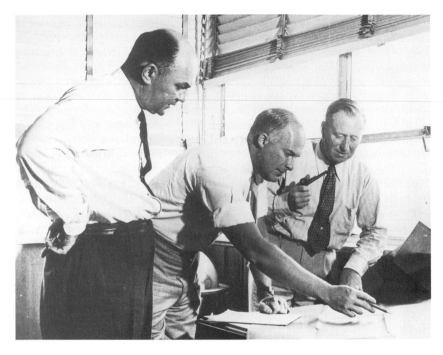

The three principal founders of the Grumman Aircraft Engineering Corporation in 1940: from the left, Leon A 'Jake' Swirbul, William T Schwendler, and Leroy Randle 'Roy' Grumman. *(Grumman)*

As detailed here, Grumman and his associates succeeded in their venture and the Grumman Aircraft Engineering Corporation was incorporated on 6 December, 1929. Leroy Grumman, who invested $16,950 from his savings and his severance pay from the Loening Aeronautical Engineering Corporation to acquire 46.7 per cent of the voting shares of the new company, became chairman of the board and president, a dual position he held until July 1946, when he relinquished the position of president. For the next twenty years Roy Grumman continued to serve as chairman of the board, a position from which he stepped down on 16 May, 1966. He was then elected honorary chairman for his lifetime and remained a director on the board until 15 June, 1972.

Even though he was a quiet and reserved, almost shy, person, Roy Grumman was nevertheless awarded many honours and awards during his lifetime as a result of the outstanding contributions made by the company which bore his name and which he led for thirty-seven years. First and foremost was the Presidential Medal of Merit, the nation's highest civilian award, which was presented in March 1948 by Navy Secretary James Forrestal on behalf of President Harry Truman both to Roy Grumman and to his colleague Jake Swirbul '... for exceptionally meritorious conduct in the performance of outstanding service... in the design and production of several of the most efficient types of aircraft supplied to the Navy. [As heads of the Grumman Company] . . . an organization which by outstanding initiative in researching and making improvements, maintained its aircraft constantly at the forefront of operational and combat efficiency . . . and contributed greatly to the effectiveness of United States Naval Aviation.' In 1948, the Daniel Guggenheim Fund for the Promotion of Aeronautics also awarded its medal to Roy Grumman 'for outstanding achievement in successfully advancing aircraft design for naval and peacetime use.' In 1966, it was the turn of the National Aeronautics Association to recognize Grumman by citing him 'in recognition of his significant and enduring contributions over the years to the progress of aeronautics, and his demonstrated qualities of patriotism, integrity, and moral courage worthy of emulation' while, in 1968, the National Academy of Sciences gave him the first Hunsaker Medal 'for his contribution to aeronautical engineering.'

Other honours and awards received by Roy Grumman include an honorary Doctor of Engineering degree from the Polytechnic Institute of Brooklyn (in 1949), the nineteenth annual Frank M Hawks Memorial from the American Legion Air Service Post 501 (in 1959), and an honorary Doctor of Law degree from Adelphi College (in 1961). In 1953, he was elected to the Board of Trustees of his alma mater, Cornell University. In 1972, shortly after resigning as director of the board from the Grumman Corporation, he was enshrined in the Long Island Hall of Fame and in the Aviation Hall of Fame in Dayton, Ohio. In 1973, he was invested in the International Aerospace Hall of Fame in San Diego, California, and in 1984 he was posthumously inducted into the Naval Aviation Hall of Honor in Pensacola, Florida. In December 1988, he was further honoured when the US Navy had a fleet oiler christened the USS *Leroy Grumman* (T-AO-195) by his three daughters.

Leroy Randle Grumman was married to Rose Marion Werther, with whom he had three daughters and one son. He died in his eighty-eighth year on 4 October, 1982.

The Grumman Aircraft Engineering Corporation 1929-1969

After deciding during the autumn of 1929 to go into the aircraft manufacturing business for themselves, Roy Grumman, Bill Schwendler, and Jake Swirbul obtained a commitment to help finance their venture from Grover and Albert Loening and were joined by Edmund W Poor, a moderately wealthy accountant working as the Loenings' assistant treasurer, and his friend, E Clinton Towl. Furthermore, they were confident that some of the most skilled Loening employees, who also had roots on Long Island and in New York and did not wish to move to Pennsylvania following the merger of Loening and Keystone, would be available to staff a new company.

The first plant of the Grumman Aircraft Engineering Corporation on Railroad Avenue, Baldwin, Long Island. (*Grumman*)

On that strength, six initial investors agreed on 5 December, 1929 to invest a total of $81,325 by subscribing to 450 non-voting preferred shares with a par value of $100 and 1,453 common shares with a par value of $25. Grover Loening pledged $20,000 for preferred shares and purchased 200 common shares for $5,000 to help launch a company in whose management he was not to play a role* and Roy Grumman took $16,950 in common shares to become the largest voting stockholder and gain operating control of the company. The other investors were Albert Loening and Ed Poor who both provided $10,000 for preferred and $2,500 for common shares, Jake Swirbul who invested $8,125 in common shares, and Clint Towl who contributed the remaining $6,250 ($5,000 for preferred shares and $1,250 for common shares)†. On 6 December, one day after the founders had subscribed to these shares, the Grumman Aircraft Engineering Corporation was incorporated.

* Later, he organized the Grover Loening Aircraft Company and pressed a patent claim on the Grumman Aircraft Engineering Company regarding the use of his retractable undercarriage design. The suit was settled out of court for $25,000 and Loening did some consulting work for Grumman, notably when the G-21 was under development.

† With the exception of Grover Loening, the initial associates of Roy Grumman remained closely associated with the comapny for their entire lives. Jake Swirbul was president at the time of his death in June 1960; Ed Poor was treasurer when he died in January 1966; Albert Loening retired as a director in 1969 but remained as a director emeritus until September 1974; Bill Schwendler was still a director when he died in January 1978; and Clint Towl retired as chairman of the board in December, 1975, remained on the board until 1977, and was a director emeritus until 1985.

6

A Grumman crew recovering a damaged Loening Commuter from Lake Champlain. After being rebuilt, this aircraft was sold for a handsome profit, thus helping the fledgeling company to survive until it sold the first aircraft of its own design. *(Grumman)*

First renting an 11,465 sq ft (1,065 sq m) building located on Railroad Avenue in Baldwin on the south shore of Long Island (previously used by the Cox-Klemin Aircraft Company and by an automobile agency as a combination garage and showroom), the Grumman investors hired the company's first employee, Joseph A Stamm*, as a purchasing agent/company secretary in December 1929 and assembled a 15-man shop crew to begin operations on 2 January, 1930. While Bill Schwendler and Roy Grumman worked on the company's first proposals (an amphibian for the Army Air Service as described in Appendix B, a twin-engined flying-boat for the Coast Guard, and an amphibian float design and a two-seat fighter for the Navy), Jake Swirbul and the shop crew set about rebuilding a damaged Loening Air Yacht amphibian and repairing a car which had crashed into the amphibian which protruded from the shop on to Railroad Avenue. Other aircraft repair projects followed including that of a Loening Commuter which the company purchased for $450 as it lay wrecked in Lake Champlain and which, after being rebuilt, was sold for $20,000. However, aircraft repair was not enough to keep the small shop team busy on a steady basis and Roy Grumman and his colleagues were forced to seek non-aviation work. They obtained an initial contract for the manufacture of four aluminium truck bodies for Motor Haulage Corporation. Additional orders for truck bodies and aluminium trailers followed, thus marking the

* Joe Stamm served as secretary of the Grumman Corporation until 1966.

beginning of a diversification programme which, after a lapse between 1932 and 1946, went on to play an important role for the Grumman Corporation and was still significant nearly sixty years later.

The company's first aviation product was developed as a result of Roy Grumman's contacts with Naval Aviation personnel, which gave him advance information about a new requirement. To avoid having to replace the fixed undercarriage of its O2U-1 observation biplanes with a single float when switching from land or carrier operations to operations at sea from battleships or cruisers, Vought had developed an amphibious float with wheels folding upward. Tested in 1928, the Vought float had proved only moderately successful. The Navy, therefore, wished to obtain better amphibious floats. To meet this known need Bill Schwendler designed in 1930 the Model A float with a monocoque aluminium structure in which the mainwheels and struts retracted fully and which was fitted with a tail hook for carrier landings. Although the Navy awarded a $33,700 contract to Grumman for two Model A float prototypes for trial installation on the Vought O2U-4, it also expressed reservations regarding the float's strength. To alleviate this doubt, Roy Grumman and Jake Swirbul had to fly in the back seat of the floatplane during catapult trials! Satisfied, the Navy ordered eight more Model A floats. In 1931, following carrier trials aboard the uss *Lexington* and catapult trials aboard the uss *Tennessee* during which Model A floats proved superior to Brewster stainless steel floats and to improved Vought floats, the Navy awarded to Grumman a follow-on order for fifteen Model B amphibious floats. Slimmer and characterized by their straight top

Eight Model A floats in the Baldwin plant before being delivered to the US Navy. (*Grumman*)

A8836, a Vought O3U-1 fitted with a Grumman Model B float. (*USN/National Archives*)

where Model A floats had sloped lines, the Model B floats were fitted with wheels of smaller diameter and had a slightly wider track (6 ft 4 in versus 5 ft 10 in) to improve carrier landing characteristics. Ordered in December 1931, the Model B floats were delivered in 1932 to be fitted to the Vought O3U-1s of Observation Squadrons VO-3B and VO-4B.

During initial discussions of the Model A float with personnel from the Bureau of Aeronautics, Roy Grumman and Jake Swirbul had been asked whether it would be feasible to fit the same type of retractable undercarriage design to existing naval fighters, particularly to the Boeing F4B-1, which had recently entered service. Feeling that such modifications would not be satisfactory and moreover not being keen on the idea of having the company's gear design used to improve the performance of aircraft built by others, Grumman submitted an informal proposal in March 1930 for a new design, the High Performance Two-Seater Fighter, the aircraft which was ordered one year later as the XFF-1. Details on the development of this epochal machine – the first Grumman aircraft and the first Navy fighter to be fitted with a retractable undercarriage – are provided in the main body of the book.

The first year of operations ended with a profit of just under $5,500 on revenues of $109,700 – a rate of return which is two and a half times that averaged during the following fifty-seven years. Shortly before that, the company's financial structure had been modified when the number of preferred shares (subscribed but not all paid for) was reduced from 450 to 225. As 225 additional common shares had been purchased during the previous March by Bill Schwendler, Ed Poor, and two of the shop employees, Julie Holpit and Ed Weick, the control exercised by Roy Grumman and his working partners was strengthened as they now held a greater percentage of the $64,325 paid-in capital. For the company as a whole, prospects were encouraging as Navy orders for Model B floats and the High Performance Two-Seater Fighter were thought likely to be obtained during the second year of operations.

Major corporate events and significant technical achievements in that

9

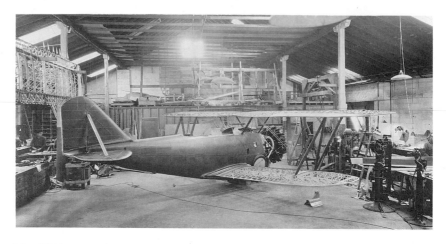

The XFF-1, the first aircraft designed and built by Grumman Aircraft Engineering Corporation, shortly before its completion in the Baldwin plant in December 1931. (*Grumman*)

second year of operations and in subsequent years are summarized chronologically. Annual employment, gross sales, and net income are given in a table appearing on pages 48 and 50. Annual aircraft deliveries by types are given in Appendix A.

1931: Although the shop team continued working on aircraft repair projects and other sundry jobs, the main emphasis during the year was on designing and building the XFF-1 ordered on 28 March under a $46,875 Navy contract stipulating that it must be completed within 200 days. The tight schedule could not quite be maintained and the first Grumman aircraft flew on 29 December. During 1931, work was also initiated on the XSF-1, an aircraft differing from the XFF-1 in having greater fuel capacity as it was intended for use in the scout (fighter reconnaissance) role, for which a $29,850 contract had been awarded on 9 June.

With two prototypes on order and hopes for production contracts, the company needed a larger facility on an airport site; the Baldwin plant was far too small and located about 8 miles from the nearest aerodrome. Grumman, however, was not yet ready to move into its own facility and the decision was made to lease a factory at Valley Stream for one year. Located on Long Island on the edge of Curtiss Field, the new home into which the Grumman Aircraft Engineering Corporation moved in November consisted of a vacant Naval Reserve hangar measuring 200 ft by 100 ft and a small adjacent building which was used to house the engineering department and office. At the end of the year the contract for Model B floats was received, the XFF-1 had been flown, and employment stood at 42, a near two-fold increase in one year.

1932: The year's key technical and business events included the first flight of the XSF-1 on 20 August, the winning of a contract for the third type

10

The Grumman XJF-1 at NAS Anacostia on 24 May, 1933. (*USN/National Archives*)

of Grumman aircraft – the XJF-1 amphibian, the completion of the floatplane production, and the receipt of a $641,250 contract for twenty-seven FF-1 fighters in December.

After a year at Curtiss Field, the company was forced to move to still larger quarters and in November, at the expiry of its lease on the Valley Stream facilities, Grumman relocated to Farmingdale, further out on Long Island. Built for the Fulton Truck Company and later acquired by Sherman M Fairchild, the plant on Hempstead Turnpike had been leased briefly by the American Airplane and Engine Company before becoming Grumman's third location in as many years.

1933: Business expanded quickly during the fourth year of operations with employment passing the 100 mark early on and reaching 207 at the end of December. All twenty-seven FF-1s were delivered, the XJF-1 first flew on 24 April, and thirty-four SF-1s were ordered in August. However, the most important step toward securing the company's future was the first flight and delivery on 18 October of a new single-seat carrier fighter prototype, the XF2F-1.

1934: Production of SF-1s and JF-1 Ducks for the Navy and of JF-2s for the Coast Guard kept the Farmingdale plant busy, with employment reaching 292 by the end of the year. The other noteworthy event was the maiden flight on 28 September of the first civil-registered Grumman aircraft, the GG-1 demonstrator which was built with available FF-1 and SF-1 components. For the first time, annual gross sales exceeded $1,000,000.

1935: Consolidating the dominance of the naval fighter market it had achieved remarkably quickly, Grumman delivered the first of fifty-five F2F-1s in January and flew the prototype of its third type of fighter, the XF3F-1, on 20 March. Unfortunately, Jimmy Collins, a noted pilot specially contracted to fly the new fighter, became the first pilot to lose his

11

The XF3F-2 was first flown on 27 July, 1936. It is seen here during a Navy test flight from NAS Anacostia on 6 October, 1936. (*USN/National Archives*)

life while testing a Grumman aircraft when the F3F-1 crashed on 22 March. The first flight of the XSBF-1 two-seat scout, dive-bomber biplane took place on 24 December; however, this aircraft was destined to become the first Grumman aircraft not to be put into quantity production, as the Navy chose instead to order the Curtiss SBC-3 biplane and Northrop BT-1 monoplane.

1936: During the year, Grumman received its first export contracts (eight G-20 amphibians ordered by the Argentine Government for delivery in February 1937 and the GG-1 modified and sold to Canadian Car & Foundry). It also delivered F3F-1s and J2F-1s to the Navy, first flew the XF3F-2, and built a civil version of the F3F for Al Williams, the demonstration pilot for Gulf Oil Company. The company received a contract for a new fighter, the XF4F-1 biplane, in March, but four months later this contract was replaced by one for the XF4F-2 monoplane, the prototype of the Wildcat of Second World War fame.

In October, Grumman purchased 120 acres alongside the Long Island Railroad in Bethpage on which to build its own Plant 1 and where room was available for later expansion and development of a proper aerodrome. As completed in April of the following year, Plant 1 had a total floor area of nearly 65,000 sq ft.

Capitalizing on the knowledge of the luxury aircraft civil market gained by its officers while they worked for Loening Aeronautical Engineering Corporation and benefiting from some marketing assistance from Grover Loening, the firm also began work on the G-21 Goose twin-engined commercial amphibian. By the year's end, employment had risen to 362.

1937: Booming operations (with J2F-1s and F3F-2s being built for the

One of the eight G-20s which were shipped to Argentina in February 1937. *(Grumman)*

Navy, G-20s for Argentina, and G-21s for civil customers), fast rising employment (with 511 employees at the year's end), and the move to its own facilities in Bethpage nearly bankrupted the company and led to a major financial restructuring, undertaken in two phases.

In June and July the Preferred Stock was eliminated, the authorized number of shares of Common Stock was increased to 600,000 and their par value was reduced from $5 to $1 (each $5 share being exchanged for five $1 shares), and a 300 per cent stock dividend was paid. The net result was to increase paid-in capital to $368,060. In December, a public offering of 95,000 shares was made by an underwriter, 60,000 of which were issued at $7.50 per share having a par value of $1. An additional 5,000 shares (of which 3,805 were issued) were offered by the company to its employees. At the end of the year there were 431,865 shares outstanding and, including Capital Surplus and Earned Surplus, Stockholders' Equity stood at $916,391 as against $740,626 in Current Liabilities and Deferred Credits, to reflect once again a healthy balance sheet. Gross sales went over the $2-million mark and a 6.1 per cent profit margin resulted in net income of $139,602.

Significant first flights in 1937 were those of the G-21 prototype on 29 May, when it became the first new aircraft to fly at Bethpage, and the XF4F-2 on 2 September.

1938: In April, the month during which Grumman stock was first listed for public trading, Grumman lost to Brewster a production contract for the Navy's first monoplane fighter to be ordered in large quantity, as development of the XF4F-2 had run into troubles. However, in October the company was awarded a contract to continue work on its monoplane and to develop it into the XF4F-3. At the end of the year, when all Navy and Marine fighter squadrons were flying either F2Fs or F3Fs, Grumman received a contract for twenty-seven F3F-3s, the last of its biplane fighters.

13

The first aircraft built by Grumman for the Army Air Corps, an OA-9 amphibian derived from the civil G-21, was delivered on 21 November.

Grumman aircraft went to war in July when CC&F-built G-23s were put into Spanish Republican service by Grupo Núm 28 and first drew blood nine months later when a G-23 shot down a Heinkel He 59B-2 off the Murcia coast.

Plant expansion, a constant occurrence until close to the end of the Second World War, added 10,000 sq ft of floor space while airfield facilities were improved and enlarged. Sales more than doubled to nearly $4,905,000 and net income more than quadrupled to $617,074 with profit margin reaching 12.6 per cent.

1939: Although gross sales dropped off slightly, Grumman ended the year with gratifying results as the backlog was boosted from $3.5 to $5.2 million as the result of sustained sales of Goose amphibians and the receipt of large Navy and export orders for the F4F. Good mark-up on commercial sales resulted in net income increasing by almost 45 per cent and profit margin reaching 19.9 per cent, the highest ever recorded by the company, and an exceptional result by any standards.

1940: The first F4F-3 was delivered to the Navy on 24 February and Grumman's first twin-engined fighter, the XF5F-1, first flew on 1 April. Other new projects were the XTBF-1, which was ordered in April, and the XG-44, the prototype of the small Widgeon amphibian, which was first flown on 28 June. Boosted by US preparations for war (during the year Congress authorized the procurement of 15,000 naval aircraft) and large export orders for F4F variants (G-36As for France and Martlets for Britain), gross sales nearly doubled from $4,482,350 to $8,811,295, profit margin remained exceptionally high at 16.1 per cent, and employment at year's end increased by 250 per cent from 813 in 1939 to 2,034 in 1940.

NC20648, the eighteenth Goose, was delivered to Texaco in July 1938. (*Grumman*)

14

Roy Grumman and Jake Swirbul standing by the Widgeon prototype in June 1940. (*Grumman*)

Construction of Plant 2, the main production facility during the war, was begun.

1941: Net income dropped from $1,415,964 in 1940 to $1,066,683 as profit margin plummeted from 16.1 per cent in 1940 to 4.9 per cent after profitable civilian contracts were all but replaced by wartime production contracts. Other factors contributing toward the reduction in earnings were increased labour rates, higher material costs, and the indirect cost of the intensive plant and personnel expansion programme carried on throughout the year (with employment more than tripling to reach 6,650 employees in December). On 10 December, three days after the Japanese attack against Pearl Harbor, Grumman delivered its last non-military aircraft, a G-44 Widgeon.

The XP-50, which was first flown on 18 February, 1941, was Grumman's first aircraft to be fitted with a nosewheel undercarriage. *(Grumman)*

The XP-50 and the first XTBF-1 first flew respectively on 18 February and 7 August but both were lost in accidents. Fortunately, the two pilots and the test engineer involved in these accidents baled out successfully. Not so fortunate were Wildcat pilots from VMF-211, who were overwhelmed by superior Japanese forces during the fight for Wake Island in December 1941; the first Medal of Honor won by pilots of Grumman aircraft was awarded posthumously to Capt Henry T Elrod of that unit.

1942: With America now at war against all the Axis Powers and doing most of the fighting in the vast Pacific area, Grumman concentrated its energy on building carrier aircraft for the USN and the Royal Navy, with Wildcats/Martlets and Avengers/Tarpons being joined on 26 June by the prototype of the Hellcat. Each month during the year, aircraft were delivered to the Navy in quantities in excess of the schedule and at a fast increasing rate (for example, during the last two weeks of November more aircraft were delivered by Grumman than during the entire year of 1940!). On 16 April, the company was presented with the Navy 'E' Award for excellence in production achievement; six months later it received a first star to that award.

As the Navy and the Allies needed more Grumman-designed aircraft than could be produced in the company's fast growing facilities in Bethpage (Plant 3 was opened in March), the Navy Department instructed Grumman to transfer production of Wildcats and Avengers to the Eastern Aircraft Division of the General Motors Corporation and that of Ducks to Columbia Aircraft Corporation. Accordingly, Grumman provided drawings, manufacturing data, shop methods, materials, sets of parts and sub-assemblies, and complete aeroplanes to Eastern and Columbia. As a result of this programme, the last Grumman-built Duck, Wildcat, and Avenger were delivered respectively in March 1942, May 1943, and December 1943.

During Operation Torch in November 1942, Widcats operated from the decks of the USS *Ranger* (CV-4), USS *Sangamon* (ACV-26), USS *Suwanee* (ACV-27), and USS *Santee* (ACV-29) off the Moroccan coast, while Martlets flew from those of HMS *Formidable* and HMS *Victorious* off the Algerian coast. (*USN/National Archives*)

Early in the year, to replace men leaving the employ of the company to join the armed services, Grumman encouraged women to enter its training schools. By the end of the year, over 20 per cent of the nearly 20,000 employees were women.

Even though sales rose dramatically from $21,858,681 in 1941 to $143,155,931 – a near seven-fold increase in one year – net income increased only slightly more than four times as the profit margin on wartime contracts continued dropping. Employment again nearly tripled. Acting prudently and wisely, the board of directors had the company set aside a reserve of $1,200,000 out of 1942 income to provide for the funds which would be needed to re-establish normal business after the war.

1943: Production was again accelerated and in April and October Grumman was presented with the second and third stars to its Navy 'E' Award for excellence in production achievement. In November the company attained the distinction of producing the largest number of combat aircraft per month ever built in a single plant. To support increased delivery schedules, two large additions to existing plants were made, additional land was purchased for a new engineering and experimental building, employment was increased, and employees were given new benefits.

Continuing its progressive approach to employee relations (which dated back to the first year of operations, when Christmas bonuses were first paid), Grumman established one of the nation's most generous non-

17

contributory employee pension programmes for the benefit of those of its record 25,094 employees (30 per cent of whom were women) who would retire after twenty years of service. It also implemented an incentive plan through which all employees, up to a certain salary bracket, could receive additional remuneration in proportion to the increase in plant output per man-hour.

During the year, at the request of the Navy Department, cost-plus-fixed fee contracts were supplanted by fixed price incentive contracts to encourage cost reductions. This resulted in a reduction of profit margin to 2.8 per cent, the lowest yet experienced by Grumman. However, as sales nearly doubled, net income reached a new high of $7.9 million.

With Eastern Aircraft now working at a fast pace, the last Grumman-built Wildcat and Avenger were respectively delivered on 29 May and 31 December. The XF7F-1 was first flown at Bethpage on 3 November.

1944: Although the Navy had imposed a reduction in fighter aircraft production for a few months in mid-year before reinstating the original maximum schedule, the total number of aircraft delivered in 1944 exceeded that of 1943 by 44 per cent and a fifth Navy 'E' star was received in May. Gross sales reached $324 million, a level not exceeded until 1960, and net income topped the $11.5 million mark, a figure not exceeded until 1965. Conversely, employment was reduced by almost 14 per cent during the year.

Providing positive proof that the company was preparing for a return to peacetime operations, two of the three aircraft making their debut during 1944, the G-63 Kitten I and the G-65 Tadpole, which were first flown respectively on 18 March and 7 December, were intended for the civilian market. The third was the XF8F-1, which first flew on 31 August.

Non-business development of note included the establishment during the year of the corporate Grumman Enginering Scholarship Program. Since then ten full-expense four-year college scholarships in engineering or

The first XF7F-1 (BuNo 03549) at Bethpage on 12 November, 1943, ten days after its first hop and nine days after its official first flight. (*Grumman*)

After the war had ended, USN carrier-based aircraft briefly bore fuselage codes similar to those in use before the war. Coded 5-F-1, this F6F-5 was the Hellcat assigned to the commander of Fighter Squadron Five (VF-5). (*USN*)

business have been awarded every year to Long Island high school graduates with high scholastic records.

1945: During the first seven months, work continued at maximum wartime capacity and exceeded previously set records to earn a sixth Navy 'E' star for the company. However, in August the end of the war was followed immediately by the receipt of notices of termination or partial termination of contracts to the extent of reducing the $380-million backlog by slightly more than 80 per cent. Compared with record results in 1944, gross sales dropped 27 per cent and net income was halved.

Faced with the need to cut back its large wartime workforce and not wanting to cause uncertainty by slowly reducing the number of employees, the company took the unusual step of terminating the employment of all 20,511 of its personnel and briefly closed all plants before recalling 5,411 key personnel considered essential to the new requirements*. By the year's end the number of employees had been reduced further to 4,670.

Most of the factories, hangars, warehouses, and related buildings built during the war on Grumman property had been funded by the Government and were owned by the Defense Plant Corporation. However, as following contract cancellations the company only needed portions of these plant assets, negotiations were opened with the Government for a lease-with-purchase option covering the facilities which were to be retained by Grumman.

From February 1940, when it had gone into war production tempo, until the end of the war, 17,573 aircraft were built at the Bethpage plant (12,275 Hellcats, 2,293 Avengers, 1,978 Wildcats, 248 Tigercats, 151 Bearcats, and 628 Ducks, Goose, and Widgeons) and 13,803 Grumman-designed aircraft were produced by others (7,546 Avengers and 5,927 Wildcats by GM's Eastern Aircraft Division and 330 Ducks by Columbia).

* Those who were re-hired did not lose previously earned pension fund benefits as the temporary termination was not considered to have ended their employment.

19

To offset the mass cancellation of wartime contracts, Grumman, like other manufacturers, hoped to succeed in the light aircraft market. Development of the twin-tailed Kitten II was initiated in November 1944, but only a prototype was built. This photograph was taken at Bethpage on the day of the Kitten II's first flight, 4 February, 1946. (*Grumman*)

The last Hellcat was delivered on 21 November and no new aircraft was first flown during the year. However, Grumman initiated another diversification programme by developing a line of aluminium canoes using materials and methods of fabrication similar to those employed in the manufacture of aircraft. A limited number of canoes were produced and sold in the last months of the year.

1946: The full impact of military contract cancellations was felt during the year with gross sales and net income plummeting respectively to $37.6 million (almost one tenth what they had been two years earlier) and $337,772 (a paltry 2.9 per cent of the 1944 income). Employment, however, was up slightly.

New aircraft flown during the year were the G-72 Kitten II (on 4 February), the G-73 Mallard (on 30 April), and the XTB3F-1 (on 23 December). The company was also awarded contracts for its first jet – the XF9F-1 night fighter – which was ordered in April but was replaced in October by the XF9F-2 day fighter, the Panther prototype, and for the Rigel ramjet-powered missile which was to have been launched from surfaced submarines and to carry a conventional or nuclear warhead over distances up to 500 nautical miles. Moreover, diversification undertakings were expanded, with work on canoes being complemented by aircraft repair and overhaul and by efforts to produce a new line of aluminium truck bodies.

The first significant management change in the company's history took place in July when Roy Grumman resigned as president, but not as chairman of the board, and was replaced by Jake Swirbul.

1947: While sales dropped to less than two-thirds of those achieved during the preceding year and employment reached a new nadir, net income

20

After receipt of Approved Type Certificate 783 on 8 September, 1947, the registration of the first Mallard was changed from NX41284 to NC41284. (*Grumman*)

and profit margin rose substantially. At the end of the year Grumman purchased for $3.5 million most of the plant facilities built during the war and previously owned by the United States Government; it also signed a lease agreement for the engineering building which had been built in 1943.

New aircraft flown during the year were the XJR2F-1 Pelican utility amphibian* on 1 October and the XF9F-2 Panther jet fighter on 21 November. These two types brought much work to the company in following years.

1948: This was primarily a year of consolidation during which no new aircraft were introduced but production of the Panther, the first jet designed by Grumman, was initiated. The company's capitalization was increased from $500,000 to $5,000,000 by transferring funds from capital and earned surplus and increasing the number of shares outstanding to one million through a two-to-one split. A subsidiary, Aerobilt Bodies Inc, was organized to continue the manufacture of aluminium truck bodies at a small plant acquired in Athens, New York.

1949: The last Bearcat, the ultimate Grumman propeller-driven fighter, was delivered on 9 July. Thereafter, as no new types was introduced, the company only had four types in production, the Albatross, Guardian, and Panther for the armed forces and the Mallard for civil customers. Sales of non-aeronautical products (canoes and trucks) remained small and constituted only about 4 per cent of total sales. Nevertheless, gross sales during

---

* This aircraft was soon renamed Albatross, a name under which it gained much fame in the rescue role during the Korean and Southeast Asia wars. With a span of 80 ft, the XJR2F-1 had a larger span than any previous Grumman aircraft; in its final form, the SA-16B, the aircraft grew even larger with the span reaching 96 ft 8 in. Although this span is short when compared to that of such behemoths as the Hughes H-4 flying-boat or the Lockhed C-5, the SA-16B remains the largest aircraft built by Grumman.

21

BuNo 122562, the third J33-powered F9F-3, dumping fuel. In service, most of the fifty-four F9F-3s were re-engined with J42 turbojets. *(Courtesy of Jay Miller)*

the year were nearly seven times higher than they had been in 1940, the last year before the United States entered the war. At the end of the year, there were 6,313 employees, of whom three-quarters had been with the company at the war's end.

1950: Plant and tooling modernization and runway extension at Bethpage resulted in substantial expenditures. In addition, the company leased facilities at Witham Field near Stuart, Florida, to take advantage of the better weather to accelerate engineering flight test programmes especially during winter months. Following the start of fighting in Korea, the production rate on military aircraft was accelerated and was mostly responsible for a 70 per cent increase in gross sales. Net income almost doubled to $6.2 million but employment remained almost constant. The number of shares was increased to two million by a distribution made in November of an additional share for each share outstanding.

Although in the period 1945-1950 over 22,000 aluminium canoes, pleasure boats, and dinghies had been built, dollar volume generated by this diversification programme remained small compared to that generated by aircraft.

1951: After forty-six months during which no new types were flown, the prototype of the Cougar made its maiden flight on 20 September. Orders for three military types already in production were increased and, as its

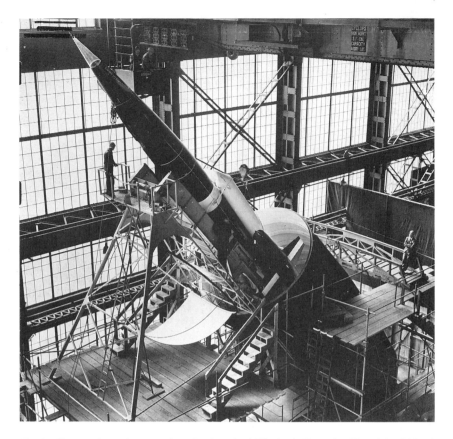

The loading mock-up for the submarine-launched Rigel missile at the Mare Island Naval Shipyard, Vallejo, California, on 12 March, 1952. *(USN/Grumman)*

plant facilities were in need of changes, replacement and/or improvements and as it had to comply with the Government's economic policies to spread defence work among other industries, Grumman increased its reliance on sub-contracting. Thus, approximately 50 per cent of the year's volume of work was obtained from outside sources, notably from the Plymouth Division of the Chrysler Corporation in Evansville, Indiana, which began fabricating Albatross fuselages. Gross sales increased from $102.3 million in the previous year to $167.6 million, but net income dropped 12.6 per cent, due mainly to higher tax rates imposed under the Federal Revenue Act of 1951 and to higher sub-contract costs.

During the year, test firing of the Rigel ramjet-powered missile began under tight security at the Naval Air Missile Test Center, Point Mugu, California. Despite encouraging results, this technologically advanced programme was cancelled before the end of the following year.

23

When it initiated its Evening Student Scholarship programme during that year, Grumman became one of the pioneers of tuition reimbursement programmes for the benefit of employees taking evening classes at local colleges and universities.

1952: The prototype of the the XF10F-1 swing-wing fighter was airlifted from Bethpage to Edwards AFB in an Air Force C-124 and was first flown in California on 19 May. Thus, it became the first Grumman to make its maiden flight away from the company's plant. The other prototype making its debut during the year, the XS2F-1, was first flown at Bethpage on 4 December.

As volume of business had more than doubled in the previous two years, Grumman had to increase its personnel (from 6,633 at the end of 1950 to 11,367 at the end of 1952), to reactivate Plant 3 in 1952, to enlarge and modernize other existing facilities, and to start work on a new facility. Located at Calverton, about 40 miles east of Bethpage, the $23.5 million Peconic River Facility was financed by the Government and consisted of an aerodrome and assembly plant on a 4,000-acre site.

1953: Although the last Panther was delivered in January and the last Guardian followed in May, Grumman was kept busy with production of Cougars and Albatrosses and with the start of the Tracker line (nineteen S2F-1s were built between March and the end of the year). Gross sales reached $240.9 million, the third highest results yet achieved by the company, and net income was up 33 per cent to $7.1 million.

During the autumn, the Metal Boat Division was moved from the main plant to Marathon, New York.

1954: The F9F-9, the prototype of the first Grumman aircraft to reach supersonic speeds in level flight, made its first flight on 30 July. Sales declined slightly but net income rose 57 per cent to $11.2 million, a level nearly matching the record set in 1944 and not to be exceeded until 1965.

Between 1949 and 1954, sales of Aerobilt Bodies Inc, the Grumman subsidiary manufacturing truck bodies for Chevrolet, Dodge, Ford, and

The XS2F-1 Sentinel taxi-ing before its first flight on 4 December, 1952, with Norm Coutant in the left-hand seat and Fred Rowley in the right-hand seat. (*Grumman*)

24

During its 208th flight, BuNo 126670, the first F9F-6 prototype, lost the top of its tail surfaces but was landed safely. As it handled well during this emergency, Grumman fitted a temporary fairing over the truncated vertical tail surfaces and flew the aircraft twice more to evaluate the effect of this configuration on directional stability. *(Grumman)*

An F9F-6P (BuNo 127480) from VMJ-2. *(USMC)*

GMC chassis, increased from $850,000 to $2,500,000, forcing the company to initiate a doubling of the floor space at the Athens plant.

Other significant events during the year were the opening of the Peconic River Facility, to which was transferred the final assembly, flight testing, and flight delivery of jet aircraft, and the signing by the Canadian Government of a Licence and Royalty Agreement for the manufacture of the S2F-1 in Canada.

1955: Employment continued to increase slowly as Grumman now had four types under production (the Albatross, Cougar, Tiger, and Tracker) and was preparing for production of the TF-1, which had first flown on 19 January. Eighteen of the original employees, including four of the principal founders but excluding Roy Grumman who was only serving as chairman of the board and thus was no longer a salaried employee, were among the 12,483 employees on the payroll at the end of the twenty-sixth year of operations.

In December, a 10 per cent stock dividend was declared, thus increasing the number of shares outstanding to 2,200,000. With capital stock and retained earnings exceeding liabilities by more than 50 per cent, the company remained financially healthy.

1956: Although not an entirely new type, the F9F-8T, which first flew on 29 February, deserves mention as this two-seat trainer version of the Cougar went on to make significant contributions to sales during the following four years. To lessen the dependency of its aeronautical activities on the Department of Defense, the company started the initial development and design of a twin-propeller-turbine executive transport.

Non-aeronautical developments of note were the incorporation of the former Metal Boat Division under the name Grumman Boats Inc, and the acquisition of 50 per cent of the stock of Dynamic Developments Inc, a small company with extensive hydrofoil experience. Coupled with hydrofoil research which had been initiated earlier by Grumman, this acquisition gave the company a strong base from which to pursue the developments of hydrofoil vehicles for the Office of Naval Research.

1957: Two new types were flown during the year, the prototype of the WF-2 Tracer airborne early warning aircraft on 1 March and the prototype of the Grasshopper (later renamed Ag-Cat) crop-dusting and -spraying aircraft on 27 April. Production continued on six types (the Albatross,

BuNo 136792, the last TF-1, was modified as the aerodynamic prototype for the WF-2 airborne early warning aircraft. *(Grumman)*

26

The first Grasshopper prototype, with the original short nose and a 50-lb lead weight added in front of the engine to correct a cg problem. *(Grumman)*

Cougar, Tiger, Tracer, Trader, and Tracker), and sub-contract work for other manufacturers (including Boeing, General Electric, McDonnell, and Vought) was undertaken to make better use of existing facilities. Grumman also won two major design competitions, those which led to the development of the Mohawk surveillance aircraft for the Army and the Intruder all-weather attack aircraft for the Navy and Marines. Non-aeronautical product lines also showed signs of promising growth.

1958: The Gulfstream executive transport first flew on 14 August, production of the Ag-Cat by Schweizer Aircraft Corporation under Grumman direction was initiated, and Grumman won the Navy competition for a new propeller-turbine-powered AEW aircraft. However, some of the most significant events of the year were in the field of space and missiles.

In July, Grumman organized a Space Steering Group to consolidate company efforts in participating in national programmes for the exploration of space. This resulted in the submittal in December of an unsuccessful proposal for the Mercury capsule (the winning bid was that submitted by McDonnell Aircraft). In December, the Department of Defense announced that a Bendix Systems Division-Grumman team was the winner of a design competition for the Eagle long-range air-to-air missile (unfortunately cancelled in December 1960).

1959: The thirtieth year in the company's existence proved to be relatively quiet. The only aeronautical development of note was the first flight of the Mohawk on 14 April. Company diversification efforts were rewarded when Dynamic Developments Inc, in which Grumman still held a 50 per cent interest, was awarded a contract for the design and construction of an 80-ton hydrofoil craft for the Maritime Administration.

A YAO-1A flying over a suburban development on Long Island. (*Grumman*)

1960: On 29 June, Leon 'Jake' Swirbul, the popular president, became the first of the founders to die. He was succeeded as president by Clint Towl, another of the founders.

On 16 April, two months after delivering the last aircraft in the Panther/Cougar series at the end of a record-setting 12-year production life, Grumman first flew the prototype of its Intruder, an aircraft which was to remain in production for two and a half times as long. The first flight of an equally long-lived aircraft, the Hawkeye propeller-turbine AEW aircraft, took place on 21 October. In that same month, Grumman won its first major NASA contract for the design, development, and production of the unmanned Orbiting Astronomical Observatory (OAO), a research satellite to be used for observation of stars outside of the earth's polluted atmosphere.

The major non-aerospace development of the year was the merger of Grumman Boats Inc with Pearson Boat Corporation, a manufacturer of fibreglass power and sailing boats. Upon completion of the merger, Grumman owned a controlling interest in the surviving company, Pearson Corporation.

Gross sales, which had remained in the $198- to 289-million range during the preceding years and were split roughly 90 per cent to the Government and 10 per cent to commercial customers, increased to over $325 million.

However, at 2.2 per cent, net income to gross sales remained at a disappointing level.

1961: The last Albatross was delivered to Japan in May and Ag-Cat, Gulfstream, Hawkeye, Intruder, Mohawk, and Tracker production generated most of the earnings.

A second NASA contract, for the design and manufacture of canisters to house the Echo II satellite, was won in June. However, in October the more important bid for the Apollo Command and Service Modules, which had been included by Grumman as part of the proposal submitted by a team led by General Electric, lost to that submitted by the North American team.

The world's first open-water hydrofoil craft, the HS *Denison*, built by Grumman for the Maritime Administration, was completed at the Bethpage plant in July.

The third Gulfstream I was first flown in February 1959. In 1970, it was fitted with a magnetometer boom in the tail and was then used for geophysical surveying by Grumman Ecosystems. Formed in January 1971, this wholly-owned subsidiary was in existence for just over six years. (*Grumman*)

BuNo 148149, the third W2F-1, ended its life mounted on a pedestal at NAS Miramar. (*Gordon S Williams*)

1962: Still not discouraged after losing a feasibility study contract in January for the LOR (Lunar Orbiting Rendezvous), Grumman saw its persistence rewarded on 7 November when NASA selected the company as the prime contractor for the Lunar Module. The importance of this win is evidenced by the initial contract value, $387 million, which exceeded by 20 per cent the highest annual sales previously realized by the company.

What was considered to be another potentially lucrative contract award was also announced in November when the Department of Defense selected the General Dynamics-Grumman team as the winner of the TFX competition for the F-111 tactical fighter with variable-sweep wings. As part of the team arrangement, Grumman was to be responsible for producing the aft sections, stabilizers, and undercarriage for all versions of the F-111 for the Air Force and the Navy, for the entire assembly of the F-111B version for the Navy, and for integration of all Navy electronics.

As a consequence of these two major awards, employment, which during the preceding ten years had remained in the 11,000 to 14,500 range, began rising rapidly and addition to plant facilities again became necessary.

1963: Early in the year, Aerobilt Bodies Inc and Pearson Corporation were merged into Grumman Allied Industries Inc, with the new subsidiary opening plants in Sturgis, Michigan and Sherman, Texas, and getting ready to start operations at a plant in Portsmouth, Rhode Island. In April, an electronic countermeasures version of the Intruder, the EA-6A, flew for the first time.

Gross sales reached a new high, $468.2 million, but profit margin remained low and net income was only $7.6 million or 1.6 per cent of gross sales. For the first time since 1944, employment exceeded the 20,000 mark at the end of the year.

1964: The C-2 Greyhound COD transport was first flown on 18 November and the General Dynamics F-111, for which Grumman was principal sub-contractor, first flew on 21 December. Investment in facilities amounted to approximately $15 million as both aerospace and other industrial activities were growing at a rapid pace. In November, the company announced that it would develop a turbofan-powered executive transport.

1965: In many ways, 1965 was a banner year for Grumman as gross sales ($852.0 million) and net income ($20.9 million) set new records. Moreover, in mid-year, employment exceeded the record set in the middle of the Second World War and kept rising during the last months of the year. The number of outstanding shares, which had grown slowly to 2,246,700 as a result of the Incentive Stock Option Plan which had been authorized in 1958, increased to 4,539,700 following a two-to-one split in May.

The F-111B was first flown on 18 May, production of the Ag-Cat and Super Ag-Cat, Greyhound, Hawkeye, Intruder, Mohawk, and Tracker continued throughout the year, and work on the OAO and LM proceeded on schedule. With ten years of experience in the design and development of hydrofoil craft, Grumman entered the European market when it reached an

30

agreement with Blohm und Voss for the the construction of its 90-passenger *Dolphin*, intended to link Barcelona and Majorca at a speed of 50 knots.

1966: Despite production increases on A-6s and OV-1s, the Vietnam war exercised only a very nominal influence on the company's overall volume. Sales, which reached the billion-dollar mark for the first time, net income, and employment grew for the fifth consecutive year as space and commercial activities increased in importance. Major aerospace achievements during the year were the launching in April of the first Grumman-built satellite, the OAO designated Spacecraft A-1, and the first flight of the Gulfstream II on 2 October.

In January, Ed Poor, one of the founders, died. In July, Roy Grumman stepped down as chairman of the board and chief executive officer and Clint Towl was elected as his successor. In turn, Towl was succeeded as president and chief operating officer by Llewellyn J Evans. Significantly, Lew Evans,

Bob Smyth and Carl Alber first flew the Gulfstream II from Bethpage to Calverton on 2 October, 1966. (*Grumman*)

BuNos 155725 and 155730 were delivered to VA-42 at NAS Oceana, Virginia, in 1968. This photograph was taken twenty years later at NAS Whidbey Island, Washington, where these two TC-4Cs were then operated by VA-128. (*René J Francillon*)

31

who had joined Grumman in 1951 as an assistant counsel, was the first senior officer not to have been a founder.

1967: The company's last piston-powered military aircraft, an S-2E, was completed in December and production of the Greyhound was terminated (however, C-2A deliveries were to be resumed 17 years later). Overall, sales of aircraft and related goods and services to the Department of Defense accounted for only 59 per cent of total sales (the lowest ever recorded by the company), sales to NASA added another 37 per cent, and commercial aircraft sales (Gulfstream I and Ag-Cat) and non-aerospace product represented but 4 per cent.

Expenditure for new plant, existing plant modernization, and equipment exceeded $30 million, nearly half the year's net income after taxes. Included in this expenditure was work in Stuart, with this Florida plant delivering its first Mohawk in November. An even larger plant, construction of which had begun during the previous year, was leased from the City of Savannah and the Savannah Airport Commission. Located at Travis Field, Georgia, this plant became the home of the Gulfstream II assembly line.

Gross sales and net income were down slightly but employment, which had risen by a factor of 2.5 in six years, reached its year's end record, 35,755. A three-to-two stock split was declared and, with additional stock options being exercised during this and preceding years, resulted in a further increase in the number of outstanding shares to 7,106,933 on 31 December.

1968: Employment continued to rise during the first quarter but, after reaching the all-time record of 37,121 in April, edged downward as work on NASA contracts began to decrease. Department of Defense contracts now accounted for 65 per cent of sales, but the company received bad news in this area when the F-111B was cancelled in May. Nevertheless, Grumman's

Photographed during a test flight in 1969, the first YOV-1D, 67-18898, shows the long radome housing the antenna for the AN/APS-94F side-looking airborne radar. (*Grumman*)

future appeared promising as commercial sales rose sharply following the introduction of the Gulfstream II and as other diversification programmes started yielding results (with the PX-15 *Ben Franklin* deep-diving research submersible and the PG(H)-1 *Flagstaff* hydrofoil patrol gunboat undergoing sea trials during the year).

The Grumman Corporation since 1969

1969: In July, in the middle of the fortieth year of operations, the name of the company was changed to Grumman Corporation to reflect the changing nature of its business. At that time, four major subsidiaries were organized. Grumman Aerospace Corporation became responsible for aircraft and space systems, including development of the F-14; production of Gulfstream IIs, Hawkeyes, Intruders, Prowlers, Mohawks, and the Schweizer-built Ag-Cat; sub-contract work on the F-111; support of previously built aircraft; the Lunar Module and Orbiting Astronomical Laboratory programmes; and the activities of the Ocean Systems group. Grumman Allied Industries provided a broad diversity of consumer and allied products, including glass fibre and aluminium pleasure boats, motor homes and buses, and modular vacation homes. Grumman Data Systems was organized to provide end-to-end computer services for business and scientific clients. Although Grumman had obtained its first export order in 1936 and many of its aircraft had since been delivered to foreign customers through Lend-Lease, Mutual

Astronaut Edwin Aldrin photographed at Tranquility Base during deployment of the Passive Seismic Experiment Package in front of LM-5 *Eagle* on 21 July, 1969. (*Neil Armstrong/NASA*)

Assistance Program, and other government-to-government undertakings, the company had not actively attempted to sell its products abroad. To correct this deficiency and boost foreign sales, Grumman International was set up as the fourth subsidiary of Grumman Corporation.

In January, Grumman was announced the winner of the VFX competition and a contract was awarded for the development of that design as the F-14. Then unsuspected, this award proved to be the last for a totally new combat aircraft type to be received by the company.

Preceded in January by the first unmanned Lunar Module mission, the Grumman-designed and -built LM was used for two manned landings on the moon. On 20 July, two of the Apollo 11 astronauts, Neil Armstrong and Edwin Aldrin, Jr, were brought to the surface of the moon by *Eagle* (LM-5, the fifth Lunar Module). Four months later, on 19 November, LM-6 made the second manned landing on the moon.

1970: In April, flawless performance by *Aquarius* (LM-7) saved the Apollo 13 astronauts after a component failure in the Apollo Service Module threatened to maroon them in space, and this gained much public acclaim for the company.

Net income decreased 8 per cent to $20.2 million while gross sales and employment both dropped by about 16 per cent respectively to $993.3 million and 28,112. Moreover, it was already becoming evident that the F-14 was going to be the source of headaches for management: the prototype crashed on 30 December, nine days after its first flight, and inflation was increasing faster than had been forecast when entering into a fixed-price incentive contract.

1971: The year started with the organization of a fifth subsidiary, Grumman Ecosystems Corporation, to seek solutions to environmental problems (notably doing resource survey work with a specially-modified Gulfstream I and a similarly modified Douglas A-26). It ended with the first loss being posted by the company and, for the first time since 1930, without

First assigned for training to VF-124 in 1973, the F-14A Tomcat became operational with VF-1 and VF-2 during the following year. (*Grumman*)

34

any dividends being paid. Gross sales decreased by almost 20 per cent to $799 million and earnings plummeted in one year from a net income of $20.2 million to a net loss of $18.0 million. Fortunately, the $65 million loss on the Tomcat programme was offset to a large extent by positive earnings from other programmes. Additional worries came from the fact that more losses were expected on the F-14A programme while two profitable contracts came to an end, the last Lunar Module being delivered in June and sub-contract work on the F-111 ending in September.

1972: Following the death of Lew Evans in July, John C Bierwirth was elected the fourth president at a particularly difficult time in the company's history. A second and greater financial loss, a whopping $70 million on sales of $683.5 million, was posted at the end of the year.

1973: On 8 March, Grumman and the government reached a settlement with regard to the F-14A contract. The company agreed to accept the previously rejected Lot V order under the original terms of the contract and the government agreed to cancel options under that unfavourable contract and to place future orders under contracts to be priced on the basis of current estimated costs.

After the Grumman/Boeing team had lost the NASA competition in 1972 for the Space Shuttle, Grumman recovered partially in 1973 when it obtained a contract for the design, production, and testing of five sets of wings for the Rockwell Space Shuttle.

Struggling to eliminate its losses on military contracts by finding new work in non-military markets, Grumman began the year by reaching an agreement with American Aircraft Corporation, a general aviation manufacturer which in 1972 had produced 450 single-engined aircraft in its small plant at the Cuyahoga County Airport, Cleveland, Ohio. On 2 January, a new 80 per cent owned subsidiary, Grumman American Aviation

The Tr-2 was the de luxe trainer version of the AA-1 Yankee, one of the light aircraft for which Grumman obtained the rights when it acquired 80 per cent of the capital of American Aviation. N1438R was photographed at the Mojave Airport in January 1984. (*René J Francillon*)

35

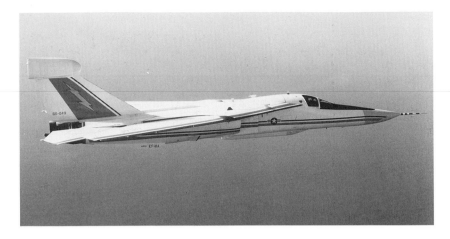

66-0049, one of the two F-111As modified by Grumman as EF-111A prototypes. *(Grumman)*

Corporation, was formed by merging Grumman's civil aircraft activities with those of American Aviation. Operations of the new company were to be concentrated in the Savannah plant. Meanwhile, Ag-Cat production by Schweizer continued at a record pace with the 1,000th aircraft being delivered during the year.

In further diversification moves, Grumman entered in a joint venture with VFW-Fokker to build Aviobridge passenger-loading systems in facilities located in Grand Prairie, Texas. It also formed Grumman Houston Corporation, a wholly-owned subisdiary, to operate primarily as a NASA contractor for specialized hardware and services.

Profitability was restored as $28.2 million was earned on sales of $1.1 billion. Although sales from Grumman American were only $86.8 million, the new organization contributed $6.4 million in regular net income and an additional $5.3 million in extraordinary income. Furthermore, employment rose slightly to cope with increased F-14 production and civil aircraft work.

1974: In June, as the result of the Shah's personal interest in the Tomcat, Iran placed an initial order for thirty F-14As. In addition, this Middle Eastern monarch was influential in having Bank Melli Iran contribute 37.5 per cent of a $200 million line of credit obtained by Grumman from a group of banks. As, moreover, gross sales and net income increased during the year – the latter setting a new record of $32.9 million – the company was well on the way to financial recovery.

1975: At the end of the year, E Clinton Towl retired from active management and John Bierwirth and Joseph G Gavin, Jr, were respectively elected chairman of the board and president. Thus, for the first time none of the company's founders occupied the two top positions; however, Clint

BuNo 155600 was delivered as an A-6A in June 1968, modified as an A-6E in 1976 (in which form it is illustrated in the markings of VMA(AW)-533), and modified as an A-6E TRAM in 1982. *(Courtesy of Jay Miller)*

Towl and Bill Schwendler were still on the Board of Directors and Roy Grumman remained as honorary chairman of the board.

1976: While employment and net income levelled off, gross sales increased 13 per cent to $1.5 billion. Much of that increase, however, was due to inflation. In February, Grumman broadened its diversification programme by acquiring the Howe Fire Apparatus Company, a well-established manufacturer of fire engines, emergency rescue vehicles, and related products.

In common with other major US aircraft manufacturers with overseas operations, Grumman came under scrutiny during 1976 regarding the use of commissioned sales representatives and alleged payments to foreign officials. In a 24 March letter to shareholders, Chairman Bierwirth and President Gavin denied that the company's use of commissioned sales representatives in Iran were 'in violation of any provision of US law or procurement regulations nor did it serve as a cover for bribes or kickbacks to Iranian governmental officials or for political contributions.' They added, 'We have obtained written statements from our sales representatives that neither the services performed nor the commissions paid violated in any way the laws, rules and regulations of the Government of Iran.'

Notwithstanding this statement, rumours persisted and an Audit Committee composed of five outside members of the board of directors requested an investigation of foreign sales activities and policies. As a result of an investigation initiated in March, the Securities and Exchange Commission (SEC) expressed the view that violations of the laws and regulations had occurred (1) through a failure to make timely disclosure of both the sales commission arrangements and the initial payments there-under associated with the sale of F-14 aircraft and spares to the Government of Iran and (2) in connection with commission payments made on foreign sales of Gulfstream II commercial jet aircraft. In the end, on 4 January, 1979, Grumman settled an SEC complaint alleging that the company had

37

violated federal securities laws by failing to disclose commission payments on certain foreign sales of Gulfstream II and F-14s. In addition, also during January 1979, Grumman agreed to reimburse the $120,000 fine imposed by the Department of Justice on Gulfstream American Corporation after that company pleaded guilty to twelve counts of making false statements to agencies of the United States Government in connection with foreign sales of Gulfstream II business jets between 1974 and 1977.

1977: The company's recovery continued at a satisfactory pace with gross sales setting a new high, over $1.5 billion, and net income being at a near record $32.4 million.

1978: At the beginning of the year, Grumman acquired from Rohr Industries for $54.2 million the Flxible Company, one of three American firms manufacturing city and suburban buses. Then, in a surprise move, the company announced in September the sale of its 80 per cent interest in the profitable Grumman American Aviation Corporation to American Jet Industries (subsequently merged into Gulfstream American). Grumman received $15 million in cash and $20.5 million in preferred Gulfstream American Stock. In addition, the sales agreement provided for a fee to be paid to Grumman for each of the first 200 Gulfstream IIIs* sold after December 1979. However, the combination of the acquisition of the Flxible Company and the sale of its profitable commercial aircraft business† soon proved to have been ill-advised for Grumman.

Diversification programmes expanding the company's activities into such non-aerospace fields as municipal waste disposal and energy recovery systems and wind and solar energy systems proved equally disappointing. Likewise, a 1978 Israeli order for two 85-ton missile-armed hydrofoils also proved to be unsatisfactory; four years later Grumman was forced out of the hydrofoil business after being unable to recover fully R & D costs on the Israeli order.

1979: In August, two million shares of a new cumulative preferred stock were issued for $50 million, with proceeds being used to repay borrowings from the line of credit. Nevertheless, the company ended the decade in a far less advantageous position as on 31 December total liabilities were $521.1 million versus $276.3 million in capital and retained earnings. At $19.6 million, net income was virtually unchanged from the previous year. It would have been substantially higher had it not been for operating losses of $16.1 million due to production problems with Flxible buses.

During the decade which ended on 31 December 1979, the company had realized a net income averaging a dismal 0.9 per cent on gross sales of nearly

---

* Design of a first Gulfstream III model had been initiated by Grumman in 1974 but was abandoned in 1977 when the general aviation market was in a downturn. A less ambitious design was launched in April 1978 and it was on the sales of this aircraft that Grumman was to be paid a fee.

† Between 1973 and August 1978, Grumman American Aviation Corporation earned $38.7 million in income before taxes on sales totalling $717.6 million.

$12 billion. This represented an average annual profit contribution of only $410 per employee, whereas, during the first year of operations, the initial group of employees had contributed an average of $238. When considering the decrease in purchasing power of the dollar between 1930 and 1979, this, in fact, represented a drastic reduction in profit contribution.

1980: By the end of the year, production of Flxible buses was performed at a profitable rate. However, in November, cracks were discovered in structural members of some of the buses, a disconcerting development for a company which had always been known for the toughness and durability of its products. Grumman took full responsibility, helped customers inspect their fleets, designed reinforced structures for installation in buses already in service, and was forced to set aside $7 million to cover repair costs. Overall, however, the year's results were quite satisfactory with income

The first X-29A being towed back to a NASA hangar at the Hugh L. Dryden Flight Research Center, Edwards AFB, California, on 15 November, 1988. *(René J Francillon)*

An A-4PTM, a version of the Douglas Skyhawk rebuilt and fitted with modern avionics by the St Augustine Division in Florida. *(Grumman)*

increasing 57 per cent to $30.7 million on sales virtually unchanged from a year earlier. Increased aerospace sales (with production work continuing on A-6Es, E-2Cs, EA-6Bs, EF-111As, and F-14As) were the primary reasons for improved operating results.

1981: Rising interest rates (a problem affecting everyone in the early 1980s), higher than anticipated bus repair costs, and increased foreign competition in the transit bus business (the latter two combining to generate a $68.9 million loss in the Flxible bus business) resulted in net income dropping to $20.5 million in spite of a 14 per cent increase in gross sales to $1.7 billion.

At the end of the year, Design 712 was selected by the Defense Advanced Research Projects Agency (DARPA) and the Air Force Flight Dynamics Laboratory as the winner of the Forward Swept Wing (FSW) technology aircraft competition, with Grumman receiving a contract for two X-29As.

1982: For the first time, gross sales exceeded the $2-billion mark while net income jumped 59 per cent to $32.6 million despite substantial bus losses.

The year saw Grumman establish the business base for its new aircraft overhaul and refurbishing facility in St Augustine, Florida. The first contract was from the Navy for the conversion of A-6Es as KA-6D tankers and was followed by a contract from the Government of Malaysia to modernize forty Douglas A-4 Skyhawks.

1983: Sales and backlog increased again but it was the 239 per cent increase in net income to the all-time record of $110.7 million which was the most remarkable.

The troubled Flxible bus subsidiary was sold in July and Grumman filed a lawsuit to attempt recovery from Rohr Industries of some of the damages caused by their defective bus design.

1984: Once again, despite near record net income of $108.4 million and rising sales and employment, problems with Flxible buses caused concern as the New York City Transit Authority discovered cracks in the front-end assembly of some of its buses. Despite the previous year's sale of its Flxible business, Grumman retained the warranty responsibility for buses it had manufactured and the company faced additional losses. Moreover, the City of New York and three public authorities filed suit against Grumman for actual and punitive damages of up to $324 million.

Positive developments during the year included the first flight of the X-29A on 14 December and increases of 50 per cent and 30 per cent respectively in sales of aluminium truck bodies and aluminium boats.

1985: During the year which ended with sales exceeding the $3-billion mark for the first time and net income starting a new downward spiral, the company was restructured into operating divisions. Still in use four years later, this organization is described at the end of the chapter. The only other significant corporate change was the retirement of Joseph Gavin after more than thirty years with Grumman and his replacement as president by George M Skurla.

The new Melbourne Systems Division won a contract valued at $657 million, the largest ever received by Grumman from the Air Force, to develop the Joint Surveillance Target Attack Radar System (Joint STARS), with prototype systems to be installed in two modified Boeing 707-320s. Award of other aerospace and non-aerospace contracts helped Grumman to end the year with a funded backlog double its annual sales, the highest ratio in the industry.

1986: Non-aerospace operations provided the main news with Grumman selling its unprofitable Pearson Yacht product line and winning a major contract from the US Postal Service to build 99,150 mail delivery trucks. Together with an option for another 59,490 trucks, this award was expected to generate revenues of $1.8 billion by the mid-1990s.

Aerospace sales increased by 6 per cent during the year but the loss in October of the contract for the concept demonstration/validation phase for the Advanced Tactical Fighter (ATF) was a major blow as, in addition to being planned as the new Air Force fighter, the ATF may be developed as a Tomcat replacement.

After only one year as president of Grumman Corporation, George M Skurla retired and was replaced by John O'Brien, who had been serving as president of the Data Systems Division.

1987: The year 1987 was a difficult one for the Grumman Corporation. Gross sales decreased by a little over 3 per cent to $3.3 billion while net income was cut by 55 per cent to $35.7 million. Contributions to sales and income made by each of the major business segments were as follows:

	Percentage of total sales	Percentage of total operating profit (loss)
Aerospace	73.5	41.6
Electronics systems	18.9	8.4
Special purpose vehicles	7.4	8.5
Information and other services	13.4	50.8
Corporate items and others	(13.2)	(9.3)

At the end of the year, total liabilities were $1,485 million and capital and retained earnings totalled $770 million.

Although the backlog was up to a record $7.9 billion, the future appeared unpromising in the company's traditional mainstay, naval aircraft, after Grumman-Northrop-LTV had lost the Navy competition for the ATA (Advanced Tactical Aircraft, the likely replacement of the Intruder) to a General Dynamics-McDonnell Douglas team.

Quite remarkably in the light of the many business ups and downs experienced by the company, management had succeeded during the preceding twenty years in avoiding the massive layoffs which so frequently occur in the aerospace industry. During the period, employment remained fairly stable with a high of 35,588 at the end of 1968 and a low of 25,115 at

41

the end of 1971. At the end of 1987, there were 33,700 employees on the Grumman payroll.

1988: Grumman's fifty-ninth year of operations began with new rumours of a take-over by large firms including some with limited experience in the aerospace business. Meanwhile operations continued under a revised senior management as, following John C Bierwirth's retirement in August, John O'Brien was elected chairman of the board and chief executive officer while retaining the presidency of Grumman Corporation. Mr O'Brien's former post of chief operating officer then remained vacant.

During the year, reductions in the military aircraft acquisition budget prompted the US Navy to contemplate terminating the production of A-6s and EA-6s and reducing the number of new F-14Ds to be built. To offset this potential loss of business, the company agreed with Agusta to propose Grumman-built SIAI-Marchetti S.211 jet trainers, plus simulators, support equipment, and training materials, as replacements for Cessna T-37Bs under the Air Force's Primary Aircraft Training System (PATS).

In early 1989, the Grumman Corporation still had its headquarters in Bethpage. It had four subsidiaries (Grumman Credit Corporation, Grumman International Inc, Grumman Ventures Inc, and Paumanock Development Corporation) and was organized into the following operating divisions:

Aircraft Systems Division

As the direct descendant of Grumman Aircraft Engineering Company, the Aircraft Systems Division was manufacturing F-14A(Plus) and F-14D fighters and C-2A COD transports for the USN, A-6E attack aircraft and EA-6B ECM aircraft for the USN and USMC, and E-2C AEW aircraft for the USN and export customers. Work was done at facilities in Bethpage, Calverton, and other less important locations.

The division was also working on the Air Force-managed *Peace Pearl* contract to provide a modern fire control system for the Shenyang J-8 II fighter (two prototypes of which were scheduled to be flight tested at Mojave, California, in late 1989) and on a preliminary design contract from the China National Aero Technology Import-Export Corporation (CATIC) to develop an advanced version of the Xian F-7M fighter (Chinese-built MiG-21) with a General Electric F404/RM12 turbofan with side intakes, increased fuel capacity, an AN/APG-66 radar, and enlarged wings with two additional store stations. Moreover, since Fairchild went out of business in 1987, the Aircraft Systems Division has provided product support for the A-10A. Finally, the division was known to be working on the development of new advanced airborne early warning systems to meet joint Air Force/Navy requirements.

Two previously independent divisions, the Aerostructures Division and the St Augustine Division, were placed under the Aircraft Systems Division in January 1989 to improve efficiency and reduce administrative costs. Using facilities in Bethpage, Calverton, and Melville, New York; Milledgeville, Georgia; and Stuart, Florida, Aerostructures Operations is a major sub-contractor to aerospace companies for the design and production of structural assemblies for aircraft, missiles, and space vehicles. Major work in 1989 included composite spoilers and centre wing beam and keel assembly for the Boeing 767, composite transcowls for General Electric CF6-80C2 nacelles, Tay nacelles for the Gulfstream IV and Fokker 100, empennages for the Bell Helicopter Textron/Boeing Helicopter V-22 Osprey, and composite flight control surfaces for the McDonnell Douglas C-17.

St Augustine Operations continued as an overhaul and modification facility serving the military and commercial aircraft markets. In 1989, its principal projects were the S-2T re-engining and updating programme for export customers and the overhaul and modification of A-6s and KA-6s for the USN and USMC. It also provided logistic and service support for out-of-production Grumman aircraft, primarily HU-16s and S-2s.

Another entity reporting to the Aircraft Systems Division, Grumman Houston Operations in Webster, Texas, operated primarily as a NASA contractor for specialized hardware and services.

Side-by-side assembly lines for A-6s and EA-6s, on the left, and F-14s, on the right, in Calverton in 1986. (*Grumman*)

43

Allied Division

In its first year of operations, the Grumman Aircraft Engineering Corporation produced its first aluminium truck bodies and in the autumn of 1945, the company built its first aluminium canoes. In 1989, the Allied Division of the Grumman Corporation was delivering a broad range of non-aerospace products including postal delivery vans – (the so-called Long Life Vehicles (LLV) mounted on General Motors chassis) aluminium truck bodies, and a full line of fire fighting equipment, as well as a line of fishing and sports boats and canoes from plants located in several states.

Subsidiaries of the Allied Division were Boats, LLV, Grumman Olson, and Grumman Emergency Products Inc.

Corporate Services Division

This division was organized to centralize overhead activities (such as Business Operations, Counsel, Corporate Procurement, Human Resources Planning, and Facilities Management) for Grumman Corporation, its Operating Divisions, and its subsidiaries.

Data Systems Division

From its new facility in Holtsville, New York, the Data Systems Division pursued work in five major segments: Command, Control, Communications, and Intelligence systems (C^3 & I); computerized test systems;

A Grumman LLV delivery truck of the US Postal Service in Vallejo, California, in November 1988. (*René J Francillon*)

44

engineering and scientific systems; management information systems; and integrated manufacturing systems. Its subsidiaries were Grumman Data Systems Institute, InfoConversion, and Systems Support.

Electronics Systems Division

In its Bethpage headquarters and in facilities located in Maryland, New Jersey, New York, and Texas, the Electronics Systems Division designed, manufactured, and integrated sophisticated electronics for aircraft, computerized test equipment and other defence-related products, and products for the broadcasting and communications industries. Major military projects underway in 1988 were the Integrated Family of Test Equipment, or IFTE, which will be used by the Army to diagnose electronic problems of equipment in the field, and the Teleoperated Mobile Antiarmor Platform, or TMAP, a four-wheeled remotely operated vehicle that will carry many mission payloads (such as anti-tank missiles) and will be operated by infantrymen through a fibreoptic link from locations many miles away. Associated with Northrop, the Electronics Systems Division was also developing an inexpensive guidance device which could give standard bombs an accuracy similar to that achieved by guided missiles.

A subsidiary, Tachonics Corporation, designed and built integrated circuits on gallium arsenide. Gallium arsenide was said to have better frequency performance and substantially increased resistance to heat and radiation than silicon and was thus well-suited for the manufacture of EMP (electro-magnetic pulse) -hardened military electronics.

The E-8A prototype on the day of its first flight at Melbourne, Florida, in April 1988. (*Grumman*)

Melbourne Systems Division

Taking its name from its location in Melbourne, Florida, this division was primarily responsible for the Air Force/Army Joint STARS programme which provided for the development and testing of two 707s modified by Boeing. Designated E-8As, these two test bed aircraft carry Grumman-designed systems to detect, locate, classify, and track large numbers of stationary and moving targets and to provide real-time battlefield surveillance and attack management for air and land battles. Adoption of the Joint STARS by the USAF, the US Army, and NATO could result in a $10-billion programme.

Space Station Program Support Division

Spun off from the Space Systems Division, this division assisted NASA with programme control and management, information systems, operations, programme requirements and assessment, systems engineering, safety, reliability, quality assurance, and international integration for the Space Station Program. The initial contract awarded in July 1987 had a value of over $800 million and provided for work during more than ten years; additional options may increase contract value to $1.2 billion.

Space Systems Division

The Space Systems Division was working as a sub-contractor on various packages to develop NASA's Manned Space Station. As a member of a Boeing-led team, it was designing and building the station's crew quarters; teamed with TRW and Robotics Research Corporation, it was competing for the preliminary design of a space station robot; and associated with TRW it was working on the Orbital Maneuvering Vehicle, a so-called space tug which will be used to deliver and retrieve orbiting satellites.

The division was also taking part in the final phase of an Air Force competition to develop the Boost Surveillance Tracking System (BSTS) to detect and track ballistic missiles just after launch as part of the Strategic Defense Initiative. Should Grumman be selected to produce the BSTS and to develop a military satellite supporting this system, potential revenue could reach $10-20 billion and this program would become the cornerstone of the company's activities at the beginning of the twenty-first century.

Technical Services Division

This division serviced and maintained military flight simulators and trainers, provided product support for Grumman aircraft, and, as a Lockheed sub-contractor, helped ready the Space Shuttle for successive flights.

The Goose was in production between 1937 and 1945. RCAF 926, a Goose Mk. II, was struck off strength on 25 June, 1942, after serving briefly in Canada with No.121 (Communications) Squadron. (*Public Archives of Canada*)

Annual employment, gross sales, and net income1930-1988

Year	Number of employees	Gross Sales US$	Net Income US$
1930	23	109,724	5,476
1931	42	146,971	N.A.
1932	64	276,184	44,871
1933	207	862,697	132,094
1934	292	1,810,775	208,185
1935	293	1,640,094	228,277
1936	362	1,719,043	79,509
1937	511	2,284,764	139,062
1938	710	4,904,946	617,074
1939	813	4,482,350	892,063
1940	2,034	8,811,295	1,415,964
1941	6,650	21,858,681	1,066,683
1942	19,556	143,155,931	4,654,654
1943	25,094	278,695,001	7,898,287
1944	21,607	323,749,331	11,550,001
1945	4,670	236,846,862	5,713,528
1946	5,369	37,615,541	337,772
1947	3,379	24,241,248	2,291,121
1948	4,564	41,031,662	2,393,311
1949	6,313	59,756,838	3,191,520
1950	6,633	102,312,498	6,242,064
1951	9,287	167,581,568	5,456,246

NASA's Mohawk is an OV-1B which was modified in 1980 by Grumman in Stuart for engine noise monitoring tests at the Langley Research Center. *(NASA)*

Year	Number of employees	Gross Sales US$	Net Income US$
1952	11,367	220,547,193	5,348,900
1953	11,092	240,857,669	7,129,341
1954	11,815	235,318,223	11,214,853
1955	12,483	213,353,647	9,756,500
1956	13,074	197,504,602	7,702,892
1957	12,788	205,159,921	5,235,774
1958	13,789	225,055,032	2,492,061
1959	14,378	288,978,628	4,938,308
1960	14,437	325,555,488	7,194,292
1961	14,454	316,714,782	6,103,088
1962	16,178	357,099,282	6,245,600
1963	20,118	468,175,408	7,607,962
1964	22,659	598,375,676	10,659,766
1965	29,201	852,032,800	20,936,064
1966	33,556	1,059,379,320	27,622,252
1967	35,755	968,596,157	21,450,858
1968	35,588	1,152,571,091	19,037,286
1969	33,804	1,180,328,130	22,087,714
1970	28,112	993,260,754	20,271,704
1971	25,115	799,021,180	(17,989,580)
1972	26,527	683,456,819	(70,026,223)

Artist's rendering of the Super-7. Grumman and Chengdu Aircraft Corporation began preliminary design work for this derivative of the Xian F-7M during the autumn of 1988. *(Grumman)*

Year	Number of employees	Gross Sales US$	Net Income US$
1973	27,372	1,082,569,646	28,243,317
1974	29,850	1,112,855,955	32,929,307
1975	27,949	1,328,622,338	23,547,199
1976	28,101	1,502,058,385	23,553,936
1977	26,901	1,552,694,634	32,396,577
1978	26,372	1,455,448,285	19,969,170
1979	27,827	1,476,009,578	19,571,272
1980	27,640	1,515,452,000	30,668,000
1981	28,354	1,726,986,000	20,486,000
1982	27,158	2,003,244,000	32,600,000
1983	28,680	2,220,162,000	110,746,000
1984	30,866	2,557,807,000	108,418,000
1985	32,177	3,048,520,000	81,535,000
1986	33,400	3,440,125,000	78,690,000
1987	33,700	3,375,260,000	35,650,000
1988	31,980	3,648,892,000	86,465,000

The XFF-1 flying near NAS Hampton Roads, Virginia, on 4 February, 1932. (*USN/National Archives*)

Grumman FF and SF

In September 1922, the Naval Aircraft Factory had fitted a retractable undercarriage designed by J V Martin to a modified Vought VE-7. In November 1930, the Navy had acquired the privately-developed Curtiss Helldiver Cyclone Command which was powered by a Wright Cyclone and had tandem enclosed cockpits. Initially designated XF8C-7, this aircraft was assigned as the personal transport of a Naval Aviator of note, First World War Ace David S Ingalls, who was then Assistant Secretary of the Navy for Aviation. Therefore the retractable undercarriage, the new and powerful Wright R-1820 Cyclone nine-cylinder air-cooled radial, and fully enclosed cockpits were not totally new to US Naval Aviation when William H McAvoy first flew the XFF-1 at Curtiss Field, Valley Stream, on 29 December, 1931. The XFF-1, however, was the first to combine all three of these features. Moreover, it had a fully retractable undercarriage (whereas the Martin undercarriage fitted to the VE-7 left most of the wheels exposed) and became the first naval fighter to exceed 200 mph in level flight.

Development of this epochal aircraft began almost by accident. During discussions of the proposed Model A amphibian floats in February 1930, Bureau of Aeronautics (BuAer) personnel asked Roy Grumman and Jake Swirbul whether they thought their retractable undercarriage design could be adapted to existing carrier fighters such as the single-seat Boeing F4B-1, which had entered service in June 1929, or the two-seat Curtiss F8C-4, which was about to do so. Grumman and Swirbul also learned that the Navy would soon order new two-seat carrier fighter prototypes. As they were not keen on the idea of letting others benefit from their development of a practical retractable undercarriage design and as they wanted to put their

50

new company on a stronger footing, Roy Grumman and his chief engineer, Bill Schwendler, set out to design a two-seat fighter. On 10 March 1930, barely three months after the company had been organized and less than a month after becoming aware of the Navy's interest, Grumman submitted preliminary data on the High Performance Two-Seater Fighter (HPTSF) to the Bureau of Aeronautics. BuAer immediately saw merit in this proposal and on 29 March informally notified Grumman of its interest. After this rapid start, however, the project moved forward slowly as the Navy did not yet have funds with which to order two-seat fighter prototypes and as, notwithstanding Roy Grumman's personal reputation and the fact that he was well-known to many Naval Aviators, the Navy had to proceed carefully before awarding a contract to an untried contractor.

The HPTSF design evolved as a small single-bay biplane, with fabric-covered, staggered two-spar wings and ailerons on the upper wing only. Its semi-monocoque fuselage was characterized by a deep forward section in which the mainwheels were raised vertically by means of thirty-five turns of a hand crank. Pilot and rear gunner were accommodated in tandem under an enclosed canopy and armament was to consist of the then standard pair of forward-firing guns (with a 0.50-in Browning M-3 machine gun being offered as a substitute for one of the two 0.30-in Browning M-2 machine guns normally fitted) and one rear-firing 0.30-in flexible gun. Power was to be supplied by one of the new Wright Cyclone nine-cylinder radials, with a 575-hp R-1820-E driving a ground-adjustable two-blade propeller being initially selected for the prototype.

As adoption of the HPTSF for Service use would introduce several features novel to carrier aircraft designs, notably a retractable undercarriage and an aluminium alloy semi-monocoque fuselage, and as calculated performance appeared over-optimistic, conservative elements within BuAer insisted that Grumman first provide drawings on a 12:1 scale to enable the Navy to build a wind tunnel test model. Further delays resulted from protracted discussions regarding the design of the flexible rear gun installation. Ultimately wind tunnel tests validated the company's claims and a satisfactory flexible rear gun design was provided (the gun being provided with a swivel mount and the gunner's seat being allowed to tilt back to provide better defence against aircraft attacking from above). Finally, as budgetary matters were resolved, the Navy requested Grumman to submit a quotation for the design, construction, and testing of one prototype. A $73,975 quotation was submitted by Grumman on 6 March, 1931, and accepted on 28 March when the Navy ordered one XFF-1 and reserved an option for a second prototype (which was exercised on 9 June when an order for an XSF-1 was placed). Contractual guarantees included a top speed of 190 mph at sea level and a service ceiling of 22,000 ft; moreover, delivery was to take place within 200 days.

This delivery date represented a risky undertaking for a firm which then had a work force of less than thirty and would have to move from its converted garage into larger rented facilities before completing the

This view of the XFF-1 flying near NAS Hampton Roads on 4 February, 1932, adds useful details on the aircraft's retractable undercarriage. (*USN/National Archives*)

experimental aircraft. Despite strenuous efforts to meet this challenge and make up time lost during its move from Baldwin to Valley Stream in November 1931, Grumman could do no better than to have the aircraft ready to fly just before the end of 1931, seventy-six days behind schedule. The second prototype, the XSF-1, took even longer to build and was first flown on 20 August, 1932, 437 days after it had been ordered. Fortunately for Grumman, the other type of two-seat carrier fighter ordered by the Navy in 1931, the Berliner-Joyce XF2J-1, which had a non-retractable undercarriage and open cockpits, was only delivered in May 1933 and was slower than the XFF-1 and XSF-1.

Production history

Production contracts for twenty-seven FF-1 two-seat fighters and thirty-four scout aircraft (thirty-three delivered as SF-1s and one as the XSF-2) were obtained respectively in December 1932 and August 1933, thus firmly placing Grumman in the naval aircraft business. In addition, Grumman built a GG-1 civil demonstrator derived from the two naval aircraft prototypes and produced fifty-seven fuselages for G-23 export models assembled by Canadian Car & Foundry.

XFF-1: Started as the HPTSF design and later given the same company designation as production models – Design 5, or G-5 – the XFF-1 (BuNo A8878) was built in the Baldwin garage and completed in the Valley Stream plant. It was powered by a 575-hp Wright R-1820-E radial fitted with a Townend ring cowling and driving a two-blade ground-adjustable propeller

The XSF-2 photographed on 14 March, 1935, with undercarriage and arrester hook lowered and locked. The muzzle for the forward-firing 0.30-in machine-gun can be seen on the starboard side of the cowling, just aft the lip. (*USN/National Archives*)

when it was first flown at Curtiss Field on 29 December, 1931, by Bill McAvoy. Following initial Navy trials at NAS Anacostia, District of Columbia, during which it encountered only minor problems and was found highly manoeuvrable for a two-seat aircraft, the XFF-1 was returned to Valley Stream in May 1932, where it was fitted with a 750-hp R-1820-F (military designation R-1820-78). Additional Navy testing revealed the need for some modifications including a minor redesign of the canopy, the fitting of horn-balances to the ailerons, the relocation further aft of the arrester hook, and a strengthening of the undercarriage locking mechanism to prevent accidental retraction during heavy landings or while taxi-ing on rough ground.

Powered by the R-1820-E engine, the XFF-1 had already demonstrated sprightly performance. Its top speed of 195 mph at sea level exceeded both the contractual guarantee and the 188 mph speed achieved by the F4B-4, the single-seat carrier fighter delivered by Boeing beginning in June 1932. With that engine, however, the XFF-1 took 4.3 minutes to climb to 5,000 ft whereas the F4B-4 reached that altitude in 2.9 minutes. Following its re-engining with the R-1820-F, the Grumman prototype matched the climb performance of the Boeing fighter and increased its speed advantage at sea level by 13 mph, reaching 201 mph.

After receiving the modifications noted above, the aircraft had the X removed from its designation and was successively assigned to the San Diego Battle Fleet, to VF-5B, and to NAS Anacostia. There the aircraft was modified during the summer of 1936, to test the effectiveness of a Bureau of Aeronautics proposal to reduce the visibility of an aircraft in flight by using lights to lower the contrast between those parts of an aircraft in the shadow

FF-1 (BuNo 9365), aircraft number 15 of VF-5B in August 1934. (*USN/National Archives*)

and those in full light. To that end, BuNo A8878 was fitted with twelve landing lights beneath the fuselage to provide uniform illumination of the portion of the fuselage normally in shadow. Four batteries in the rear cockpit provided electrical power for the lights. Tests began on 1 October, 1936, but proved inconclusive, and lights and batteries were removed before the aircraft was assigned to NAS Norfolk, Virginia. It was damaged beyond repair in a crash landing on 4 March, 1937, after running out of fuel.

FF-1: Preceded by the XSF-1 and XJF-1 prototypes, the twenty-seven production FF-1 two-seat fighters (BuNos 9350/9376) were built in the Farmingale plant and were delivered between April and November 1933. They were essentially similar to the modified XFF-1 and like that aircraft were powered by R-1820-78 engines. A total of 120 US gallons of fuel could be carried internally; an 82-gal main tank was fitted beneath the pilot's seat and a 38-gal auxiliary tank was provided between the wheel wells. Armament consisted of two synchronized 0.30-in guns in the upper fuselage decking (with provision being made for substituting a 0.50-in weapon for the starboard gun) and one similar weapon on a flexible mount in the rear cockpit.

FF-2: In 1935, twenty-two of the twenty-five surviving FF-1s were modified by the Naval Aircraft Factory in Philadelphia before being assigned as fighter trainers to Naval and Marine reserve units. For that purpose, they were fitted with dual controls and retained the gun camera mounted slightly to starboard of the centreline in the upper wing (an optional feature for the FF-1 fighters), but all guns were removed.

XSF-1: First flown at Curtiss Field on 20 August, 1932, the XSF-1 scout prototype (BuNo A8940) differed from the XFF-1 in having the two forward guns removed to enable the internal fuel capacity to be increased

54

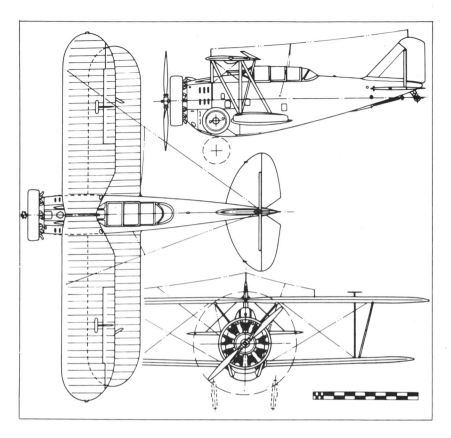

Grumman FF-1

from 120 to 165 US gal by enlarging the tank located between the wheel wells. Armament consisted of one forward-firing 0.30-in gun mounted in the starboard upper wing, a flexible weapon of the same calibre installed in the rear cockpit, and two 100-lb bombs carried beneath the lower wings. From the onset it was powered by a 750-hp R-1820-78 but the Townend ring cowling and short exhaust pipes which had been fitted by Grumman were later replaced by the Navy with a NACA cowling and and exhaust collector ring.

SF-1: Like the FF-1, the thirty-three SF-1s (BuNos 9460/9492) were produced in the Farmingdale plant. However, manufacture of the wings and control surfaces was sub-contracted to Brewster Aeronautical Corporation in Long Island City to avoid hiring temporary help or increasing staff beyond the number considered prudent by Grumman's conservative management. The SF-1s were delivered between February and July 1934 and were powered by the 750-hp R-1820-84 (a few initially being powered

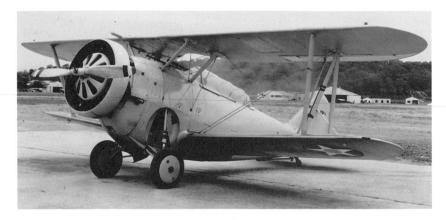

The XSF-1 at NAS Anacostia, District of Columbia, on 16 September, 1932. (*USN/National Archives*)

The carriage of a 1,000-lb bomb beneath the starboard wing of an SF-1, well aft of the cg and well outboard of the centre line, was probably one of the most harebrained schemes proposed by the Navy in 1934. (*USN/National Archives*)

560

The bomb & Dolly are on the ground & the handle is not connected to anything; this is an optical illusion!

by the R-1820-78) with NACA cowling and exhaust collector ring. One of these aircraft was used in April 1934 in rather hazardous bomb-carrying trials, during which a 1,000-lb bomb was carried on a sway brace beneath and aft of the port wing. A skid was fitted beneath the aft end of the brace as

56

clearance between the bomb and the ground was minimal. In Grumman's nomenclature, both the XSF-1 prototype and the SF-1 production aircraft were Design 6, or G-6.

XSF-2: Powered by a 700-hp Pratt & Whitney R-1535-72 fourteen-cylinder radial, this aircraft (BuNo 9493) matched the SF-1 airframe with the powerplant installation of the XF2F-1. This Design 13, or G-13, also differed from the SF-1 in having the forward-firing 0.30 in gun relocated on the right side of the cowling. It was first flown on 26 November, 1934, and was used for sundry development projects until assigned to the Machinist's Mates School for ground instruction.

GG-1: Assembled from major components remaining after production of FF-1s and SF-1s had ended, the GG-1 was an unarmed company-owned demonstrator which was initially powered by a 450-hp Pratt & Whitney Wasp radial and fitted with modified canopy. Registered X12V, the GG-1 first flew on 28 September, 1934, and was retained by Grumman until 1936. It was then re-engined with an 890-hp Wright R-1820-F52 radial and, after its US registration was changed to NR12V, it was sold in November 1936 to Canadian Car & Foundry to be used in promoting the 'Canadian Grumman Fighter,' an export version which was to be assembled in Canada. In December, the aircraft was flown back to the United States, by Howard Frederick Klein, where it was demonstrated at Floyd Bennett Field, not far from Grumman's Bethpage plant, to aircraft purchasing agents of the Spanish Republican Government. In 1937, Canadian Car & Foundry sent the aircraft on a demonstration tour of Central America, during which it was lost at sea on 29 September while flying off San Juan del Norte on the Nicaraguan-Costa Rican border.

G-23: Under rather mysterious conditions, and quite possibly to avoid an arms embargo imposed in January 1937 by the United States against both Nationalists and Republicans during the Spanish Civil War, Canadian Car & Foundry suddenly acquired in 1936 rights to assemble the G-23 (also

Powered by a 450-hp Pratt & Whitney Wasp, the GG-1 demonstrator was the first civil registered aircraft built by Grumman. It was first flown on 28 September, 1934. (*Grumman*)

called GE-23, or Grumman Export 23), the production version of the re-engined GG-1.

Lacking any experience in aircraft manufacturing, Canadian Car & Foundry had been better known as the largest manufacturer of rolling stock in the British Commonwealth with headquarters in Montreal, CC&F planned to have G-23s assembled in Ontario at its Fort William plant, using fuselages built by Grumman*, wings and tail surfaces built by Brewster, and engines, undercarriages, and other components and equipment imported from the United States.

Apparently, Canadian Car & Foundry obtained an order for a single aeroplane from both Nicaragua and Japan (these G-23s being respectively flown on 2 and 12 February and delivered shortly after) and two orders for fifty aircraft then believed to have been placed by Turkey. These aircraft, however, were ordered by agents of the Spanish Government using false Turkish Government documentation. Be that as it may, thirty-four aircraft were shipped to the Spanish Republicans in April and May 1938 before the subterfuge was discovered. The remaining sixteen aircraft were kept in Canada, one being sold to Mexico later in 1938 as a pattern aircraft for intended production there and fifteen eventually taken on charge by the Royal Canadian Air Force in the autumn of 1940.

Service history

The first FF-1 was delivered to NAS Anacostia on 24 April, 1933, and was initially retained at that station for Service evaluation. The next twenty-five aircraft were sent to NAS North Island, California, where between May and November 1933 they were used to replace the Boeing F4B-2s of VF-5B, one of the two fighter squadrons assigned to the uss *Lexington* (CV-2). The final aircraft went to VF-1B to be flown alongside the Curtiss F11C-2 single-seat fighters then operated by this squadron from North Island and aboard the uss *Saratoga* (CV-3).

Before receiving its FF-1s, which inevitably were nicknamed 'Fifis,' VF-5B had gained some experience with the type as it had briefly evaluated the XFF-1 under operational conditions in mid-1933. Both the XFF-1 and the FF-1s were praised by the Red Rippers for their high speed, exceptional manoeuvrability, good handling characteristics, and sturdiness; however, they were criticized for their restricted forward vision and difficult landing characteristics resulting from the use of a hard and narrow-track undercarriage. Moreover, most pilots experienced difficulties in getting used to flying with the canopy closed, a problem common to all early types of enclosed-cockpit aircraft.

Upon entering service in the spring of 1934, single SF-1s were first delivered to VF-1B, VF-2B, and VF-6B to serve as command aircraft. This

---

* Grumman built fifty-seven fuselages for delivery to Canadian Car & Foundry. However, five of these fuselages appeared not to have been used by the Canadian firm and nothing is known about their final disposition.

An FF-1 of VF-5B. While equipped with Fifis, this squadron served first aboard the USS *Lexington* (CV-2), with yellow tail surfaces, and then aboard the USS *Ranger* (CV-4), with green tail surfaces. (*Courtesy of Hal Andrews*)

practice was later extended to VB-2B and VB-5B, but the bulk of the SF-1s went to VS-3B with which they replaced Vought SU-2s and SU-3s for service at NAS North Island and aboard *Lexington*. Like the FF-1s, the SF-1s were generally well liked by their crews. Both the SF-1s and FF-1s, however, were rapidly overtaken by newer aircraft with higher performance. Furthermore, unlike Great Britain's Fleet Air Arm, the US Navy had already lost interest in two-seat carrier fighters and scout fighters. Accordingly, after being reassigned to the USS *Ranger* (CV-4), VF-5B partially exchanged its FF-1s for F2F-1s in the autumn of 1935 and fully converted to F3F-1s during the following spring. In the same period, VS-3B converted to Vought SBU-1s. Twenty-two FF-1s were then fitted with dual controls and redesignated FF-2s before to being distributed to various Naval Reserve Air Bases or assigned to Marine Reserve Squadrons and ending their career as ground instructional airframes. The last flyable FF-2s were finally grounded in the second half of 1942. A similar fate befell the unmodified SF-1s.

Several of the G-23s assembled by Canadian Car & Foundry and surreptitiously acquired by the Spanish Republican Government had a much longer life than the Grumman-built aircraft, and the G-23 sold to Nicaragua became the sole surviving example of the Grumman two-seat fighter biplane. Brief details of the G-23's operational career with military air arms of five countries are given in alphabetical order.

CANADA: When in June 1938 the final shipment of G-23s consigned to the Turkish Ministry of Defence but actually intended for Spain was

Three SF-1s from VN-6R, a Reserve unit based at NRAB Anacostia, in 1937. *(USN)*

declared illegal by the Canadian Government, the sixteen crated aircraft were disembarked at St John and returned to Canadian Car & Foundry at Fort William. Subsequently, CC&F sold one aircraft to Mexico *(qv)* and assembled c/n 143 to be used as a demonstrator registered CF-BLK. No new foreign customers could be found for that aircraft and, in spite of CC&F's sustained attempts to gain Royal Canadian Air Force interest in these 'fighter trainers,' the remaining G-23s (c/ns 137/142, 144/147, and 149/152) remained unsold until the autumn of 1940 when it became evident that Great Britain could not supply fighters to the RCAF. These fourteen aircraft and the Canadian-registered demonstrator were then taken on charge by the RCAF. Named Goblins and given Canadian serials 334 to 348, they were assigned to No 118 Squadron. After training at Rockliffe, Ontario, No 118 moved to Dartmouth, Nova Scotia. When this squadron began receiving Curtiss Kittyhawks, five of its Goblins remained at Rockliffe and were used briefly by No 123 Army Co-operation Squadron. The last Goblins were struck of charge on 21 April 1942.

JAPAN: The second G-23 (c/n 102) was acquired in 1938 to obtain information on the Grumman retractable undercarriage mechanism. The G-23 proved of little interest as by then Japan had obtained other foreign aircraft equipped with more modern retractable undercarriages and had developed its own undercarriage retraction mechanisms.

RCAF 342, one of the CCF-assembled Goblins assigned to No 118 (Fighter) Squadron in 1941, was struck off strength on 21 April, 1942. *(Public Archives of Canada)*

MEXICO: One of the sixteen G-23s embargoed before being shipped to Spain was delivered to Mexico in the autumn of 1938. It was to have served as a sample for intended sub-licence production, but Mexico did not proceed with this plan and nothing is known of the fate of this aircraft (CC&F c/n 148).

NICARAGUA: The first G-23 (CC&F c/n 101) was among the trio of aircraft obtained by the Fuerza Aérea de la Guardia Nacional de Nicaragua when that service was formed in June 1938. Bearing the serial number GN-3, it saw little service before being consigned to the scrap heap in 1942. It remained there until 1962, when the airframe was acquired by J R Sirmons and was fitted with a Pratt & Whitney R-1340 Wasp engine before being flown back to the United States in 1966. It was then acquired by Grumman, restored in the markings of an FF-1 from VF-5B, and presented to the US Naval Aviation Museum in Pensacola, Florida, where it is now on display as BuNo 9351 with the code 5-F-1.

SPAIN: Covering up their action by using forged Turkish documents, arm dealers working on behalf of the Spanish Republican Government, ordered fifty CC&F-assembled G-23s in two batches, one of forty and one of ten aircraft. Thirty-four crated aircraft (CC&F c/ns 103 to 136) were shipped from St John's, Newfoundland, to Le Havre, France, from where they were trucked to Catalonia, but as previously indicated the second shipment was embargoed.

In Spain the type was named Delfin, and the thirty-four aircraft were assembled at Vich, Catalonia, and given serials AD-001 to AD-034 before being assigned to equip two flights of Grupo Núm 28 at Cardegeu-La Garriga, north of Barcelona. Primarily intended for use in the ground attack role, for which two 110-lb or twelve 22-lb bombs could be carried beneath the wings, the Delfins of Grupo Núm 28 made their combat debut in July 1938. Before the Republican forces surrendered on 30 March, 1939, one of

Well-known view of a *Pedro Rico* operated by the Ejército del Aire after the Spanish Civil War had ended. *(Grumman)*

the Delfins gained the distinction of claiming the only victory credited to Grumman biplanes when its crew shot down a Legión Cóndor Heinkel He 59B. Overall, however, the Delfins did not perform well: three were shot down by enemy aircraft, six were captured by the Nationalists, and twenty were lost in combat and operational accidents. Five escaped to France on the last day of the war but were soon returned to Spain. After the war, these five aircraft along with the six previously captured Delfins were designated R.6s by the newly organized Ejército del Aire and were assigned to Grupo 5W. This unit later moved to Spanish Morocco where the last R.6s, by then nicknamed *Pedro Ricos* on account of their corpulence, were scrapped in 1955, more than twenty-four years after the maiden flight of the first Grumman.

PRODUCTION: A total of 116 aircraft was built, including 64 delivered by Grumman between December 1931 and November 1934 and 52 assembled by Canadian Car & Foundry in 1938-39, as follows:

1	XFF-1		1	XSF-1
27	FF-1		33	XSF-1
(22)	FF-2		1	XSF-2
1	GG-1		52	CC&F G-23

They were assigned the following BuNos, foreign serial numbers, and civil registrations:

XFF-1:	A8878	CC&F G-23:	Nicaraguan serial GN-3
FF-1:	9350/9376		Unknown Japanese serial
XSF-1:	A8940		Spanish serials AD-001/
			AD-034
SF-1:	9460/9492		RCAF serial 334/348
XSF-2:	9493		Unknown Mexican serial
GG-1:	NX12V		

	XFF-1	**FF-1**	**SF-1**	**XSF-2**
DIMENSIONS:				
Span, ft in	34 6	34 6	34 6	34 6
(m)	(10.52)	(10.52)	(10.52)	(10.52)
Length, ft in	24 6	24 6	24 11	24 81/2
(m)	(7.47)	(7.47)	(7.59)	(7.53)
Height, ft in	9 8	11 1	11 1	10 11
(m)	(2.95)	(3.38)	(3.38)	(3.33)
Wing area, sq ft	310	310	310	310
(sq m)	(28.80)	(28.80)	(28.80)	(28.80)
WEIGHTS:				
Empty, lb	2,667	3,098	3,259	2,970
(kg)	(1,210)	(1,405)	(1,478)	(1,347)
Loaded, lb	3,933	4,677	5,072	4,783
(kg)	(1,784)	(2,121)	(2,301)	(2,170)
Wing loading*, lb/sq ft	12.7	15.1	16.4	15.4
(kg/sq m)	(61.9)	(73.6)	(79.9)	(75.3)
Power loading*, lb/hp	6.8	6.7	7.0	6.8
(kg/hp)	(3.1)	(3.0)	(3.2)	(3.1)
PERFORMANCE:				
Max speed, mph/ft	195/sl	207/4,000	206/4,000	215/8,900
(kmh/m)	(314/sl)	(333/1,220)	(331/1,220)	(346/2,715)
Climb rate, ft/min	5,000/4.3	5,000/2.99	1,650/1	5,000/3.2
(m/sec)	(5.9)	(8.8)	(8.4)	(7.9)
Service ceiling, ft	23,600	22,100	22,500	24,100
(m)	(7,195)	(6,735)	(6,860)	(7,345)
Normal range, miles	818	685	800	934
(km)	(1,315)	(1,100)	(1,285)	(1,505)

* wing and power loadings are calculated at normal loaded weight and maximum take-off power.

A JF-1 from VJ-1 with green tail surfaces and main float tip. *(USN/National Archives)*

Grumman JF and J2F Duck

In 1928, the US Navy first assigned the type or class letter J to identify transport aircraft and subsequently ordered single examples of the Atlantic XJA-1, the Fairchild XJQ-1 and XJ2Q-1, and the Ford XJR-1, which were respectively military versions of the single-engined Fokker Super Universal, and the Fairchild FC-2 light transports, and the Ford Tri-Motor transport. Then, in 1931, the Navy re-assigned the letter J to identify a new category of aircraft intended as a general utility type for assignment to utility flights aboard carriers and to newly organized Utility Squadrons (VJ). The distinction of becoming the first type of aircraft to be designed as a general utility aircraft to meet specific Navy requirements went to the Grumman Design 7 single-engined amphibian. Preliminary design work began in Baldwin during the summer of 1931, and a prototype was ordered as the XJF-1 in 1932 just as Grumman was about to vacate its leased hangar in Valley Stream. The first flight was made in Farmingdale in April 1933, and the last Grumman-built aircraft in the series was completed in Bethpage in March 1942.

Conceptually, Design 7 was a descendant of the Loening OL amphibians on which the principal Grumman founders had worked during their days with the Loening Aeronautical Engineering Corporation. Technically, it combined features of the XFF-1, particularly the semi-monocoque fuselage design, with those of the Model B float. When first proposed to the Navy, Design 7 was also offered as landplane with a retractable undercarriage similar to that fitted to the XFF-1. Furthermore, its equal-span single-bay wings were similar in design to those of the XFF-1 but had greater overall span and area and were fitted with ailerons on all four outboard panels.

Some sixteen months went by between the time Grumman first discussed its proposed utility landplane or amphibian and the ordering of the XJF-1

64

prototype (c/n 103, BuNo 9218) under Contract 26467, as the Navy did not have funds immediately available. During this period, requirements were refined until the need to stress the aircraft for catapult launch from warships was eliminated from the specification. Construction of the prototype was undertaken immediately after the move to the Farmingdale plant and was completed in April 1933 with Paul Hovgard making the first flight on the 24th from the grass field in front of the plant.

Production history

The Grumman utility amphibian was first ordered into quantity production in early 1934 when the Navy Department awarded Contract 32111 for twenty-seven JF-1s. Three other JF variants were then built for the Navy, the Marine Corps, the Coast Guard, and for export to Argentina. An enlarged and more versatile variant of the Duck, the J2F-1, was first ordered in 1935 with subsequent orders resulting in the production of four additional models for the US military and, again, one model for Argentina. Finally, to enable Grumman to concentrate on the production of fighters and torpedo bombers, manufacture of the Duck was transferred in 1942 to Columbia Aircraft Corporation in Valley Stream.

XJF-1: Powered by a 700-hp Pratt & Whitney R-1830-62 fourteen-cylinder radial driving a three-blade propeller, the XJF-1 had a crew of two sitting in tandem under a fully enclosed canopy. In addition, accommodation was provided in the rear of the float for two passengers sitting side-by-side in a lower compartment accessible through folding doors in the floor of the rear cockpit. Armament consisted of one flexible 0.30-in machine-gun firing aft and two 100-lb bombs on wing racks. The amphibian float was faired into the lower fuselage, much as had been done before on Loening amphibians, with the mainwheels and struts retracting upward by means of chains and sprockets. A non-retractable tailwheel/water-rudder combination was mounted at the aft end of the float. Whereas the arrester hook in Model A and B floats had been attached at the rear of the float, that of the XJF-1 was attached beneath the rear fuselage.

The XJF-1 taking off from Farmingdale for its first flight, on 24 April, 1933. (*Grumman*)

65

J2F-3 (BuNo 1587) alongside the USS *Wasp* (CV-7) on 25 August, 1940. *(USN/National Archives)*

When first flown on 24 April, 1933, and as delivered on 4 May, for evaluation by the Navy at NAS Anacostia, District of Columbia, the XJF-1 had been characterized by triangular vertical tail surfaces with a rather pointed rudder. This arrangement, however, resulted in some longitudinal instability and the aircraft had to be returned several times to Grumman to be fitted with modified surfaces. After first trying the simple expedient of broadening the chord of the upper portion of the fin, Grumman had to redesign entirely the vertical tail surfaces which then took on the broader and squarer appearance found on production aircraft. The XJ-1 was then redelivered to NAS Anacostia in January 1934 and, as the new surfaces solved the earlier directional problem, the aircraft was almost immediately accepted for service. Sent to NAS Norfolk, Virginia, BuNo 9218 crashed in the James River on 8 March, 1934.

JF-1: The twenty-seven JF-1s (BuNos 9434/9455 and 9523/9527) built in the Farmingdale plant and delivered to the Navy and the Marine Corps beginning in May 1934 were similar to the XJF-1 with its redesigned vertical tail surfaces. Although retaining provision for the installation of the dorsal gun and bomb racks, the JF-1s were normally not fitted with armament and were often operated as three-seaters with the addition of a radio operator.

JF-2: Built in two batches (c/ns 188/196 and 263/268) and designated Design 9 by the manufacturer, the fifteen JF-2s were unarmed utility aircraft ordered for the US Coast Guard for use from shore bases and aboard cutters. In addition to being unarmed, the JF-2s differed from the JF-1s in being powered by a 700-hp Wright R-1820-102 nine-cylinder radial fitted with a narrow-chord cowling and driving a three-blade propeller. They were also distinguished by the installation of a radio direction finder with a loop antenna aft of the canopy. The first fourteen aircraft were delivered in

A J2F-5 'trapping' aboard the USS *Charger* (AVG-30) during training operations in Chesapeake Bay on 2 August, 1942. (*USN/National Archives*)

1934-35 and initially received USCG serial numbers 161 to 174. On 13 October, 1936, they were renumbered V135 to V148. The fifteenth JF-2, which would have been serialled 175 in the original Coast Guard system, was transferred to the Navy for assignment to the Marine Corps and given BuNo 0266. Later on, at least three other JF-2s were transferred to the Navy with which they became BuNos 00371/00372 and 01647.

JF-3: Five unarmed JF-3s (BuNos 9835/9839) were delivered in 1935 for use by Navy and Marine reserve units. They were powered by a 750-hp R-1820-80 and, like the JF-2s, did not have an arrester hook. In the Grumman nomenclature, this model was known as Design 10, or G-10.

G-20: Although they were essentially similar to the JF-2s of the Coast Guard, the eight unarmed aircraft (c/ns 357 to 364) ordered by Argentina came out of the Farmingdale plant after the J2F-1s and were given a separate Design Number, G-20. C/n 357, the first Grumman aircraft built for export, first flew on 18 December, 1936. All G-20s were shipped in February 1937. In service with the Aviación de la Flota de Mar, these R-1820-powered aircraft carried the serials 0068/0074 (plus one unknown serial) and were initially coded M-0-1/M-0-8.

J2F-1: Designated G-15 by Grumman, as were all subsequent Duck models, the J2F-1 was a more polyvalent development of the JF-1 which could be used not only for the usual utility/light transport duties but also for target towing, smoke laying, photographic surveying, and medical evacuation (in which case a stretcher was carried in the float in place of the two passenger seats). The J2F-1 was characterized by the use of a float with greater length and was powered by a 750-hp Wright R-1820-20. Twenty-

67

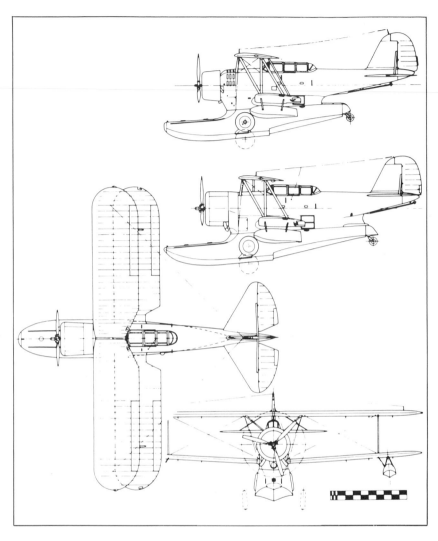

Grumman J2F-5 Duck. Side view of JF-1 (top)

nine were built for the Navy before Grumman moved to Bethpage. The first (BuNo 0162) was delivered to NAS Anacostia in April 1936 and, after the Navy completed its evaluation of that aircraft, BuNos 0163/0190 followed between January and June 1937. Provision was made for the installation of a flexible dorsal gun and the carriage of two bombs on wing racks but armament was seldom installed. The tailhook was again fitted.

J2F-1A: The first G-15, BuNo 0162, was later modified by the Navy and was experimentally fitted with full span flaps on the upper wings. It may then have been unofficially known as the J2F-1A.

J2F-2: Differing from the J2F-1s in being powered by the 790-hp R-1820-30 and in being armed with a forward-firing 0.30 in gun and a flexible 0.30 in gun in the rear cockpit, thirty J2F-2s (BuNos 0780/0794 and 1195/1209) were built in the Bethpage plant and were delivered to the Navy and the Marine Corps between June and November 1938.

J2F-2A: This designation identified nine Marine J2F-2s (BuNos 1198/1206) which were modified in 1939 to be used by VMS-3 in providing Neutrality Patrol over the Caribbean Sea. For that purpose, they had their single rear defence gun replaced by twin guns and were fitted with two bomb racks beneath each lower wing.

J2F-3: Twenty unarmed J2F-3s (BuNos 1568/1587) were ordered as 'admiral barges' and for use by US Naval Attachés. Powered by a 790-hp R-1820-36 driving a constant-speed propeller instead of the previously used variable pitch unit, they were delivered between February and June 1939.

J2F-4: The J2F-4 was a utility version with provision for armament and various operational gear, such as target towing and smoke laying equipment. Thirty-two (BuNos 1639/1670) were delivered to the Navy between September 1939 and June 1940.

J2F-5: This was Grumman's main production version of the Duck with 144 (BuNos 00659/00802) being delivered between July 1941 and March 1942. The J2F-5s differed from the J2F-4s in having a more powerful Cyclone engine, the 950-hp R-1820-50, fitted within a broader chord cowling in which the oil cooler was incorporated. Stronger bomb racks were fitted to enable two 325-lb depth charges to be carried. The J2F-5s had no forward-firing guns but usually had a flexible rear-firing gun.

J2F-6: At the behest of the Navy Department, Grumman transferred

This J2F-3 (BuNo 1569) was operated as an 'admiral's barge' for Rear Admiral Wilson Brown, Superintendent of the US Naval Academy at Annapolis, Maryland, in 1939. (*USN/National Archives*)

responsibility for the J2F production to Columbia Aircraft Corporation, a small company which had its plant in Valley Stream, near the facility which had housed Grumman from November 1931 until November 1932. With the exception of the two XJL-1 prototypes described on pages 274-275 the only aircraft built by Columbia were 330 J2F-6s (BuNos 32637/32786, 33535/33614, and 36935/37034). Production ended in August 1945 following contract cancellation at the end of the war. These last Ducks were essentially similar to the J2F-5s but were powered by 1,050-hp R-1820-54 radials.

OA-12: This designation was given to the second J2F-5 (BuNo 00660) after it was transferred to the Army Air Forces in 1942. In AAF service, it carried the serial 42-7771.

OA-12A: This was the designation given by the USAF to five ex-USN J2F-6s which were acquired in 1947. These aircraft were overhauled at the Warner Robins AMC, Georgia, and given Air Force serials 48-563/48-567 before being assigned to the 10th Rescue Squadron in Alaska.

OA-12B: This was the designation given to three surplus J2F-6s which were overhauled and modified by the USAF at the Warner Robins AMC. For administrative purposes, they received the Air Force serials 48-1373/48-1375 before being transferred to the Fuerza Aérea Colombiana in 1948.

G-15: Similar to the J2F-4s, except for the removal of the tailhook, these four aircraft ordered by Argentina (c/ns 612/615, Argentine naval serials 0090/0093) were simply known by their Grumman Design Number, G-15. They were shipped to Argentina in November 1939.

Service history

The first JF-1 was delivered to NAS Norfolk, Virginia, in May 1934. All twenty-seven JF-1s, including some handed over to the Marine Corps, were in service by the beginning of February 1935. With the Navy, these aircraft were distributed among Utility Squadron One (VJ-1, the principal user of JF-1s), Utility Units assigned to the carriers *Lexington*, *Ranger*, and *Saratoga*, and Utility Units at various Naval Air Stations on the mainland and at Fleet Air Bases outside the forty-eight contiguous states (Cavite in the Philippine Islands, Coco Solo in the Canal Zone, and Pearl Harbor in the Territory of Hawaii). The next Ducks to enter service with the Navy were the JF-3s which were flown by reservists from six Naval Air Reserve Bases.

When deliveries of J2F-1s began in January 1937, these improved Ducks were used to replace JF-1s with VJ-1 and Utility Units aboard older carriers and to equip Utility Units aboard new carriers (*Yorktown*, *Enterprise*, and *Wasp*). In service with Navy Utility Units and Squadrons, the JF-1s and J2F-1s were supplemented by J2F-2s and J2F-4s between 1938 and 1940 and by the first J2F-5s during the second half of 1941. In addition, during the first six months of 1939, the Navy received its plusher J2F-3s and

70

The first of four Argentine G-15s at Bethpage on 30 October, 1939, before being exported. The Argentine G-15s differed from US G-15s notably in being completed without arrester hooks as Argentina did not then have an aircraft carrier. *(Grumman)*

In December 1935, this Marine JF-2 (BuNo 0266) was flown by a VJ-6M crew to set an unofficial speed record of 191 mph in the single-engined amphibian class. *(USMC/National Archives)*

assigned them to flag officers at various bases (including BuNo 1569 which was provided to the Commandant of the US Naval Academy at Annapolis, Maryland) and to US Naval Attachés.

The Marine Corps first obtained four JF-1s and one JF-2 in 1935 for assignment to VJ-6M and VJ-7M (these two utility squadrons being respectively redesignated VMJ-1 and VMJ-2 in July 1937). Noteworthy is the fact that in December 1935, when based at Quantico, Virginia, the sole JF-2 operated by the Marines (BuNo 0266) was flown by a VJ-6M crew at a speed of 191 mph to set an unofficial speed record for single-engined amphibians. In 1939, these early Ducks were followed in the Marine Corps by nine J2F-2As carrying armament and assigned to VMS-3 at Bourne Field, Charlotte Amalie, on St Thomas in the Virgin Islands, to fly on Neutrality Patrol over the Caribbean Sea.

At the end of 1941, the Navy and Marine Corps had a total of 184 Ducks on hand (13 JF-1s, 3 JF-3s, 23 J2F-1s, 28 J2F-2/J2F-2As, 17 J2F-3s, 32 J2F-4s, and 68 J2F-5s). This represented a low attrition rate as, since the XJF-1 had been delivered in January 1934, only 213 Ducks had been assigned to the Navy and Marine Corps. Wartime production added seventy-six Grumman-built J2F-5s and 330 Columbia-built J2F-6s which were distributed among Navy, Marine, and Coast Guard units.

Although most Navy and Marine Ducks were retained at bases in the continental United States or away from the front, others distinguished themselves in the Pacific during often dangerous rescue and combat support operations. Among such activities, mention ought to be made of those undertaken by the two J2F-5s which had been assigned to Cavite when Japanese forces attacked the Philippines. After these two aircraft brought in supplies and evacuated wounded personnel for several weeks during the siege of Bataan, one finally flew out from Cabcaben on 8 April, 1942, to bring to safety six VIP passengers, including Carlos Romulo who later became President of the Philippines.

Beginning at the onset of the long battle for Guadalcanal in August 1942, and continuing for three years until Japan was defeated, a small number of Ducks were put to good use by the Marines, and to a lesser extent by Navy crews, to pick up downed flyers at sea or from Japanese-held islands. However, this work remained mostly unheralded. Then, after the war had ended, the Navy and the Marine Corps quickly disposed of their remaining J2F-5s and J2F-6s; some were scrapped, others sold as surplus, and a few transferred to the Coast Guard.

Of course, the Duck was no stranger to Coast Guard crews. In 1934 the USCG, then part of the Treasury Department, had ordered fifteen JF-2s. One of these aircraft was exchanged for a Lockheed XR3O-1 but the fourteen others were given USCG serial numbers 161/174 and delivered for operations from shore stations (San Diego and San Francisco, California; Miami and St Petersburg, Florida; Cape May, New Jersey; Salem, Oregon; and Port Angeles, Washington) and aboard cutters (*Northland* and the seven ships in the *Treasury* class). In addition, the Coast Guard had also obtained one of the plusher J2F-3s, but this aircraft was not assigned an USCG serial number.

On 1 November, 1941, the Coast Guard was placed under the operational control of the Navy and thereafter its prewar Ducks were supplemented by J2F-5s and J2F-6s and were used mainly for rescue operations along the Atlantic seaboard, in the Gulf of Mexico, and from cutters operating in the North Atlantic. After the Coast Guard was returned to the control of the Treasury Department at the end of the war, some Ducks were retained until

A J2F-5 aboard the 2,065-ton cutter USCGC *Northland* (PG-49) in 1943. *(US Coast Guard)*

the early fifties when the type was finally phased out of service some seventeen years after being first operated by the Navy.

Ducks entered USAF service in 1948 when five OA-12As were assigned to the 10th Rescue Squadron for operations in Alaska from Elmendorf AFB in Anchorage and Ladd AFB in Fairbanks. One of these aircraft, 48-563, crashed in Chekatna Lake in August 1948 but was subsequently recovered by collectors. The four others were withdrawn from use in the early fifties.

Although in 1937 eight G-20s had become the first new aircraft to be exported by Grumman, Ducks only saw limited service outside the United States, as follows:

ARGENTINA: The eight G-20s shipped by Grumman in February 1937 replaced Vought O2U-1As in service with the Escuadrilla Aeronaval de Observación at BAN Comandante Espora and for detachment aboard the cruisers *Almirante Brown* and *Veinticinco de Mayo*. After being supplemented in the autumn of 1939 by four G-15s (one of which had been ordered as a replacement for a G-20 which had been lost on 27 May, 1938), the Argentine Ducks were distributed among two observation escadrilles, one at BAN Comandante Espora and one at BAN Punta Indio. Few of the G-15s and G-20s remained airworthy when Argentina obtained twenty-two J2F-5s and nine J2F-6s from US surplus stocks in 1948. In September 1955, some of these aircraft took part in operations leading to the ousting of Juan Peron. The Escuadrilla Aeronaval de Observación was disbanded during the

73

An Air Force OA-12A (48-566) of the 10th Air Rescue Squadron in Alaska. (*R B Hamel, courtesy of David W Menard*)

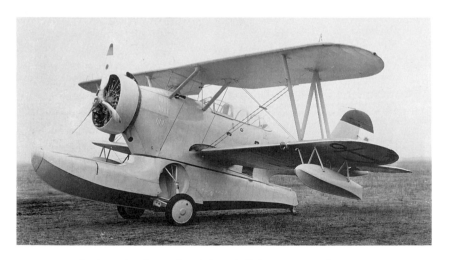

An Argentine G-20 before delivery in February 1937. (*Grumman*)

following year, but at least one of the Ducks remained operational in Argentina until 1959.

COLOMBIA: In 1948, after that nation became a signatory of the 1947 Inter-American Treaty of Reciprocal Assistance ('Rio Pact'), three OA-12Bs were transferred by the USAF to the Fuerza Aérea Colombiana. Nothing is known about the use made by the Colombians of these ex J2F-6s.

MEXICO: Two J2F-6s were acquired by the Aviación Naval Mexicana in 1947 and, carrying the AVM codes MV-07 and MV-08, were operated from

Vera Cruz until 1951. The survivor, MV-08, was then sold in the United States.

A number of surplus J2F-5s and J2F-6s went onto the US civil register but saw little use. The best known was a J2F-6 (N67790, ex-BuNo 33587) which starred in a 1974 Hollywood production, *Murphy's War*. At least four Ducks – including a J2F-6 (N67790, ex-BuNo 33587) which had been used for aerial fire fighting – ended up in US civilian and military museums. Abroad, two Ducks of unknown origin were included in 1946 in the initial fleet of Aerovias Nacionales del Ecuador SA (ANDESA), a small Ecuadorian company which went bankrupt in 1948.

PRODUCTION: A total of 645 aircraft was built, including 315 produced by Grumman between April 1933 and March 1942 and 330 produced by Columbia Aircraft Corporation in 1942-45, as follows:

1	XJF-1	32	J2F-4
27	JF-1	144	J2F-5
15	JF-2	330	J2F-6
5	JF-3	(1)	OA-12
29	J2F-1	(5)	OA-12A
30	J2F-2	(3)	OA-12B
(9)	J2F-2A	4	G-15
20	J2F-3	8	G-20

They were assigned the following BuNos and military serial numbers:

XJF-1:	BuNo 9218	J2F-4:	BuNos 1639/1670
JF-1:	BuNos 9434/9455	J2F-5:	BuNos 00659/00802
	BuNos 9523/9527	J2F-6:	BuNos 32637/32786
JF-2:	USCG 161/175		BuNos 33535/33614
QT			
JF-3:	BuNos 9835/9839		BuNos 36935/37034
J2F-1:	BuNos 0162/0190	OA-12:	(AAF 42-7771)
J2F-2:	BuNos 0780/0794	OA-12A:	(AF 48-563/48-567)
	BuNos 1195/1209	OA-12B:	(AF 48-1373/48-1375)
J2F-2A:	(BuNos 1198/1206)	G-15:	0090/0093
J2F-3:	BuNos 1568/1587	G-20:	0068/0074 plus one unknown

	JF-1	J2F-2A	J2F-6
DIMENSIONS:			
Span, ft in	39 0	39 0	39 0
(m)	(11.89)	(11.89)	(11.89)
Length, ft in	33 0	34 0	34 0
(m)	(10.06)	(10.36)	(10.36)
Height, ft in	14 6	12 4	12 4
(m)	(4.42)	(3.76)	(3.76)
Wing area, sq ft	409	409	409
(sq m)	(38.00)	(38.00)	(38.00)

WEIGHTS:			
Empty, lb	4,133	4,300	5,445
(kg)	(1,875)	(1,950)	(2,470)
Loaded, lb	5,375	6,180	7,290
(kg)	(2,438)	(2,803)	(3,307)
Wing loading,* lb/sq ft	13.1	15.1	17.8
(kg/sq m)	(64.2)	(73.8)	(87.0)
Power loading,* lb/hp	7.7	7.8	6.9
(kg/hp)	(3.5)	(3.5)	(3.1)
PERFORMANCE:			
Max speed, mph/ft	168/sl	179/sl	190/14,000
(kmh/m)	(270/sl)	(288/sl)	(306/4,265)
Cruising speed, mph	–	150	155
(kmh)	(–)	(241)	(249)
Climb rate, ft/min	–	1,500/1	1,330/1
(m/sec)	(–)	(7.6)	(6.8)
Service ceiling, ft	18,000	21,600	26,700
(m)	(5,485)	(6,585)	(8,140)
Normal range, miles	–	780	675
(km)	(–)	(1,255)	(1,085)
Max range, miles	–	–	850
(km)	(–)	(–)	(1,370)

* wing and power loadings are calculated at normal loaded weight and maximum take-off power.

BuNo 9652, an F2F-1 from VF-2 over Southern California on 7 July, 1939. The tail surfaces are white, indicating that the squadron was assigned to the USS *Saratoga* (CV-3). (*USN/ National Archives*)

Grumman F2F

During the late 1920s, when it was confronted with tight budget constraints and hence needed to find ways to limit unnecessary losses, the US Navy found considerable merit in a proposal from Hall Aluminum Aircraft Corporation to develop a carrier fighter with an all-metal watertight structure capable of keeping the aircraft afloat in the event of ditching. The aircraft developed to meet this requirement, the Hall XFH-1, first flew in 1929 but proved disappointing during evaluation at NAS Anacostia. Nevertheless, the idea of having an aircraft capable of floating indefinitely following an emergency alighting on water was thought by BuAer to have much merit and the Grumman XFF-1, like other aircraft of the period, was fitted with quickly inflatable flotation bags. However, the effectiveness of these inflatable bags was considered to be marginal and the Navy sought to obtain aircraft with a watertight structure. On the other hand, the anticipated performance of the XFF-1 proved a strong incentive for the Navy to acquire single-seat fighters with substantially better performance than the Boeing F4B then under development. These two sets of considerations led BuAer to seek new designs and provided the framework for ordering a new Grumman single-seat fighter.

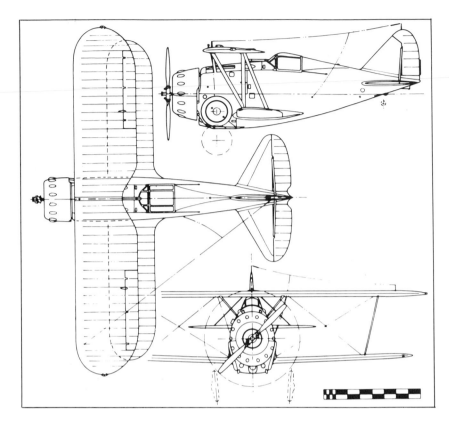

Grumman F2F-1

First discussed in the autumn of 1932, while the XFF-1 was undergoing trials at NAS Anacostia but before the FF-1 was ordered into production, Design 8 was proposed as a diminutive single-seater with a watertight monocoque fuselage which, on the power of a Pratt & Whitney R-1535 fourteen-cylinder radial, would exceed the performance of both the Boeing F4B single-seat carrier fighter and the XFF-1 two-seat fighter. The Grumman G-8 proposal further specified that the aircraft would be carefully streamlined, with the tailwheel and arrester hook retracting into the rear fuselage, and that the hook would be located in such a way that it would eliminate the tail rise experienced by most aircraft during arrested landings.

Smaller and lighter than the FF-1, with span of 28 ft 6 in versus 34 ft 6 in and loaded weight of 3,490 lb versus 4,677 lb, Design 8 was to be more streamlined than Grumman's earlier fighter as it was to be powered by a closely-cowled Pratt & Whitney Twin Wasp Jr twin-row radial instead of a Wright Cyclone single-row engine with a Townend cowling ring. Hence, although its engine developed 100 less hp at low altitude, the G-8 was

78

expected to be nearly 15 per cent faster than the G-5. The promise of this proposal was such that an XF2F-1 prototype was ordered on 2 November, 1932.

Production history

Although the XF2F-1 displayed some difficult handling characteristics during Navy evaluation in 1933-34, its performance was such that a contract for the production of fifty-four F2F-1s was awarded on 17 May, 1934. Later, a replacement aircraft was substituted for one lost during a dust storm while being ferried to California. Follow on orders, however, were placed not for F2F-1s but for F3F-1s, which had somewhat less demanding flying characteristics.

XF2F-1: Powered by a 650-hp Pratt & Whitney R-1535-44 twin-row radial, the XF2F-1 (c/n 131, BuNo 9342) was of similar construction to the FF-1 with all-metal fuselage and tail surfaces, fabric covered single-bay wings, and retractable undercarriage. Its rear-sliding canopy fully enclosed the small cockpit. Two synchronized 0.30-in machine guns were mounted above the forward fuselage (with the usual provision for substituting a 0.50-in gun for the starboard weapon) and two 100-lb bombs could be carried beneath the wings.

Completed at Farmingdale in October 1933, BuNo 9342 was first flown by James H 'Jimmy' Collins on the 18th of that month and was ferried the same day to NAS Anacostia. There Jimmy Collins and Navy pilots found the aircraft to have excellent manoeuvrability and outstanding performance; a top speed of 229 mph was reached at 8,400 ft and an altitude of 3,080 ft was attained in one minute. They also found that it required careful handling, had marginal directional stability, and tended to go into a spin easily (fortunately, recovery was found to be quick).

Early during the evaluation programme, the smooth cowling was replaced by a slightly smaller one incorporating rocker arm blisters, a telescopic gun sight projecting through the windshield was added, and a tall

The XF2F-1 (BuNo 9342) at NAS Anacostia, on 20 October, 1933. (*USN/National Archives*)

radio mast was fitted aft of the cockpit. Following preliminary evaluation at NAS Anacostia and service evaluation at NAS Norfolk (including carrier trials undertaken by VF-2B pilots aboard *Lexington*), the XF2F-1 was permanently assigned to Anacostia. It was there that on 12 April, 1938, it was damaged beyond repair in a flying accident.

F2F-1: The fifty-four F2F-1s originally ordered (BuNos 9623/9676) and BuNo 9997, which was ordered in 1935 as a replacement for BuNo 9634, were essentially similar to the XF2F-1 as modified with revised cowling and telescopic gun sight. However, they were not fitted with the tall radio mast and were powered by the 650-hp R-1535-72. They were delivered between January and August 1935.

Service history

During most of their operational life, the F2F-1s were flown by three Fighting Squadrons. VF-2B, which was assigned to *Lexington* and was redesignated VF-2 in July 1937, converting from F4B-2s beginning in February 1935. It kept its small Grumman biplanes until September 1940 when it acquired Brewster F2A-3s. VF-3B received its F2F-1s during the spring of 1935, while assigned to *Ranger,* and retained these aircraft when its was transferred to *Yorktown* and renumbered VF-7B before becoming VF-5 in July 1937. This squadron converted to F3F-3s in late 1938. The F2F-1s relinquished by VF-5 were then given to a new squadron, VF-7, which operated them briefly aboard *Wasp* and ashore before converting to F4F-3s.

In June 1937, a pair of F2F-1s and six F3F-1s were assigned as interim equipment to VF-4M in San Diego. One month later this Marine squadron was redesignated VMF-2 and shortly thereafter received its F3F-2s. However, VMF-2 retained its two F2F-1s until the following summer.

With the Navy, the F3F-1 was phased out from first-line service in September 1940 when VF-2 transferred its eighteen aircraft to NAS Pensacola. Nevertheless, on 31 December, 1941, the Navy still had twenty-

An F2F-1 used at NAS Seattle, Washington, in 1941 to provide gunnery training for Patrol Squadrons. (*Chester W Phillips, courtesy of Hal Andrews*)

F2F-1s from the 2nd section of Fighting Squadron Two flying near NAS San Diego in July 1939. The white tail surfaces identify VF-2 as assigned to the USS *Saratoga* (CV-3). (*Grumman*)

three F3F-1s on strength, these aircraft being distributed among fighter training units at NAS Miami and NAS Pensacola. During 1942, the last F3F-1s ended their careers as ground instructional airframes.

PRODUCTION: One XF2F-1 and 55 F2F-1s were built by Grumman between October 1933 and October 1935 and were assigned the following BuNos:

XF2F-1:	BuNo 9342	F2F-1:	BuNos 9623/9676 and 9997

	XF2F-1	F2F-1
DIMENSIONS:		
Span, ft in	28 6	28 6
(m)	(8.69)	(8.69)
Length, ft in	21 1	21 5
(m)	(6.43)	(6.53)
Height, ft in	8 6	9 1
(m)	(2.59)	(2.77)
Wing area, sq ft	230	230
(sq m)	(21.37)	(21.37)
WEIGHTS:		
Empty, lb	2,525	2,691
(kg)	(1,145)	(1,221)
Loaded, lb	3,490	3,847
(kg)	(1,583)	(1,745)
Maximum, lb	3,690	4,050
(kg)	(1,674)	(1,837)
Wing loading*, lb/sq ft	15.2	16.7
(kg/sq m)	(74.1)	(81.7)
Power loading*, lb/hp	5.4	5.5
(kg/hp)	(2.4)	(2.5)
PERFORMANCE:		
Max speed, mph/ft	229/8,400	231/7,500
(kmh/m)	(368/2,560)	(372/2,285)
Cruising speed, mph	198	–
(kmh)	(319)	(–)
Climb rate, ft/min	3,080/1	2,050/1
(m/sec)	(15.6)	(10.4)
Service ceiling, ft	29,800	27,100
(m)	(9,085)	(8,260)
Normal range, miles	543	–
(km)	(875)	(–)
Max range, miles	750	985
(km)	(1,205)	(1,585)

* wing and power loadings are calculated at normal loaded weight and maximum take-off power.

An F3F-1 from VF-4 on 17 January, 1939. Assigned to the USS *Ranger* (CV-4), the aircraft has green tail surfaces. The forward portion of the cowling and the rear fuselage band are blue, indicating that the aircraft is that of the leader of the 3rd section. *(USN/National Archives)*

Grumman F3F

Basically, Design 11 was nothing more than an improved Design 8, incorporating relatively simple modifications to correct the directional stability problem and excessive tendency to spin which had been encountered during initial trials with the XF2F-1. Yet, this slightly larger aircraft received a new military designation, XF3F-1, instead of being designated F2F-2 as would have been logical. At first this new designation proved inauspicious for the third type of Grumman carrier fighter. On 22 March, 1935, two days after its maiden flight in Farmingdale, the first prototype crashed and its pilot was killed. On 13 May, seven and a-half weeks after this accident, the pilot of a hastily built replacement was forced to bale out. Grumman again had to bear the cost of a replacement.

Production history

Fortunately for Grumman, the third XF3F-1 successfully completed its initial Navy trials in August 1935 and on the 24th of that month Grumman was awarded a contract for fifty-four F3F-1s. Subsequent orders enabled the eventual re-equipment of all Navy and Marine fighter squadrons with either F2Fs or F3Fs.

XF3F-1: Ordered on 15 October, 1934, and first flown on 20 March 1935, the original prototype (c/n 257, BuNo 9727) crashed on 22 March near a Farmingdale cemetery. The pilot, Jimmy Collins, was killed after pulling 14g in an attempted recovery at the end of the tenth and final terminal velocity dive scheduled for that day. A replacement aircraft, which was given the same c/n and BuNo and had reinforced lower wing-to-fuselage fittings and a strengthened engine mount, flew at Farmingdale on 9 May and was immediately ferried to NAS Anacostia. Four days later it was lost as Lee Gehlbach had to bale out when unable to recover from a flat spin. A third XF3F-1, which with notable disregard for superstition was again given the c/n and BuNo of the first prototype, differed in having a small increase in fin area below the tailplane. It was flown to NAS Anacostia in June 1935 and after successfully completing the contractual terminal velocity dive demonstration was handed over to the Navy on 10 July. At the end of a long career at Anacostia, this aircraft was transferred to NAS Miami where in 1942 it was last used as a fighter-trainer.

Whereas the first two XF3F-1s were powered by the 700-hp Pratt & Whitney R-1535-72 as used on the F2F-1s, the third aircraft had a similarly rated R-1535-84. All three prototypes differed from the F2F-1s in having fuselages lengthened from 21 ft 5 in to 23 ft and wings of greater span and area (32 ft versus 28 ft 6 in and 261 sq ft versus 230 sq ft). Although these changes did improve directional stability, they only slightly reduced the tendency to spin. Nevertheless, the flying characteristics were sufficiently improved for the Navy to accept the type for production.

F3F-1: With the exception of a small increase in fuselage length (3 in), the fifty-four F3F-1s (BuNos 0211/0264) built in Farmingdale and delivered between January and September 1936 were similar to the third XF3F-1.

The third XF3F-1 to bear BuNo 9727 was delivered to NAS Anacostia in June 1935. (*Grumman*)

84

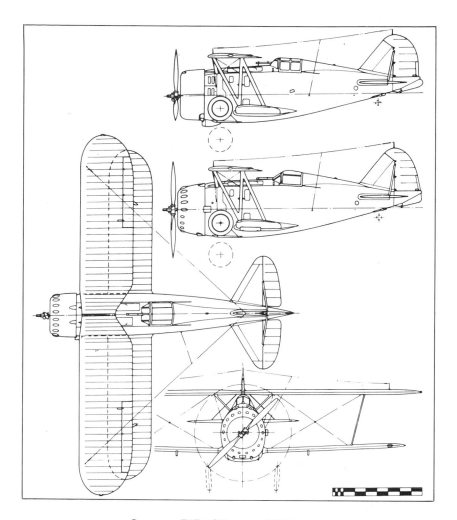

Grumman F3F-1 Side view of F3F-2 (top)

Like this prototype, they were armed with one 0.50-in gun on the starboard side of the fuselage decking and one 0.30-in gun on the opposite side and could be fitted with wing racks for two 100-lb bombs.

XF3F-2: Proposed by Grumman in June 1936, Design 19 was a development of Design 11 with the small twin-row Twin Wasp Jr radial and two-blade propeller of Design 11 replaced by a single-row Cyclone G driving a three-blade propeller. As calculated performance with a 950-hp Wright XR-1820-22 closely approximated that predicted for Design 16 (then under development as the XF4F-1), the Navy quickly agreed with Grumman's recommendation of abandoning Design 16 in favour of Design 18, the monoplane fighter which became the XF4F-2, and ordering a Design 19 prototype as the XF3F-2. First flown on 27 July, 1936, and delivered on that date to NAS Anacostia, the XF3F-2 (c/n 354, BuNo 0452) immediately demonstrated sprightly performance with top speed being increased to 254 mph (a 10 per cent gain over that achieved by the F3F-1). Fuel tank capacity was increased from 110 US gal, as provided for the F2F-1s and F3F-1s, to 130 gal. In April 1938 this aircraft was brought to full F3F-2 standards for assignment to operational squadrons.

F3F-2: Charactized by a broader rudder and powered by a 950-hp Wright R-1820-22, the eighty-one F3F-2s (BuNos 0967/1047) were built in Bethpage and delivered between July 1937 and May 1938.

XF3F-3: In an attempt to achieve the best possible performance without the need for a major redesign, the sixty-fifth F3F-2 (BuNo 1031) was returned to Grumman in May 1938 to be fitted with a new windshield, a more closely streamlined cowling, and revised wing leading edges. It was then tested in flight at Anacostia and in the NACA wind tunnel at Langley. In October 1938, BuNo 1031 was modified once again so that the Navy could evaluate the split flaps being developed by Grumman for the G-32 and G-32A. Fitted beneath the upper wing, inboard of the ailerons, the flaps did reduce approach and landing speeds but not enough for the Navy to request that they be fitted to production F3F-2s.

F3F-3: The final production version of the Grumman biplane fighter differed almost imperceptibly from the XF3F-3. The main external difference was a return to the F3F-2 windshield design and the addition of framing on the rear-sliding canopy. Twenty-seven (BuNos 1444/1470) were delivered between December 1938 and May 1939.

G-22: During the 1930s, several major oil companies in the United States retained the services of well-known pilots and purchased special aircraft to help promote their sales. This was notably the case of the Gulf Oil Company

The XF3F-3, with underwing bomb racks, at Bethpage in the late spring of 1938. *(Grumman)*

Al Williams's Gulfhawk II in December 1936. This aircraft is now in the National Air and Space Museum in Washington, DC. (*Grumman*)

which in 1936 bought the sole Design 22 for its demonstration pilot, Al Williams.

Powered by a 940-hp Wright GR-1820-G1, the G-22 was an hybrid using the wings of the F2F-1, the fuselage and powerplant installation of the XF3F-2, and the enlarged vertical tail surfaces of the F3F-2s but without the increase in fin area below the tailplane. Bearing c/n 355, registered NR1050, and named *Gulfhawk II*, this aircraft first flew on 6 December, 1936. Twelve years later, it was donated to the National Air and Space Museum.

G-24: Design 24 was an advanced trainer which was proposed in February 1937 and was to have used the F3F-2 wings.

G-32: To complement its G-22, Gulf Oil obtained a two-seat demonstration aircraft powered by a 950-hp GR-1820-G5 radial. Unlike the G-22, the two-seater was fitted with the longer wings of the F3F and had split flaps beneath the upper wings. Bearing c/n 446, registered NR1051, and named *Gulfhawk III*, it was first flown on 6 May, 1938. In 1942, it was impressed into USAAF service as an UC-103.

G-32A: Registered NC1326 and nicknamed *The Red Ship*, c/n 447 was a two-seat demonstrator which combined features of the F3F-2 and F3F-3, was powered by a 775-hp Wright SR-1820-F52 and, like the G-32, was fitted with split flaps. It was first flown on 1 July, 1938, and was owned by Grumman until impressed into AAF service in November 1942. In 1945, after being used by the AAF as an UC-103, c/n 447 was returned to the US civil register as NC46110. It was then sold several times before being re-registered N7F and painted to look like an F3F-2. It was destroyed in a crash at Oskosh, Wisconsin, on 7 August, 1971.

G-37: Design 37 was an export version of the F3F-2 which was proposed in

September 1938 when Grumman attempted to capitalize on the notoriety gained by its small biplane as the result of Al Williams's tour of Europe in the *Gulfhawk II*.

UC-103: In November 1942 the G-32 and the G-32A were impressed by the Army Air Forces at Homestead Army Airfield, Florida, where they were designated UC-103s and given serial numbers 42-97044 and 42-97045. They were used by the Air Transport Command as utility light transports and to train ferry pilots. The first made a forced landing in the Everglades and was subsequently scrapped at Homestead AAF. In January 1945, the second was transferred for disposal to the Reconstruction Finance Corporation and then sold to Clayton Long.

Service history

F3F-1s were first assigned in March and April 1936 to replace the FF-1s in service with VF-5B, the fighter squadron assigned to *Ranger*. Others then went to VF-6B aboard *Saratoga* and to VF-4M* at San Diego. Similarly, upon delivery, most F3F-2s were distributed to VF-6 aboard *Enterprise*, VMF-1, and VMF-2 and most F3F-3s went to VF-5 aboard *Yorktown*.

With Navy squadrons, the F3Fs began to be replaced with monoplane fighters in 1940, when Brewster F2A-1s were first assigned to replace F3F-1s in service with VF-3. They were finally phased out from carrier-based squadrons in June 1941. In the meantime, however, F3F-1s had been assigned to a new squadron, VF-7, until that unit was redesignated VF-72

When impressed during the Second World War, the G-32A demonstrator was designated UC-103 and assigned the military serial 42-97045. *(Grumman)*

* In July 1937, VF-5B, VF-6B, and VF-4M were respectively redesignated VF-4, VF-3, and VMF-2.

An F3F-2 in the markings of Marine Fighting Squadron Two (VMF-2). *(Courtesy of Hal Andrews)*

and received its Grumman F4F-3s for service aboard *Wasp*. With the Marines, F3Fs were still in service with VMF-1 and VMF-2 when these squadrons were redesignated VMF-111 and VMF-211 in July 1941. However, VMF-111 was re-equipped with F2A-3s in July and VMF-211 converted to F4F-3s in October. Thus, when the United States went to war in December 1941, seventy-six F3Fs were serving with training units at NAS Corpus Christi and NAS Miami, Florida, and 101 were about to be transferred to these and other Transition Training Units and to Naval Technical Training Units. The last of these aircraft to be flyable, an F3F-2, was struck off in November 1943.

While the F3F was certainly well liked by its crews and compared favourably with contemporary biplane fighters (such as the Fiat C.R.42 or Gloster Gladiator), it was nevertheless obsolete by world standards as truly modern land-based monoplane fighters were by then operated by several European air forces. Moreover, as a carrier fighter, the F3F-3 was outclassed by the Mitsubishi A5M4, a Japanese Navy monoplane fighter which was faster than the last Grumman fighter in spite of being fitted with a non-retractable undercarriage and powered by a less powerful engine. That is not to say that the F3F was anachronistic, as in other ways it was ahead of its time, notably in terms of manoeuvrability.

With today's pilots pulling 9g in F-16s or F/A-18s and complaining that 'g-lock' has become a problem, it is easy to forget that F3Fs stressed for 9g manoeuvres were already in service fifty years ago. The XF3F-1 and F3F-1 had indeed been designed to perform highly stressed manoeuvres and the XF3F-1 had demonstrated this capability but, following three accidents involving F3F-1s from VF-6B, the type had to be limited temporarily to 6g. After the upper wing spars were strengthened and aileron bell cranks reinforced, F3F-1s were cleared to 8.44g while F3F-2s and F3F-3s went to the full 9g limit. Needless to say, these aircraft gave thrilling and long-remembered aerobatic experiences to their pilots and helped make Grumman a favourite with Naval Aviators.

PRODUCTION: A total of 169 aircraft was built by Grumman between March 1935 and May 1939 as follows:

3	XF3F-1		1	G-22
54	F3F-1		1	G-32
1	XF3F-2		1	G-32A
81	F3F-2			
(1)	XF3F-3			
27	F3F-3			

They were assigned the following BuNos and civil registration numbers:

XF3F-1:	BuNo 9727 (assigned to three different aircraft)		
F3F-1:	BuNos 0211/0264	G-22:	NR1050
XF3F-2:	BuNo 0452	G-32:	NC1051
F3F-2:	BuNos 0967/1047	G-32A:	NC1326
XF3F-3:	(BuNo 1031)	UC-103:	(42-97044/42-97045)
F3F-3:	BuNos 1444/1470		

Registered NC1326 and nicknamed *The Red Ship*, the Grumman-owned G-32A demonstrator was photographed at Floyd Bennett Field, New York, on 8 February, 1938. *(Grumman)*

	XF3F-1	F3F-1	F3F-2	F3F-3
DIMENSIONS:				
Span, ft in	32 0	32 0	32 0	32 0
(m)	(9.75)	(9.75)	(9.75)	(9.75)
Length, ft in	23 0	23 3	23 2	23 2
(m)	(7.01)	(7.09)	(7.06)	(7.06)
Height, ft in	10 6	9 4	9 4	9 4
(m)	(3.20)	(2.84)	(2.84)	(2.84)
Wing area, sq ft	261	261	260	260
(sq m)	(24.25)	(24.25)	(24.15)	(24.15)
WEIGHTS:				
Empty, lb	2,868	2,952	3,254	3,285
(kg)	(1,301)	(1,339)	(1,476)	(1,490)
Loaded, lb	4,094	4,170	4,498	4,543
(kg)	(1,857)	(1,891)	(2,040)	(2,061)
Maximum, lb	4,327	4,403	4,750	4,795
(kg)	(1,963)	(1,997)	(2,155)	(2,175)
Wing loading,* lb/sq ft	15.7	16.0	17.3	17.5
(kg/sq m)	(76.6)	(78.0)	(84.5)	(85.3)
Power loading,* lb/hp	5.8	6.0	4.7	4.8
(kg/hp)	(2.6)	(2.7)	(2.1)	(2.2)
PERFORMANCE:				
Max speed, mph/ft	226/7,500	231/7,500	260/17,250	264/15,200
(kmh/m)	(364/2,285)	(372/2,285)	(418/5,260)	(425/4,635)
Climb rate, ft/min	5,000/2.5	1,900/1	2,800/1	2,750/1
(m/sec)	(10.2)	(9.7)	(14.2)	(14.0)
Service ceiling, ft	29,500	28,500	32,300	33,200
(m)	(8,990)	(8,685)	(9,845)	(10,120)
Normal range, miles	910	882	975	980
(km)	(1,465)	(1,420)	(1,570)	(1,575)
Max range, miles	–	1,000	1,130	1,150
(km)	(–)	(1,610)	(1,820)	(1,850)

* wing and power loadings are calculated at normal loaded weight and maximum take-off power.

The sole XSBF-1, at Bethpage in December 1935. *(Grumman)*

Grumman XSBF-1

By the mid-1930s, most airliners being built or developed in the United States were of monoplane configuration and were fitted with retractable undercarriages, variable-pitch propellers, and other modern equipment. The Bureau of Aeronautics, however, was more conservative and kept fluctuating between monoplanes and biplanes. Traditionalists insisted that biplanes had better handling characteristics for operations aboard carriers, while more forward-thinking officers stressed that monoplanes would be needed if the performance of carrier aircraft were to keep up with those of land-based aircraft then under development. Nowhere was this dichotomy more evident than among officers at the Class Desk 'B', the BuAer organization responsible for developing requirements for the new class of scout bombers needed by the Navy and for ordering aircraft to meet these requirements.

The first scout bomber was the Vought SBU-1, a biplane with non-retractable undercarriage which was ordered in prototype form in February 1934 and entered service in November 1935. By the latter date, BuAer had also initiated a competition for scout bombers of monoplane configuration by ordering prototypes of the Brewster XSB2A-1 and Vought XSB2U-1 in October 1934 and of the Northrop XBT-1 in November 1934. A second competition, for aircraft of biplane configuration, was initiated by ordering a single prototype of the Vought XSB3U-1 in February 1935, of the Grumman XSBF-1 in March 1935, and of the Curtiss XSBC-2 in April 1935. For Grumman, this plethora of competitors resulted in the company's first loss of a competition.

To a great extent, the XSBF-1 (Design 16) was a refinement of the XSF-2 (Design G-13) and was characterized by wings of reduced span and

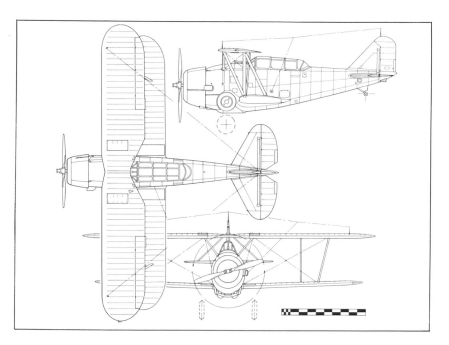

Grumman XSBF-1

increased chord and a rudder without mass balance. Built in the Farmingdale plant and powered by a 700-hp Pratt & Whitney R-1535-72
fourteen-cylinder radial, the XSBF-1 had provision for either one 0.50-in
and one 0.30-in engine-mounted forward-firing guns or two forward-firing
0.30-in guns. A flexible 0.30-in gun was installed in the rear cockpit and a
500-lb bomb was carried beneath the fuselage on a swinging arm to clear the
propeller arc during dive-bombing operations.

First flown by B Allison 'Bud' Gillies on 24 December, 1935, the XSBF-1
(BuNo 9996) was ferried to NAS Anacostia on 12 February, 1936, after
completing uneventful manufacturer's trials in Farmingdale. Navy trials
proceeded equally smoothly and were completed in August. Although the
XSBF-1 was found just as satisfactory as the Curtiss XSBC-3 (a development of the XSBC-2 with the Wright R-1510-12 replaced by the Pratt &
Whitney R-1535-94) and had comparable performance to the Curtiss
prototype, the Navy elected to give the contract for scout bomber biplanes
to Curtiss as Grumman was already busy with the production of fighters. In
any case, the real winner was the Northrop XBT-1 monoplane which, after
a small production batch of BT-1s had been built, was developed into the
Douglas SBD Dauntless of Second World War fame.

After failing to win a production contract, the XSBF-1 was retained at
NAS Anacostia where it was used as a hack and for sundry development

work. Damaged slightly in accidents in October 1937, September 1938, and May 1939, BuNo 9996 was finally struck from the inventory in July 1939.

PRODUCTION: One XSBF-1 was completed by Grumman in December 1935 and was assigned BuNo 9996.

Span 31 ft 6 in (9.60 m); length 25 ft 9 in (7.85 m); height 11 ft 3 in (3.43 m); wing area 310 sq ft (28. 80 sq m).

Empty weight 3,395 lb (1,540 kg); loaded weight 5,002 lb (2,269 kg); maximum weight 5,442 lb (2,468 kg); wing loading 16.1 lb/sq ft (78.8 kg/sq m); power loading 7.1 lb/hp (3.2 kg/hp).

Maximum speed 215 mph at 15,000 ft (346 kmh at 4,570 m); climb to 5,000 ft (1,525 m) in 3.2 minutes; service ceiling 26,000 ft (7,925 m); range with 500 lb (227 kg) bomb 688 miles (1,105 km); range without bomb 987 miles (1,590 km).

CF-EXA was built as a JRF-5 (BuNo 37997), went to the RCAF as a Goose Mk.II (receiving the Canadian serial 385 and serving with the Eastern Air Command), and was acquired by the British American Oil Co Ltd after being struck off strength by the RCAF in October 1946.

Grumman G-21 Goose

Although its development was started after that of Design 18, the XF4F-2 single-engined fighter, the G-21 became, on 29 May, 1937, the first Grumman monoplane to fly. It was also Grumman's first twin-engined aircraft (Design 3 had been proposed to the Coast Guard in early 1930 but had remained on the drawing board), its first expressly built for the civil market (the GG-1, G-22, G-32, and G-32A were derivatives of military aircraft), its first to be used by scheduled airlines, and its first to operate from land, water, and snow. The G-21 also proved to be long-lived, with several extant more than fifty years after the first flight.

Work on this outstanding aircraft was initiated in 1936 to meet the needs of ten wealthy aircraft-owner businessmen who were seeking a modern successor to the Loening Air Yacht and Commuter amphibians. Organized in a loose syndicate led by Wilton Lloyd-Smith, these businessmen had asked Grover Loening either to design such an aircraft or to recommend a company which could do so. As his own Grover Loening Aircraft Company was too small to undertake this assignment and as he was also then providing consulting services to the Grumman Aircraft Engineering Corporation, Loening naturally suggested the company he had helped to finance as that likely to design a good amphibian. On his recommendation, Roy Grumman and Bill Schwendler began work on Design 21.

With hydrodynamicist Ralston Stalb designing a two-step hull, the aircraft evolved into a clean monoplane powered by a pair of Pratt & Whitney Wasp Jr nine-cylinder radials which were mounted on the wing leading edge, forward of the cabin, and fitted with collector rings exiting above the wings to reduce cabin noise. Accommodation was provided for

NX16910, the G-21 prototype, at the time of its initial trials in May 1937. (*Grumman*)

two pilots in a cockpit situated forward of the wing and for four-to-six passengers in a roomy cabin located beneath the high-mounted wing and entered via a door on the port side just aft of the wing. A small galley and a lavatory were provided in the rear of the cabin and baggage was carried in a bow compartment and aft of the cabin.

Other distinguishing features of the G-21 included its hand-cranked retractable undercarriage which was used for land operations or could be extended in the water during beaching. The mainwheels retracted upward into the fuselage sides, as in earlier Grumman aircraft, and the steerable tailwheel retracted aft into the hull just behind the second step. For land operations, the wing floats could be removed, thus reducing drag and increasing performance. For operations from snow covered fields, the main and tail wheels could be replaced with skis.

Built in Bethpage, the first G-21 (c/n 1001, NX16910) began its flight trials on 29 May, 1937, when Bud Gillies and Robert L Hall took it up from the field in front of the new plant. At the end of a 65-minute flight Gillies and Hall alighted the G-21 on Manhasset Bay to take up Roy Grumman on a 15-minute demonstration flight. Three more flights were made on that day and two were made on both 30 and 31 May to bring total flight time to 6 hr 10 min in just three days. Subsequent flights, during which Roy Grumman contributed his long experience and expertise in seaplanes, revealed the need to move the step aft by $4^{1}/_{2}$ in. The effectiveness of this modification was first tested on 3 June, 1937, by temporarily fitting wooden blocks and all G-21 models had it incorporated during production.

Production history

As flight testing proceeded quickly and smoothly Grumman was able to deliver the first aircraft only thirty-five days after it had first been flown and before receipt of the Approved Type Certificate which was issued on 29 September, 1937. The ease of handling, good stability, and satisfactory

96

One of the four G-21As delivered in December 1938 and January 1939 to the Fuerza Aérea del Peru for service with Escuadrón de Transporte No.2. *(Grumman)*

performance demonstrated during the trials soon made the Goose a very popular aircraft with civil and military customers alike. Moreover, it proved to have a very strong airframe, thus endowing many of the 345 aircraft built by Grumman between May 1937 and October 1945 with a long service life.

G-21: Twelve of these commercial amphibians (c/ns 1001/1012) each powered by two 450-hp Pratt & Whitney Wasp Jr SB radials driving two-blade propellers were built in 1937. Nine were initially registered in the United States, one was acquired by Lord Beaverbrook and registered in the United Kingdom, and two went to Asiatic Petroleum and were registered in Australia. Shortly after being delivered, the first eleven aircraft were brought up to G-21A standards while the twelfth was modified to that standard before delivery.

G-21A: Thirty G-21As (c/ns 1013/1020, 1048/1062, 1080/1084, 1175, and 1188) differed from the G-21s in being powered by 450-hp Wasp Jr SB-2 radials, in being fitted with a modified tailwheel and with a slightly redesigned hull to reduce water spray on take-off and alighting, and in having their certificated gross weight increased from 7,500 lb to 8,000 lb. They were delivered between May 1938 and September 1942 to private customers, oil companies, the Canadian and Peruvian air forces, an airline (KNILM), the Ford Motor Company, and Columbia University. Some were later re-engined with 450-hp Wasp Jr SB-3 radials using higher octane fuel and driving three-blade propellers.

G-21B: The twelve G-21Bs (c/ns 1088/1099) ordered by the Portuguese Government as coastal patrol flying-boats were the only aircraft in the Goose series not to be fitted with a land undercarriage. Defensive armament – one flexible 0.30-in machine gun in the bow and a similar weapon in a dorsal hatch aft of the wings – was provided and a rack was mounted just outboard of the engine nacelles to carry one 100-lb bomb beneath each wing. Their Portuguese naval serials, 97 to 108, were prefixed by the letters NX when used as temporary US registration.

97

The XJ3F-1, the twenty-first Goose built by Grumman, was delivered to the US Navy at NAS Anacostia on 9 September, 1938. *(Grumman)*

G-21C to **G-21G:** These McKinnon conversions are described under the 'Odds and Mods' heading at the end of this chapter.

XJ3F-1: The sole Design 26 aircraft was an unarmed eight-seat utility amphibian (c/n 1021, BuNo 1384) for the US Navy. Powered by two 450-hp Pratt & Whitney R-985-48 radials, it was delivered to NAS Anacostia, in September 1938.

JRF-1: These five Design 38 aircraft (BuNos 1674/1677 and 1680) were basically similar to the XJ3F-1 but were intended to be used primarily in the light transport role. They were delivered to the Navy between November 1939 and January 1940. Two civilian G-21As (c/ns 1014 and 1017) were impressed as JRF-1s in 1942 and were given BuNos 07004 and 09782. Neither survived the war.

JRF-1A: The five JRF-1As (BuNos 1671/1673 and 1678/1679) differed from the JRF-1s in having a camera hatch in the hull bottom and in being fitted with target towing gear. They were delivered to the Navy between September 1939 and January 1940.

JRF-2: Seven Design 39 amphibians were built to meet Coast Guard requirements. Powered by 450-hp Wasp Jr SB-2 radials, they were equipped to have the passenger seats replaced when needed by stretchers. Bearing USCG serials V174/V176 and V184/V187, they were delivered between July 1939 and May 1940.

JRF-3: Bearing USCG serials V190/V192 and delivered to the Coast Guard in November 1940, the three JRF-3s differed from the JRF-2s in being fitted with an autopilot and with de-icing boots on the leading edge of their wing and tail surfaces.

JRF-4: The ten JRF-4s (BuNos 3846/3855) differed from earlier Design 38 amphibians in being powered by 450-hp R-985-50 radials and in being fitted to carry a 250-lb bomb or a 325-lb depth charge on a rack mounted outboard of each engine nacelle. They were delivered to the Navy between December

In Flygvapnet service, the ex-RAF Goose IA received the Swedish military designation Tp 81.
(Flygvapnet courtesy of the Swedish Air Attaché in Washington)

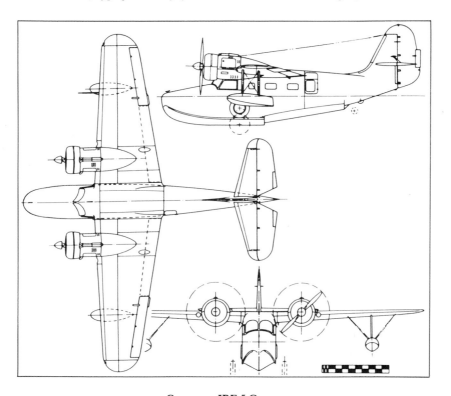

Grumman JRF-5 Goose

99

1940 and April 1941. The two civil G-21As (c/ns 1060 and 188) impressed in 1942 as BuNos 07004 and 09782 were modified as JRF-4s by installation of wing racks and other military equipment; both were returned to the US civil register after the war.

JRF-5: This was the main version of the Goose and the last to remain in production. A total of 184 JRF-5s (BuNos 6440/6454, 04349/04358, 34060/34094, 37771/37831, 39747/39748, 84790/84818, and 87720/ 87751) was delivered between July 1941 and October 1945; eleven more (BuNos 87752/87762) were cancelled after VJ-Day. Powered by 450 hp R-985-AN-6 radials and still listed under the Design 38 nomenclature, the JRF-5s incorporated features from the JRF-1A (camera hatch in the hull and provision for target towing gear), the JRF-3 (de-icing boots and provision for the installation of an autopilot), and JRF-4 (wing racks).

JRF-5G: The G suffix identified JRF-5s operated after the war by the Coast Guard.

JRF-6B: Fifty Design 38 navigation trainers were ordered in 1939 by the British Purchasing Commission and assigned serials FP475/FP524. The contract was transferred to Lend-Lease before deliveries began in January 1942 and only forty-four Goose IAs were delivered to the Royal Air Force while five went to the Army Air Forces as OA-9s and one was supplied to Bolivia.

OA-9: Twenty-six Design 31 amphibians (c/ns 1022-1047) were ordered in June 1938 by the Army Air Corps to replace its Douglas OA-3s and OA-4s used in the staff transport and air-sea rescue roles. Powered by 450-hp Pratt & Whitney R-985-17s and designated OA-9s, these six-seat aircraft (38-556/38-581) were delivered between November 1938 and October 1939. Rather confusingly, the OA-9 designation was used again in 1942 to identify five Design 38 aircraft diverted from the Lend-Lease contract for JRF-6Bs and assigned serials 42-106979/42-106983 for service with the AAF. In

38-564, an OA-9 of the 91st Observation Squadron, at Ft Lewis, Washington. (*USAF*)

1948, the survivors from these two batches were redesignated A-9s and then ZA-9s (the prefix Z indicating their obsolete status) before becoming surplus to requirements.

OA-13A: This designation identified three G-21As (c/n 1058, 1006, and 1062) which were taken over by the AAF and given serials 42-38214, 42-38215, and 42-97055. The first two were assigned to Pan American Airways as support/administrative aircraft for operations in Africa and the Middle East and 42-97055 was operated by the AAF in the United States (Bolling Field and Laredo) and Latin America (Peru and Brazil). The second of these aircraft, 42-38215, was written off but the other two were returned to the US civil register at the end of the war.

OA-13B: Two G-21As (c/ns 1175 and 1188) were taken over by the Navy and were later assigned AAF serials 45-49088 and 45-49089 and given OA-13B designations. However, this appears only to have been a paper transaction.

Service history

The first G-21 was delivered to co-owners Wilton Lloyd-Smith and Marshall Field, III, on 3 July, 1937, only five weeks after its maiden flight. Thereafter, G-21As were operated as luxury transports by wealthy owners in the United States, Canada, and the United Kingdom. Other prewar civil operators included several oil companies with aircraft registered in Australia, the Netherlands East Indies, the United States, and Venezuela.

The first airline to order a Goose was Lloyd Aéreo Boliviano but apparently this Bolivian carrier did not put c/n 1015 into service. KNILM, the KLM subsidiary in the East Indies, acquired two G-21As (c/ns 1080/1081, PK-AFR/PK-AFS) in March 1940. Unfortunately, both aircraft were short-lived as PK-AFR was destroyed during the first year of operation and PK-AFS was shot down by Japanese aircraft at Koepang, Timor, on 26 January, 1942. Thus, it was only during the 1950s and 1960s, long after the type was last produced, that it was operated in respectable numbers by airlines and third level carriers. Alaska Coastal Airlines, which in 1968 had thirteen Goose and one Turbo-Goose, and Reeve Aleutian Airways both used their aircraft for scheduled operations in Alaska. Mackey Airlines operated G-21As between Miami and the Bahamas until it was absorbed by Eastern Air Lines in 1967. Avalon Air Transport, which was renamed Catalina Airlines in 1963, flew its aircraft between the Long Beach Municipal Airport and Avalon Harbor at Catalina Island, off the coast of Southern California, in competition with Catalina Seaplanes which operated the Goose from San Pedro Harbor. Antilles Air Boats in St Croix, Virgin Islands, put its first Goose into service in February 1964 and went on to operate eighteen of the Grumman amphibians on short sectors in the Caribbean.

The Royal Canadian Air Force became the first military customer when it took delivery of the sixteenth Goose (c/n 1016, RCAF 917) in June 1938. It

N329 of Catalina Air Lines, an ex-Coast Guard JRF-5G (BuNo 87725) modified with retractable floats, photographed in August 1968 at Long Beach, California. *(Warren M Bodie)*

was followed by the US Navy, which accepted the XJ3F-1 in October; the Army Air Corps, which received its first OA-9 in November; and the Fuerza Aérea del Peru, which took delivery of its first two G-21As in December. In September of the following year the Coast Guard received its first JRF-1 and in 1940 Portugal's Aviação Naval joined the growing list of Goose operators.

It was the Army Air Corps, however, which first operated the type in quantity as, by October 1939, it had all of its twenty-six OA-9s in service. Eleven of these aircraft had crashed or had been damaged beyond repair before the United State's entry into the war and two OA-9s were destroyed on the ground at Wheeler Field during the Japanese attack against military facilities on Oahu Island on 7 December, 1941. The thirteen remaining aircraft were supplemented during the war by five more OA-9s, three OA-13As, and, possibly, two OA-13Bs. Only eight were on hand at the end of the war. Finally, soon after being redesignated A-9s and then ZA-9s in 1948, the four aircraft remaining from the original batch of OA-9s and one of the ex JRF-6Bs were sold as surplus and went onto the US civil register.

At the end of 1941, the US Navy had thirty-five Goose amphibians (the XJ3F-1, four JRF-1 transports and five JRF-1As utility aircraft, as well as ten JRF-4s and fifteen JRF-5s which could be used in the anti-submarine role) and the Coast Guard had seven JRF-2s and three JRF-3s. During the war, when the Coast Guard and the Navy operated side-by-side and exchanged aircraft, 169 JRF-5s were added to the naval inventory and four G-21As were taken over from civil operators. The Navy and the Coast Guard used these amphibians for utility duty, light transport, and coastal anti-submarine patrols. The Navy disposed of its remaining JRFs shortly

A JRF-1A of Utility Squadron One (VJ-1) on 6 December, 1939. *(USN/National Archives)*

after the end of the war while the Coast Guard retained some of its JRF-5Gs until the mid-1950s.

Abroad, the Grumman Goose was operated by the air forces and naval air arms of the following eleven nations.

ARGENTINA: After Argentina became a signatory of the 1947 Rio Pact, a small number of JRF-4s and JRF-5s were transferred by the United States. They were used in the utility role by the Servicio de Aviación Naval (Naval Aviation Service) and the Prefectura Naval Argentina (the latter being Argentina's Coast Guard) for nearly twenty years until the last three survivors were given to Paraguay.

BOLIVIA: In 1942, at least one JRF-2 and one of the Lend-Lease JRF-6Bs (serial FP500) were given by the United States to be used in the Amazon area by the Cuerpo de Aviación (Bolivian Aviation Corps). After the war, the JRF-6B was sold in the United States.

BRAZIL: Ten JRFs (model unknown) were supplied by the United States some time after Brazil declared war on Germany and Italy on 22 August, 1942. They were apparently used for anti-submarine patrols by the Força Aérea Brasileira (Brazilian Air Force) along the Brazilian coast, but no further details are known.

CANADA: Altogether, the RCAF obtained thirty-one Goose Mk I and IIs. The first of these aircraft (RCAF 917, a G-21A ordered by the Canadian Government) was taken on strength in July 1938 and the last two (RCAF 387 and 391 which were ex-USN JRF-5s) were struck off charge in February 1956. Twenty-nine Goose Mk IIs – three delivered new to the RCAF in 1938 and 1940, ten ex-US - or Canadian-registered G-21As taken on charge in 1940-42, and sixteen ex-USN JRF-5s delivered in 1944-45 – were given Canadian military serials (383/397, 796/798, 917, 924/926, and 939-944). Two Goose Mk Is, which were taken on charge in 1944, retained

A JRF-4 taxi-ing at NAS Anacostia at the start of its delivery flight to Bolivia in 1942. *(USN/ National Archives)*

their British serials (FP471 and FP473). Over the years, these aircraft served in the communications and training roles with No.13 Operational Training Unit; Nos.2 (AC), 12 (Comm), 118, 121 (Comp), 167, and 412 Squadrons; No.6 (Training) Group; and the Western Air Command.

CUBA: During the Second World War, the Aviación de la Marina de Guerra (Cuban Naval Aviation) received two JRF-5s. One was lost in Cuban service but the other was sold to commercial interests and successively appeared on the US and Canadian civil registers.

FRANCE: In March 1952, ten (or possibly twelve) JRF-5s were handed over to the Aéronautique Navale (French Naval Aviation) to re-equip Escadrille 85 at Cat-Laï, Indochina. A second batch of five JRF-5s was obtained in 1954. During the Indochina War, Escadrille 85 and its detachments flew the Goose on river and maritime reconnaissance missions, casualty evacuation, and communications duties from various bases and from the seaplane tenders *Robert Giraud* and *Paul Goffeney*. In addition, some of the JRF-5s were used on armed reconnaissance operations for which they carried four 100-lb bombs. At least one had a pair of forward-firing guns mounted in the nose and a few acquired the distinction of becoming the primitive precursors of Vietnam War-era gunships when twin 7.62mm machine guns were fitted on a fixed mount in the port side door to fire sideways.

After French forces withdrew from Vietnam, four JRF-5s were shipped to New Caledonia and eleven were taken by Escadrille 85 to Algiers-Maison Blanche. Most then flew anti-smuggling patrols over the Mediterranean during the Algerian War but others released by Escadrille 85 were used for communications duties from Saint-Mandrier, France; Dakar, Sénégal; and Casablanca, Morocco. Following the crash of one of the aircraft operated by

104

A JRF-5 of the Aéronautique Navale. (*ECPA-Marine, courtesy of Alain Pelletier*)

Flotille 27F from Dakar, the JRF-5s were finally withdrawn from French service in the spring of 1961.

JAPAN: Four ex-USN JRF-5s were delivered to the Nihon Kaijyo Jieitai (Japanese Maritime Self-Defence Force or JMSDF) shortly after the naval air arm of the Japanese Self Defence Forces came into existence on 1 July, 1954. Bearing Japanese serials 9011/9014, they were operated for a few years in the utility role.

PARAGUAY: One JRF-4 and two JRF-5s were obtained from Argentina in 1967 and, respectively numbered 0128 and 0126/0127, were briefly used by the Servicio de Aeronáutica de la Marina (Naval Aviation Service) before being resold to US owners.

PERU: Four G-21As were delivered to the Fuerza Aérea del Peru (Peruvian Air Force) in 1938-9 and, bearing Peruvian serials 2TP-1H to 2TP-4H, served with Escuadrón de Transporte No2. Supplemented during the late 1940s by at least one ex-USN JRF-5, two of these G-21As survived until 1950 when they were renumbered 323 and 324 in the new Peruvian military serial system. Subsequently, they were sold in the United States.

PORTUGAL: The twelve G-21B flying-boats ordered by the Portuguese Government in December 1939 were crated and shipped between April and May 1940. Although they had been provided with bow and dorsal flexible guns and with two racks for 100-lb bombs, these aircraft were operated by the Aviação Naval (Naval Aviation) in the transport role from Bom Sucesso, Lisbon. A few were apparently transferred to Macau. By May 1952, when the Aviação Naval and the Aeronáutica Militar (Military Aviation) were merged to form the Força Aérea Portuguesa (Portuguese Air Force), none of the G-21Bs was airworthy.

105

The first of twelve G-21Bs built for Portugal's Aviação Naval. (*Grumman*)

SWEDEN: A single Goose was operated by Kungliga Svenska Flygvapnet (Royal Swedish Air Force) between 1951 and 1962. Assigned the Swedish military designation Tp 81 and the serial 81001, this aircraft was an ex-RAF Goose IA (FP484, c/n 1134) which after the end of the war had been returned to the US Navy and sold as surplus. Before being acquired by Flygvapnet, this aircraft was registered N9293H in the United States and LN-SAB in Norway. With Flygvapnet the sole Tp 81 was primarily operated by F21 in the aeromedical evacuation role and was fitted with skis for land operations during the winter.

UNITED KINGDOM: The JRF-5s and JRF-6Bs obtained during the war by the Royal Air Force had been preceded in Great Britain by two G-21As purchased by Lord Beaverbrook. The ninth Goose (c/n 1009) had been registered G-AFCH in October 1937 but had been sold as PK-AER in July 1938. Five months later, this G-21A was replaced by c/n 1049, G-AFKJ. Impressed as HK822 in February 1941, this aircraft served with the RAF until it sank off Benghazi on 9 December, 1942.

Fifty Design 38 amphibians had been ordered by the British Purchasing Commission. However, before delivery could begin, the contract was absorbed into Lend-Lease and only forty-four were taken on charge by the Royal Air Force. Forty of these Goose IAs (FP475/FP495, FP501/FP504, and FP510/FP524) were equipped for navigational training and had a larger blister window on the starboard fuselage side. The four others (FP496/FP499) were fitted with additional radio equipment. In addition, the RAF was assigned seven JRF-5s which were designated Goose Is and were given serials FP470/FP474, MV989, and MV993. Two of these, FP471 and

FP474, were transferred to the RCAF before being taken on strength by the RAF.

During the war, both versions were used for air-sea rescue duty, particularly from Piarco, Trinidad, and for ferry duty by the Air Transport Auxiliary. Thirty-eight surviving aircraft were returned to the United States at the end of the war.

Odds and Mods

What the Goose lacked in colourful service history it more than made up in having a long and fruitful 'after life' during which its rugged construction and pleasant handling characteristics led to its repeated modification, either for experimental purposes or to extend its commercial usefulness.

Modifications undertaken under military contracts were performed by Edo Corporation in College Point, New York, and by Kaman Aerospace in Windsor Locks, Connecticut. Sponsored by the Air Force, the first Edo conversion was intended to demonstrate the 'Pantobase' system which had been conceived to enable amphibious aircraft to operate not only from airfields and water surfaces but also from semi-prepared fields, ice and snow. To that end, a JRF-5 (BuNo 37795) was acquired from the Navy and given the Air Force serial 48-128 when it was fitted with a main hydro-ski beneath the hull and auxiliary hydro-skis beneath the tail and the wing floats. Flight tests revealed that the combination of tip floats and available aileron control provided adequate roll stability, thus eliminating the need for the hydro-skis beneath the floats. Moreover, the tail hydro-ski was found unnecessary because of inherent stability of the aircraft during

Although most reference documents indicate that serial 48-128 was cancelled, it was in fact assigned to an ex-JRF-5 (BuNo 37795) acquired by the USAF to serve as the prototype for a 'pantobase aircraft' capable of operating from water, ice, snow, and unprepared fields. Bearing the buzz number OA-128 and fitted with four hydro-skis by Edo Corporation, the modified aircraft is seen during snow landing trials. (*Edo*)

107

unporting* until it was planing on the main hydro-ski. Tests data were later incorporated in the design of the triphibian gear for the Grumman SA-16.

The second Edo conversion was undertaken under a Navy contract to explore the operational characteristics of a single hydro-ski configuration and was intended solely for water operation. The hydro-ski, which was fitted to an unidentified Navy JRF-5, was reconfigured for hydro-dynamic optimum drag because of the elimination of any solid surface operational requirements. Later the aircraft was evaluated with twin hydro-skis. The success of this programme then led to the installation of a single hydro-ski on a modified Martin PBM-5.

As part of the Navy seaplane research programme, the Bureau of Weapons also funded the testing of a Gruenberg super-cavitating hydrofoil system. A single hydrofoil was fixed beneath a modified JRF-5G (BuNo 37782, USCG 7782), small hydro-skis were attached to slanted attachments projecting beneath the bow, and the two-blade propellers were replaced by three-blade units. The practicality of the concept was successfully demonstrated during the summer of 1962 but by then the Navy was fast losing interest in flying-boats and no further development was funded.

When the Navy and the Air Force showed interest in the development of V/STOL aircraft during the mid- and late-1950s, Kaman obtained a contract from the Office of Naval Research (ONR) to modify an existing aircraft into a V/STOL research vehicle and to undertake ground tests. The aircraft selected for modification by Kaman was a JRF-5 which was fitted with low aspect ratio wings (span and area respectively were 34 ft and 251 sq ft) which tilted through 50 degrees. The K-16B, as it was designated, also received lateral control spoilers, aileron servo flaps along the entire trailing edge, and enlarged vertical tail surfaces. Power was provided by two 1,024

Fitted with a single hydro-ski by Edo Corporation, this modified JRF-5 was intended solely for water operation as part of a Navy-funded research programme. This photograph was taken on 11 June, 1957, during Edo trials. (*Edo*)

* Term used by Edo Corporation to describe the action of changing from hull to ski support as the speed of the aircraft increases during a water take-off.

The JRF-5G modified by Edo Corporation for testing of a Gruenberg super-cavitation hydrofoil system. *(Edo)*

shp General Electric T-58-GE-2a propeller-turbines driving 14 ft 10-in diameter three-blade propellers. The Kaman K-16B (the much modified Goose) underwent ground testing at Windsor Locks in 1960. However, as bearings in the propulsive rotors were found inadequate, the ONR did not fund further development.

Most of the modifications undertaken for commercial purposes were due to McKinnon Enterprises Inc, of Sandy, Oregon, and to its Canadian successor, McKinnon-Viking Enterprises of Sidney, British Columbia. This firm had first developed several minor modifications for the Goose, including an electrical undercarriage retraction mechanism and retractable wingtip floats, which were adopted by several operators. McKinnon then engineered the G-21C, a four-engined conversion of the G-21A in which the Wasp Jr radials were replaced by four 340-hp Lycoming GSO-480-B2D6 six-cylinder air-cooled engines driving three-blade propellers. The modified aircraft, which was registered N150M and had a lengthened forward hull with provision for weather radar, was approved in 1958 under a Supplemental Type Certificate. Later, the control surfaces were enlarged and the forward hull extended again and fitted with windows to provide the G-21D with accommodation for four additional passengers. However, the four-engined conversions did not generate much interest among prospective buyers. Consequently, McKinnon decided to follow the lead of Strato Engineering Corporation, a small firm from Burbank, California, which in 1966 had helped Alaska Coastal to re-engine one of its Goose amphibians with two 550-shp Pratt & Whitney of Canada PT6A-6 propeller-turbines.

Confusingly, the G-21C and G-21D designations were retained for the McKinnon intermediate and long hull conversions powered by two 550-shp PT6A-20s. These turbines were installed in long slim nacelles which projected further forward of the wings, were mounted 1 ft 3 in closer to the aircraft centreline, and were canted outboard to provide adequate propeller

A McKinnon G-21C with four Lycoming GSO-480 flat-six engines replacing the pair of Wasp Jr radials originally fitted by Grumman. (*Grumman*)

clearance. Fuel tankage was increased from 220 to 337 US gal both to offset the increased fuel consumption of the turbines (this being particularly marked as, lacking cabin pressurization, the G-21C and G-21D had to cruise at an altitude too low for effective turbine engine operation) and to augment range.

McKinnon also offered a simple conversion package to fit PT6As without many other modifications and projected G-21E and G-21F versions. The first was to have been a G-21A conversion with PT6As and wing and flap modifications, whereas the the G-21F was to have been re-engined with AiResearch TPE 331 propeller-turbines. Finally, after moving to British Columbia and being re-organized as McKinnon-Viking Enterprises, the firm developed the G-21G powered by 680-hp PT6A-27s and combining most of the G-21D features with further improvements (such as a metalizing treatment for the fabric wing covering).

Another noteworthy civil conversion was that which saw an aircraft being re-engined by Volpar Inc of Van Nuys, California, with a pair of 715-shp AiResearch TPE 331-2U-203 propeller-turbines. Registered N780, this aircraft was also fitted with a long dorsal fin extension.

PRODUCTION: A total of 345 aircraft was built by Grumman between May 1937 and October 1945 as follows:

12	G-21		3	JRF-3
(12)	G-21A		10	JRF-4
30	G-21A		184	JRF-5
12	G-21B		50	JRF-6B
1	XJ3F-1		26	OA-9
5	JRF-1		(3)	OA-13A
5	JRF-1A		(2)	OA-13B
7	JRF-2			

A PT6A-powered McKinnon G-21C of Alaska Coastal Airlines. *(Grumman)*

They were assigned the following BuNos, military serial numbers, and construction numbers:

G-21:	Civil-registered c/ns 1001/1012
G-21A:	(Civil-registered c/ns 1001/1012)
	Civil-registered c/ns 1013/1015
	RCAF 917 (c/n 1016)
	Civil-registered c/ns 1017/1020
	Civil-registered c/ns 1048/1049
	Peruvian Air Force 2TP-1H/2TP-4H (c/ns 1050/1053)
	Civil-registered c/ns 1054/1062
	Civil-registered c/ns 1080/1081
	RCAF 925/926 (c/n 1082/1083)
	Civil-registered c/n 1084
	Civil-registered c/n 1175
	Civil-registered c/n 1188
G-21B:	Portuguese naval serial numbers 97/108
XJ3F-1:	BuNo 1384
JRF-1:	BuNos 1674/1677 and 1680
JRF-1A:	BuNos 1671/1673 and 1678/1679
JRF-2:	USCG V174/V176 and V184/V187
JRF-3:	USCG V190/V192
JRF-4:	BuNos 3846/3855
JRF-5:	BuNos 6440/6454, 04349/04358, 34060/34094, 37771/37831, 39747/39748, 84790/84818, and 87720/87751
JRF-6B:	FP475/FP524
OA-9:	38-556/38-581
OA-13A:	(42-38214/42-38215 and 42-97055)
OA-13B:	(45-49088/45-49089)

	G-21	**JRF-5**	**G-21G**
DIMENSIONS:			
Span, ft in	49 0	49 0	50 10
(m)	(14.94)	(14.94)	(15.49)
Length, ft in	38 3	38 4	39 7
(m)	(11.66)	(11.68)	(12.07)
Height, ft in	12 2	15 0	–
(m)	(3.71)	(4.57)	(–)
Wing area, sq ft	375	375	377.64
(sq m)	(34.84)	(34.84)	(35.08)
WEIGHTS:			
Empty, lb	5,320	5,425	6,700
(kg)	(2,413)	(2,461)	(3,039)
Loaded, lb	7,500	7,955	12,500
(kg)	(3,402)	(3,608)	(5,670)
Wing loading, lb/sq ft	20.0	21.2	33.1
(kg/sq m)	(97.6)	(103.6)	(161,6)
Power loading, lb/hp	8.3	8.8	9.2
(kg/hp)	(3.8)	(4.0)	(4.2)
PERFORMANCE:			
Max speed, mph/ft	195/sl	201/5,000	243/8,000
(kmh/m)	(314/sl)	(323/1,525)	(391/2,440)
Cruising speed, mph	175	191	–
(kmh)	(282)	(307)	(–)
Climb rate, ft/min	1,490/1	1,100/1	–
(m/sec)	(7.6)	(5.6)	(–)
Service ceiling, ft	24,000	21,000	20,000
(m)	(7,315)	(6,400)	(6,095)
Normal range, miles	795	640	1,600
(km)	(1,280)	(1,030)	(2,575)
Max range, miles	1,150	–	–
(km)	(1,850)	(–)	(–)

The sixth Wildcat V (JV330) during an acceptance test after being brought up to Fleet Air Arm standards by Blackburn Aircraft Ltd. (*Blackburn*)

Grumman F4F Wildcat

Conceived when aircraft design technology was progressing by leaps and bounds, the Wildcat had by standards of the day an inordinately long and trying gestation period. An XF4F-1 biplane prototype was ordered in March 1936 but was not built. The XF4F-2 monoplane prototype was ordered in July 1936, first flew on 2 September, 1937, was heavily damaged on 11 April, 1938, and, after being rebuilt as the XF4F-3 production prototype, was returned to flight status on 12 February, 1939. Finally, the F4F-3 entered squadron service in November 1940. Thus, thirty-seven months had elapsed from first flight to initial assignment to an operational squadron.

Similarly, the P-36 developed by Curtiss for the Army Air Corps entered service thirty-five months after first flying on 13 May, 1935. Abroad, however, development of single-engined monoplane fighters with retractable undercarriages proceeded somewhat more speedily and, in some cases, significantly more so. For example, in Germany, the Messerschmitt Bf 109 was operational thirty months after first flight; and in Britain, the Spitfire went into RAF service twenty-nine months after its maiden flight. Even more remarkable were the achievements of the often-berated Japanese and Soviet industries. The Mitsubishi A6M2, soon to be the Wildcat's nemesis, was flying combat sorties over China sixteen months after the first flight of its A6M1 prototype on 1 April, 1939, and the Polikarpov I-16 went into V-VS service barely over one year after the first flight of its TsKB-12 prototype on 31 December, 1933. Notwithstanding its slow development, the Wildcat was an aeroplane of which Grumman could justly be proud, for it compiled an enviable combat record and remained effective until the end of the war.

113

The XF4F-2 after it had been fitted with a cleaner cowling and a small propeller spinner.
(Grumman)

Work on Design 18, Grumman's first monoplane fighter, was initiated in June 1936 when it had become obvious that Design 16, then on order as the XF4F-1 biplane described in Appendix B, was not going to be a match for the Brewster B-139 monoplane which was on order as the XF2A-1. Moreover, as replacing the 700-hp Pratt & Whitney R-1535-72 of the F3F-1 with a 950-hp Wright R-1820-22 would result in the XF3F-2 being nearly as fast as the XF4F-1, BuAer willingly agreed to Grumman's suggestion to terminate development of the XF4F-1 and to order a Design 18 prototype. Accordingly, on 28 July, 1936, Contract 46973 was amended to provide for the substitution of an XF4F-2 monoplane for the previously ordered XF4F-1 biplane. Immediately, Roy Grumman, Bill Schwendler and their engineering team set about detailing Design 18. The manufacture of components was initiated in Farmingdale with final assembly taking place in Bethpage where the prototype (BuNo 0383) was completed in September 1937.

As could have been expected since the XF4F-2 was designed in a relatively short time, this monoplane bore an undeniable family resemblance to Grumman's earlier biplanes. True, the fabric-covered biplane wings and braced tailplane had been replaced with mid-mounted cantilever all-metal wings and unbraced tail surfaces. However, like the earlier aircraft, the XF4F-2 had a small rotund fuselage in which the manually-operated undercarriage was retracted and was powered by a radial engine, that of the XF4F-2 being a 1,050-hp Pratt & Whitney R-1830-66 (Twin Wasp SC-G).

First flown by Robert L Hall at Bethpage on 2 September, 1937, the XF4F-2 underwent manufacturer's trials for more than two months before being delivered to NAS Anacostia on 23 December. During the next six months, Bob Hall, Navy pilots, and a NACA pilot flew BuNo 0383 at NAS

114

Martlet Is in the Bethpage plant before receiving their wings and horizontal tail surfaces.
(Grumman)

Anacostia and at the Naval Proving Ground at Dahlgreen, Virginia. All was not well, however, as the R-1830-66 experienced teething troubles including repeated crankshaft failures. Then, on 14 February, 1938, the XF4F-2 was nearly lost when Bob Hall had to make an emergency landing after ballast bags in the rear fuselage caught fire. A more serious accident occurred on 11 April during catapult trials at the Naval Aircraft Factory in Philadelphia when the aircraft was forced down after its engine stopped, possibly after running out of fuel. BuNo 0383 was quickly repaired so that it could take part in comparative trials against the Brewster XF2A-1 and the Seversky NF-1.

Although the XF4F-2 was the fastest of the three by a comfortable margin (its top speed of 290 mph exceeded that of the Brewster by 10 mph and that of the Seversky by 40 mph) and handled better than either of its competitors, it was not selected for production as the Navy apparently wished to spread its contracts among several manufacturers. As BuAer was about to order the XF5F-1 prototype and twenty-seven F3F-3s from Grumman, Brewster was awarded a contract for fifty-four F2A-1s on 11 June, 1938. Disappointed but undaunted, the Grumman team set out to modify its single-engined carrier fighter prototype to achieve better performance while at the same time working on the new twin-engined fighter.

The redesign undertaken during the summer of 1938 was, to say the least, major, as it was proposed that only the fuselage and undercarriage of Design 18 (XF4F-2) be retained for the Design 36 prototype. New wings, with span and area respectively increased from 34 ft to 38 ft and from 232 sq ft to 260 sq ft, were to be fitted and given square tips instead of rounded tips. The tail surfaces were to be enlarged and also given square tips. The most important modification, however, was that affecting the powerplant installation with the 1,050-hp R-1830-66 with a single-stage, single-speed supercharger and its Hamilton Standard propeller being planned for replacement by a 1,200-hp Pratt & Whitney XR-1830-76 with a two-stage, two-speed supercharger driving a Curtiss Electric propeller. Calculated performance included a top speed of at least 330 mph thus increasing the speed advantage

115

The XF4F-3 in its original configuration returning from a gun-firing test in 1939. *(Grumman)*

over the XF2A-1 to more than 50 mph. It did not take long for BuAer to become interested in the Grumman proposal and, in October 1938, a contract was awarded for the modification of the XF4F-2 into the XF4F-3.

First flown by Bob Hall on 12 February, 1939, the modified prototype soon showed that it would exceed performance guarantees. However, it required further modifications to solve some stability problems and improve engine cooling. Over the next six months, BuNo 0383 was modified several times. First, wing dihedral was increased, aileron area was reduced, and rudder horn balance area was increased. Next, various modifications (such as the fitting of a large propeller spinner, the addition of propeller cuffs, and the testing of several configurations of cowling flaps) were incorporated in an attempt to solve engine cooling difficulties. Finally, however, Grumman's perseverance was rewarded with a first production contract for the F4F-3.

Production history

After the XF4F-3 had undergone preliminary evaluation at NAS Anacostia and carrier suitability trials at the Naval Aircraft Factory in Philadelphia, the Navy placed an initial order for fifty-four F4F-3s (BuNos 1844/1897) in August 1939. Three of these aircraft were completed as prototypes for other variants (BuNo 1897 as the XF4F-4 delivered in May 1941 and BuNos 1846 and 1847 as the XF4F-5s delivered in July 1940) and the first two F4F-3s (BuNos 1844 and 1845) were not up to initial production standards when first delivered in August 1940. Thereafter, additional orders were quickly placed and production fast gained tempo in the Bethpage plant. In early 1942, the Navy also placed large orders with Eastern Aircraft which went on to produce FM-1s and FM-2s in Linden, New Jersey. Altogether, a total of 7,825 Wildcats was produced in the following versions:

116

The XF4F-2 at Bethpage in March 1938. *(Grumman)*

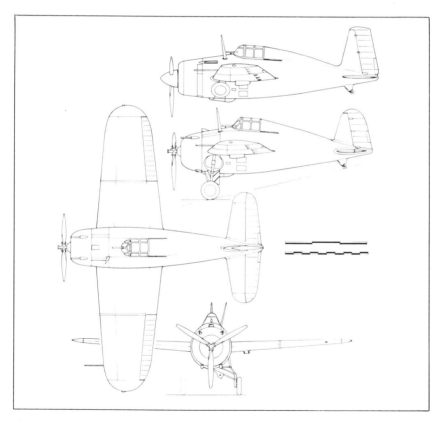

Grumman XF4F-2 Wildcat   XF4F-3 side view at top

117

XF4F-2: The Design 18 prototype (c/n 356, BuNo 0383) had mid-mounted cantilever wings, a fully enclosed cockpit, and a retractable main undercarriage with a single-stage, single-speed supercharger. It was powered by a 1,050-hp Pratt & Whitney R-1830-66 fourteen-cylinder radial. Normal armament consisted of two synchronized 0.50-in machine-guns mounted in the upper engine cowling but could be supplemented by two wing-mounted 0.50-in guns and/or two 100-lb bombs. This aircraft was first flown at Bethpage by Bob Hall on 2 September, 1937. During trials, the originally-fitted 10-ft propeller was replaced by a unit having a diameter of 9 ft 9 in and a small spinner was added. After failing to win a production order, it was rebuilt as the Design 36 prototype ordered as the XF4F-3.

XF4F-3: This prototype retained the XF4F-2 fuselage and main undercarriage (as well as its c/n and BuNo) but was fitted with enlarged wings and redesigned tail surfaces and was powered by a 1,200-hp XR-1830-76 radial with a two-stage, two-speed supercharger. First flown at Bethpage by Bob Hall on 12 February, 1939, the XF4F-3 was modified several times, as already described. In addition, several months after the F4F-3 had been ordered into production, the XF4F-3 underwent full-scale wind tunnel testing at Langley Field, Virginia. As a result, NACA recommended that the vertical tail surfaces be redesigned again and the tailplane be raised approximately 20 in, thus leading to the adoption of a shape which was to characterize the tail surfaces of all production versions until the advent of the FM-2. The prototype crashed at NAS Norfolk on 17 December, 1940, as the apparent result of a pilot error.

F4F-3: As construction of the first two F4F-3s (BuNos 1844 and 1845) was started by Grumman in anticipation of the production order, they were not to the full production standards. They differed from the next forty-nine aircraft (BuNos 1848/1896) delivered under the first production contract notably in being fitted with a propeller spinner and in being armed with a pair of cowl-mounted 0.30-in guns and two wing-mounted 0.50-in guns instead of four wing-mounted 0.50-in machine guns. Following completion of the first two aircraft, production deliveries began in August 1940 and

An F4F-3 of VF-3 from the uss *Lexington* (CV-2) during the spring of 1942. (*USN*)

118

continued until May 1943 as follow-on contracts first added 134 fighters (BuNos 2512/2538, 3856/3874, and 3970/4057) in three batches delivered before the end of 1942, and then added a batch of 100 fighter-trainers (BuNos 12230/12329) delivered in 1943. The latter, originally ordered as F4F-7 long-range reconnaissance aircraft, were then to have been built as F4F-3S floatplane fighters, but were finally delivered as F4F-3 fighter-trainers. Whereas the XF4F-2/XF4F-3 had a telescopic sight, all production fighter models were fitted with a reflector gun sight.

After the Chief of Naval Operations suggested to BuAer on 1 March, 1941, that some of the new fighters be given longer range so that they could be more effective when used for 'off-shore operation in defense of shipping' or could be transfered 'in flight over greater distance of open water,' Grumman was requested to increase the range of the F4F-3. To that end, a number of F4F-3s and F4F-3As were modified to carry a 42-US gal Grumman-designed, non-jettisonable tank flush-mounted beneath each wing to supplement the internal fuel tankage (one 117-gal main tank and a 27-gal auxiliary tank in the rear fuselage). Except as later modified in Pearl Harbor for use as a jettisonable ventral tank (see details under Service history), these tanks do not appear to have been used by the Navy.

During the course of production, and as a result of operational experience, the F4F-3s received numerous modifications and improvement including the fitting of an armoured windshield, self-sealing tanks, and armour plates to improve combat survivability and the replacement of the two cowl flaps with eight-segment flaps to improve engine cooling. Most aircraft had the carburettor intake on the upper cowling lip but others had the intake incorporated in the cowling. In addition, starting with about the one-hundredth F4F-3, the 1,200-hp R-1830-76 engine was replaced by the similarly-rated R-1830-86 which had two nose-mounted magnetos.

F4F-3A: As a precautionary measure when it was feared that production of two-stage engines would fall below requirements, BuAer ordered 95 aircraft

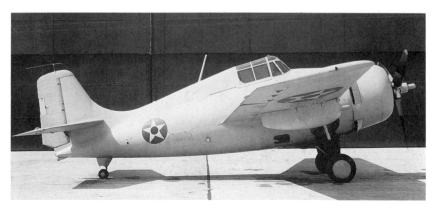

An F4F-3 fitted with a non-jettisonable 42-gallon external tank beneath each wing. (*Grumman*)

(BuNos 3875/3969) powered by 1,200 hp R-1830-90 radials with single-stage, two-speed supercharger. In other respects, these F4F-3As were similar to F4F-3s from the third production batch.

At the request of the Government of Greece, the US Government authorized the diversion of the first thirty for delivery to the Greek Air Force. Shipped in March 1941, these thirty aircraft were still at sea when Greece fell. They were then taken over by Great Britain, given the serials BJ501/BJ530, and designated Martlet IIIs. The remaining sixty-five were delivered to the USN in April and May 1941 for service alongside F4F-3s.

F4F-3P: This designation identified a number or early production F4F-3s (including BuNos 1849, 1852, 1856, 1865, 1867, 1870/1872, 1875, 1880, 1894, 2512, 2517, 2524, 2526, 2530, and 2537) which in 1942 were modified by the Navy and fitted with two cameras in place of the rear fuselage tank, thus reducing fuel capacity to 117 US gal. The four wing-mounted 0.50-in guns were retained.

F4F-3S: In October 1942, following the lead of the Imperial Japanese Navy, which had obtained a floatplane version of the Mitsubishi A6M2 fighter (type coded Rufe by the Allies, the A6M2-N was first encountered in June 1942 during operations in the Aleutians, and met in some number during the Guadalcanal landing in August 1942), the US Navy amended a contract for one-hundred F4F-7s to have these aircraft delivered as F4F-3S floatplane fighters. A Wildcatfish prototype was obtained by fitting a pair of Edo single-step floats and tailplane-mounted auxiliary fins to an F4F-3 (BuNo 4038). During trials, which began on 28 February, 1943, when T F 'Hank' Kurt first flew the F4F-3S from the East River at College Point, the addition of auxiliary tailplane fins proved insufficient to achieve satisfactory yaw stability and a ventral fin was provided. As the performance of the F4F-3S was disappointing, with a top speed of 266 mph being achieved at 20,300 ft, as more carriers were placed in operation, and as construction

The excessive drag of its twin Edo floats reduced the top speed of the F4F-3S to 266 mph whereas the carrier-based F4F-3 flew at a maximum speed of 328 mph. *(Grumman)*

battalions (the famed Seabees) were able to build air strips in a very short time, the Navy saw no further need for seaplane fighters to provide air cover during amphibious landing operations. The one hundred aircraft which had been ordered as F4F-7s but had later been scheduled for delivery as F4F-3S floatplane fighters were, in the end, delivered as fighter trainers with the F4F-3 designation.

XF4F-4: By a contract change issued in March 1940, Grumman was instructed to complete the last F4F-3 in the initial order (BuNo 1897) with hydraulically-operated folding wings. Conceived by Roy Grumman to increase by 150 per cent the number of aircraft which could be embarked aboard a carrier, this so-called 'sto-wing' reduced span to a mere 14 ft 4 in after the outboard panels rotated almost vertically while swinging aft. In fully folded position, the outboard panels rested, bird-like, parallel to the fuselage with the leading edge turned downward and the wing tips braced to the aft fuselage with jury struts*. When spread to flying position, the wings were safely latched by means of a lock-lock procedure (*ie*, a steel bolt latched each folding wing panel to its fixed stub and a second bolt passed through the first at a right angle).

A folding geometry very similar to that of the 'sto-wing' – but with the leading edge turned upward instead of downward – was used for the Blackburn Skua single-engined carrier fighter and dive-bomber. This two-seat monoplane first flew on 9 February, 1937, more than fifty months before the XF4F-4, and was first deployed aboard *Ark Royal* in November 1938.

The XF4F-4 was first flown on 15 April, 1941, delivered on 14 May, and later tested by VF-42 aboard *Yorktown*.

F4F-4: Whereas the wings of the XF4F-4 folded hydraulically, those of the 1,168 F4F-4s (BuNos 4058/4098, 5030/5261, 01991/02152, 03385/03544, and11655/12227) built in Bethpage folded manually. Each folding wing panel contained three 0.50-in machine-guns, two close to the wing fold and one further outboard. All F4F-4s were powered by the 1,200-hp R-1830-86 radial. During the course of production, the inboard wing section was fitted with a rack and related piping to enable a 58-US gal drop tank to be carried on each side. With these external tanks, total capacity was increased from 144 to 260 gal. The first F4F-4 flew on 7 November, 1941, and the last was delivered on 31 December, 1942.

An unidentified F4F-4 was fitted with extended wingtips bringing the span to approximately 42 ft. Details concerning this 1942 modification and its purpose cannot be found in Grumman's archives. Another unidentified F4F-4 was used in 1944 to test break-away wingtips such as those planned for the F8F Bearcat. For that purpose, the aircraft was fitted with redesigned folding wing panels reducing the span by 2 ft and incorporating 3-ft 6-in panels designed to break during violent manoeuvers. NACA tests

---

* Folding wings, of course, were not new to naval aviation. A patent had been taken out by Horace Short in 1912, and wings folding back alongside the fuselage had first been fitted to the Short S.41 when this tractor biplane was rebuilt in September 1912.

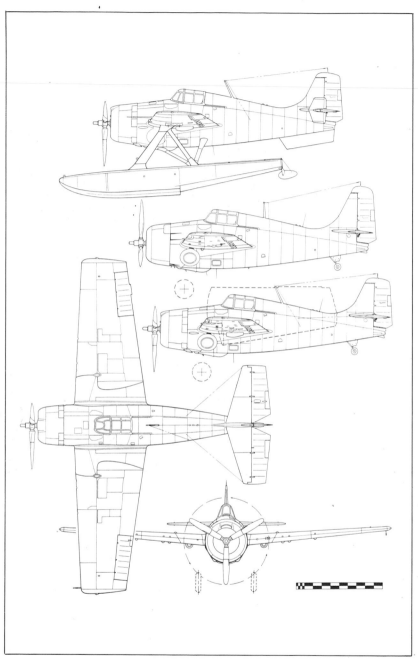

Grumman F4F-4 Wildcat. Side views of F4F-3S (top) and FM-2 (middle)

The XF4F-4 (BuNo 1897) was the first Wildcat to be fitted with folding wings. *(Grumman)*

BuNo 1846, the first of two XF4F-5s ordered by the US Navy to evaluate the nine-cylinder Wright Cyclone as an alternative power plant for its Wildcats. *(Grumman)*

were encouraging and led to the incorporation of break-away tips in early Bearcats.

F4F-4B: This USN designation identified F4F-4s delivered to Britain under Lend-Lease. Designated Martlet IVs in Fleet Air Arm service and assigned serials FN100/FN319, 220 of these aircraft were produced between February and November 1942, but six were lost in transit.

F4F-4P: One F4F-4 (BuNo 03386) and probably a few others were modified by the Navy as reconnaissance fighters with a rear fuselage camera installation similar to that of the F4F-3P.

XF4F-5: After France had ordered G-36As powered by the Wright Cyclone nine-cylinder radial, the Navy decided that for evaluation purposes the third and fourth F4F-3s (BuNos 1846 and 1847) should be completed as XF4F-5s powered by the 1,200-hp R-1820-40, the military version of the Cyclone G205A single-stage, two-row radial. Both were delivered in July 1940 to NAS Anacostia, where evaluation proved them to have performance very close to that of the F4F-3 except above 15,000 ft, where the two-stage R-1830-76 gave a definite edge to the F4F-3.

During the winter of 1942, BuNo 1846 was experimentally re-engined with an R-1820-54 turbo-supercharged engine with which it reached a top speed of 340 mph at 26,400 ft to become the fastest Wildcat. For comparive trials, BuNo 1847 was re-engined with an XR-1820-48 with two-stage supercharger, oil cooler integrated within the cowling (instead of the oil cooler mounted beneath the wings of all production Wildcats), and jet exhaust stacks.

XF4F-6: First flown on 11 October, 1940, and delivered to NAS Anacostia two weeks later, BuNo 7031 differed from F4F-3s in being powered by a 1,200-hp Pratt & Whitney R-1830-90 radial. It served as a prototype for the F4F-3As.

F4F-7: Almost eleven months before the Japanese attack against Pearl Harbor, the US Navy realized that it would soon need a long-range photographic-reconnaissance aircraft with performance sufficient to render its interception difficult when used to gather intelligence throughout much of the central and southwest Pacific. To fill this need, BuAer first requested on 13 January, 1941, that Grumman provide cost and time estimates to modify two F4F-3s for special long-range use and then on 29 January asked that this conversion be undertaken on a high priority basis. Design 52 was developed to that requirement and provided for the removal of guns, wing racks and gun sight, the fitting of a rounded windshield similar to that installed on early production aircraft before the adoption of a flat panel

The unarmed F4F-7 long-range reconnaissance version of the Widcat could be identified easily by the use of a rounded windshield and the installation of twin, upward-canted, fuel-venting pipes in the tail. (*Grumman*)

124

armoured windshield, and the installation of two cameras in place of the 27-gal aft fuselage tank of the F4F-3. Furthermore, Design 52 called for the use of non-folding wings housing 555 gal of fuel. Total capacity rose to 672 gal and range was expected to be increased more than fourfold to 3,700 miles.

Before work on the requested F4F-3 conversions was begun, BuAer increased its request for long-range reconnaissance aircraft and instructed Grumman to drop the conversion of the two F4F-3s in favour of completing twenty-one F4F-4 airframes (BuNos 5263/5283) as F4F-7s. The first F4F-7 was flown on 30 December, 1941, and all twenty-one were delivered before the end of the following year. Gross weight had increased from 7,952 lb for the F4F-4 to 10,328 lb for the fully fuelled F4F-7 and wing loading had also increased by 30 per cent to 39.7 lb/sq ft. The F4F-7s, however, had exceptionally long range and endurance as was demonstrated when one of these aircraft flew nonstop across the United States in just under 11 hours while being delivered to NAS San Diego. Some operational flights in the Solomons are said to have been even longer.

XF4F-8: In July 1942, after Grumman had studied ways to tailor the Wildcat for operations from the small deck of escort carriers, BuAer ordered two XF4F-8 prototypes (BuNos 12228/12229). The first flight was made on 8 November, 1942, and both prototypes were delivered at the end of the following month, one on the 30th and the other on the 31st. In addition to being powered by a 1,350-hp Wright XR-1820-56 nine-cylinder radial with jet exhaust pipes, the XF4F-8s differed from F4F-4s in having only four wing guns and slotted flaps instead of split flaps. It was found that with slotted flaps the aircraft would have to be fitted with enlarged horizontal tail surfaces and that increased engine torque required larger vertical surfaces. Later, BuNo 12228 was refitted with split flaps, thus eliminating the cost and time of redesigning the tailplane, and BuNo 12229

XF4F-8 (BuNo 12229), the second prototype for a Widcat version specially intended for operation from escort carriers, on 27 April, 1943, after it had been fitted with revised vertical tail surfaces as subsequently adopted for Eastern-built FM-2s. (*Grumman*)

125

was used to test the enlarged tail surfaces adopted for the Eastern Aircraft FM-2, the production version of the XF4F-8.

On BuAer instruction, in early 1943 the Naval Aircraft Factory undertook to study the feasibility of a radar installation for the F4F-8/FM-2 as the Navy then felt the need to operate night fighters from escort carriers as a means of intercepting German aircraft shadowing convoys under cover of darkness. Probably in part because it was realized that night operations from the small decks of carriers would be difficult, the study did not lead to actual radar installation on one of the XF4F-8s.

FM-1: Parts and components for 1,060 FM-1s (BuNos14992/15951 and 46738/46837) were built in three General Motors plants in New Jersey with final assembly taking place at Linden in a plant operated by the Eastern Aircraft Division of General Motors. These aircraft differed from the Grumman-built F4F-4s in having only four wing-mounted 0.50-in guns, but they carried a total of 1,720 rounds versus 1,440 rounds for the six-gun F4F-4s. Deliveries were made between August 1942 and September 1943 with 312 FM-1s being diverted to Britain as Martlet Vs (JV325/JV636)

FM-2: The Eastern production version of the Grumman XF4F-8 had split flaps, as retrofitted to BuNo 12228, and taller vertical tail surfaces, as first applied to BuNo 12229. It had the same gun installation as the FM-1 but its two wing racks were strengthened for 250-lb bombs.

The first FM-2s were powered by 1,350-hp Wright R-1820-56 radials with single-stage, two-speed supercharger. Later FM-2s were powered by R-1820-56As or R-1820-56Ws and -56WAs with water injection. Several other changes were introduced during the course of production. Beginning with BuNo 57044, internal fuel tank capacity was increased from 117 to 126 US gal. Starting with BuNo 74359, three Mk.5 zero-length launchers were fitted beneath each wing to enable late production FM-2s to carry 5-in (127-mm) HVAR projectiles.

A total of 4,777 FM-2s (BuNos 15952/16791, 46838/47437, 55050/55649, 56684/57083, 73499/75158, and 86297/86973) was built by Eastern Aircraft between September 1943 and August 1944. Of this total, 370 were delivered to the Fleet Air Arm with which they were designated Wildcat VIs (JV637/JV924, JW785/JW836, and JZ860/JZ889).

FM-2P: A small number of FM-2s were modified by the Navy as reconnaissance fighters with a rear fuselage camera installation similar to that of the F4F-4P.

XF2M-1: At the behest of BuAer and with assistance from their colleagues at Grumman, Eastern engineers studied various ways of increasing the FM-2's level speed and climb performance by substituting more powerful engines in cleaned-up airframes. The use of two types of twin-row radials, the Pratt & Whitney R-2000 and Wright R-2600, was quickly rejected and plans were made to use more powerful versions of the Cyclone single-row radial, either the R-1820-62 or the R-1820-70W. Although design work on the XF2M-1 had been started in October 1942, it had almost immediately been slowed down as the Bureau of Aeronautics wanted to avoid delays

An Eastern FM-2 with 'double-nut' Air Group Commander markings. *(USN)*

This French-ordered G-36A appears already to have received British-style fuselage roundels with yellow outline, but retains French-style rudder striping. *(Grumman)*

which would result from a production switch from FM-2s to F2M-1s. Three XF2M-1s (BuNos 82855/82857) had been ordered but the contract was cancelled in the spring of 1945 before the completion of a prototype.

G-33: Design 33 was a Grumman-funded preliminary study undertaken in February 1938 to determine performance gains which could be obtained by replacing the R-1830 of the F4F with a 1,600-hp Wright R-2600 two-row radial. Within one month Grumman also started work on Design 35, an all-new aircraft powered by the R-2600 engine. Neither Design 33 nor Design 35 proved sufficiently promising to warrant further work, but information gained at that time was put to use in September 1940 when the company began working on Design 50, the aircraft which gained fame as the Hellcat.

G-36A: The French Purchasing Commission became interested in the Grumman carrier fighter soon after the war started in Europe and initially wanted to order one hundred aircraft for the Aéronautique Navale. It was intended that these aircraft would be similar in most respects to the F4F-3. However, fear that Pratt & Whitney could not keep up with the demand for Twin Wasp (US military designation R-1830) twin-row radials led to the Commission ordering fewer aircraft (eighty-one in fly-away condition plus spare parts equivalent to ten additional aircraft) and requesting that they be powered by the 1,200-hp Wright Cyclone G205A nine-cylinder radial with single-stage, two-~~row~~ speed supercharger. The French-ordered G-36As were also to differ from the F4F-3s in being armed with four to six 7.5-mm Darne machine guns, two being fuselage-mounted and one being mounted in each wing (with provision for a second gun in each wing).

Bearing the temporary US civil registration (NX-G1), the first G-36A flew on 10 May, 1940, on the very first day of the German invasion; none had been delivered by the time France surrendered on 23 June. Without wasting time, representatives of the French and British Purchasing Commissions ~~agreed~~ to have all completed and all yet to be built G-36As transferred to Britain as Martlet Is. All ninety-one aircraft, including the ten which had been ordered as spare parts by France, were completed in flyable condition and were given British serials in the following sequences AL231/AL262, AX725/AX747, AX753/AX754, AX761, AX824/AX829, BJ554/BJ570, and BT447/BT456.

Before being flown to Canada for subsequent shipment to the United Kingdom, the aircraft were fitted with revised armament (two 0.50-in Colt-Browning guns in each wing and no fuselage guns), reverse operation throttle, and some British instrumentation and radio equipment. Deliveries began on 27 July, 1940, and were completed three months later. However, ten Martlet Is were lost at sea when the ship in which they were carried was torpedoed in the North Atlantic.

G-36B: Like its French counterpart, the British Purchasing Commission initially ordered aircraft with non-folding wings but selected the 1,200-hp Twin Wasp S3C-4G with two-speed, single-stage supercharger as the powerplant for one-hundred G-36Bs. However, almost immediately after placing this order, the Commission became aware of the folding wings being developed for the XF4F-4. As the Royal Navy was planning to operate a number of escort carriers with small decks and no hangars, the Commission negotiated a contract amendment to have the first ten aircraft (AM954/AM963) delivered with fixed wings and fitted later with folding wings, while the next ninety (AM964/AM999 and AJ100/AJ153) were to be delivered with folding wings. Both fixed and folding wing versions, which were respectively fitted with four and six 0.50-in guns, were designated Martlet IIs in British service.

The first fixed-wing G-36B (AM954) was flown at Bethpage in October 1940; the first G-36B with folding wings (AM964) first flew on 8 July, 1941.

128

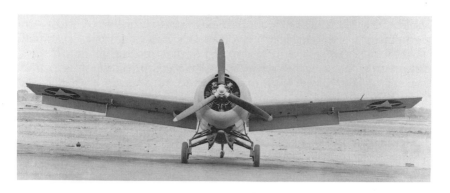

The experimental G-53 (BuNo 5262) with full-span (duplex) flaps. *(Grumman)*

Deliveries were made between March 1941 and April 1942, but five were lost at sea.

G-53: This experimental aircraft was obtained by fitting non-folding wings with full-span (duplex) flaps to the 274th F4F-4 (BuNo 5262). The inboard split flaps were the same as those used on standard Wildcats and were pneumatically operated whereas the outboard flaps were electrically actuated. The G-53 first flew on 5 May, 1942.

Service history

While the first two F4F-3s (BuNos 1844 and 1845) initially were respectively retained by Grumman for additional testing and sent to the Naval Aircraft Maintenance Unit in Philadelphia, the next forty-nine aircraft were delivered to three operational squadrons: eighteen went to VF-41 in November–December 1940 for service aboard *Ranger* (CV-4), twenty-one went to VF-72 in December 1940 and January 1941 for service aboard *Wasp* (CV-7), and, in January 1941, the last ten went to VF-71 also assigned to *Wasp*. These three squadrons first deployed aboard their carriers in March 1941 for a training cruise in the Caribbean Sea from which pilots returned generally pleased with the performance and handling characteristics of their new mounts. However, they also reported fuel venting problems, windshield failures, and gun jamming occurrences. Flotation bags were the source of other difficulties, as on at least two occasions they popped out from their wing storage compartment during flights. Moreover, these early aircraft were not yet fitted with self-sealing fuel tanks and armour plate and hence were not yet combat ready. Fortunately, most difficulties and deficiencies were corrected during the summer and autumn of 1941.

On 1 October, 1940, just over two months before the United States was drawn into the war, the F4F was officially named Wildcat, thus starting the Grumman 'cat' line which has remained unbroken until now. When Japan launched its multi-pronged offensive stretching from Pearl Harbor to

Malaya, less than 230 F4F-3s and F4F-3As had been delivered. Most were then assigned to seven Navy squadrons (VF-3, VF-5, VF-6, VF-8, and VF-42 which were respectively assigned to the carriers *Saratoga*, *Ranger*, *Enterprise*, *Hornet*, and *Yorktown*, and VF-71 and VF-72 which were both assigned to the *Wasp*) and three Marine squadrons (VMF-111 and VMF-121, based at Quantico, Virginia, but on manoeuvres at New Bern, North Carolina and VMF-211 which had aircraft at Ewa, Hawaii, and on Wake Island), with a few others serving with the Advanced Carrier Training Group or being held in reserve or undergoing repair.

The war began badly for VMF-211. On the very first day (7 December, 1941, at Pearl Harbor but 8 December on Wake as that island is on the other side of the International Date Line) sixteen Wildcats were destroyed on the

BuNo 1850, an F4F-3 of VF-41, with Neutrality Patrol star on the forward fuselage. (*Grumman*)

An F4F-3 of VF-41 in early wartime markings. (*USN/National Archives*)

130

ground, nine at Ewa and seven on Wake. The next day, Lt David S Kliever and Tech Sgt William Hamilton shot down two Mitsubishi G3M2s (twin-engined Japanese bombers which soon thereafter acquired the Allied code name of *Nell*), the first to fall to the guns of US Wildcats. Over the next thirteen days, until the last two F4F-3s were shot down by Mitsubishi A6M2 Zero fighters from the carriers *Hiryu* and *Soryu,* the Wake defenders fought on against overwhelming odds. They are believed to have shot down eight Japanese aircraft and to have contributed to the sinking of one, or possibly two, destroyers on 11 December. For his part in the sinking of the *Kisaragi,* for shooting down two enemy aircraft, and for the action on the ground during which he was killed shortly before the defenders were forced to surrender on 23 December, 1941, Capt Henry T Elrod was posthumously awarded the Medal of Honor.

In US Navy service, Wildcats claimed their first victory during operations in the Gilbert Islands when, on 1 February, 1942, an aircraft from VF-42 operating from *Yorktown* shot down a Kawanishi H6K2 (a four-engined Japanese flying-boat later coded *Mavis* by the Allies). Less than three weks later, on 20 February, Lt Edward H 'Butch' O'Hare from VF-3 became the first USN ace by shooting down five Mitsubishi G4M1 twin-engined bombers which were attacking *Lexington* during operations by Task Force 11 against Rabaul. For this action, Lt O'Hare became the second Wildcat pilot to be awarded the Medal of Honor.

After the XF4F-4 had been evaluated aboard *Yorktown* by VF-42 pilots, folding-wing Wildcats began reaching operational squadrons in the Pacific

An F4F-3P of VMO-251 being refuelled at Kirby Schuessler Field in the New Hebrides on 19 November, 1942. (*USN/National Archives*)

131

during the month of March and were first taken on a combat deployment when VF-6 and VF-8 operated a mix of F4F-3s and F4F-4s from *Enterprise* and *Hornet* during the Doolittle raid against Tokyo and other Japanese cities on 16 April. Only fixed-wing F4F-3s were flown by VF-2 and VF-42 from *Lexington* and *Yorktown* on the occasion of the world's first carrier battle on 7-8 May in the Coral Sea. Four weeks later, on 3-6 June during the momentous Battle of Midway, the three squadrons embarked aboard *Enterprise*, *Hornet*, and *Yorktown* (VF-6, VF-8, and VF-3) all flew F4F-4s. As is well-known, the Japanese suffered a crushing defeat off Midway, but the US price paid, including the loss of many Wildcats and their pilots, was also high.

In air combat against the Imperial Japanese Navy's nimble and well armed Mitsubishi A6M2 carrier fighters, F4F-3s and F4F-4s had by then been found less manoeuvrable and to have slightly lower performance (notably in terms of level speed, climb, and ceiling) but were acknowleged to be superior in push-overs and rolls at high speeds, to have superior armament (particularly the F4F-4s which had six 0.50-in guns), and to offer better protection for their pilots, as production F4F-3s and F4F-4s had adequate armour and fuel tank protection. Accordingly, Wildcat pilots avoided dogfights with the Zero and relied extensively for mutual protection on the 'Thach Weave,' the manoeuvre developed by Lt-Cdr John S 'Jimmy' Thach and which called for two fighters to fly a repeated criss-cross pattern to cover each other's six o'clock position.

When US forces went on the offensive in August 1942, Wildcats were in the lead. Ninety-nine F4F-4s were embarked aboard *Enterprise*, *Saratoga*, and *Wasp* to provide cover during Operation *Watchtower*, the amphibious landing on Guadalcanal. In the early hours of 7 August, VF-71 pilots destroyed a dozen A6M2-N floatplane fighters based at Tulagi, VF-5 pilots worked over Japanese installations on Guadalcanal, and VF-6 pilots

Taken in September 1942 at NAS Norfolk, Virginia, this photograph shows one of the first Tarpon Is of the Fleet Air Arm sharing the ramp with a Wildcat of VGS-30. (*USN/National Archives*)

provided air cover. The first Japanese air raid, launched from Rabaul, developed in early afternoon and ended unfavourably for VF-5 and VF-6 as they lost nine F4F-4s while claiming five enemy aircraft destroyed and three damaged. Later in the day, the score was more than evened as fifteen Japanese aircraft were shot down for the loss of six Wildcats. A long and costly campaign had started, during which carrier-based Wildcats (including those from VGF-27 and VGF-28 which were the first in the Pacific to fly combat sorties from the decks of escort carriers, in this instance *Suwanee* (ACV-27) and *Chenango* (ACV-28)) fought against land-based Japanese aircraft and took part in several major sea actions.

Wildcats first operated from Guadalcanal on 20 August after nineteen F4F-4s from VMF-223 were launched from the escort carrier *Long Island* (ACV-1) to begin operations from Henderson Field. From then until 8 February, 1943, when the island was secured, six Marine Fighting Squadrons (VMF-112, -121, -122, -212, -223, and -224) equipped with F4F-4s and one Marine Observation Squadron (VMO-251) with F4F-3Ps, occasionally reinforced by Navy squadrons, fought with distinction. An idea of their achievements can be gauged from the fact that six of the eleven Marine pilots who won the Medal of Honor during the Second World War did so while flying Wildcats from Guadalcanal and over the Solomons. They were: Lt-Col Harold W Bauer, who at war's end was credited with the destruction of eleven Japanese aircraft; First Lt Jefferson J DeBlanc, who scored nine victories, including five on 21 January, 1943, before he had to bale out from his Wildcat (Jeff DeBlanc remained hidden with coast-watchers on Japanese-held Kolombangara for thirteen days and then was returned to Guadalcanal by a Duck); Capt Joseph J Foss, with twenty-six victories); Maj Robert Galer, thirteen victories; Maj John L Smith, nineteen victories; and First Lt James E Swett, who claimed 16.5 victories including eight in a single action over Tulagi on 7 April, 1943.

As soon as US Naval Aviation went to war, the desirability of extending

Admittedly of poor quality, this rare photograph shows a Marine F4F-4 with a jury-rigged 42-gallon ventral drop tank. This Wildcat was photographed from the cockpit of an Army Air Forces Douglas C-47 during a ferry flight from Esperitu Santo to Guadalcanal in October 1942. *(John Cairns, courtesy of Fred C Dickey Jr and Grumman)*

the Wildcat's range, if not for combat at least for ferry purposes, was demonstrated as F4F-3s could not be flown from Hawaii to reinforce VMF-211 on Wake Island. As noted earlier, Grumman had provided non-jettisonable tanks but, unfortunately, none had been sent to Pearl Harbor. Without these tanks, F4F-3s did not have sufficient range to reach Wake. In early 1942, in answer to an urgent request from the fleet, some of these tanks were shipped by Pan American Airways Clipper from North Island, California, to Pearl Harbor. There, engineers jury-rigged fittings so that a Grumman 42-gal tank could be carried beneath the fuselage of the F4F-4. Unlike the wing installation on the F4F-3, this ventral installation enabled the tank to be jettisoned.

Fittings were first installed in May 1942 on BuNo 5050, one of the F4F-4s with which VF-3 was being re-equipped, and the ventral drop tank installation was tested by the squadron C O, Lt-Cdr John S Thach. Although somewhat crude, this installation worked satisfactorily and other F4F-4s were modified before Operation *Watchtower* began. There is no evidence that belly tanks were used in combat. However, they were frequently used in 1942-43 when Wildcats were ferried from Guadalcanal to Espiritu Santo, where they were overhauled and repaired before being returned to Guadalcanal. Subsequently, the availability of late production F4F-4s with provision for carrying a 58-gal drop tank beneath each wing eliminated the need for the ventral drop tank.

Other means of extending range were investigated in the Continental United States, thus leading to flight tests in May 1942 during which a Wildcat was towed behind a Douglas BD-1 and a pair of Wildcats was towed by a Boeing B-17. During towing trials, with at least one flight lasting eight hours, the Wildcat's engine was shut off and its propeller feathered. Before being released from tow, the Wildcat's pilot started the engine by allowing the propeller to windmill. Having been towed, the Wildcat in turn was used

An FM-1 making a jet assisted take-off (JATO) from the deck of a USN escort carrier on 18 March, 1943. (*USN/National Archives*)

during the same year for towing a Cessna UC-77 from Philadelphia to Bolling Field, Washington, D C, to demonstrate the feasibility of towing disabled aircraft. However, operational use of the Wildcat either to tow a single-engined aircraft or to be towed behind a multi-engined aircraft was never seriously considered.

In the war against the European Axis powers, Wildcats were first in action in April and May 1942 when those from *Wasp* (CV-7) flew combat air patrols over the North Atlantic and Western Mediterranean on the two occasions that this carrier was used to ferry RAF Spitfires to Malta. Then, during Operation *Torch* in November 1942, Wildcats operated from the deck of *Ranger* (CV-4), *Sangamon* (ACV-26), *Suwanee* (ACV-27), and *Santee* (ACV-29) to provide air cover for the transports and warships and air support for Army troops during landings in French Morocco. As these landings were initially opposed by French forces loyal to the Vichy Government, six Wildcats were lost in the first encounter with French fighters on the morning of 8 November. Quickly recovering the initiative, the Wildcats had the upper hand by the time the Vichy French surrendered on 11 November. F4F-4s took part in their only other offensive operations outside the Pacific when *Ranger* joined the British Home Fleet in several operations between August and December 1943. The most notable of these was a successful strike flown on 3 October against German shipping in Bodø in Norway.

During the second half of 1943 and throughout the following year, Wildcats were rapidly supplanted aboard fast carriers by Hellcats and in service with land-based Marine squadrons by Corsairs. However, FM-1s and FM-2s remained the most important fighters aboard escort carriers. In

An FM-2 of VC-12 on the deck of the USS *Core* (CVE-13) during anti-submarine operations in the North Atlantic on 10 April, 1944. *(USN/National Archives)*   ·

135

the Atlantic, they operated alongside Avengers on anti-submarine operations (not always with impunity as a VC-13 Wildcat from the USS *Core* (CVE-13) was shot down on 13 July, 1943, by anti-aircraft guns from U-487) and against Luftwaffe maritime patrol aircraft shadowing convoys. In the Pacific, Wildcats operated from escort carriers primarily to provide close air support during amphibious landings. This was notably the case in October 1944 when Army troops were landed on Leyte Island under the protective cover of Wildcats, Hellcats, and Avengers embarked aboard the seventeen escort carriers of Task Group 77.4. On that occasion, Wildcats from VF-76 and from fourteen Composite Squadrons (VC-3, -4, -5, -10, -20, -21, -27, -65, -66, -75, -76, -78, -80, and -81) not only provided close air support for the troops and fought off enemy aircraft (including kamikazes, which made their appearance on 25 October) but also put up a determined defence against Japanese battleships and other surface vessels during the Battle of Samar. Remaining embarked aboard *Savo Island* (CVE-78) after that battle, pilots from VC-27 were credited with the destruction of 62.5 Japanese aircraft during four months of operations in Philippine waters, thus making their squadron the top-scoring CVE unit.

During the war, no fewer than 1,123 of Grumman's first monoplane fighters were obtained by the Royal Navy, including one hundred ordered by Great Britain, 127 taken over from French and Greek contracts, and 902 delivered under Lend-Lease. They were known as Martlets until 13 January, 1944, when the name was changed to Wildcat to conform to US Navy nomenclature. The ninety-one Martlet Is were G-36A aircraft taken over by Great Britain following the fall of France. One hundred Martlet IIs were Grumman G-36Bs ordered by the British Purchasing Commission; only the first ten of which were completed with non-folding wings. Thirty Martlet IIIs with non-folding wings were taken over from a Greek contract.

Bearing identification markings as applied during the summer of 1945 to aircraft embarked on the USS *Natoma Bay* (CVE-62), this beautifully restored FM-2 was photographed in 1980.
(Peter Kirkup)

AM958, one of ten Martlet IIs delivered with non-folding wings. *(Air Ministry)*

Aircraft delivered under Lend-Lease included 220 Martlet IVs, 312 Martlet Vs, and 370 Wildcat VIs. Most of these aircraft were taken on charge in the United Kingdom, where Lend-Lease Martlet IVs and Vs and Wildcat VIs were fitted with British equipment by Blackburn Aircraft Ltd. Others were taken on charge in Africa (notably seventeen Martlet IVs which had been shipped to Mombasa), in India (where fifty-four Martlet IIs had been shipped), in Australia (where a number of Wildcat VIs were shipped for embarkation aboard carriers operating in the Indian and Pacific Oceans) and in the United States (notably the Martlet IVs which carried US markings when going aboard HMS *Victorious* to take part in joint US-British operations in the Southwest Pacific from May to July 1943).

The first to reach the United Kingdom were the ex-French Martlet Is which entered Fleet Air Arm (F A A) service with No.804 Squadron at Hatston in Orkney in October 1940. Two pilots of this squadron, Lt L V Carter and Sub-Lt A Parker, forced down a Junkers Ju 88A which, on 25 December, 1940, was attempting to bomb the Home Fleet at Scapa Flow. Theirs was the first victory to be credited to an American-built fighter in British service.

The first to go to sea aboard a carrier of the Royal Navy were a pair of Martlet IIs from B Flight, No.802 Squadron, which in August 1941 went on convoy escort duty to Russia aboard HMS *Argus**. During the return voyage from Murmansk aboard HMS *Victorious,* these two Martlet IIs escorted Fairey Albacores during shipping strikes off the coast of Norway in September and October. From carriers and escort carriers of the Home Fleet, Martlets and Wildcats later provided air cover for Arctic convoys to Murmansk (Nos.811, 813, 816, 819, 824, 825, 835, 842, 846, and 853 Squadrons), flew air cover and anti-flak sorties during Operations *Tungsten* and *Goodwood* against the *Tirpitz* in April and August 1944 (Nos.842, 846,

* It is worth noting that the initial deployment of Market IIs with folding wings took place three months before the US Navy took delivery of its first folding-wing F4F-4s.

137

852, 881, 882, 896, and 898 Squadrons) and during anti-shipping strikes in Norwegian coastal waters from April 1944 until May 1945 (Nos.813, 821, 824, 835, 842, 846, 852, 853, 856, 881, 882, 896, and 898 Squadrons). On 26 March, 1945, during one of the last strikes of the war, Wildcats from No.882 Squadron embarked on HMS *Searcher* shot down five Messerschmitt Bf 109Gs, thus proving that the obsolescent Grumman fighter still had quite a bite.

In the Mediterranean and North African theatre of operations, Martlet IIIs were first assigned in September 1941 to No. 805 Squadron for operations over the Western Desert with the Naval Fighter Wing. In the Western Mediterranean, Martlet IIs were first operated by No. 806 Squadron aboard HMS *Indomitable* during Operation *Pedestal* in August 1942. Thereafter carrier-based Martlets, and later Wildcats, took part in numerous operations in the Mediterranean and Aegean and notably supported landings in Algeria during Operation *Torch* in November 1942 (Nos. 882, 888, and 893 Squadrons), in Sicily during Operation *Husky* in July 1943 (No. 888 Squadron), in Southern Italy during Operation *Avalanche* in September 1943 (Nos. 878 and 890 Squadrons), and in Southern France during Operation *Dragon* in August 1944 (No. 881 Squadron, which also took part in mopping-up operations in the Aegean in September 1944).

In the Indian Ocean, Martlet IIs made their debut in May 1942 during Operation *Ironclad*, when Britain feared that the Vichy Government would let Japan establish bases on the French-controlled island of Madagascar. In three days of operations, Nos. 881 and 882 Squadrons operating from HMS *Illustrious* claimed six confirmed victories (four Morane M.S.406 fighters and two Potez 63.11 reconnaissance aircraft) and eleven probables for the loss of a single Martlet II. Following this operation, *Illustrious* and her Martlets remained in the Indian Ocean but saw little action until withdrawn in January 1943. Wildcats returned to this theatre of operations in 1944 with

A June 1943 recognition photograph of a Martlet V. *(Air Ministry)*

138

Nos. 832, 834, 851, and 890 Squadrons providing trade protection from the escort carriers *Begum, Battler, Shah,* and *Atheling* beginning that summer.

Above all, however, it was in the Battle of the Atlantic that Martlets and Wildcats distinguished themselves while operating aboard escort carriers. The first to do so had been six Martlet IIs from No. 802 Squadron aboard HMS *Audacity* which shot down five Focke-Wulf Fw 200C patrol bombers and shared in the destruction of the submarine U-231 during two escort voyages to and from Gibraltar in September-November 1941. Unfortunately, *Audacity* was sunk on 21 December while returning to Britain. No other escort carriers were available until April 1943 when HMS *Biter* joined the fray with No. 811 Squadron. During the next sixteen months, until the Battle of the Atlantic was won, Martlets and Wildcats from Nos.811, 813, 819, 824, 833, 842, 846, 881, 882, 892, 896, and 898 Squadrons hunted Heinkel He 177s, Focke-Wulf Fw 200s, and Junkers Ju 88s and Ju 290s (with at least one example of each falling to the guns of Wildcats) and strafed surfaced U-boats to distract flak gunners during rocket, bomb, or depth charge attacks by strike aircraft.

Virtually none of the British-, French-, or Greek-ordered Martlets were operational at the end of the war but a Martlet I, AL246, survived and is now in the FAA Museum at Yeovilton. The Lend-Lease Wildcats were dumped after the war as Great Britain had no need to purchase them and the United States already had too many aircraft to dispose of.

PRODUCTION: A total of 7,825 Wildcats was built, including 1,988 F4Fs produced by Grumman between September 1937 and May 1943 and 5,837 FMs produced by Eastern Aircraft between August 1942 and August 1945, as follows:

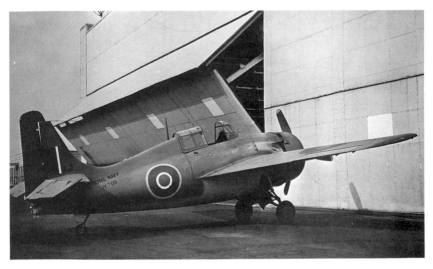

Wildcat VI (JV708) awaiting shipment to Great Britain.

139

A Marine FM-2 aboard the USS *Solomons* (CVE-67) during training operations off the East Coast of the United States in May 1945. *(USN/National Archives)*

1	XF4F-2	2	XF4F-5
(1)	XF4F-3	1	XF4F-6
285	F4F-3	21	F4F-7
95	F4F-3A	2	XF4F-8
(1)	F4F-3S	91	G-36A
1	XF4F-4	100	G-36B
1,168	F4F-4	1,060	FM-1
220	F4F-4B	4,777	FM-2
1	G-53		

The Grumman-built aircraft were assigned the following BuNos (including Lend-Lease aircraft which were later given British serials) and British military serials:

XF4F-2:   BuNo 0383
XF4F-3:   (BuNo 0383)
F4F-3:   BuNos 1844/1845, 1848/1896, 2512/2538, 3856/3874,
          3970/4057, and 12230/12329
F4F-3A: BuNos 3875/3969
F4F-3S: (BuNo 4038)
XF4F-4:   BuNo 1897
F4F-4:   BuNos 4058/4098, 5030/5261, 01991/02152,
          03385/03544, and 11655/12227

140

F4F-4B: FN100/FN319
XF4F-5:   BuNos 1846/1847
XF4F-6:   BuNo 7031
F4F-7:   BuNos 5263/5283
XF4F-8:   BuNos 12228/12229
G-36A: AL231/AL262, AX725/AX747, AX753/AX754, AX761,
           AX824/AX829, BJ554/BJ570, and BT447/BT456
G-36B: AJ100/AJ153 and AM954/AM999
G-53:   BuNo 5262

The Eastern-built aircraft were assigned the following BuNos (including Lend-Lease aircraft which were later given British serials):

FM-1:   BuNos14992/15951 and 46738/46837
FM-2:   BuNos 15952/16791, 46838/47437, 55050/55649,
         56684/57083, 73499/75158, and 86297/86973

	XF4F-2	F4F-3	F4F-4	FM-2
DIMENSIONS:				
Span, ft in	34 0	38 0	38 0	38 0
(m)	(10.36)	(11.58)	(11.58)	(11.58)
Span (wings folded), ft in	N.A.	N.A.	14 4	14 4
(m)	(N.A.)	(N.A.)	(4.37)	(4.37)
Length, ft in	26 5	28 9	28 9	28 11
(m)	(8.05)	(8.76)	(8.76)	(8.81)
Height, ft in	–	9 2½	9 21/2	9 11
(m)	(–)	(2.81)	(2.81)	(3.02)
Wing area, sq ft	232	260	260	260
(sq m)	(21.55)	(24.15)	(24.15)	(24.15)
WEIGHTS:				
Empty, lb	4,036	5,342	5,758	5,448
(kg)	(1,831)	(2,423)	(2,612)	(2,471)
Loaded, lb	5,535	7,002	7,406	7,487
(kg)	(2,511)	(3,176)	(3,359)	(3,396)
Maximum, lb	–	8,152	7,952	8,271
(kg)	(–)	(3,698)	(3,607)	(3,752)
Wing loading,* lb/sq ft	23.9	26.9	28.5	28.8
(kg/sq m)	(116.5)	(131.5)	(139.1)	(140.6)
Power loading,* lb/hp	5.3	5.8	6.2	5.5
(kg/hp)	(2.4)	(2.6)	(2.8)	(2.5)
PERFORMANCE:		*330/22000*	*Same*	*402/15000*
Max speed, mph/ft	288/10,000	~~328/21,000~~	~~318/19,400~~	~~332/28,800~~
(kmh/m)	(463/3,050)	(528/6,400)	(512/5,915)	(534/8,780)
Cruising speed, mph	–	147	148	164
(kmh)	(–)	(237)	(238)	(264)
Climb rate, ft/min	–	*3,265/1*	~~1,950/1~~ *Same*	~~3,650/1~~ *5,000/1 min*
(m/sec)	(–)	(11.5)	(9.9)	(18.5)
Service ceiling, ft	29,450	37,500	34,000	34,700
(m)	(8,975)	(11,430)	(10,365)	(10,575)
Normal range, miles	740	845	910	900
(km)	(1,190)	(1,360)	(1,465)	(1,450)
Max range, miles	–	1,690	1,250	1,310
(km)	(–)	(2,720)	(2,010)	(2,110)

* wing and power loadings are calculated at normal loaded weight and maximum take-off power.

141

The XF5F-1 climbing over Long Island during an early test flight. *(Grumman)*

Grumman XF5F-1 Skyrocket

On 30 June, 1938, when the US Navy ordered the XF5F-1 as its first twin-engined fighter intended for shipboard operations, the award of this contract was not as spontaneous and momentous a decision as it has since been made to appear. Indeed, it was the result of considered planning dating back to the summer of 1935 when BuAer first contemplated sponsoring the development of a single-seat, twin-engined carrier fighter. Moreover, the Navy had first ordered a twin-engined carrier aircraft in 1926, the Douglas XT2D-1 torpedo bomber biplane, but carrier trials planned for April 1927 aboard the uss *Langley* did not take place. Abroad, the first shipboard operations of a twin-engined monoplane took place in September 1936, when the Potez 56E made several arrested landings and take-offs aboard the *Béarn* during trials off the coast of southern France.

By early 1937, BuAer had come to believe that engines of higher horsepower than the 1,000-hp Pratt & Whitney R-1830 would not give any increase in speed over that expected to be reached by the XF4F-2, then still under construction. Thus, considering it necessary to resort to a twin-engined design for fighters to reach speed in excess of 300 mph, BuAer sent out a request on 18 March, 1937, for twin-engined fighter proposals. In answer, Grumman submitted a proposal for its Design 25, a high-altitude fighter powered by a pair of turbosupercharged Allison V-1710 liquid-cooled engines. BuAer, however, felt that neither Design 25 nor the twin-engined proposals submitted by Brewster, Curtiss, Lockheed, Seversky, and Vought offered sufficient performance improvements over new single-engined fighters to warrant awarding a development contract.

After rejecting these industry proposals, BuAer undertook its own preliminary study to determine the best performance that could be expected

The XF5F-1 after installation of new propeller hubs and revised exhaust system. *(Grumman)*

from shipboard fighters powered by either two turbosupercharged R-1535 or R-1830 radials or one turbosupercharged V-1710 liquid-cooled engine. BuAer also explored the benefits which could be derived from allowing the stalling speed of the twin-engined aircraft to increase from the then standard 65 mph limit to 70 mph. Based on its Design 144 calculations, on 1 February, 1938, BuAer sent to the industry a request for designs and informal proposals for (1) a single-engined fighter designed around the Allison mechanically supercharged engine, and (2) a twin-engined fighter weighing less than 9,000 lb. These aircraft were to be armed with two 20-mm cannon, two 0.30-in machine guns, and 200 lb of anti-aircraft bombs. Performance requirements included highest possible speed, take-off distance of 200 ft with wind-over-deck of 25 knots, and stalling speed of not more than 70 mph.

On 11 April 1938, Bell, Brewster, Curtiss, Grumman, and Vought submitted proposals for either or both single-engined and twin-engined fighters with the specified powerplants. Vought also proposed a fighter to be powered by a new Pratt & Whitney R-2800 eighteen-cylinder radial. This time BuAer was satisfied, and on 30 June it awarded contracts to Vought, for the XF4U-1 with an 1,850-hp Pratt & Whitney XR-2800-4 radial, and to Grumman, for the XF5F-1 then expected to be powered by a pair of 750-hp Pratt & Whitney R-1535-96 radials. A third contract was awarded, on 8 November, to Bell for the XFL-1 powered by an 1,150-hp Allison V-1710-6 liquid-cooled engine.

As detailed work on Design 34 was progressing, Grumman was forced to substitute Wright R-1820 nine-cylinder radials for the much smaller R-1535-96 fourteen-cylinder engines as Pratt & Whitney was no longer offering a development of this powerplant with the two-speed super-charger* which had been specified in the April 1938 proposal. Although the greater diameter of the Wright engines was bound to affect adversely forward and downward visibility, the Navy agreed reluctantly to this change to avoid an excessively long wait for its first twin-engined fighter. Nevertheless, as priority was given to ironing out teething difficulties encountered by the F4F-3 single-engined fighter, the XF5F-1 (c/n 505, BuNo 1442) was not completed until March 1940. Late as it was, the XF5F-1 was Grumman's first aircraft to be fitted with folding wings, the panels outboard of the engine nacelles folding upward, and to be planned for a heavy armament. Four 23-mm Madsen guns were to be mounted in the abbreviated nose just aft of the wing leading edge and forty 5-lb anti-aircraft bomblets were to be carried in the wing outer panels. The non-availability of the Madsen cannon later led to a proposal to use a quartet of 0.50-in machine-guns, but armament was never fitted.

Powered by two 1,200-hp Wright XR-1820-40 and -42 engines driving three-blade propellers rotating in opposite directions BuNo 1442 was first flown at Bethpage on 1 April, 1940, with B A 'Bud' Gillies at the controls. Almost immediately it ran into trouble. Engine oil cooling was inadequate, drag was excessive, and the three-segment doors enclosing each main undercarriage unit seldom closed properly.

Seventy flights were made at Bethpage before the XF5F-1 could be delivered to NAS Anacostia, on 22 February, 1941, for preliminary evaluation by Navy personnel. By then, however, the XF4U-1, which had

Intended as the prototype for a carrier fighter, the XF5F-1 was fitted with upward-folding wings. (*Grumman*)

* Without two-speed supercharger the R-1535-96 had a normal rating of 750 hp at 9,000 ft. With the two-speed supercharger installed, it was expected that that rating could be maintained up to an altitude of 17,500 ft.

been ordered on the same day as the XF5F-1, had already been flown at speeds in excess of 400 mph and the Navy had requested that Vought submit details on the production configuration of its single-engined fighter. As the XF5F-1 was slower than its single-engined competitor, it was already becoming evident that it would not be ordered into production. Nevertheless, the aircraft was returned to Bethpage at the end of April 1941 to have its hydraulic system overhauled and several major changes incorporated. However, when the XF5F-1 was returned to NAS Anacostia on 24 July, 1941, neither the redesign and aftward extension of the engine nacelles, nor the reduction in height of the canopy, nor the addition of wing fillets, nor the lengthening of the nose to project forward of the wing leading edge were found to have reduced drag or to have improved cooling to acceptable levels. Moreover, the new two-segment main undercarriage covers had not solved fully the defect noted earlier.

After evaluation at Anacostia, the XF5F-1 was sent to the Naval Aircraft Factory in Philadelphia, for simulated carrier landings during which its undercarriage was damaged twice. Following repair in Philadelphia and refurbishing at Grumman, the little used prototype suffered two more undercarriage failures. Finally, one day after that last accident, the XF5F-1 was struck off charge at NAS New York on 11 December, 1944. It had been flown less than 156 hours in just over fifty-six months.

The XF5F-1 was not one of the most felicitous designs from the Bethpage manufacturer and its contributions have since been frequently overrated. The XF5F-1's strongest point was its outstanding rate of climb, 4,000 ft/min versus 2,660 ft/min for the XF4U-1 and 2,630 ft/min for the Bell XFL-1, which justified its Skyrocket name. Level speed and range

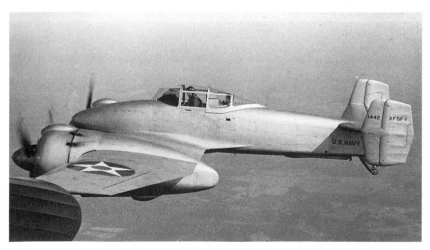

Fitted with wool tufts to evaluate the effectiveness of modifications incorporated during the spring of 1941 to reduce drag and improve engine cooling, BuNo 1442 was photographed from *The Red Ship* (Grumman G-32A demonstrator). (*Grumman*)

145

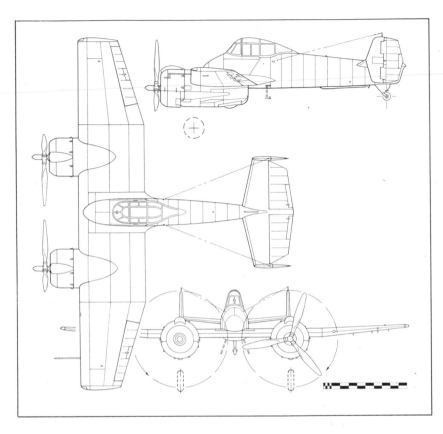

Grumman F5F-1 Skyrocket

performance, however, were no match for those of the Vought F4U, or even those of its F6F stablemate. As a shipboard aircraft it would have been handicapped, both in combat and during carrier approach, by dismal side and downward visibility due to the forward location of its wings and the position and diameter of its engine nacelles. Furthermore, and notwithstanding what has often been written, its only contribution to the XF7F-1, Grumman's next twin-engined carrier fighter, was of the negative type, *ie* where not to locate the wings and how not to design vertical tail surfaces.

PRODUCTION: One XF5F-1 was completed by Grumman in March 1940 and was assigned BuNo 1442.

Span 42 ft (12.80 m); span (wings folded) 21 ft 2in (6.45 m); length 28 ft 81/2 in (8.75 m); height 11 ft 4 in (3.45 m); wing area 303.5 sq ft (28. 20 sq m).
    Empty weight 8,107 lb (3,677 kg); loaded weight 10,138 lb (4,599 kg); maximum weight 10,892 lb (4,941 kg); wing loading 33.4 lb/sq ft (163.1 kg/sq m); power loading 4.2 lb/hp (1.9 kg/hp).

Maximum speed 383 mph (616 kmh) at sea level; rate of climb, 4,000 ft/min (20.3 m/sec); service ceiling 33,000 ft (10,060 m); normal range 780 miles (1,255 km); maximum range 1,170 miles (1,885 km).

The XF5F-1 flying above Long Island during manufacturer's trials. *(Grumman)*

Still carrying the experimental registration NX28633, the XG-44 was photographed before the issue of Approved Type Certificate 734 on 5 April, 1941. (*Grumman*)

Grumman G-44 Widgeon

Despite the precarious economic conditions prevailing in the late 1930s, the G-21 Goose sold well in 1937 and 1938 and contributed significantly to the company's profitability during those two years. Nevertheless, Grumman realized that the market for this expensive aircraft was relatively limited. Moreover, contacts with prospective amphibian customers indicated a need for a smaller aircraft to complement the Goose. Accordingly, the company started work on Design 44 in August 1939.

Powered by a pair of inline engines and looking much like a scaled-down G-21, the XG-44 prototype (c/n 1201, NX28633) was first flown by Bud Gillies and Roy Grumman at Bethpage on 28 June, 1940. Although its trials proceeded slowly, they proved generally satisfactory. The only modification required before the issuance of an Approved Type Certificate on 5 April, 1941, consisted of adding elevator horn balances.

Production history

After the G-44 received its ATC, the programme speeded up with fifty-one aircraft being delivered in 1941 to civil customers and the Portuguese naval air arm before production switched to J4F-1s and J4F-2s for the USCG and USN. An upgraded civil prototype, the XG-44A, was flown in August 1944 and deliveries to civil customers were resumed in February 1945 and continued until February 1949. In addition, forty-one aircraft were built in France under licence.

XG-44: Except for its angular tail surfaces and inline engines, the Widgeon prototype looked much like the G-21 except that it was smaller and much lighter. Its empty and gross weights were three-fifths of those of the larger aircraft. Likewise accommodation and power were reduced; seats were provided for a pilot and three or four passengers, and a pair of 200-hp Ranger 6-440C-5 six-cylinder, air-cooled engines driving two-bladed propellers were fitted.

G-44: Between February and December 1941, Grumman delivered thirty G-44s (c/ns 1202/1221 and 1230/1239) to private and corporate operators in the United States (including three to Pan American Airways), one to a Canadian customer (c/n 1240, CF-BVN), and twelve to Portugal's Aviação Naval (c/ns 1241/1252, Portuguese serials 119 to 130). All were basically similar to the XG-44 and were powered by the same Ranger 6-440C-5 engines. During the 1950s, several were modernized and re-engined as described below under 'Odds and Mods.'

XG-44A: First flown in August 1944, the prototype (c/n 1401, NX41818) of the postwar civil variant featured minor improvements including a revised electrical panel, a relocated pitot tube, and a deeper forward keel and revised hull step to reduce spray. Engines and other features were unchanged from those characterizing the prewar G-44s.

G-44A: Production of civil Widgeons was resumed before the end of the war with no fewer than twenty-five G-44As (c/ns 1402/1426) being delivered to US customers between February and July 1945. Fifty more (c/ns 1427/1476) were delivered between December 1945 and May 1949. All but three initially went to customers in the United States, the exceptions being

This G-44A (c/n 1402) was initially registered NC41971 in the United States and was later registered EC-AJU in Spain. *(Courtesy of Alain Pelletier)*

149

V197, the first J4F-1, was delivered to the US Coast Guard in July 1941. *(USCG)*

c/n 1466 which was registered VH-AZO to the Australian Petroleum Company, and c/ns 1471 and 1476 which went to the Pakistan Government as AP-ADV and AP-ADW. Most G-44As differed from the G-44s and the XG-44A in being fitted with oil coolers, exhaust mufflers, soundproofing, and cabin heater. In addition, some had an HF radio reel antenna with drogue cone attached to a small mast atop the rudder.

J4F-1: Ordered as utility aircraft, twenty-five J4F-1s were built for the US Coast Guard in two batches (V197/V204 delivered in 1941 and V205/V221 delivered during the following year). They were powered by 200-hp Ranger L-440-5 engines and initially differed from the civil aircraft in having an upper fuselage hatch just behind the wing to enable easy loading and unloading of stretchers. Later, a rack was added beneath the starboard wing to carry either a 200-lb depth charge or a raft and rescue gear.

J4F-2: The Navy ordered a total of 131 J4F-2s (BuNos 09789, 09805/09816, 30151, 32937/32986, 33952/33957, 34585, and 37711/37770) as utility amphibians and transferred fourteen of these aircraft to Brazil and fifteen to the United Kingdom. All were delivered between February 1942 and February 1945. They lacked the dorsal hatch of the J4F-1s but were otherwise similar to the Coast Guard aircraft.

Gosling: The name Gosling I was initially used by the Royal Navy for the fifteen J4F-2s (British serials FP455/FP469) which were supplied under Lend-Lease in 1942-43. The American name Widgeon I was adopted in early 1944. Another aircraft, believed to be the twelfth G-44, was acquired for use by the Foreign Commision in Miami and was given the British serial JS996.

UC4F-2: The UC4F-2 designation, which was not an official US Navy designation, was used in Brazil to identify fourteen J4F-2s used by the Força Aérea Brasileira in the utility transport role.

150

OA-14: Early during the war, fifteen G-44s were impressed into USAAF service as OA-14s and were assigned serial numbers 42-38216/42-38223, 42-38285, 42-38339/42-38340, 42-38355/42-38356, 42-43460, and 42-53003. Later, c/n 1208 was transferred from the Corps of Engineers and given the serial 44-52997. Nine OA-14s were written off or surveyed during the war and seven were returned to the civil register after the war.

OA-14A: This designation has been used unofficially to identify the last OA-14, 44-52997, but does not appear to be correct.

SCAN 30: In 1948, Société de Constructions Aéro-navales (SCAN) acquired components, tooling, and a manufacturing licence from Grumman for the Widgeon. Designated SCAN 30 and powered by two 190-hp Mathis 8G40 eight-cylinder engines, the first French-built Widgeon (c/n 01, F-WFDM) flew in January 1949 at La Rochelle. Six months later, on 11 July, the aircraft crashed into the Seine during a low altitude demonstration near Les Mureaux. All four occupants were pulled from the wreck but the noted French aviatrix, Jacqueline Auriol, who had been sitting in the co-pilot's seat while the aircraft was demonstrated by Mr Mingam, had to undergo several operations before resuming her career and going on to set several world air speed records.

Notwithstanding this accident and the lack of firm orders, SCAN went ahead with production and, to attract customers, offered the twin-engined amphibian in three versions: the SCAN 30A with 240-hp Salmson 8AS-00 eight-cylinder inverted vee engines, the SCAN 30G with 200-hp de Havilland Gipsy Queen 2 six-cylinder inline engines, and the SCAN 30L with 260-hp Lycoming GO-435-C2 flat-six engines. Unfortunately for the small company, the hoped for order from the Aéronautique Navale failed to materialize. Furthermore, by February 1952, only three amphibians had

The SCAN 30 prototype in which noted aviatrix Jacqueline Auriol came close to being killed when another pilot flew the amphibian into water after failing to judge its altitude accurately during a demonstration flight over the Seine. (*SCAN, courtesy of Stéphane Nicolaou*)

been delivered to the French Service de la Santé (Health Administration) in Indochina, one had gone to Emperor Bao-Dai in that country, and four were operated by government agencies in French Guiana. Thirty-three unsold airframes, most in various stages of completion and still without engines, were subsequently auctioned off by the French Government. The majority of these aircraft went to the United States and Canada where, like many Grumman-built Widgeons, several were re-engined with Continental IO-470-Ds or with Lycoming GO-435-C2Bs, GO-480-B1Ds, or R-680Es. A number of re-engined SCAN 30s were extant in 1988. The sole Gipsy Queen-powered SCAN 30G eventually found its way to Britain where, registered G-ARIX, it was written off in an alighting accident at Southampton on 19 May, 1961.

Service history

In civilian service, Widgeons were mostly owned by private individuals and had long but mostly unremarkable careers. In addition, before and during the Second World War, Pan American operated three G-44s (NC28675,

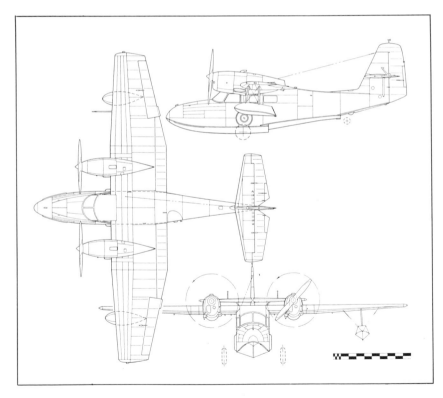

Grumman G-44A Widgeon

152

NC28676, and NC37189, which respectively were the fourteenth, fifteenth, and thirty-ninth Widgeons), as seaplane trainers. They were later resold to private operators.

In US military service with the Coast Guard, the Navy, and the Army Air Forces, J4F-1s, J4F-2s, and OA-14s were mostly used for search and rescue in coastal waters and as utility transports in the United States, Alaska, the Caribbean, and Central America. Early during the war, the Coast Guard and, to a much lesser extent, the Navy, also used their J4Fs for anti-submarine patrols. Thus, on 1 August, 1942, a Widgeon of Coast Guard Patrol Squadron 212, based at Houma, Louisiana, and flown by Chief Aviation Pilot Henry C White, scored the first Coast Guard kill of an enemy submarine with the sinking of U-166 off the Passes of the Mississippi in the Gulf of Mexico. The Navy and the AAF disposed of their last Widgeons at the end of the war and the Coast Guard did so shortly thereafter.

Abroad, Widgeons were operated by the air arms of the following nations:

BRAZIL: Among the aircraft supplied by the United States after Brazil declared war on Germany and Italy on 22 August, 1942, were fourteen J4F-2s. These aircraft were initially serialled FAB 01 to FAB 14 but were later renumbered 2667 to 2680 and were designated UC4F-2s by the Força Aérea Brasileira (Brazilian Air Force). The last five were withdrawn from use in the mid-1950s, with at least one then being transferred to the Brazilian civil register.

PORTUGAL: Twelve G-44s were shipped to Portugal in December 1941 and were put into service by the Aviação Naval (Naval Aviation). Details regarding their use and subsequent fate are not available, but it is known that at least two eventually went onto the Portuguese civil register.

THAILAND: The Royal Thai Air Force apparently acquired the third G-44A (c/n 1403, ex NC41972) and used it briefly before transferring it to a civil flying school in Thailand. No further details are available.

UNITED KINGDOM: The fifteen Lend-Lease Gosling Is/Widgeon Is obtained by the Royal Navy during the war served in the communications role, primarily in the West Indies. All but three which had been written off while in British service were returned to the United States and went on to the civil register.

URUGUAY: A Widgeon of unknown origin (either a civil G-44 or a Navy J4F-2) was interned in Uruguay in 1942. Given the naval serial A-751, it was then operated from the Isla Libertad naval station by the Servicio Aeronáutico de la Armada (Naval Aviation Service).

Odds and Mods

Much like the Goose, the Widgeon proved quite adaptable and was both modified as a research aircraft and re-engined to improve its single-engined performance. The most drastic series of modifications were those made by Edo Corporation to BuNo 32976. Intended as a testbed for evaluating seaplane hulls of different length-to-beam ratio of up to 12.5:1, this J4F-2 was also fitted with a new main undercarriage which for water operations swung upward but remained in the airstream while in flight. Windows were provided in the hull afterbody to view water flow characteristics aft of the step. Data obtained with this research aircraft, which first flew in May 1948 with a half-scale replica of the Martin XP5M-1 hull having a length-to-beam ratio of 8.5:1, led to significant gains in hull design, but by the late 1940s and early 1950s the flying-boat era was rapidly coming to an end. Nevertheless, the modified J4F-2 was considered of sufficient interest to be preserved and is now kept in the collection of the National Air and Space Museum in Washington, DC.

With 200-hp Ranger engines, in the case of G-44s and J4Fs, or 220 hp Mathis and Salmson engines, in the case of SCAN 30s, Widgeons were somewhat underpowered and had marginal single-engined performance. Thus, after the Federal Aviation Agency imposed more stringent certification requirements, numerous Widgeons of various origins (including some SCAN 30s) were re-engined by a number of contractors. The most numerous were the Super Widgeons which were fitted by McKinnon-Hickman Company (later McKinnon Enterprises) with Lycoming flat-six engines (either 260-hp GO-435-C2B or 270-hp GO-480-B1D) and three-bladed fully-feathering propellers. The McKinnon Super Widgeons also had strenghtened hulls and undercarriages, larger passenger windows, additional soundproofing, modernized instrumentation, and increased fuel capacity (from 108 to 154 US gal). Some were fitted with retractable wingtip floats. In New Zealand, three Widgeons were similarly re-engined with 260-hp Continental IO-470-D flat-six engines.

More drastic in appearance was the fitting of radial engines in place of the

J4F-2 (BuNo 32976) modified by Edo Corporation as a test-bed for a half-scale replica of the Martin XP5M-1 hull. *(Edo)*

Re-engined with Continental IO-470-D flat-six engines, this G-44A (c/n 1466, ZK-AVM) was used in New Zealand for a service linking Invercargill with Stewart Island. *(H L James)*

Ranger, Mathis or Salmson inline engines initially fitted to G-44s, J4Fs, and SCAN 30s. At least one aircraft was re-engined with a pair of 220-hp Lycoming W-670 radials while several were fitted with two 300-hp Lycoming R-680-E3 nine-cylinder radials. The latter conversion was marketed as the PACE Gannet by Pacific Aircraft Engineering Corporation.

PRODUCTION: A total of 317 Widgeons was built, including 276 produced by Grumman between June 1940 and January 1949 and 41 produced by Société de Constructions Aéro-navales in 1949-52, as follows:

1	XG-44	25	J4F-1
43	G-44	131	J4F-2
1	XG-44A	(16)	OA-14
75	G-44A	(15)	Gosling
41	SCAN 30		

They were assigned the following BuNos, military serial numbers, and construction numbers:

XG-44:	Civil registered c/n 1201
G-44:	Civil registered c/ns 1202/1221, 1230/1240
	Portuguese naval serial numbers 119/130
XG-44A:	Civil registered c/n 1401
G-44A:	Civil registered c/ns 1402/1476
J4F-1:	V197/V221
J4F-2:	BuNos 30151, 32937/32986, 33952/33957, and 37711/37770
	Brazilian Air Force serial numbers FAB-01/FAB-14
Gosling:	British military serials FP455/FP469

| | **OA-14:** | (42-38216/42-38223, 42-38285, 42-38339/42-38340, 42-38355/42-38356,42-43460, 42-53003, and 44-52997) |
| | **SCAN 30:** | Civil registered c/ns 01 and 1/41 |

	G-44	**McKinnon Super Widgeon**
DIMENSIONS:		
Span, ft in	40 0	40 0
(m)	(12.19)	(12.19)
Length, ft in	31 1	31 1
(m)	(9.47)	(9.47)
Height, ft in	11 5	11 5
(m)	(3.38)	(3.38)
Wing area, sq ft	245	245
(sq m)	(22.76)	(22.76)
WEIGHTS:		
Empty, lb	3,240	–
(kg)	(1,470)	(–)
Loaded, lb	4,525	5,500
(kg)	(2,053)	(2,495)
Wing loading,* lb/sq ft	18.5	22.4
(kg/sq m)	(90.2)	(109.6)
Power loading,* lb/hp	11.3	10.2
(kg/hp)	(5.1)	(4.6)
PERFORMANCE:		
Max speed, mph/ft	153/sl	190/sl
(kmh/m)	(246/sl)	(306/sl)
Cruising speed, mph	138	175
(kmh)	(222)	(282)
Climb rate, ft/min	700/1	1,750/1
(m/sec)	(3.6)	(8.9)
Service ceiling, ft	14,600	18,000
(m)	(4,450)	(5,485)
Normal range, miles	800	–
(km)	(1,285)	(–)
Max range, miles	920	1,000
(km)	(1,480)	(1,610)

* wing and power loadings are calculated at normal loaded weight and maximum take-off power.

Neither the Grumman XP-50 nor its competitor, the Lockheed XP-49, were put into production. *(Grumman)*

Grumman XP-50 and XP-65

After receiving contracts from the Navy Department for the development of seven different types of aircraft from the XFF-1 to the XF5F-1, after putting into production two civil types--the G-21 and G-44, and after obtaining export contracts from Argentina, Canada, and Portugal, Grumman finally succeeded in obtaining a contract from the War Department when the Army Air Corps ordered a twin-engined fighter prototype on 25 November, 1939. Unfortunately, this XP-50 was destroyed after flying only some 20 hours between 18 February and 14 May, 1941. Thereafter until the advent of the X-29 research aircraft in 1981, no other Grumman aircraft specially conceived for either the Army Air Corps, Army Air Forces, or USAF was ordered.

Development of Grumman's only Army or Air Force fighter was begun in answer to Circular Proposal 39-775 issued by the Materiel Division on 11 March, 1939, and calling for a new generation of interceptor fighters which would match existing airframes with more powerful engines and other refinements. To that end, Bill Schwendler and his team proposed Design 41 which was essentially identical to Design 34 (the XF5F-1 which was then under construction for the Navy) but was to be powered by two Wright R-1820 radials fitted with turbosuperchargers. Submitted to the Army Air Corps in June 1939, Design 41 came in second to the Lockheed Model 522, a proposed development of the P-38 with either Pratt & Whitney XH-2600 or Wright R-2160 turbosupercharged engines. However, the Army had seen sufficient merits in the Grumman proposal, notably finding its powerplant installation less risky than that of the Lockheed design, to

157

The XP-50 during an engine run-up test. The retractable ladder on the port side of the fuselage aft of the wing can just be seen. *(Grumman)*

encourage the Bethpage manufacturer to submit Design 45, a revised Design 41 incorporating a nose wheel undercarriage, lengthened nose, and other minor improvements. Proposed armament consisted of two 20-mm cannon and two 0.50-in machine guns in the nose and two 100-lb bombs beneath the fuselage.

Although the Materiel Division still preferred the Lockheed Model 522 and did order an XP-49 prototype, it decided to play it safe by also ordering a prototype of the Grumman Design 45 as the XP-50. The contract for that aircraft was awarded on 25 November, 1939, and detail design and construction of the prototype proceeded swiftly. Powered by two 1,200 hp Wright R-1820-67/79 nine-cylinder radials fitted with turbosuperchargers and driving three-blade propellers, the XP-50 (c/n 643, 40-3057) was first flown by Robert L Hall at Bethpage on 18 February, 1941. During early tests, it handled better than the XF5F-1 and, as its engines were turbosupercharged, showed markedly better performance at medium and high altitudes. Unfortunately for Grumman, the XP-50 was damaged in a landing accident on 14 March and, after being repaired and returned to flight status, experienced an inflight turbosupercharger explosion on 14 May, 1941. On that occasion, as a result of the damage caused by the inflight explosion, Bob Hall was unable to retract the aircraft's right wheel to attempt a belly landing or to lower the nosewheel to make a normal landing. The pilot was left with no alternative but to bale out over Long Island Sound.

Following the loss of the XP-50, Grumman succeeded in attracting the Army interest in its Design 46, a larger twin-engined fighter to be powered by 1,700-hp Wright R-2600 radials with either two-stage mechanical superchargers or turbosuperchargers. Work on that project, begun in October 1939, led to Design 49, an export version proposed in February

1940, and to Design 51, a naval fighter proposal which was submitted on 24 March, 1941. Eventually, the Army and Navy agreed to seek the development of similar twin-engined fighters differing only in details, with the Army version being powered by turbosupercharged engines whereas the Navy version was to have mechanically-supercharged engines. Moreover, the Army version was to have a pressurized cockpit and two 37-mm cannon in place of the four 20-mm cannon of the naval fighter. Both versions were also to be armed with four 0.50-in machine guns.

The Army Air Forces ordered two XP-65 prototypes on 16 June, 1941, and two weeks later the Navy awarded a contract for two F7F-1 prototypes. Subsequently, however, both Services concluded that a single design would not meet their specific requirements and, on 16 January, 1942, the Army dropped out of the programme to enable Grumman to optimize the design of the new twin-engined fighter to satisfy naval requirements.

PRODUCTION: One XP-50 was built by Grumman in 1941 and assigned the AAF serial 40-3057.

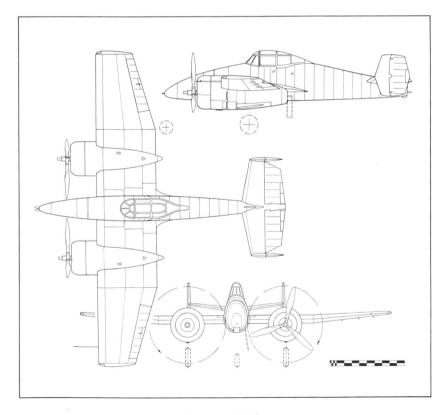

Grumman XP-50

XP-50 (Grumman's estimates)

Span 42 ft (12.80 m); length 31 ft11 in (9.73 m); height 12 ft (3.66 m); wing area 304 sq ft (28.24 sq m).

Empty weight 8,307 lb (3,768 kg); loaded weight 10,558 lb (4,789 kg); maximum weight 13,060 lb (5,924 kg); wing loading 34.7 lb/sq ft (169.6 kg/sq m); power loading 4.4 lb/hp (2.0 kg/hp).

Maximum speed 424 mph at 25,000 ft (682 kmh at 7,620 m); cruising speed 317 mph (510 kmh); climb to 20,000 ft (6,095 m) in 5 minutes; service ceiling 40,000 ft (12,190 m); normal range 585 miles (940 km); max range 1,250 miles (2,010 km).

XP-65 (Grumman's estimates)

Span 52 ft 6 in (16.00 m); length 46 ft 5 in (14.15 m); height 15 ft 2 in (4.62 m); wing area 463 sq ft (43.01 sq m).

Empty weight 15,943 lb (7,232 kg); loaded weight 21,425 lb (9,718 kg); wing loading 46.3 lb/sq ft (225.9 kg/sq m); power loading 6.3 lb/hp (2.9 kg/hp).

Maximum speed 427 mph at 25,000 ft (687 kmh at 7,620 m); cruising speed 180 mph (290 kmh); service ceiling 42,000 ft (12,800 m); normal range 825 miles (1,325 km).

TBM-3s of VMTB-232 during the Okinawa campaign in April 1945. *(USMC)*

Grumman TBF Avenger

First flown exactly four months before the Japanese bombed Pearl Harbor, this soon-to-be-famous Grumman carrier-based torpedo-bomber received the appropriate name of Avenger in early 1942. Although at first it failed to live up to that name when making its combat debut during the Battle of Midway and seemed to deserve better the *Turkey* nickname by which it was later affectionately known to its crews, the Avenger went on to justify its name fully by sinking large numbers of Japanese warships, oilers, and freighters during the last three years of the Second World War. Interestingly enough, Avengers became the first combat aircraft operated by the Nihon Kaijyo Jieitai in 1954, when Japan was again authorized 'defensive' forces by the allied powers.

On 25 March, 1939, the Bureau of Aeronautics asked manufacturers to submit design proposals for a VTB (carrier-based torpedo-bomber) intended to undertake the following missions: (1) attack against heavy surface ships with bombs or torpedoes; (2) heavy smoke laying; (3) scouting; and (4) strafing light surface vessels. Principal performance requirements included: (1) top speed of 300 mph with normal fuel load; (2) range of not less than 1,000 miles while carrying one torpedo or three 500-lb bombs; (3) service ceiling of not less than 30,000 ft; (4) take-off distance when carrying a torpedo and fuel for a combat range of 1,000 miles not to exceed 325 ft with a 25-knot wind-over-deck; and (5) stalling speed when carrying a torpedo and less than half the fuel load not to exceed 70 mph. Overall span and length were limited respectively to 60 ft and 39 ft while maximum height with wings folded was not to exceed 17 ft. Finally, BuAer specified that the aircraft was to carry its torpedo or bombs internally.

161

In answer to this request, the Navy received a total of thirteen design proposals on 24 August, 1939, as six manufacturers (Brewster, Douglas, Grumman, Hall, Vought, and Vultee) each submitted one or more configurations. For its part, Grumman had entered two G-40 designs differing in the type of Wright R-2600 radial engine to be fitted, one featuring a two-speed engine while the other was offered with a two-stage engine. Preliminary review during the late summer and early autumn of 1939 led BuAer to eliminate from further consideration ten of the proposed designs and to concentrate its evaluation on the Grumman design with the two-stage engine, one of the Vought designs with a Pratt & Whitney R-2800, and one of the Brewster designs with an R-2600. By 3 November, BuAer had completed its evaluation and recommended the procurement of two prototypes from Grumman and one prototype from Vought. However, contract execution was delayed for six months and Contract 72974 covering the design, construction, and testing of two Grumman XTBF-1s (BuNos 2539 and 2540, c/ns 644 and 645) was only awarded on 8 April, 1940.

When its mock-up was inspected on 6 July, 1940, the XTBF-1 was shown to bear a strong family resemblance to the Wildcat. Substantially larger than the single-seat fighter and having a deeper belly, the torpedo-bomber designed by a team led by William T Schwendler had mid-mounted wings folding alongside the fuselage sides in the 'sto-wing' manner which had just been developed for the XF4F-4. Beneath the centre section of the wings was an internal bomb bay with hydraulically operated doors which could house either a 22-in Mk. XIII torpedo or four 500-lb bombs while above the wings the crew of three (pilot, navigator/ventral gunner, and radio-operator/dorsal gunner) sat in line beneath a large canopy. For horizontal bombing, provision was made for the installation of a Norden bombsight in production aircraft. Defensive armament consisted of a forward-firing 0.50-in machine gun mounted on the starboard side of the upper engine cowling, a 0.50-in gun offset to starboard in a Grumman-designed, electrically-operated dorsal turret, and a 0.30-in rear-firing flexible gun in a ventral step.* Although the Navy had wanted to procure the aircraft with a two-stage engine as proposed in August 1939, the late-availability of this powerplant forced Grumman to switch to a two-speed version of the Wright R-2600, the 1,700-hp Wright R-2600-8 fourteen-cylinder air-cooled radial driving a three-blade Curtiss Electric propeller being selected for the prototypes and first production models. The conventional main undercarriage retracted outboard into the wings and the tailwheel and 'stinger' arrester hook were also fully retractable. While work on the prototypes progressed at a steady pace, the Navy increasingly felt an urgency to boost its air strength, notably by supplementing as quickly as possible its limited inventory of obsolescent Douglas TBD-1 torpedo-bombers. Hence, on 30 December, 1940, more than seven months before the first XTBF-1 was

---

* Illustrations submitted with the proposal showed the fixed gun and dorsal gun on the port side and a glazed fairing aft of the turret.

The first XTBF-1 without the large dorsal fin which characterized all other TBFs and TBMs. *(Grumman)*

ready to begin flight trials, Grumman was awarded Contract 76928 for 285 TBF-1s and one XTBF-2. The latter was to differ in being powered by a two-stage R-2600-10 engine.

Flight trials, which began on 7 August, 1941, when Bob Hall took BuNo 2539 for an abbreviated first flight at Bethpage, were initially plagued by a series of problems due mainly to the engine being mounted too far aft for proper cg location, insufficient engine cooling, and vertical tail surfaces which were too small. The first three flights totalled less than one hour and, as the XTBF-1 spent much time in the shops to have its engine relocated forward and numerous changes made to its cowling and tail surfaces, it had only been flown less than 25 hours when it was lost on 28 November, 1941. Fortunately, Hobart Cook and Gordon Israel baled out successfully after fire erupted during a full power climb stability check near Brentwood, Long Island. Furthermore, the development programme was not set back too much as the second prototype was ready to fly three weeks later and the first production TBF-1 (BuNo 00373) was rolled out on 3 January, 1942. Both of these aircraft differed from the first prototype in minor details and in having a large dorsal fin, a feature retained for all production aircraft.

Production history

In early 1942, with urgent demand from the fleet for more and better aircraft, the Navy instructed Grumman to give priority to the F4F and F6F production programme and sought a new contractor initially to supplement and eventually to supplant Grumman as the TBF manufacturer. The choice soon fell on General Motors Corporation, which had just formed the Eastern Aircraft Division using the facilities and personnel of five of its plants in the Middle Atlantic States. Grumman was instructed to co-operate

Close-up of the first XTBF-1, with wool tufts on the forward fuselage during tests undertaken to solve a cooling problem and reduce drag. *(Grumman)*

with Eastern to set up a production line for the Avenger in a GM hardware plant located in Trenton, New Jersey.

Contract 98837 for 1,200 TBM-1s (the manufacturer letter M for Eastern Aircraft replacing F for Grumman) was awarded to Eastern on 23 March, 1942, and the first TBM-1 assembled in Trenton from parts delivered by Grumman was delivered on 12 November, 1942. Subsequently, Eastern took full responsibility for the production of Avengers, building wings and cowlings in Tarrytown, New York; rear fuselages in Baltimore, Maryland; and electric and hydraulic systems in Bloomfield, New Jersey. Manufacturing of forward and centre fuselage sections, final assembly, and acceptance trials took place at the Trenton plant. Production peaked in March 1945, when 400 aircraft were delivered from the Trenton line, and Eastern Aircraft delivered its 7,546th and last TBM in September 1945. With Grumman, Avenger production in Plant Number 2 quickly gained tempo. Sixty TBF-1s were delivered in June 1942, the month in which the Avenger made its combat debut. Production peaked fifteen months later, in September 1943, when 163 aircraft were delivered, and ended in December with the delivery of the 2,293rd TBF.

In addition to twelve prototypes, Grumman and Eastern built 9,827 production aircraft in four basic versions (TBF-1/TBM-1, TBF-1C/TBM-1C, TBM-3, and TBM-3E). As detailed here, many of these aircraft were modified either by the manufacturers or in Navy facilities to adapt them to a variety of missions.

XTBF-1: Two prototypes (BuNos 2539 and 2540) were built by Grumman and were powered by the 1,700-hp Wright R-2600-8 radial engine. The crew of three was housed under a large canopy ending with an electrically-powered dorsal turret. The aircraft were armed with one forward-firing 0.50-in machine gun in the engine cowling, one 0.50-in machine gun in a dorsal turret, and one flexible 0.30-in machine gun in a ventral position and could carry an offensive load of up to 2,000 lb in a fully enclosed bomb bay. The second XTBF-1 had a large dorsal fin added to improve directional stability.

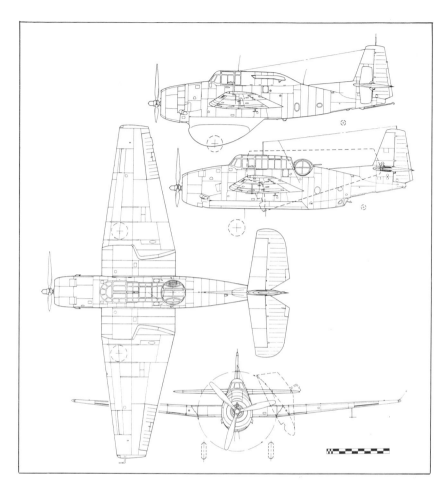

Grumman TBF-1 Avenger, side view of F7F2N (top)

TBF-1 and **TBM-1:** Grumman and Eastern respectively first built 1,524 and 500 Avengers similar to the second prototype. Many of these aircraft were modified in service for a variety of duties as identified by special purpose suffix letters. Some were fitted with underwing rails or zero-length launchers for up to eight rockets, while others were equipped with ASB radar (Air to Surface Type B) and related Yagi antennae; however, in both cases the modified aircraft retained their TBF-1 or TBM-1 designations.

Noteworthy experiments included the modification at Quonset Point, Rhode Island, in 1943 of a TBF-1 which was fitted with fourteen sealed-beam lights (four around the cowling and five on the leading edge of each wing) as part of Project *Yehudi*. This Navy programme sought ways of

One of the first TBF-1s fitted with ASB radar and a Yagi aerial beneath each wing. (*USN/ National Archives*)

A TBM-3D with six Yehudi lights around the cowling and ten of these lights on the wing leading edges. (*USN/Grumman*)

reducing the visibility of an aeroplane in flight by illuminating those parts of its surface which normally were in shadow and, hence, contrasted with the lighter sky background. Tests indicated that the distance at which the modified aircraft could be detected visually was reduced from 12 to 2 miles

166

when the lights were switched on. Plans were made to have an Avenger squadron fitted with *Yehudi* lights for operational evaluation in the Atlantic and to that end a few TBM-3Ds were fitted with lights but the planned evaluation did not take place.

BuNo 00550 was modified by Grumman in July 1942 to evaluate performance gains which could be derived from modifying the Avenger into a single-seater by removing the dorsal turret and installing fairings aft of the

BuNo 00550 modified as a single-seater in July 1942 and fitted with a temporary fairing aft of the pilot's cockpit. *(Grumman)*

The G-56 was a proposed Avenger version with a two-gun Martin turret and R-2800 engine. This TBF-1 (BuNo 01746), photographed in Bethpage on 14 October, 1942, was modified to test the Martin turret installation. *(Grumman)*

167

pilot's cockpit and beneath the rear fuselage. In 1943, BuNo 01746 was fitted with a Martin dorsal turret to test the twin-gun installation planned for Design 56, a proposed Avenger development to be powered by a Pratt & Whitney R-2800 radial. Tests, however, revealed that the twin-gun turret had a lower effective rate of fire than the standard single-gun installation as firing had to be interrupted more than twice as frequently to avoid hitting the tail surfaces.

TBF-1B: The suffix B identified 402 aircraft included in the previous total but reserved for delivery to the Fleet Air Arm and completed by Grumman in British markings and camouflage. These aircraft were initially designated Tarpon T.R. Mk. Is, but later the Royal Navy adopted the US name and the TBF-1Bs were redesignated Avenger T.R. Mk. Is.

TBF-1C and **TBM-1C:** Aircraft from this second production variant differed mainly from the TBF-1/TBM-1s in having the engine-mounted gun replaced by one 0.50-in gun in each wing. For ferry or long-range scouting, these aircraft could carry a 275-gal auxiliary tank installed in the bomb bay and two 58-US gal underwing tanks, thus increasing maximum fuel capacity from 335 to 726 US gal. Like aircraft from the earlier production model, many TBF-1Cs and TBM-1Cs were modified in service to carry rockets beneath their wings or were fitted with ASB radar and related Yagi antennae without being redesignated. Other TBF-1Cs and TBM-1Cs were more extensively modified and were redesignated as detailed below.

TBF-1CP and **TBM-1CP:** This designation was given to a small number of TBF-1Cs and TBM-1Cs (*eg* BuNo 17060) which were modified as photographic-reconnaissance aircraft with cameras installed in the bomb bay.

TBF-1D and **TBM-1D:** This designation was given to TBF-1Cs and TBM-1Cs (*eg* BuNo 17091) optimized for use in the anti-submarine role and fitted with an ASD radar (Air to Surface Type D, later designated AN/APS-3) in a radome on the starboard wing leading edge and underwing rocket launching rails or pylons. Some of the TBF-1Ds and TBM-1Ds were

TBF-1D (BuNo 47670) with a radome for the AN/APS-3 on the starboard wing leading edge. (*Grumman*)

168

Experimental AN/APS-3 installation in a radome atop the centre cockpit of an Avenger. (*USN courtesy of Hal Andrews*)

BuNo 00393, the sole XTBF-2, prior to its first flight on 1 May 1942. Note additional intake on the left side of the cowling for the intercooler installation of the Wright XR-2600-10 engine. (*Grumman*)

also fitted with the ASB radar with Yagi antennae atop both wings. At least one TBF-1D had its AN/APS-3 radome relocated above the cockpit and was tested by the Naval Experimental Station at Philadelphia.

TBF-1E and **TBM-1E:** The TBF-1Es and TBM-1Es were late production TBF-1Cs and TBM-1Cs which were fitted with ASH radar (Air to Surface Type H, later designated AN/APS-4) in a radome beneath their starboard wing.

TBF-1J and **TBM-1J:** The J suffix identified early production aircraft fitted

The first XTBF-3 (BuNo 24141) during a flight on 12 March, 1945, while serving as a test-bed for the Halford H-1B turbojet. *(Curtiss Wright, courtesy of Hal Andrews)*

with special equipment and systems, including boosted cabin heaters, for operations under Arctic conditions.

TBF-1L and **TBM-1L:** A few TBF-1Cs and TBM-1Cs were fitted experimentally with a retractable searchlight in the bomb bay to illuminate surfaced submarines during night attacks by other aircraft. This scheme, however, was not used much operationally as searchlight-equipped aircraft became easy prey for anti-aircraft guns of U-boats.

TBF-1P and **TBM-1P:** This designation was given to a small number of TBF-1s (*eg* BuNo 06307) and TBM-1s modified as photographic-reconnaissance aircraft with cameras installed in the bomb bay.

XTBF-2: Ordered at the same time as the first production batch of TBF-1s, this prototype (BuNo 00393) was the twenty-second production airframe which was powered by a Wright XR-2600-10 radial. The XTBF-2 was first flown on 1 May, 1942; however, as the use of a two-stage engine was by then considered unnecessary since Avengers were anticipated to be operating mainly at low altitudes, this powerplant installation was not retained for production aircraft.

XTBF-3 and **XTBM-3:** As late production TBM-1Cs weighed nearly 2,750 lb more than early TBF-1s when normally loaded, performance had progressively deteriorated. In particular, take-off at high gross weight had become marginal when operating from the small decks of escort carriers. Consequently, after briefly considering the use of the 2,000 hp Pratt & Whitney R-2800 in place of the 1,600-hp Wright R-2600-8, Grumman and the Navy agreed to retain the Wright engine but to switch to its 1,900 hp R-2600-20 variant. To test the new powerplant installation, which featured multiple cowl flaps and an oil cooler intake on the lower cowling lip, Grumman and Eastern respectively built two XTBF-3s (BuNos 24141 and 24341) and four XTBM-3s (BuNos 25175, 25521, 25700, and 45645). The XTBF-3 first flew on 20 June, 1943. Two of these aircraft gained further

170

TBM-3D (BuNo 83506) with rockets on Mk. 5 zero-length launchers and a searchlight for night ASW operation. (*USN/National Archives*)

distinction: BuNo 25700 became the prototype of the airborne early warning version described under the TBM-3W heading and BuNo 24141 became the first Grumman aircraft to be fitted with a turbojet. The latter came about in the spring of 1944, when after completing NATC evaluation, the first XTBF-3 was chosen by the Navy to become a flying test bed for the 2,700-lb thrust Halford H-1B turbojet being imported from Great Britain for installation in the Curtiss XF15C-1 composite fighter. For that purpose, the H-1B turbojet was fitted in a faired housing beneath the fuselage of BuNo 24141. Intakes for the turbojet were located on both sides of the forward fuselage, just beneath the R-2600 cowling gills, and the exhaust was located beneath the centre fuselage, forward of the ventral step. All armament was removed and the dorsal turret was replaced with a partially glazed fairing. Ground testing began in November 1944 and XTBF-3 flights with the H-1B installed were begun during the following month. Nicknamed *Fertile Myrtle,* as had been the XFF-1 and as later was the XTB3F-1, BuNo 24141 was thus the first Grumman to be powered, albeit partially, by a turbojet.

TBM-3: Built exclusively by Eastern, the production version powered by the R-2600-20 began rolling off the Trenton line in April 1944. Including aircraft completed as TBM-3Es or modified as detailed below, Eastern built a total of 4,657 TBM-3s. A few detail changes were made during the course of production, the most significant being the replacement of the Norden bombsight with an automatic pilot as Avenger crews had found that horizontal bombing was useless against manoeuvring ships and less accurate than glide bombing when attacking small land targets or anchored vessels.

TBM-3D: This designation identifies TBM-3s modified for use in the anti-submarine role and fitted with the same radar equipment as TBF-1Ds and

171

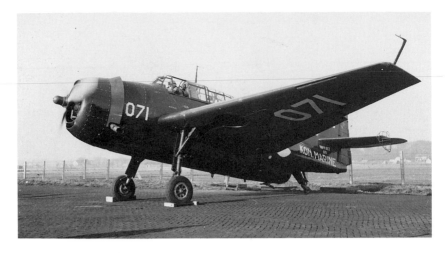

Bearing the Netherlands serial 071, this TBM-3E-2 (BuNo 91131) was acquired by the Koninklijke Luchtvaart Dienst in 1958 after it had served with the Fleet Air Arm as an Avenger A.S. Mk. 4 (serial XB379). *(G Kamphius, courtesy of Alain Pelletier)*

TBM-1Ds. In addition, a searchlight was often fitted beneath the port wing. The dorsal turret was frequently removed and the canopy extended rearward.

TBM-3E and **TBM-3E2:** The TBM-3E, the last Avenger model put into production during the war, had a fuselage lengthened by $11\frac{1}{2}$ in and carried an AN/APS-4 search radar in a radome beneath the starboard wing. By paying attention to details and deleting some equipment (notably wing and tail de-icing gear), Eastern managed to reduce empty weight by nearly 300 lb in spite of the addition of the APS-4 radar and other systems. These changes were introduced on the production line in December 1944. Later on, additional weight reduction was made possible by dispensing with the ventral tunnel gun and replacing the aft armour plate with a flak suit and two flak curtains. Late production aircraft could carry twin 0.50-in gun packages beneath the wings and had two ultraviolet fluorescent spotlights installed in the pilot's cockpit to ease night operations. The TBM-3E2 designation identified aircraft which were modernized after the war had ended; most then had the original 'stinger' arrester hook replaced by an external hook attached further forward beneath the tail.

TBM-3H: This unconfirmed designation may have been given to a few TBM-3s fitted with special search radar.

TBM-3J: This 'winterized' version of the early production TBM-3 was similar to the TBF-1J/TBM-1J but used the R-2600-20 engine.

TBM-3L: A few TBM-3s were fitted with a retractable searchlight as were TBF-1Ls and TBM-1Ls.

TBM-3M: This designation was given after the war to a small number of TBM-3/3Es used for missile and rocket testing.

A TBM-3U of Utility Squadron Five (VU-5) in flight near Guam in February 1952. *(USN/ National Archives)*

TBM-3N: Development of a night torpedo bombing version was begun in July 1945 when modification of a TBM-3 airframe was undertaken at NAS Norfolk, Virginia. After the war ended, more than forty additional aircraft were modified as TBM-3Ns with their rear turret removed and a radar operator station fitted beneath a glazed canopy. These aircraft served until the early fifties with NightDevRonPac (Night Development Squadron Pacific, later redesignated VCN-1 and then FAWTUPac), Night-DevRonLant (then VCN-2 and FAWTULant), VA-1E, and VA-2E.

TBM-3Q: In an October 1945 directive, BuAer provided for the modification of ninety-five TBM-3s for use in the radar counter measures role with conversion work to be undertaken at NAS Norfolk and NAS San Diego. However, it appears that only a few of these TBM-3Qs were actually completed. They were externally identical to the better-known TBM-3W version with AN/APS-20 in a large ventral radome.

TBM-3R: Postwar modification of a small number of TBM-3 airframes resulted in a seven-seat 'carrier-onboard-delivery' (COD) version from which the dorsal turret and all other combat equipment were removed. Cargo was carried in a wire mesh basket fitted in the bomb bay. Most TBM-3Rs also had the original 'stinger' arrester hook replaced by an external hook attached further forward beneath the tail.

TBM-3S and **TBM-3S2:** To obtain an Avenger version better suited to postwar ASW operations, the Navy had the turret, ventral, and wing guns removed from a fair number of TBM-3/TBM-3Es. Specialized ASW equipment – including a searchlight beneath the port wing and a data link antenna atop the fin – was fitted, with that of the TBM-3S2 being more advanced. Many of these aircraft had the modified arrester hook as installed on TBM-3E2s and TBM-3Rs.

TBM-3U: Postwar modification of TBM-3s to fullfil sundry utility duties including target-towing. Most often, combat equipment and guns were removed and the TBM-3Us flown with a crew of two.

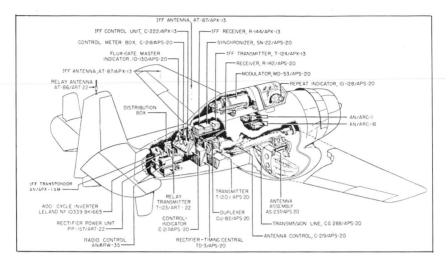

IFF ANTENNA, AT-87/APX-13
IFF CONTROL UNIT, C-222/APX-13
CONTROL METER BOX, C-218/APS-20
FLUX-GATE MASTER INDICATOR, ID-130/APS-20
IFF ANTENNA, AT-87/APX-13
RELAY ANTENNA AT-86/ART-22
DISTRIBUTION BOX
IFF TRANSPONDOR AN/APX-1 AM
400 CYCLE INVERTER LELAND N° 10339 BKI665
RECTIFIER POWER UNIT PP-157/ART-22
RADIO CONTROL AN/ARW-35
RELAY TRANSMITTER T-123/ART-22
CONTROL-INDICATOR C-217/APS-20
RECTIFIER-TIMING CENTRAL TD-3/APS-20
TRANSMITTER T-120/APS-20
DUPLEXER CU-82/APS-20
IFF RECEIVER, R-144/APX-13
SYNCHRONIZER, SN-22/APS-20
IFF TRANSMITTER, T-124/APX-13
RECEIVER, R-142/APS-20
MODULATOR, MD-53/APS-20
REPEAT INDICATOR, ID-128/APS-20
AN/ARC-1
AN/ARC-18
ANTENNA ASSEMBLY AS-237/APS-20
TRANSMISSION LINE, CG-288/APS-20
ANTENNA CONTROL, C-219/APS-20

AEW installation in the TBM-3W. (*Research Laboratory of Electronics/MIT*)

TBM-3W: Project *Cadillac*, the development of an airborne early warning system capable of detecting enemy aircraft or ships far beyond the horizon of existing shipborne radar, was initiated by the Radiation Laboratory of the Massachussetts Institute of Technology (MIT-RL) in February 1944 to meet Navy requirements. By combining previously developed relay radar and radio control equipment with a powerful S-band radar transmitter fitted with an 8 ft by 3 ft somewhat eliptical antenna, MIT-RL sought to develop an aircraft capable of detecting low-flying aircraft formations at ranges of 90 to 100 miles and to relay the radar picture to the Combat Information Centre of warships.

The first aircraft fitted with Project *Cadillac* equipment was an XTBM-3 (BuNo 25700) which was modified at NAMU (Naval Aircraft Maintenance Unit) Johnsville in Pennsylvania during the spring of 1944. All armament and armour were removed, and the aircraft was fitted with a large ventral radome to house the 8 ft by 3 ft quasi-eliptical antenna for the AN/APS-20 radar and with auxiliary fins on the tailplane. First flown in August 1944, the modified aircraft was delivered to the Special Project Unit *Cast* at Bedford AAF, Massachussetts, the closest field to the MIT-RL. Notwithstanding the advanced nature of the equipment, trials progressed remarkably swiftly. Forty sets of electronic equipment were ordered in June 1944, two months before the prototype first flew, thus enabling delivery of TBM-3Ws to begin in March 1945. Altogether, between thirty-six and forty TBM-3s were modified by the Navy as TBM-3Ws, and many were later fitted with the modified arrester hook as installed on some of the TBM-3Rs.

As shown in the accompanying internal arrangement drawing, the TBM-3W was quite packed with electronic gear and festooned with numerous aerials. The aircraft was a two-seater with the pilot in the

174

standard cockpit and an electronic equipment operator housed in a claustrophobic rear fuselage station.

TBM-3W2: Externally identical to the TBM-3W, the TBM-3W2s had their AN/APS-20 radar optimized for detecting the snorkel of submerged submarines. Modified from existing TBM-3 airframes, TBM-3W2s entered service in 1950 and, at peak strength in the spring of 1953, the USN had 156 of these aircraft in service. Most were fitted with the modified arrester hook as installed on some of the TBM-3Rs.

XTBM-4: As the standard TBM-3 structure had been found to be insufficiently strong to withstand stresses associated with dive bombing operations, three uncompleted airframes (BuNos 97673/97675) were strengthened to withstand 5g manoeuvres at 16,000 lb by using high-

The first XTBM-4 (BuNo 97673), in the markings of the Engineering Test Division at the Naval Air Test Center Patuxent River, Maryland. (*Hal Andrews*)

A two-seat XTBM-5 prototype modified from a TBM-3E airframe. Note wheelwell's doors and longer span. (*USN/National Archives*)

strength aluminium alloy in structural members and fitting revised wing hinges. Static tests were begun in April 1945 and flight trials began two months later.

TBM-4: This proposed production version had strengthened airframes as used in the XTBM-4s. Eastern had initially planned to switch from TBM-3 to TBM-4 production in August 1945 but had not yet done so when all Avenger contracts were cancelled following the defeat of Japan.

XTBM-5: This little known experimental version was realized by NAMU Johnsville as part of the Navy's endeavour to improve the Avenger's performance by reducing airframe weight and wing loading. The turret was removed, the ventral step was faired smoothly into the rear fuselage, the crew was reduced to two, the cockpit and canopy were modified to accommodate the second crew member in the location previously used for the dorsal turret and to house twin flexible rear-firing 0.30-in guns, the fixed leading edge slots were sealed, jet augmentation exhaust pipes were fitted, wheelwell doors were added, and span was increased by 3 ft. Two XTBM-5 prototypes, modified from existing TBM-3E airframes, were tested beginning in June 1945, but the end of the war ended further work.

Service history

Making its debut during the Battle of Midway – when six Midway-based TBF-1s of VT-8 attacked the Japanese fleet on 4 June, 1942, with disastrous results to themselves (five aircraft shot down and one damaged beyond repair) and without scoring a single torpedo hit, the Avenger came into its own two months later when forty-one aircraft from VT-3, VT-7, and VT-8 flew from *Enterprise, Wasp,* and *Saratoga* to provide support during the

An early production TBF-1 with red and white rudder striping as used on naval aircraft between 5 January, 1942, and 15 May, 1942. (*C G B Stuart Collection/National Air and Space Museum*)

landing at Guadalcanal. Less than three weeks later, on 24-25 August, these three squadrons helped to sink the carrier *Ryujo* during the Battle of the Eastern Solomons. Thereafter, Avengers took part in all the major air-sea battles in the Pacific while operating from fast carriers, and provided effective support during all amphibious operations while operating from escort carriers. A synopsis of their role in major actions follows:

BATTLE OF THE SANTA CRUZ ISLANDS (26-27 October, 1942): Even though twenty-nine TBF-1s from VT-6 (*Hornet*) and VT-10 (*Enterprise*) were available at the start of this battle, no Avenger was able to score a hit on any of the four Japanese carriers challenging the American Task Force.

OPERATIONS IN THE GILBERT ISLANDS (10 November-10 December, 1943): During landings on Makin and Tarawa, 199 Avengers embarked aboard five fleet carriers, five light carriers, and eight escort carriers played a major part in providing air support for the Marines. During operations in the Gilberts, VT-6 crews used the ASB radar of their Avengers to guide Hellcats in an attempt to intercept Japanese night bombers and reconnaissance aircraft. The first night interception, on 25 November, proved unsuccessful, and during the following night two Hellcats failed to locate the enemy aircraft. However, the lead Avenger was luckier as its pilot, Lt-Cdr John Philips, shot down two Mitsubishi G4M

A TBF-1 of the US Navy, with warships and transport vessels anchored in the Marshall Islands during the spring of 1944. *(USN)*

177

Betty bombers with his single forward-firing 0.50-in gun. Tragically, the aircraft shot down by the Avenger's turret gunner appears to have been the F6F-3 flown by Lt-Cdr Edward H 'Butch' O'Hare, the well-known fighter ace who was then the *Enterprise* Air Group Commander and who had conceived the plan of using radar-equipped Avengers to lead Hellcats during night interception sorties.

CONQUEST OF THE MARSHALL ISLANDS (29 January-23 February, 1944): In support of the landings on Majuro, Kwajalein, and Eniwetok, the USN deployed 247 Avengers aboard six fleet carriers, six light carriers, and eight escort carriers.

STRIKES AGAINST TRUK (17-18 February, 1944): Operating from five fleet carriers and four light carriers, 126 Avengers took part in a major strike against the Japanese stronghold at Truk. During the night, twelve radar-equipped TBF-1Cs from VT-10 aboard *Enterprise* flew the first night carrier attack of the war; one Avenger was shot down but the others sank or damaged thirteen Japanese ships.

FIRST BATTLE OF THE PHILIPPINE SEA (19-24 June, 1944): On the eve of the 'Great Marianas Turkey Shoot,' 194 Avengers were among the 896 aircraft embarked aboard the fifteen fast carriers of Task Force 58. After first bombing airfields on Guam to neutralize Japanese land-based aircraft, Task Force 58 aircraft attached the carriers of the First Mobile Fleet in the late afternoon of 20 June. During this epic battle, fifty-four Avengers contributed to the sinking of the carrier *Hiyo* and to the damaging of the carriers *Chiyoda* and *Zuikaku*.

SECOND BATTLE OF THE PHILIPPINE SEA AND BATTLE OFF SAMAR (24-26 October, 1944): In preparation for the liberation of the Philippines, 236 Avengers were embarked aboard the fast carriers of Task Force 38 and 199 Avengers were aboard the eighteen escort carriers assigned to Task Group 77. In three days of heavy fighting, TBFs and TBMs contributed to the sinking of the battleship *Musashi* (hit by eighteen torpedoes and eleven bombs), the carriers *Chitose, Chiyoda, Zuiho,* and *Zuikaku,* and twenty-six other warships. Worthy of admiration was the gallant defence put up by aircrews operating from escort carriers off Samar on 25 October.

In 1945, USN Avengers continued to take part in pre-invasion strikes and provided air support during amphibious operations at Iwo Jima and Okinawa. They hunted Japanese shipping and flew their first mission against the Japanese mainland on 10 February and their first radio countermeasures (ECM in modern parlance) sorties during the night of 16 February. On 7 April, they obtained their last major success of the war when they achieved ten torpedo hits on *Yamato* to help sink this 68,000-ton battleship.

Although twenty-seven TBF-1s from the *Sangamon, Santee,* and *Suwanee* took part in Operation *Torch*, the Allied landings in North Africa in November 1942, the most important contribution made by Avengers in the war against the European Axis powers was their anti-submarine

A TBM-3E flying over the USS *Sangamon* (CVE-26) before the invasion of Okinawa in the spring of 1945. Shortly after, on 4 May, this escort carrier was badly damaged by Kamikaze attack. (*USN/C G B Stuart Collection/National Air and Space Museum*)

A TBM-3D in the non-specular dark and light gull grey scheme adopted in 1944 for ASW operations in the North Atlantic. (*C G B Stuart Collection/National Air and Space Museum*)

operations from the decks of escort carriers. The first use of TBF-1s in this role was made by Composite Squadron Nine (VC-9) which embarked aboard the USS *Bogue* (CVE-9) in March 1943 to take part in convoy escort operations in the North Atlantic. The first two crossings were uneventful but on the third, convoy ON-184 from the United Kingdom to Nova Scotia, VC-9 Avengers first damaged U-569 on 21 May and sank her the next day.

From then on, Composite Squadrons and their escort carriers proved increasingly effective not only during daylight operations but also at night. In the latter case, to prevent U-boats from taking advantage of the night to surface and recharge their batteries while trailing convoys, some Avengers were stripped of much equipment and were flown with two-man crews. By this expedient, weight was reduced and endurance increased to as much as 14 hours, thus enabling Avengers to be launched at dusk and remain airborne until after dawn.

The effectiveness of the TBF/TBMs in the ASW role can be gauged from the fact that they destroyed, or shared in the destruction of thirty U-Boats, twelve Japanese submarines (I-52 sunk on 23 June, 1944, in the Atlantic and the others in the Pacific and Indian Oceans), and a Vichy French submarine. The top scoring Composite Squadrons flying Avengers and Wildcats were those from the USS *Bogue,* which were credited with the destruction of twelve U-boats, those from the USS *Card* and USS *Anzio,* which respectively destroyed eight German and eight Japanese submarines, and those from the USS *Core,* which sank five German submarines. These successes, however, were obtained at a high cost, not only in terms of aircraft and crews lost during operations in treacherous North Atlantic weather but also as the result of enemy action, with the USS *Block Island* being torpedoed northwest of the Canary Islands on 29 May, 1944.

Working with surface vessels from hunter-killer groups, Avengers used radar and sonobuoys to locate submarines and bombs, Mk. 54 depth charges, Mk. 24 Fido homing torpedoes, and rockets to hit them. The latter weapons were first tested in early 1943 when a few Avengers were fitted with a retractable MAD (magnetic anomaly detector) boom in place of the ventral gun and were armed with retro rockets which were carried beneath the fuselage. Developed by the California Institute of Technology (Cal Tech), these retro rockets were designed to be fired rearwards in a spread while the aircraft was flying at a precise speed so that it cancelled out the speed of the rockets and caused them to drop vertically. Although this scheme did work, it held less promise than conventional forward-fired rockets such as the 3½-in British rocket projectile mounted on Mk.I rail-type launchers. Accordingly, after successful trials of the British Mk.I installation were conducted in July 1943 at the Naval Proving Ground with a specially modified TBF-1, a US-developed Mk.4 installation with shorter launching rails was used operationally by relatively few Avengers. The US Navy then adopted the Cal Tech 5-in High Velocity Aircraft Rocket (HVAR) which did not require the installation of heavy and drag inducing launching rails as did the British Mk.I or American Mk.4 installations, as they were carried on Mk.5 zero-length launchers. HVARs were first used in combat on 11 January, 1944, when TBF-1Cs from VC-58 aboard the USS *Block Island* attacked a surfaced U-boat.

Following the Japanese surrender, the number of Torpedo Squadrons in service with Carrier Air Groups decreased rapidly but this was partially offset by the transfer of Avengers to the Naval Air Reserve. Then, on 15

November, 1946, the VT designation of the eighteen Avenger squadrons still serving with Carrier Air Groups was replaced by that of VA (Attack Squadron). By that time, however, the TBM-3s and TBM-3Es operated by these squadrons were scheduled to be replaced as soon as possible by Douglas Skyraiders. Finally, Avengers were last flown by three Attack Squadrons in 1949. In the anti-submarine role, TBM-3Es and TBM-3S/-3S2s equipping Composite Squadrons and Anti-Submarine Warfare Squadrons lasted until the Autumn of 1954 when the type was phased out by VS-27.

After being tested operationally aboard the USS *Ranger* in May and June 1945, TBM-3Ws were first assigned either directly to six Carrier Air Groups (CVG-3, CVG-20, CVG-153, and CVLG-58 in the Atlantic Fleet and to CVG-5 and CVG-81 in the Pacific Fleet) or to two Fleet Airborne Electronic Training Units, FAETULANT in the Atlantic Fleet and FAETUPAC in the Pacific Fleet. Later they equipped two specialized units, Carrier Airborne Early Warning One (VAW-1, later redesignated Composite Squadron Eleven or VC-11) at NAS Ream Field in California and VAW-2/VC-12 at NAS Quonset Point in Rhode Island. The last four TBM-3Ws were phased out by VC-11 during the summer of 1951. The externally similar TBM-3W2s, which had entered service with ASW squadrons during the summer of 1950, became the last Avengers in US military service and were finally phased-out by the Naval Air Reserve at the end of 1956.

During the war, the first of twenty-three Marine Torpedo Bomber Squadrons to be equipped with Avengers was VMSB-131 (later properly redesignated VMTB-131) which obtained TBF-1s in September 1942. On 13 November, shortly after beginning operations from Henderson Field on Guadalcanal, VMSB-131 scored a torpedo hit on *Hiei* (hit again by USN and

A TBM-3W-2/TBM-3S-2 hunter-killer team of VS-26 in the early 1950s. (*USN/Grumman*)

USMC aircraft, this Japanese battleship was scuttled during the following night). Even though Marine Avengers used torpedoes for their combat debut, this proved an exceptional event as thereafter they were primarily operated against land targets with bombs and rockets or on anti-submarine patrols with depth charges and rockets. Major operations included the landing at Torokina, Bougainville, in November 1943, for which air support was provided by Avengers from VMTB-143, -232, and -233. In early 1944, the same three squadrons bombed five airfields and harbour installations during the campaign to isolate Rabaul. Later, during operations in the Marianas in July 1944, VMTB-131 provided air support to ground forces on Guam and VMTB-242 did likewise on Tinian. Shortly after, VMTB-134 took part in the Peleliu landing. Finally, during the battle for Okinawa, the last major amphibious operation of the war, Avengers from VMTB-131 and VMTB-232 flew both air support sorties and anti-submarine patrols.

Following the organization of Marine Carrier Groups to provide squadrons for operations from escort carriers, Marine Avengers also operated at sea. The first to do so were those of VMTB-233 which embarked aboard the uss *Block Island* in March 1945 to provide air support during the Okinawa landing and to fly strike missions against targets in the Ryukyus. Before the war ended, VMTB-143 went aboard the uss *Gilbert Island* (Okinawa campaign and Balikpapan landings), VMTB-234 embarked aboard the uss *Vella Gulf* (strikes on Pagan and Rota), and VMTB-132 took part in operations in the East China Sea from the uss *Cape Gloucester*. Four

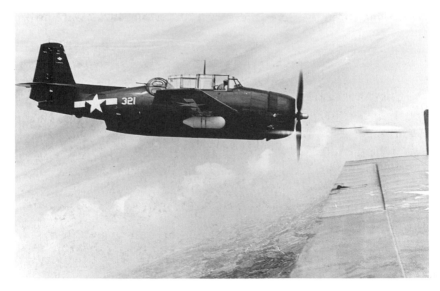

A TBM-3E of VMTB-232 launching HVAR rockets while providing air support for Marines on Okinawa. (*USMC*)

182

more Marine escort carriers, each with its Avenger squadron, were to be added for Operation *Olympic*, the planned invasion of Japan in late 1945, but the Japanese surrender rendered this project unnecessary.

The end of the war brought a rapid reduction in the number of Avengers in USMC service. By the time war started in Korea in June 1950, only a few TBM-3Rs and TBM-3Us remained in service as personnel transports and 'hack' aircraft.

During the Second World War, Avengers were also operated by the Royal Navy's Fleet Air Arm and the Royal New Zealand Air Force, and in the 1950s Avengers served with eight non-US naval air arms.

BRAZIL: In early 1960, Brazil obtained six ex-Dutch Avenger A.S. Mk. 4s, including two which had been modified as target-tugs, as initial equipment for the light carrier *Minas Gerais*. Shortly after being transferred to the Aviação Naval (Naval Aviation) in June 1960, these aircraft (Brazilian naval serials N-501 to N-506) were briefly used for carrier qualifications in the North Sea following the reconstruction of *Minas Gerais* in Rotterdam. However, when responsibility for providing aircraft for *Minas Gerais* was transferred to the Força Aérea Brasileira (Brazilian Air Force) in 1961, the Brazilian Avengers were placed in storage at the Quartel dos Marinheiros (Naval Barracks) in Rio de Janeiro and quickly deteriorated.

CANADA: The Royal Canadian Navy first acquired 114 ex-USM TBM-3S anti-submarine aircraft in May 1950. Two more followed one month later and another was obtained in May 1952. These aircraft, which were designated Avenger A.S. Mk. 3s in Canada, retained their BuNos. Sixteen (BuNos 53072, 53109, 53119, 53420, 53545, 53554, 53626, 53632, 53696/53697, 53802, 53804, 53845, 53908, 86281, and 91426) were

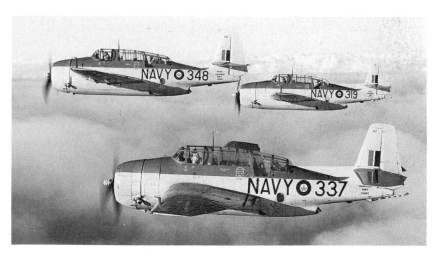

TBM-3S anti-submarine aircraft in service with the Royal Canadian Navy in the early 1950s.
(RCN/C G B Stuart Collection/National Air and Space Museum)

modernized by Fairey Aviation Co of Canada Ltd in Halifax, Nova Scotia, and were redesignated Avenger A.S.Mk. 3Ms after being fitted with a MAD (Magnetic Anomaly Detection) boom retracting into a cylindrical fairing on the port side of the fuselage. Fairey also modified a few aircraft (*eg*, BuNo 53078) for target towing with stepped-up 'greenhouse' canopy and towing gear in a cylindrical fairing similar to that housing the MAD gear of A.S. Mk.3Ms. In addition to the ASW strike aircraft, the RCN obtained eight TBM-3W2 anti-submarine search aircraft in September 1952.

In RCN service, Avengers were operated by eight squadrons (Nos.825 and 826 Squadrons, VC 920, VS 880, VS 881, VT 40, VU 32, and VX 10) from shore bases or aboard HMCS *Magnificent*. The last Canadian TBM-3W2s were struck off strength in March 1959, but the last A.S. Mk. 3s and 3Ms continued in operation until July 1960.

FRANCE: Between May 1951 and April 1958, the United States delivered 140 Avengers (including TBM-3Es, TBM-3S/3S2s, TBM-3Us, and TBM-3W2s) as part of the Mutual Assistance Program. In addition, a small but undetermined number of Avenger A.S. Mk. 4s were transferred by Great Britain in 1957. The unofficial designations TBM-53, TBM-57and TBM-UT were used in France to identify respectively TBM-3Es, TBM-3S/-3S-2s and TBM-3Us fitted with French equipment.

In service with the Aéronautique Navale, TBM-3S/TBM-3W2 hunter-killer teams first entered service with Flottille 4F in September 1951 and were used by that unit until February 1960. They also equipped Flottilles 6F (until November 1959) and 9F (until September 1960). In addition to routine operations from shore bases and aboard the carriers *Arromanches*, *Bois Belleau* and *Lafayette*, Avengers from Flottille 4F and 9F took part in

This TBM-3E of Flottille 4F is one of the 140 Avengers supplied to France under MAP between 1951 and 1958. (*Courtesy of Alain Crosnier*)

TBM-3S2 (JMSDF serial 2347) of the Nihon Kaijyo Jieitai with a searchlight pod beneath the port wing and an AN/APS-4 radar beneath the starboard wing. (*JMSDF courtesy of the Japanese Defense & Naval Attaché*)

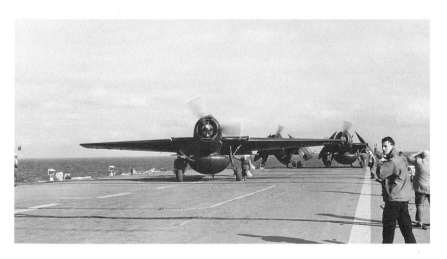

TBM-3W2s aboard the French Navy light carrier *Arromanches* in January 1956. (*ECPA-Marine, courtesy of Alain Crosnier*)

the Suez Operation in October-November 1956. Avengers were also operated in the training and support roles by Escadrilles 2S, 3S, 4S, 5S, 10S, 15S, 54S and 56S. The last of these aircraft was retired in April 1966.

JAPAN: The first combat aircraft of the newly created Nihon Kaijyo Jieitai (Japanese Maritime Self-Defence Force) were ten TBM-3W2s (2101 to 2110) delivered in 1954 and ten TBM-3S2s (JMSDF serials 2341 to 2350) delivered in 1955. They were operated in the ASW role from Omura until 1962.

NETHERLANDS: As did France, the Netherlands received Avengers both from the United States, under the MAP, and as transfers from Great Britain. Twenty-four ex-USN TBM-3W2s received Dutch naval serials 16-101 to 16-124 upon being delivered to the Marine Luchtvaart Dienst (MLD, the Naval Air service of the Koninklijke Marine/Royal Netherlands Navy) in September 1953 and were followed by thirty-four TBM-3Ss (Dutch naval serials 1-1 to 1-34) delivered between January 1954 and May 1955. Twenty ex-Royal Navy Avenger A.S. Mk. 4s delivered in 1958 were given Dutch serials 21-20 to 21-39. In MLD service, five TBM-3Ss and five Avenger A.S. Mk. 4s were converted as target tugs and were operated by 1 Squadron from Valkenburg. Also based at Valkenburg were the two operational ASW units, 2 and 4 Squadrons, which regularly operated their Avengers aboard the carrier HRMS *Karel Doorman*. The MLD phased out its Avengers in late 1960.

NEW ZEALAND: Starting in the summer of 1943, the RNZAF received six TBF-1s (NZ2501/NZ2506) and forty-two TBF-1Cs (NZ2507/NZ2548). These aircraft were initially assigned to No. 30 Squadron, formed in September 1943, and to No. 31 Squadron, formed two months later. Both squadrons completed a tour of duty in the Solomons before being disbanded in 1944. At the end of the war, nine of the surviving Avengers were subsequently transferred to the Royal Navy for disposal while sixteen others were returned to the USN. A few remained in RNZAF service as target-tugs (with dorsal turret and other armament removed) and as vehicles for aerial top-dressing trials. The last two aircraft (NZ2504 and NZ2527) were finally retired in 1960.

UNITED KINGDOM: Initially named Tarpon by the Royal Navy but renamed Avenger on 13 January, 1944, to conform to the designation already adopted by the USN, the Grumman-designed torpedo-bomber became one of the most important types of carrier-based aircraft operated by the Fleet Air Arm during the last three years of the war.

Between 1943 and 1945, the Royal Navy was allocated a total of 958 Tarpons and Avengers under Lend-Lease, including 402 Grumman TBF-1Bs (Tarpon or Avenger T.R. Mk. Is, serials FN750/FN949, JT773, and JZ100/JZ300), 334 Eastern-built TBM-1Cs (Avenger T.R. Mk. IIs, serials JZ301/JZ634), and 222 Eastern-built TBM-3s and TBM-3Es (Avenger T.R. Mk. IIIs, serials JZ635/JZ746 and KE430/KE539). Most Avenger squadrons of the Fleet Air Arm operating in the Pacific formed up in the United States and were equipped with aircraft straight off the Grumman or Eastern lines or modified by Blackburn Aircraft Ltd at Roosevelt Field, New York. Squadrons operating in the Atlantic and Arctic were equipped with Avengers modified in the United Kingdom by Blackburn to meet British requirements. Major modifications included the installation of British gun sights, oxygen system and radio equipment; the substitution of an F.24 camera for the ventral gun; the relocation of the navigator closer behind the pilot; and the use of a folding radio mast rendered necessary by the lower ceiling of hangar decks aboard British

Avenger T.R. Mk. IIs awaiting delivery to the Fleet Air Arm. *(General Motors/Aero Digest)*

An *Avenger* T.R. Mk. II showing the characteristic bulged window, forward of and below the fuselage roundel, fitted to most British *Tarpons* and *Avengers*. *(Imperial War Museum courtesy of Alain Pelletier)*

carriers. One of the T.R. Mk. Is, JZ146, was modified even more extensively and served as a test bed for the Frazer Nash F.N.95 remotely-controlled twin-gun barbette intended for the Fairey Spearfish.

No. 832 Squadron, the first Fleet Air Arm unit to be equipped with Tarpons, was formed in January 1943 at NAS Norfolk, Virginia, and trained in the United States before embarking aboard the USS *Saratoga* for operations in the Pacific. The squadron first went into action on 27 June, 1943, when it provided support during the American landing on New

Georgia in the Middle Solomons. Shortly after, No. 832 Squadron transferred to HMS *Victorious* before embarking successively aboard HMS *Illustrious* and HMS *Begum* for operations in the Pacific and in the Indian Ocean (where Avengers of Nos. 832 and 851 Squadrons worked with HMS *Findhorn* and RINDN *Godavari* to sink U-198 on 12 August, 1944). Other Avenger squadrons which served aboard armoured and escort carriers of the East Indies Fleet and the British Pacific Fleet were Nos. 820, 828, 845, 848, 849, 854, 857, and 885. Their greatest successes were achieved in 1945 during operations against Japanese oil refineries in the Netherlands East Indies and against enemy bases on Formosa, Truk, the islands south of Japan, and the Japanese mainland.

In home waters, Avengers flew anti-submarine and anti-shipping patrols and mine-laying sorties from shore bases. Others operated from escort carriers on strikes against shore targets, coastal shipping and naval facilities in Norway (notably sinking U-711 and its depot ship at Kilbotn just four days before VE-Day) and on convoy escort duty, mainly in the Arctic where they shared in the destruction of two U-boats (U-288 and U-355). Squadrons involved in these operations between the summer of 1943 and VE-Day were Nos. 846, 850, 852, 853, 855, and 856. In addition, during the last war years Avengers served along with other aircraft with an Anti-Submarine Warfare Development Unit (No. 703 Squadron at Thorney Island), a Tactical Trials Unit (No. 711 Squadron at Crail), the Operational Training Unit (No. 732 Squadron at Squantum), four Telegraphist/Air Gunner Training Units (Nos. 743, 744, 745, and 754 Squadrons), and a Target Towing Unit (No. 785 Squadron at Crail). A Royal Air Force target-towing and army co-operation squadron, No. 567, is also reported as having received at least one Avenger III. After the war, the Lend-Lease Avengers were either returned to the United States or, as they were no longer needed and their transport back to the US was costly, were simply destroyed. The

Recognition photograph of an Avenger T.R. Mk.III taken in July 1945. (*Ministry of Aircraft Production/C G B Stuart Collection/National Air and Space Museum*)

first career of the Avenger in British service came to an end in June 1946 when No. 828 Squadron was disbanded.

The one hundred TBM-3Es and TBM-3Ss delivered in 1953 received the serials XB296/XB332, KB355/XB404, and XB437/XB449 and were designated Avenger A.S. Mk. 4s (TBM-3Es operated as received from the US), Avenger A.S. Mk. 5s (TBM-3Ss fitted with British equipment including radar in a large radome beneath the starboard wing), and Avenger A.S. Mk. 6s (TBM-3Ss fitted with British equipment including radar in a radome beneath the forward section of the bomb bay). Avenger A.S. Mk. 4s were first assigned to No. 815 Squadron in May 1953 and A.S. Mk. 4s, Mk. 5s and Mk.6s subsequently served with Nos. 814, 820, 824, and 831 Squadrons until 1955 and then were flown by Nos. 1830, 1841, and 1844 Squadrons of the Royal Voluntary Reserve until 1957. However, a few were attached to No. 831 Squadron at Culdrose until 1962 and were used for development work.

URUGUAY: The Aviación Naval Uruguaya (Uruguayan Naval Aviation) received ten Avengers in December 1949 and nine more five months later. Assigned serials A-501 to A-510 and A-551 to A-559, these TBF-1s, TBM-1s and TBM-1Cs were operated from Lagune del Sauce until withdrawn in 1960.

Forest fire-fighting and crop-dusting

Although a few surplus TBF-1s and TBM-1s did find their way on to the US civil register shortly after the end of the War, it was not until the mid-1950s that large numbers of TBM-3s became available to civil operators. In the United States and Canada, surplus Avengers found a ready market as they were easily converted for firefighting and agricultural spraying duties. Over

N7833D, a forest fire-fighting TBM of Hemet Valley Flying Service at Ryan Field, Hemet, California. (*René J Francillon*)

189

the years, these aircraft were extensively modified, some being converted as single-seaters, and most were fitted with an enlarged ventral bay to carry up to 6,000 lb of fire retardant chemicals – enough to cover a 50 ft by 260 ft swath – or 625 US gal of chemical compound. At least one, which was registered N9598C and was operated under contract from the US Department of the Interior, carried fire-retardant in underwing tanks.

Following the conversion of a TBM-1C by Otto Timm in 1954 and its initial use as an air tanker on 1 September of that year, converted TBM-3Us were used by the United States Forestry Service beginning in 1957. Thereafter the principal commercial US operators of firefighting and crop-spraying Avengers were Aerial Applicators, Air Tankers Inc, Hemet Valley Flying Service, Johnson Flying Service, Reeder Flying Service, Sis-Q Flying Service, and TBM Air Tanker. By the mid-1960s, as many as seventy Avengers were operated by these companies under contract from several federal and state agencies, notably the California Division of Forestry. However, following a series of accidents which led to a decision no longer to contract single-engined aircraft for tanker duty, most US-registered Avengers were withdrawn from fire-fighting use at the end of the 1973 season. Nevertheless, forty-five Avengers, all ex-TBMs, were still carried on the March 1987 United States Civil Aircraft Registry.

In Canada, where seventy-three TBMs received civil registrations, Skyway Air Services and Wheeler Airlines first operated Avengers for crop and forest spraying in 1959 and shortly after started using them to fight forest fires. Other operators were Airspray, Conair Aviation, Evergreen Air Service, Forest Protection Ltd, Hicks & Lawrence, Maritime Air Service, Miramich Air Service, and Richel Air. At least twenty-eight Canadian TBMs were still in operation as late as 1982.

PRODUCTION: 9,839 Avengers were built, including 2,293 TBFs delivered by Grumman between August 1941 and December 1943 and

A TBM-3 from NAS Boca Chica near the Florida Keys. (*USN/National Archives*)

Photographed at the Hayward Municipal Airport, California, on 24 February, 1989, this TBM-3E of the Confederate Air Force displays a dubious mix of markings and paint schemes. Unfortunately, inaccurate markings have become the trademark of a great number of 'warbirds' flying in the United States. (*René J Francillon*)

7,546 TBMs delivered by Eastern between November 1942 and September 1945, as follows:

2	XTBF-1	550	TBM-1
1,524	TBF-1	2,332	TBM-1C
764	TBF-1C	4	XTBM-3
1	XTBF-2	4,657	TBM-3/TBM-3E
2	XTBF-3	3	XTBM-4
	(2)	XTBM-5	

The Grumman-built aircraft were assigned the following BuNos:
XTBF-1: BuNos 2539/2540.
TBF-1:   BuNos OO373/00392; 00394/00658; 01731/01770; 05877/06491; 23857/24140; 24142/24241; and 47438/47637.
TBF-1C: BuNos 24242/24340; 24342/24520; and 47638/48123.
XTBF-2: BuNo 00393.
XTBF-3: BuNo 24141 and 24341.

The Eastern-built aircraft were assigned the following BuNos:
TBM-1:   BuNos 24521/25070.
TBM-1C: BuNos 16792/17091; 25071/25174; 25176/25520; 25522/25699; 25701/25720; 34102/34105; 45445/45644; 45646/46444; and 73117/73498.
XTBM-3: BuNos 25175; 25521; 25700; and 45645.
TBM-3:   BuNos 22857/2365; 53050/53949; 68062/69538; 85459/86292; and 91107/91752.
XTBM-4: BuNos 97673/97675.

A TBM-3R (BuNo 86143) with the AZ tail code identifying aircraft of HEDRON-1 (Headquarters Squadron, First Marine Air Wing). *(Clay Jansson)*

	TBF-1	TBF-1C	TBM-3E	TBM-3W
DIMENSIONS:				
Span, ft in	54 2	54 2	54 2	54 2
(m)	(16.51)	(16.51)	(16.51)	(16.51)
Span (wings folded), ft in	19 0	19 0	19 0	19 0
(m)	(5.79)	(5.79)	(5.79)	(5.79)
Length, ft in	40 0	40 0	40 11½	41 0
(m)	(12.19)	(12.19)	(12.48)	(12.50)
Height, ft in	16 5	16 5	16 5	16 6
(m)	(5.00)	(5.00)	(5.00)	(5.03)
Wing area, sq ft	490	490	490	490
(sq m)	(45.52)	(45.52)	(45.52)	(45.52)
WEIGHTS:				
Empty, lb	10,080	10,555	10,545	11,893
(kg)	(4,572)	(4,788)	(4,783)	(5,395)
Loaded, lb	13,667	16,412	14,160	13,994
(kg)	(6,199)	(7,444)	(6,423)	(6,348)
Maximum, lb	15,905	17,364	17,895	14,798
(kg)	(7,214)	(7,876)	(8,117)	(6,712)
Wing loading,* lb/sq ft	27.9	33.5	28.9	28.6
(kg/sq m)	(136.2)	(163.5)	(141.1)	(139.5)
Power loading,* lb/hp	8.0	9.65	8.3	7.4
(kg/hp)	(3.65)	(4.38)	(3.38)	(3.34)
PERFORMANCE:				
Max speed, mph/ft	271/12,000	257/12,000	276/16,500	260/16,450
(kmh/m)	(436/3,660)	(414/3,660)	(444/5,030)	(418/5,015)
Cruising speed, mph	145	153	147	144
(kmh)	(233)	(246)	(237)	(232)
Climb rate, ft/min	1,430/1	10,000/13	2,060/1	1,695/1
(m/sec)	(7.3)	(3.9)	(10.5)	(8.6)
Service ceiling, ft	22,400	21,400	30,100	28,500
(m)	(6,830)	(6,525)	(9,175)	(8,685)

Range with torpedo, miles	1,215	1,105	1,130	–
(km)	(1,955)	(1,780)	(1,820)	(–)
Range as scout, miles	1,450	2,335	1,920	845
(km)	(2,335)	(3,755)	(3,090)	(1,360)

* wing and power loadings are calculated at normal loaded weight and maximum take-off power.

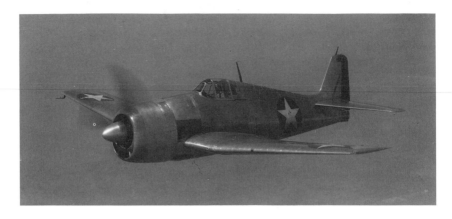

The first XF6F-3 photographed before its forced landing on 17 August, 1942. *(Grumman)*

Grumman F6F Hellcat

There is no denying that the Hellcat was neither the fastest nor longest ranged fighter of the Second World War. Nor was it the most heavily armed, nor the most manoeuvrable fighter of the time. Yet, in terms of kill-to-loss ratio, it was clearly the most successful. From the time it went into action on 31 August, 1943, until VJ-Day, the F6F achieved and maintained air superiority to an extent never matched by friend or foe. In just short of two years of combat operations, its pilots claimed 55 per cent of all enemy aircraft destroyed by the USN and USMC during the War and were credited with 5,156 victories (4,947 by carrier-based units and 209 by land-based units) for the loss of 270 Hellcats. Numerical superiority and good training certainly helped Hellcat pilots achieve this remarkable 19.1:1 kill-to-loss ratio, but much of the credit goes to the F6F itself. Its design blended adequate performance with heavy armament and protection. It had an immensely strong airframe capable of taking much punishment and was powered by the most reliable engine then available. Finally, it was easy to fly and handled well during carrier operations.

Contrary to what has often been written, design of this superlative fighter neither emerged fortuitously nor was undertaken in answer to the Japanese Zero threat. Its development can be traced back to February 1938, when Grumman began working on Designs 33 and 33A, which were proposed derivatives of the XF4F-2 in which the Pratt & Whitney R-1830 radial was to be replaced by a Wright R-2600 radial, and to March 1938, when work on Design 35, an all-new naval fighter with the R-2600, was initiated. From these three studies, the team led by William Schwendler and Richard Hutton concluded that to take full advantage of the 33 per cent increase in power resulting from a switch from the R-1830 to the R-2600 it would be necessary to proceed with a new design, as the heavier weight of the new

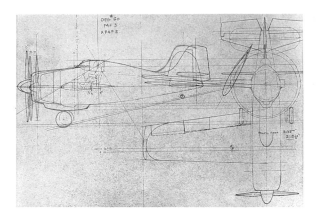

Comparative drawing of XF4F-2, F4F-3 and Design 50. *(Grumman)*

engine and the greater diameter of its propeller could not be easily accommodated in a simple revision of the F4F airframe. However, during the summer of 1938, following the Navy's selection of the Brewster XF2A-1 in preference to the XF4F-2, priority had to be given to the development of the XF4F-3, and Grumman temporarily suspended further work on an all-new fighter.

In September 1940, after a two-year lapse, work on a new carrier-based fighter to be powered by a 1,600- to 1,700-hp Wright R-2600 fourteen-cylinder radial was resumed, as by then reports from the war in Europe made it clear to Grumman that fighters with performance much better than that of the F4F-3 would be needed soon. As the Navy then had high hopes that its requirement for high performance fighters would be met by the production version of the Vought XF4U-1 (first flown on 29 May, 1940), BuAer gave Grumman a free hand in developing its Design 50, thus ensuring that an alternative to the F4U would be available in time of need. Time proved this decision to have been wise; the F4U-1 was initially found unsatisfactory as a carrier fighter, whereas the F6F-3, the initial production version of Design 50, proved highly suitable for carrier operations.

After again briefly attempting to retain some F4F design features to save time and cost, the project team proceeded with a larger and heavier aircraft retaining only a slight family ressemblance to the Wildcat. Moreover, it emphasized ease of production and maintenance and introduced several improvements, notably a wider track undercarriage and better forward and downward visibility through the use of a humped fuselage. The resulting Design 50 mock-up was first inspected on 12 January, 1941, when a number of minor changes were recommended. Notably, length, span, and wing area were increased respectively from 31 ft 4 in to 33 ft 6^{1}/$_{2}$ in, 41 ft 6 in to 42 ft 10 in, and 290 sq ft to 334 sq ft. So modified, Design 50 proved sufficiently promising for the Navy to order two XF6F-1 prototypes (BuNos 02981/02982) on 30 June, 1941, the same date on which the Vought F4U-1 was ordered into production. Both prototypes were initially intended to be powered by the 1,700 hp Wright XR-2600-10 fourteen-cylinder radial with two-stage mechanical supercharger but BuAer modified the contract on 26 April, 1942, to have the second prototype fitted with a turbosupercharged version of the R-2600-10. In the end, only the first aircraft flew with the Wright engine – and this briefly starting on 26 June, 1942. All other F6Fs were powered by the more powerful and more reliable Pratt & Whitney R-2800 eighteen-cylinder radial as first installed on the second airframe in July 1942.

Production history

With the war on, the need for large numbers of F6Fs quickly arose and an initial contract for 1,080 F6F-1s, to be powered by Wright R-2600-10s and delivered beginning in September 1942, was placed on 7 January, 1942, more than five months before the maiden flight of the XF6F-1. Subsequent orders brought Hellcat production to a total of 12,275 aircraft, all built in Bethpage. Most were F6F-3s and F6F-5s as described here along with prototypes and less proliferous variants.

XF6F-1: Powered by a Wright XR-2600-10 radial rated at 1,700 hp on take-off and 1,380 hp at 21,500 ft, the only XF6F-1 (c/n 3188, BuNo 02981) was fitted with a three-blade Curtiss propeller and large spinner when it was first flown at Bethpage by Robert L Hall on 26 June, 1942. Provision was made for six wing-mounted 0.50-in machine guns but initially these were not installed. Trials continued until 8 August, 1942, when the XF6F-1 was grounded to be modified to the XF6F-3 configuration with a Pratt & Whitney R-2800-10 eighteen-cylinder radial replacing the lower powered R-2600 fourteen-cylinder radial.

The XF6F-1 photographed at Bethpage on 25 June, 1942, on the eve of its first flight. (*Grumman*)

196

A four-blade propeller and deeper cowling housing a turbosupercharged XR-2800-16 characterized the XF6F-2 (BuNo 66244). *(Grumman)*

XF6F-2: Initially ordered as an XF6F-1 with a two-stage XR-2600-10 engine, the second prototype (c/n 3189, BuNo 02982) was to have been completed as the XF6F-2 with a turbosupercharged version of the XR-2600-10. However, before completion this airframe was fitted with a Pratt & Whitney engine and became the first XF6F-3 to fly.

The XF6F-2 designation was resurrected in 1944 when the last F6F-3 airframe (c/n A-4403, BuNo 66244) was experimentally fitted with a turbosupercharged Pratt & Whitney XR-2800-16 radial. The engine was rated at 2,000 hp for take-off as well as at 25,000 ft, drove a four-blade propeller with wide-chord blade cuffs, and was housed in a deeper cowling. This prototype first flew in January 1944 but its further development was not warranted as by then the Navy had little or no need for a high-altitude fighter with turbosupercharged engine as most combat operations in the

The second F6F airframe, on 1 October 1942, after it had been re-engined with an R-2800-27 to become the XF6F-4. (*Grumman*)

Pacific were taking place at low or medium altitudes. Following completion of trials, BuNo 66244 was re-engined with an R-2800-10W and delivered as an F6F-3.

XF6F-3: On 3 June, 1942, 23 days before the first flight of the XF6F-1, the Navy decided that the second prototype (c/n 3189, BuNo 02982) should be completed as an XF6F-3 with a Pratt & Whitney R-2800-10 two-stage radial driving a Curtiss three-blade propeller and rated at 2,000 hp for take-off, 1800 hp at 15,500 ft, and 1,650 hp at 22,500 ft. Modifications were undertaken without delay and this first XF6F-3, which also differed from the XF6F-1 in having horizontal tail surfaces of slightly greater span and narrower chord, was first flown by Bob Hall on 30 July, 1942. Quite confusingly, its Bureau Number was soon changed to 02981 – the BuNo originally assigned to the XF6F-1, while the first prototype, then still being re-engined, became BuNo 02982.

The first XF6F-3 (BuNo 02981, ex-BuNo 02982) was damaged on 17 August, 1942, when an engine seizure due to lack of lubrication forced Bob Hall to make a belly landing. It was then rebuilt as the XF6F-4.

The first airframe (c/n 3188, now BuNo 02982 but originally numbered 02981) flew as an XF6F-3 on 13 September, 1942. Trials proceeded smoothly and, with the exception of teething troubles with the R-2800-10 engine, the only significant problem – tail flutter encountered during high-speed dives –was easily solved by strengthening the rear fuselage. Later the Curtiss propeller was replaced by a Hamilton Standard, and the aircraft was brought up to full F6F-3 production standard. Nevertheless, it was still designated XF6F-3 when it was accepted by the Navy on 22 November, 1943. From December 1943 until July 1944, it was bailed to Pratt & Whitney in Hartford, Connecticut, and was finally struck off at Norfolk, Virginia, on 30 November, 1944.

198

Reserve F6f-5s from Floyd Bennett Field, NAS New York. *(Grumman)*

This F6F-3 (BuNo 42874) was transferred to the National Advisory Committee for Aeronautics in June 1945 and, as illustrated after being modified, was used by NACA as a variable stability research aircraft. *(NACA/Grumman)*

199   *Photo taken early 1950's*

F6F-3: First flown on 3 October, 1942, the initial production version of the Hellcat differed mainly from the first XF6F-3 in being fitted with a Hamilton Standard propeller without spinner and, with the exception of a handful of early production aircraft, in having a cleaned-up cowling and simplified main undercarriage fairings. During the course of production, a number of minor improvements were progressively introduced, including additional cleaning up of the cowling and the removal of small fairings which had initially been fitted to the protruding barrels of the inboard guns. More importantly, from August 1943, all Hellcats were fitted to carry a 150-US gal (568-liter) drop tank beneath the fuselage. Beginning in January 1944, 60 per cent of the F6F-3s were delivered with R-2800-10W engines in place of the R-2800-10s which lacked water injection.

A total of 4,402 F6F-3s (BuNos 04775/04958, 08798/09047, 25721/26195, 39999/43137, and 65890/66243) were built in Bethpage with production rates increasing steadily and exceeding 500 aircraft a month after January 1944. The last F6F-3 was delivered on 20 April, 1944. As indicated elsewhere, eighteen were completed as F6F-3Es, 229 as F6F-3Ns, and a few were modified as F6F-3Ks and F6F-3Ps. All F6F-3/-3E/-3N/-3Ps were armed with six wing-mounted 0.50-in machine guns with 400 rounds per gun; late production aircraft were also fitted with a single bomb rack. Although trials conducted in August 1943 with an aircraft carrying two 1,000-lb bombs and a ventral tank had proved satisfactory, production F6F-3s delivered beginning in September 1943 were fitted to carry only the ventral tank and one bomb on a rack beneath the starboard wing, close to the fuselage.

In answer to a December 1942 request from the Navy, Grumman and Edo Corporation jointly undertook studies to fit a pair of 29-ft floats to the F6F-3. Wind tunnel and hydrodynamic tests were conducted with a $\frac{1}{16}$th scale model but the availability of escort carriers and the ability of construction battalions (Seabees) to build airstrips in less than a week eliminated the need for floatplane fighters before the completion of an F6F-3 floatplane prototype.

F6F-3E: Whereas F6F-3Ns were optimized for the night interception role, F6F-3Es were intended as night intruders and fitted with a Westinghouse AN/APS-4 radar in a radome hung beneath their starboard wing. In other respects – including a flat windshield, the installation of radar altimeter and IFF, and red instrument lighting – the eighteen F6F-3Es delivered by January 1944 were similar to the F6F-3Ns.

F6F-3F: This designation is believed to have been given to an F6F-3 which was used as a powerplant development aircraft.

F6F-3K: Beginning in 1946, the Navy modified a small number of F6F-3s as remotely-controlled drones for use in special programmes such as air sampling during nuclear weapons testing.

F6F-3N: As the fleet had an urgent need for night fighters and as the Vought F4U-2 was considered to be marginal for carrier operations, Grumman was asked in early 1943 to study ways of installing night fighter

F6F-3Ns of VMF(N)-534 at Orote Field, Guam, on 21 August, 1944. *(USMC/DOD Still Media Records Center)*

equipment on the F6F-3. By the end of April, wind tunnel tests confirmed that the installation of a Sperry AN/APS-6 radar set in a radome on and below the leading edge of the starboard wing would result in minimal drag and satisfactory operation. The study further determined that the F6F-3 night fighter version would have to be fitted with an AN/APN-1 radar altimeter, an IFF transponder, a flat front windshield serving as the gunsight reflector, and redesigned instrument panel with red lighting and a centrally mounted radar screen. The first F6F-3 modified to the night fighter configuration was delivered by Grumman to the Project *Affirm* team in Quonset Point, Rhode Island, in June 1943, but the first radar sets were not available until September, by which time eighteen additional aircraft had been modified. The modified aircraft were designated F6F-3Ns in March 1944 and two months later were operating aboard carriers in the Pacific. A total of 229 Hellcats were modified by Grumman as F6F-3Ns. At least one aircraft (BuNo 65950) was experimentally fitted with a searchlight installed in a fairing beneath the port wing.

F6F-3P: This designation was given to a small number of F6F-3s which were modified in service by installation of a long focal length camera in the lower port fuselage, aft of the wing. The high-altitude phototographic reconnaissance F6F-3Ps retained the standard armament of the fighters.

XF6F-4: After being damaged in a belly landing on 17 August, 1942, BuNo 02981 (the second airframe, ex-BuNo 02982) was re-engined with a 2,000-hp R-2800-27 single-stage radial driving a three-blade Hamilton Standard propeller, and was redesignated XF6F-4. It first flew in this form on 3 October, 1942, and was accepted by the Navy seven days later. Subsequently, the XF6F-4 was used to test the four 20-mm cannon arrangement on which Grumman had begun working in November 1942 after being

201

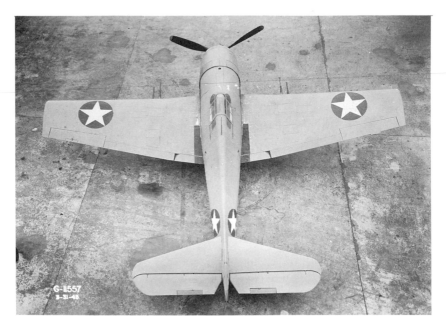

The XF6F-4 on 31 March, 1943, after it had been fitted with four 20-mm cannon. *(Grumman)*

asked by the Navy to develop a heavier armament for the Hellcat. The cannon wing was not retained for production but the XF6F-4 kept this armament until struck off at Quonset Point, Rhode Island, on 31 October, 1946.

F6F-4: This designation was used by the Navy to identify a projected version for which preliminary studies were prepared in July 1943. Intended for operations aboard escort carriers (CVEs), this variant was to have been lightened, through removal of two of the six 0.50-in guns and the 75-US gal rear fuel tank and to have been fitted with wings of increased span and area. Although the proposed aircraft would have been better than the F6F-3 for operations aboard CVEs, its superiority over the FM-2 was questionable. Since the FM-2 was smaller, allowing more aircraft to be carried aboard a CVE, and was already in production, BuAer concluded that the F6F-4's speed advantage and probable lower attrition rate due to its wider track undercarriage did not justify the engineering and productive efforts required to put it into production.

F6F-5: Including aircraft delivered as F6F-5Es and F6F-5Ns and aircraft modified as F6F-5Ds, F6F-5Ks, and F6F-5Ps, a total of 7,868 F6F-5s were built (BuNos 58000/58999, 69992/70187, 70189/70912, 70914/72991, 77259/80258, and 93652/94521). The first flew on 5 April, 1944, and the last was delivered on 21 November, 1945. In addition to incorporating most of the improvements which had been introduced during the course of F6F-3 production, all F6F-5 variants were powered by R-2800-10Ws with water

An F6F-5 of Escadrille 3S from BAN Cuers in southern France. *(Courtesy of Alain Crosnier)*

injection and featured numerous additional refinements. Notably, they were fitted with spring tabs on the ailerons, additional armour protection, strengthened assembly, a closer fitting cowling, and a revised windshield.

Development of an improved windshield had been begun by Grumman in compliance with a request made by BuAer in October 1943 after operational units had complained that dust was accumulating between the bullet-proof plate and the curved windshield of F6F-3s. Accordingly, and on the strength of the experience gained during the development of the F6F-3N when the curved windshield had been dispensed with and the flat bullet-proof plate modified to double as a windshield, this arrangement was retained for the F6F-5. In addition, the bullet-proof plate and the side panels were enlarged to eliminate the need for the small upper windshield panel. Conversely, the contemplated redesign of the Hellcat's upper rear fuselage fairing and the use of a sliding bubble-type canopy to improve rearward vision were both rejected as they would have entailed much work and resulted in a significant production slowdown. In fact, quite the opposite happened as rearward vision was reduced in late production F6F-5s following the deletion of the windows aft of the sliding canopy.

Early production F6F-5s were fitted with a single bomb rack beneath the starboard wing as developed for late F6F-3s; however, late production F6F-5s had a rack beneath each wing's inboard section for bombs of up to 1,000 lb or 11¾-in *Tiny Tim* rockets and three Mk 5 zero-length launchers beneath each outer wing panel for 5-in HVAR rockets.

F6F-5D: This designation identified a small number of F6F-5s which were modified by the Navy after the war to serve as drone directors.

F6F-5E: Along with F6F-5N night interceptors, Grumman produced a smaller number of F6F-5E night intruders by modifying F6F-5 airframes before completion and fitting them with an AN/APS-4 radar in a radome beneath the starboard wing.

F6F-5K: Between 1949 and 1957, a fair number of F6F-5s were modified

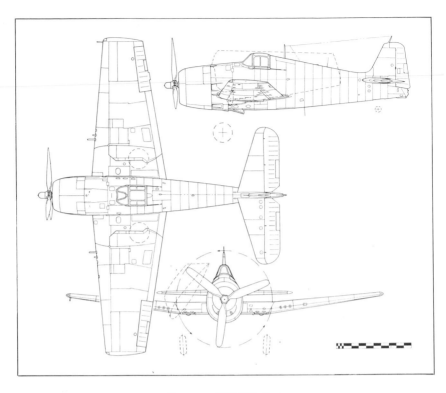

Grumman F6F-5 Hellcat

into radio-controlled drones by O & R Pensacola in Florida. Controls and instrumentation were retained for use during check-out and ferry flights.

F6F-5N: Some 1,432 F6F-5s were completed by Grumman as night fighters and were fitted with the same AN/APS-6 radar installation and other specialized equipment as the F6F-3Ns. Late production aircraft had the inboard 0.50-in gun in each wing replaced by a 20-mm cannon to increase the probability of kills during brief night engagements when pilots seldom could stay for long behind their intended victims. At least two F6F-5Ns (BuNos 70729 and 79139) were fitted with an airborne searchlight pod on the port wing leading edge and were evaluated in the night ASW role late in the war and during the immediate postwar period.

F6F-5P: An undetermined number of F6F-5s were modified by the Navy as fighter reconnaissance aircraft with cameras in the rear fuselage.

XF6F-6: Two prototypes of a better performing aircraft were obtained by fitting a 2,100-hp R-2800-18W radial driving a four-blade propeller in uncompleted F6F-5 airframes (BuNos 70188 and 70913). The first XF6F-6 flew on 6 July, 1944, and reached a top speed of 417 mph at 21,900 ft during trials. The F6F-6 had been scheduled to go into production beginning in

An F6F-5E with an AN/APS-4 radar in a radome beneath the starboard wing.

Although substantially faster than F6F-5s powered by R-2800-10W engines, the F6F-6 powered by the R-2800-18W was not put into production. This photograph of one of the two XF6F-6s was taken on 31 October, 1944. The wartime censor has air-brushed all details behind the aircraft. (*Grumman*)

September 1944 but, as the R-2800-18W engine was in great demand for the better-performing Vought F4U-4, this did not materialize.

Design 54: In February 1942, four months before the first flight of the XF6F-1, Grumman initiated the preliminary design for a version to be fitted with laminar-flow wings. Calculated performance did not justify a

205

switch to this version as rapid delivery of large numbers of aircraft was of the utmost importance.

Designs 59 and **60**: These were studies undertaken in August 1943 to see if the installation of a 3,000 hp Pratt & Whitney R-4360 28-cylinder engine would result in sufficient performance improvement to justify production. Design 59 was planned around an engine with a single-stage variable-speed supercharger whereas Design 60 was to have had a two-stage engine. The installation of the big Wasp Major necessitated too many modifications to be practical.

Design 61: Prelimary design work for a mixed-power version of the Hellcat was begun in August 1943. The R-2800 was to have been supplemented by a General Electric I-20 turbojet installed in the rear fuselage. However, calculated performance gains were insufficient to warrant construction of a prototype, and Design 61 remained on the drawing board.

Design 69: During the spring and summer of 1944, BuAer showed much interest in single-seat fighter-bombers with which to replace two-seat dive bombers and three-seat torpedo bombers. To meet this requirement, in July 1944 Grumman unsuccessfully proposed a development of the Hellcat, Design 69, to be powered by a 2,100-hp R-2800-22 engine.

Service history

On 16 January, 1943, sixteen days after the commissioning of the USS *Essex* (CV-9) as the first ship in a new class of fast aircraft carriers, F6F-3s were assigned to VF-9 at NAS Oceana, Virginia, to start training before going aboard the new carrier. During the following seven months, additional Hellcat squadrons were established to serve aboard *Essex*-class (CV) and *Independence*-class (CVL) carriers which were commissioned at a rapid rate. Aircraft, ships, and men participated in shakedown and training cruises in preparation for the impending offensive in the Pacific.

The US Navy unleashed its new weapons on 31 August, 1943, when Task Force 15 struck Japanese installations on Marcus Island. Joining other carrier aircraft, F6F-3s from VF-9 (*Essex*), VF-5 (*Yorktown*), VF-6 (*Independence*), and VF-22 (*Independence*) destroyed four Japanese aircraft on the ground during a dawn mission and later in the day Lt Richard Loesch of VF-6 claimed the first air combat victory for the Hellcat. From then on, carrier-based F6F-3s took part in a series of strikes against Japanese bases designed to paralyse the Imperial Japanese Navy while American amphibious forces landed in the Solomons (New Georgia, Choiseul, and Bougainville) and in the Gilbert and Marshall Islands (Tarawa, Makin, Roi, and Namur). While providing escort for the carrier bombers and strafing Japanese ships and ground installations, the Hellcat then quickly asserted its superiority over the Mitsubishi Zero, with Ens Robert W Duncan of VF-5 becoming the first Hellcat pilot to down two of the much-vaunted Japanese fighters during a mission against the naval base at Truk in the Caroline Islands on 5 October, 1943.

The Allied offensive gained tempo in the early months of 1944 and

These F6F-3s, with crudely painted three-digit identification numbers on their cowlings, were photographed before delivery. (*Grumman*)

Hellcats based aboard Task Force 58 carriers inflicted telling damage on Japanese land-based aircraft in a series of attacks. On 17 and 18 February, when major strikes were again flown against the Japanese stronghold at Truk, F6F-3s from nine squadrons (VF-5, -6, -9, -10, -18, -24, -25 , -30, and-31) and F6F-3Ns from VF(N)-76 destroyed 127 enemy aircraft in the air and 86 on the ground. On 29 and 30 March, Hellcats from eleven air groups were credited with the destruction of some 150 Japanese aircraft during operations in the Palau Islands. Notwithstanding the magnitude of these successes, the Hellcat's most celebrated contribution to the Allied war efforts was yet to come.

For Operation *Forager* in the Marianas Islands, Task Force 58 deployed fifteen carriers with 896 aircraft, of which more than half were Hellcats (443 F6F-3s and 24 F6F-3Ns). After flying strikes against Guam, Saipan, and Tinian between 11 and 14 June, and against Iwo Jima and Chichi Jima on 15 and 16 June, during which great numbers of Japanese land-based aircraft were destroyed, the Hellcats were called to intercept the first waves of aircraft coming from Guam and from the carriers of the First Mobile Fleet on the morning of 19 June. Thirty-five land-based attackers and forty-two carrier-based aircraft were shot down for the loss of only two F6F-3s. These engagements were followed by other equally one-sided fights during the remainder of the day as Hellcats annihilated their opponents and, in the words of Lt-Cdr Paul Buie, the CO of VF-16, turned the First Battle of the Philippine Sea into the 'Marianas Turkey Shoot.'

Thereafter, Hellcats (F6F-5s supplanted F6F-3s during the summer of 1944 and fully replaced the older version in early 1945) and the USN continued to enjoy a series of remarkable successes paving the road to Japan: an air-sea battle off Formosa on 12-14 October, 1944; Second Battle of the Philippine Sea on 24 and 25 October; Iwo Jima in February 1945; and Okinawa in March 1945. Finally, carrier-based Hellcats provided air cover for the bombers attacking the remnants of the Imperial Japanese Navy which were taking refuge in the Inland Sea. Despite the qualitative improvements of Japanese fighter aircraft, notably following the introduction of the Kawanishi N1K1-J/N1K2-J *George* and Nakajima Ki-84 *Frank*, the Hellcats continued to enjoy an unbroken stream of triumphs, as by then they had an overwhelming numerical superiority. Moreover, at this stage of the war, the F6F pilots were better trained than their opponents, who were being thrown into battle after flying only a minimum number of hours.

In 1945, to deal with the threat of Japanese kamikazes, the complement of air groups aboard *Essex*-class carriers was revised to add a fighter-bomber squadron (VBF) and reduce the number of aircraft assigned to bomber and torpedo bomber squadrons (VB and VT). Although Vought Corsairs equipped several of the VBFs, others flew F6F-5s and several VBF Hellcat pilots emulated their VF colleagues by becoming aces. Altogether, according to the American Fighter Aces Association, the Hellcat produced more aces than any other type of aircraft. Many were aces-in-a-day, including seven who achieved this distinction during the 'Marianas Turkey Shoot.' All top-scoring Navy carrier aces were F6F pilots, namely Cdr

An F6F-5P of Marine Photographic Squadron 354 (VMD-354) on Guam in 1945. (*USMC/ DOD Still Media Records Center*)

F6F-5s of VF-11 aboard the USS *Hornet* (CV-12) off Japan in February 1945. *(USN/National Archives)*

David McCampbell of VF-15 (34 victories), Lt-Cdr Cecil Harris of VF-18 and -27 (24), Lt-Cdr Gene Valencia of VF-9 (23), Lt-Cdr Alex Vraciu of VF-6, -16, and -20 (19), and Lt-Cdr Pat Fleming of VF-80 (19 each).

Although, as noted in the Avenger chapter, Hellcats had first been used at night when F6F-3s had been guided by radar-equipped TBF-1Cs during operations in the Gilbert Islands in November 1943, the true debut of Hellcat night fighters took place in February 1944 when detachments of F6F-3Ns from VF(N)-76 began operating aboard *Essex*-class ships. This squadron was soon joined by VF(N)-77 and -78, and all three accounted for fifteen to twenty kills during night operations in the spring of 1944. Thereafter, four-aircraft detachments of F6F-3Es/-3Ns/-5Es/-5Ns were added to most Fighting Squadrons operating aboard *Essex*-class ships and to some of the squadrons assigned to escort carriers. In addition, Night Fighting Squadrons, notably VF(N)-41 and VF(N)-90 which respectively claimed twenty seven and nineteen night kills plus additional victories during daytime operations, operated as part of specialized Night Air Groups aboard *Enterprise* and *Independence*. At least five Hellcat pilots became nocturnal aces.

While Navy Hellcats are best remembered for their operations in the Pacific, F6F-5s and F6F-5Ns also fought against German forces. In August 1944, aircraft from VOF-1 (Observation Fighting Squadron One) aboard the USS *Tulagi* (CVE-72) and VF-74 aboard the USS *Kasaan Bay* (CVE-69) provided air cover during Operation *Dragoon* in southern France. On that occasion, they directed naval gunfire, flew armed reconnaisance, interdiction, strafing, and bombing sorties, and shot down three Heinkel He 111 bombers before the two escort carriers were re-assigned as aircraft transports or sent to the Pacific.

After the end of the war, the number of naval fighter squadrons was

An F6F-5N of NightDevRonPac over Honolulu in 1946. The aircraft has an AN/APS-6 radar beneath the starboard wing and a searchlight beneath and in front of the port wing. (*USN, courtesy of Leonard Skreba and Tailhook Photo Service*)

F6F-5 Hellcats were the first aircraft flown by the *Blue Angels* when this demonstration squadron was formed in July 1946. (*Grumman*)

Bearing the alpha-numeric identification V1 and V6 on their cowling, these two F6F-5K drones of GMU-90 were guided against North Korean targets by operators aboard AD-4Ns of VC-35. Carrying a 1,000-lb bomb beneath their fuselage and a television camera and transmitter in a pod beneath the starboard wing, these two drones were photographed just before being launched from the USS *Boxer* (CV-21) in August or September 1952. *(USN/ National Archives)*

rapidly reduced. Nevertheless, F6F-5s and -5Ps continued to serve aboard carriers until 1948, when they were replaced by Corsairs and Bearcats, while others served with reserve units for five more years. During the spring and summer of 1953 reserve F6F-5s were briefly re-assigned to fleet squadrons when delivery of F9F-5 Panthers was delayed by engine teething troubles. Moreover, F6F-5s briefly equipped the *Blue Angels* after the soon

211

famous US Navy aerial demonstration team was organized in July 1946. In the night fighting role, Hellcats were longer lived, as the last F6F-5Ns were only retired by Composite Squadron Four (VC-4) during the summer of 1954. During the postwar years and well into the 1950s, F6F-3K and F6F-5K drones were put to many uses. In July 1946, several F6F-3Ks were flown through radio-active clouds during Operation *Crossroad*, when atomic bombs were tested against naval vessels anchored in Bikini lagoon. Between 28 August and 2 September, 1952, six F6F-5Ks of GMU-90 (Guided Missile Unit 90) were launched from the USS *Boxer* (CV-21) against a bridge, a railway tunnel, and a power plant in North Korea. In these instances, the F6F-5Ks were guided by AD-4Ns from VC-35. Each carried a 1,000-lb bomb beneath its fuselage and a television camera and transmitter in a pod beneath the starboard wing. They scored two direct hits and one near miss for a disappointing success rate of less than 50 per cent. Most F6F-5Ks, however, were used as target drones, notably during air-to-air missile testing at NOTS Inyokern, California, and for that role were often fitted with recording cameras in wingtip pods. A few F6F-5K drones survived into the late 1950s to become the last Hellcats in US service.

With the Marine Corps, Hellcats were used principally by night fighter squadrons, with the F6F-3Ns of VMF(N)-534 being the first to reach the combat zone when they arrived on Guam in early August 1944. Remaining in the Western Pacific until the end of the war, VMF(N)-534 was credited with the destruction of only one enemy aircraft, a Nakajima C6N1 *Myrt* reconnaissance aircraft which was brought down in daylight while allegedly carrying a high-ranking Japanese officer. Also equipped with F6F-3Ns, VMF(N)-541 arrived in September 1944 on Peleliu, in the Palau Islands, where it claimed its first enemy aircraft. It then was credited with the destruction of twenty-two aircraft in the air and five on the ground during operations from Tacloban, on Leyte in the Philippines, from 3 December, 1944, until 11 January, 1945. VMF(N)-541 made no further kills after returning to Peleliu and later sending detachments to Ulithi. During the Okinawa campaign, when they flew F6F-5Ns, pilots from VMF(N)-533, -542, and 543 respectively claimed thirty-five, eighteen and fifteen night air victories. All three squadrons were on Okinawa when the war ended. By early 1946, Hellcat night fighters were serving with eight squadrons on Okinawa and in China, Japan, and the United States. Soon afterwards the number of squadrons was reduced, and by the end of the decade the last Marine F6F-5Ns had been replaced by more modern aircraft.

Although during the last two years of the war most of the Marine Fighting Squadrons (VMFs) flew F4U Corsairs, a few were equipped with F6F-5s. This was notably the case of squadrons from MAG-51 (Marine Air Group 51) which in 1944 trained with Tiny Tim rockets in preparation for deployment to Europe (Project *Danny*) and operations against V 1 flying-bomb launching sites. As these sites were captured by Allied ground troops before Project *Danny* got underway, the MAG-51 squadrons supplemented

During the war, and unlike the AAF, the USN and the USMC discouraged its personnel from applying nose art on their aircraft. These F6F-5Ns of VMF(N)-541 at Falalop Island, Ulithi, on 30 May, 1945, prove once again that there are exceptions to almost every rule. *(USMC/National Archives)*

The F6F-3 variable stability research aircraft operated by the Ames Research Center at Moffett Field, California. *(NASA/Grumman)*

MAG-31 squadrons being trained for operations aboard Marine Corps escort carriers. The VMF (CVS) squadrons which deployed before the end of the war – VMF-351 aboard the uss *Cape Gloucester* (CVE-109), VMF-511 (*Block Island*, CVE-106), VMF-512 (*Gilbert Islands*, CVE-107), VMF-513 (*Vella Gulf*, CVE-111), and VMF-514 (*Salerno Bay*, CVE-110) – flew a mix of Hellcats and Corsairs during operations off Okinawa, Leyte, Balikpapan, and Japan.

In addition to the land-based F6F-3N and F6F-5N night fighters and to the F6F-5/-5Ns aboard escort carriers, the only Hellcats known to have been used by the USMC in combat operations were those of VMD-354 (Marine Photographic Squadron 354). Equipped with F6F-5Ps, this squadron was sent to Guam in May 1945 and operated until the end of the war from Peleliu, Ulithi, and Okinawa. Less well-known is the experimental use made by the National Advisory Committee for Aeronautics of the small number of F6F-3s and F6F-5s it acquired in the immediate postwar period.* Foremost among these Hellcats was an F6F-3 (BuNo 42874) which was operated by NACA from 22 June, 1945, until 9 September, 1960, and given the tail number 158. During the intervening years, NACA 158 was modified to become the world's first variable stability research aircraft and to simulate the handling characteristics of a variety of aircraft then under development. While assigned to the Ames Research Center at Moffett Field, California, this variable stability research aircraft was flown by Grumman's test pilot Corky Meyer to gain a feel of the likely handling characteristics of the XF10F-1 before the first flight of that aircraft in May 1952, and by Lockheed's test pilot Tony LeVier to gain a similar experience before the first flight of the XF-104 in February 1956.

During the war the United Kingdom was the only foreign recipient of Hellcats, with a total of 1,177 F6F-3s, F6F-5s, F6F-5Ns, and F6F-5Ps delivered to the Fleet Air Arm. During the 1950s, F6F5s and F6F-5Ns were also flown in combat by France's Armée de l'Air and Aéronautique Navale and were operated by the air arms of three Latin American nations, with Uruguay's Aviación Naval becoming, in 1961, the last service to fly Hellcats.

ARGENTINA: Ten F6F-5s were transferred to the Servicio de Aviación Naval (Argentine Naval Aviation Service) by the United States after Argentina became a signatory of the 1947 Rio Pact. No details regarding their service use are available but it is known that a few were later handed over to Paraguay.

FRANCE: Following the signature of the treaty establishing the North Atlantic Treaty Organization (NATO) in April 1949 and the recognition by the US government less than a year later that France was fighting in Indochina against Communist forces not just anti-colonialism insurgents, much military help was received by France from the United States. France received 179 F6F-5s and F6F-5Ns to equip both units of the Armée de l'Air operating in Indochina and units of the Aéronautique Navale based in France and deployed to Indochina aboard carriers.

In the spring of 1950, while an initial group of Aéronautique Navale pilots received conversion training in the United States, the first F6F-5s were ferried to Bizerte, Tunisia, aboard the escort carrier *Dixmude* to replace Supermarine Seafire IIIs and XVs in service with Flottilles 1F and 12F. Including subsequent deliveries, the Aéronautique Navale eventually received 124 F6F-5s and fifteen F6F-5Ns, with the last being received in 1953. The Armée de l'Air received forty F6F-5s and F6F-5Ns (the latter

---

* The Hellcat had first been evaluated by NACA between February and May 1944 when, at the request of the Navy, BuNo 04776 was used for a series of handling and stalling tests.

An F6F-5 of Flottille 11F about to be catapulted from the deck of the *Bois Belleau* during operations in the Gulf of Tonkin on 5 May, 1954. (*ECPA, courtesy of Alain Crosnier*)

F6F-5s from an unidentified unit of the Aéronatique Navale aboard *La Fayette* in December 1954. Aircraft No.6 is ready for launch on the port of the light carrier. (*ECPA courtesy of Alain Crosnier*)

were armed with two 20-mm cannon and four 0.50-in guns but did not have their AN/APS-6 radar and distinctive radome) which were delivered to Saïgon aboard *Dixmude* in October 1950 and were operated in Indochina by three Groupes de Chasse.

After training for over a year and taking part in exercises in home waters, Flottille 1F deployed in August 1951 aboard the light carrier *Arromanches* for operations in Indochina. It left the F6F-5Ns of its section de nuit (night flight) in France. The first combat sorties were flown on 6 October and the carrier and her Hellcats and Curtiss Helldivers remained in operation until returning to France in May 1952. *Arromanches* went back to Indochina in October 1952, but on that occasion her Hellcats were those of Flottille 12F. When the carrier had to be sent back to France for refit in early 1953, Flottille 12F was transferred ashore and continued flying combat operations from Haiphong-Cat Bi until embarking aboard the light carrier *La Fayette*. Flottille 12F returned to France aboard the *La Fayette* in May 1953 and then began its conversion to Vought F4U-7s. Meanwhile, Flottille 1F had been renumbered 11F. With this new designation, the unit returned to Indochina aboard *Arromanches* for combat operations from October 1953 until after the fall of Dien Bien Phu on 7 May, 1954. Flottille 11F, which had lost four of its Hellcats during operations in support of the Dien Bien Phu garrison, began its conversion to Sud Aquilons immediately upon its return home.

In addition to equipping Flottilles 1F, 11F and 12F, Hellcats were operated at Hyères by the Section d'Entraînement à la Chasse de Nuit (SECN), which had a number of radar-equipped F6F-5Ns, and by Escadrilles de Servitude 3S, 54S, 57S, and 59S. The last of these, which had been formed in February 1956 when the SECN was redesignated, sent a four-aircraft detachment to Algeria in 1960 in an attempt to intercept light aircraft flying guerilla supplies and cadres across the border with Tunisia. Soon after, the last Hellcats of the Aéronautique Navale ended their useful life as training airframes at the Section 'Marine' de l'Ecole de Rochefort.

In Indochina, the carrier-based Hellcats of the Aéronautique Navale had been preceded by those of the Armée de l'Air, with that Service assigning some of the first aircraft offloaded in Saïgon to replace the war-weary Supermarine Spitfire IXs of Groupe de Chasse I/6 'Corse.' This unit then first used its Hellcats to provide air support to French troops and to interdict Viet Minh lines of communication during operations from Tourane (better known since as Da Nang) in early December 1950. Later in the month, F6F-5s were also assigned to supplement the Bell P-63Cs of GC II/6 'Normandie Niemen.' Both GC I/6 and GC II/6 sent Hellcat detachments to Hanoi for operations in the Tonkin area where they helped stop a major Viet Minh offensive. In March 1951, GC I/6 converted to Bearcats and in April 1951, before being sent back to France without equipment, GC II/6 began transferring its F6F-5s to GC II/9 'Auvergne.' This latter unit then flew Hellcats until the end of 1952, when it converted to Bearcats and transferred its last F6F-5s to the Aéronautique Navale.

PARAGUAY: A handful of ex-Argentine F6F-5s saw limited service with the Servicio de Aeronáutica de la Marina (Naval Aviation Service).

UNITED KINGDOM: Next to the Vought Corsair, of which 1,977 were delivered to Britain under Lend-Lease, the Hellcat was the most numerous

American aircraft operated by the Fleet Air Arm during the war years. The first 252 aircraft were F6F-3s which were to have been designated Gannet Is in British Naval service but were redesignated Hellcat Is before deliveries began in May 1943. They were followed by 849 F6F-5s and seventy-six F6F-5Ns which respectively became Hellcat F. Mk. IIs and Hellcat N.F. Mk. IIs with the Fleet Air Arm. Most Hellcats were operated as received from the United States, but Blackburn Aircraft fitted British rocket projectile launchers to a number of F6F-3s and modified some F6F-5s as Hellcat F.R. Mk. II fighter-reconnaissance aircraft and others as Hellcat P.R. Mk. II unarmed photographic-reconnaissance aircraft.

The first two squadrons to be equipped with Hellcat Is were Nos.800 and 804 which began their training at RNAS Eglington, Derry, in the early summer of 1943. After first deploying in December 1943 for North Atlantic convoy duty aboard HMS *Emperor*, the two squadrons went on the offensive during Operation *Tungsten* on 3 April, 1944, when they provided cover for strikes against the German battleship *Tirpitz* anchored in Kaafjord, in Norway. From then until the end of the war, Hellcats took part in several operations in Norwegian waters. Those from Nos. 800 and 804 Squadrons flew anti-shipping strikes in May 1944, with No. 800 claiming three enemy aircraft for the loss of two Hellcats during a dogfight against Bf 109Gs and Fw 190As on the 8th. Those from No. 1840 Squadron provided cover during two further strikes against the *Tirpitz:* Operation *Mascot* on 17 July, 1944, when they operated from HMS *Furious*, and Operation *Goodwood* on 22-29 August when they were aboard HMS *Indefatigable*. The only other significant operations against German forces in which Hellcats took part were those which saw No. 800 Squadron provide cover for a convoy to

Hellcat Is of the Fleet Air Arm. JV163 in the foreground with JV117 beyond. (*IWM*)

Gibraltar, in June 1944, and air support for the landings in Southern France, in August 1944, while operating from HMS *Emperor*.

In the war against Japan, British Hellcat squadrons went into action on 29 August, 1944, when Nos. 1839 and 1844 aboard HMS *Indomitable* provided cover during strikes against a cement plant at Indaroeng and the Emmahaven harbour in the Netherlands East Indies. These two squadrons scored their first victories against Japanese aircaft during operations over the Nicobar Islands in October 1944 and took part in strikes against Belawan Deli in December 1944, and Pladjoe and Soengi Gerong in January 1945. Remaining aboard *Indomitable* until May 1945, when this carrier was withdrawn for refitting, Nos. 1839 and 1844 Squadrons provided Hellcat F. Mk. IIs and N.F. Mk. IIs for operations with the British Pacific Fleet. Their N.F. Mk. IIs then went aboard *Formidable* to continue providing the British Pacific Fleet with its only night fighter defence during the final operations of the war. Other Hellcat squadrons which saw service in the Indian Ocean and the Pacific Ocean were Nos. 800 (aboard *Emperor* and *Shah*), 804 (*Ameer, Empress,* and *Shah*), 808 (*Khedive*), 885 (*Ruler*), 888 (with Hellcat P.R. Mk.IIs aboard *Indefatigable* and *Empress*), 896 (*Ameer* and *Empress*), and 898 (*Attacker* and *Pursuer*). FAA squadrons which formed up too late to see action were Nos. 881, 889, 891, and 1847. After the war, all airworthy Hellcats were returned to the United States. The last two squadrons to fly the type were No.892 and No.888 which disbanded in April and August 1946 respectively. However, at least one Hellcat F. Mk. II

A Royal Navy Hellcat II operating with the British Pacific Fleet. With undercarriage, flaps and hook lowered, this Hellcat appears to be executing a missed approach. (*IWM*)

A late production F6F-5 at the Hayward Municipal Airport, California, on 24 February, 1989, after it had been rebuilt for a Texas museum. The glossy finish and highly polished propeller and fittings are historically inaccurate but the workmanship is superb. Markings reproduce quite well those of the F6F-3 flown by Lt Alex Vraciu after he gained his nineteenth and final victory while flying with VF-16 from the USS *Lexington* (CV-16) in June 1944. *(René J Francillon)*

(KE209) was retained in the United Kingdom and was airworthy as late as April 1953.

URUGUAY: Ten F6F-5s were ferried from the United States in April 1952 and received the serials A-401/A-406 and A-451/A-454 in service with the Aviación Naval (Uruguayan Naval Aviation). The last Hellcats were withdrawn from use in 1961.

Unlike two of its contemporaries, the Mustang and the Corsair, the Hellcat has had relatively little success with private owners (though at least one surplus F6F-3 was evaluated in the crop spraying role, with chemicals carried in large underwing tanks, it was found to be uneconomical) and warbird enthusiasts. True, the F6F never compared with the P-51 as far as aerodynamic cleanliness and beauty were concerned nor did it have the imaginative lines of the F4U, but it was truly a most successful and efficient beast. Thus, only eleven Hellcats were listed in March 1987 on the United States Civil Aircraft Registry. Fortunately, museums in the United States and abroad have recognized the importance of the Hellcat in military aviation history and have preserved quite a few of this outstanding naval fighter.

PRODUCTION: 12,275 Hellcats were built by Grumman between June 1942 and November 1945 as follows:

1	XF6F-1	(1)	XF6F-4
1	XF6F-2	7,868	F6F-5/F6F-5E/F6F-5N
1	XF6F-3	2	XF6F-6
4,402	F6F-3/F6F-3E/F6F-3N		

219

They were assigned the following BuNos and British serial numbers:

XF6F-1:	BuNo 02981 (later renumbered O2982)
XF6F-2:	66244
XF6F-3:	BuNo 02982 (later renumbered O2981)
F6F-3/-3E/-3N:	BuNos 04775/04958, 08798/09047, 25721/26195, 39999/43137, and 65890/66243
XF6F-4:	(BuNo 02981)
F6F-5/-5E/-5N:	BuNos 58000/58999, 69992/70187, 70189/70912, 70914/72991, 77259/80258, and 93652/94521
XF6F-6:	BuNos 70188 and 70913
Hellcat I:	FN320/FN449 and JV100/JV221
Hellcat II:	JV222/JV324, JW700/JW784, JW857/JW899, JX670/JX964, JX968/JX999, JZ775/JZ827, JZ912/JZ946, JZ960/JZ964, JZ968/JZ994, KD118/KD152, KD158/KD160, KE118/KE159, KE170/KE214, and KE220/KE265
Hellcat NF II:	JX965/JX 967, JZ890/JZ911, JZ947/JZ959, JZ965/JZ967, JZ995/JZ999, KD108/KD117, KD153/KD157, KE160/KE169, and KE215/KE219.

	F6F-3	F6F-5	F6F-5N	XF6F-6
DIMENSIONS:				
Span, ft in	42 10	42 10	42 10	42 10
(m)	(13.06)	(13.06)	(13.06)	(13.06)
Span (wings folded), ft in	16 2	16 2	16 2	16 2
(m)	(4.93)	(4.93)	(4.93)	(4.93)
Length, ft in	33 7	33 7	33 7	33 7
(m)	(10.24)	(10.24)	(10.24)	(10.24)
Height, ft in	13 1	13 1	13 1	13 1
(m)	(3.99)	(3.99)	(3.99)	(3.99)
Wing area, sq ft	334	334	334	334
(sq m)	(31.03)	(31.03)	(31.03)	(31.03)
WEIGHTS:				
Empty, lb	9,101	9,238	9,421	9,526
(kg)	(4,128)	(4,190)	(4,273)	(4,321)
Loaded, lb	12,441	12,740	13,190	12,768
(kg)	(5,643)	(5,779)	(5,982)	(5,791)
Maximum, lb	15,487	15,413	14,250	13,823
(kg)	(7,025)	(6,991)	(6,464)	(6,270)
Wing loading,* lb/sq ft	37.2	38.1	39.5	38.2
(kg/sq m)	(181.9)	(186.2)	(192.8)	(186.6)
Power loading,* lb/hp	6.2	6.4	6.6	6.1
(kg/hp)	(2.8)	(2.9)	(3.0)	(2.8)
PERFORMANCE:				
Max speed, mph/ft	375/17,300	380/23,400	366/23,200	417/21,900
(kmh/m)	(603/5,275)	(611/7,130)	(589/7,070)	(671/6,675)
Cruising speed, mph	160	168	166	171
(kmh)	(257)	(270)	(267)	(275)
Climb rate, ft/min	3,500/1	2,980/1	2,840/1	3,070/1
(m/sec)	(17.8)	(15.1)	(14.4)	(15.6)

Service ceiling, ft	38,400	37,300	36,700	39,000
(m)	(11,705)	(11,370)	(11,185)	(11,885)
Normal range, miles	1,090	945	880	1,170
(km)	(1,755)	(1,520)	(1,415)	(1,885)
Max range, miles	1,590	1,355	1,260	1,730
(km)	(2,560)	(2,180)	(2,030)	(2,785)

* Wing and power loadings are calculated at normal loaded weight and maximum take-off power.

F7F-3N (BuNo 80590) flying near Cherry Point, North Carolina, on 24 April, 1950. *(USMC)*

Grumman F7F Tigercat

The United States Navy's long quest for twin-engined carrier fighters appeared to bear fruit with the award of a contract for 650 F7F-1s. Unfortunately, as a carrier-borne aircraft, the Tigercat proved disappointing and, except during repeated attempts at getting carrier qualified, it was mostly operated ashore. When operating from land bases, however, the Tigercat was without peer among piston-powered night fighters. Its many attributes included outstanding performance, heavy armament, generally pleasant handling characteristics, and good manoeuvrability, especially when compared to most other types of twin-engined fighters. Nevertheless, the end of the war and the appearance of jet aircraft curtailed its development and its operational career was brief.

As detailed in the XP-50 chapter, in October 1939 Grumman had begun working on Design 46, a large twin-engined Army fighter to be powered by 1,600-hp Wright R-2600 radials with either two-stage mechanical superchargers or turbosuperchargers, and had offered a derivative of that proposed aircraft, Design 49, to export customers in February 1940. Thus, preliminary design work on these two projects came in handy when Grumman decided to submit a twin-engined proposal in answer to a request for designs in accordance with specification SD-112-18 which was issued by the VF Design Branch of the Bureau of Aeronautics on 21 December, 1940. Seeking to satisfy both Army and Navy requirements with a common design, Grumman incorporated most features of Designs 46 and 49 into the Design 51 proposal which was submitted to BuAer on 24 March, 1941, and emerged as the winner of the Navy competition on 14 May. By then, the Army and Navy had agreed to seek the development of twin-engined fighters differing only in details, with the Army version to be powered by turbosupercharged engines whereas the Navy version was to have mechanically-supercharged engines. Moreover, the Army version was to have a pressurized cockpit and to be armed with two 37-mm cannon and four 0.50-in machine guns whereas the Navy fighter, which had been initially proposed with two nose-mounted and four wing-mounted 0.50-in machine guns, was to have an unpressurized cockpit and four 20-mm cannon in place of the two 37-mm guns.

Grumman's efforts were soon rewarded; the Army Air Forces ordered two XP-65 prototypes on 16 June, 1941, and, two weeks later, the Navy awarded a contract for two F7F-1 prototypes. Subsequently, however, both Services concluded that a single design would not meet their specific requirements, and on 16 January, 1942, the Army dropped out of the programme to enable Grumman to optimize the design to satisfy naval requirements for twin-engined fighters intended to operate from soon-to-be-ordered 45,000-ton *Midway*-class carriers and from land bases. Changes made during the ensuing months were incorporated in the mock-up, which passed inspection in September 1942, and included a switch from mid-mounted to shoulder-mounted wings.

Detail design and construction of the XF7F-1 prototypes (c/ns C-01/C-02, BuNos 03549/03550) progressed slowly as, at the Navy's

The first XF7F-1, at Bethpage on 12 November, 1943. (*Grumman*)

223

BuNo 03550, the second XF7F-1, at Bethpage five weeks before being delivered to the Navy. (*Grumman*)

request, Grumman gave priority to Hellcat development and production*
and because the powerplant installation remained unsettled until the
summer of 1943. After first concurring with Grumman's recommendation
to use a pair of 1,600-hp Wright R-2600-14 radials driving three-blade
Curtiss propellers rotating in the same direction, the Navy requested that
R-2600s driving propellers rotating in opposite directions be substituted.
Soon after, the Navy recommended the selection of '**B**' series Pratt &
Whitney R-2800-18 radials. In the end, non-availability of 2,100-hp
R-2800-18s with two-stage superchargers led to the prototypes being
powered by 'B' series engines with single-stage superchargers: two 2,000-
hp R-2800-27s for the first XF7F-1 and two 2,100-hp R-2800-22s for the
second.

Production history

Almost from the outset of the programme, Grumman had suggested that
the single-seat F7F be used as a night fighter and, as the Navy found
considerable merit to this suggestion, it was agreed that production aircraft
would be fitted with an AN/APS-6 radar installed in the nose. Thus, the
F7F-1 gained the seldom recognized distinction of being the world's first
single-seat aircraft to be fitted with an internally-mounted radar. Later
night fighter variants of the Tigercat were completed as two-seaters and,
whether retaining the original AN/APS-6 installation or fitted with the
SCR-720 radar in an enlarged radome, had the N suffix added to their
designation. Single-seat variants were produced as F7F-2 and F7F-3 day
fighters and F7F-3P photographic-reconnaissance fighters.

Although contract negotiations covering the production of 650 F7F-1s

---

* Although prototypes of the XF6F-1 and XF7F-1 were ordered on the same day, 30 June,
1941, the first flight of the XF7F-1 took place more than 16 months after that of the XF6F-1
and two months after Hellcats had made their combat debut in the Pacific.

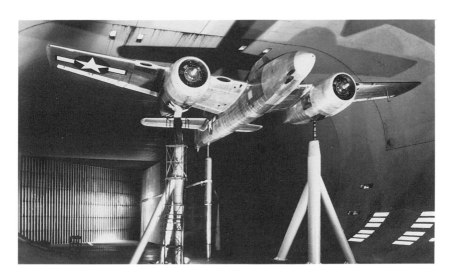

The second Tigercat prototype in the wind tunnel of the Ames Laboratory at Moffett Field, California, on 27 September, 1944. *(NACA/Grumman)*

had begun before the first flight of the XF7F-1 on 3 November, 1943, the programme underwent numerous changes and was cut back drastically after the war ended. Consequently, only 364 Tigercats were built in, or modified into, the following versions.

XF7F-1: The first XF7F-1 (BuNo 03549) was powered by two Pratt & Whitney R-2800-27 eighteen-cylinder single-stage radials which were rated at 2,000 hp for take-off and 1,600 hp at 13,500 ft and which each drove a three-blade propeller fitted with a large spinner. The second XF7F-1 differed in having R-2800-22s rated at 2,100 hp for take-off and 1,600 hp at 16,000 ft. Both aircraft were fitted with a single-piece windshield and a small window on each side of the fuselage just aft of the single-piece rear-sliding canopy. Both had provision for armament (four nose-mounted 0.50-in machine guns and four wing-mounted 20-mm cannon) and a nose-mounted AN/APS-6 radar, but neither guns nor radar were initially installed.

Following high-speed taxi-ing tests, during which BuNo 03549 had first become briefly airborne for 15 seconds on 2 November, 1943, Robert Hall made the first official, 21-minute flight at Bethpage on 3 November. The second XF7F-1 followed it into the air exactly three months later. For the most part early trials fulfilled sanguine hopes held by the Navy and the contractor, as the XF7F-1 proved faster at low altitudes than either the Hellcat or the Corsair and as it was quite manoeuvrable in spite of its size and weight. Further tests , however, confirmed wind tunnel data which had predicted that the F7F would have marginal spin characteristics. The aircraft was also found to be directionally unstable and, in an attempt at

was a death trap if one engine failed on T.O. or go around.

225

The first production F7F-1 (BuNo 80259), on 12 April, 1945, 17 days before being accepted by the USN. (*Grumman*)

correcting this deficiency, the first prototype was fitted with a dorsal fin extension in January 1944.

The first XF7F-1 was damaged in an accident on 1 May, 1944, never again to be flown, and was struck off at the end of August. The other prototype was accepted by the Navy on 2 August, was tested in the wind tunnel at the NACA Ames Laboratory at Moffett Field, California, from September 1944 to February 1945 and from April 1945 to October 1946, and was struck off on 30 November, 1946.

F7F-1: The thirty-four F7F-1s (BuNos 80259/80260 & 80262/80293) differed from the prototypes mostly in being powered by two 2,100-hp R-2800-22Ws with water injection and in having a three-piece windshield in place of the single-piece molded unit. The propeller spinners, as initially fitted to the prototypes and first production aircraft, were later dispensed with. Provision was made for carrying a 150- or 300-US gal ventral drop tank.

Although the F7F-1s were delivered with provision for the full gun armament, Service trials revaled a number of problems. Notably, the nose-mounted machine-guns were prone to jamming and the inboard wing panels were easily damaged by the blast of the wing-mounted cannon. Accordingly, only short bursts could be fired with the nose guns, and the 20-mm cannon had to be temporarily replaced by 0.50-in guns until minor modifications and local strengthening eliminated the problem. The aircraft was also found to suffer from marginal control forces harmonization and to have poor directional stability characteristics, thus prompting the Navy to request Grumman to design an enlarged vertical fin in an effort to increase the directional stiffness. Moreover, severe longitudinal oscillations were encountered during terminal velocity testing at NAS Patuxent River, Maryland, and prevented the aircraft from reaching the required maximum diving speed until rib spacing on the elevators was reduced by half.

As the British Fleet Air Arm was interested in evaluating the single-engined handling characteristics of large twin-engined carrier aircraft, the thirtieth and thirty-fourth F7F-1s (BuNos 80289 and 80293) were flown at RAE Farnborough in 1946. During this brief evaluation, both aircraft retained their US markings but were assigned the British serial numbers TT348 and TT349. Both were returned to the US Navy in 1947.

F7F-1N: The fact that F7F-1s were fitted with radar and could be used as night fighters led to some confusion. Thus, the F7F-1 and F7F-1N designations were used in both Navy and Grumman documents to identify aircraft from the first production batch. Moreover, the F7F-1N designation was actually painted on a number of single-seaters while others retained the F7F-1 designation.

XF7F-2: Even though consideration had been given as early as August 1943 to adding a radar operator aft of the pilot, the Navy did not formally request a design study of a two-seat F7F version until January 1944. However, a request from the Marine Corps for the addition of a navigator was not approved by the Bureau of Aeronautics as provision for a third crew member would have entailed a major redesign and resulted in delays.

As a result of the Navy request, Grumman proposed to provide space for a radar operator by reducing the size of the reserve fuel tank located in the upper fuselage decking aft of the pilot, thus decreasing internal fuel capacity from 426 to 375 US gal. A mock-up of this installation was approved in March, and construction of a prototype, to be obtained by completing the third F7F-1 airframe (BuNo 80261) as a two-seater, was authorized. Completed at the end of July 1944, the resulting XF7F-2 prototype was found satisfactory, and Grumman was instructed to deliver all aircraft beginning with the thirty-sixth production airframe to the two-seat configuration.

F7F-2: Designation confusion prevailed once more as two-seat night fighters were indifferently reported as F7F-2s and F7F-2Ns initially. Later, however, the F7F-2 designation was set aside for aircraft modified, before delivery or in service, as single-seaters by replacing the radar operator station with an 80-gal auxiliary tank covered by a metal fairing. The four nose-mounted 0.50-in guns and four wing-mounted 20-mm cannon were supplemented by Mk 5 launchers for eight 5-in HVAR rockets.

F7F-2D: Following successful operations by a few F7F-2Ns which had been modified by the Naval Aircraft Factory in 1946 to serve as two-seat drone directors, all available F7F-2N airframes were modified to that configuration in 1948. Armament was removed, an ADF fairing was added above the nose, and a pylon and sway brace were attached beneath each wing, near the tip, to carry Globe KD2G target drones. The drone director was seated in the aft cockpit and was provided with a raised seat protected by a windshield and sliding canopy similar to those of the F8F Bearcat.

F7F-2N: Except for incorporating a radar operator station and minor airframe improvements (including a revised tailskid arrangement and a small strake beneath the rear fuselage), the sixty-five F7F-2Ns (BuNos 80294/80358) were essentially similar to the F7F-1s. The one-piece canopy over the radar station, which was hinged on the port side, was initially flat-

F7F-2D (BuNo 80352) carrying a KD2G-2 drone beneath each wing. *(USN/National Archives)*

topped, but later a small bulge was added aft to provide more space over the radar operator's head. In service, the nose-mounted guns were frequently removed.

One of the F7F-2Ns (BuNo 80330) was used by the NATC at Patuxent River for a radio control test programme in 1947. Another (BuNo unknown) was modified as a test vehicle to evaluate a supine pilot position during tests conducted at NATC Patuxent River in the early 1950s. To that end, the aft cockpit was fitted with a swivelling seat, a periscopic sight, and a limited set of controls to enable the supine test pilot to fly the aircraft under the careful supervision of a check/safety pilot riding in the conventional forward cockpit. There were no accidents during the brief evaluation programme but the far-fetched concept of a supine pilot position did not gain acceptance!

F7F-3: A total of 250 Tigercats (BuNos 80359/80608) was built in three -3 versions, the single-seat F7F-3 fighter, the two-seat F7F-3N night fighter, and the single-seat F7F-3P reconnaissance fighter. All versions were characterized by larger vertical tail surfaces of revised shape, as the area of the fin and rudder were increased respectively by 29.2 per cent and 2.5 per cent, and were powered by 2,100-hp R-2800-34W radials with military rating at 16,000 ft increased from 1,600 hp to 1,700 hp. The single-seat models were fitted with improved cooling and blast tubes for the 0.50-in nose guns, and single- and two-seat variants eventually had long-barrel 20-mm wing cannon. Armament changes made during the course of F7F-3/F7F-3N production included the replacement of the four Mk.5 launchers for 5-in HVAR rockets beneath the wing outboard panels by Mk.9 racks for HVARs or bombs of up to 250 lb. In addition, Mk.51 rack and pylons were provided beneath the fuselage and beneath each wing between the fuselage and engine nacelles. A 2,000-lb bomb or a Mk.13 torpedo could be carried

F7F-3 (BuNo 80530) flying near NAS Patuxent River on 13 August, 1948. There is a Mk. 51 store pylon beneath each wing inboard panel and five Mk.9 pylons are fitted beneath each outboard panel. (*USN/National Archives*)

The two-seat F7F-3N had a longer nose housing the SCR-70 radar but did not have 0.50-in guns as mounted in the nose of the F7F-3 single-seat version. (*Grumman*)

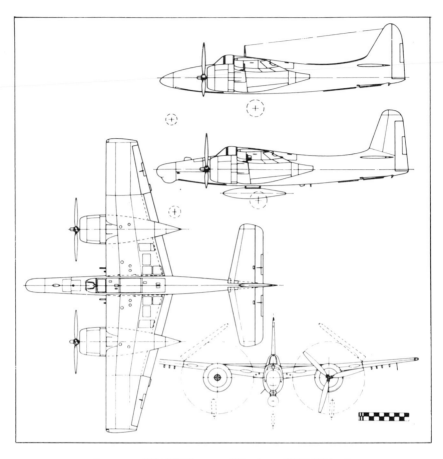

Grumman F7F-3N Tigercat. Side view of F7F-2N (top)

on the centreline but the wing racks were limited to carrying 1,000-lb
bombs.

Reversing its earlier decision to have all but the first thirty-four Tigercats
completed as two-seat night fighters, the Navy instructed Grumman to
complete most aircraft from the third production variant as single-seat
F7F-3s for delivery beginning in March 1945. Like the single-seat F7F-2s,
the F7F-3s had an 80-gal auxiliary tank installed in place of the radar
operator station. For ferry purposes, their ventral 300-gal external tanks
could be supplemented by two 150-gal drop tanks, one beneath each wing.
On at least one occasion, 300-gal wing drop tanks were carried to bring total
fuel capacity to 1,335 gal and thus enable an F7F-3 to fly nonstop across the
country from Cherry Point, North Carolina, to San Diego, California.
F7F-3E: This designation was set aside in 1946 for a proposed version
which was to have been optimized for night intruder operations and fitted

with a specialized radar set and a bombsight. Apparently, the planned conversion of three F7F-3s (Bunos 80375, 80455, and 80487) as F7F-3E development aircraft was not realized.

F7F-3K: At least one F7F-3 (BuNo 80411) was modified by Bell Aircraft in 1946 as a radio control drone.

F7F-3N: Essentially similar to single-seat F7F-3s, two-seat F7F-3Ns were fitted with SCR-720 radar in a bulbous nose from which provision for the four 0.50-in guns was deleted. The necessary airframe modifications were incorporated before delivery by Grumman and an initial batch of forty-nine of these aircraft was sent to the Lockheed Modification Center at the Van Nuys Airport in California to be modified as F7F-3Ns. As many as fifty-seven additional aircraft were later brought to F7F-3N standards.

F7F-3P: The only reconnaissance fighter version of the Tigercat was obtained in the spring and summer of 1945 when the Lockheed Modification Center fitted cameras to fifty-eight F7F-3s. At least three more F7F-3s were later modified to this configuration. Camera ports were provided beneath and on both sides of the rear fuselage and sighting was made by the pilot through use of a periscopic sight. Most F7F-3Ps were also fitted with an ADF antenna above the centre fuselage.

XF7F-4N: This two-seat prototype was completed in June 1945 when a two-seat F7F-3 airframe (BuNo 80548) was fitted with an AN/APS-19 radar housed in a nose radome similar to that of the AN/APS-6 set as fitted to early production Tigercats. There was no provision for nose-mounted guns, but the wing-mounted cannon and Mk.9 and Mk.51 racks were retained.

Although all versions of the Tigercat were cleared to carry a Mk. 13 torpedo on the centreline, operational squadrons did not train to launch this weapon. (*Grumman*)

231

F7F-4N: The last Tigercat production version differed from the prototype in having a strengthened airframe, a modified tail hook, and a longer stroke undercarriage as dictated by the results of early carrier qualification trials. The twelve F7F-4Ns (BuNos 80609/80620) were delivered in the autumn of 1946 and, like all -3 versions and the XF7F-4N prototype, were powered by R-2800-34W engines.

F7F-5: The F7F-5 designation was reserved for aircraft to be powered by R-2800-30W engines rated at 2,300 hp for take-off and 1,600 hp at 22,000 ft. It is not known whether both single- and two-seat versions were planned; however, none were built before Tigercat production was terminated in November 1946.

Design 66: This designation was given to a torpedo bomber proposal, the XTSF-1, which is described in Appendix B.

Design 67: In June and July 1944, Grumman conducted a feasibility study for a mixed-power version of the F7F-2. The engine nacelles were to be extended aft to house an I-20 turbojet aft of the R-2800-22W radials and jet intakes were provided on the wing leading-edge on both sides of the nacelles. At a comparable loading, the mixed-power Design 67 was expected to reach a top speed of 473 mph at sea level as opposed to 399 mph for the piston-only F7F-2. At 20,000 ft, calculated top speed was 505 mph for Design 67 and 432 mph for the F7F-2. Maximum rate of climb was predicted to be 6,290 ft/min for Design 67 and 4,650 ft/min for the F7F-2. BuAer, however, felt that these estimates were too optimistic and did not authorize further development of Design 67.

Design 80: In March 1946, Grumman briefly considered the feasibility of developing a high-speed executive transport using the wings and powerplant installation of the F7F. However, development, manufacturing, and operating costs were found too high to justify further work on this project.

Service history

Although field carrier landing tests conducted with the XF7F-1 had revealed that the 'Y' tail hook had to be moved forward and allowed to swivel in order to reduce damage to the rear fuselage, and that the single-engined approach speed was higher than desired, neither of these discrepancies would have prevented the F7F from being cleared for regular carrier operations. However, the need for higher capacity arresting gear – as first fitted to *Essex*-class carriers commissioned after October 1944, beginning with the uss *Randolph* (CV-15) – and for special barriers, which resulted from the aircraft's heavy landing weight and its nosewheel undercarriage configuration, were more serious. Nevertheless, BuNo 80291 satisfactorily completed initial carrier qualification trials aboard the uss *Shangri-La* (CV-38) on 15 November, 1944. In later years, F7F-2Ns, F7F-3Ns and F7F-4Ns were operated from carriers for brief periods on a number of occasions notably when Navy and Marine pilots from VF(N)-52, VCN-1, VCN-2, and VMF(N)-534 became carrier qualified on the

Tigercat. However, even the F7F-4N version with its strengthened airframe, modified tail hook, and longer stroke undercarriage remained marginal when operating aboard carriers.

With land-based units, the Tigercat made its debut when F7F-1s were assigned to VMF-911 at MCAS Cherry Point, North Carolina, to begin crew training during the summer of 1944. Additional F7F-1s and the first F7F-2Ns were then delivered to VMF(N)-531 at MCAS Eagle Mountain Lake, Texas, where this squadron trained in preparation for overseas deployment. Crews, maintenance personnel, and F7F-2Ns were shipped in July 1945. After being unloaded on Guam, the Tigercats were flown to Okinawa where they arrived on the penultimate day of the war. Soon after,

BuNo 80291, the 32nd F7F-1, aboard the USS *Shangri-La* (CV-38) during initial carrier trials on 15 November, 1944. (*USN/National Archives*)

An F7F-3N of VMF(N)-533 taxi-ing on the Chimu airstrip, Okinawa, on 20 August, 1945. (*USMC/DOD Still Media Records Center*)

233

the squadron exchanged identity with VMF(N)-533 and was then sent to China where it remained until January 1947.

In its F7F-3P version, the Tigercat was initially assigned to a training squadron, VMD-954, and to two operational squadrons, VMD-254 and VMD-354. VMD-354, the first to deploy, was shipped to Guam in May 1945 and flew a few operational sorties from Peleliu, Ulithi, and Okinawa during the closing weeks of the war. A fate similar to that of VMF(N)-533 befell VMD-254 as it arrived on Okinawa too late for combat operations and went on to China before being returned to the United States.

With the Marine Corps, postwar Tigercat use in the United States was limited to VMF-312 and -911 (F7F-3s), VMP-254 and -354 (F7F-3Ps), and VMF-461 and VMF(N)-531, -533, -534, and -542 (F7F-3Ns and -4Ns). When fighting began in Korea in June 1950, most of these squadrons had been re-equipped and most airworthy F7F-3Ns had been assigned to VMF(N)-542 at MCAS El Toro, California. This squadron was shipped to Japan at the end of August and flew to Kimpo, Korea, on 19 September. From then until March 1951 when its personnel were sent back to the United States, VMF(N)-531 provided combat air patrols and flew night interdiction missions both on their own and with Firefly flare-dropping aircraft. In fact, the F7F-3Ns proved so successful in the latter role that the Tigercats were kept in Korea to supplement the F4U-5Ns of VMF(N)-513. With this last squadron, the F7F-3Ns continued flying night interdiction sorties, took part in early attempts at providing close air support at night, and fought a frustrating war against slow-flying Polikarpov Po-2 biplanes which North Korean pilots used for night harassment operations against Allied ground troops. Finally, during the summer nights in 1951, VMF(N)-513 crews succeeded in shooting down two Po-2s, one on 30 June and one on 23 September. The Tigercats of VMF(N)-513 flew their last combat sorties in April 1952. However, a few F7F-3N/-4N/-3Ps continued to be operated in Korea by Headquarters Squadrons from the First Marine Air Wing and from Marine Air Group 33 until the fighting ended. They

An XF7F-1 carrying a 150-gallon auxiliary tank. (*Grumman*)

234

were last used in support of USAF Boeing B-29 night operations during which they dropped flares and markers to designate targets for the bombers.

With the Navy, the Tigercat had a lack-lustre career. The first operational unit was VF(N)-52 which briefly operated F7F-2Ns in 1945 before being disbanded. It was followed by Night Composite Squadrons One and Two (VCN-1s and VCN-2s) which flew F7F-3Ns and F7F-4Ns alongside other types beginning in 1946 but these units no longer operated Tigercats when they were redesignated Fleet All-Weather Training Units (respectively FAWTUPAC and FAWTULANT) in June 1950. Tigercats were also used by the Navy for a variety of experimental activities. However, it was as a drone director that the type proved the longest lived and the most useful while operated by several units including Air Development Squadrons One and Two (VX-1 and VX-2) and Utility Squadrons Two and Four (VU-2 and VU-4).

Civil Tigercats

During the summer of 1948, less than a year after the last F7F-2Ds had been struck off by the Navy, a surplus F7F-3 was used as an air tanker in Oregon, where Kreitzberg Aviation fitted modified drop tanks beneath each wing, inboard of the engine nacelles, to carry fire retardant. This scheme did not prove successful as drop patterns were ineffective. Later Tigercat air tanker conversions were fitted with a large tank faired beneath the centre fuselage and containing 800 gal of fire retardant. In that form at least fifteen Tigercat air tankers were used in the United States during the 1960s and -70s, notably by Cal-Nat Airways, Sis-Q Flying Service, and TBM Air Tankers.

In the 1980s, several air tankers had the slurry tank removed and were restored as warbirds. At the end of 1988, there were five civil-registered Tigercats in the United States, one F7F-3 had just been flown to Great Britain (ex-BuNo 80843 owned by Paul Wilson), and four Tigercats were kept in US museums.

An F7F-3 tanker of Sis-Q Flying Service at Santa Rosa, California. The ventral tank contained 800 gallons of fire retardant slurry. (*C Waldenmaier, courtesy of Alain Pelletier*)

235

PRODUCTION: A total of 364 Tigercats was built by Grumman between October 1943 and November 1946 as follows:

2	XF7F-1	250	F7F-3/-3N/-3P
34	F7F-1	(1)	XF7F-4N
1	XF7F-2	12	F7F-4N
65	F7F-2N		

They were assigned the following BuNos:

XF7F-1:	BuNos 03549/03550
F7F-1:	BuNos 80259/80260 and 80262/80293
XF7F-2:	BuNo 80261
F7F-2N:	BuNos 80294/80358
F7F-3/-3N/-3P:	BuNos 80359/80608
XF7F-4N:	(BuNo 80548)
F7F-4N:	BuNos 80609/80620

	F7F-1	F7F-2N	F7F-3	F7F-4N
DIMENSIONS:				
Span, ft in	51 6	51 6	51 6	51 6
(m)	(15.70)	(15.70)	(15.70)	(15.70)
Span (wings folded), ft in	32 2	32 2	32 2	32 2
(m)	(9.80)	(9.80)	(9.80)	(9.80)
Length, ft in	45 4$^{1}/_{2}$	45 4$^{1}/_{2}$	45 4$^{1}/_{2}$	46 9$^{1}/_{4}$
(m)	(13.83)	(13.83)	(13.83)	(14.26)
Height, ft in	15 2	15 2	16 4	16 4
(m)	(4.62)	(4.62)	(4.98)	(4.98)
Wing area, sq ft	455	455	455	455
(sq m)	(42.27)	(42.27)	(42.27)	(42.27)
WEIGHTS:				
Empty, lb	15,943	16,321	16,270	16,954
(kg)	(7,232)	(7,403)	(7,380)	(7,690)
Loaded, lb	21,425	21,857	21,720	21,960
(kg)	(9,718)	(9,914)	(9,852)	(9,961)
Maximum, lb	22,560	26,194	25,720	26,167
(kg)	(10,233)	(11,881)	(11,666)	(11,869)
Wing loading*, lb/sq ft	47.1	48.1	47.7	48.3
(kg/sq m)	(229.9)	(234.5)	(233.1)	(235.7)
Power loading*, lb/hp	5.1	5.2	5.2	5.2
(kg/hp)	(2.3)	(2.4)	(2.4)	(2.4)
PERFORMANCE:				
Max speed, mph/ft	445/16,000	431/20,600	450/21,500	436/24,500
(kmh/m)	(716/4,875)	(693/6,280)	(724/6,555)	(702/7,470)
Cruising speed, mph	177	183	222	235
(kmh)	(285)	(294)	(357)	(378)
Climb rate, ft/min	4,360/1	4,540/1	6,040/1	4,100/1
(m/sec)	(22)	(23)	(31)	(21)
Service ceiling, ft	36,200	39,800	40,700	37,600
(m)	(11,035)	(12,130)	(12,405)	(11,460)
Normal range, miles	1,170	960	1,200	810
(km)	(1,885)	(1,545)	(1,930)	(1,305)
Max range, miles	1,485	1,250	1,900	1,360
(km)	(2,390)	(2,010)	(3,055)	(2,190)

* wing and power loadings are calculated at normal loaded weight and maximum take-off power.

The Kitten I during an engine run-up test at Bethpage on 13 March, 1944. This light aircraft was first flown five days later. (*Grumman*)

Grumman G-63 Kitten I

Like most other major aircraft manufacturers in the United States, Grumman expected that after demobilization many wartime aircrews would want to acquire their own aircraft, thus creating a demand for large numbers of light aircraft. As mass cancellation of military aircraft contracts was expected to take place immediately after war's end, preparing to tap this incipient market appeared to be prudent business. Unfortunately for Grumman and the other manufacturers who went after that market, the expected demand for light aircraft did not materialize for many years.

Preliminary development work on Design 63 was authorized by Roy Grumman during the summer of 1943, a full two years before the war ended, to explore the use of all-metal spot-welded construction in small aircraft. Entrusted to a small team led by Dayton T Brown and Franklin T 'Hank' Kurt, it was hoped that this work would lead to the production of a 'quality personal airplane with sufficient load, speed, range, simplicity and ruggedness to bring big ship features to a two-place personal airplane'.

First known as the Hepcat but renamed Kitten I after a similar aircraft with a nosewheel undercarriage was started in November 1944 as the G-72 Kitten II, the G-63 prototype was a low-wing monoplane with conventional retractable undercarriage. Powered by a 125-hp Lycoming O-290-A flat-four air-cooled engine driving a two-blade propeller, this two-seat aircraft could be fitted with an auxiliary third seat and, in its production form, was intended to have folding sto-wings so that it would require minimum hangaring space. However, as completed during the first quarter of 1944, the G-63 wings lacked the required forged hinges and locking pins and could not be folded.

Registered NX41808, the G-63 was first flown at Bethpage by Hank Kurt on 18 March, 1944. Trials, which proceeded at a sedate pace as priority had to be given to military projects while the war was still on, revealed a number

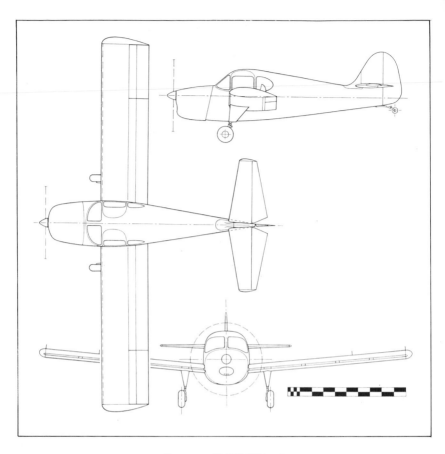

Grumman G-63A Kitten I

of problems. Notably, controls were quite sensitive, with the aircraft responding too quickly to directional and longitudinal changes, the wing stalled abruptly on landing, and latches for the mechanically operated retractable undercarriage failed repeatedly, with the aircraft making two belly landings and one one-wheel landing before accumulating 15 hours in the air. Fortunately, undercarriage problems were quickly solved by redesigning the latches and installing a hydraulic retraction system, while the abrupt stall was almost totally eliminated when the engine cowling was deepened to divert the flow of air over the wing. Control problems were more persistent as several revisions to geometry of the tail surfaces (the rudder chord was increased while the chord, area and span of the tailplane and elevator were increased) failed to result in significant improvements.

Finally, after 21 hours of testing, the Kitten I was fitted with a new set of wings with span and area increased respectively from 28 ft to 31 ft 4 in and from 117 sq ft to 130 sq ft. This modification, which resulted in a change of designation to G-63A, proved quite effective and almost completely eliminated the previously encountered tendency to spin after a power-on stall. Moreover, it was confidently expected that other minor modifications would result in an entirely satisfactory design. However, as the anticipated postwar market for light aircraft failed to materialize, Grumman was forced to abandon plans to put into production either the G-63A or its derivative, the G-72. Nevertheless, both aircraft were kept as company hacks and in June 1946 the Kitten I was modified once again. Fitted with a ducted wing and renumbered Design 81, it took part in 1947 in a brief and inconclusive test programme to evaluate a ducted wing configuration as a means of increasing the lift over drag ratio.

PRODUCTION: One Kitten I was completed by Grumman in March 1944 and received the civil registration number NX41808.

G-63A with larger wings
    Span 31 ft 4 in (9.55 m); length 19 ft 10.75 in (6.06 m); height 5 ft 9 in (1.75 m); wing area 130 sq ft (12.08 sq m).
    Empty weight 1,280 lb (581 kg); loaded weight 1,950 lb (885 kg); wing loading 15.0 lb/sq ft (73.3 kg/sq m); power loading 15.6 lb/hp (7.1 kg/hp).
    Maximum speed 159 mph (256 kmh) at sea level; cruising speed 134 mph (216 kmh).

The G-81 ducted wing test aircraft on 12 May, 1947. (*Grumman*)

F8F-1s flown by naval reservists from NAS Anacostia prepare to leave Webster Field, Maryland, for gunnery practice over Chesapeake Bay on 22 August, 1952. (*USN/National Archives*)

Grumman F8F Bearcat

Aware that the only new types of military aircraft then being designed by his company, the XF7F-1 and XTB2F-1, were too large and heavy to operate from most carriers and worried that his design team was too confident that twin-engined aircraft were what the Bureau of Aeronautics wanted for the future, Roy Grumman sent a confidential memorandum to his chief engineer, Bill Schwendler, on 28 July, 1943. Clearly spelling out his misgivings about over-reliance on twin-engined designs, Roy Grumman proposed the addition of an experimental programme to develop 'a small fighter plane, which could (without question) be used on large or small carriers, and with a performance superior to the F6F.' He provided the following specifications for that aircraft: (a) same size and dimension as the Wildcat; (b) normal gross weight of 8,500 lb; (c) two-speed R-2800 engine; (d) armament consisting of four 0.50-in guns; (e) internal fuel capacity of 170 gallons; (f) bubble-type canopy; (g) wide-track undercarriage providing adequate propeller clearance; (h) performance superior in every way to that of the Hellcat; and (i) power loading at normal gross weight of 4 lb/hp and wing loading of 33 lb/sq ft. Also noteworthy were his recommendations that a design study should be made before approaching BuAer and that this study should be given priority over jet propulsion studies. Finally, in a hand-written and quite revealing postscript, Roy Grumman added: 'In

240

order to *check* Bureau tendency to overload, this design should be sold as a "converted-carrier" fighter.'

Funded by the company, preliminary work on Design 58 began at once and continued until the early autumn when an unsolicited proposal submitted to BuAer got immediate attention. Although prototypes of the Navy's first jet interceptor, the McDonnell XFD-1, had been ordered in January 1943, BuAer still harboured doubts about the feasibility of using jets aboard carriers and consequently considered the development of a fast climbing piston-powered fighter to be one of its highest priorities. Accordingly, as the proposed Grumman fighter was expected to have sprightly climb performance as its power-to-weight ratio was 40 to 50 per cent better than that of contemporary carrier fighters (Grumman F6F-3s and Vought F4U-1s), BuAer at once began contract discussions with Grumman. Even though agreement regarding the fee to be paid to the manufacturer could not initially be reached, a letter of intent for two experimental XF8F-1 carrier fighters (c/ns D-01/D-02, BuNos 90460/90461) was signed on 27 November, 1943. The first was to be ready within eight months and was to be powered by a 2,100-hp Pratt & Whitney 'C' series R-2800 radial with a two-speed supercharger. The second was to follow two months later and was to receive a 2,250-hp 'E' series R-2800 with a variable speed supercharger. BuAer further specified that, unlike Roy Grumman's initial insistence that the aircraft be small enough to be sold as a 'converted carrier' fighter, small carrier limitations would not be allowed to compromise the performance of the new fighter as the Navy wanted the F8F for use aboard *Midway*-class carriers.

Cockpit and engine mock-ups passed inspection respectively in January and March 1944, thus enabling detailed design to progress at a steady pace. Nevertheless, the schedule agreed upon in November 1943 proved a somewhat optimistic, and completion of the prototypes was late. BuNo 90460 began flight trials one month behind schedule when flown by Robert L Hall on 31 August, 1944. Even though it was powered by the same 2,100 hp R-2800-22W 'C' series engine as the first XF8F-1 and not by an 'E' series engine as planned, the second prototype was even further behind and was airborne for the first time on 2 December. Outstanding performance and handling characteristics, however, more than made up for schedule delays and Grumman and the Navy had reason to be jubilant.

Production history

A contract for two thousand F8F-1s (including twenty-three development aircraft which in some official documents are listed as XF8F-1s but in others are designated F8F-1s) was awarded in October 1944. It was amended in April 1945 to cover twice as many aircraft, while plans were made for the F8F to supplant the F6F on Grumman's lines in March 1946. Moreover, a letter of intent issued in February 1945, called for Eastern Aircraft to build 1,876 F3M-1s.

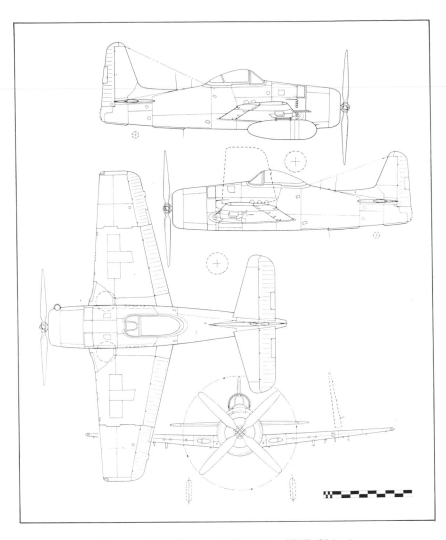

Grumman F8F-1B Bearcat; Side view of F8F-2N (top)

Although postwar contract cancellations affected the Bearcat programme much less than others, the Eastern contract was terminated before the completion of a single F3M-1 and the Grumman contract was cut back by more than 70 per cent. In the end, Grumman produced 1,265 Bearcats (including two civil-registered G-58As) in ten experimental and production versions described here. Other variants were obtained by modifying existing airframes.

XF8F-1: The XF8F-1 designation officially identified two prototypes

BuNo 90438, the fourth Bearcat, during initial carrier trials. (*Grumman*)

(BuNos 90460/90461) and was often used to identify 23 development aircraft (BuNos 90437/90459). The prototypes, which were powered by R-2800-22W radials, respectively flew on 31 August and 2 December, 1944, and the first of the 23 development aircraft, which were powered by 2,100-hp R-2800-34W radials, flew on 6 January, 1945.

Although initial trials were exceptionally promising, they revealed the need for minor improvements and modifications. In particular, the span of the horizontal tail surfaces was increased by 1 ft and a dorsal fin was added. Afterward, BuNo 90460 was used for field arrested trials at Philadelphia in December 1944, BuNo 90438 went aboard the USS *Charger* (CVE-30) for initial carrier trials in February 1945, and BIS (Board of Inspection and Survey) trials began during the following month.

Following brief wind tunnel evaluation by NACA to help find a solution to directional instability problems, the first XF8F-1 was used by the Navy for preliminary armament testing. By the time it crashed in March 1945, the second prototype and several of the development aircraft had been accepted by the Navy. Three of these aircraft were later modified as the F8F-1D, the F8F-1E, and the XF8F-1N as described here.

F8F-1: Ultimately, due to postwar contract reductions as well as the completion of four aircraft as prototypes for the XF8F-1N and XF8F-2 versions and of 226 others as cannon-armed F8F-1Bs, only 654 aircraft were delivered as F8F-1s. These aircraft incorporated all the changes progressively introduced during trials with the prototypes and development aircraft and, notably, were fitted with a wider tailplane and a dorsal fin and had less fin offset. Unlike the Wildcats, Avengers, and Hellcats which had

243

F8F-1 development aircraft (BuNo 90438) aboard the USS *Charger* (CVE-30) on 17 February, 1945. (*Grumman*)

Grumman 'sto-wings,' they were fitted with more conventional upward-folding wings. They were powered by 2,100-hp R-2800-34Ws and had internal fuel capacity increased from 162 to 183 US gal. An external rack was provided beneath the fuselage for a 150-gal centreline drop tank. Another rack was fitted beneath each wing, just outboard of the undercarriage, and could be used to carry either a 100-gal tank, a 1,000-lb bomb, an 11.75-in Tiny Tim rocket, or a Mk.I twin 0.50-in gun pod. Beginning with the 201st production aircraft (BuNo 94929), two Mk. 9 racks for HVAR rockets or 100-lb bombs were added beneath each wing outboard of the main rack.

Service trials with early production aircraft and NACA tests with the first XF8F-1 had revealed that the Bearcat was directionally unstable, particularly when flying at high speeds with a ventral tank. Some improvements came about when fins were fitted to the tank, but Grumman and the Navy nevertheless accepted a NACA recommendation calling for taller tail surfaces. BuNo 94873 was the first to receive a 12-in taller fin and rudder. After initially flying without a dorsal fin as fitted on other aircraft ever since the second XF8F-1 had been so modified, BuNo 94873 served as a development aircraft for the F8F-2 tail configuration.

An unusual design feature incorporated in both the prototypes and production aircraft was the provision of break points in the wingtips. Thus, if a pilot exceeded operating g restrictions, the outboard 3 ft of each wing would fail nearly simultaneously, thus maintaining a symmetrical configuration. Notwithstanding earlier tests with a modified F4F-4, the so-called 'Safety Wing Tip' was not as safe as expected. Following a December 1945 accident in which an F8F-1 crashed after only one breakaway tip separated during violent manoeuvring, the fittings were modified and brazier head

244

F8F-1s of a Reserve unit based at NAS Glenview, Illinois, in 1950. *(Grumman)*

rivets replaced countersunk rivets in the 251st and subsequent aircraft. Notwithstanding a later modification providing for the use of explosive bolts to ensure simultaneous separation of the tips, the breakaway tips continued to be a source of concern. In 1949, a service change provided for local strengthening of the wing to eliminate the break points.

F8F-1B: Cannon-armed Bearcats, which had been ordered under the F8F-1C designation were, with the exception of the first aircraft, delivered as F8F-1Bs as the suffix 'B' was re-assigned in March 1945 to identify naval aircraft with special armament instead of aircraft intended for Lend-Lease delivery to Great Britain as had been the case. Including the aircraft which was initially designated F8F-1C, a total of 226 F8F-1Bs were delivered by Grumman. The first one hundred were built at random alongside the more numerous F8F-1s, but the last 126 were built consecutively in two batches before the switch to F8F-2s was finalized. The last F8F-1Bs were delivered in August 1947.

F8F-1C: As the Navy judged the fixed armament of the F8F-1 to be too light, consideration was given early during the programme to increasing the number of 0.50-in machine-guns from four to six. However, as this could not be accomplished without major modifications, it was decided that increased hitting power would best be achieved by substituting 20-mm T-31 cannon for the 0.50-in guns. Trial installation of the four-cannon armament was first made on BuNo 94803 in June 1945. After the cannon were installed, this aircraft was redesignated F8F-1C before becoming the first F8F-1B under the new nomenclature already mentioned.

245

BuNo 94803, the F8F-1C used in June 1945 as the trial aircraft for the four-cannon installation. (*Grumman*)

F8F-1E (BuNo 90445), with AN/APS-4 radar beneath the starboard wing, at Bethpage on 22 June, 1945. (*Grumman*)

F8F-1D: This designation was first applied to BuNo 90446 which in 1949 was modified as a drone control aircraft by the Naval Air Development Center in Johnsville, Pennsylvania. Following this experimental modification, a few other F8F-1s may have been similarly converted.

The F8F-1D designation has frequently been used to identify F8F-1s delivered to the French and Thai Air Forces. However, this designation appears to have been unofficial as this use of the suffix 'D' does not fit into

246

the US Navy nomenclature. 'D' normally indicated the addition of drop tanks (a standard feature in all Bearcats), the fitting of special search radar, or the conversion to drone control.

F8F-1DB: This unofficial designation has been used, quite possibly erroneously, to identify cannon-armed F8F-1Bs delivered to the Armée de l'Air for use in Indochina.

F8F-1E: BuNo 90445, the ninth development aircraft, was fitted in 1945 with an AN/APS-4 radar installed in a radome beneath the starboard wing to serve as prototype for a proposed night intruder version. No other Bearcats were modified or built to this standard.

XF8F-1N: In view of the successful adaptation of the Hellcat to the night fighting role, it was logical that a night fighter version of the Bearcat be considered early during the programme. Unfortunately, there was insufficient space between the guns and the wing fold to mount a radome on the leading edge as had been done with the F6F-3Ns and F6F-5Ns. Consequently, the AN/APS-19 had to be installed in a nacelle hung on the bomb rack beneath the starboard wing, thus greatly increasing drag. Trial installations were made in the summer of 1945 using BuNos 94812 and 94819.

F8F-1N: Twelve F8F-1 airframes were modified to F8F-1N standards and fitted with AN/APS-19 radar before completion. As the installation of the AN/APS-19 radar in an underwing nacelle drastically reduced performance and significantly affected handling characteristics, the night fighter version of the Bearcat was operated only briefly by VCN-1 and VCN-2 and was not adopted for Service use.

F8F-1P: The fifth development F8F-1 (BuNo 90441) was modified by the Naval Aircraft Factory in 1946 to evaluate alternative installations of vertical and oblique cameras in the rear fuselage.

XF8F-2: Use of 'E' series engines with a variable-speed supercharger and an automatic engine control (AEC) had been planned from the onset of the programme but, as Pratt & Whitney encountered difficulties with the development of this powerplant, installation of 'E' series engines had to be postponed several times. Finally, semi-production 2,300-hp R-2800-30Ws were installed in an F8F-1 airframe (BuNo 95049) and in a cannon-armed F8F-1B airframe (BuNo 95330) which then served as XF8F-2 prototypes. The first flight of an XF8F-2 was made at Bethpage on 11 June, 1947.

F8F-2: The 293 F8F-2s delivered between November 1947 and April 1949 were powered by 2,250-hp R-2800-34Ws and were fitted with the tall vertical tail surfaces and dorsal fin as tested on BuNo 94873. Even though the 'B' suffix was not included in their designation, these aircraft were armed with four 20-mm cannon. The F8F-2s had provision for carrying the same external stores as late production F8F-1s and F8F-1Bs.

F8F-2D: A few F8F-2s may have been converted by the Navy as drone directors, but the use of the F8F-2D designation cannot be confirmed.

F8F-2N: Twelve F8F-2 airframes were fitted with an AN/APS-19 radar in

BuNo 121549, the first of twelve F8F-2Ns delivered between December 1947 and March 1948. *(Grumman)*

Completed in March 1959, the second G-58A was used by Grumman as a demonstrator and hack until sold to Cornell Laboratories in 1960. *(Grumman)*

an underwing nacelle and were delivered as F8F-2Ns. In service with advanced training units, the radar nacelle was seldom carried.

F8F-2P: The sixty F8F-2Ps delivered by Grumman between February 1948 and May 1949 combined the airframe and power-plant of the F8F-2 with the camera installation developed by the Naval Aircraft Factory and fitted to the F8F-1P in 1946. Fixed armament was reduced to two 20-mm cannon, one in each wing.

F3M-1: Plans to have Eastern Aircraft terminate FM-2 production and manufacture the Bearcat under the F3M-1 designation were elaborated early in 1945. A letter of intent for the production of 1,876 F3M-1s, which were to be powered by 2,100-hp R-2800-34WAs or -40Ws and armed with four machine-guns, was issued in February. Grumman and Eastern began planning work during the following month. The thirty-seventh F8F-1 (BuNo 94765) was delivered to Eastern to serve as a pattern aircraft, but the contract was canceled at the end of the war before the completion of the first F3M-1.

G-58A: As a replacement for the prewar Gulfhawk II biplane used by its demonstration pilot, Al Williams, Gulf Oil Company ordered a civil version of the F8F-1. All armament and military equipment, including the tail hook, were removed and a 2,100-hp Pratt & Whitney Double Wasp CA-15 eighteen-cylinder radial was installed. Registered NX120IV, the Gulfhawk 4 was flown on 23 July, 1947. It was later re-registered NL3025, but shortly after it was destroyed in a landing accident at Elizabeth City, New Jersey.

A second civil Bearcat, also powered by a 2,100-hp Pratt & Whitney Double Wasp CA-15, was built as a company demonstrator. Registered N700A when it was completed in March 1949, this aircraft differed from the first G-58A in being fitted with the taller vertical tail surfaces of the F8F-2, more comprehensive radio and navigation equipment, and a ventral tank modified to carry spares, tools, or baggage. Re-registered N7700C, this

Three F8F-2Ps of VC-61 in April 1949. Aircraft PP 2 is BuNo 121583. (*USN/National Archives*)

aircraft was subsequently transferred to Cornell Laboratories, and finally acquired by a private owner.

Service history

Highly praised by Navy, Marine, and Army pilots who had flown the XF8F-1 during the Joint Fighter Conference held at NATC Patuxent River in October 1944 and getting through its Service trials without encountering major difficulties, the Bearcat was rushed to the fleet. On 21 May, 1945, less than nine months after the first prototype was flown, F8F-1s were delivered to VF-19 at NAAS Santa Rosa, California, where operational training was begun in preparation for deployment aboard the uss *Langley* (CVL-27) in early August 1945. *Langley* and VF-19 were en route to the Western Pacific when the Japanese surrendered; US Bearcats were destined not to be flown in combat. They were, however, to become one of the main types to operate from carriers during the late 1940s. F8F-1s, F8F-1Bs, and F8F-2s equipped thirty-two squadrons at one time or another (with a maximum of twenty-four squadrons operating at the end of 1948) and F8F-2Ps were flown by VC-61 and VC-62 beginning in January 1949, but F8F-1Ns and F8F-2Ns only saw limited service with VCN-1 and VCN-2.

In service, most pilots gloated over the Bearcat's manoeuvrability (the aircraft was cleared for 7.5 positive g and 3.7 negative g) and flying characteristics and considered it to be the best propeller-driven fighter. Maintenance officers, on the other hand, were less enthusiastic and found problems with its powerplant installation. Deck officers were quick to note that Bearcats were very compact aircraft and that fifty could be spotted in the space taken by thirty-six Hellcats, even though with folded wings the span of the F8F was still 23 ft 3 in whereas that of the F6F was only 16 ft 2 in.

When the Korean war began, the Bearcat was being replaced as an

The *Blue Angels'* Bearcats at Oakland, California, in the late 1940s. (*Grumman*)

250

interceptor by jet fighters as, notwithstanding its superb handling qualities and outstanding level and climb performance* at low and medium altitudes, it was no match for jet fighters. Moreover, the Bearcat had been found less suited to the close support role than the Corsair due to its lesser warload/radius of action (drag rose markedly when Bearcats carried bombs and/or rockets but no external tanks and the internal fuel capacity of the F8F-2 was less than four-fifths of that of the F4U-5). Consequently, no Bearcats operated from Seventh Fleet carriers off Korea and those in service in the Mediterranean aboard Sixth Fleet carriers were rapidly replaced by Panthers and Banshees.

In addition to being flown by test units and by Navy development and operational squadrons, Bearcats were operated by the *Blue Angels* aerial demonstration team (from 1946 until the summer of 1949, when they were replaced by F9F-2 Panthers), by advanced training units (beginning in 1949), and by reserve units. The last F8F-2s in service with reserve squadrons were phased out by VF-859 and VF-921 during the first quarter of 1953 and the last Bearcats in the inventory were struck off in 1956.

Outside the Navy, the Bearcat was little used in the United States. A few F8F-2s were assigned to the Marine Corps Schools at Quantico, Virginia, for ground crew training in the early 1950s but none were assigned to Marine operational squadrons. Earlier, the seventy-sixth F8F-1 (BuNo 94804) was lent to the Army Air Forces for evaluation at Wright Field,

During the Indochina War, Bearcats equipped ten Groupes de Chasse of the French Air Force.
(ECPA)

* The Bearcat's exceptional climb performance had been demonstrated on 20 November, 1946, during the National Air Races in Cleveland, Ohio, when an F8F- flown by Lt-Cdr M W Davenport set an unofficial time-to-height record by reaching 10,000 ft (3,048 m) in 1 minute 34 seconds.

251

Ohio, in 1945, and at Eglin Field, Louisiana, in 1946-47. With NACA, Bearcats were first used when the first XF8F-1 was briefly tested in Langley, Virginia. At least two F8F-1s (BuNos 90461 and 94873) later took part in NACA programmes intended to find a permanent solution to the Bearcat instability problems when carrying external loads.

Bearcats were not exported until early 1951, when a first batch of F8F-1s and F8F-1Bs were provided to re-equip French fighter squadrons operating against Communist insurgents in Indochina. Beginning in 1953, Bearcats were provided to Thailand under the Mutual Assistance Defense Programme and in 1956, were given to South Vietnam to equip that nation's first combat squadron.

FRANCE: Over 140 F8F-1s and F8F-1Bs were operated by the Armée de l'Air in Indochina from March 1951, when the type made its combat debut with GC III/6 'Roussillon' based at Cat Bi, until January 1956, when GC II/21 'Artois' transferred its last aircraft to the Vietnamese Air Force. The first batch of Bearcats was delivered directly to Saïgon by the USS *Windham Bay* (CVE-92) in February 1951. Additional batches followed two months later aboard the USS *Sitkoh Bay* (CVE-86), aboard the freighter *Groton Trail* in July 1953, and aboard the freighter *Nutmeg Mariner* in the spring of 1954.

Ten Groupes (squadrons), designated sequentially as Groupes de Chasse (GC I/6 'Corse' and III/6 'Roussillon'), Groupes de Marche (GM I/8 'Saintonge', II/8 'Languedoc, I/9 'Limousin,' II/9 'Auvergne,' and I/21 'Artois'), and then again GCs (GC II/21 'Auvergne,' I/22 'Saintonge,' and II/22 'Artois'), flew Bearcats at one time or another on ground support duty. However, peak strength never exceeded four Groupes even at the height of the fighting around Dien Bien Phu in the spring of 1954. In addition, Bearcats were operated by two reconnaissance units: Escadrille de Reconnaissance d'Outre-Mer 80 (EROM 80) flying F8F-1s and F8F-1Bs fitted with field-modified ventral tanks housing two cameras (from May 1951 until September 1955) and Escadrille de Reconnaissance Photographique II/19 (ERP II/19) 'Armagnac,' which was primarily equipped with Douglas RB-26 Invaders but which had also obtained a pair of Bearcats in November 1951.

Following the signing of the Geneva Agreement on 21 July, 1954, the war in Indochina ended. Thereafter, the Groupes de Chasse were dissolved one by one and their Bearcats were either scrapped or transferred to South Vietnam and Thailand. Finally, only GC II/21 'Artois' remained. Based at Bien Hoa, it trained Thai and Vietnamese pilots assigned to fly Bearcats until dissolved on 31 January, 1956.

SOUTH VIETNAM: As agreed with the United States, France's Armée de l'Air left twenty-eight F8F-1s to the fledgling Vietnamese Air Force and twenty-two of these aircraft were taken on strength by the 1er Groupe de Chasse (1st Fighter Squadron) when this unit was activated at Bien Hoa in June 1956. The Bearcats were mainly used for training but also took part in

F8F-1s of the 1st Fighter Squadron, Vietnamese Air Force, at Bien Hoa in 1958. *(Colonel N'Guyen Than Tong, courtesy of Marc Rostaing)*

An F8F-1 Bearcat of the 23rd Fighter Squadron, Royal Thai Air Force. *(Courtesy Gordon Swanborough)*

small scale operations against politico-religious rebel groups and against Communist insurgents. Serviceability, however, was poor due to the lack of spare parts and to the insufficient number of trained mechanics available to the VNAF. Finally, following an operational loss during a strike against Communist elements in August 1959, the remaining Bearcats were grounded by the VNAF.

THAILAND: Bearcats were first delivered to the Royal Thai Air Force in 1953. Eventually the RTAF received a total of twenty-nine F8F-1Bs and one hundred F8F-1s, including many ex-French aircraft transferred in 1955-56. The F8F-1Bs were broken up to serve as a source of spares for the F8F-1s assigned to the 13th Fighter Squadron of the 1st Fighter Wing and

NL14HP, the last airworthy F8F-1, at Reno, Nevada, in September 1988. *(Peter B Lewis)*

N777L *Rare Bear*, the much modified F8F-2 powered by a boosted Wright R-3350-18EA engine, won the Reno Unlimited Race in 1988 at an average speed of 456.8 mph and on that occasion set a new lap record of 474.6 mph. *(Jim Dunn)*

to the 22nd and 23rd Fighter Squadrons of the 2nd Fighter Wing. In Thai service, Bearcats were first supplemented by Republic F-84G Thunderjets beginning in 1957 and then supplanted by North American F-86F Sabres in 1961. The last Bearcats were struck off in 1963.

Civilian Bearcats

In addition to the two previously described G-58As specially built as civil aircraft, at least three F8F-1s and more than a dozen F8F-2s have been registered in the United States. While most civil Bearcats were used and

254

Carrying four HVAR rockets, this F8F-1 (BuNo 94759) bears the markings of the Naval Ordnance Test Station at NAF Inyokern, California. *(Warren M Bodie)*

Bearing the last three digits of its Bureau Number on its cowling, this Bearcat is the eighth F8F-2N. The nacelle beneath the starboard wing houses an AN/APS-19 radar. *(Grumman)*

continue to be used as glamorous air racers, mention must be made of a more workaday F8F-2 which was operated for aerial surveying. Registered N212KA, this aircraft was fitted with cameras and with an extra seat for a camera operator. It was destroyed after its engine lost power on take-off.

As air racers, Bearcats moved to the fore in 1964 when unlimited air races were once again organized in the United States. The winner in that first year was a surplus F8F-2, N9885C, flown by Mira Slovak and sponsored by Smirnoff Vodka. Better known, however, is the F8F-2 (BuNo 121646) in which Darryl Greenamyer first won in Reno in 1965 and set the current world's speed record for piston-powered aircraft in 1969. After first making relatively small modifications before entering the aircraft in the 1964 Reno National Air Races from which he was disqualified after being forced to land at another field, Greenamyer and his associates progressively incorporated a series of major modifications. Notably, wing span was reduced to 28 ft 6in, a tiny bubble canopy replaced the windshield and sliding canopy of the military aircraft, the hydraulic system was removed, and filler was used extensively to reduce drag. In addition, high octane fuels with special additives were used and the powerplant installation was greatly modified – with the standard 12 ft 7 in propeller being replaced by a 13 ft 6 in propeller fitted with a modified P-51 Mustang spinner. After four consecutive wins in the Reno National Air Races proved the effectiveness of these modifications, Greenamyer was ready for his attempt at breaking the 469.22-mph (754.97-kmh) speed record set by Flugkapitän Fritz Wendel in the Messerschmitt Me 209 V1 in April 1939. Flying four times over a 3-km (1.87-mile) course at Edwards AFB, California, Darryl Greenamyer averaged 483.041 mph (777.213 km/h) on 16 August, 1969, to set a new record. During the following month, Greenamyer and his N1111L *Conquest I* won the National Air Races once more. Pilot and aircraft repeated their feat a record sixth time in 1971.

After winning nine of the first twelve National Air Races held in Reno between 1964 and 1975 as well as other unlimited races held elsewhere in the United States, it appeared that F8Fs had lost all chance of winning against much modified and re-engined North American Mustangs and Hawker Sea Furies. However, those betting against the Bearcat were proved to have lost faith prematurely. In September 1988, Lyle Shelton, flying N777L *Rare Bear*, an extensively modified F8F-2 rebuilt from parts of several Bearcats and powered by a Wright R-3350, set a new lap record of 474.622 mph (763.667 kmh) to take first place in the unlimited category at the record average speed of 456.821 mph (735.025 kmh).

PRODUCTION: A total of 1,265 Bearcats was built by Grumman between August 1944 and May 1949 as follows:

2	XF8F-1	2	XF8F-2
654	F8F-1	293	F8F-2
226	F8F-1B/F8F-1C	12	F8F-2N
2	XF8F-1N	60	F8F-2P
12	F8F-1N	2	G-58A

They were assigned the following BuNos and civil registration:

XF8F-1:   BuNos 90460/90461
F8F-1:   BuNos 90437/90459, 94752/94802, 94804/94811,
             94813/94818, 94820/94971, 94973/94981,
             94983/94986, 94988/94998, 95000/95001,
             95003/95008, 95010/95014, 95016/95021,
             95023/95027, 95029/95032, 95035/95038,
             95040/95043, 95045/95048, 95051/95055,
             95057/95061, 95063/95067, 95069/95073,

	95075/95079, 95081/95085, 95087/95092,
	95094/95097, 95099/95102, 95104/95107,
	95109/95112, 95114/95117, 95119/95122,
	95124/95127, 95129/95132, 95134/95137, 95139,
	95141/95142, 95144/95147, 95149, 95151/95155,
	95157/95160, 95163/95165, 95167/95170,
	95173/95175, 95177/95180, 95183/95189,
	95192/95194, 95196/95197, 95199, 95201/95204,
	95207/95209, 95211/95213, 95216/95220,
	95223/95226, 95228/95229, 95231, 95233/95236,
	95238/95241, 95243/95246, 95248/95252,
	95254/95259, 95261/95264, 95266/95270,
	95272/95274, 95276/95280, 95282/95284,
	95286/95289, 95291/95294, 95296/95299,
	95301/95304, 95306/95309, 95311/95314,
	95316/95318, 95320/95323, 95325/95329,
	95331/95333, 95335/95339, 95341/95343,
	95345/95348, 95350/95353, 95355/95358,
	95360/95362, 95364/95367, 95369/95372,
	95374/95377, 95379/95382, 95384/95386,
	95388/95390, 95392/95395, 95397/95400,
	95402/95405, 95407/95410, 95412/95415,
	95417/95419, 95421/95424, 95426/95429,
	95431/95434, 95436/95439, 95441/95444,
	95446/95449, 95451/95453, 95455/95458,
	95460/95462, 95464/95467, 95469/95471,
	95473/95476, 95478/95481, 95483/95486,
	95488/95491, and 95493/95497

F8F-1B/F8F-1C:	BuNos 94803, 94972, 94982, 94987, 94999, 95002,
	95009, 95015, 95022, 95028, 95033, 95039, 95044,
	95050, 95056, 95062, 95068, 95074, 95080, 95086,
	95093, 95098, 95103, 95108, 95113, 95118, 95123,
	95128, 95133, 95138, 95143, 95148, 95156, 95162,
	95166, 95172, 95176, 95181, 95190, 95195, 95200,
	95205, 95210, 95215, 95221, 95227, 95232, 95237,
	95242, 95247, 95253, 95260, 95265, 95271, 95275,
	95281, 95285, 95290, 95295, 95300, 95305, 95310,
	95315, 95319, 95324, 95334, 95340, 95344, 95349,
	95354, 95359, 95363, 95368, 95373, 95378, 95383,
	95387, 95391, 95396, 95401, 95406, 95411, 95416,
	95420, 95425, 95430, 95435, 95440, 95445, 95450,
	95454, 95459, 95463, 95468, 95472, 95477, 95482,
	95487, 95492, 95498, & 121463/121522, and
	122087/122152

| F8F-1D: | (BuNo 90446) |
| F8F-1E: | (BuNo 90445) |

XF8F-1N:	BuNos 94812 and 94819
F8F-1N:	BuNos 95034, 95140, 95150, 95161, 95171, 95182, 95191, 95198, 95206, 95214, 95222, and 95230
F8F-1P:	(BuNo 90441)
XF8F-2:	BuNos 95049 and 95330
F8F-2:	BuNos 121523/121548, 121551/121574, 121586/121600, 121612/121631, 121638/121657, 121664/121683, 121690/121708, 121715/121733, 121740/121757, 121764/121769, 121776/121784, 121791/121792, and 122614/122708
F8F-2N:	BuNos 121549/121550, 121575/121579, and 121601/121605
F8F-2P:	BuNos 121580/121585, 121606/121611, 121632/121637, 121658/121663, 121684/121689, 121709/121714, 121734/121739, 121758/121763, 121770/121775, and 121785/121790
G-58A:	NX120IV and N700A

	XF8F-1	F8F-1	F8F-2
DIMENSIONS:			
Span, ft in	35 6	35 6	35 6
(m)	(10.82)	(10.82)	(10.82)
Span (wings folded), ft in	23 3	23 3	23 3
(m)	(7.09)	(7.09)	(7.09)
Length, ft in	27 6	27 6	27 8
(m)	(8.38)	(8.38)	(8.43)
Height, ft in	13 8	13 8	13 8†
(m)	(4.17)	(4.17)	(4.17)
Wing area, sq ft	244	244	244
(sq m)	(22.67)	(22.67)	(22.67)
WEIGHTS:			
Empty, lb	6,733	7,070	7,690
(kg)	(3,054)	(3,207)	(3,488)
Loaded, lb	8,788	9,386	10,426
(kg)	(3,987)	(4,257)	(4,729)
Maximum, lb	9,537	12,947	13,494
(kg)	(4,326)	(5,873)	(6,121)
Wing loading,* lb/sq ft	36.0	38.5	42.7
(kg/sq m)	(175.8)	(187.8)	(208.6)
Power loading,* lb/hp	4.2	4.5	4.5
(kg/hp)	(1.9)	(2.0)	(2.1)
PERFORMANCE:			
Max speed, mph/ft	424/17,300	434/19,800	447/28,000
(kmh/m)	(682/5,275)	(698/6,055)	(719/8,535)
Cruising speed, mph	170	163	182
(kmh)	(274)	(262)	(293)
Climb rate, ft/min	4,800/1	4,570/1	4,420/1
(m/sec)	(24.4)	(23.20)	(22.5)
Service ceiling, ft	33,700	38,900	40,700
(m)	(10,270)	(11,855)	(12,405)
Normal range, miles	955	1,105	865
(km)	(1,535)	(1,780)	(1,390)

| Max range, miles | 1,450 | 1,965 | 1,435 |
| (km) | (2,335) | (3,160) | (2,310) |

* Wing and power loadings are calculated at normal loaded weight and maximum take-off power.

† Although the F8F-2 had 1-ft taller vertical tail surfaces, overall height – an important consideration for carrier-based aircraft being handled in the confined space of hangar decks – was identical to that of the F8F-1 as in both cases the tallest point when in a three-point attitude was the tip of the propeller.

The Tadpole at Bethpage on 25 May, 1945. *(Grumman)*

Grumman G-65 Tadpole

Development of Design 65 was begun in May 1944 to investigate the feasibility of producing a small, low-cost, single-engined amphibian. The configuration adopted by the design team led by Dayton T Brown and Franklin T 'Hank' Kurt was quite advanced and featured all-metal, spot-welded construction and mid-mounted wings with split flaps and 6 degrees of dihedral to keep the tips as far above the water as possible. For water operations, the G-65 was provided with a single-step hull and aerofoil-shaped underwing floats. For land operations, it received an hydraulically operated tricycle undercarriage with the main units retracting inboard into the wings and the nose gear retracting into the hull without hull bottom doors. The engine, which drove a pusher propeller, was mounted aft and above the cabin. Access to the cabin was by means of upward-hinged doors. When in the water, access to the anchor housed in the bow was by means of a hinged, chain-supported plate on either side of the hull.

Trials began on 7 December, 1944, when the Tadpole, which was registered NX41828, was first flown as a landplane at Bethpage by Hank Kurt. On that occasion, the small amphibian was powered by a 125-hp Lycoming O-290-A four-cylinder air-cooled engine driving a four-blade 64-in diameter pusher propeller by means of a 28-in extension shaft. However, this arrangement resulted in excessive vibration and unsatisfactory airflow around the rear of the cowling. Accordingly, the length of the extension shaft was increased to 36-in. Later, various four- and two-blade propellers were tested while the engine cowling, fairing, and location were revised several times to reduce drag. Finally, the Lycoming four-cylinder engine was replaced by a 125-hp Continental C125-3 six-cylinder engine driving a two-blade pusher propeller by means of a 37-in extension shaft.

Whether operating from the water or on land, the Tadpole possessed pleasant taxi-ing, take-off, and landing characteristics but required extremely long take-off runs. In the air, handling characteristics were

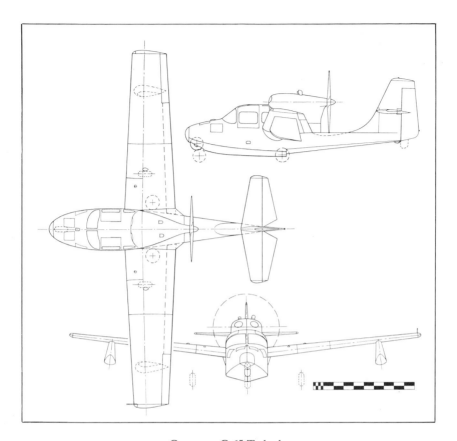

Grumman G-65 Tadpole

generally satisfactory and only a few minor changes would have been required to turn the proposed production version into an excellent two-seat amphibian. Likewise, pilot visibility was judged outstanding and, with the exception of the desirability of replacing the upward-hinged doors with conventional doors, the cabin arrangement was considered satisfactory.

Seats had been provided for a pilot and two passengers, but tests revealed that with a 125-hp engine water take-off performance was marginal when carrying three people. Hence, as Grumman believed that there was no market for a two-seat amphibian and that redesigning the Tadpole to provide more seats and more power would be expensive, development of the G-58 was terminated at the end of 1946. The fact that in 1946 – 47 the other major Long Island-based manufacturer, Republic Aircraft, sold over 1,000 of its similar Seabee amphibians might lead one to conclude that Grumman was over-conservative. However, the heavy losses incurred by the Seabee programme vindicated the prudent management of the Bethpage firm.

261

PRODUCTION: One Tadpole was completed by Grumman in November 1944 and received the civil registration number NX41828.

Span 35 ft (10.67 m); length 23 ft 6 in (7.16 m); height 8 ft 3 in (2.51 m); wing area 155 sq ft (14.40 sq m).Empty weight 1,450 lb (658 kg); loaded weight 2,100 lb (953 kg); wing loading 13.5 lb/sq ft (66.2 kg/sq m); power loading 16.8 lb/hp (7.6 kg/hp).Maximum speed 125 mph (201 kmh) at sea level; cruising speed 103 mph (166 kmh).

First flown before the end of the Second World War, the Tadpole was a bold but unsuccessful attempt by Grumman to find a new market. (*Grumman*)

The twin-finned Kitten II two/three-seater was first flown on 4 February, 1946. *(Grumman)*

Grumman G-72 Kitten II

Experience gained during initial flight testing of the G-63 Kitten I prompted Dayton T Brown and Hank Kurt to initiate in November 1944 a major redesign of their light aircraft. The resulting Design 72, which was named Kitten II, retained the 125-hp Lycoming O-290-A flat-four engine, two- to three-seat accommodation, and most of the fuselage of Design 63. However, to improve the stall characteristics and cure the directional instability problems encountered with the earlier design, the G-72 was fitted with twin fins and rudders and with wings of modified section and without chord-line twist or provision for folding. In addition, the G-72 differed from the G-63 in having slotted instead of split flaps, a tricycle retractable undercarriage in place of a conventional retractable landing gear, and cabin doors hinged at the top edge and lifting up in lieu of conventional-opening doors hinged at their forward edge.

Registered NX41858, Design 72 was first flown by Hank Kurt on 4 February, 1946, and quickly demonstrated stalling characteristics markedly improved over those of the G-63. While it was found to be nearly unspinnable in power-off condition, with power-on it still tended to get into a spin rather easily when flown at maximum gross weight and with full rear cg. However, after the cg was moved slightly forward by relocating the battery, spin recovery became satisfactory.

After being flown for some 28 hours, the G-72 was brought back to the shop in June 1946 to have the twin fins and rudders replaced by a single vertical surface with 1 degree of fin offset. At that time, a two-control system eliminating the necessity for rudder pedals and enabling the aircraft to be flown solely with the control wheel was substituted for the conventional controls as initially installed. With the two-control system,

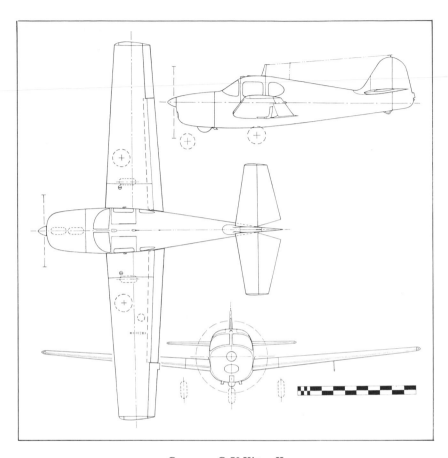

Grumman G-72 Kitten II

the G-72 handled exceptionally well in cruise and only minor adjustments in fin offset and rudder setting were found necessary to reduce right wheel force and displacement on take-off and during the climb.

Many improvements were planned for the proposed production version including the use of power-operated undercarriage and flaps; the installation of conventional entrance doors and access steps on the wing; the provision for ventilating, heating, and soundproofing; the adoption of a revised instrument panel layout; etc. However, as demand for light aircraft was insufficient in the immediate postwar period, the project was terminated at the end of 1946 before any of these modifications could be evaluated on the prototype.

PRODUCTION: One Kitten II was completed by Grumman in February 1946 and received the civil registration number NX41858.

Span 32 ft (11.14 m); length 20 ft 11.5 in (6.36 m); height 6 ft 4 in (1.93 m); wing area 130 sq ft (12.08 sq m).Empty weight 1,215 lb (551 kg); loaded weight 1,900 lb (862 kg); wing loading 14.6 lb/sq ft (71.4 kg/sq m); power loading 15.2 lb/hp (6.9 kg/hp).Maximum speed 154 mph (248 kmh) at sea level; cruising speed 132 mph (212 kmh).

The Kitten II at Bethpage on 19 June, 1946, after being fitted with single fin and rudder. (*Grumman*)

The ninth Mallard (NC2946) at the Downtown Skyport, New York, in 1947. (*Grumman*)

Grumman G-73 Mallard

Notwithstanding the fact that only three Goose amphibians had been sold to airlines before the war, a group of Grumman executives and engineers confidently felt that a twin-engined 10- to 15-seat amphibian would find a ready market after the war among feeder airlines. Moreover, they believed that a sound design to fit that market could be developed and produced at minimum cost by redesigning the G-21 and incorporating new production techniques. Accordingly, development of a fourth type of aircraft for the postwar civil market, the Design 73 twin-engined amphibian, was begun in December 1944 by a team led by Project Engineer Gordon Israel*. Unfortunately for Grumman, airlines did not show the expected interest in the G-73 and total sales were disappointing. Although Design 73 did much better than the G-63, G-65, and G-72 (which had not gone past the prototype stage), that success was only relative; only fifty-nine G-73s were built, whereas market studies on which Roy Grumman had based his go-ahead authorization had forecast a potential market for at least 250 twin-engined amphibians of that size and power.

As design progressed, the G-73 evolved into a larger, cleaner version of the G-21 with a tricycle undercarriage in place of the conventional undercarriage of the Goose. Normal accommodation was provided for a cockpit crew of two (although the Mallard was later certificated for single-pilot operation) and for ten passengers in a cabin located beneath the wings, with access through a door on the port fuselage side, aft of the wings. A mooring hatch and a baggage compartment were provided in the bow, and a lavatory and another baggage compartment were located in the rear fuselage. Luxury accommodation with a couch, tables, and 'overstuffed chairs' were offered as an option. Alternatively, five additional seats could be installed in place of the lavatory and rear baggage compartment.

As the G-73 was to be larger and heavier than the G-21, Grumman thought to replace the 450-hp engines of the earlier amphibian with engines in the 700 to 800-hp class. However, as no such suitable engines were available, Gordon Israel selected the Pratt & Whitney Wasp nine-cylinder radial to power its new amphibian. Most received Wasp S3H1s with take-off rating of 600 hp up to an altitude of 3,000 ft and normal rating of 550 hp at 5,000 ft, but some had Wasp S1H1s with take-off and normal ratings respectively maintained up to 6,200 ft and 8,000 ft. In both cases, the engines drove three-blade fully-feathering propellers. While reliable, these powerplant installations left the Mallard slightly underpowered. However, this was the only real shortcoming of the design as, on the water, on the ground, or in the air, the G-73 handled extremely well.

---

* A preliminary study for a fifth postwar civil project, Design 74, was also initiated during that month. However, additional work on this proposed redesign of the Widgeon was not authorized as the G-74 would not have offered significant improvements over the G-44A.

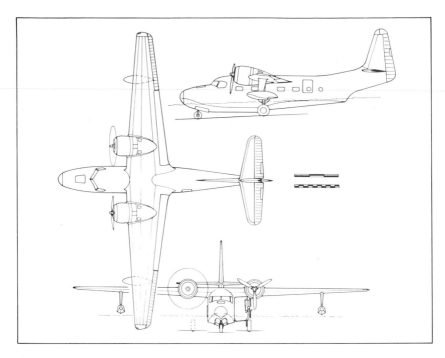

Grumman G-73 Mallard

Registered NX41824 and bearing the c/n J-1, the prototype Mallard was first flown on 30 April, 1946, with Frederick C Rowley at the controls. It was retained as a demonstrator by Grumman until January 1949 when it was sold to Avalon Industries Ltd, in St John's, Newfoundland. Two months later, by which time it was re-registered as CF-GPA, ownership of this aircraft was transferred to Canada Veneers Ltd. Still owned by this company, the first Mallard crashed and burned at St John's on 4 December, 1951.

Following the issue of an Approved Type Certificate on 8 September, 1946, the first production aircraft (c/n J-2, CF-BKE) was delivered to the McIntyre Porcupine Mines in Toronto, Ontario, Canada, on 27 September. From then until March 1951 Grumman delivered fifty-six additional Mallards, mainly to private and industrial customers in the United States, Canada, Egypt, and Great Britain*. Resales saw Mallards registered in Australia, Fiji, French Polynesia, Gabon, Indonesia, Japan, New Guinea,

* The only Mallards to appear on the British civil register were c/n J-41 and c/n J-55. The former was acquired by Shell Refining and Marketing Co Ltd in 1949 and was registered G-ALLJ. It was almost immediately sold to an affiliated company, NV Bataafsche Petroleum Maattschappij and registered PK-AKE in Indonesia. The latter was purchased on the second-hand market by Dennis Ferranti Meters Ltd, and was on the British register as G-ASCS from September 1962 until April 1969, when it was sold and re-registered in Canada.

N2973, the thirty-fifth Mallard, was delivered to J J Ryan of Arlington, Virginia, in May 1948. Soon after it went to Indonesia with the Asiatic Petroleum Company (as PK-AKD) and in 1963 it was acquired by the Indonesian Police Force. *(Grumman)*

New Zealand, and Panama. The fifty-ninth and last Mallard was at first retained by Grumman but was later sold to Robertson & O'Connell Ltd, and registered CF-HPN in Canada.

The only military operator was the Egyptian Air Force which received two Mallards (c/n J-47 and J-48, Egyptian military serials F7 and F8) in 1949. However, these were not genuine military aircraft; they had been selected in preference to the smaller Short Sealand to equip the Royal Flight. Luxuriously appointed, they were used by HRM King Farouk until his overthrow in 1952. Later they were used by General Mohammed Naguib, Colonel Gamal Abdel Nasser, and visiting dignitaries.

Much to the dismay of those who had predicted that Mallards would sell well to air carriers, only one, c/n J-11, was sold by Grumman to an airline customer. Even then, the Mallard only had a short first career as an airliner, as Air Commuting went out of business within a year and its Grumman amphibian was sold to Texaco. More luck attended the second coming of Mallard airliners as some of the aircraft acquired on the second-hand market beginning in the mid-1950s remained in service into the 1980s. They were operated in limited numbers by small regional carriers in the United States (mainly in Alaska but also in the lower forty-eight states), Canada, the Caribbean, Australia, Japan, and French Polynesia.

To solve the chronic lack of power which had limited the usefulness of the Mallard, c/n J-36 was fitted by Northern Consolidated Airlines with a 578-ehp Pratt & Whitney PT6A-6 propeller-turbine in place of its starboard Wasp radial engine. After some 50 hours of flying in 1964-65, this test bed was brought back to standard configuration. However, in 1968 c/n J-36 was once again modified, and this time J Fred Frakes had both Wasps replaced by 652-ehp PT6A-27 propeller-turbines. The resulting TurboMallard conversion was technically successful but only met with limited commercial

The fourteenth Mallard, at the Hollywood-Fort Lauderdale Airport in May 1982. (*René J Francillon*)

N2974, the TurboMallard prototype, was fitted with two PT6A-27 propeller-turbines in 1968. (*Grumman*)

success. Nevertheless, by the mid-1980s five TurboMallards were still operated from Watson Island in Miami by Chalks International Airline.

After experiencing disappointing Mallard sales for four years, mainly due to the availability of low-priced surplus transport aircraft, Grumman was finally forced to terminate production of its twin-engined executive amphibian in 1951 due to restrictions on the use of aluminium and other strategic materials imposed as a result of the war in Korea.

PRODUCTION: 59 Mallards were built by Grumman between April 1946 and May 1951 and were assigned construction numbers J-1 to J-59.

Span 66 ft 8 in (20.32 m); length 48 ft 4 in (14.73 m); height 18 ft 9 in (5.72 m); wing area 444 sq ft (41.25 sq m).

270

Empty weight 9,350 lb (4,241 kg); loaded weight 12,750 lb (5,783 kg); wing loading 28.7 lb/sq m (140.2 kg/sq m); power loading 10.6 lb/hp (4.8 kg/hp).

Maximum speed 215 mph at 6,000 ft (346 kmh at 1,830 m); cruising speed 180 mph (290 kmh); climb rate 1,290 ft/min (6.6 m/sec); service ceiling 23,000 ft (7,010 m); range with 1,950-lb (885-kg) payload 730 miles (1,175 km); range with 810-lb (367-kg) payload 1,380 miles (2,220 km).

N2945, c/n J-8, at Clear Lake, California, in September 1988. (*Peter B Lewis*)

The first XJL-1 (BuNo 31399), at NAS Patuxent River, Maryland, on 17 September, 1948, shortly before being stored at the conclusion of Navy trials. *(USN/National Archives)*

Columbia XJL-1

Work on Design 42, a proposed single-engined amphibian monoplane intended as a successor for the J2F-1, was begun at Bethpage in June 1939. However, more pressing work kept Grumman fully occupied and the project lay dormant until after Columbia Aircraft Corporation began manufacturing J2F-6s. At that time, Grumman and the Navy agreed that development of a monoplane successor to the Duck would be a worthwhile project, provided that design work would not interfere with Grumman's more important projects and provided that manufacture of this amphibian be entrusted to Columbia. Accordingly, design work was resumed in Bethpage in late 1942 and progressed slowly until the later part of 1943, when the project was transferred to Valley Stream for final detailing by Columbia engineers.

Even after the transfer of design responsibility to Columbia, from which two prototypes (BuNos 31399/31400) had been ordered as XJL-1s, progress was slow and neither of the prototypes was completed by the end of the war. Work on these aircraft, however, was sufficiently advanced for Columbia to be instructed during the summer of 1946 to proceed with their completion even though no production contract would be awarded.

Retaining the typical float/fuselage arrangement which had first been developed by Grover Loening, Design 41 differed from the Duck not only in its monoplane configuration but also in being fitted with a tricycle undercarriage instead of a conventional one. Furthermore, the main units no longer retracted vertically into the float but, being attached to the centre section of the wings, retracted laterally after their unusually long struts were compressed. The nosewheel and strut retracted into the forward portion of the float. Accommodation was similar to that in the Duck, with the crew of two sitting in tandem and seats for four passengers being provided in the fuselage/float combination, beneath and aft of the cockpit. Power was provided by a 1,350-hp Wright R-1820-56 nine-cylinder radial driving a three-blade propeller.

BuNo 31399 was first flown at Valley Stream on 25 October, 1946, and the second XJL-1 was airborne shortly before the end of that year. Both were evaluated by the Navy at NATC Patuxent River in 1947 before being stored in Norfolk, Virginia. The two XJL-1s were sold as surplus in 1959, when they were respectively registered N54207 and N54205. Various restoration schemes, including one under which a surplus XJL-1 was to be used for a round-the-world flight, did not materialize.

PRODUCTION: Two XJL-1s were completed by Columbia Aircraft Corporation in 1946 and were assigned BuNos 31399/31400.

Span 50 ft (15.24 m); length 45 ft 11 in (14.00 m); height 16 ft (4.88 m); wing area 413 sq ft (38.37 sq m).
Empty weight 7,250 lb (3,289 kg); loaded weight 13,000 lb (5,897 kg); wing loading 31.5 lb/sq ft (153.7 kg/sq m); power loading 9.6 lb/hp (4.4 kg/hp).
Maximum speed 200 mph (322 kmh) at sea level cruising speed 119 mph (191 kmh); climb rate 1,110 ft/min (5.6 m/sec); max range 2,070 miles (3,330 km).

AF-2S (BuNo 129209) of the Reserve unit based at NAS Oakland, California, flying near the Golden Gate Bridge on 14 February, 1953. (*USN/National Archives*)

Grumman XTB3F and AF Guardian

By the middle of 1944, weight increases began severely to affect the Avenger's performance, prompting Grumman and the US Navy to seek ways of increasing the TBF/TBM performance and to accelerate plans for the development of a new torpedo bomber. Unfortunately, the new aircraft programme ran into delays when, on 14 June, 1944, the Bureau of Aeronautics was forced to instruct Grumman to stop work on the twin-engined XTB2F as the size of that aircraft would have precluded its use from all but the larger carriers. At that time, however, BuAer requested that Grumman prepare and submit design studies for a smaller twin-engined torpedo bomber based on the F7F-2 and for a cleaned-up and lighter two-seat version of the TBF. The former became Design 66 as described in Appendix B and the latter was the starting point for the development of Design 70.

At the onset of the study in July 1944, Design 70 was planned as a straightforward development of the TBF powered by a 'C' series R-2800 and incorporating various improvements to reduce drag. However, the proposed weight reduction failed to satisfy BuAer and, after Grumman dropped all consideration of retaining some commonality with the Avenger, the project evolved into a totally new design. Five preliminary designs for a new two-seat torpedo bomber were submitted to BuAer on 19 September, 1944. The base case Design 70 called for the use of an R-2800 engine and the installation of a dorsal turret. Alternate designs were the G-70A with a

The XTB3F-1 (BuNo 90504) after removal of the turbojet. The wing root air intakes for the turbojet have been faired over. *(Grumman)*

Wright R-3350 engine, the G-70B with a Pratt & Whitney R-4360 radial and a General Electric remotely-controlled turret, the G-70D with an R-3350 supplemented by an I-20 turbojet but without turret, and the G-70F with a Westinghouse 24C replacing the I-20 turbojet of the G-70D.

With both engines running, calculated performance for the G-70F included a top speed of 394 mph at sea level, an initial rate of climb of 4,880 ft/min, and a take-off distance of 204 ft. As this was a sizeable improvement over the performance of the TBM-3, the current production version of the Avenger, and was better than the calculated performance for other Design 70 versions, on 25 October, 1944, BuAer recommended the procurement of three G-70F prototypes and one static test airframe. The programme was assigned high priority and arrangements were made immediately for Grumman to be supplied with a mock-up of a 24C jet unit, a new four-bladed Curtiss propeller, and a new 0.60-in machine-gun for installation in the XTB3F-1 mock-up. At that time, first flight was optimistically expected to take place in July 1945.

The expected late availability of both the R-3350-26 radial and 24C turbojet prompted BuAer in January 1945 to request Grumman to prepare revised performance data based on the installation of lower powered engines (R-2800-34W radial and Westinghouse 19XB turbojet). Mock-up inspections took place in February (basic installation) and March (revised wing armament installation to enable the carriage of larger external loads and substitution of a single 20-mm cannon in each wing for the 0.60-in gun initially provided).

Although with the R-2800-34W and W-19XB engines top speed at sea level was going to be reduced 7 per cent to 367 mph and take-off distance increased 62 per cent to 330 ft, Grumman was instructed in February to complete the three XTB3F-1s (BuNos 90504/90506) with this revised powerplant installation. In July 1945, these instructions were again revised

275

The XTB3F-1S (BuNo 90506), nearer the camera, and XTB3F-2S (BuNo 90505) served as prototypes for the Guardian ASW hunter-killer team. *(Grumman)*

to provide for the completion of the second prototype as the XTB3F-2 with an R-3350-26W radial and a 24C turbojet. Meanwhile, additional engine delivery delays kept pushing back the first flight date and by the time Japan surrendered in August 1945 neither the two XTB3F-1s nor the XTB3F-2 had been completed. With the return to peace, the programme lost its priority and work on the first prototype proceeded at a slow pace, while completion of the other two was held back pending review of Navy requirements. With its turbojet installed but not operative, BuNo 90504 was finally flown at Bethpage by Pat Gallo on 23 December, 1946. The next day, the Navy sent a stop-work order.

By then more versatile single-seat, single-engined attack aircraft (Douglas AD-1s and Martin AM-1s) were planned to operate in both the bombing and torpedo bombing roles and the Navy no longer had a requirement for large multi-seat torpedo bombers. Conversely, a requirement for multi-seat aircraft to replace the TBM-3W/TBM-3S hunter-killer team in the carrier-based anti-submarine role was high on the Navy priority list. Accordingly, on 20 February, 1947, Grumman was instructed to complete the second airframe (BuNo 90505) as the XTB3F-2S prototype for an ASW attack version and the third airframe (BuNo 90506) as the XTB3F-1S prototype for an ASW search aircraft. Space made available by the removal of the turbojet (jet engine boost not being required for the ASW mission) was to be used to accommodate three equipment operators.

Production history

Mock-ups of the search and attack versions respectively passed inspection from 28 April to 2 May and 2 to 6 June, 1947. An initial contract for sixteen search aircraft and fourteen attack aircraft was awarded in May 1948 before

The XTB3F-1 at Bethpage on 28 April, 1947, after it had been fitted with a large dorsal fin. *(Grumman)*

the completion of prototypes. The first of the revised prototypes to fly, the XTB3F-1S, was airborne in November 1948 and was followed two months later by the XTB3F-2S. The first AF-2W and AF-2S (as the production versions of the XTB3F-1S and XTB3F-2s were eventually designated) respectively flew in November and December 1949. In addition to the three XTB3F-designated prototypes, Grumman built 386 AF-designated production aircraft. The following designations were given to prototypes and production aircraft.

XTB3F-1: This designation was successively used to identify three torpedo bomber prototypes (BuNos 90504/90506), which were to be powered by the 2,700-hp Wright R-3350-26 radial driving a four-blade propeller and a 3,000-lb thrust Westinghouse 24C turbojet, and was then given to two prototypes (BuNos 90504 and 90506) which were to be completed as two-seaters (with pilot and bomb-aimer/navigator sitting side-by-side) and each powered by a 2,100-hp Pratt & Whitney R-2800-34W radial driving a four-blade propeller and a 1,600-lb thrust Westinghouse 19XB turbojet. In the end, only BuNo 90504 was completed with the R-2800 radial and the W-19XB turbojet. It was first flown by Pat Gallo on 23 December, 1946.

The turbojet, which was fitted but not used, was fed by intakes on the wing leading edges next to the fuselage and exhausted at the tail, but intakes and exhaust were faired over after the turbojet was removed. For carrier storage, sto-wings were again used as the low height of hangar decks made conventional upward folding wings impractical. Armament, which was not installed in BuNo 90504, was to have consisted of two Mk. 13-2 torpedoes or two 2,000-lb bombs carried in a fuselage bomb bay, one Tiny Tim or three 5-in HVAR rockets beneath each wing, and one 20-mm cannon in each wing. After development of the torpedo bomber version was terminated, BuNo 90504 was used to explore the basic handling characteristics of the ASW production version and to evaluate the effectiveness of a number of proposed modifications. Notably, in April 1947, it was fitted with a dorsal fin extension. It was struck from the inventory on 31 March, 1949.

The XTB3F-1S with its large ventral radome housing the semi-elliptical antenna of the AN/APS-20A radar. The geometry of the main undercarriage leg is noteworthy. *(Grumman)*

XTB3F-1S: As instructed by the Navy in February 1947, Grumman completed the third airframe (BuNo 90506) as the prototype of the ASW search version. First flown in November 1948, this prototype was powered by a 2,300-hp Pratt & Whitney R-2800-46W radial with a single-speed supercharger. The aircraft had no provision for armament (although the carriage of sonobuoys and the installation of sonobuoy receivers were proposed) and the bomb bay, as fitted to the XTB3F-1 torpedo-bomber prototype, was faired over to provide attachment for the large ventral radome housing an AN/APS-20A search radar. The crew consisted of a pilot in the cockpit above the wing leading edge and two radar operators in a cabin located above and behind the trailing edge. A fourth crew member was provided later to operate the radio countermeasures (RCM) equipment which was added in the rear fuselage.

The XTB3F-1S was evaluated at NATC Patuxent River beginning in February 1949 and was used for carrier suitability trials. As a result of these tests, its 13 ft 2 in diameter propeller was replaced by a 12 ft 2 in unit to increase clearance during arrested landings until a modification to the hook attachment reduced the aircraft's tendency to nose over slightly after catching a wire. The XTB3F-1S was struck off in January 1951.

XTB3F-2: In accordance with a July 1945 programme change, the second prototype was to have been completed as a torpedo bomber powered by a Wright R-3350-26W and a Westinghouse 24C-4B. Its construction was halted at the end of the war and BuNo 90505 was later completed as the XTB3F-2S.

XTB3F-2S: BuNo 90505, the prototype of the ASW attack version, was first flown in January 1949. Also powered by an R-2800-46W, it did not have the AN/APS-20A radar characterizing the search version but did retain the bomb bay of the XTB3F-1 torpedo bomber. Its crew consisted of a pilot in the forward cockpit and a radar operator and a bomb-aimer/

navigator in the aft fuselage compartment. During the course of its evaluation, the XTB3F-2S was fitted with spoiler ailerons (flaperons) to improve lateral control. Armament proposed for the production version consisted of a homing torpedo in the fuselage weapon bay and/or six 5-in HVAR rockets, four 500-lb bombs, or four Mk.54 depth charges beneath the wings. ASW search equipment was to have included an AN/APS-31 radar in a nacelle beneath the starboard wing, an AN/AVQ-2 searchlight in a nacelle beneath the port wing, and sonobuoys, but most of it had not yet been installed when the aircraft was lost in an accident during a propeller vibration test on 4 October, 1949.

AF-1S: Confusingly, this designation was first used between March 1948 and May 1949 to identify the planned search production version and was then used between May and July 1949 to identify the planned attack version. In the end, no aircraft was actually built with this designation.

AF-1W: The same confusing designation changes saw the proposed search production version being designated AF-1W between May and July 1949. Again, no aircraft was actually built with this designation as search aircraft with AN/APS-20A radar were redesignated AF-2W on 6 July, 1949, four months before the maiden flight of this version.

AF-2S: The AF-2S designation was adopted in March 1948 to identify the attack version of the Guardian. The designation of this version was then temporarily changed to AF-1S between May and July 1949 but the use of the AF-2S designation was confirmed on 6 July, 1949, five months before the first flight of a production attack aircraft.

Basically similar to the XTB3F-2S, the AF-2S attack version was fitted

An AF-2S (BuNo 123090) with full external load consisting of an AN/APS-31 radar and an AN/AVQ-2 searchlight in underwing nacelles, two 150-gallon drop tanks, and six HVAR rockets. *(Grumman)*

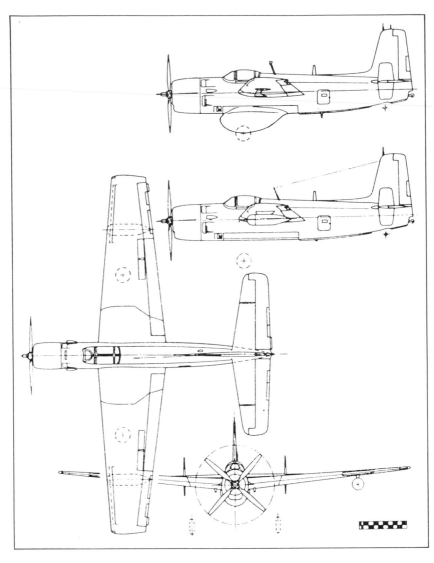

Grummans AF-2S Guardian. Side view of AF-2W (top)

with AN/APS-31 and AN/AVQ-2 searchlight in underwing nacelles and
carried the previously described offensive stores. In service, some of these
aircraft were retrofitted with an AN/APA-70C ECM set with a distinctive
inverted Y dorsal antenna. The 193 aircraft of this variant were powered by
either 2,300-hp R-2800-46W or -48 radials and, like the AF-2Ws and
AF-3Ss, were Design 82s in the Grumman nomenclature whereas the
prototypes were Design 70s.

AF-2W: This designation was adopted in July 1949 to identify the production version of the search aircraft with AN/APS-20A radar which had earlier been designated AF-1S and then AF-1W. Like some of the search aircraft, most AF-2Ws were retrofitted with an AN/APA-70C ECM set while others received an AN/APA-69A ECM set with a dorsal radome. A total of 153 AF-2Ws was built with R-2800-46W or -48 radials.

AF-3S: The AF-3S version, of which forty were built as the last of the ASW attack Guardians, differed from the AF-2S in being fitted with an AN/ASQ-8 magnetic anomaly detector (MAD) with a retractable boom housed in the rear fuselage and extended during search operations.

Service history

Initial deliveries were made to VX-1 at NAS Key West, Florida, in June 1950, and this development squadron received the first AF-2S and AF-2W

This AF-2W (BuNo 123095) was modified as a test-bed for the retractable APS-33 radar installation as proposed for Design 91 (*see* Appendix B) and for the S2F-1. (*Grumman*)

The first AF-3S (BuNo 129243) with MAD boom extended. (*Grumman*)

to develop hunter-killer tactics before Guardians were assigned to operational squadrons. Soon after, AFs were delivered to FAETULANT and FAETUPAC, the training units with the Atlantic and Pacific Fleets, and to the first operational squadrons, VS-24 at NAS Norfolk, Virginia, and VS-25 at NAS San Diego, California, with which the AF-2W/AF-2S hunter-killer team replaced the TBM-3W2/TBM-3S2 team.

In service, the AF-2W was nicknamed *Guppy* on account of its large belly radome, whereas the more bellicose AF-2S was known to its crews as the *Scrapper*. As previously done by TBM-3W2 and as validated during the VX-1 evaluation, the *Guppy* typically patrolled at an altitude of 1,000 ft to 1,500 ft, seeking to obtain a radar echo from surfaced submarines or from snorkels of submerged vessels. Upon obtaining a possible submarine contact, the *Guppy* crew guided the *Scrapper* crew toward the target. The latter then sought to confirm the contact with its own AN/APS-31 radar and sonobuoys. Contacts which were confirmed as enemy submarines were to be attacked by the *Scrapper* with torpedoes or depth charges, if submerged, or with rockets, if on the surface.

While ASW tactics were easily developed, carrier operations proved the source of many difficulties. Some of these difficulties were relatively short-lived as minor modifications (*eg*, a redesign of the hook attachment and substitution of non-retractable dual tailwheels for the retractable single wheel as fitted during production) were made following BIS carrier trials aboard the uss *Wright* (CVL-49) in November 1950 and initial carrier operations aboard the uss *Palau* (CVE-122) by VS-24 in December 1950. Other difficulties were inherent in the large size of the aircraft. Notably, when operating aboard CVEs and CVLs, there was little clearance between the Guardian's starboard wingtip and the island, thus rendering night

An AF-2W of VS-37 off the coast of Japan in March 1955 while operating from the uss *Princeton* (CVS-37). (*USN/National Archives*)

N9995Z (ex-AF-2S, BuNo 126792), a fire fighting tanker of Aero Union, at Chico, California, on 27 January, 1973. (*J Whitehead, courtesy of Alain Pelletier*)

operations in a high-sea state very tricky. For the deck crew, however, the use of typical Grumman sto-wing folding which reduced span from 60 to 24 ft greatly eased spotting aboard these small carriers.

Notwithstanding tricky carrier operations, Guardians were assigned to eleven fleet squadrons between the autumn of 1950 and August 1955, when the last fleet Guardians were transferred to the reserve. With deployable squadrons, Guardians not only took part in normal peacetime operations with the Atlantic Fleet and the Pacific Fleet but they also provided effective ASW support to Task Force 77 during combat operations off Korea in 1951-53. With the Naval Air Reserve, AFs were operated from January 1953, when the first were flown by reservists in Oakland, California, until June 1957, when New York reservists flew the last Navy Guardians.

Civil Guardians

After being placed in storage at NAF Litchfield Park, Arizona, all but five Guardians were eventually scrapped. The five survivors, two AF-2Ss and three AF-2Ws less ventral radome and other military equipment, were modified in the late 1950s as air tankers and operated by Aero Union Corporation of Chico, California, until 1973. One of these aircraft (N3144G, ex BuNo123100) was restored as an AF-2S in 1974 and later donated to the Naval Air Museum in Pensacola, Florida.

PRODUCTION: A total of 389 XTBFs and AFs was built by Grumman between December 1946 and May 1953 as follows:

1	XTB3F-1	193	AF-2S
1	XTB3F-1S	153	AF-2W
1	XTB3F-2S	40	AF-3S

They were assigned the following BuNos:
XTB3F-1:   BuNo 90504
XTB3F-1S: BuNo 90506

XTB3F-2S: BuNo 90505
AF-2S: BuNos 123088/123116 even numbers only,
             124188/124208 even numbers only, 124778/124848 even
             numbers only, 126720/126737, 126756/126821, and
             129196/129242
AF-2W: BuNos 123089/123117 odd numbers only,
             124187/124209 odd numbers only, 124779/124849 odd
             numbers only, 126738/126755, 126822/126835,
             129258/129299, and 130389/130404
AF-3S: BuNos 129243/129257 and 130364/130388

	XTB3F-1	AF-2S	AF-2W
DIMENSIONS:			
Span, ft in	60 0	60 0	60 0
(m)	(18.29)	(18.29)	(18.29)
Span (wings folded), ft in	24 0	24 0	24 0
(m)	(7.32)	(7.32)	(7.32)
Length, ft in	42 1	43 5	43 1
(m)	(12.83)	(13.23)	(13.13)
Height, ft in	13 2	13 2	13 2
(m)	(4.01)	(4.01)	(4.01)
Wing area, sq ft	549	549	549
(sq m)	(51.00)	(51.00)	(51.00)
WEIGHTS:			
Empty, lb	13,306	14,658	16,256
(kg)	(6,036)	(6,649)	(7,374)
Loaded, lb	19,065	20,298	20,018
(kg)	(8,648)	(9,207)	(9,080)
Maximum, lb	21,465	22,565	22,220
(kg)	(9,736)	(10,235)	(10,079)
Wing loading,* lb/sq ft	34.7	37.0	36.5
(kg/sq m)	(169.6)	(180.5)	(178.0)
Power loading,* lb/hp	9.1	8.8	8.7
(kg/hp)	(4.1)	(4.0)	(3.9)
PERFORMANCE:			
Max speed, mph/ft	341/sl	275/4,000	273/4,000
(kmh/m)	(549/sl)	(442/1,220)	(439/1,220)
Max speed (with jet on), mph/ft	393/sl	N.A.	N.A.
(kmh/m)	(632/sl)	(N.A.)	(N.A.)
Cruising speed, mph	160	166	–
(kmh)	(257)	(267)	(–)
Climb rate, ft/min	2,433/1	2,300/1	2,112/1
(m/sec)	(12)	(12)	(11)
Climb rate (with jet on), ft/min	3,629/1	N.A.	N.A.
(m/sec)	(18)	(N.A.)	(N.A.)
Service ceiling, ft	35,200	22,900	–
(m)	(10,730)	(6,980)	(–)
Service ceiling (with jet on), ft	35,500	N.A.	N.A.
(m)	(10,820)	(N.A.)	(N.A.)
Normal range, miles	1,280	915	–
(km)	(2,060)	(1,470)	(–)
Max range, miles	2,880	1,140	–
(km)	(4,635)	(1,835)	(–)

* Wing and power loadings are calculated at normal loaded weight and maximum take-off power.

BuNo 126756, an AF-2S from the reserve unit at NAS Jacksonville, Florida. *(USN)*

HU-16A (M.M. 50-177) of the 84° Gruppo, 15° Stormo SAR, during a rescue exercise. (*Stato Maggiore Aeronautica, AMI, courtesy of the Italian Air Attaché in Washington*)

Grumman UF and SA-16 (HU-16) Albatross

Following protracted and frequently acrimonious inter-Service negotiations, the National Security Act of 1947 became law on 26 July and the United States Air Force was established on 18 September, 1947. At that time, the newest branch of the Armed Services was given responsibility for worldwide air rescue operations. For Grumman, this meant that its Design 64, which had been initiated in April 1944 for the Navy would gain a new primary customer, the USAF.

As initially conceived by a team led by project engineer William Wange, the G-64 was intended as a replacement for the Navy's JRF Goose utility amphibian. Of similar twin-engined configuration, but larger and more powerful than its predecessor, the new amphibian was intended for all-weather operations. Moreover, it was to have better water and land handling characteristics, the former being improved as the result of the work undertaken by Ralston Stalb, a noted hydrodynamicist, and the latter coming about through the adoption of a tricycle undercarriage with a wider track main gear attached beneath the engine nacelles and retracting into the fuselage sides.

Ordered in November 1944, the XJR2F-1 prototypes (BuNos 82853 and 82854) survived the rash of postwar contract cancellations, but their construction proceeded at a leisurely pace. Finally, the first Pelican* (BuNo 82853) first lifted off from the Bethpage runway on 1 October, 1947, with Fred Rowley and Carl Alber at the controls. No significant problems were encountered in this or subsequent flights, and the new utility amphibian could have been put into service rapidly had it not been for the fact that the Navy could not immediately afford ordering more than a few new utility amphibians and quickly lost interest in the proposed PF-1 patrol

---

* Although the name Pelican was used for the XJR2F-1 prototypes, the name Albatross was retained for all production versions.

An SA-16A (50-181) of the 129th Air Resupply Squadron, California ANG, at Oakland in September 1956. *(William T Larkins)*

amphibian version. Fortunately for Grumman, the Air Force had an urgent requirement for amphibians to equip rescue squadrons, the Coast Guard selected the type as its standard rescue aircraft, and foreign customers were also interested. In the end, Grumman built 464 production Albatrosses (with the Plymouth Division of the Chrysler Corporation in Evansville, Indiana, manufacturing hulls for the 116th to 364th aircraft) and deliveries extended over a 12-year period.

Production history

The Albatross production history is the most complex of any Grumman types. In numerous instances, aircraft which had been ordered by one branch of the Armed Forces, and given appropriate designations and serials, were delivered to another branch and assigned new designations and serials as required (*eg*, c/n G-27 was ordered by the Navy as a PF-1A and assigned BuNo 124292 but was delivered to the Air Force as an SA-16A with the serial 49-069). In other cases, aircraft were given new designations and serials upon being transferred from one branch of the Armed Forces to another (*eg*, c/n G-88 was delivered to the Air Force as an SA-16A with the serial 51-015 but was later transferred to the Coast Guard with which it was designated UF-1G and numbered 1015). Added confusion came with the transfer of surplus or modified aircraft to foreign air forces and naval air arms (*eg*, c/n G-321, was delivered to the USAF as an SA-16A with serial 51-7235. It retained this serial when converted as an SA-16B and later when redesignated as a HU-16B. Still carrying this designation when it was transferred to the Royal Thai Navy under the jurisdiction of the USN, it was then given BuNo 151265; however, this Bureau Number was not painted on the aircraft and appeared only on transfer papers and US Navy documents). Finally, more confusions and misidentifications came about when surplus military aircraft ended up on civil registers.

287

The XJR2F-1 Pelican was first flown, from the Bethpage runway, on 1 October, 1947.
(Grumman)

As all Albatrosses were delivered before the adoption of a new tri-Service designation system on 18 September, 1962, all versions are listed here under their original designations. Whenever applicable, the corresponding post-1962 designations are provided in parentheses.

XJR2F-1: These two utility amphibian prototypes (BuNos 82853 and 82854) were ordered by the US Navy in November 1944. Powered by two 1,425-hp Wright R-1820-76 nine-cylinder, single-stage, two-speed radials driving constant speed, reversible-pitch three-blade propellers, BuNo 82853 was first flown on 1 October, 1947, by Fred Rowley and Carl Alber. The second prototype, BuNo 82854, was accepted by the Navy in May 1948.

SA-16A (HU-16A): First ordered in May 1948 under a USN contract covering twenty SA-16A rescue amphibians for the Air Force (AF serials 48-588/48-607), six UF-1 utility amphibians for the Navy (BuNos 124374/124379), and thirty-two PF-1 patrol amphibians for the Navy (BuNos 124292/124323), the SA-16As differed from the XJR2F-1s in being fitted with Air Force instrumentation and communications equipment. They were powered by 1,425-hp R-1820-76A engines and, for shorter take-offs notably when operating in open sea conditions or from short fields, could be fitted with one or two JATO bottles on each side of the aft fuselage.

The normal crew consisted of a pilot, co-pilot, navigator, and radio operator, with two observers being added during search sorties. The main cabin could be configured to carry either ten passengers or twelve stretcher patients plus one attendant, or a mix of passengers and stretcher patients. Alternatively, twenty-two troops could be carried on canvas seats or up to 5,000 lb of cargo could be loaded through a 5 ft 3 in by 4 ft 10 in overhead fuselage hatch and secured to tie-down points on the cabin floor and side walls. External store racks on each wing, usually reserved for 295-US gal drop tanks, could be used to carry items weighing up to 2,000 lb, such as rescue kits and supplies.

During the course of production, the AN/APS-31A search radar, which

48-588, the first Albatross fitted with triphibian gear, demonstrates the feasibility of water take-offs in spite of the addition of a skid beneath the floats. *(Grumman)*

initially was carried in a nacelle beneath the port wing, was relocated to the nose of the aircraft. More significantly, following tests conducted with 48-588 in 1950 at the request of the Air Materiel Command, the Air Force ordered 154 conversion kits for installation on some of its SA-16As which were to be used in Alaska and Greenland. Designed to enable the aircraft to operate from snow or ice surfaces as well as from paved runways or water, the triphibian gear consisted of a centreline ski beneath the hull and a small shock-absorbing swivelling skid attached to each float. The centreline ski was 12-in wide and 15-ft long with the forward 8-ft section being fixed to the keel, whereas the last 7-ft section of the ski was hinged at its forward end and fitted with a shock-absorbing strut at its aft end. Most Triphibian SA-16As were fitted with the full ski/skid equipment (the so-called winter configuration) but later Triphibian SA-16As were delivered in the summer configuration with only the forward fixed element of the ventral ski and the attachments for the float skids.

The first SA-16A was the first production Albatross and was flown on 20 July, 1949. A total of 290 SA-16As were delivered to the USAF between July 1949 and December 1953 and were assigned Air Force serial numbers (48-588/48-607, 49-069/49-100, 50-172/50-182, 51-001/51-071, 51-471/51-476, 51-5278/51-5306, 51-7140/51-7255, and 52-136/52-137). Three were built under MDAP contracts and delivered to Portugal (51-5277 and 51-15270/51-15271). In addition, fifteen aircraft ordered as SA-16As and assigned Air Force serial numbers 52-121/52-135 were transferred to the Coast Guard before completion and delivered as UF-1Gs (USCG serials 2121 to 2135). Air Force serial numbers 60-9301/60-9310 were given for administrative purposes to surplus Albatrosses of various models being transferred to foreign air forces under MDAP.

SA-16B (HU-16B): Design 111 was initiated in April 1955 to meet specific

289

A triphibian SA-16B of the 55th Air Rescue Squadron at Thule AB, Greenland, in May 1958.
(David W Menard)

operational requirements of the Air Rescue Service, and demonstrated significantly improved performance at minimum additional cost. Notably, single-engine ceiling at 29,500 lb was increased from sea level to 8,000 ft, stalling speed at the same weight was reduced from 70 kt to 64 kt, and normal range went up from 1,150 to 1,715 miles. However, this increase in range was derived only in part from aerodynamic improvements and was mainly the result of the addition of a 206-US gal fuel tank in the wing floats to bring internal capacity up from 676 to 1,088 gal. In addition, like the SA-16A, the SA-16B could carry one 295-gal drop tank beneath each wing.

Modifications incorporated in the G-111 included (1) the insertion of a 70-in panel outboard of the engine nacelles and the addition of 30-in tip extensions, thus increasing span from 80 ft to 96 ft 8 in and area from 833 sq ft to 1,035 sq ft; (2) the substitution of a cambered leading edge and chordwise high-pressure de-icing boots for the SA-16A arrangement of wing slots and spanwise boots; (3) the use of increased area ailerons fitted with a geared tab; (4) the fitting of broader-chord horizontal tail surfaces with span increased from 29 ft to 31 ft; and (5) the heightening of the vertical surfaces by 1 ft 7 in to 25 ft 10 in and the widening of the chord of the rudder. Other modifications included flush-mounting a number of high-drag antennae and making minor avionic changes.

The first Albatross to be modified to the SA-16B configuration (c/n G-267, Air Force serial 51-7200) was flown on 16 January, 1956. In addition to this prototype, Grumman's records list eighty-six SA-16As as having been brought up to SA-16B standards for the USAF, either during the course of IRAN (Inspect and Repair As Necessary) visits or during a special modification programme. In addition, five other SA-16As were modified as SA-16Bs for use in Argentina in the air rescue role and were given a separate design number, G-333.

SA-16B/ASW (SHU-16B): Development of an ASW version was initiated

290

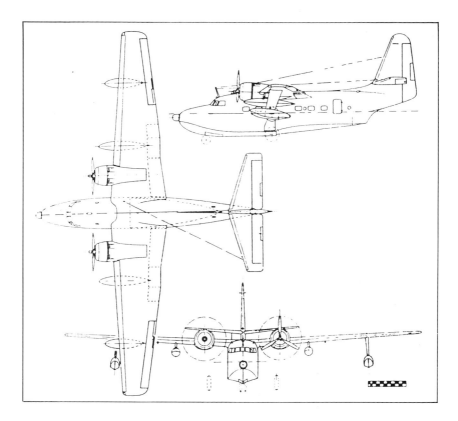

Grumman SA-16B (HU-16B) Albatross

in 1960 as part of MDAP to provide smaller air arms with a suitable replacement for the wartime Consolidated Catalina. As the number of aircraft in the programme was small, the decision was made neither to develop a new aircraft nor to build a new Albatross version, but rather to modify existing airframes and incorporate some of the features planned a few years earlier for the PF-1 version of the Albatross. The aircraft selected to serve as the SA-16B/ASW prototype, 51-070, was an Air Force SA-16B which was returned to Grumman for modification.

To suit the aircraft to the ASW role, the following systems were installed: (1) an AN/APS-88 search radar in an enlarged nose radome in place of the AN/APS-31A of the SAR version; (2) a retractable MAD (magnetic anomaly detection) boom in the aft fuselage; (3) a six-sonobuoy launcher mounted externally on the main cabin entrance door on the port side of the rear fuselage which could be swung inside to be reloaded in flight; (4) an AN/AVQ-2C searchlight beneath the starboard wing; and (5) ECM antennae housed within the wingtips. Armament, including HVAR and Zuni rockets, Mk. 43 homing torpedoes, or Mk. 54 depth charges, was to be

291

Although painted in Colombian markings, this SA-16B/ASW was not delivered to the Fuerza
Aérea Colombiana. It went instead to Chile. *(Grumman)*

hung on two racks beneath each wing. Internal ordnance carried within the fuselage as part of the ASW search equipment were a Retro-Ejector Unit for rearward ejection of marine markers and a dispenser for Signal, Underwater Sound (SUS) charges or Marine Location Markers. Storage units for sonobuoys, SUS charges, and marine markers were also provided. The crew consisted of a pilot, co-pilot, flight engineer, navigator, ASW operator, and a weapons loader.

The first SA-16B/ASW was flown by a Grumman crew on 11 May 1961. After completing company and military acceptance trials, this aircraft and a second SA-16B modified as an ASW prototype (51-048) were handed over to Patrol Squadron 31 (VP-31) at NAS North Island, California, so that the Navy could undertake operational trials before the start of delivery to five foreign customers.

Thirty-seven SA-16Bs/HU-16Bs were modified as SA-16B/ASWs (redesignated SHU-16Bs in September 1962) with the last of these aircraft being redelivered in March 1964. The SHU-16Bs were given distinct Design Numbers depending on the intended customer: twenty aircraft modified for Norway (51-040, 51-044, 51-048, 51-050, 51-060, 51-068, 51-070, 51-474, 51-5281, 51-5283, 51-5289, 51-5300, 51-7177, 51-7183, 51-5190, 51-7201/51-7204, and 51-7207) were G-251s; an additional G-251 (51-7196) was modified for Greece; the five aircraft for Chile (49-097, 49-099, 49-100, 51-014, and 51-024) were G-315s; the single G-340 (51-7191), intended for Colombia, was delivered to Chile; the three G-341s (51-038, 51-041, and 51-7174) went to Peru; and the seven G-342s (51-069, 51-7147, 51-7148, 51-7165, 51-7167, 51-7170, and 51-7172) were for Spain.

UF-1 (HU-16C): The first UF-1 utility amphibian for the Navy was the tenth production Albatross. It was first flown on 30 December, 1949, more than five months after the first SA-16A. Except for minor equipment changes, the UF-1s were similar to the SA-16As, and initial production aircraft were fitted with an AN/APS-31A search radar in a nacelle beneath the port wing whereas late production UF-1s had the radar housed in a

292

thimble radome in the nose. Like the SA-16 variants, all UF versions were powered by 1,425 hp R-1820-76A or -76B radials.

In addition to ninety-four UF-1s ordered by and delivered to the USN (BuNos 124374/124379, 131889/131913, 137899/137933, 141261/141283, and 142358/142362), five additional aircraft (BuNos 141284/141288) were ordered by the Navy as UF-1s but were delivered to the USCG as UF-1Gs (Coast Guard serials 1313/1317). Moreover, BuNos 149822/149824 and 149836 and 149837 were assigned to ex-USAF SA-16As/HU-16As being transferred to foreign air arms under Navy cognizance as part of MDAP; however, designations and BuNos were only assigned for administrative purposes and were not actually painted on these last aircraft.

UF-1G: The US Coast Guard received a total of eighty-three UF-1Gs including thirty-one ordered as such with specifications closely matching those of Navy UF-1s (USCG serials 1240/1243, 1259/1267, 1271/1280, 1293/1294, 1311, and 1313/1317), fifteen ordered by the USAF and transferred before completion (52-121/52-135 which were renumbered 2121/2135 in USCG service), and thirty-seven SA-16As (51-015/51-016, 51-026, 51-030, 51-7188, 51-7209, 51-7213/51-7216, 51-7218, 51-7223, 51-7226/51-7230, 51-7232/51-7234, 51-7236/51-7243, 51-7245/51-7251, and 51-7254/51-7255) which were transferred after first seeing service with the Air Force. In USCG service, these later aircraft used serial numbers corresponding to their Air Force serial numbers without the first digit and the hyphen (*eg*, 51-015 became 1015). The UF-1G was ordered in April 1950 and first flown in May 1951. All but five of the UF-1Gs were later brought up to UF-2G standards.

UF-1L (LU-16C): This designation identified two aircraft ordered by the USAF as SA-16As (51-7162 and 51-7164) but completed for the Navy with triphibian gear for use in Antarctica during Operation *Deep Freeze*. In USN service the two UF-1Ls were given BuNos 142428 and 142429.

BuNo 142429, a UF-1L of VXE-6 at Peoria, Illinois, during the summer of 1958. (*David H Brazelton, courtesy of David W Menard*)

UF-1T (TU-16C): Five UF-1s (BuNos 131914/131918) were specially outfitted as navigation trainers prior to completion and, designated UF-1Ts, were delivered to the US Naval Academy in Annapolis, Maryland.

UF-2 (HU-16D): The thirty-three UF-2s were generally similar to the Air Force SA-16Bs but were given a separate Design Number, G-211. In addition to these aircraft which were obtained through modification of existing UF-1s and redelivered to the Navy, eight additional aircraft were designated UF-2s (HU-16Ds after September 1962) and given BuNos 148240/148245 and 151264/151265. They apparently were ex-USAF SA-16Bs/HU-16Bs being transferred to foreign air and naval forces under MDAP; however, in this instance, designations and BuNos were only assigned for administrative purposes and were not actually painted on the aircraft. The designation UF-2 was also given to five new aircraft (BuNos146426/146430) which were built for Germany and carried the Design Number G-191. Six other new UF-2s (BuNos 148324/148329) were built for Japan under the G-262 Design Number and differed in being powered by a pair of 1,525 hp R-1820-82 radials.

UF-2G (HU-16E): This designation identified seventy-eight UF-1Gs brought up to SA-16B/UF-2 standards with longer wings and other aerodynamic improvements, as well as an ex-Air Force SA-16B (51-023) which became 1023 in USCG service. Minor equipment changes and systems improvements resulted in three batches of UF-2Gs being given distinct Design Numbers, G-234, G-270, and G-288.

UF-2S: The UF-2S designation appears to have been the Navy equivalent of the Air Force SA-16B/ASW designation, but the introduction in 1962 of the tri-Service system eliminated this possible duplication as the ASW aircraft became SHU-16Bs.

UF-XS: The UF-XS was a much modified Albatross designed in Japan as a six-engined, dynamically-similar flying scale model of the Shin Meiwa PS-1

The Shin Meiwa UF-XS research aircraft was an extensively modified Albatross (BuNo 149822). Given the JMSDF serial 9911, the UF-XS was first flown on 20 December, 1962.
(Shin Meiwa)

flying-boat. The basic airframe used by Shin Meiwa Industry to realize this research aircraft was that of BuNo 149822, an unidentified SA-16A which was given a Bureau Number before being transferred to Japan under Navy cognisance. In Japan, the hull was lengthened and given an increased length-to-beam ratio and deeper afterbody. In addition, new T-tail surfaces with swept fin and rudder were fitted and the undercarriage was removed. To achieve STOL performance, the wings were fitted with a boundary-layer control system and large leading-edge slats. The complex powerplant installation comprised two original Wright R-1820-76A radials inboard and two 600-hp Pratt & Whitney R-1340-AN-10 radials outboard, which all drove conventional propellers, and two 1,000-hp General Electric T58-GE-6 turbines in a humped fairing above the hull, which provided compressed air for the boundary-layer control system.

Given the Japanese Maritime Self Defense serial number 9911, the UF-XS was first flown on 20 December, 1962. It provided much useful data for the PS-1 programme and was later put on permanent display at Shimofusa. Quite extensively modified, it had the following principal characteristics and performance: span 80 ft 0^1/$_4$ in (24.40 m); length, 75 ft 5^1/$_2$ in (23.00 m); height 25 ft 3 in (7.70 m); basic operating weight 29,450 lb (13,400 kg); maximum take-off weight 35,495 lb (16,100 kg); and maximum speed 207 mph (333 kmh).

PF-1A: This designation was given to thirty-two patrol amphibians (BuNos 124292/124323) ordered by the USN. However, as the PF-1A would have been less well suited to maritime reconnaissance than the more powerful and better armed Martin P5M-1 Marlin, the Navy lost interest in the PF-1A and the contract was amended to have the aircraft paid for by the Air Force and delivered as SA-16As (49-069 to 49-100).

CSR-110: Except for the installation of RCAF-specified equipment and of 1,525-hp Wright R-1820-82A engines (distinguished externally by an

An SA-16A (48-606) of the Air Rescue Service, USAF. (*W J Balogh Sr, courtesy of David W Menard*)

295

additional cooling intake above the cowling), the ten G-231s ordered by Canada were essentially similar to the SA-16Bs with triphibian undercarriage. They were delivered between September 1960 and March 1961. In service with the Royal Canadian Air Force, these aircraft received the CSR-110 designation and were assigned serials 9301/9310.

Service history

First delivered in late 1949 to the Air Rescue Service at its Orlando AFB headquarters in Florida, SA-16As quickly replaced Consolidated OA-10A Catalina amphibians and supplemented other fixed-wing aircraft (Douglas SC-47s and Boeing SB-17s and SB-29s) assigned to USAF rescue units in the United States and abroad. Notably, two SA-16As were added to the inventory of the 3rd Air Rescue Squadron at Johnson AB, Japan, one month after North Korea had crossed the 38th parallel. Soon after, Albatrosses made their first combat rescue. Operating at various times from bases in Japan (Ashiya, Johnson, and Misawa) and in Korea (K-2 Taegu, K-3 Pohang, K-16 Seoul, K-24 Pyongyang, etc), the 3rd ARS was elevated to group status in November 1952 and one month later was joined by the 2nd ARG. Together these two units rescued eighty-one US and allied flyers during wartime operations. In addition, SA-16As were used by the 581st Air Resupply and Communications Wing to insert and extract special units operating behind North Korean lines.

Following the Korean Armistice, Albatrosses continued to fly peacetime air rescue missions in support of CONUS-based units and those assigned to USAFE and to Far East Air Forces (FEAF). Activities ranged from the polar regions, where Triphibian SA-16As replaced ski-equipped SC-47s, to Lebanon and Asia where SA-16As provided coverage for air transport and

An SA-16A of the 74th Air Rescue Squadron at Ladd AFB, Alaska, in May 1957. The attachments for JATO bottles partially mask the national star on the rear fuselage. (*David W Menard*)

296

An SA-16A of the 130th Air Resupply Squadron, West Virginia ANG, over Charleston, West Virginia, on 8 May, 1957. *(USAF)*

tactical aircraft during emergency operations in 1958. Moreover, SA-16As frequently rescued civilian victims, as was the case on 23 July, 1954, when an SA-16A from the 31st ARS at Clark AB in the Philippines picked up nine survivors of a Cathay Pacific Douglas DC-4 which had been shot down by Chinese fighters over international waters off the island of Hainan.

Before taking part once again in combat rescue operations, the Albatross gained additional renown when Air Force crews broke two world class records aboard an HU-16B (51-7211) of the 48th ARS in March 1963. On the 19th, the crew of Capt Glenn A Higginson flew at an average speed of 153.65 mph (247.28 kmh) over a 1,000-km (621.4-mile) course while carrying a 5,000-kg (11,023-lb) payload. Carrying the same payload, the crew of Capt Henry E Irwin climbed to a new record height of 19,747 ft (6,019 m) on the 20th.

The first HU-16Bs assigned to Southeast Asia for combat rescue operations were two aircraft from the 33rd ARS sent from Naha AB on Okinawa to Korat RTAFB in Thailand in June 1964 to be used as airborne rescue control ships during *Yankee Team* operations in Laos. Three aircraft from the 31st ARS were sent during the same month from Clark AB in the Philippines to Da Nang AB in South Vietnam for rescue duties in the Gulf of Tonkin. Replaced in 1965 in the airborne rescue control role first by Douglas HC-54s and then by Lockheed HC-130s, HU-16Bs of the 37th ARS continued to operate from Da Nang until 30 September, 1967, when the Albatross flew its last rescue sortie in Southeast Asia. Frequently hit during daring rescue operations close to North Vietnamese shores and flying under often appalling weather conditions, the HU-16Bs took exceptionally heavy losses in spite of the small number of aircraft involved in combat operations. Nine crew members were killed and four aircraft

297

were lost, two in combat and two in operational accidents. Conversely, in three years SA-16B crews saved forty-seven US airmen during combat operations over the Gulf of Tonkin.

To replace units which were relocated when their bases could not be extended for jet aircraft operations, the Air National Guard was authorized to organize four new Air Resupply Squadrons in 1955: the 129th at the Hayward Municipal Airport in California, the 130th at the Kanawha County Airport in West Virginia, the 135th at Harbor Field in Maryland, and the 143rd at the T. F. Green Airport in Rhode Island. In addition to being equipped with Curtiss C-46 Commando twin-engined transports, these squadrons received Grumman SA-16As in 1955-56. Successively redesignated Troop Carrier Squadrons (Medium), Air Commando Squadrons, and Special Operations Squadrons, these units operated Albatrosses (with HU-16Bs supplementing the HU-16As) in support of Army Special Forces and for rescue duties. The last Albatrosses in ANG service were phased out by the 143rd SOS, Rhode Island ANG, in September 1971.

With the Air Force Reserve, Albatrosses served with the 301st Air Rescue Squadron (later Aerospace Rescue and Recovery Squadron) at Homestead AFB, Florida; the 302nd ARS at Williams AFB and Luke AFB, Arizona; the 303rd ARS at the Long Beach Municipal Airport and March AFB, California; the 304th ARS in Portland, Oregon; and the 305th ARS at Selfridge AFB, Michigan. Before being retired from AFRES service, the last Air Force HU-16B (51-5282) was flown by Lt-Col C H Manning and his crew to 32,883 ft (10,022 m) to set a world altitude record without payload on 4 July, 1973. The aircraft was then sent to the Air Force Museum at Wright-Patterson AFB, Ohio.

Even though the Navy received no fewer than ninety-four UF-1s (of which thirty-three were modified as UF-2s), five UF-1Ts, and two UF-1Ls, which thirty-three were modified as UF-2s), five UF-1Ts, and two UF-1Ls, the only Albatrosses known to have carried squadron markings were the two UF-1Ls which were operated by Antarctic Development Squadron Six (VXE-6) and two SA-16B/ASWs which were temporarily assigned to Patrol Squadron Thirty-one (VP-31) for operational testing before delivery to Norway. Mainly, the Navy assigned its Albatrosses to Naval Air Stations in the continental United States, Alaska, Guam, Hawaii, Kwajalein, Midway, and Puerto Rico and to Naval Stations abroad (Lajes, Azores; Bermuda; Guantanamo Bay, Cuba; Reykjavik, Iceland; Sigonella, Italy; Iwakuni and Oppama, Japan; Port Lyautey, Morocco; Argentia, Newfoundland; Naha, Okinawa; Cubi Point, the Philippines; and Rota, Spain) where they were used as general utility aircraft. Similar duties were performed by Albatrosses assigned to seaplane tenders, Fleet Aircraft Services Squadrons (FASRONs), and to various headquarters (eg ASWLANT). At least one HU-16C (137927) was used by the Naval Test Pilot School at Patuxent River, Maryland, to provide students with some flying boat/amphibian experience while at the same location other Albatrosses were used as utility aircraft by the Naval Air Test Center. Other UF-1s and UF-2s (respectively

A civil-registered Albatross repainted as a utility aircraft from NAS Guantanamo Bay, Cuba. It was photographed at Clear Lake, California, in September 1988. *(Peter B Lewis)*

HU-16Cs and HU-16Ds after September 1962) were assigned to Naval Attachés in Greece, Indonesia, Norway, and Peru. The UF-1Ts (TU-16Cs) were assigned to the Naval Academy in Annapolis, Maryland, to provide air navigation training and familiarization flights for midshipmen. The UF-1Ls (LU-16Cs) were operated by VXE-6 in support of Operation *Deep Freeze* in Antarctica. The last UF-2 was flown from Guantanamo Bay to Pensacola on 13 August, 1976.

Altogether, the United States Coast Guard operated eighty-three UF-1Gs and seventy-eight of these Albatrosses were modified as UF-2Gs before being redesignated HU-16Es in 1962. The first UF-1G (serial 1240) was delivered in April 1951 and the last HU-16E (serial 7250, ex SA-16A 51-7250) was retired at Cape Cod, Massachusetts, in March 1983. In the intervening years, Albatrosses flew rescue, fishery patrol, and pollution surveillance missions from Coast Guard Air Stations in Alaska (Annette and Kodiak), California (San Diego, San Francisco, and Sacramento), Florida (Miami and St Petersburg), Hawaii (Barber's Point), Massachusetts (Cape Cod), Michigan (Traverse City), Mississippi (Biloxi), Oregon (Salem), Texas (Corpus Christi), Puerto Rico (San Juan), Washington (Port Angeles), and the Philippines (Sangley Point). In addition to their regular duties, Coast Guard Albatrosses were often flown as transports for the benefit of various government agencies and VIPs. An HU-16E (7246) was

299

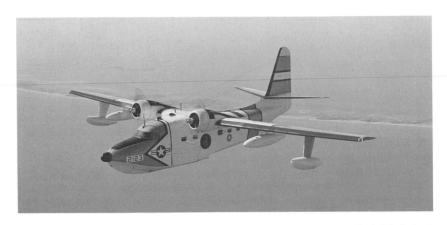

HU-16E (USCG 2123, ex-USAF 52-123) assigned to the USCG Station at Biloxi, Mississippi, over the Gulf of Mexico. *(USCG)*

modified in 1975 to test the AOSS (Airborne Oil Spill Surveillance) system with a SLAR (Side-Looking Airborne Radar) housed in a fairing on the rear of the starboard hull side and with other pollution detection equipment mounted in the bow, in a nacelle attached beneath the cockpit on the port side, and in a modified external tank beneath the starboard wing.

Whereas their numerous humanitarian deeds mostly went unheralded, Coast Guard and Navy Albatross crews received more attention when in August and September 1962 they broke seven world class records for amphibians. On 13 August, Cdr W C Dahlgreen, USCG, and his crew flew at an average speed of 373.22 km/h (231.96 mph) over a 1,000 km (621.5 miles) course to break records without payload and with 1,000-kg (2,205-lb) and 2,000-kg (4,409-lb) payloads. On 11 September, it was the turn of the crews commanded by Lt-Cdr D E Moore, USN, to set a new altitude record of 8,984 m (29,475-ft) with a 1,000-kg payload, and for Lt-Cdr F A W Franke, Jr, and his Navy crew to break that with a 2,000-kg payload by reaching 8,353 m (27,405 ft). On 16 September, Lt-Cdr R A Hoffman, USN, and his crew set a new world speed record over a 5,000-km (3,107.5-miles) course by flying at an average speed of 243.59 km/h (151.39 mph) while carrying a 1,000-kg payload. Finally, Cdr W Fenlon, USCG, and his crew flew 5,746.78 km (3,571.65 miles) on 25 October, 1962, to set a new straight-line distance record without payload. With the exception of this straight-line distance record, which entailed a flight from NAS Kodiak, Alaska, to NAS Pensacola, Florida, all record flights were flown at Floyd Bennett Field, NAS New York. The record aircraft was an UF-2G (USCG 7255 which was redesignated HU-16E before setting the last record) which took off on land and alighted on water as required for FAI homologation.

In addition to twenty-nine aircraft built by Grumman for export to Canada, Germany, Indonesia, and Japan, large numbers of Albatrosses were either transferred to foreign military forces by the United States or

300

USCG 7209, a HU-16E assigned to the USCG Station at Port Angeles, Washington, passing Mt Rainier in March 1970. *(USCG)*

specially rebuilt for foreign governments by Grumman. More than thirty years after the first export UF-1s were delivered, small numbers of military Albatrosses remained operational in Greece, Mexico, and the Philippines.

ARGENTINA: Under a Military Assistance Program contract issued in 1961, Grumman modified five ex-USAF SA-16As to a modified SA-16B configuration (Design Number 333). Three of these aircraft were delivered to the Fuerza Aérea Argentina (Argentine Air Force) and the two others (later supplemented by two SA-16Bs transferred directly by the USAF) went to the Servicio de Aviación Naval. In naval service, the Argentine Albatrosses were first operated by the Escuela Aeronaval de Búsqueda y Salvamento at BAN Punta del Indio and were later operated by the 2ª Escuadrilla Aeronaval de Propósitos Generales at BAN Comandante Espora until withdrawn from use in 1978. With the Fuerza Aérea Argentina, the three Albatrosses were used by the Escuadrón de Búsqueda y Salvamento at BAM El Palomar (Buenos Aires) and by LADE (Líneas Aéreas del Estado, the military airline operating with military cockpit crews and civil cabin crews) for service to Port Stanley in the Falklands. Two of the FAA aircraft were fitted with triphibian gear and were also operated at one point by FATA (Fuerza Aérea de Tareas Antárticas) for service between Rio Gallegos and two Antarctic bases, BAM Vice-Comodoro Marambio and BAM Benjamin Matienzo. The last Argentine Albatross was withdrawn from use in the early 1980s.

BRAZIL: Fourteen SA-16As were transferred from the USAF in 1959. In service with the Força Aérea Brasileira (FAB or Brazilian Air Force), these aircraft were successively given the designation A-16, U-16, M-16,

301

and S-16 and were assigned Brazilian serials 6530/6543. The last S-16s were phased out by the 2°/10°GAv (2° Esquadrão, 10° Grupo de Aviação) of the Serviço de Busca e Salvamento (Search and Rescue Service) at Florianopolis in August 1980.

CANADA: Ten new G-231s with airframes similar to those of SA-16Bs but fitted with triphibian undercarriages and powered by R-1820-82s were delivered to the Royal Canadian Air Force in 1960-61. Dispersed to Greenwood in Nova Scotia, Trenton in Ontario, Winnipeg in Manitoba, and Comox in British Columbia, they remained in service with the Canadian Armed Forces until 1971.

CHILE: The Fuerza Aérea de Chile (Chilean Air Force) received three ex-USAF SA-16As (49-097, 49-099, and 49-100) in 1958 and subsequently had them brought up to the SA-16B/ASW configuration. It also obtained three additional SHU-16Bs (51-014, 51-024, and 51-7191) in 1963. Numbered 566 to 571, these six ASW aircraft were operated until 1979 by Grupo No. 2 at Santiago-Los Cerrillos.

The Servicio de Aviación Naval de Chile (Chile's Naval Aviation Service) received four ex-Canadian Armed Forces CSR-110s (9301/9303 and 9310) in 1971. These aircraft were used in the SAR role until the late 1970s. Two were later resold to Grumman and modified in St Augustine, Florida, before going to Malaysia.

COLOMBIA: One SA-16B/ASW (51-7191) was modified for Colombia and was painted in the markings of the Fuerza Aérea Colombiana (Colombian Air Force) but was not taken on charge by this air force. The aircraft became the sixth Chilean SHU-16B.

GERMANY: Five G-191s were ordered by Germany in 1956 and, built to a standard corresponding to that of the UF-2, were delivered in 1958-59. Given BuNos 146426/146430 for contractual purposes, these five aircraft were numbered SC501/SC505 before entering service with the Marine Seenotstaffel at Kiel. The German Albatross were first renumbered RE501/RE505 and, after being supplemented by three ex-USAF SA-16As (49-088,

The first German G-191 before its delivery to the Marine Seenotstaffel at Kiel in December 1958. (*Grumman*)

302

A UF-1 of the Tentara Nasional Indonesia - Angkatan Udara (TNI-AU, Indonesian National Armed Forces - Air Force). (*Grumman*)

49-095, and 49-096 which became RE506/RE508 and then 6001/6003 in Bundesmarine service) became 6004/6008. They last served with a staffel of Marinefliegergeschwader 5 (MFG5) before being sold as surplus in 1972.

GREECE: A single SA-16B/ASW (51-044) was modified for Greece and was joined in 1970 by eleven ex-Norwegian SHU-16Bs (51-068, 51-070, 51-5289, 51-7177, 51-7183, 51-7196, 51-7201/51-7204, and 51-7207) and still later by an ex-Spanish SHU-16B (51-5283). In addition, Greece received an HU-16C (ex-BuNo 137909) and possibly an HU-16D (ex-BuNo137915) to be used as sources of spares for its SHU-16Bs. In 1988, the surviving SHU-16Bs of the Hellinikí Aeroporía (Greek Air Force) were still operated by 353 Mira at Elefsís.

ICELAND: Íslenska Landhelgisgaeslan (the Icelandic Coast Guard) obtained two HU-16Cs (c/ns G-368 and G-423, BuNos 142361 and 141276) on lease in 1969, but the Albatross was not adopted as a Service type.

INDONESIA: First export customer to order new Albatrosses from Grumman, the Tentara Nasional Indonesia - Angkatan Udara (TNI-AU or Indonesian National Armed Forces - Air Force) received eight aircraft in 1957-58. Assigned serials PB 517/PB 524, these aircraft were similar to late production UF-1s of the US Navy. They were later supplemented by two ex-USN UF-2s (BuNos 137907 and 142359), four ex-German G-191s (German serials 6005/6008), and one ex-Japanese G-262 (JMSDF serial 9056 which had earlier been modified as a civil G-111 and registered in Indonesia as PK-PAM). Some of these aircraft were later transferred to the Tentara Nasional Indonesia - Angkatan Laut (TNI-AL or Indonesian National Armed Forces - Naval Aviation). Apparently, the five surviving Indonesian Albatrosses were last operated in 1987.

ITALY: The Aeronautica Militare Italiana (AMI or Italian Air Force) received six ex-USAF SA-16As (with US serials 50-174, 50-175, 50-177, 50-179, 50-180, and 50-182 prefixed by MM, Matricola Militare, in Italian service) in 1958 to replace Cant Z.506 floatplanes of the Comando Soccorso Aereo (140ª Squadriglia, 84º Gruppo) at Vigna di Valle. In 1965, when it became part of the 15º Stormo, the 84º Gruppo took delivery of six additional HU-16As (51-035, 51-037, 51-7157, 51-7175, 51-7252, and 51-7253). By the mid-1970s, the Italian Albatrosses were coming to the end of their useful life and were increasingly difficult to maintain. Withdrawal began in 1976, and the last five HU-16As were struck off charge three years later.

JAPAN: Six G-262s (UF-2s built for Japan and powered by 1,525-hp R-1820-82s) were delivered to the Nihon Kaijyo Jieitai (JMSDF or Japanese Maritime Self-Defence Force) in 1961. Assigned BuNos

The fifth G-262 for the Nihon Kaijyo Jieitai (JMSDF), seen off Long Island before delivery.
(Grumman)

148324/148329 for contractual purposes, they were numbered JMSDF 9051/9056 before delivery. They were operated by the Omura Kokutai until 1976 when the five survivors were sold and then modified in the United States as civil G-111s. In 1963-64, the Omura Kokutai also undertook operational evaluation of the unique UF-XS research flying-boat.

MALAYSIA: Two Albatrosses were refurbished by Grumman in St Augustine, Florida, before being delivered in 1986 to the Tentera Udara Diraja Malaysia (TUDM or Royal Malaysian Air Force) and received the Malaysian military serials M35-01 and M35-02. Both were ex-Canadian CSR-110s (RCAF serials 9303 and 9310) which had also served in Chile. The first was fitted with an executive interior for use by the Prime Minister and the other was delivered without interior furnishing.

An ex-Canadian Armed Forces CSR-110 refurbished by Grumman for the Aviación de la Armada Mexicana. (*Grumman*)

A refurbished Albatross before delivery to the 27th SAR and Reconnaissance Squadron of the Philippine Air Force at Sangley Point. (*Grumman*)

MEXICO: The Aviación de la Armada Mexicana (Mexican Naval Aviation) first obtained four ex-Canadian CSR-110s (9305, 9306, 9307, and 9309 which after being refurbished by Grumman became MP-101/MP-104) in 1974. They were later supplemented by nine ex-USN HU-16Cs (BuNos 137913, 137914, 137917, 137920, 141270, 141273, 141274, 141280, and 141283) and one more ex-Canadian aircraft (9308 which earlier had been refurbished as a civil G-111). These aircraft were used to equip the 3º Escuadrón Aeronaval with detachments at Ensenada and La Paz. This unit still had some Albatrosses on strength in 1988.

NORWAY: Kongelige Norske Luftforsvaret (Royal Norwegian Air Force) was the largest operator of SHU-16Bs and received twenty of these ASW amphibians to equip Skv 330 at Bodø and Skv 333 at Andoya. In 1969, when Luftforsvaret replaced its SHU-16Bs with Lockheed P-3Bs and Westland Sea Kings, ten went to Greece, six to Spain, and two to Peru.

PAKISTAN: Four ex-USAF SA-16As were delivered in 1958 to the Pakistan Fiza'ya (Pakistan Air Force). They were operated first by No. 12 (Composite) Squadron and then by No. 4 Squadron until phased out during the early 1970s.

PERU: Three SHU-16Bs (51-038, 51-041, and 51-7174) were delivered to the Fuerza Aérea Peruana (Peruvian Air Force) in 1963 and were supplemented in 1970 by two ex-Norwegian aircraft (51-048 and 51-050). They were operated in the ASW role by Grupo 4 from Lima-Callao for some twenty years.

PHILIPPINES: The Philippine Air Force has over the years received twelve Albatrosses including four ex-USAF SA-16As (48-589, 48-599, 48-605, and 48-607) delivered in the mid-1950s and supplemented in the

Bearing the Spanish serial AN1-B-12, this SHU-16B (ex-51-5295) of Escuadrón 221 had previously been operated by Kongelige Norske Luftforsvaret. (*Ejercito del Aire, courtesy of Christian Boisselon*)

1970s by four ex-USAF HU-16Bs (51-019, 51-473, 51-7151, and 51-7184), two ex-USCG HU-16Es (1267 and 7248), and two ex-USN HU-16Cs (BuNos 137906 and 137922). Although serviceability was low in 1988, some of these aircraft were still on strength with the 27th SAR and Reconnaissance Squadron at Sangley Point.

PORTUGAL: Under MDAP the Força Aérea Portuguesa (FAP or Portuguese Air Force) received three SA-16As (51-5277, 51-15270, and 51-15271). They served alongside Boeing SB-17Gs and Douglas SC-54Ds with Esquadra 4 at Base Aérea 4 (Lajes) in the Azores until phased out of service in 1962.

SPAIN: The five SA-16As (49-091, 49-092, 49-098, 52-136, and 52-137) supplied to the Ejército del Aire (EdA or Spanish Air Force) under MDAP in 1954 were supplemented in the early 1960s by seven HU-16As and HU-16Bs including one and possibly three ex-Portuguese HU-16As. In Spanish service these aircraft were numbered 1 to 12 with the SA-16As/ HU-16As prefixed by AD.1 (*eg*, AD.1-1 which formerly was 52-136) and the HU-16Bs prefixed AD.1B (*eg*, AD.1B-12, ex 51-7182). They were assigned to units of the Servicio de Búsqueda y Salvamento at Son San Juan in Palma de Mallorca (Escuadrilla 55 which was redesignated Escuadrón 55 in 1963 and Escuadrón 801 in 1967) and at Gando in the Canary Islands (Escuadrilla 56, then Escuadrón 56 and Escuadrón 802). They were replaced by CASA 212s in the late 1970s.

For ASW duty, in 1963 EdA received seven SHU-16Bs from the United States (51-069, 51-7147, 51-7148, 51-7165, 51-7167, 51-7170, and 51-7172 which became AN.1A-1 to AN.1A-7) and in 1969 obtained six ex-Norwegian aircraft (which became AN.1A-8 to AN.1A-13). These aircraft were based at Jerés de la Frontera and were operated by the Ala de Cooperación Aeronaval 61 (Escuadrón 611 which was renumbered

N9944F, an ex-Air Force SA-16A operated by Transocean Airlines on behalf of the US Department of the Interior in the Trust Territory of the Pacific. (*Grumman*)

Escuadrón 206 in 1967 and Escuadrón 211 in 1973). The SHU-16Bs were phased out in 1978.

TAIWAN: Having received its first ex-USAF SA-16As in 1958 and replacing its last HU-16Bs with Sikorsky S-70C helicopters in 1987-88, the Republic of China Air Force (formerly the Chinese Nationalist Air Force) operated Albatrosses for three decades. Over the years, fourteen SA-16As (one of which was shot down by a People's Republic of China MiG in January 1966 during a rescue operations off the island of Matsu) and at least three HU-16Bs were transferred to the CNAF/RoCAF and were operated in the SAR role from Chiayi.

THAILAND: Two ex-USAF HU-16Bs were delivered in 1968 under MDAP to the Royal Thai Navy via the USN as BuNos 151264/151265. They were used for search and rescue until 1981.

VENEZUELA: Six unidentified ex-USAF HU-16As are believed to have been operated by the Servicio de Aviación de la Marina Venezolana (Aviation Service of the Venezuelan Navy) for nearly two decades. The last were phased out in 1982.

Civil Guardians

Even though no allowances were made in its design for commercial requirements, the Albatross nevertheless had a civil career which spanned a third of a century. This career began in 1955 when the ninth, eleventh, and twentieth aircraft (48-596, 48-597, and 48-603) were transferred by the Air Force to the Department of the Interior to provide air services in the Caroline, Marianas (excluding Guam), and Marshall Islands. Collectively known as the Trust Territory of the Pacific and comprised of more than

Photographed on 10 January, 1973, at the Military Aircraft Storage & Disposition Center, Davis-Monthan AFB, Arizona, this HU-16B had previously been operated by Pan American Airways to link the satellite tracking station in the Seychelles with Mombassa in Kenya. (*Ben Knowles, courtesy of Alain Pelletier*)

2,000 islands in the western Pacific, the US-administered area was first served in 1949 by Transocean Airlines under contract from the Department of Interior with converted Consolidated PBY-5 Catalina amphibians. Modified to carry fifteen passengers, the three Albatrosses replaced Catalinas in the autumn of 1955. Less than five years later, Transocean Airlines went bankrupt and the Trust Territory Air Services and its three converted Albatrosses were taken over by Pan American World Airways. The construction on several Micronesian islands of airports suitable for jet operations and the award of a contract to Air Micronesia in 1968 finally ended Albatross commercial operations in the western Pacific. During the late 1960s and early '70s, Pan American again operated Albatrosses on contract from the US Government when the airline provided a weekly service linking the satellite tracking station in the Seychelles with Mombassa in Kenya. Bearing the Pan American logo but retaining their Air Force serials, the HU-16Bs used until the end of 1972 on that unusual route were successively 51-7163 and 51-7219.

In the Caribbean, where other ex-military HU-16s were apparently used for drug smuggling, four civilianized Albatrosses were used briefly by Antilles Air Boats to supplement Grumman Goose twin-engined amphibians and a Sikorsky VS-44 four-engined flying-boat during part of the 1970s. Following a 1979 agreement providing for the acquisition of Antilles Air Boats by Resorts International, these aircraft joined others which were being modified by Grumman to the specifications of Resorts International and its division, Chalks International Airlines of Miami, Florida. The extensive modification programme involved four phases: inspection and replacement to obtain a zero-time airframe; overhaul and modification of the military engines for FAA-certification as 1,475-hp Wright 982C9HE3 radials driving auto-feathering propellers; installation of twenty-eight non-reclinable passenger seats; and modernization of the aircraft's cockpit and instrumentation. The first of these commercial Albatrosses flew on 13

N112FB, a G-111 of Chalk International Airlines, Miami, was an ex-JMSDF G-262 (c/n 463, Japanese serial 9055). *(Grumman)*

309

February, 1979, and, like the next five, was modified by Grumman in Stuart, Florida, whereas the last seven were modified in St Augustine, Florida. Even though all were referred to as G-111s, the modified Albatrosses were in fact ex-Japanese G-262s (c/n 463, ex-JMSDF 9055, which became N112FB; c/n 464, ex 9056, N114FB; c/n 462, ex 9054, N115FB; c/n 460, ex 9052, N116FB; and c/n 461, ex 9053, N117FB), ex-Canadian G-231s (c/n 452, ex-RCAF 9304, N118FB and c/n 456, ex 9308, N119FB), ex-USAF HU-16Bs (51-7168, N122FB; 51-7243, N120FB; 51-7244, N113FB; and 51-7249, N121FB), or ex-USN HU-16Ds (BuNo 137901, N124FB and BuNo 141282, N125FB). One of these aircraft, N114FB, was repurchased by Grumman and sold to Pelita Air Services as PK-PAM to provide offshore oil platform support for Conoco in Indonesia. The remaining 'G-111s' were again offered for sale in 1988.

Grumman St Augustine Corporation had anticipated a strong market for civilianized Albatrosses and by early 1983 had acquired fifty-seven aircraft through US surplus sales, from a broker, and from Chile. Unfortunately, many of these aircraft were damaged during a desert storm before being taken out of the Military Aircraft Storage & Disposition Center at Davis-Monthan AFB, Arizona, and had to be scrapped; the others were then stored at the nearby Bob's Air Park. However, the market for converted aircraft did not materialize and the only other Albatrosses modified in St Augustine have been two for the Government of Malaysia and two for the Smithsonian Institution. The latter (N693S and N695S which were ex UF-2s, BuNos 141266 and 146426) were used for four years for an exploration project sponsored by the Coral Reef Museum of Natural History and for a geological survey of the coast of Labrador. Those for Malaysia are described under Service History. The HU-16s stored for

Still bearing the Rescue tail stripe as applied while serving with the Aerospace Rescue and Recovery Service, this HU-16B was operated by the 354th TFW at Korat RTAFB for R&R (rest and recuperation) flights to the Thai coast during the early 1970s. The diagonal stripes on the forward hull are in the colours used for the wing's emblem, azure, or, vert, and gules.
(*Norman E Taylor, courtesy of David W Menard*)

Grumman St Augustine Corporation at Bob's Air Park were sold to Jim Robinson of Hollywood, Florida. After forming Island Flying Boats, Robinson then offered Albatrosses for sale and in 1988 advertised an inventory of thirty-three of these amphibians. In mid-1989, most of these aircraft were in open storage at the Pinal County Air Park in Arizona.

Propeller-turbine conversion was long thought to offer exceptional potential to extend the useful life of the Albatross. In fact, as long ago as 1957, Grumman had proposed to the Air Force a development of the SA-16B with 2,200-shp Lycoming T55 propeller-turbines and in 1961 had offered to the Navy a UF-2 version to be powered by 2,850-shp General Electric T64s, but neither Service was interested. For the next twenty years various propeller-turbine-powered Albatross developments were elaborated by Grumman (including a version with four Pratt & Whitney T74s and one with two Garrett TPE331s) and by other contractors, but the only one which reached the hardware stage was the Conroy Turbo Albatross. Using a surplus SA-16A airframe (c/n G-77, ex 51-004 and N459U) as a prototype, Conroy Aircraft Corporation in Santa Barbara, California, installed two 1,740-ehp Rolls-Royce Dart R.Da.6 Mk. 510 engines. The engine nacelles, which came from a Vickers Viscount, were canted 3 degrees down and 5 degrees outboard to compensate for the increased thrust during single-engine operations. Registered N16CA, the Turbo Albatross prototype first flew on 25 February, 1970, but remained without progeny.

PRODUCTION: A total of 466 Albatrosses was built by Grumman between September 1947 and May 1961 as follows:

2	XJR2F-1
94	UF-1 (HU-16C)
46	UF-1G
5	UF-1T (TU-16C)
5	G-191 (UF-2 for Germany)
6	G-262 (UF-2 for Japan)
290	SA-16A (HU-16A)
8	UF-1 (with Indonesian serials)
10	G-231 (CSR-110)

They were assigned the following BuNos and military serials:

XJR2F-1:	BuNos 82853/82854
UF-1 (HU-16C):	BuNos 124374/124379, 131889/131913, 137899/137933, 141261/141283, and 142358/142362
UF-1G:	USCG serials 1240/1243, 1259/1267, 1271/1280, 1293/1294, 1311, 1313/1317, and 2121/2135
UF-1T (TU-16C):	BuNos 131914/131918
Indonesian UF-1:	Indonesian military serials PB 517/PB 524
G-191 (German UF-2):	SC-101/SC-105 (BuNos 146426/146430)

Grumman G-262 Albatross (JMSDF serial 9065, ex-BuNo 148329) of the Omura Kokutai Japanese Maritime Self-Defense Force. *(JMSDF courtesy of the Japanese Defense & Naval Attaché in Washington)*

G-262 (Japanese UF-2):	9051/9056 (BuNos 148324/148329)
SA-16A (HU-16A):	AF 48-588/48-607, 49-069/49-100, 50-172/50-182,51-001/51-071, 51-471/51-476, 51-5278/51-5306,51-7140/51-7255, 51-15270/51-15271, and 52-136/52-137
CSR-110:	Canadian military serials 9301/9310

	SA-16A	HU-16B
DIMENSIONS:		
Span, ft in	80 0	96 8
(m)	(24.38)	(29.46)
Length, ft in	60 8	62 10
(m)	(18.49)	(19.15)
Height, ft in	24 3	25 10
(m)	(7.39)	(7.87)
Wing area, sq ft	833	1,035
(sq m)	(77.39)	(96.15)
WEIGHTS:		
Empty, lb	20,815	22,883
(kg)	(9,442)	(10,380)
Loaded, lb	28,670	30,353
(kg)	(13,004)	(13,768)
Maximum, lb [water operations]	29,500	34,000
(kg)	(13,381)	(15,422)
Maximum, lb [land operations]	33,000	37,500
(kg)	(14,969)	(17,010)
Wing loading,* lb/sq ft	34.4	29.3
(kg/sq m)	(168.0)	(143.2)
Power loading,* lb/hp	10.1	10.7
(kg/hp)	(4.6)	(4.8)

PERFORMANCE:

Max speed, mph/ft	238/s.l.	236/s.l.
(kmh/m)	(383/s.l.)	(380/s.l.)
Cruising speed, mph	150	171
(kmh)	(241)	(275)
Climb rate, ft/min	1,430/1	1,170/1
(m/sec)	(7.3)	(5.9)
Service ceiling, ft	24,800	23,500
(m)	(7,560)	(7,165)
Normal range, miles	1,150	1,715
(km)	(1,850)	(2,760)
Max range, miles	2,680	3,465
(km)	(4,310)	(5,575)

* Wing and power loadings are calculated at normal loaded weight and maximum take-off power.

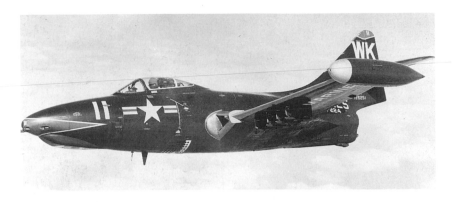

F9F-5 (BuNo 126251) of VMF-224 based at MCAS El Toro, California, in 1956. *(USMC)*

Grumman F9F (F-9) Panther

As its manufacturing and enginering teams were busy during the war with production of the much needed F6F and with the development of the high performance but still piston-powered XF7F and XF8F and as its chairman and president, Roy Grumman, gave priority to the F8F over jet propulsion studies, the Bethpage manufacturer was almost left out of the development of jet fighters. First, BuAer selected the less busy McDonnell team to develop the first Navy jet, the XFD-1, ordered in January 1943. Then the next Navy contracts for jet fighters went to the larger Vought and North American teams, with the single-engined XF6U-1 and XFJ-1 being ordered respectively on 29 December, 1944, and 1 January, 1945, and to the experienced McDonnell team, with the twin-engined XF2H-1 being ordered on 2 March, 1945. Thus, it was only on 22 April, 1946, five years after the Heinkel He 280 had become the world's first turbojet powered aircraft to fly, that Grumman finally obtained a contract for a prototype of the two-seat, four-jet XF9F-1 night fighter. However, even then, fate was not kind to Grumman. The XF9F-1 (Design 75) remained unbuilt and the first jet to fly at Bethpage, the prototype of the single-seat, single-jet XF9F-2 day fighter (Design 79), only did so on 21 November, 1947. For the US Navy, however, the resulting Panther was well worth the long wait as the F9F-2 and F9F-5 were the best of the first generation of naval jet fighters.

Between July 1943 and November 1944 Grumman had half-heartedly undertaken preliminary work on various designs powered by either a combination of piston engines and turbojets, turbojets only, or propeller-turbines. The G-57 was an all-new design initiated in July 1943 which was to have been powered by an R-2800 and a small turbojet while the G-61, on which work began during the following month, was a derivative of

314

BuNo 123564, the 215th F9F-2, in an experimental two-tone finish applied in 1950. *(Grumman)*

the F6F with an auxiliary turbojet in the tail. However, work on these two projects was almost immediately abandoned in favour of the G-58 (XF8F-1). The G-67, a derivative of the F7F-2 proposed in July 1944 with an auxiliary turbojet mounted in the rear of both piston engine nacelles, was also rejected by BuAer. The G-63 and G-71 were small single-jet designs on which work had started respectively in August 1943 and November 1944 but which also failed to generate interest. Similarly, work on the G-68 single-seat fighter design with a TG-100 propeller-turbine was terminated almost immediately after being started in June 1944.

Work on the G-75 was begun in September 1945 in answer to a Navy RFP for a jet-powered, two-seat, carrier-borne night fighter capable of detecting enemy aircraft flying at 500 mph and 40,000 ft from a distance of 125 miles. The resulting four-engined design, as described in Appendix B, was submitted in competition with proposals from Curtiss, Douglas, and Fleetwings. BuAer's evaluation led to the award to Grumman on 11 April, 1946, of a letter of intent for two XF9F-1s as back-ups for three XF3D-1s which had been ordered from Douglas eight days earlier. On the basis of additional design data submitted during the summer of 1946, the larger and heavier Grumman design was judged less promising than its Douglas competitor and in August the Navy was ready to cancel the XF9F-1 contract. Fortunately for Grumman, preliminary design work on a single-seat jet fighter had been initiated in Bethpage a month before the two night fighter jet prototypes had been ordered, and the resulting G-79 was sufficiently promising for Grumman to convince the Navy to revise the existing contract rather than cancel it outright.

As first informally proposed to the Navy in June 1946, Design 79 was planned to be powered by either a 3,750 to 4,000-lb thrust US-designed centrifugal-flow turbojet, such as the Allison J33 or the General Electric J35, with wing root intakes and a single exhaust beneath the rear fuselage, or by two wing-mounted 3,000-lb thrust Westinghouse J34 axial flow turbojets or Rolls-Royce Derwent centrifugal-flow turbojets. Alternatively, during the early summer of 1946, Grumman proposed the use of a 5,000-lb thrust Rolls-Royce Nene centrifugal-flow turbojet which Taylor Turbine Corporation was proposing to build under licence in the United States. However, when the XF9F-1 contract was amended on 9 October to provide for the construction of three single-seat prototypes (BuNos 122475/122477), a static-test airframe, and design data for a swept-wing version, the Navy was not yet ready to make an engine selection. BuAer considered the Nene to be the most promising powerplant but was concerned that the newly-organized Taylor Turbine Corporation would not be able to produce enough engines in a timely fashion. Thus, while encouraging Taylor Turbine Corporation to negotiate an agreement by which the Nene manufacturing licence would be transferred to one of the three leading American engine manufacturers*, the Navy specified in November 1946 that two of the G-79 prototypes should be completed as XF9F-2s and powered by imported Nene turbojets and that the third should be powered by an Allison J33 and designated XF9F-3.

By the time the XF9F-2/XF9F-3 mock-up was inspected in January and February 1947, Design 79 had been revised with the cockpit being moved further aft, the exhaust extended aftward, and the tail surfaces redesigned.

---

* On 30 June, 1946, the Naval Air Material Command ordered from Rolls-Royce two Nene turbojets for testing at the Aeronautical Engine Laboratory in Philadelphia. One of these engines completed its Navy 150-hour test at 4,500 lb of thrust in December of that year. Although Taylor Turbine Corporation and Rolls-Royce had signed a licensing agreement on 8 August, 1946, Pratt and Whitney started negotiations in April 1947 to take over manufacturing and sales rights and received a letter of intent from the US Navy on 29 May for production of J42 engines. Pratt & Whitney received the drawings from Rolls-Royce on 15 July and immediately after began redesigning the accessory section of the Nene to use standard American accessories and replace the Lucas fuel control system with a Bendix unit designed to Navy standards. As the J42 was not going to be ready in time to be installed in the XF9F-2 prototypes, Taylor Turbine Corporation supplied six imported Rolls-Royce Nene turbojets to Grumman. Pratt & Whitney first ran an experimental J42 in March 1948, completed the first production engine on 23 September, and went on to build a total of 1,139 J42-P-4s, -6s, and -8s between March 1948 and June 1951 for installation in F9F-2s and re-engined F9F-3s.

The first XF9F-2 (BuNo 122475), with speed brakes partially deployed. (*Grumman, courtesy of Dave Anderton*)

No major changes resulted from the mock-up inspection and the first Nene-powered XF9F-2 prototype (BuNo 122475) was ready to begin engine ground running tests in October 1947. A first flight attempt in mid-November was abandoned after the aircraft got stuck in the mud when test pilot Corwin H 'Corky' Meyer taxied through a grassy area in his haste to get to the runway. BuNo 122475 then spent a few days in the shops to be cleaned and checked before the next attempt. At last the first take-off was made in Bethpage on 21 November and Corky Meyer made a precautionary landing on a long runway at Idlewild Airport in New York as the runway at the plant was considered too short for the first landing of a Grumman jet.

During company and Navy trials, the two XF9F-2s and the XF9F-3 (first flown on 16 August, 1948) were found to snake markedly at all speeds and to be unstable longitudinally at low speed. The first problem was partially eradicated by increasing the area of the fin and rudder; the other was cured by adding baffles in the fuel tanks. Trials also revealed the need for strengthening the rear fuselage as one of the prototypes had shed its tail during an arrested landing at NATC Patuxent River. Moreover, during trials the Panther was found to have a rather high stalling speed for a carrier-based aircraft in spite of the use of leading-edge flaps. Notwithstanding these problems and shortcomings, the Panther was better in most respects than jet fighters previously evaluated at the NATC and hence was accepted for service use in both its Nene-powered F9F-2 and J33-powered F9F-3 variants.

Engine development and production problems delayed the initial flight of the first production F9F-2 and F9F-3 respectively until August 1949 and January 1949. By then Grumman had received two production contracts, one for nine F9F-2s and twenty-one F9F-3s and one for thirty-eight F9F-2s and thirty-three F9F-3s. Later contracts brought total production to 1,385 Panthers in the versions described here.

317

BuNo 122475 after 120-gallon tip tanks were added in February 1948. (*Grumman, courtesy of Dave Anderton*)

Production history

XF9F-1: This designation identified the two-seat night fighter prototype (Design 75) described in Appendix C.

XF9F-2: Two of the single-seat prototypes (Design 79) ordered in the summer of 1946 were powered by 5,000-lb thrust Rolls-Royce Nene turbojets imported for Grumman by the Taylor Turbine Corporation and bearing the US military designation J42-TT-2. BuNo 122475 was first flown by Corky Meyer on 21 November, 1947, and BuNo 122477 first flew five days later. Neither was initially fitted with the planned armament nor equipped with an ejector seat. The wing folded upward hydraulically and a sting tail hook retracted into the rear fuselage beneath the jet exhaust. Non-jettisonable 120-US gal tanks were attached to the wingtips of the first prototype in February 1948 and this feature became standard beginning with the thirteenth production aircraft.

F9F-2: Externally similar to the XF9F-2 with wingtip tanks, the F9F-2 was substantially heavier with empty, loaded, and maximum weights being increased respectively by 31 per cent, 52 per cent, and 57 per cent. Most of the weight increase came from added fuel (total capacity went from 597 to 923 US gal, from the fitting of a Martin-Baker ejector seat, and from the installation of four 20-mm cannon with 190 rounds per gun. After the first F9F-2s began trials with J42-P-4 engines running on 100/130-octane

318

aviation fuel mixed with 3 per cent lubricating oil, initial production F9F-2s were powered by J42-P-6s dispensing with the addition of oil to the fuel. However, most F9F-2s received J42-P-8s with modified ignition system. All J42 versions had a maximum wet take-off thrust of 5,750 lb and a dry take-off rating of 5,000 lb.

A total of 564 Panthers were delivered as F9F-2s (BuNos 122563, 122567, 122569/122570, 122572, 122586/122589, 123016/123019, 123044/123067, 123077/123083, 123397/123713, 125083/125155, and 127086/127215). In addition, three airframes which had started down the line as F9F-2s (BuNos 123084/123086) were completed as the XF9F-4, XF9F-5, and as the static test airframe for the XF9F-4/XF9F-5. Moreover, in service most F9F-3s were re-engined by the Navy with J42-P-6 turbojets and were redesignated F9F-2s. Late in their Service life, a number of F9F-2s and re-engined F9F-3s were fitted with a UHF homing antenna in a fairing beneath the nose cone.

F9F-2B: In service, the Navy modified a substantial number of early production F9F-2s as fighter-bombers by fitting four racks beneath each wing. The inboard rack was stressed for bombs of up to 1,000 lb or 150-gal drop tanks, whereas the three outboard racks could be used to carry 250-lb bombs or 5-in HVAR rockets. Maximum external load was 3,000 lb. These racks were fitted during assembly beginning with the 365th F9F-2 built by Grumman (BuNo 125083). After most F9F-2s had been brought up to F9F-2B standard, the B suffix was normally dropped from the aircraft designation painted on the sides of the rear fuselage.

F9F-2D: This designation was given to a few F9F-2s which were modified by the Navy as unarmed radio-controlled drones with the necessary remote

A bomb-laden F9F-2B of VMF-115 departing for a combat sortie in Korea on 15 March, 1953.
(USMC)

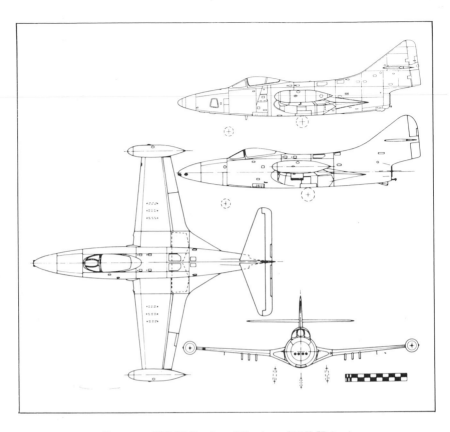

Grumman F9F-2B Panther. Side view of F9F-5P (top)

control equipment installed in place of the cannon, and antennae protruding beneath the nose.

F9F-2KD: This designation identified a small number of F9F-2s which were modified by the Navy as drone directors.

F9F-2P: When the Korean War started in June 1950, the Navy found itself without jet-powered reconnaissance aircraft as the first of the McDonnell F2H-2Ps it had on order was still four months from entering flight trials. Accordingly, the Navy modified a small number of F9F-2s as unarmed photographic-reconnaissance aircraft by substituting oblique and vertical cameras for the four 20-mm cannon in the nose of the aircraft. The fact that the entire nose cone of the F9F slid forward on beams for servicing greatly eased this modification and provided easy access to the cameras.

XF9F-3: The second Panther airframe (BuNo 122476) was fitted with a 4,600-lb thrust J33-A-8 as the prototype for the less powerful Allison-powered version which the Navy ordered as a precautionary measure against possible delays with the Americanization of the Nene and the setting

Having previously flown fifty photographic-reconnaissance sorties, as evidenced by the scoreboard beneath its windshield, BuNo 123706, an F9F-2P of VC-61, crosses the North Korean coast on its way back to its carrier in the Sea of Japan. *(USN/National Archives)*

up of a J42 production line by Pratt & Whitney. The XF9F-3 first flew on 16 August, 1948.

F9F-3: The fifty-four F9F-3s (BuNos 122560/122562, 122564/122566, 122568, 122571, 122573/122585, 123020/123043, and 123068/123076) delivered by Grumman between August 1948 and November 1949 differed from the F9F-2s in being powered by the 4,600-lb thrust Allison J33-A-8 turbojet. In service, virtually all F9F-3s were re-engined by the Navy with the 5,750-lb thrust Pratt & Whitney J42 turbojet and became indistinguishable from the F9F-2s.

During the summer of 1950, a re-engined F9F-3 (BuNo 122562) was fitted with an electro-hydraulically driven Emerson Aero X17A roll-traverse turret housing four 0.50-in machine-guns. Tests began on 21 September, 1950, and proved quite promising, but delays with the development of the required radar and fire control systems led to the project being cancelled in early 1954. During flight evaluation at NATC Patuxent River, the turret had been rolled 100 degrees per second and the guns traversed at up to 200 degrees per second. The traverse range was from dead ahead to 20 degrees aft and the roll range was 360 degrees in either direction from the stow position.

XF9F-4: The 99th and 101st production airframes (BuNos 123084 and 123086) were modified respectively as the XF9F-4 prototype and the static-test airframe for the XF9F-4/XF9F-5. The fuselage was extended 19.5 in forward of the wing to enable internal fuel capacity (including the fixed tip tanks) to be increased from 923 to 1,003 gal, and the height and area of the vertical tail surfaces were increased to offset the loss of directional stability

321

BuNo 122562, the F9F-3 which served as a test-bed for the Emerson Aero X17A roll-traverse turret. (*Grumman*)

The first F9F-4 (BuNo 125081) after it had been modified as a test-bed for a boundary layer control system. Note absence of cannon and plain nose cone stemming from the earlier use of this aircraft to test photographic-reconnaissance camera installations. Note also the open trap door beneath the tailpipe in which a spin recovery chute was fitted during trials of the boundary-layer control system. (*Grumman*)

resulting from the lengthening of the fuselage. Powered by a 6,250-lb thrust Allison J33-A-16 turbojet, BuNo 123084 first flew on 5 July, 1950.

F9F-4: Ordered simultaneously with F9F-5s, the F9F-4s (BuNos 125081, 125156/125227, and 125913/125948) were intended to be powered by the J33-A-16. However, as this turbojet proved unreliable, many were delivered as J48-powered F9F-5s and most of the others were re-engined with J48-P-6As. In early 1954, BuNo 125081 became the most noteworthy F9F-4 when it was modified as a test-bed for the high-lift boundary-layer control system developed by John D Attinello of the NATC.

XF9F-5: The 100th production airframe (BuNo 123085) was modified as the XF9F-5 prototype. Featuring a lengthened fuselage and revised tail

F9F-5 (BuNo 125240) with experimental air refuelling probe installation in the nose. (*Grumman*)

surfaces similar to those of the XF9F-4, the XF9F-5 was powered at various times by either the XJ48-P-6 (the Pratt & Whitney version of the British-developed Tay turbojet with Rolls-Royce manufactured power section and Pratt & Whitney installed accessories) or the similarly rated YJ48-P-6 (which was entirely manufactured by Pratt & Whitney). Both variants had maximum wet and dry take-off thrusts of 7,000 lb and 6,250 lb. The XF9F-5 was first flown on 21 December, 1949.

F9F-5: This was numerically the most important version of the Panther with 616 aircraft (BuNos 125080, 125082, 125228/125313, 125414/125443, 125489/125499, 125533/125648, 125893/125912, 125949/126256, and 126627/126669) being delivered between November 1950 and January 1953. Similar to the XF9F-5, they were powered by the 7,000-lb wet thrust Pratt & Whitney J48-P-6 or P-6A. Like the F9F-4s, the F9F-5s were armed with four 20-mm cannon and had four external store pylons beneath each wing as first fitted to F9F-2Bs; however, like those of the F9F-4s, the three outboard pylons were stressed to carry bombs of up to 500 lb to increase maximum external load to 3,465 lb. During the course of production an anti-stall fence was added just outboard of the wing root intakes to control the spanwise airflow and reduce landing speed. Service modifications also included installation in some aircraft of a UHF homing antenna in a fairing beneath the nose cone.

323

At least one F9F-5 (BuNo 125240) was fitted with a nose-mounted inflight refuelling probe for trials during the summer of 1952, with a North American XAJ-1 modified as a tanker. The success of this experiment led the Navy to announce in September 1955 that henceforth all its jet-powered fighters and attack aircraft would be fitted with probes for inflight refuelling.

F9F-5K: The F9F-5K designation identified a small number of F9F-5s which were modified by the Navy in the mid-1950s as remotely-controlled drones.

F9F-5KD (DF-9E): This designation identified F9F-5s modified by the Navy as drone directors. The radio control equipment was installed in the nose in place of the guns and associated radar-ranging equipment. Being the only Panthers still in the inventory when the tri-Service designation system was adopted in 1962, the F9F-5KDs were redesignated DF-9Es.

F9F-5P: Unlike the F9F-2Ps, which were Service modified from existing fighter airframes, the thirty-six F9F-5Ps (BuNos 125314/125321, 126265/126290, and 127471/127472) were built by Grumman as unarmed reconnaissance aircraft. The modified nose housing vertical and oblique cameras gave the F9F-5Ps an overall length of 40 ft versus a length of 38 ft $10\frac{1}{2}$ in for the F9F-5s. In addition to the installation of cameras and the removal of cannon and wing racks, the F9F-5Ps differed from the fighters in being fitted with a General Electric G-3 autopilot.

Service history

Following BIS trials and initial carrier qualifications, both the F9F-2 and F9F-3 versions of the Panther were declared ready for Service use in the spring of 1949. However, initial slow delivery of J42s resulted in J33-powered F9F-3s preceding J42-powered F9F-2s into service. Thus, F9F-3s were first delivered to VF-51 at NAS San Diego, California, on 8 May, 1949, while F9F-2s were first assigned to the *Blue Angels* demonstration team at NAS Pensacola, on 20 August and, later in that month to a Marine squadron, VMF-115 at MCAS Cherry Point, North Carolina. The first Navy squadron to fly J42-powered Panthers was VF-111, also at NAS San Diego, which received F9F-2s during the early autumn of that year.

On 25 June, 1950, when President Truman and his military advisers began planning the US response to the North Korean invasion of South Korea, the US Navy only had seven jet-capable carriers in commision: the USS *Leyte* (CV-32), *Midway* (CVB-41), *F.D. Roosevelt* (CVB-42), and *Coral Sea* (CVB-43) with the Atlantic Fleet and the USS *Boxer* (CV-21), *Valley Forge* (CV-45), and *Philippine Sea* (CV-47) with the Pacific Fleet. Furthermore, most of the aircraft embarked aboard these carriers were piston-powered and the Navy only had eight first-line squadrons equipped with jets (six with Panthers and two with McDonnell F2H Banshees). Two of these squadrons, VF-51 and VF-52 (both equipped with F9F-3s) were aboard *Valley Forge* at Hong Kong, which immediately put to sea in

The *Blue Angels* were first equipped with F9F-5s in November 1951. *(USN/Grumman)*

A J33-powered F9F-3 of VF-51 aboard the USS *Valley Forge* (CV-45) during early operations off Korea in the summer of 1950. *USN/National Archives)*

preparation for operations along with HMS *Triumph*. Eight Panthers from VF-51 provided cover for the first strike against Pyongyang airfield on 3 July and on that occasion drew first blood when Ens E W Brown and Lt(jg) L H Plog both shot down a Yak-9, while the Air Group Commander and two other *Screaming Eagles* pilots destroyed three North Korean aircraft on the ground.

On 1 November, 1950, MiG-15s based in Antung, China, first crossed the Yalu River to challenge US aircraft. For the Navy, this was a particularly serious development as its highest-performance aircraft, the F9F-2 then operating with six squadrons aboard the carriers *Leyte*, *Philippine Sea*, and *Valley Forge*, appeared to be markedly inferior to the

Soviet-built aircraft. Though the F9F-2 and MiG-15 were powered by virtually the same engine (like the J42 of the F9F-2, the RD-45 and VK-1 powering the MiG were derivatives of the Rolls-Royce Nene), the Soviet fighter had a decisive edge in terms of performance as it was lighter and was fitted with swept wings. Fortunately, US naval aviators were much better trained than their North Korean and Chinese adversaries and consequently succeeded in defeating their opponents. In the first encounter between Panthers and MiG-15s, the CO of VF-111 operating from the USS *Philippine Sea*, Cdr W T Amen, shot down one of the enemy jets on 9 November, 1950. Before the armistice was signed in July 1953, four more MiG-15s (including two Soviet Air Force aircraft flying from Vladivostok) were shot down by Panther pilots who suffered no air-to-air combat losses.

For most of the war, however, Panther pilots were not allowed to seek out enemy fighters and instead provided cover for carrier-based attack aircraft and flew in the ground attack role*. In this role, active and reserve fighter pilots from VF-23, -24, -31, -34, -51, -52, -71, -72, -91, -93, -111, -112, -113, -191, -721, -781, -821 -831, and -837 mainly flew F9F-2 fighters and F9F-2B fighter-bombers. The latter were first used on 2 April, 1951, by VF-191 from the USS *Princeton* (CV-37) during an attack on railway bridges near Songjin, North Korea. More powerful F9F-5s first went to war in Korea with VF-781 and VF-783, reserve squadrons which had been placed

An F9F-2B (BuNo123624) of VF-191 over Korea during this squadron's first combat deployment aboard the USS *Princeton* (CV-37) from 5 December, 1950, until 29 May, 1951. (*USN/National Archives*)

---

* Two of the first seven astronauts were shot down while flying Panthers in Korea. Ens Neil A Armstrong from VF-51 baled out over friendly troops after his aircraft was hit by AAA near Wonsan. Maj John H Glenn from VMF-311 brought back badly damaged Panthers on two occasions: the first had been hit by a 75-mm AAA shell and the second by a 90-mm AAA shell.

on active duty and deployed aboard the USS *Oriskany* (CVA-34)† in October 1952, and were also flown by VF-51, -52, -53, -111, -153, and -154 during the final phases of the war. Unarmed photographic-reconnaissance F9F-2Ps were first deployed by VC-61 Detatchment E aboard *Princeton* in December 1950 and were supplanted by F9F-5Ps two years later.

While the Panther is better known for its wartime service in Korea and was outnumbered with Atlantic Fleet squadrons by the McDonnell Banshee, Grumman's first jet was nevertheless extensively used by active and reserve units of the Atlantic and Pacific Fleets during the first half of the fifties. Phased out from service with operational fighter squadrons in 1956, Panthers continued to serve with Advanced Training Units and to provide jet experience for heavy attack crews transitioning to the Douglas A3D Skywarrior until finally supplanted by more modern types in 1958. As drones and drone directors, Panthers were used extensively by Utility Squadrons, Guided Missile Squadrons, and at NAS Point Mugu and NOTS China Lake.in California, until the mid-1960s when the last DF-9Es were struck off.

As indicated earlier, the *Blue Angels* also flew Panthers while in transition from Bearcats to new F9F-2s in August 1949, and then to new F9F-5s in November 1951. They began their conversion to F9F-6s in 1953 but were almost immediately re-equipped with overhauled F9F-5s as the fleet needed the new Cougars. Finally, in 1954, the *Blue Angels* exchanged their Panthers for F9F-8s.

With the Marine Corps, the first Panthers were the F9F-2s delivered in August 1949 to VMF-115. The first jets to enter combat operations were the F9F-2Bs from VMF-311 which, based at Yonpo, North Korea, supported the withdrawal of besieged troops from the Chosin Reservoir area in

F9F-5Ps of VMJ-3 prepare to take-off at MCAS Cherry Point, North Carolina, in 1954. (*USN/ National Archives*)

† The previously used CV carrier designation was replaced by the CVA designation on 1 October, 1952

An F9F-2 of the 1ª Escuadrilla Aeronaval de Ataque, 3ª Escuadra Aeronaval, at BAN Commandante Espora, Argentina, in the mid-1960s. *(Courtesy of A Reinhard and Jay Miller)*

December 1950. For the next two and a half years, VMF-311 and VMF-115 flew F9F-2Bs, F9F-4s, and then F9F-5s in Korea in the ground support role. Other active and reserve Marine Fighter Squadrons (notably VMF-122, -211, -213, -214, -223, -224, -232, -234, -235, -312, -314, -323, -334, and -451, and two training squadrons, VMFT-10 and -20) and two reconnaissance squadrons (VMJ-1 and VMJ-3, the latter still flying F9F-5Ps when it was redesignated VMCJ-3) flew Panthers in the United States. The last Marine Panther units in 1958 were the two reserve squadrons in Minneapolis, VMF-213 and VMF-234.

The only foreign air arm to receive Panthers was Argentina's Servicio de Aviación Naval, which obtained twenty-four refurbished F9F-2s (some with and some without the UHF homing antenna in a nose fairing) in 1958. Bearing Argentine military serials in the 0417 to 0461 range, these aircraft were assigned to the 1ª Escuadrilla Aeronaval de Ataque when this attack squadron was established in December 1958 as part of 2ª Escuadra Aeronaval at BAN Comandante Espora in Puerto Belgrano. In April 1963, after the unit had been transferred to BAN Punta del Indio, four Panthers were destroyed on the ground and one collided with an F4U-5 during a three-day coup pitting naval forces against the Army (Ejército Argentino) and the Air Force (Fuerza Aérea Argentina). Shortly after, the 1ª Escuadrilla Aeronaval de Ataque was transferred to 3ª Escuadra Aeronaval at BAN Comandante Espora and continued to remain land based, as the catapult of the ARA *Independencia* light carrier was not powerful enough to launch the F9F-2 at normal operating weights. In 1965, the Panthers were back in action when they flew patrols during a border clash between Argentina and Chile. Finally, lack of spares forced the Argentine Navy to ground its surviving F9F-2s in 1969 and to re-equip the 1ª Escuadrilla Aeronaval de Ataque with Macchi MB.326GB training and light attack aircraft.

As a warbird, the Panther has gained little acceptance and only a few surplus aircraft were purchased by civilian owners. Nevertheless, three were listed in March 1987 on the United States Civil Aircraft Registry.

PRODUCTION: A total of 1,385 Panthers was built by Grumman between November 1947 and January 1953 as follows:

2	XF9F-2
564	F9F-2/F9F-2B
1	XF9F-3
54	F9F-3
1	XF9F-4
1	XF9F-4/XF9F-5 static test airframe
109	F9F-4
1	XF9F-5
616	F9F-5
36	F9F-5P

They were assigned the following BuNos:

XF9F-2:	BuNos 122475 and 122477
F9F-2/F9F-2B:	BuNos 122563, 122567, 122569/122570, 122572, 122586/122589, 123016/123019, 123044/123067, 123077/ 123083, 123397/123713, 125083/125155, and 127086/127215
XF9F-3:	BuNo 122476
F9F-3:	BuNos 122560/122562, 122564/122566, 122568, 122571, 122573/122585, 123020/123043, and 123068/123076
XF9F-4:	BuNo 123084
F9F-4:	BuNos 125081, 125156/125227, and 125913/125948
XF9F-5:	BuNo 123085
F9F-5:	BuNos 125080, 125082, 125228/125313, 125414/125443, 125489/125499, 125533/125648, 125893/125912, 125949/126256, and 126627/126669
F9F-5P:	BuNos 125314/125321, 126265/126290, and 127471/127472
XF9F-4/XF9F-5:	BuNo 123084 (static test airframe)

	XF9F-2	F9F-2	F9F-5
DIMENSIONS:			
Span, ft in	35 3	38 0	38 0
(m)	(10.74)	(11.58)	(11.58)
Span (wings folded), ft in	23 5	23 5	23 5
(m)	(7.14)	(7.14)	(7.14)
Length, ft in	37 8	37 5³/₈	38 10¹/₂
(m)	(11.48)	(11.41)	(11.85)
Height, ft in	11 3	11 4	12 4

329

(m)	(3.43)	(3.45)	(3.76)
Wing area, sq ft	250	250	250
(sq m)	(23.23)	(23.23)	(23.23)
WEIGHTS:			
Empty, lb	7,107	9,303	10,147
(kg)	(3,224)	(4,220)	(4,603)
Loaded, lb	10,840	16,450	17,766
(kg)	(4,917)	(7,462)	(8,059)
Maximum, lb	12,442	19,494	18,721
(kg)	(5,644)	(8,842)	(8,492)
Wing loading,* lb/sq ft	43.4	65.8	71.1
(kg/sq m)	(211.7)	(321.2)	(346.9)
Power loading,* lb/lb st	2.2	2.9	2.5
(kg/kgp)	(2.2)	(2.9)	(2.5)
PERFORMANCE:			
Max speed, mph/ft	594/sl	575/sl	604/sl
(kmh/m)	(956/sl)	(925/sl)	(972/sl)
Cruising speed, mph	350	487	481
(kmh)	(563)	(784)	(774)
Climb rate, ft/min	7,700/1	6,000/1	6,000/1
(m/sec)	(39)	(30)	(30)
Service ceiling, ft	–	44,600	42,800
(m)	(–)	(13,595)	(13,045)
Normal range, miles	1,100	1,353	1,300
(km)	(1,770)	(2,175)	(2,090)

* Wing and power loadings are calculated at normal loaded weight and maximum take-off power.

An F9F-8 (BuNo 131072) from NOTS China Lake, California, carrying a pair of AAM-N-7A infrared-guided missiles during a sidewinder flight test over the Sierra Nevada on 22 March 1956. (*USN courtesy of NWC China Lake/PA*)

Grumman F9F (F-9) Cougar

When BuAer and Grumman discussed the Design 79 proposal for a single-seat, single- or twin-jet, carrier-based fighter during the summer and early autumn of 1946, both parties were fully aware of the higher critical Mach number which could be achieved by adopting a swept instead of a straight wing configuration. Accordingly, the XF9F-2/XF9F-3 contract awarded in October 1946 included a clause by which, in addition to designing, manufacturing, and testing three straight-wing prototypes, Grumman was to provide design data for a swept-wing version.

When work on Design 79 started in earnest, the Bethpage project team naturally gave priority to the development of the straight-wing aircraft which was on firm order. Nevertheless, whenever feasible, features which would facilitate the eventual development of a swept-wing version were incorporated in the basic design. Thus, changes made in Design 79 between contract award and mock-up inspection were in part dictated by such considerations. All along, however, Grumman engineers were concerned by the apparent incompatibility of swept wings with carrier requirements as sweeping the wing introduced undesirable stability effects at low-speed and increased stalling speed. As early as January 1946, Grumman had proposed to BuAer the building of a research aircraft to obtain data on low-speed handling characteristics of highly swept wings. Unfortunately, this Design 77 proposal (see Appendix C) did not find acceptance. Hence, deprived of acquiring the data it considered to be badly needed, Grumman prevailed upon the Navy to postpone work on a swept-wing development of Design 79 until ways could be found to eliminate or offset the poor low-speed behaviour of swept-wing aircraft.

331

BuNo 126670, the first Cougar prototype, photographed before its maiden flight on 20 September, 1951. The horizontal tail surfaces with tab-geared elevators fitted to this aircraft were later replaced by an hydraulically-operated flying tail. (*Grumman*)

By the time Grumman was ready to submit the Design 83 swept-wing proposal,the concept had evolved away from the XF9F-2 without getting any closer to solving low-speed handling problems. Nevertheless, the Navy saw development potential in the Grumman proposal and a letter of intent covering additional Design 83 engineering data and drawings was issued in December 1947. Eventually, any pretence at developing Design 83 as a swept-wing version of the XF9F-2 was dropped and additional work led to an all-new aircraft, the XF10F-1 described in the next chapter. Nearly three years later, however, work on a swept-wing Panther was resumed on a high priority basis when the surprise appearance of the swept-wing MiG-15 in November 1950 suddenly rendered obsolete the straight-wing Grumman F9F-2 and McDonnell F2H-2, the Navy's most advanced fighters then in squadron service.

Necessity being the mother of invention, BuAer and Grumman agreed in December 1950 to expedite the development of a swept-wing version of the Panther. A contract for the modification of three F9F-5 airframes was awarded on 2 March, 1951, the Cougar prototype first flew six and a half months later, and the first F9F-6s were delivered to VF-32 in November 1951, just one year after the MiG-15's debut in Korea.

Conceived as a straightforward derivative of the Panther, Design 93 retained the fuselage, vertical tail surfaces, powerplant, and undercarriage of the F9F-5 and was fitted with wings swept at 35 degrees at quarter chord and with swept horizontal tail surfaces. To compensate for the increase in approach and stalling speeds resulting from the use of swept wings, the chord of the leading-edge slats and that of the trailing-edge flaps were

This photograph of BuNo 1266670 proves that the first F9F-6 initially flew with horn-balanced ailerons. White wool tufts have been added above the starboard wing, forward of the aileron, to help visualize the air flow in an attempt to correct the control reversal problem which prevailed until the ailerons were replaced by 'flaperon/flaperette' spoilers. *(Grumman)*

increased and much larger split flaps were fitted beneath the centre section. Other modifications included the lengthening of the forward fuselage by 2 ft, the forward extension of the intake-housing wing centre section, the enlargement of the wing root fillets, and the use of a broader chord lower rudder section linked to the rudder pedals and of an upper rudder section of unchanged dimension but linked to a yaw damper. Furthermore, as the tip tanks had to be dispensed with, the resulting reduction in fuel capacity was made up partially by increasing the size of the forward fuselage fuel tank and adding bladder-type tanks in the wing leading-edge. (Nevertheless, total internal fuel capacity decreased from 1,003 to 919 US gal.)

As completed and first flown by Fred C Rowley at Bethpage on 20 September, 1951, BuNo 126670 had conventional horn-balanced ailerons for lateral control and conventional tab geared elevators for longitudinal control. However, with these surfaces, the F9F-6 experienced control reversal at high speed and poor lateral and longitudinal control. The use of an hydraulically-operated 'flying tail' easily cured the longitudinal control deficiency but lateral control remained unsatisfactory until the horn-balanced ailerons were replaced by 'flaperon/flaperette' spoilers fitted on the wing upper surface at about 75 per cent of the chord line. The flaperon was ahead of the flaperette and under normal flight conditions both of these spoiler sections were hydraulically operated as a single surface. In an emergency, the flaperette section was operated independently by means of a separate hydraulic system. Large fences were also added during trials to inhibit spanwise flow and preserve lateral control effectiveness. So modified, the F9F-6 demonstrated better carrier handling characteristics than the F9F-5 while critical Mach number was increased from 0.79 to 0.86 at sea level and to 0.895 at 35,000 ft.

In spite of the need to develop and evaluate these major control system changes, and much to the credit of the Grumman engineering team, flight trials proceeded remarkably quickly and production F9F-6s were ready for squadron delivery only fourteen months after the first flight of the prototype. Equally impressive were the ease with which this stop-gap design was further developed and its longeivity. The 1,988th and last Cougar, a two-seat F9F-8T advanced trainer, was delivered in February 1960, and the last TF-9Js were phased out by VT-4 in February 1974.

Production history

F9F-6 (F-9F): Two flying prototypes (BuNos 126670 and 126672) and a static test airframe (BuNo 126671) were obtained by fitting swept wings and horizontal tail surfaces to three uncompleted F9F-5 airframes. The first prototype (BuNo 126670) was completed and initially flown with conventional horn-balanced ailerons but was later fitted with the previously described flaperon/flaperette spoilers. Powered by a Pratt & Whitney J48-P-6 turbojet with take-off ratings of 7,000 lb with water injection and 6,250 lb dry, it first flew on 20 September, 1951, and was later re-engined with a YJ48-P-8 rated at 7,250 lb without the need for water injection.

In addition to 646 ordered and delivered with flaperon/flaperette spoilers as F9F-6s (BuNos 126257/126264, 127216/127470, 128055/128294, and 130920/131062), the last fifty aircraft ordered as F9F-7s (BuNos 130870/130919) were delivered as F9F-6s with J48-P-8 turbojets. The 7,000-lb thrust J48-P6A was used to power the first 30 F9F-6s, but the 7,250-lb thrust J48-P-8 was adopted for later aircraft and for the re-engined F9F-7s. Some aircraft later received J48-P-8Bs which were modified J48-P-8s with titanium impeller inducers. All were armed with four 20-mm cannon and had two wing racks for 1,000-lb bombs or, more usually, 150-US gal drop tanks. In service, a number of F9F-6s were fitted with a UHF homing antenna in a fairing beneath the nose and a few had an inflight refuelling probe installed in the nose.

F9F-6D (DF-9F): The F9F-6Ds were F9F-6s which were modified by the Navy as drone directors for use in various RDT&E (Research, Development, Test, and Evaluation) programmes.

F9F-6K (QF-9F): The F9F-6K drones were obtained through Service modification of F9F-6s and re-engined F9F-7s after these aircraft were phased out by fighter squadrons.

F9F-6K2 (QF-9G): This designation identified F9F-6Ks fitted with modernized equipment, as well as a number of F9F-6s and F9F-7s which were directly modified to this improved drone configuration.

334

F9F-7 (BuNo 130912) during a test flight over the Atlantic Coast. *(Grumman)*

F9F-6P: Sixty F9F-6 airframes (BuNos 127473/127492, 128295/128310, 131252/131255, and 134446/134465) were fitted by Grumman with a vertical and oblique camera installation in place of the cannon and were delivered as F9F-6Ps between June 1954 and March 1955.

F9F-7 (F-9H): Contracts were placed for 168 F9F-7s (BuNos 130752/130919) which were to be identical to the F9F-6s with the exception of the substitution of a 6,350-lb thrust Allison J33-A-16 turbojet for the J48 powering other Cougar versions. However, as the J33 was less powerful and reliable, the last fifty were delivered as J48-powered F9F-6s, and in service most F9F-7s were re-engined with the J48. Like the F9F-6s, F9F-7s were frequently fitted in service with a UHF homing antenna in a fairing beneath the nose.

To evaluate the feasibility of flexdeck operations, a British-devised concept calling for carrier-aircraft to be landed intentionally undercarriage up on an inflated rubber mat, Grumman was asked to modify two F9F-7s (BuNos 130862 and 130863). To that end, work on Design 94A was begun in February 1954 and resulted in the aircraft being fitted with a 3-in deep false bottom under the centre fuselage and being re-engined with J48-P-8s. Other modifications included bolting the leading-edge slats in the down position and the centre flap section in the shut position, limiting the travel

335

The first flexdeck F9F-7 (BuNo 130862) being towed on the experimental deck at NATC Patuxent River in early 1955. *(Grumman)*

of the outboard flap sections to avoid contact with the deck, and deactivating the flying tail. In addition, Grumman developed a handling dolly to be used on the ground when the undercarriage was in the up position. The first wheels-up arrested landing was made on a 570-ft by 80-ft flexdeck at NATC Patuxent River on 18 February, 1955. Tests continued until August 1955 and proved relatively satisfactory. However, the flexdeck concept itself was found impractical as the use of aircraft without undercarriage (as envisioned to derive full benefit from the flexdeck by dispensing with the unneeded weight and complexity of a retractable undercarriage) would have caused numerous operational problems (*eg*, no possibility of diverting to airfields or carriers without flexdeck) and the project was terminated in March 1956.

F9F-8 (F-9J): To reduce stalling speed, improve control at high angles of attack, and increase the Cougar's range, Grumman initiated work on Design 99 in April 1953. Changes included an 8-in extension of the centre fuselage, the fitting of extended and cambered leading edges in place of the slats outboard of the fences, and the aft extension of the trailing edges. The 15 per cent greater wing chord increased wing area from 300 to 337 sq ft and also resulted in a relatively thinner section and an improvement in critical Mach number. Internal fuel tankage was increased from 919 to 1,063 gal by adding a 30-gal tank in the extended leading edge and enlarging the forward fuselage tank.

The first F9F-8 flew on 18 January, 1954, and 601 F9F-8s (BuNos

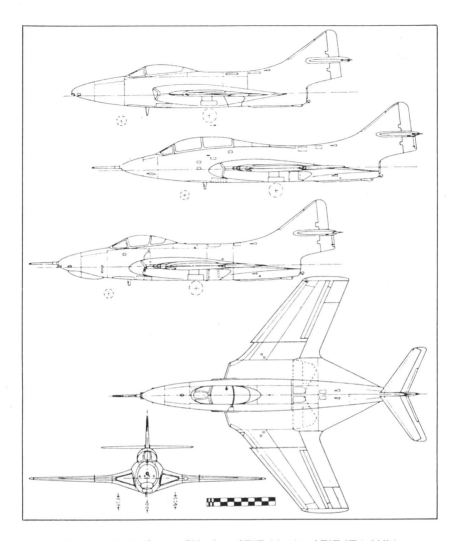

Grumman F9F-8 Cougar. Side view of F9F-6 (top) and F9F-8T (middle)

131063/131251,   134234/134244,   138823/138898,   141030/141229,
141648/141666, and 144271/144376) were delivered between April 1954
and March 1957. They were fitted with a reinforced sliding canopy and
powered by the 7,250-lb thrust J48-P-8As or P-8Cs. During the course of
production, a fixed inflight refuelling probe was added in the nose and most
aircraft were fitted with a UHF homing antenna in a fairing beneath the
nose. Provision for carrying a Sidewinder infrared guided missile beneath
each wing was also incorporated in late production aircraft and retrofitted to
earlier F9F-8s.

337

An F9F-8B (BuNo 132149) of VMA-311 carrying a training shape during a flight from MCAS El Toro, California, on 12 May, 1958. *(USMC)*

F9F-8P (BuNo 141722) of VMCJ-3 on the ramp at MCAS El Toro, California, on 1 August, 1957. *(MSgt Clay Jansson/USMC)*

F9F-8B (AF-9J): When tactical nuclear bombs were developed, the Cougar was one of the aircraft types selected by the Navy to be modified to carry special stores. For that purpose, F9F-8s were fitted with LABS (Low Altitude Bombing System), additional instruments, and the required control and arming devices for the special stores. In service, however, most F9F-8Bs were operated by squadrons assigned conventional fighter-bombing duties and were fitted with six underwing weapon pylons. Later when used as advanced trainers, some of these aircraft were redesignated TAF-9Js.

F9F-8P (RF-9J): Whereas the nose of the photographic-reconnaissance and fighter versions of the F9F-6 were almost identical, the flat-sided droop nose of the unarmed F9F-8P was substantially larger and longer than that of the F9F-8. It housed forward, vertical, and oblique cameras and incorporated provision for a fixed inflight refuelling probe. The first F9F-8P was flown on 18 February, 1955. Including the prototype, 110 F9F-8Ps (BuNos 141668/141727 and 144377/144426) were delivered between August 1955 and July 1957.

338

A QF-9J drone of Utility Squadron Eight (VC-8) at NAS Point Mugu on 5 January, 1973. *(Ben Knowles, courtesy of Alain Pelletier)*

QF-9J: The final drone version of the Cougar was obtained through Service modification of re-engined F9F-7s, F9F-8s, and AF-9Js.

F9F-8T (TF-9J): Development of a two-seat version was initiated by Grumman in November 1953 as Design 105 to meet anticipated Navy requirements for a combat capable check-out trainer to serve in fleet squadrons alongside single-seat Cougars. In addition, Grumman offered the two-seat Cougar as an advanced trainer which could also be used as a carrier landing trainer and to provide inflight refuelling instruction. This Grumman proposal initially failed to gain much support as the Navy saw little need for combat-capable or inflight refuelling trainers and preferred to order Lockheed T2V-1s to fill its requirements for advanced trainers which could also be used to provide initial jet carrier-landing experience to student naval aviators. Nevertheless, Grumman was eventually authorized to complete an F9F-8 airframe (BuNo 141667) as a two-seat prototype. It first flew on 29 February, 1956. Later, the failure of the T2V-1s to live up to expectations boosted requirements for F9F-8Ts.

To provide space for a second cockpit, the forward fuselage was extended by 34 in. A large rear-sliding canopy covered the tandem cockpits and an auxiliary windshield was provided internally ahead of the instructor's seat to enable the aircraft to be flown with partially opened canopy. To offset the resulting weight increase, two of the four cannon were removed and the ammunition supply was reduced. Powered by J48-P-8As (often replaced in service by P-8C engines), 399 production F9F-8Ts (BuNos 142437/142532, 142954/143012, 146342/146425, and 147270/ 147429) were delivered between July 1956 and February 1960. They featured some structural strengthening to enable repeated arrested landings at high weights. Most were fitted with a nose-mounted inflight refuelling probe increasing overall length from 44 ft 4^1/$_4$ in to 48 ft 8^3/$_4$ in. Provision for carrying two Sidewinders beneath each wing was incorporated in late production aircraft, but the necessary wiring was seldom retained in service.

339

Bearing the Thunderbird tail markings applied to aircraft assigned to the Naval Weapons Evaluation Facility, Kirtland AFB, New Mexico, this NTF-9J was fitted with an experimental radar installation in the nose. *(Courtesy of Cloud 9 Photography)*

Several F9F-8T developments were considered, including night fighter and night fighter trainer versions proposed in 1955 with AN/APQ-50 radar and missile armament (Sparrows or Sidewinders) and a trainer proposed in 1961 with more modern systems and a Pratt & Whitney J52 in place of the J48. The performance of the night fighter versions was found insufficient to warrant production, and the Navy selected the Douglas TA-4F in preference to the modernized, J52-powered Cougar trainer.

NTF-9J: This designation identified a number of F9F-8Ts which were modified for use in a variety of RDT&E programmes.

Service history

Developed in great haste during the Korean War as a stop-gap design to provide the Navy with a fighter having performance comparable to that of the MiG-15, the Cougar was made ready for squadron assignment in a remarkably short time. Beginning in November 1952, when VF-32 became the first fleet squadron to convert to Cougars, F9F-6s and F9F-7s quickly re-equipped no fewer than twenty Navy fighter squadrons. Eight of these squadrons later converted to the more capable F9F-8, and this variant was also assigned to seven other squadrons which had not previously been flying Cougars. In addition, four Navy attack squadrons were equipped with Cougars before converting to Douglas A4D Skyhawks and three reconnaissance squadrons flew F9F-6Ps and/or F9F-8Ps.

Too late to fly combat sorties in Korea, Cougars made numerous deployments to the Pacific, the Atlantic, and the Mediterranean during which their pleasant handling characteristics and strong airframe well suited to the rigours of carrier operations earned praise from their pilots. Most cruises were routine but that made between July 1956 and February 1957 by the F9F-8s from VA-46 as part of Air Task Group 202 (ATG-202) aboard the USS *Randolph* (CVA-15) was noteworthy as it marked the first

340

overseas deployment of a unit equipped with aircraft armed with Sidewinder missiles. Notable non-operational occurences during that period were two record US transcontinental crossings. Flying probe-equipped F9F-6s and refuelling in flight over Kansas, three VF-21 pilots made the first such flight in less than four hours on 1 April, 1954, with Lt-Cdr F X Brady clocking the fastest time, 3 hr 45 min 30 sec, for a distance of 2,438 miles. On 5 October, 1956, three VF-144 pilots set an unofficial round trip record by flying their F9F-8s from NAS Miramar, California, to Long Island, New York, and back with fuelling stops each way at NAS Olathe, Kansas. Total time was 10 hr 49 min 11 sec.

By the mid-1950s, Cougars were the most numerous carrier-based fighters. However, it was already evident that these aircraft had been rendered obsolete by rapid technological development and would only have abbreviated lives as front-line aircraft. Supersonic aircraft, notably Grumman Tigers and the LTV Crusaders, were about to replace them in the fighter and reconnaissance roles and Douglas Skyhawks were destined to become the Navy's standard jet-powered light attack aircraft. Conversions to more modern types were undertaken at a rapid rate during the late 1950s. The F9F-8s and F9F-8Bs were phased out of the Pacific and Atlantic Fleets respectively in 1958 and 1959, and the last Cougars to serve with a fleet squadron were the F9F-8Ps, which were retained by VFP-62 until February 1960. With reserve units at naval air stations throughout the United States as well as in the drone and drone director roles, single-seat Cougars remained in service until the mid-1960s.

Two-seat F9F-8Ts/TF-9Js had a distinguished 17-year career with the Naval Air Training Command, and equipped five squadrons until finally phased out by VT-4 in February 1974. The Cougars thus played a vital role in training most of the pilots who flew combat operations in Vietnam. Other two-seat Cougars were used for a variety of experimental purposes. Notably, it was from the aft cockpit of an F9F-8T flying at ground level at 120 mph that Flight Lt Sydney Hughes, RAF, ejected on 28 August, 1957, to make the first demonstration of the Martin-Baker ground level ejector seat. Later, F9F-8Ts were operated by the Naval Parachute Facility at NAS El Centro, California, for additional ejector seat trials with the rear section of their canopies removed.

After transitioning from F9F-5s to F9F-6s in 1953, the *Blue Angels* were forced to re-equip briefly with Panthers as the fleet needed Cougars for operational squadrons. Finally, the *Blue Angels* exchanged their F9F-5s for F9F-8s in 1954 and flew Cougars until converting to F11F-1s during the summer of 1957. After converting to Tigers, the Navy aerial demonstration team still retained an F9F-8T and disposed of this aircraft only when it was re-equipped with McDonnell Phantom IIs in 1969.

None of the Fleet Marine Force squadrons were equipped with F9F-6s but, after being phased out by Navy fleet squadrons, the type was assigned in the mid- to late-1950s to at least twenty-three reserve squadrons at eleven air stations as well as to Marine Reserve Air Training Detachments sharing

Aircraft No. 7 of the *Blue Angels* (F9F-8T, BuNo 142470) dumping fuel over NAS Pensacola, Florida, in April 1959.*(USN)*

aircraft with Navy reservists at other stations until the early 1960s. Photographic reconnaissance Cougars were operated by two Fleet Marine Force squadrons, F9F-6Ps being assigned to VMJ-2 at MCAS Cherry Point, North Carolina, and F9F-8Ps equipping VMCJ-3 at MCAS El Toro, California. Also in the second half of the 1950s, F9F-8s and F9F-8Bs were flown by VMCJ-2, VMF-311, VMA-533, and VMFT-10. As was the case with Navy two-seat Cougars, Marine F9F-8Ts had a longer life than the single seaters. They were mainly used as instrument trainers by VMIT-10 and for a variety of duties by Headquarters & Maintenance Squadrons (notably H&MS-11, -13, -15, and -37). In 1966-67, four TF-9Js were even used by H&MS-13 in the Tactical Air Control (Airborne) role to direct strike aircraft against enemy positions in South Vietnam, thus marking the only time that Cougars were used in combat.

Four years after becoming the only foreign air arm to fly straight-wing Panthers, Argentina's Servicio de Aviación Naval became the sole non-US operator of swept-wing Cougars. Two ex-USN F9F-8Ts were delivered in 1962 and, given serials 0516 and 0517, served with the 1ª Escuadrilla Aeronaval de Ataque, 3ª Escuadra Aeronaval, at BAN Comandante Espora until withdrawn from use in 1971.

Surplus F9F-8Ps were used by the Federal Aviation Administration for a variety of ground tests at NAFEC and one of these aircraft was registered N474 in the mid-1960s. Another Cougar was listed on the United States Civil Aircraft Registry in March 1987, but this F9F-6 was not airworthy at the time.

PRODUCTION: A total of 1,988 Cougars was built by Grumman between September 1951 and February 1960 as follows:

F9F-8P (BuNo 141683) used by the Federal Aviation Agency for non-flying tests at the National Aviation Facilities Experimental Center, NAFEC Atlantic City, New Jersey. *(FAA)*

An F9F-6 used by Grumman to fly a model of the F9F-9 mounted on an instrumented nose boom. *(Grumman)*

3	XF9F-6	601	F9F-8
696	F9F-6	110	F9F-8P
60	F9F-6P	400	F9F-8T
118	F9F-7		

They were assigned the following BuNos:
XF9F-6:   BuNos 126670/126672

| | F9F-6: | BuNos 126257/126264, 127216/127470, 128055/128294, and 130870/131062 |

F9F-6: BuNos 126257/126264, 127216/127470, 128055/128294, and 130870/131062

F9F-6P: BuNos 127473/127492, 128295/128310, 131252/131255, and 134446/134465

F9F-7: BuNos 130752/130869

F9F-8: BuNos 131063/131251, 134234/134244, 138823/138898, 141030/141229, 141648/141666, and 144271/144376

F9F-8P: BuNos 141668/141727 and 144377/144426

F9F-8T: BuNos 141667,142437/142532, 142954/143012, 146342/146425, and 147270/147429

	F9F-6	F9F-8	F9F-8P	F9F-8T
DIMENSIONS:				
Span, ft in	34 6	34 6	34 6	34 6
(m)	(10.52)	(10.52)	(10.52)	(10.52)
Span (wings olded), ft in	14 2	14 2	14 2	14 2
(m)	(4.32)	(4.32)	(4.32)	(4.32)
Length, ft in	40 10	42 2	44 9	44 4¼
(m)	(12.45)	(12.85)	(13.64)	(13.52)
Height, ft in	12 4	12 3	12 3	12 3
(m)	(3.76)	(3.73)	(3.73)	(3.73)
Wing area, sq ft	300	337	337	337
(sq m)	(27.87)	(31.31)	(31.31)	(31.31)
WEIGHTS:				
Empty, lb	11,255	11,866	12,246	12,787
(kg)	(5,105)	(5,382)	(5,555)	(5,800)
Loaded, lb	18,450	20,098	18,421	16,698
(kg)	(8,369)	(9,116)	(8,356)	(7,575)
Maximum, lb	21,000	24,763	22,697	20,574
(kg)	(9,525)	(11,232)	(10,295)	(9,331)
Wing loading,* lb/sq ft	61.5	59.6	54.7	49.5
(kg/sq m)	(300.3)	(291.2)	(266.9)	(241.9)
Power loading,* lb/lb st	3.0	2.8	2.5	2.3
(kg/kgp)	(3.0)	(2.8)	(2.5)	(2.3)
PERFORMANCE:				
Max speed, mph/ft	654/sl	647/2,000	637/5,000	630/5,000
(kmh/m)	(1,052/sl)	(1,041/610)	(1,025/1,525)	(1,014/1,525)
Cruising speed, mph	541	516	508	475
(kmh)	(870)	(830)	(817)	(764)
Climb rate, ft/min	6,750/1	5,750/1	4,700/1	4,800/1
(m/sec)	(34)	(29)	(24)	(24)
Service ceiling, ft	44,600	42,000	41,500	43,000
(m)	(13,595)	(12,800)	(12,650)	(13,105)
Normal range, miles	932	1,208	960	600
(km)	(1,500)	(1,945)	(1,545)	(965)
Max range, miles	–	1,312	1,045	–
(km)	(–)	(2,110)	(1,680)	(–)

* Wing and power loadings are calculated at normal loaded weight and maximum take-off power.

With Joshua trees in the background, the XF10F-1 Jaguar touches down on Muroc Dry Lake, Edwards AFB, California, on 19 May, 1952. *(Grumman)*

Grumman XF10F-1 Jaguar

Development of this unique aircraft – the world's first variable-sweep fighter* – was begun in November 1946, to satisfy contractual requirements for the provision of design data for a swept-wing version of the XF9F-2/XF9F-3. As submitted on 3 September, 1947, however, Design 83 already retained little but the forward fuselage, cockpit, and J42 turbojet of the F9F-2 and was proposed with clipped delta-wing, T-tail with swept surfaces, and conventional tail exhaust. Nevertheless, BuAer saw sufficient merit in the Design 83 proposal to issue letters of intent first in December 1947 to cover additional design work and then on 7 April, 1948, to provide for the design and manufacture of two XF10F-1 prototypes. At that time, rather optimistically as it turned out, flight trials were projected to begin in August 1949. What followed was a long evolutionary gestation during which frequently changing Navy requirements and the selection of an unreliable powerplant (the Westinghouse J40 turbojet which was also the downfall of several other contemporary Navy projects) doomed this overly ambitious project.

In the three years between the issue of the initial letter of intent and December 1950, when Grumman and the Navy finally reached an agreement on the Detailed Specification for a new naval fighter, the design was entirely revised and the resulting design for a variable geometry aircraft ended without commonality with either the straight-wing F9F-2 or the original Design 83 proposal with a modified delta-wing.

All along, the project team, led by Gordon Israel, strove to design a carrier-based fighter capable of achieving the then-elusive twin goals of

* The Messerschmitt P.1101 and the Bell X-5 were both research aircraft. The P.1101 was not completed before the end of the war, and was not a true variable-sweep aircraft as sweep could only be changed on the ground between 35 degrees and 45 degrees. The X-5, which first flew on 20 June, 1951, only eleven months before the XF10F-1, had wings that could be swept in flight between 20 deg and 60 deg.

transonic speeds and good low-speed handling qualities. Difficult as it was, this task was further complicated by a steady stream of Navy-dictated changes and demands for radar, increased range, heavier armament, etc, which led to size and weight increases; span increased from 32 ft 4 in for the original Design 83 proposal to 50 ft 7 in for the December 1950 XF10F-1 specification, and normal take-off weight increased from 18,730 lb for the former to 31,255 lb for the latter. In the process, to achieve the desired low-speed characteristics, Grumman first proposed the use of variable incidence wings in the autumn of 1948 and finally proposed variable-sweep wings in July 1949.

As provided in the Detailed Specification issued in December 1950, the shoulder-mounted wings of the XF10F-1 were to translate hydraulically fore and aft by means of a single pivot-point to change sweep from a minimum of 13.5 deg to a maximum of 42.5 deg. The maximum sweep was to be used at the top-end of the performance envelope, and good low-speed handling characteristics were to be obtained by flying with the wings at the minimum sweep angle, and through the use of full-span slats and Fowler

The XF10F-1 at Bethpage on 12 April, 1952. The wings are shown in the fully aft (top) and fully forward (bottom) positions with leading-edge slats down. *(Grumman)*

flaps extending over 80 per cent of the trailing edge. Lateral control was to be provided by ailerons supplemented by spoilers (four above and four below each wing) and longitudinal control by a delta tailplane driven by a servoplane tab at the front of a long acorn fairing. The main undercarriage was to retract into the deep-bellied fuselage, beneath the compressor section of the engine. The Westinghouse J40 turbojet was to be fed by cheek intakes, and fuel tanks in the wings and fuselage were to have a total capacity of 1,573 US gal. In addition, a 300-gal drop tank was to be carried beneath each wing on a swivelling pylon which remained parallel to the fuselage regardless of sweep angle. Production aircraft were to be fitted with an AN/APS-25 radar in the nose and armed with four 20-mm cannon in the forward fuselage and two rocket packs (each containing twenty-four 2.75-in FFARs or six 5-in HPAGs) or bombs of up to 2,000 lb on swivelling wing pylons.

Even before the first prototype was completed, the future of the Jaguar appeared safely assured, as the outbreak of fighting in Korea brought with it a new urgency. In August 1950 the order for two prototypes (BuNos 128311/128312) to be powered by the 7,310/10,900-lb military/afterburning thrust Westinghouse XJ40-WE-6 was supplemented by one for ten pre-production aircraft (BuNos 128313/128322) with either the XJ40-WE-6 or, if available, the 7,400/10,900 lb thrust J40-WE-8. Later contracts were placed for 123 F10F-1s (BuNos 131256/131378) and eight F10F-1Ps (BuNos 131379/131386), all to be powered by J40-WE-8s. However, after the XF10F-1 encountered overwhelming stability and control problems and its Navy-specified J40 engine proved totally inadequate, the entire programme for what had been intended to be the world's first variable-sweep fighter had to be cancelled.

As the J40 programme was already running behind schedule, no afterburning XJ40-WE-6 was available when the first XF10F-1 was completed. Thus this aircraft was fitted with a non-afterburning XJ40-WE-6 with an installed maximum thrust of only 6,800 lb before undergoing systems checks and low-speed taxi-ing runs at Bethpage. On 16 April, 1952, BuNo 128311 was partially dismantled and loaded aboard a Douglas C-124 to be airlifted to Edwards AFB, California, where initial trials of this advanced aircraft could be made safely over the Mojave Desert and away from prying eyes.

With Corwin H 'Corky' Meyer at the controls, the first flight on 19 May, 1952, lasted 16 minutes. It was marred by the failure of the slats to retract, excessive change in trim with flap movement, and rudder buffet. Two days later, the second flight ended with a dead stick landing due to a defective electronic fuel control unit. As taxi-ing trials earlier had confirmed wind-tunnel and control-line tests predicting major longitudinal control difficulties with the initial horizontal tail design, it was painfully clear that the XF10F-1 trials were going to be anything but routine. Later tests revealed more airframe and engine problems. On the positive side, however, tests proved the wing sweep mechanism to be reliable and effective.

347

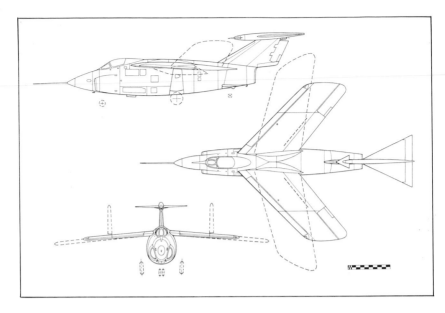

Grumman XF10F-1 Jaguar

The XF10F-1 after it had been fitted with powered F9F-6 horizontal tail surfaces. *(Grumman)*

While Grumman had no control over engine-related deficiencies, the company did try to correct the numerous stability and control problems plaguing the trials. Noteworthy changes included the fitting of 'horsal' (horizontal ventral) fins on the rear fuselage sides (first tried on 9 September, 1952), the testing of larger horizontal tail surfaces (in January 1953), and the substitution of powered F9F-6 swept horizontal surfaces for the originally fitted delta tailplane (in April 1953). The last of these changes

348

appeared to hold much promise but nevertheless on 1 April, 1953, the Navy cancelled production contracts. The subsequent grounding of all J40-powered aircraft spelled the end for the Jaguar. The second XF10F-1 prototype which was then 90 per cent complete was shipped to the Naval Air Material Center in Philadelphia where, together with the first prototype, it was used for barrier testing.

When trials ended on 25 April, 1953, with the thirty-second flight, the XF10F-1 had never been airborne for more than 67 minutes at a time. It had never reached an altitude of more than 31,500 ft nor gone past Mach 0.86 in level flight or Mach 0.975 in a dive as, fitted with a non-afterburning engine, it was grossly underpowered. Even with their intended afterburning engines, however, it is doubtful that production F10F-1s could have achieved predicated performance as their power loading would still have been higher than desired.

PRODUCTION: Only one of the two XF10F-1s was completed. It was assigned BuNo 128311.

Calculated data for production F10F-1s with afterburning J40-WE-8 turbojet:

Span (minimum sweep) 50 ft 7 in (15.42 m); span (maximum sweep) 36 ft 8 in (11.18 m); span (wings folded) 24 ft 9 in (7.54 m); length 54 ft 5 in (16.59 m); height 16 ft 3 in (4.95 m); wing area (minimum sweep) 467 sq ft (43.39 sq m); wing area (maximum sweep) 450 sq ft (41.81 sq m).

Empty weight 20,426 lb (9,265 kg); loaded weight 27,450 lb (12,451 kg); maximum weight 35,450 lb (16,080 kg); wing loading 58.8 to 61.0 lb/sq ft (287.0 to 297.8 kg/sq m); power loading 2.5 lb/lb st (2.5 kg/kg st).

Maximum speed 710 mph (1,142 kmh) at sea level; cruising speed 478 mph (769 kmh); climb rate 13,350 ft/min (68 m/sec); service ceiling 45,800 ft (13,960 m); normal range 1,670 miles (2,685 km); maximum range 2,090 miles (3,365 km).

An S-2D of VS-36 passing the island of the USS *Randolph* (CVS-15). *(Grumman)*

Grumman S2F (S-2) Tracker

Conceived in 1950, when jet aircraft were rapidly replacing piston-powered aircraft aboard carriers, the Tracker nevertheless went on to have a remarkably long service life both in the United States and abroad. With the US Navy, S-2Gs were last deployed in the ASW role aboard the USS *Kitty Hawk* (CV-63) in 1975 and TS-2As were retired by the Naval Air Training Command in 1979. Abroad, in the late 1980s these venerable piston-powered aircraft were not only soldiering on with the air forces or naval air arms of eleven nations – including those of Argentina and Brazil, which were still flying their Trackers from carriers – but also many were being modernized, while others were expected to have their radial engines replaced by propeller-turbines. Quite possibly, some of these re-engined aircraft will thus still be operated in their original role in 2002, fifty years after the maiden flight of the XS2F-1 on 4 December, 1952, while others will then be operated in the forest fire-fighting role, much as modified Trackers started doing during the 1970s. Although piston- and turbine-powered Trackers will then look decidedly elderly in the midst of jet aircraft, their exceptional longevity will be a glowing tribute to the skill and care of design and production personnel from the 'Bethpage Iron Works.'

Seeking both to conserve deck space aboard carriers by replacing its AF-2S and AF-2W ASW team with a single aircraft and to improve operating efficiency by placing the detection and attack crews in the same ASW aircraft, the US Navy issued an Invitation to Bid on 20 January, 1950. In addition to specifying that the new anti-submarine aircraft had to carry the necessary search equipment and weapons to detect and destroy enemy submarines without assistance from other aircraft or from ships, the Bureau of Aeronautics also stipulated that the aircraft should be small enough to operate from CVE-105 escort carriers. In answer to these demanding requirements, eighteen manufacturers submitted twenty-four proposals for single- or twin-engined aircraft on 27 April, 1950, with those submitted by Grumman, Douglas, and Vought subsequently being considered the most promising by the evaluation team. In the end, the Douglas proposal for Models D-603 and D-604 was eliminated, that from Vought was considered to warrant further evaluation (a subsequent contract for two XS2U-1s was later cancelled before completion of the first aircraft), and Grumman's Model 89 emerged winner of the competition on 2 June, 1950.

Of fairly conventional twin-engined design with shoulder-mounted wings and nosewheel undercarriage, the G-89 incorporated numerous advanced features to solve control problems previously associated with the operation of twin-engined aircraft aboard carriers and to provide sufficient volume for accommodating a crew of four and housing a large amount of ASW detection equipment and weapons within an airframe small enough for operations aboard escort carriers. Of particular interest were the measures adopted to achieve adequate control during single-engined carrier approach and landing. To that end, the rudder was split vertically into two sections, with the forward section being hydraulically-actuated during take-off, landing, and single-engined operations to supplement the main manually-operated rudder section. Wing control surfaces included flaps extending over 85 per cent of the trailing edge and circular arc spoilers supplementing relatively small ailerons. The multi-spar wings which, after folding hydraulically upward from a point just outboard of the engine nacelles, overlapped longitudinally above the fuselage, incorporated leading-edge slots. Also noteworthy was the use of large underwing nacelles to house Wright R-1820 nine-cylinder radial engines and to provide space for the main undercarriage and rear-launched sonobuoys.

One of the key factors in the selection of the G-89 as the winner of the 1950 competition for a hunter-killer ASW aircraft was Grumman's early adoption of the AN/APS-33G search radar (which was powerful enough to detect snorkels but yet used an antenna small enough to fit into a retractable 'dustbin' radome beneath the rear fuselage) in preference to the heavier and bulkier AN/APS-20 radar, which forced both Douglas and Vought to propose large radomes generating drag and complicating the design of wing fold and undercarriage. Other non-acoustic detection equipment proposed by Grumman included ECM direction-finding gear mounted atop the fuselage, a retractable 'stinger' MAD (magnetic anomaly detector) boom,

S2F-1 (BuNo 133237) with the ventral radome for the AN/APS-33G search radar and the tail boom for the AN/ASQ-8 magnetic anomaly detector in the extended position as during ASW search operations. The inverted Y antenna atop the cockpit is for the AN/APA-70C ECM set. (*USN/National Archives*)

and a steerable searchlight in a fairing beneath the starboard wing. In addition to housing most of the detection gear, the fuselage incorporated a cabin forward of the wings with accommodation for a crew of four (pilot, co-pilot/navigator, radar operator and MAD operator, all of whom sat on conventional, forward-facing seats) and the main weapons bay on the port side.

Although a Letter of Intent dated 30 June, 1950, had been followed on 31 October, 1950, by the award of Contract NOa(s)-12242 for two XS2F-1s (BuNos 129137 and 129138) and a mock-up inspection in December 1950 had resulted in only a few requests for modifications, detailed design and manufacturing of the first aircraft proceeded slowly, as combat operations in Korea had by then rendered more urgent the production of Panthers and the development of the Cougar. Consequently, contracts for fifteen YS2F-1s and the first 284 production S2F-1s were not executed until the spring of 1952, by which time the vertical tail surfaces had been enlarged and the horizontal tail surfaces given marked dihedral, and construction of the two prototypes proceeded slowly until after the end of the Korean War. Finally, however, the first XS2F-1, BuNo 129137, was ready to begin flight trials. Following a successful 22-minute first flight made at Bethpage on 4 December, 1952, with Norman J Coutant and Fred C Rowley at the controls, trials and development proceeded smoothly and rapidly before the first operational S2F-1s were assigned to VS-26 in February 1954. Contractor demonstration flights started in February 1953 and ended thirteen months later; BIS (Board of Inspection and Survey) trials were initiated in February 1953; carrier suitability evaluation was undertaken later in the year aboard the uss *Mindoro* (CVE-120) and uss *Coral Sea* (CVA-43); static tests were performed between February 1953 and October 1955; and service trials were undertaken by VX-1.

Production history

Between 1953 and 1967, Grumman built four production models – the S2F-1, S2F-2, S2F-3, and S2F-3S, respectively redesignated S-2A, S-2C, S-2D, and S-2E in September 1962; de Havilland Aircraft of Canada produced two models under licence, the CS2F-1 and CS2F-2. As detailed here, numerous other variants appeared, and in the late 1980s continue to appear, as a result of modification programmes in the United States and abroad.

XS2F-1: Two prototypes (BuNos 129137 and 129138) were built in 1952-53 and were each powered by a pair of 1,425-hp Wright R-1820-76 radials driving three-blade Hamilton Standard propellers. BuNo 129138 was accepted by the Navy on 3 July, 1953, but BuNo 129137, was retained by Grumman for development work and was not delivered until 17 August, 1956, more than forty-four months after its maiden flight on 4 December, 1952.

YS2F-1: The fifteen pre-production YS2F-1s (BuNos 129139/129153) differed from the prototypes in being powered by 1,525-hp Wright R-1820-82s and in being fitted with additional operational equipment. The YS2F-1 first flew on 30 July, 1953, and the pre-production aircraft were used for preliminary carrier suitability trials at NATC Patuxent River and aboard the USS *Mindoro* (CVE-120).

S-2A (S2F-1): Grumman built a total of 740 S2F-1s for the US Navy and for export customers (Brazil, Italy, Japan, and The Netherlands). All were powered by R-1820-82s and most were basically similar to the YS2F-1s. During the course of production, internal fuel capacity was increased from 377 to 544 US gal. On some of the aircraft built for Italy and Japan, the wing

The fourth YS2F-1 (BuNo 129142) over NAS Patuxent River on 7 May, 1954. The aircraft bears the markings of the Flight Test Division, Naval Air Test Center. (*USN/National Archives*)

353

folding mechanism was dispensed with and internal fuel capacity was increased to 753 gal, thus extending combat range from 968 to 1,351 miles; moreover, catapult and arrester hooks were not fitted to these aircraft, which were intended solely for operations from land bases. The typical electronic fit of late production S2F-1s included an AN/APS-38 search radar replacing the original AN/APS-33G set in a retractable ventral radome beneath the rear fuselage, an AN/ASQ-8 magnetic anomaly detector in a retractable tail boom, and an AN/APR-9B ECM search receiver. Beginning with BuNo 133240, this equipment also included an AN/APA-69A ECM set in a radome above the forward fuselage in lieu of an AN/APA-70C and its inverted Y dorsal antenna. Other operational equipment included a 70-million candlepower AN/AVQ-2A searchlight beneath the starboard wing, sonobuoys (two AN/SSQ-1s or eight AN/SSQ-2s) in the rear of each engine nacelle, and a Retro Ejector Unit in the fuselage for rearward ejection of Mk. 7 Marine markers. By retrofit to early aircraft and during manufacture for late production aircraft, the outboard side of each engine nacelle was modified to provide for the carriage of three Mk. 6 Marine Location Markers and, following installation of early Julie explosive echo-ranging equipment, a dispenser for thirteen PDCs (Practice Depth Charges). PDCs, which provided the underwater sound source for the Julie detection system, were eventually replaced by specially designed SUS (Signal, Underwater Sound) charges.

The S2F-1 could carry either one Mk. 34 torpedo, one Mk. 41 torpedo, two Mk. 43 torpedoes, or one Mk. 24 mine in the ventral bomb bay, and either four Mk. 19 mines, four Mk. 43 torpedoes, four Mk. 54 depth charges, or six HVAR rockets beneath its wings. In US service a number of S2F-1s were modified to the S2F-1S, S2F-1S1, S2F-1T, S2F-1U, and US-2B configurations. Abroad, two Japanese S2F-1s became S2F-Cs and four were modified as S2F-Us, two Brazilian aircraft became UP-16As, and

Built as an S2F-1, BuNo 136616 was later modified as a five-passenger US-2A utility transport and is illustrated in that configuration as operated by Air Development Squadron Five (VX-5). *(Peter B Lewis)*

eighteen Dutch S-2As were modified as S-2Ns with two of the latter being further modified as US-2Ns.

S2F-C: This non-USN designation was given to two Japanese S2F-1s modified in service as transport aircraft. At that time, their original Japanese serial numbers, 4110 and 4105, were changed to 9061 and 9062.

TS-2A (S2F-1T): This designation identifies multi-engined advanced trainers obtained by removing armament, radar, and ECM gear from 228 S2F-1s and fitting dual controls for pilot training.

US-2A (S2F-1U): At least sixty-four S-2A airframes were converted for target towing and utility transport duties. All ASW equipment was removed.

S2F-U: This non-USN designation was given to four Japanese S2F-1s modified in service as target-towing aircraft. At that time, their original Japanese serial numbers, 4160, 4159, 4137, and 4158, were changed to 9151/9154.

S-2B (S2F-1S): In service with the US Navy, 138 S2F-1s were upgraded to the S2F-1S configuration by installation of the AN/AQA-3 Jezebel long-range acoustic search equipment and improved Julie explosive echo-ranging system. The Julie/Jezebel system was also retrofitted to a number of non-US operated aircraft. A number of S-2Bs were later modified as S-2Fs or US-2Bs.

US-2B: This designation was given to sixty-four S-2As, S-2Bs, TS-2As, and US-2As converted to a five-passenger configuration with removal of electronics and installation of seats and modified nacelle aft ends. The torpedo bay was used for carrying cargo.

S-2C (S2F-2): The S2F-2 version, of which sixty were built for the US Navy, differed from the first production model in having an enlarged bomb bay with an asymmetrical extension on the port side of the fuselage to enable internal carriage of a Mk. 90 nuclear depth charge. The span of the horizontal tail surfaces was increased from 22 ft 4 in to 27 ft 2 in. Contrary to

US-2C target-towing aircraft (BuNo 133347) of Utility Squadron Five (VC-5).

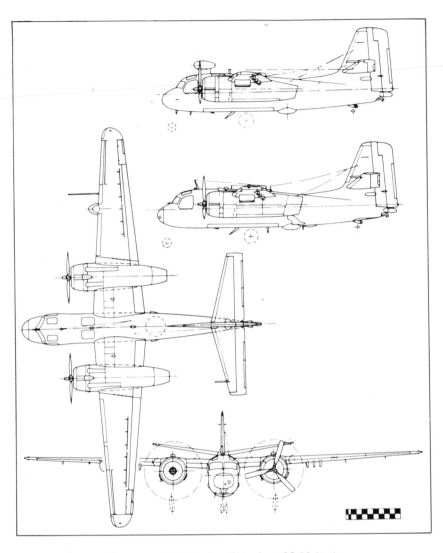

Grumman S-2D Tracker. Side view of S-2A (top)

previously published data, BuNos 140103/140120 were not built. BuNo 133329, the first S2F-2, flew on 12 July, 1954, and S2F-2 deliveries began in November of that year.

The enlarged bomb bay was no longer required when the large-size Mk. 90 nuclear depth charge was replaced by the smaller Mk. 101 (Lulu) nuclear weapon. Accordingly, S2F-2 production was terminated in November 1955 after the completion of the sixtieth aircraft, whereas the S2F-1 with the originally sized torpedo bay remained in production for another sixty-six months.

S2F-1 (JMSDF serial 4152, BuNo 144705) of the Nihon Kaijyo Jieitai in August 1970. After becoming surplus to JMSDF requirements, this aircraft was sold in the United States and registered N214AK. (*Toshiyuki Toda, courtesy of Alain Pelletier*)

RS-2C (S2F-2P): These post- and pre-September 1962 designations were given to an S2F-2 which was modified for photographic work.

US-2C (S2F-2U): A total of fifty S2F-2s were modified by the Navy as S2F-2U target-towing utility aircraft.

S-2D (S2F-3): Grumman Design 121 was an enlarged and modernized version which was proposed in October 1957 and ordered two months later under the S2F-3 designation. Compared with the S2F-1, the S2F-3 was 18 in longer, had enlarged wings (the span was increased by 2 ft 11 in and area by 11 sq ft with rounded tips), larger horizontal tail surfaces, roomier cabin area, and enlarged weapons bay. The 1,525-hp R-1820-82A or -82WA radials were housed in revised nacelles which each provided space for twice the number of sonobuoys (sixteen versus eight in the S2F-1 and S2F-2 versions) in the rear and thirteen Mk. 25 Marine Markers on the outboard side. Internal fuel capacity was increased to 728 US gal. New electronic equipment included the AN/APS-88A search radar, which replaced the AN/APS-38 in the ventral radome, an AN/ALD-2B ECM direction finder, an AN/APN-122 doppler, and an AN/ASQ-10A magnetic anomaly detector. Other ASW equipment and systems, including Julie/Jezebel, were similar to those in the S2F-1S. Internally-carried weapons included either two torpedoes (Mk. 34, Mk. 43, Mk. 44, or Mk. 46), one special store (Mk. 57 or Mk. 101), one Mk. 54 depth charge, or one Mk. 52 mine. Externally-carried weapons included either torpedoes (one or two beneath each wing), six HVAR rockets, six rocket pods, or four depth charges. An internal dispenser aft of the fuselage entrance door carried twenty-seven SUS charges. The dispenser had two release doors and two vertical rows of SUS charges permitting the release of a shallow and a deep charge at the same time. Additional charges could be loaded in flight from a 35-SUS storage

357

unit. Corrosion control was improved by substituting chemical milling for spot welding in the manufacture of the wing centre section and of the rudder trimmer. The first S2F-3 (BuNo 147531) flew on 20 May, 1959, and production for the US Navy totalled 100 aircraft.

YAS-2D: This designation identified the proposed conversion of an S-2D to a self-contained night attack (SCNA) prototype configuration for evaluation by the US Air Force. Work on Design 325 was undertaken in the spring of 1966 in response to a request from the Office of the Deputy Chief of Staff for Research and Development. Specifically, the request called for feasibility and cost estimates for the procurement of twenty-four S-2D or S-2E aircraft modified for night visual attack against trucks and sampans. As proposed in June 1966, all Navy ASW, communications, IFF, and navigation equipment was to be replaced by Air Force-specified systems. Principal new systems were to include LLLTV (Low-Light-Level Television installed in the rear fuselage on the retracting system used for the AN/APS-88 search radar of standard Navy S-2s), LORAN D (Long-Range Navigation Doppler Inertial), TACAN (Tactical Air Navigation), radar altimeter, and doppler. Armament was to consist of ten anti-personnel munitions canisters in the bomb bay and two bomblet dispensers beneath each wing. Armour against light ground fire was to be added around the cockpit and beneath the engines and wing fuel tanks.

With a crew of pilot and observer-bombardier, the proposed SCNA-configured night attack aircraft was to have a take-off gross weight of 27,403 lb when carrying 3,508 lb of bomblets. Typical sorties were to include 6.4 hours on station at a radius of 115 miles from base and a loiter speed of 127 mph. However, at this speed the aircraft was considered by the Air Force to be too vulnerable to ground fire. Accordingly, the Air force dropped its projected acquisition of twenty-four ex-Navy Trackers modified to the AS-2D configuration.

Based at NAS Point Mugu and fitted with loud speakers in underwing nacelles, this ES-2D was used to warn off vessels sailing in the restricted Pacific Missile Range off the coast of California.
(Ben Knowles, courtesy of Alain Pelletier)

358

ES-2D: This designation was given to at least six S-2Ds and one S-2E (BuNos 147531/147532, 147554, 147872, 148726, 149245, and 151667) modified by the Navy for special electronic operations and development work.

US-2D: This designation was given to S-2Ds modified by the Navy as target-towing utility aircraft.

S-2E (S2F-3S): The S-2E differed from the S-2D mainly in being fitted with the AN/ASN-30 tactical navigation system featuring memory, display, and automatic computations for the solution of tactical and navigational problems. These functions were accomplished separately and, in many cases, manually in the S-2D and earlier models. A total of 252 S-2Es, including fourteen aircraft for the Royal Australian Navy, was built between 1962 and 1967.

S-2F (S2F-1S1): These were respectively post- and pre-September 1962 designations given to 244 S-2A/S2F-1s and S-2B/S2F-1Ss fitted with updated electronics and further improved Julie detection equipment.

US-2F: This designation was given to at least one S-2F modified as a utility transport.

YS-2G and **S-2G:** In the early 1970s, with the impending decommissioning of its last Antisubmarine Warfare Support Carriers (CVSs) and while awaiting delivery of its Lockheed S-3As, the US Navy needed to adapt a number of Trackers for operations aboard Multi-purpose Aircraft Carriers (CVs). Having won the competition for modernizing S-2Es, Martin Marietta modified an aircraft as the YS-2G prototype in 1971 and manufactured kits to enable the Navy's Quonset Point Rework Facility to convert forty-nine S-2Es to S-2G standard. Equipment and armament changes included installation of AN/AQA-7 DIFAR (Direction Low-Frequency Analyzer and Ranging) processing equipment and provision for carrying the Martin AGM-12B Bullpup anti-ship missile.

An S-2G (BuNo 153576) of VS-24 assigned to Carrier Antisubmarine Warfare Air Group 56 (CVSG-56) for deployment aboard the USS *Intrepid* (CVS-11) before the decommissioning of this carrier in March 1974.

359

S-2N: The S-2N designation, which was not an official US Navy designation, was given to eighteen Dutch S-2As overhauled by Fairey Canada in 1968-70 and fitted with modernized equipment. Their Marine Luchtvaart Dienst serial numbers were 149, 151, 153, 155/162, 164/169, and 171.

US-2N: This non-USN designation identifies four S-2Ns (MLD serial numbers 151, 159, 160, and 168) which were modified as utility transports in 1972.

S-2T: This unofficial designation was used in 1987-88 to identify Trackers which were to be modernized and re-engined with 1,650-shp Garrett TPE331-15AW propeller-turbines. In addition to new engines, proposed new equipment includes AN/ASQ-504(V) magnetic anomaly detector, AN/APS-128D search radar, MAPADS 902F acoustic processor, AN/ASN-150 tactical navigation system, AN/ARR-15 acoustic receivers, and Collins avionics. The first of two prototype conversions made for Grumman St Augustine by Tracor Aviation Inc was scheduled to fly early in 1989 with most of the testing being done at Mojave, California. Thereafter, S-2Es and S-2Gs are to be modified for a number of overseas customers including the Republic of China and Turkey.

S-2 Turbo: Also re-engined with Garret propeller-turbines (TPE331-14s flat rated at 1,250 shp) driving five-blade propellers, the S-2 Turbo conversion was realized by Marsh Aviation Company, in Mesa, Arizona, for the California Forestry Department. In addition to its new engines, the S-2 Turbo differs from other Trackers modified earlier for forest fire-fighting in incorporating a number of aerodynamic improvements to reduce drag and computerized engine controls to reduce pilot workload and improve

The Marsh Aviation S-2 Turbo (N426DF, ex-BuNo 133245) at Fresno, California, on 22 July, 1988, during its evaluation by the California Department of Forestry and Fire Protection. *(René J Francillon)*

reliability. The first S-2 Turbo (N426DF, ex TS-2A BuNo133245) flew on 21 November, 1986. Following evaluation of this prototype during the 1988 and 1989 fire seasons, the California Department of Forestry and Fire Protection will decide whether to proceed with further conversions.

CS2F-1: Selected in 1954 to replace the Grumman Avenger in Royal Canadian Navy service, the Tracker was built under licence by de Havilland of Canada. Work done by Grumman to adapt the S2F-1 to Canadian requirements was undertaken under Design Number 103 beginning in December 1953. More than fourteen years later, Grumman did some preliminary design work on Design Number 103A to fit Mohawk-type surveillance equipment in ex-RCN CS2F-1s for possible use in support of land operations by the Canadian Armed Forces.

Grumman provided some parts and components for the first CS2F-1 (initially numbered X500 and later assigned the RCN serial number 1501 when brought up to full CS2F-1 standard) and the US Navy lent an S2F-1 (BuNo 136519) to the Royal Canadian Navy for one year. Forty-two CS2F-1s (RCN 1502/1543) built in Downsview, Ontario, differed from Grumman built S2F-1s in being fitted with Julie/Jezebel acoustic search and echo-ranging equipment, in incorporating minor equipment details, and in being powered by R-1820-82s built under licence by Pratt & Whitney of Canada. The first Canadian-built Tracker flew at Downsview on 31 May, 1956. Seventeen CS2F-1s were transferred to The Netherlands in 1960-61 and two others, RCN 1534 and 1540, were modified as COD transports in 1964.

CS2F-2: The last fifty-seven Canadian-built Trackers (RCN 1544/1600) were fitted with Litton Industries tactical navigation equipment and were designated CS2F-2s. These aircraft, however, did not have the asymmetri-

CS2F-1 (RCN 1517) built under licence by de Havilland of Canada. (*Grumman*)

cal bomb bay extension and other improvements characterizing US -built S2F-2s.

CS2F-3: This designation was given to forty-five CS2F-1s and CS2F-2s modernized to a common standard with AN/ASN-501 tactical computer and navigation system, updated Julie/Jezebel, and AN/APN-503 doppler.

CP-121: When the new Canadian military aircraft designation system was adopted, the CS2F-1s, CS2F-2s, and CS2F-3s respectively became CP-121 Mk. 1s, Mk. 2s, and Mk. 3s. At that time, their RCN serials 1501 to 1599 were replaced by Canadian military serial numbers 12101 to 12199. Since then most CP-121s have been disposed off, ten have been placed in storage, and twenty have been stripped of their ASW equipment. With crew complement reduced to three (two pilots and an Airborne Electronic Sensor operator), the modified aircraft are now fitted to carry either six 36-rocket underwing pods for use in the sea surveillance role or a day/night photographic pod beneath the starboard wing for pollution detection and fishery patrol. In 1987, the Canadian Department of National Defence announced that the IMP Group of Dartmouth, Nova Scotia, would re-engine a CP-121 with 1,509-eshp Pratt & Whitney PT6A-67AF propeller-turbines driving six-blade propellers and that this experimental conversion was likely to be followed by the re-engining of twenty-seven additional aircraft. The re-engined CP-121s will probably be fitted with Spar Falcon FLIR (Forward Looking Infra-Red), Litton Canada APS-504(V) radar, and Marconi Canada ARV-509(V) Omega very low frequency navigation equipment.

P-16: This is a Brazilian designation for the S-2A/S2F-1.

UP-16: This is a Brazilian designation identifying two P-16s (S-2As) modified as utility transports.

P-16E: This is a Brazilian designation for the S-2E.

Service history

Initially named Sentinel but renamed Tracker before entering USN service and unofficially nicknamed *Stoof* (S-two-F), the S2F-1 was first assigned in February 1954 to VS-26 at NAS Norfolk, Virginia, to replace Avengers. Nine months later the S2F-1 was joined in service by the S2F-2. Over the next two and a half years the rapidly increasing production rate enabled the Navy to re-equip fourteen additional squadrons, with VS-23, -32, and -38 converting from Avengers to Trackers and VS-20, -21, -22, -24, -25, -27, -30, -31, -36, -37, and -39 exchanging Guardians for Trackers. Later, with the S2F-3 and S2F-3S versions joining the fleet respectively in May 1961 and August 1962, Trackers were also assigned to five other deployable squadrons (VS-28, -29, 33, -34, and -35), to twenty-one Reserve squadrons, and to several NARESTRACOM (Naval Reserve Training Command) units.

Initial operations proved remarkably trouble-free as the *Stoof* – the first twin-engined aircraft to be operated routinely and in large numbers from

S2F-1s of VS-26 aboard the USS *Antietam* (CVS-36) on 8 March 1955. *(USN)*

small carriers – encountered no significant problems and proved easier to operate from the decks of escort carriers than the Guardian it replaced. Operations from the short and narrow deck of escort and light carriers, however, were limited and of short duration as CVEs and CVLs were progressively replaced during the mid-1950s by unmodernized *Essex*-class carriers and modernized SCB 27A carriers, which were redesignated CVSs (Antisubmarine Warfare Support Carriers). Typically, each CVS embarked two 12-Tracker squadrons, an ASW helicopter squadron, and a detachment of AEW aircraft. Following the establishment in April 1960 of the first two Antisubmarine Warfare Carrier Air Groups, CVSG-53 and CVSG-59, these formerly independent squadrons were teamed together so that at peak strength in 1961-62 the Atlantic Fleet had twelve deployable Tracker squadrons in six CVSGs while the Pacific Fleet had eight Tracker squadrons in four CVSGs. Two other squadrons, VS-30 in the Atlantic Fleet and VS-41 in the Pacific Fleet, operated several S-2 models to provide conversion and operational training for personnel assigned to the deployable squadrons.

During the Vietnam War, eight S-2 squadrons (VS-33 and VS-38 aboard *Bennington*, VS-35 and VS-37 aboard *Hornet*, VS-21 and VS-29 aboard *Kearsarge*, and VS-23 and VS-25 aboard *Yorktown*) made a total of thirteen deployments to the Gulf of Tonkin, during which they flew ASW patrols, provided sea surveillance, and performed *Sea Dragon* naval gunfire spotting duty. Most sorties were fairly routine; nevertheless, an S-2D from VS-35 was lost due to an unknown cause during a combat sortie on 21 January, 1966, and three S-2Es were lost in operational accidents before the completion of the last CVS war cruise by *Kearsarge* in September 1969. By then, the huge cost of the war was forcing the Navy to decommission its

S2F-3 (BuNo 148736) of VS-30, an ASW training squadron assigned to Replacement Carrier Antisubmarine Warfare Air Group Fifty (RCVSG-50) at NAS Key West, Florida, in the early 1960s. *(Grumman)*

ASW carriers, and *Intrepid* made the last CVS deployment to the Mediterranean in 1972-73. Concurrent with the CVS phase-out, the number of Tracker squadrons was also reduced, but at a slower rate, as, following a 1971 Mediterranean cruise aboard *Saratoga* during which S-2Es from VS-28 were attached to an Attack Air Wing, squadrons equipped with specially-modified S-2Gs operated from the decks of CVs. The last to do so, VS-37, which had made its final deployment aboard the *Kitty Hawk* in 1975, retired its last S-2Gs on 27 August 1976, more than twenty-two years after VS-26 had received the first operational S2F-1s.

In addition to their long and distinguished ASW career with the US Navy, Trackers served even more years as trainers, utility, and support aircraft, and test and development vehicles. In the crew training role, Trackers replaced Beech SNB-5s and were first assigned in 1955 to Advanced Training Units (ATUs) at NAS Hutchinson, Kansas, and NAS Kingsville, Texas, and to an ATU at NAS Corpus Christi, Texas, in 1958. Following a number of station changes and the redesignation of ATUs as Training Squadrons (VTs) in May 1960, S2F-1Ts were assigned to VT-27, VT-28, and VT-31 to provide twin-engined familiarization, instrument, cross country navigation, and carrier qualification training, with all three squadrons being based at NAS Corpus Christi after October 1965. The situation remained unchanged for eight years; however, in 1973, VT-27 was re-organized as a basic training squadron and four years later VT-31 converted to the Beech T-44A. The last TS-2As were retired by VT-28 at the end of February 1979.

Over the years, various US-2 models replaced Douglas JD-1 target-tugs operated by Utility Squadrons and Beech JRB-4 light transports assigned to

364

Navy and Marine station flights in the United States and abroad. Other modified Trackers performed a variety of test and development activities at the Naval Air Test Center at Patuxent River; the Naval Air Test Facility at Lakehurst; the Naval Missile Center/Pacific Missile Center at Point Mugu; the Naval Ordnance Test Station/Naval Weapons Center at China Lake; and the Pacific Missile Range Facility at Barking Sands in Hawaii. Noteworthy among these experiments were those conducted in 1964 at the Naval Air Test Center with an S-2A (BuNo 133061) which was fitted with a nose yoke and a winching device for development trials of the Skyhook-Aerotriever system. With this system, aircrewmen or loads of up to 1,000 lb which were held aloft by a line hooked to a helium-filled balloon could be retrieved in flight*. The last Tracker in USN service, an ES-2D (BuNo 147870) from the Pacific Missile Range Facility at Barking Sands was ferried to Davis-Monthan AFB in March 1986.

First operated outside of the United States by the Royal Canadian Navy in 1957, the Tracker went on to serve with the air forces or naval air arms of the following nations:

ARGENTINA: The Servicio de Aviación Naval (the Naval Aviation Service which was later renamed Comando de Aviación Naval Argentina, CANA, Argentine Naval Aviation Command) first obtained six ex-USN S-2As in February 1962. These aircraft were assigned the Argentine naval serials 0510/0515 and equipped the 1ª Escuadrilla Aeronaval Antisubmarina when this unit was activated at BAN Punta del Indio in May 1962 as part of the 3ª Escuadra Aeronaval. One year later, the 1ª Escuadrilla Aeronaval Antisubmarina was transferred to the 2ª Escuadra Aeronaval at

Modified S-2A (BuNo 133061) used at the Naval Air Test Center, NAS Patuxent River for *Skyhook-Aerotriever* trials in 1964. (*USN, courtesy of Robert E Kling*)

* The Skyhook system was later demonstrated at NAS North Island, California, where a Tracker was used to retrieve a FAETUPAC (Fleet Airborne Electronics Training Unit, Pacific) volunteer from San Diego Bay.

A US-2B transport assigned to NAS Moffett Field, California. *(Peter B Lewis)*

An S2F-1 of the 1ª Escuadrilla Aeronaval Antisubmarine, 2ª Escuadra Aeronaval, based at BAN Comandante Espora and embarked aboard the light carriers ARA *Independencia* and ARA *Veinticinco de Mayo*. *(Grumman)*

BAN Comandante Espora in Puerto Belgrano. Normally land-based, the Argentine S-2As and a single S-2F (serial 0542), acquired in 1967 but lost eight years later in a ground fire, regularly deployed first aboard the ARA *Independencia* and then aboard the ARA *Veinticinco de Mayo*.

Six ex-USN S-2Es (Argentine naval serials 0700/0705) were obtained by CANA in 1978, and the four surviving S-2As were transferred in January 1979 to the Escuadrilla Aeronaval de Propósitos Generales at BAN Almirante Zar in Trelew. Subsequently, three of the S-2As (0510/0512) were modified locally as Trackers Utilitarios to serve as COD and target towing aircraft; all armament and ASW electronics were removed and seats were provided for a crew of two and seven passengers. In 1983, the Trackers Utilitarios were again assigned to the 1ª Escuadrilla Aeronaval Anti-submarina.

During the Falklands War in 1982, S-2Es operated from BAM Malvinas (Port Stanley), aboard ARA *Veinticinco de Mayo* (reporting a possible contact on a submarine on 5 May and, possibly, damaging HMS *Onyx* in the ensuing ASW torpedo attack), and more extensively on surface patrol duty (during which none were intercepted by Sea Harriers even though they operated close to the Task Force) from BAN Comandante Espora and the Rio Gallegos airport.

Since the war, the six S-2Es have been fitted in Argentina with tactical computers, ECM equipment, and Omega navigation sets. In 1988, CANA was seeking budgetary authorization for a more comprehensive upgrading of their avionics and ASW detection equipment and for re-engining these aircraft with TPE331 propeller-turbines. In the same year, the Instituto Forestal de la Nación was planning the re-engining of CANA's three Trackers Utilitarios with propeller-turbines and their conversion as air tankers.

AUSTRALIA: Although it had operated two squadrons of Fairey Gannets since 1955, the Royal Australian Navy was forced to replace these turbine-powered aircraft with piston-powered Trackers in the mid-1960s as Gannets were no longer in production. Fourteen S-2Es were ordered in 1965 and, bearing BuNos153595/153608 prefixed by N12-, were delivered in 1967 for service with VS-816 and VC-851 at HMAS *Albatross*, Nowra, New South Wales, and aboard HMAS *Melbourne*. The RAN also obtained a no-longer-airworthy S-2A (BuNo 133160) for use as an instructional airframe. Tragedy struck on 5 December 1976, when, as a result of a hangar fire during the night, seven S-2Es were destroyed, three were damaged beyond economical repair, and two were less severely damaged. Only the last two could later be repaired. To replace the aircraft lost in the hangar fire, a final batch of ten ex-USN S-2Gs was acquired in 1977. Fortunately, six refurbished S-2Gs which had been ordered in 1976 had not yet been delivered. Like the S-2Es, the Australian S-2Gs added the N12- prefix to their original BuNos (152333, 152337, 152800, 152805, 152807, 152809,

An S-2E of VS-816, Royal Australian Navy, aboard HMAS *Melbourne* (*Mervyn W Prime, courtesy of Alain Pelletier*)

A P-16A (Brazilian serial 7016, S2F-1 BuNo 149039) of the 2º Escuadrão do Grupo de Aviação Embarcada at Recife, Brazil, in February 1987. (*Jean-Michel Guhl*)

152811/152812, 152816, 152837, 153566/153567, 153576, 153578, 153580, and 153582). After HMAS *Melbourne* was consigned to the breaker's yard in 1983, the last three S-2Es and the sixteen S-2Gs were retained by VC-851 for a little over a year before being withdrawn.

BRAZIL: Having acquired its first carrier, *Minas Gerais*, in 1956, the Marinha do Brasil planned to operate its own aircraft, and to that effect first acquired North American T-28R-1s. However, inter-Service rivalry led to the Força Aérea Brasileira being given responsibility for providing fixed-wing aircraft for operations aboard *Minas Gerais*. Accordingly, the FAB organized the 1º GAE (Primeiro Grupo de Aviação Embarcada) in November 1958 and soon after began negotiations to acquire thirteen new S2F-1s (BuNos 149037/149049). Designated P-16s, these aircraft were delivered during the summer in 1961 and were assigned FAB serials 7014/7026 when entering service with 1º/1º GAE (1º Escuadrão do 1º Grupo de Aviação Embarcada). Shore-based at the Base Aérea de Santa Cruz, State of Rio de Janeiro, but regularly sending six-aircraft detachments for operations aboard *Minas Gerais*, the 1º/1º GAE operated its P-16s until the spring of 1976, when eight ex-USN S-2Es (Brazilian designation P-16E and FAB serials 7030/7037) replaced them in front-line service. Two P-16s (FAB 7024 and FAB 7025) were later modified as UP-16 utility/COD transports by the Parque de Material Aeronáutica de São Paulo, and in 1988 were operated alongside the P-16Es by the 2º Escuadrão do Grupo de Aviação Embarcada, Comando Costiero. Consideration was then being

368

given to having the P-16Es refurbished, fitted with modern avionics, and re-engined with propeller-turbines.

CANADA: The first Tracker in Royal Canadian Navy service was a Grumman-built S2F-1, BuNo 136519, which was on loan from 27 September, 1956, until 16 September, 1957, and was evaluated by VX-10, the RCN test and development unit. Following completion of Canadian trials, CS2F-1s were first delivered to VS-880 at Halifax-Shearwater, Nova Scotia, in February 1957 with VS-881, also based at Shearwater, converting to Trackers eight months later and becoming the first to operate from HMCS *Bonaventure* in early 1959. The two squadrons, which were progressively re-equipped with CS2F-2s and CS2F-3s, shared responsibility for providing eight-aircraft detachments for operations aboard HMCS *Bonaventure* until the last Tracker was launched on 12 December, 1969, four months before the carrier was laid up for disposal.

With VU-33 continuing for several years to provide crew training, VS-880 continued to fly ASW operations from Shearwater during the early 1970s. However, ASW progressively played a lesser part in Tracker operations and, in March 1975, VS-880 was redesignated MR-880 and moved to CFB Summerside, Prince Edward Island, where the primary missions of its CP-121s became maritime surveillance and fishery patrol. Similar duties were then assigned to VU-33 at CFB Comox, British Columbia, while CP-121s were also assigned to a reserve unit, 420 (AR) Squadron at Shearwater. The CP-121s of these three units are likely to be re-engined with PT6A-67AF propeller-turbines.

ITALY: The Aeronautica Militare Italiana obtained a total of forty-five new and ex-USN S2F-1s/S-2As. The first batch of six new Trackers, BuNos 136556-136561, which in Italian service had their BuNos prefixed

S-2F (M.M. 148303) of the 88° Gruppo Antisom at Catania Fontanarosso, Sicily. (*Stato Maggiore Aeronautica, AMI, courtesy of the Italian Air Attaché in Washington*)

by MM (Matricola Militare), was delivered in March 1957, and these aircraft were used to re-equip the 161ª Squadriglia, 86º Gruppo Autonomo Anti-Somergibili at Naples-Capodichino. Subsequent deliveries included fourteen new S2F-1s in 1959 (with BuNos/MMs 136727/136728, 136734/136735, 136741/136742, 144696/144697, 144702/144703, 144710/144711, and 144716/144717), ten new S2F-1s with long-range tanks and non-folding wings in 1961 (BuNos/MMs 148294/148303), and fifteen ex-USN S-2As in 1964 (BuNos/MMs 133069, 133073, 133078/133079, 133085, 133097, 133100, 133103, 133106/133107, 133113, 133138, 133180, 133188, and 133212).

In addition to equipping the 86º Gruppo Autonomo Anti-Somergibili until the beginning of 1973, Trackers served with the 87º Gruppo AS, beginning in the spring of 1958, and with the 88º Gruppo AS, from March 1961. After being placed under the control of the 41º Stormo Anti-Somergibili at Catania-Fontanarossa in October 1965, the 88º Gruppo AS continued to fly Trackers until 1972, when it converted to Breguet Atlantics, and the 87º Gruppo AS did so until it was disbanded in August 1978.

JAPAN: A total of sixty S2F-1s was built by Grumman for the Nihon Kaijyo Jieitai (Japanese Maritime Self-Defence Force) with deliveries beginning in 1957. In service with 11 Kokutai at Kanoya and 14 Kokutai at Atsugi, the Trackers received JMSDF serials 4101/4160. Four of these aircraft were subsequently modified as S2F-U utility aircraft for service with 61 Kokutai at Atsugi while two became S2F-C transports for service with 31 Kokutai at Iwakuni and 61 Kokutai at Atsugi. The last Japanese S2F-1s were retired from 11 Kokutai at Kanoya in March 1984.

KOREA: Thirty ex-USN S-2Es, including twenty-four delivered in 1976 and six delivered five years later, have been assigned to the Republic of

A target-towing US-2N of 5 Squadron, Marine Luchtvaart Dienst, at Soesterberg on 3 June, 1972. (*A A D Wever, courtesy of Alain Pelletier*)

Korea Navy but are flown and maintained by ROKAF personnel. These aircraft may be re-engined as S-2Ts in the late 1980s or early 1990s.

NETHERLANDS: The Marine Luchtvaart Dienst received a total of forty-five Trackers from US and Canadian sources, including twenty-six new S2F-1s delivered in 1960-61 (BuNos 147636/147645 and 147278/147293 which became MLD 146/171), two ex-USN S2F-1s delivered in 1962 (BuNos 136459 and 136576 becoming MLD 172 and 173), and seventeen ex-RCN CS2F-1s delivered in 1960-61 (ex RCN serials 1502/1507, 1511/1516, 1518, 1522/1524, and 1526 becoming MLD 180/196). Eighteen of the S2F-1s were upgraded by Fairey Canada to S-2N standards in 1968-70, with four of these aircraft (MLD 151, 159/160, and 168) being modified in 1972 as US-2N utility aircraft.

S2F-1s were first assigned to 4 and 320 Squadrons at Valkenburg, with those from 320 Squadron being transferred to 2 Squadron at the end of 1962, while the CS2F-1s went to 1 Squadron at Boch van Hato, Curaçao, Dutch Antilles. For operations aboard HRMS *Karel Doorman*, eight-aircraft detachments were regularly provided by 2 and 4 Squadrons until 1966. During 1969, 2 Squadron became an operational conversion unit for Tracker, Neptune and Atlantic crews, but 1 and 4 Squadrons continued to fly ASW operations respectively from Hato (Dr Albert Plesman Airport) and Valkenburg. Finally, 4 Squadron was disbanded in 1971, when eight of its Trackers were transferred to Turkey, and 1 Squadron, which had been re-equipped with S-2Ns in 1969, was deactivated on 1 August, 1974. In the utility role, the four US-2Ns were operated by 5 Squadron at Valkenburg

An S-2E (Peruvian serial AA-540, ex-BuNo 152831) of the Servicio Aeronaval de la Marina Peruana at Lima-Jorge Chávez in May 1977. (*René J Francillon*)

during the early 1970s, with the last two being withdrawn from use on 1 October, 1975.

PERU: Nine ex-USN S-2Es were delivered to the Servicio Aeronaval de la Marina Peruana in 1976. Based at Lima-Jorge Chávez, these aircraft have received Peruvian naval serials AA-540/AA-548 and in 1988 were still serving with Escuadrón 12.

TAIWAN: The Chinese Nationalist Navy is believed to have received thirty-seven ex-USN Trackers, including ten S-2As and two batches of S-2Es (eighteen aircraft in 1978-79 and nine in 1985) to equip a sea surveillance and ASW unit based at Pintung. In 1986, it was announced that thirty-two of these aircraft were to be modernized and re-engined as S-2Ts, the first two being modified in the United States by Tracor and Grumman International, while the remaining aircraft were to be fitted in Taiwan with US manufactured kits under the supervision of Grumman personnel.

THAILAND: Ten ex-USN S-2As and S-2Fs, as well as two US-2Cs, were delivered to the Royal Thai Navy for operations from U-Tapao RTNAB at Satahip. By 1988 few, if any, were still airworthy.

TURKEY: The Türk Deniz Kuvvetleri (Turkish Naval Force) first obtained eight ex-Dutch S-2As in 1971-72 and later two ex-USN US-2As and thirty ex-USN S-2Es. Based at Topel, Trackers are now operated for the Turkish Navy by 103 Filo of the Turkish Air Force. The last eighteen S-2Es were overhauled by Grumman in St Augustine before being delivered to Turkey in 1985, and these aircraft, as well as some of the previously acquired Trackers, are now likely to be converted as propeller-turbine-powered S-2Ts.

URUGUAY: The Aviación Naval Uruguya first obtained three ex-USN S-2As (serials A-851/A-853) in 1969-70 and supplemented them with three

An S-2E (BuNo 151652) of the Türk Deniz Kuvvetleri (Turkish Naval Force) being refurbished by Grumman in St Augustine, Florida. The last three digits of the BuNo are painted on the fin, above the tailplane, and the code TCB on the rear fuselage indicates that the aircraft is assigned to the Turkish Navy's Dardanelles Fleet. (*Grumman*)

ex-USN S-2Gs in 1981 (serials A-854/A-856). The three S-2As have since been refurbished and partially brought up to S-2G standard by Grumman in St Augustine. The Trackers of the Grupo Antisubmarino are based at BAN Capitán Curbelo in Laguna del Sauce.

VENEZUELA: Eight ex-USN S-2Es were acquired by the Aviación de la Marina Venezolana in 1974-75 and initially received serials AS-101/AS-108. Later renumbered AS-0101/AS-0108, these S-2Es were still operated in 1988 by Escuadrón Aéreo Antisubmarino 1 at BAN Puerto Cabello.

Forest fire-fighting

In 1970, the Ontario Ministry of Natural Resources, Aviation and Fire Management Branch, purchased a CS2F-1 from the Royal Canadian Navy and had it modified by Field Aviation to evaluate the Tracker in the fire-fighting role. Successful trials led Field Aviation to modify eleven additional surplus CS2F-1/CS2F-2s for use in Ontario and Saskatchewan and three more on spec. The next Tracker conversion undertaken in Canada was made by Conair Aviation Ltd which, in 1978, first flew the prototype of its Firecat. Since then, Conair has converted more than thirty ex-USN S-2/US-2/TS-2s and ex-Canadian CS2Fs for its own use or for sale to the Government of Saskatchewan and France's Sécurité Civile. The latter first obtained three Firecats in 1982 and six years later took delivery of its fifteenth. The typical Firecat conversion necessitates removing some 3,000 lb of military equipment, undertaking corrosion control and repairs as necessary, and raising the cabin floor by 8 in to provide space for an 870-US gal, four-compartment retardant tank with flush doors.

In September 1988, France's Sécurité Civile received the first Conair Turbo Firecat which had been re-engined with 1,424-shp PT6A-67AF propeller-turbines and first flown on 7 August. Thirteen other French Firecats will be re-engined over the next four years and Conair will also convert eleven of its own aircraft as Turbo Firecats.

In the United States, the primary user of surplus Trackers is the

A Conair Firecat (F-ZBET, ex-USN US-2B BuNo 147559) of the Sécurité Civile in June 1988. *(Alain Pelletier)*

373

A Tracker of the California Department of Forestry and Fire Protection starting engines at the Nevada County Airport during the disastrous 1987 fire season. (*René J Francillon*)

California Department of Forestry and Fire Protection (CDF), which first evaluated the Grumman twin-engined aircraft in 1973 (the first four were TS-2As previously operated by VT-27 and modified as air tankers by Venable Aircraft Co in Hemet, California). Since then, the CFD has acquired a large fleet of Trackers, including ex-USN S-2As, TS-2As, and US-2As, which have been fitted with an 800-US gal tank with a bulged ventral fairing by private contractors such as Aero Union, Sis-Q, and Hemet Valley Flying Service. At the end of the 1988 fire season, the eighteen Trackers (N404DF/N406DF, N411DF/N412DF, N416DF/N417DF, N420DF, N423DF, N427DF, N436DF, N442DF/N443DF, N446DF/N448DF, N450DF, and N453DF) and the Marsh S-2 Turbo (N426F) then owned by the California Department of Forestry and Fire Protection, were flown and maintained under contract by Hemet Valley Flying Service.

PRODUCTION: 1,269 Trackers were built, including 1,169 S2Fs delivered by Grumman between December 1952 and December 1967, and 100 CS2Fs delivered by de Havilland of Canada in 1956-58, as follows:

2	XS2F-1	100	S2F-3
15	YS2F-1	252	S2F-3S
740	S2F-1	43	CS2F-1
60	S2F-2	57	CS2F-2

The Grumman-built aircraft were assigned the following BuNos and Royal Canadian Navy serials:

XS2F-1:   BuNos 129137/129138
YS2F-1:   BuNos 129139/129153
S2F-1:   BuNos 133045/133328, 136393/136747, 144696/144731, 147549/147561, 147577, 147636/147645, 148278/148303, 149037/149049, and 149843/149844

S2F-2:   BuNos 133329/133388
S2F-3:   BuNos 147531/147537, 147868/147895, 148717/148752,
        and 149228/149256
S2F-3S: BuNos 149257/149275, 149845/149892, 150601/150603,
        151638/151685, 152332/152379, 152798/152845,
        153559/153582, and 153595/153608

The DHC-built aircraft were assigned the following Royal Canadian Navy serials:

CS2F-1:   RCN serials 1501/1543
CS2F-2:   RCN serials 1544/1600

	S-2A	S-2C	S-2E	S-2T
DIMENSIONS:				
Span, ft in	69 8	69 8	72 7	72 7
(m)	(21.23)	(21.23)	(22.12)	(22.12)
Span (wings folded), ft in	27 4	27 4	27 4	27 4
(m)	(8.33)	(8.33)	(8.33)	(8.33)
Length, ft in	42 0	42 3	43 6	43 6
(m)	(12.80)	(12.88)	(13.26)	(13.26)
Height, ft in	16 3½	16 3½	16 7½	16 7½
(m)	(4.97)	(4.97)	(5.07)	(5.07)
Wing area, sq ft	485	485	496	496
(sq m)	(45.06)	(45.06)	(46.08)	(46.08)
WEIGHTS:				
Empty, lb	17,357	17,640	18,820	16,783
(kg)	(7,873)	(8,001)	(8,537)	(7,613)
Loaded, lb	23,470	25,145	26,664	24,413
(kg)	(10,646)	(11,406)	(12,095)	(11,074)
Maximum, lb	24,408	25,985	29,764	27,962
(kg)	(11,071)	(11,787)	(13,501)	(12,683)
Wing loading,* lb/sq ft	48.4	51.8	53.8	49.2
(kg/sq m)	(236.3)	(253.1)	(262.5)	(240.3)
Power loading,* lb/hp	7.7	8.2	8.7	7.4
(kg/hp)	(3.5)	(3.7)	(4.0)	(3.4)
PERFORMANCE:				
Max speed, mph/ft	272/3,100	263/3,100	251/4,000	330/ –
(kmh/m)	(438/945)	(423/945)	(404/1,220)	(531/ –)
Cruising speed, mph	150	150	150	207
(kmh)	(241)	(241)	(241)	(333)
Climb rate, ft/min	2,330/1	2,040/1	1,830/1	–
(m/sec)	(12)	(10)	(9)	(–)
Service ceiling, ft	22,800	21,100	20,100	–
(m)	(6,950)	(6,430)	(6,125)	(–)
Normal range, miles	968	858	920	1,150
(km)	(1,557)	(1,380)	(1,480)	(1,850)
Max range, miles	–	1,210	1,300	–
(km)	(–)	(1,945)	(2.090)	(–)

* Wing and power loadings are calculated at normal loaded weight and maximum take-off power.

F11F-1s from the second production batch were characterized by their wing root fillets and longer nose. There four aircraft are from VF-21, one of the two Atlantic Fleet squadrons which flew Tigers. (*Grumman*)

Grumman F11F (F-11) Tiger

The early 1950s was a period of great aeronautical progress, with jet fighter performance increasing at a rapid pace. Thus, even though in its F11F-1 version it was the first Navy fighter aircraft capable of flying supersonically in level flight and in its F11F-1F version the first to exceed Mach 2 in level flight, the Tiger only served for four years with operational squadrons as the F11F-1 was quickly rendered obsolete by the appreciably faster Vought F8U-1 Crusader, and as the F11F-1F was not adopted for Service use. For Grumman, long the leading manufacturer of carrier-based aircraft, the phase-out of F11F-1s from fleet squadrons in 1961 marked the first time since 1933 that none of its fighters were embarked aboard USN carriers.*

Seeking to extract maximum performance from the basic F9F design by incorporating the NACA-developed 'Area Rule' concept to reduce transonic drag, a team led by Joseph Gavin began work on Design 98 in December 1952. Quickly, however, it became obvious that more than a redesign of the F9F would be needed to take full advantage of the NACA Area Rule. Hence, by the spring of 1953 the G-98 had evolved into an entirely new design with an area-ruled fuselage, while a more limited redesign of the F9F-6 had been started as Design 99. The revised G-98 was also notable in that, instead of using the standard wing construction technique with thin sheet aluminium riveted to a series of formed ribs, Grumman proposed to mill the main box skins from single light-alloy slabs and incorporate integral stiffeners to reduce weight while retaining full structural integrity. Other proposed features included wingtips folding manually downward, low-mounted horizontal tail surfaces, an afterburning Wright J65 turbojet (a licence-built Armstrong Siddeley Sapphire) with plain intakes on both sides of the fuselage, and an undercarriage with twin nosewheels and single main wheels retracting in the fuselage. Predicted performance indicated that the aircraft would exceed Mach 1 in level flight.

The first F9F9 prototype before its first flight on 30 July, 1954. *(Grumman)*

* It was only in 1974 that Grumman fighters finally returned to sea when VF-1 and VF-2 deployed with F-14As aboard the USS *Enterprise*.

Although it had already initiated a design competition for supersonic fighters powered by a Pratt & Whitney J57 (in which Grumman entered the G-97 described in Appendix B), BuAer was sufficiently interested in the G-98 proposal to order three prototypes on 27 April, 1953, as a potentially lighter and more manoeuvrable fighter. Notwithstanding the fact that the G-98 was no longer a derivative of the Panther/Cougar series, BuAer initially assigned the designation XF9F-8 to the prototypes. Still clinging to the commonality myth, four months later BuAer confusingly redesignated the G-98 prototypes as F9F-9s and, logically, reassigned the F9F-8 designation to identify the G-99 version of the Cougar.

While the prototypes were under construction, tests were made with a rocket-launched scale-model and with a small instrumented model mounted on the nose boom of an F9F-6. Results were encouraging and confidence ran high, thus prompting the Navy to increase its order to include not only a static-test airframe (BuNo 138603) and two flying prototypes (BuNos 138604 and 138605) but also forty-two Service test and initial production aircraft (BuNos 138606/138647). BuNo 138604 was completed in July 1954 but, owing to delays in the Americanization of the Sapphire, only a non-afterburning Wright J65-W-7 turbojet could be fitted for the initial trials which began on 30 July at Grumman's new Peconic River Facility in Calverton. On that day Corky Meyer made two flights and almost reached Mach 1 in spite of installed thrust being only 7,500 lb, thus further boosting confidence in the Tiger.

The first sign of trouble came on 20 October when the first prototype crashed at the edge of a wooded area near Peconic River following an engine flame-out. The pilot, Lt-Cdr W H Livingston, survived the crash but BuNo 138604 was too extensively damaged to be rebuilt. The second prototype, which had first flown on 2 October, was then moved to Edwards AFB to take advantage of California's better winter weather. There, after being fitted with an afterburner, BuNo 138605 finally went supersonic in level flight. However, further tests confirmed the need for modifications to solve control and stability problems.

First flown on 15 December, 1954, the third F11F-1 had redesigned vertical tail surfaces with a narrower chord rudder, a boundary layer splitter plate for the intakes, a clear sliding canopy section to improve rearward visibility, and a slighty longer nose. These modifications, as well as a partially retractable probe which was added in the nose to meet the newly specified Navy requirements for inflight refuelling, were to be incorporated in the 388 additional F11F-1s (BuNos 141728/141980 and 143232/143366) and eighty-five F11F-1Ps (BuNos 140379/140413, 141981/142009, and 143367/143387) which by then had been ordered. Furthermore, these aircraft were to be powered by 7,400/10,500-lb dry/afterburning thrust J65-W-18s instead of the slightly more powerful J65-W-6s which had been specified earlier. They were to be armed with four 20-mm cannon with muzzles on the lower edge of the air intakes and carry either four

The short-nosed F11F-1 (BuNo 138607) about to be lowered to the hangar deck of the USS *Forrestal* (CVA-59) during carrier suitability trials. (*USN/National Archives*)

Sidewinder infrared guided missiles or two Sidewinders and two 150-US gal drop tanks on underwing racks.

The first catapult launchings and arrested landings were made during carrier suitability trials aboard the USS *Forrestal* on 4 April, 1956, and these and other Service trials revealed the need for still more changes. In particular, starting with BuNo 141728, range and endurance deficiencies were to be partially corrected by fitting fuel cells in the intake walls and in the vertical fin to increase internal fuel capacity from 914 to 1,049 gal. Also starting with BuNo 141728, all F11F-1s were to be fitted with a longer nose and to have the refuelling probe relocated on the starboard side of the nose cone to provide space for an AN/APS-50 radar. However, even with the incorporation of all these changes, the F11F-1 had lower performance than the Vought F8U-1 Crusader and was a less satisfactory gun platform*. Moreover, its afterburning engine remained marginally reliable. Accordingly, the Navy drastically reduced production contracts for the Tiger and only 201 of these aircraft were built in the following versions.

Production history

F9F-8: This designation was first used in early 1953 to identify Design 98

---

* Unrelated to the Tiger's other gun-firing problems was a well-known accident in which BuNo 138620 was shot down by one of its own 20-mm projectiles during firing trials in a dive on 21 September, 1966. There were at least three hits, one on the windshield, one on the nose cone, and one on the starboard intake, and a shell was ingested by the engine. The Grumman test pilot, Tom Attridge, managed to get out of the aircraft after crash landing.

An early production F11F-1, showing the starboard spoiler in the up position. *(Grumman/National Archives)*

aircraft but was given in August 1953 to Design 99 aircraft (as described in the Cougar chapter). At the same time, Design 98 was officially redesignated F9F-9 by the Navy.

F9F-9: The F9F-9 designation was in use between August 1953 and April 1955 and was applied to the static-test airframe (BuNo 138603) and the first five aircraft (BuNos 138604/138608). The F9F-9 was first flown by Corky Meyer on 30 July, 1954, and the last of the aircraft bearing this designation was flown on 12 March, 1955.

F11F-1 (F-11A): Four F9F-9s (BuNos 138605/138608) were redesignated F11F-1s in April 1955, and subsequent production aircraft were redesignated before completion. With the exception of BuNo 138605, these aircraft were fitted with a short nose and most were equipped with an inflight refuelling probe partially retracting in the nose cone. All were powered by a 7,400/10,500-lb dry/afterburning thrust Wright J65-W-18. The last 157 F11F-1s (BuNos 141728/141884) were similarly powered but had 60 degrees leading-edge root fillets and a longer nose with a retractable refuelling probe on the starboard side of the nose and provision for an AN/APS-50. However, this radar was never installed.

YF11F-1: This designation was unofficially applied to identify a small number of early production Tigers used for development trials. This was notably the case of BuNo 138618 which had the YF11F-1 designation painted on its rear fuselage before taking part in carrier qualifications trials aboard the uss *Saratoga*.

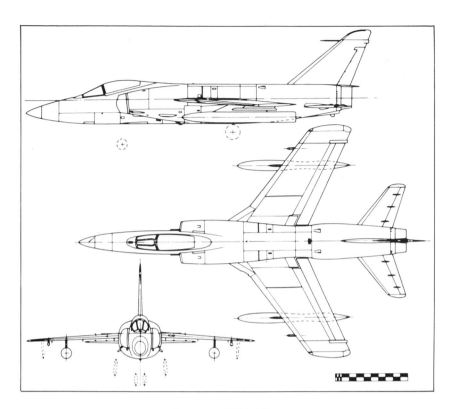

Grumman F11F-1 Tiger

F11F-1F: Before the first flight of the F9F-9, Grumman had already looked into re-engining its new fighter with a more powerful and reliable powerplant. An afterburning version of the General Electric J73 was first proposed in an October 1953 study (G-98A) and was considered again in January 1954, when the project team also looked into increasing wing sweep at the quarter chord from 35 degrees to 45 degrees (G-98D). Neither the G-98A nor the G-98D offered sufficient performance improvement to warrant further development, but the use of a General Electric J79, as incorporated in the G-98J study of January 1955, proved more promising. Accordingly, a proposal for the construction of two Super Tiger prototypes was submitted in August 1955 and during the following month the Navy authorized the completion of the last two aircraft in the initial contract (BuNos 138646/138647) as F11F-1Fs with the 9,600/15,000-lb dry/after-burning thrust General Electric YJ79-GE-3 turbojet replacing the J65-WE-18.

Flight trials began on 25 May, 1956, and ten days later BuNo 138646 flew at Mach 1.44 even though it was still fitted with a lower-rated Phase '0' J79 engine. After this, several changes, including a 13$^{1}/_{2}$-in afterbody exten-

The second F11F-1F (BuNo 138647) during trials at Edwards AFB in November 1956. (*USN/ National Archives*)

sion, the addition of 60 degrees leading-edge root fillets, and the use of a fully-rated engine, enabled the performance envelope of the two F11F-1Fs to be progressively expanded. Improved performance was demonstrated on 2 May, 1957, by Grumman test pilot John Norris, who flew BuNo 138647 to a maximum speed of Mach 2.04 and an altitude of 80,250 ft. Almost a year later, on 16 April, 1958, Lt-Cdr George Watkins set an official world altitude record of 76,831 ft (23,418 m) over Edwards AFB in the same aircraft.

Even though the Navy declined to order the F11F-1F into production, the Super Tiger attracted much interest from abroad; between May 1956 and October 1959, pilots from seven nations flew the two F11F-1Fs at Edwards AFB. Unfortunately, BuNo 138646 had to be struck from the inventory after being damaged in a non-fatal take-off accident when it was flown by a French Air Force pilot, Commandant Jean Franchi, on 23 June, 1958. In spite of this accident, and based on its evaluation of the Grumman G-98J, the Lockheed F-104A and F-104C, the North American F-100J, and the Northrop N-156F, the Japanese Air Self-Defence Force appeared ready to confirm its selection of the Super Tiger to replace its North American F-86D interceptors and F-86F fighter-bombers. Plans called for Grumman to build a small number of aircraft powered by 15,650-lb afterburning thrust J79-GE-7 turbojets and fitted with retractable ventral fins to increase stability, before a consortium would undertake licence manufacture in Japan. In the end, however, Lockheed prevailed and the JASDF adopted the F-104J.

F11F-1P: Three batches (BuNos 140379/140413, 141981/142009, and 143367/143387) were ordered, but all were cancelled before the completion of the first of these photographic-reconnaissance aircraft. They were to have used the airframe and powerplant of the F11F-1 and to have been fitted with a longer nose housing cameras.

F11F-1T: This designation was to have identified the proposed two-seat training version of the Tiger on which design work had begun in August 1954. None were built.

F11F-2: This designation was initially used to identify the J79-powered version. The F11F-1F designation was substituted when the Navy decided not to order the aircraft into production (the 'F' suffix indicating that the aircraft merely were F11F-1s with special powerplant installation).

F-11B: Although some sources indicate that the F-11B designation was given to the J79-powered Super Tiger when the tri-Service designation system was adopted in September 1962, this appears to be erroneous, as the surviving F11F-1F had been grounded and the resumption of production was not considered after 1959.

Service history

Short-nosed F11F-1s were first delivered to Air Development Squadron Three (VX-3) at NAS Atlantic City, New Jersey, in February, 1957, to enable this unit to undertake operational evaluation of the Tiger and develop operating procedures. Almost simultaneously, Attack Squadron 156 (VA-156) became the first fleet operating unit to be equipped with Tigers when three short-nosed F11F-1s were delivered to NAS Moffett Field, California, on 8 March, 1957. Soon after, VA-156 received a full complement of long-nosed F11F-1s and became the first Tiger squadron to complete carrier qualifications.

In addition to VA-156 (redesignated VF-111 in January 1959), F11F-1s equipped four other Pacific Fleet squadrons, VF-24 (redesignated VF-211 in March 1959), VF-51, VF-121, and VF-191 (which became the first F11F squadron to deploy when it embarked aboard the USS *Bon Homme Richard* in November 1958). Only two Atlantic Fleet squadrons, VF-21 and VF-33, flew Tigers.

An F-11A of VT-26 at NARF El Centro, California, on 11 March, 1967. (*Peter B Lewis*)

Compared with its main rival, the F8U-1 Crusader, which had also entered service with a fleet unit in March 1957,* the F11F-1 was slightly faster at sea level, 753 mph versus 733 mph, and had better handling characteristics. However, in most other respects the Tiger was inferior to the Crusader. Notably, it was slower at altitude (727 mph versus 1,013 mph at 35,000 ft), had a slightly slower initial rate of climb (5,130 ft/min versus 5,380 ft/min), and did not fly as far (combat range of 1,275 miles versus 1,474 miles). Moreover the Wright J65 powering the F11F-1 had a limited growth potential and was less reliable than the Pratt & Whitney J57 of the F8U-1. Consequently, the Navy was quick to cancel contracts for additional F11F-1s and for all F11F-1Ps and to cut short the Service life of the F11F-1 as an operational fighter. The last Tigers to serve with fleet units were phased out by VF-33 and VF-111 in April 1961.

Although not as sprightly as the Crusader and thus less desirable as a first line aircraft, the Tiger was nevertheless a good aircraft with pleasant handling characteristics. Hence it was well suited as an advanced trainer and demonstration aircraft. In the former role, F11F-1s were first assigned to the Jet Transition Training Unit (JTTU) at NAS Olathe, Kansas, in November 1958 and then to two Advanced Training Units in Texas, ATU-203 at NAAS Kingsville† and ATU-223 at NAS Chase Field. Redesignated respectively VT-23 and VT-26 in May 1960, these two Naval Air Training Command squadrons flew F-11As for nine years with the last being retired by VT-26 in mid-1967. As demonstration aircraft, Tigers were used by the *Blue Angels* for a longer period than any other aircraft. Short-nosed F11F-1s were first delivered in April 1957 and the last long-nosed F-11As were replaced by McDonnell F-4Js in 1969.

Two ex-*Blue Angel* F-11As which had been kept in storage at the Military

F-11A (BuNo 141824) of the *Blue Angels* at Davis-Monthan AFB, Arizona, on 17 March, 1969.
(Peter B Lewis)

* Even though its prototype had first flown eight months after that of the Tiger.

† In July 1959, the Navy announced that this unit would become the first to provide air-to-air missile training with F11F-1s carrying Sidewinders. In practice, however, few live firings were made due to the high cost of the missiles.

The F-11A (BuNo 141853) modified as a test-bed for the Rohr-developed inflight thrust reverser, at Davis-Monthan AFB, Arizona, in January 1975. *(Ben Knowles, courtesy of Alain Pelletier)*

Aircraft Storage & Disposition Center in Arizona since 1969 were refurbished by Grumman in 1973 to take part in a test programme to evaluate inflight thrust control in combat. BuNo 141853 was fitted with a thrust reverser developed by Rohr Industries and BuNo 141824 was kept in standard configuration to serve as a chase aeroplane. Inflight thrust reverser trials were made by Grumman at Calverton beginning in March 1974 and were continued by naval personnel at NATC Patuxent River until early 1975. Finally, BuNos 141824 and 141853, the last Tigers to fly, were returned to MASDC at Davis-Monthan AFB.

PRODUCTION: A total of 201 Tigers was built by Grumman between July 1954 and January 1959. They were assigned the following BuNos:

F11F-1:	BuNo 138603 (static test airframe)
F9F-9/F11F-1:	BuNos 138604/138645 (with short nose)
F11F-1:	BuNos 141728/141884 (with long nose)
F11F-1F:	BuNos 138646/138647

	F11F-1 (early production)	F11F-1 (late production)	F11F-1F
DIMENSIONS:			
Span, ft in	31 7½	31 7½	31 7½
(m)	(9.64)	(9.64)	(9.64)
Span (wings folded), ft in	27 4	27 4	27 4
(m)	(8.33)	(8.33)	(8.33)
Length, ft in	40 10	46 11	48 9
(m)	(12.45)	(14.30)	(14.86)
Height, ft in	12 9	13 3	14 4¾
(m)	(3.89)	(4.04)	(4.39)
Wing area, sq ft	250	250	250
(sq m)	(23.23)	(23.23)	(23.23)

WEIGHTS:

Empty, lb	13,307	14,330	16,457
(kg)	(6,217)	(6,500)	(7,465)
Loaded, lb	18,375	21,280	23,630
(kg)	(8,335)	(9,652)	(10,718)
Maximum, lb	23,459	24,078	26,086
(kg)	(10,641)	(10,922)	(11,832)
Wing loading,* lb/sq ft	73.5	85.1	94.5
(kg/sq m)	(358.8)	(415.5)	(461.4)
Power loading,* lb/lb st	1.8	2.0	1.6
(kg/kg st)	(1.8)	(2.0)	(1.6)
PERFORMANCE:			
Max speed, mph/ft	754/sl	753/sl	1,325/35,000
(kmh/m)	(1,213/sl)	(1,212/sl)	(2,132/10,670)
Cruising speed, mph	565	578	580
(kmh)	(909)	(930)	(933)
Climb rate, ft/min	6,300/1	5,130/1	8,950/1
(m/sec)	(32)	(26)	(45)
Service ceiling, ft	41,900	41,900	50,300
(m)	(12,770)	(12,770)	(15,330)
Normal range, miles	–	1,275	1,136
(km)	(–)	(2,050)	(1,825)

* Wing and power loadings are calculated at normal loaded weight and maximum take-off power.

The first TF-1 (BuNo 136748) during manufacturer's trials in early 1955. *(Grumman)*

Grumman TF-1 (C-1) Trader

To replace Avengers modified by the Navy as TBM-3R COD (Carrier Onboard Delivery) transports and used to fly personnel, mail, and/or small-sized priority cargo to or from carriers, in 1950 Douglas proposed the AD-5 Skyraider fitted with either four passenger seats, ten bench-type seats, or four stretchers. Alternatively, the COD-configured AD-5 was to carry a maximum of 2,000 lb of cargo. Although the Navy liked the multi-role capability of the AD-5 and ordered this Skyraider version into production, it was aware that the usefulness of the AD-5 in cargo configuration would be limited by its inability to carry often-needed bulky parts and spares such as aircraft engines.

To fill the need for a larger COD aircraft, in December 1951 Grumman first contemplated using the S2F-1 airframe and then decided to base its proposal on the S2F-2 with a deeper, more capacious fuselage and enlarged tail surfaces. Wings and powerplants were to be identical to those of the ASW aircraft, all armament and electronic equipment removed, and the fuselage deepened further to provide a compartment with a clear length of 104 in, a maximum width of 43 in, and a maximum height of 52 in. With a crew of two, the COD transport was to accomodate either nine passengers on rearward-facing seats or 3,500 lb of cargo. Primarily intended as a carrier transport, Design 96 was also offered as an instrument trainer, multi-engined trainer, carrier qualification trainer, and utility or administrative aircraft. However, this proposal did not get the immediate attention of BuAer as the Navy then had more pressing needs and plans for the COD transport were temporarily shelved.

A dummy Mk.5 special store loaded aboard BuNo 136791. Delivery of nuclear weapons to carriers operating at sea was one of the missions planned for the Trader. *(Grumman)*

In 1953, when the Navy began showing serious interest in the proposed twin-engined COD transport, it specified that the aircraft would have to be able to carry internally large special stores (the Mk. 5 was the longest at 10 ft 8 in and the Mk.6 was the heaviest at 8,500 lb and widest at 5 ft 1 in) for delivery to carriers. To that end, Grumman designed a bi-fold door on the port rear fuselage side. For passenger loading, only the rear panel swung outboard on two hinges on its forward edge; for oversize cargo loading, both panels swung outboard on the five hinges of the forward panel. After the practicality of loading bulky nuclear weapons through the resulting 67-in wide and 50-in high opening was demonstrated with a fuselage mock-up, Grumman's efforts were rewarded with a contract for forty-five COD transports (BuNos136748/ 136792), to be designated TF-1s.

With most of the airframe and the 1,525-hp Wright R-1820-82 radials being common with those of S2Fs, the Traders, as they were named, were to be built on the same line as the Trackers, and the 236th airframe on that line was selected to be completed as the first TF-1. First flown at Bethpage by Thomas 'Boots' LeBoutillier on 19 January, 1955, BuNo 136748 was accepted by the Navy nine days later. A second Trader was delivered in April. Following abbreviated BIS trials the TF-1 was cleared for Service use in October 1955.

388

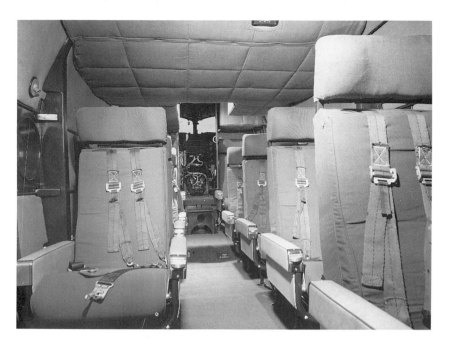

For passenger transport, the Trader was fitted with nine rearward-facing seats. (*Grumman*)

The first TF-1Q (BuNo 136783) at Bethpage. (*Grumman*)

Production history

TF-1 (C-1A): Two batches totalling eighty-seven TF-1s (BuNos 136748/136792 and 146016/146057) were ordered, but only eighty-two were operated in the standard COD configuration. Four were modified as TF-1Qs before delivery and one became the aerodynamic prototype for the WF-2. Standard and modified Traders were powered by 1,525-hp Wright

After removal of the dummy dorsal radome, the Tracer aerodynamic prototype was used as a utility transport at various stations, including NAS Cecil Field, Florida, where it was photographed in May 1977. (*Robert E Kling*)

R-1820-82 or -82A radials. The first TF-1 flew on 19 January, 1955, and the last was delivered, on 30 December, 1958.

TF-1Q (EC-1A): Following preliminary discussions between Grumman and BuAer representatives concerning requirements for an electronic surveillance and countermeasures version of the TF-1, Grumman submitted a proposal in February 1956. Soon after, the Navy approved the conversion of four new TF-1 airframes (BuNos 136783, 136785, 136787, and 136788) to the TF-1Q configuration. Modifications included the fitting of active and passive electronic reconnaissance and ECM gear within the fuselage, with antennae and sensors protruding above, below, aft, and on the sides of the fuselage as well as beneath the engine nacelles. In addition, the TF-1Qs were fitted with a dorsal radome housing a high-speed rotating antenna for an AN/APA-69A set and carried an AN/APS-31 radar, chaff dispensers, and noise jammers beneath the wings. The crew was increased to five, including three ECM operators. The first TF-1Q flew on 26 November, 1956, and completed its contractor electronic demonstration flights less than a month later.

TF-1W: This military designation was initially given to the Design 117 airborne early warning aircraft which, as described in a following chapter, was built as the WF-2 and later redesignated E-1B. To serve as an aerodynamic prototype for the Tracer AEW aircraft, the last TF-1 on the initial contract (BuNo 136792), which had been completed in July 1956, was subsequently fitted with an aluminium radome and twin fins and rudders. However, it kept its TF-1 designation and retained the shorter, upward-folding wings of the Trader. It was not fitted with the radar and other specialized electronics of the Tracer. After being modified, BuNo 136792 was first flown by Ernie von der Heyden and Fred Rowley at Calverton on 17 December, 1956. Following completion of aerodynamic trials in support of the Tracer programme, the dummy dorsal radome was removed from BuNo 136792 but the twin tail surfaces were retained. Still

390

retaining its TF-1 designation (changed to C-1A in September 1962), this unique-looking Trader was then used by Grumman as a general purpose hack before being returned to the Navy. It was successively assigned as a personnel and cargo transport to VAW-111 and to NAS Cecil Field, Florida, before being sent to MASDC at Davis-Monthan AFB, Arizona, for storage and eventual disposal.

Related projects: Proposed TF-1 derivatives included a 10- to 12-seat executive transport without or with a pressurized cabin (Designs 101 and 101A), an inflight refuelling tanker (Design 104), a photographic reconnaissance version (Design 115), a transport version to be built in Canada by de Havilland (Design 120), an airborne electronic trainer (Design 126), a propeller-turbine-powered tanker (Design 137), a test-bed for turbine engines (Design 142), and a larger COD version (Design 154). None progressed past the initial study phase.

Service history

Entering service in October 1955, TF-1s were assigned over the years to Fleet Tactical Support Squadrons (VR-21 with the Pacific Fleet and VR-24 with the Atlantic Fleet), Fleet Logistics Support Carrier Onboard Delivery Squadrons (VRC-30 and VRC-50 with the Pacific Fleet and VRC-40 with the Atlantic Fleet), and directly to attack (CVAs) and anti-submarine warfare support (CVSs) carriers.

Even though carrying special weapons to carriers at sea had been one of the TF-1 design requirements, in service Traders seldom, if ever, did so. Conversely, the ability to deliver fully assembled jet engines, which was first accomplished by a TF-1 of VR-21 on 26 June, 1958, when it flew from NAS North Island to deliver a Westinghouse J34 turbojet to the USS *Yorktown* (CVS-10) 300 miles at sea, proved a welcome improvement over the more limited capabilities of earlier COD aircraft. Moreover, for flying smaller-sized cargo, mail, and personnel to and from carriers Traders proved well-suited and had a long and safe operational career. They proved particularly useful during the Southeast Asia War, when in support of Task Force 77 in the Gulf of Tonkin, C-1As constantly shuttled between carriers and Cubi Point in the Philippines and Da Nang AB in South Vietnam.

Being the last carrier aircraft to operate on avgas and to require bridles for catapult launching (although they often made unassisted deck launches), Traders became increasingly difficult to support. In particular, when avgas was no longer stored aboard carriers, they could only be used within close proximity to shore bases as their radius of action was limited to 425 miles when carrying their maximum load of 3,500 lb. Accordingly, with the exception of the training carrier, all USN carriers lost their own CODs during the early 1980s, while the two Fleet Logistics Support Carrier Onboard Delivery Squadrons, VRC-30 and VRC-40, phased out their last C-1As in 1986. Finally, BuNo 146048, a C-1A assigned to the USS *Lexington* (AVT-16), became the last Navy piston-powered aircraft. Three days after

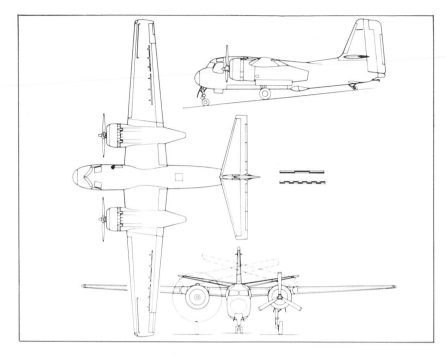

Grumman C-1A Trader

last 'trapping' on board *Lexington* on 27 September, 1988, it was delivered to the Naval Aviation Museum at NAS Pensacola.

In the electronic surveillance and training roles the TF-1Qs, first delivered to All-weather Attack Squadron 35 at San Diego on 18 January, 1957, had a shorter career. Later on, with the ECM equipment removed, they were used as utility aircraft until the last were struck from the inventory in the mid-1980s.

PRODUCTION: A total of 87 Traders was built by Grumman between January 1955 and December 1958, as follows:

    83   TF-1
      4   TF-1Q

They were assigned the following BuNos:

TF-1	BuNos 136748/136782, 136784, 136786, 136789/136792, and 146016/146057
TF-1Q	BuNos 136783, 136785, 136787, and 136788

Span 69 ft 8 in (21.23 m); span (wings folded) 27 ft 4 in (8.33 m); length 42 ft (12.80 m); height 16 ft 3½ in (4.97 m); wing area 485 sq ft (45.06 sq m).

Empty weight 16,631 lb (7,544 kg); loaded weight 23,031 lb (10,447 kg); maximum weight 24,600 lb (11,158 kg); wing loading 47.5 lb/sq ft (231.8 kg/sq m); power loading 7.6 lb/hp (3.4 kg/hp).

Maximum speed 280 mph at 4,000 ft (451 kmh at 1,220 m); cruising speed 167 mph (269 kmh); climb rate 1,950 ft/min (10 m/sec); service ceiling 24,800 ft (7,560 m); normal range 1,110 miles (1,785 km).

BuNo 136766, a C-1A from VRC-30, making a deck launch from the uss *Kitty Hawk* (CV-63) during RefTra (Refresher Training) off the coast of California on 29 March 1985. (*René J Francillon*)

N10291 with the internal leading-edge boom and external spray nozzles as fitted to early production G-164 Ag-Cats. *(Grumman)*

Grumman G-164 Ag-Cat

Among the world's major aircraft manufacturers, Grumman remains unique for its bold diversification move into the agricultural aircraft market, a field previously left to smaller manufacturers and modification shops. However, following the successful development of prototypes, Grumman was forced to sub-contract the manufacture of production aircraft to Schweizer Aircraft as in-house production would have resulted in the Ag-Cat being too expensive, due to Grumman's high overhead costs.

Development of an agricultural aircraft was suggested by Joseph Lippert Jr, an engineer in the Preliminary Design Group, in answer to a 1956 company request to employees and stockholders for suggestions for further diversification programmes. In proposing the development of this aircraft, Lippert indicated that Grumman's reputation for building sturdy aircraft would be a favourable factor in penetrating this new market, as agricultural aircraft should be able to survive collisions with trees and other small obstructions. Seeing merit in this suggestion, Roy Grumman authorized a market survey to determine requirements for an aircraft specially intended for dispersal of chemical sprays and dusts. The survey was also to ascertain whether a sufficient demand existed to warrant a development programme.

The rapidly conducted market survey confirmed the existence of a sizeable market as most of the 4,500 or so aircraft then used for agricultural work in the United States were either unsuitable or obsolete (the most numerous being converted Stearman 75 biplane trainers) and were difficult to maintain. Accordingly, Joe Lippert and Arthur Koch were authorized in September 1956 to proceed with design work on the G-164. Construction of two prototypes was approved soon afterward.

As detailed design progressed, several features were adopted to obtain a strong, manoeuvrable, and easily maintained aircraft. Notably, a biplane configuration was selected, primarily because it enabled the span to be kept relatively short, thus endowing the aircraft with the ability to fly into narrower confines while keeping wing loading low, even when carrying a heavy load. Strength was to be provided through the use of a two-spar structure. Ailerons on all four wing panels were retained to improve manoeuvrability at low airspeeds. It was also decided that the aircraft ought to have the capability for being powered by engines of various sizes in order to achieve the best possible power-to-weight ratio depending on intended use. Moreover, engines were selected on the basis of their ready and low-cost availability on the surplus market. Ease of maintenance was also stressed and led to much of the fuselage being covered by quickly removable panels. Finally, safety considerations resulted in the chemical hopper being placed forward of the pilot, extra strength being built around the cockpit, and a large reinforced fairing being provided aft of the cockpit for turnover protection.

First flown by Hank Kurt on 27 April, 1957, the G-164 prototype was named Grasshopper, registered N74054, and powered by a 220-hp

The first Grasshopper, after installation of a lead weight around the propeller shaft. (*Grumman*)

Continental W670-16 seven-cylinder air-cooled radial driving a two-blade steel propeller. While generally satisfactory, initial tests revealed that the cg was located too far aft. As a temporary answer, a lead weight was mounted around the propeller shaft, just ahead of the engine. A more satisfactory solution was provided by lengthening the engine mounting of the second prototype (N74055). Thus modified, the aircraft handled as desired. Both protypes were retained by Grumman until donated to Texas A&M University in 1961.

During a country-wide demonstration tour, the G-164 was well received by prospective operators, thus prompting Grumman to seek a way to produce the aircraft, now renamed Ag-Cat*, at a competitive price. This was achieved by entering into an agreement with Schweizer Aircraft by which the G-164 was to be manufactured in Elmira, New York. This arrangement remained in force after Grumman American Engineering Corp was organized on 2 January, 1973. After September 1978, following Grumman's sale of its 80 per cent interest in the Grumman American Aviation Corporation, Schweizer continued manufacturing Ag-Cats for Gulfstream American. Finally, Gulfstream American sold the Ag-Cat manufacturing rights to Schweizer Aircraft and that firm resumed deliveries in its own right in 1981.

The second G-164 prototype, with engine moved forward. Fuselage panels have been removed to demonstrate the ease of maintenance designed into the Grumman agricultural aircraft. (*Grumman*)

---

* The name Grasshopper, which had been suggested by Roy Grumman, was not retained for production aircraft as farmers do not like grasshoppers... The name Ag-Cat was then suggested by Dick Reade of Mid-Continent Aircraft Corp, a company which became one of the major G-164 distributors.

Production history

The Ag-Cat has appeared in the following versions:

G-164: Following certification of the Ag-Cat powered by a 220-hp Continental W670-6N, W670-16, or W670-6A radial in January 1959, the first ten production aircraft were built during that year by Schweizer in Elmira. These aircraft were fitted with a 33-cu ft glass fibre hopper for dry or liquid agricultural chemicals, and with either wing spray booms* or a dust applicator beneath the fuselage. The G-164 was later certificated with a 240-hp Gulf Coast W670-240, with a Jacobs (245-hp R-755-9, or 275-hp R-755-B2M1, or 300-hp R-755-A2M1), and with a 450-hp Pratt & Whitney R-985-AN1.

G-164A: Certificated in March 1966, the Super Ag-Cat A had a strengthened airframe with external stiffeners along the fuselage sides and was powered by either a 300-hp Jacobs R-75A2M1, a 450-hp Pratt & Whitney R-985-AN1, or a 600-hp Pratt & Whitney R-1340-AN1. Some had engine cowlings and most were fitted with an enclosed canopy and sealed cockpit.

G-164B: The Super Ag-Cat B had longer span wings (42 ft 3 in versus 35 ft 11 in) and a 33 per cent larger chemical hopper (40 cu ft). This version was certificated in November 1975 and was available with a 450-hp Pratt & Whitney R-985-AN1 or a 525-hp Continental R-975.

A Schweizer-built Super Ag-Cat C at Kingsley Field, Klamath Falls, Oregon, on 6 July, 1988.
(René J Francillon)

---

* Early aircraft had an internal leading edge boom with spray nozzles protruding from the lower surfaces. To ease maintenance, later models were fitted with an exposed trailing edge spray boom.

G-164C: Powered by the 600-hp Pratt & Whitney R-1340-AN1, the Super Ag-Cat C had enlarged tail surfaces and a 66⅔ cu ft hopper.

G-164D: The Turbo Ag-Cat D developed by Gulfstream American differed from the G-164C in being powered by Pratt & Whitney of Canada propeller-turbines (either 680-shp PT6A-15, 750-shp PT6A-34, or 850-shp PT6A-41).

G-164B Ag-Cat Super B and **G-164C Ag-Cat Super C:** These Schweizer-built versions of the G-164B and G-164C differed from the aircraft built for Grumman and for Gulfstream American in having the upper wing raised 8 in to improve forward visibility.

G-164-B/T: This was the Schweizer developed variant of the PT6A-powered Turbo Ag-Cat D. In August 1985, Ethiopian Airlines signed a licensing arrangement with Schweizer and acquired two G-164-B/Ts, one fully and one partially assembled. Subsequently, Ethiopian Airlines received and assembled knock-down components for nine more G-164-B/Ts.

Non-standard Ag-Cats

Over the years, several modified versions of the Ag-Cat and Super Ag-Cat have been offered by small firms seeking to improve the performance of the Grumman-designed agricultural aircraft or to end reliance on the rapidly diminishing supply of radial engines. Noteworthy conversions have included a Schweizer prototype powered by a 700-hp Thunder TE945-TC700 water-cooled eight-cyliner engine; the Serv-Aero Engineering conversions with either a 560-hp Alvis Leonides radial or a 1,200-hp Wright R-1820-202A radial replacing the 600-hp Pratt & Whitney R-1340-AN1

A PT6A-powered G-164B/T. (*Schweizer*)

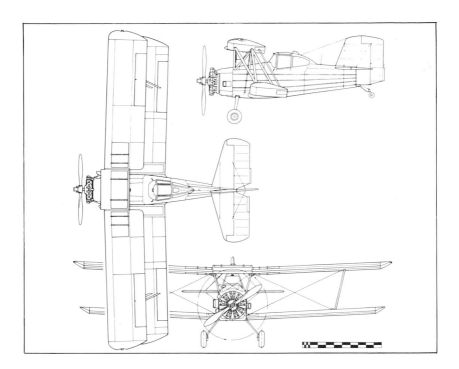

Grumman Super Ag-Cat B

(the aircraft with the R-1820 being marketed by Mid-Continent as the King Cat); the Frakes Aviation PT6A-powered Turbo-Cat; and the Marsh conversion of the Super Ag-Cat A with 778-shp Garrett TPE331 propeller-turbine. More unusual was the Twin Cat conversion developed by Chesapeake Airways and marketed by Twin Cat Corporation. In this instance, the 600-hp Pratt & Whitney R-1340-AN1 was replaced by two flat-rated 310-hp Lycoming TIO-540J flat six engines mounted on each side of a nose fairing. Also of interest were pilot training versions fitted with an open cockpit in place of the hopper and offered by Gulfstream American and by Malden Ag-Craft.

Service history

Safe, reliable, manoeuvrable, highly productive (early models could dispense 116,000 lb of dry chemical, 51 times the aircraft's own weight, in a single eight-hour day), and easy and inexpensive to maintain, the Ag-Cat gained quick acceptance with both large and small operators. Quite remarkably, by the end of 1963, when 244 aircraft had been delivered by Schweizer, the largest of these operators was NACO Spraying Company in Guatemala. Thereafter, far from tapering off, production continued at an increasing rate. The 1,000th and 2,000th Ag-Cats were delivered respectively in the fourteenth and nineteenth years of production. In 1988, with

399

Schweizer continuing production, Ag-Cats and Super Ag-Cats remained numerically the most important agricultural aircraft in the western and third world countries.

Although most of these aircraft are operated by private operators, an exception is the case of the Helliniki Aeroporia (Greek Air Force), which has acquired twenty-four Ag-Cats for use in the mosquito control, forest fire-fighting, and crop-spraying roles with the 359 Mira at Dekélia.

PRODUCTION: Two Grashopper/Ag-Cat prototypes were built by Grumman in 1957. From 1959 until September 1978, 2,214 Ag-Cats were built for Grumman by Schweizer Aircraft. Schweizer Aircraft then built 244 Ag-Cats for Gulfstream American before acquiring exclusive rights to the Ag-Cat. By 1988, over 2,600 Ag-Cats had been delivered.

(300 hp R-755)	Ag-Cat (450 hp R-985)	Super Ag-Cat A (680 shp PT6A-15)	Turbo Ag-Cat D/T
DIMENSIONS:			
Span, ft in	35 11	42 3	42 3
(m)	(10.95)	(12.88)	(12.88)
Length, ft in	24 4	25 11	34 4
(m)	(7.42)	(7.90)	(10.46)
Height, ft in	10 9	11 0	11 5
(m)	(3.28)	(3.35)	(3.48)
Wing area, sq ft	326	392	392
(sq m)	(30.29)	(36.42)	(36.42)
WEIGHTS:			
Empty, lb	2,239	3,095	3,450
(kg)	(1,016)	(1,404)	(1,565)
Loaded, lb	3,750	6,075	8,500
(kg)	(1,701)	(2,756)	(3,856)
Wing loading,* lb/sq ft	11.5	15.5	21.7
(kg/sq m)	(56.2)	(75.7)	(105.9)
Power loading,* lb/hp	12.5	13.5	12.5
(kg/hp)	(5.7)	(6.1)	(5.7)
PERFORMANCE:			
Max speed, mph/ft	110/sl	147/sl	155/sl
(kmh/m)	(177/sl)	(237/sl)	(249/sl)
Cruising speed, mph	85	98	95
(kmh)	(137)	(158)	(153)
Climb rate, ft/min	700	1,060	–
(m/sec)	(3.6)	(5.4)	(–)
Normal range, miles	–	250	–
(km)	(–)	(400)	(–)

* Wing and power loadings are calculated at normal loaded weight and maximum take-off power.

Although often identified in photograph captions as a WF-2 (or E-1B), BuNo 136792 was the forty-first Trader, modified as an aerodynamic prototype for the Tracer. In that form it retained the TF-1 designation as painted on the rear fuselage above the Bureau Number.
(Grumman)

Grumman WF (E-1) Tracer

Lying dormant for nearly four years after the XWF-1 contract was cancelled (see Design 95 in Appendix B), the idea of developing an airborne early warning aircraft based on the Tracker was resurrected by the Preliminary Design Group at Bethpage in the spring of 1955. The revised concept began almost accidentally when an avionics engineer, Samuel Rogers, and a performance and aerodynamic engineer, Joseph Lippert Jr, sought ways of installing a new Hazeltine search radar (which eventually was produced as the AN/APS-82) and its bulky rotating antenna in an aircraft small and light enough to operate from carriers.

Sixteen configurations, using either the AF Guardian, the S2F Tracker, or entirely new designs, were quickly evaluated before the conclusion was reached that a configuration based on the Tracker and a large dorsal radome was attractive. Layout and preliminary performance estimates were then prepared by Joe Lippert and appeared to validate the concept. Nevertheless wind-tunnel testing was needed to verify drag calculations and handling characteristics for the radome-equipped aircraft. However, as no immediate Navy requirements for such a system were known to exist, government funding would not be forthcoming and only limited work could be funded by the company. Fortuitously, a way was found for adding wind-tunnel testing on to S2F development work scheduled to be undertaken late in the summer of 1955. Wind-tunnel results were encouraging but indicated that a

401

rearward radome extension would be necessary to reduce drag even though there might be some loss of radar effectiveness while looking aft.

Meanwhile, planning to initiate a design competition during the following year, BuAer had begun developing requirements for a carrier-based airborne early warning/air intercept control (AEW/AIC) aircraft equipped to detect and report distant airborne targets and to vector fighters into intercept positions. Like other manufacturers, Grumman was aware of this impending design competition and during the autumn of 1955 offered a development of the S2F as an interim AEW aircraft. Preliminary performance data based on the work done by Joe Lippert were submitted by Grumman in November and soon after BuAer issued a letter of intent for two prototypes. On that strength, a team led by William Rathke began formal work on Design 117.

As the design of the AEW aircraft was being refined during the winter of 1955 and spring of 1956, numerous changes were made. Notably, the TF-1 replaced the S2F-1 as the airframe to be used for the radar platform as its more capacious fuselage provided space for additional electronic equipment and for the crew (pilot, co-pilot/tactical director, and two radar operators). Twin fins and rudders also replaced the single vertical surfaces of the Trader. Moreover, to clear the radome, wing folding had to be redesigned and, in place of the TF-1's vertically folding wings, the TF-1W (later redesignated WF-2 and then E-1B) received 'sto-wings' folding to the rear and alongside the rear fuselage as first used by Grumman on the XF4F-4. Housing a 17 ft 6 in diameter radar scanner rotating at 6 rpm, the 20 ft by 30 ft fixed aerofoil-section radome was mounted on a forward fuselage pylon, strut-braced to the wings and fuselage, and attached to a stubby central fin.

Even though wind-tunnel tests indicated that handling characteristics would not be negatively affected by the installation of the large radome, the need to confirm wind-tunnel results led to the modification of a TF-1 Trader (BuNo 136792) into an aerodynamic prototype for the Tracer as

An E-1B of VAW-111 assigned to CVSG-53 for deployment aboard the USS *Ticonderoga* (CVA-14). (*Peter B Lewis*)

402

described in the earlier chapter. Test pilots Ernie von der Heyden and Fred Rowley first flew this aerodynamic prototype on 17 December, 1956, and reported favourably on its inflight behaviour.

Trials with this aerodynamic prototype confirmed that the AEW aircraft would handle well and that its large radome would in fact contribute to lift. Nevertheless, the programme proceeded conservatively, with manufacture of the forty WF-2s (BuNos 145957/145961, 146303, and 147208/147241) on order being delayed pending further development and testing of the

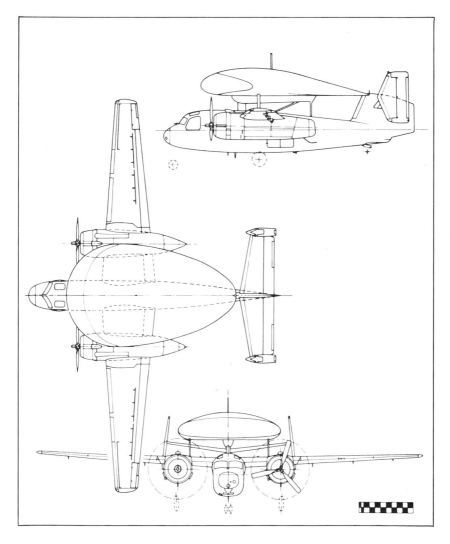

Grumman E-1B Tracer

403

complex electronics. Finally, the first WF-2 was flown on 1 March, 1958. Five more aircraft were delivered in that year, and twenty-two were accepted in 1959 before the type was cleared for Service use.

Compared with previous carrier-based aircraft fitted with the less sophisticated AN/APS-20 radar – the TBM-3W, the AF-2W, and the AD-5W – the WF-2 introduced several new capabilities. In particular, its antenna was stabilized to provide a means of determining a target's height; its displays were ground stabilized to ease detection, tracking, and intercepts; its radar relay used UHF instead of VHF; and an airborne moving target indicator (AMTI) was provided to cancel sea returns when over water. All of these features were carefully validated during a lengthy test and development programme culminating in BIS trials.

At last, nearly nine years after work on the original XWF-1 (Design 95) had begun, the first operational WF-2 was delivered to Carrier Airborne Early Warning Squadron Twelve (VAW-12) at NAS Quonset Point, Rhode Island, on 20 January, 1960. Shortly after, the type was also assigned to VAW-11 at NAS North Island, California, for service with the Pacific Fleet. All of these aircraft, as well as those from two later Tracer batches (BuNos 148123/148146, and 148900/148923), were powered by 1,525-hp Wright R-1820-82A radials.

The first deployment aboard an attack carrier was made by a detachment from VAW-11 which went aboard the USS *Constellation* (CVA-64) in April 1960, and the first deployment aboard an anti-submarine warfare support carrier was made one year later by a VAW-12 detachment aboard the USS *Randolph* (CVS-15). In service with these two squadrons, the Tracer was usually nicknamed *Willy Fudd* (a play on its WF-2 designation) but was also called *Stoof with a Roof* (S2F with a radome above the fuselage) and described as 'the only aircraft with its own umbrella.' Typical AEW sorties saw Tracers operating some 150 nm from carriers, and loitering at between 90 and 95 knots (167 to 176 kmh) for up to 4 hr 40 min, if flying at 5,000 ft, or up to 3 hr 30 min, if flying at 15,000 ft. With full tanks, a mission

An E-1B Tracer of VAW-88, a Reserve unit assigned to CVSGR-80. (*Peter B Lewis*)

duration of nearly seven hours was possible. In the anti-submarine warfare support role, Tracer detachments were embarked aboard ASW carriers and were used to control S-2s and ensure that the Trackers were flying precise search patterns.

During the Southeast Asia War, detachments of E-1Bs from VAW-11 (redesignated VAW-111* on 20 April, 1967) and VAW-12 (VAW-121 after 20 April, 1967) made fifty-six deployments aboard CVAs and CVSs. The last of these deployments was made by VAW-121 Det 38 aboard the USS *Shangri-La* (CVS-38) between March and December 1970. With the Atlantic Fleet, E-1Bs were last deployed by VAW-121 Det 42 aboard the USS *F. D. Roosevelt* (CVA-42) between October 1976 and April 1977. By then Hawkeyes had replaced Tracers aboard all other carriers and E-1Bs ended their service career with reserve squadrons. A reserve *Willy Fudd* from VAW-78 made the last E-1B flight on 19 November, 1977.

The Tracer attracted interest abroad, with Grumman notably working during the summer of 1959 on a proposal tailored to the requirements of Kungliga Svenska Flygvapnet (Royal Swedish Air Force) and incorporating some Swedish equipment. However, neither this G-117B study nor studies for other air forces led to foreign sales.

PRODUCTION: A total of 88 Tracers was built by Grumman between February 1958 and September 1961. They were assigned BuNos 145957/145961, 146303, 147208/147241, 148123/148146, and 148900/148923.

Span 72 ft 4 in (22.05 m); span (wings folded) 30 ft 5 in (9.27 m); length 45 ft 4 in (13.82 m); height 16 ft 10 in (5.13 m); wing area 506 sq ft (47.00 sq m).

Empty weight 20,638 lb (9,361 kg); loaded weight 24,800 lb (11,249 kg); maximum weight 26,600 lb (12,066 kg); wing loading 49.0 lb/sq ft (239.3 kg/sq m); power loading 8.1 lb/hp (3.7 kg/hp).

Maximum speed 227 mph at 4,000 ft (365 kmh at 1,220 m); cruising speed 163 mph (262 kmh); climb rate 1,120 ft/min (6 m/sec); service ceiling 15,800 ft (4,815 m); normal range 1,010 miles (1,625 km).

* In addition to flying standard E-1Bs, VAW-111 flew BuNo 145958, the second production Tracer as a utility aircraft after it was overstressed and had the radome removed. Thus modified, BuNo 145958 looked like BuNo 136792, the TF-1 which had been used as the Tracer aerodynamic prototype, after removal of the dummy radome. However, BuNo 136792 had upward-folding wings whereas BuNo 145958 had 'sto-wings' folding alongside the rear fuselage.

HB-LDT, the Gulfstream I modified by Eidgenössisches Flugzeugwerk at Emmen and used by the Swiss Federal Air Office to check airways navigation aids. *(Eidg. Flugzeugwerk, courtesy of the Swiss Federal Air Office)*

Grumman G-159 Gulfstream I

In its search for a successor to its long line of twin-engined executive transport amphibians, Grumman investigated a broad range of possibilities before undertaking the development of Design 159, an all-new propeller-turbine-powered aircraft. The earliest of these studies was Design 80, a May 1946 proposal for a high-speed executive transport derived from the F7F Tigercat. However, neither this nor later studies* proceeded past the conceptual phase as new piston-powered aircraft stood little chance to succeed in a market glutted with converted military aircraft (such as Douglas Skytrains and Invaders, Lockheed Lodestars and Venturas, and North American Mitchells) and as jet-powered aircraft were then uneconomic.

Toward the end of 1956, the Preliminary Design Group concluded that the use of Rolls-Royce Darts, which had been fully proven since the Vickers Viscount went into sustained service in April 1953, would enable a new executive transport to have both satisfactory operating economics and substantially better performance than converted Second World War bombers and military transports. This contention was first validated by a market survey which showed a strong interest for an aircraft cruising at a speed of 350 mph and having a range of between 1,800 and 2,200 miles. The study then was fully vindicated when customers began placing $10,000 deposits which were refundable only if the G-159's performance failed to

---

* These studies included the G-101, G-101A, and G-102 which were conceived in December 1953 as ten- to twelve-seat executive transports. The first two were to be derived from the TF-1 Trader, whereas the G-102 was a new jet-powered design.

The first Gulfstream I, with nose-mounted test boom in August 1958. *(Grumman)*

meet specifications. Confident that Grumman could sell more than the 125 to 150 aircraft needed to break even, management gave the go-ahead.

Of low wing configuration with a nosewheel undercarriage, the G-159 was designed to be flown by a crew of two and, with two 2,210-eshp Rolls-Royce Dart 529-8 propeller-turbines, to operate independently of ground services from airfields with 5,000-ft runways. Accommodation was typically to be provided for ten passengers in executive configuration and for up to twenty-four passengers in an alternative high-density version. In either case, however, Grumman planned to deliver aircraft with only minimal equipment and to have interior furnishing and customer-specified avionics installed by distributors (Atlantic Aviation in Wilmington; Pacific Airmotive in Los Angeles; Southwest Airmotive in Dallas; and Timmins Aviation in Montreal).

Although the first G-159 ran into problems during its maiden flight at Bethpage on 14 August, 1958, when the fuel boost pumps became inoperative due to a loss of electrical power, Carl Alber and Fred Rowley succeeded in making a quick landing and saving N701G. Fortunately, no further difficulties were encountered in the test programme for which the first aircraft was joined by N702G on 11 November, 1958, and by N703G on 17 February, 1959. The FAA Type Approval was granted on 21 May, 1959, and the first delivery to a distributor was made during the following month.

Production history

Remaining in production for eleven years, the G-159 was built in one civil and two military versions. Another military version and several proposed civil variants remained unbuilt.

Gulfstream I: Powered by two 2,210 eshp Rolls-Royce Dart 529-8X or 529-8E (R.Da. 7/2) turbines driving four-blade propellers, the 190 Gulfstream Is were normally fitted with ten to fourteen seats and operated as executive transports. Alternatively, nineteen to twenty-four seats could be accommodated in a corporate staff transport configuration or for feeder/regional transport operations. For cargo operations, a 62 in by 84 in door could be fitted in the port side of the fuselage, aft of the wings.

A Gulfstream I at the Mojave Airport, California, on 21 July, 1988. The aircraft, which had been used by Purolator Courier, a US small parcel carrier, is fitted with a cargo loading door on the port side of the rear fuselage. *(René J Francillon)*

No major changes were introduced during the course of production, but progressive improvements resulted in maximum take-off weight being increased from 33,600 lb to 35,100 lb and then to 36,000 lb. Maximum payload went from 4,270 lb to 4,570 lb and then to 6,070 lb. In addition, by increasing cruising altitude from 25,000 ft to 30,000 ft where fuel consumption was reduced, range with ten passengers was increased from 1,910 nm to 2,170 nm.

VC-4A: The ninety-first Gulfstream I was delivered to the US Coast Guard, by which it has been used since 1962 as a VIP/staff transport. Initially assigned the USCG serial 1380, the VC-4A was later renumbered 02. A second VC-4A on order (USCG 1381) was cancelled.

TC-4B (T-41A): This designation was given to a navigational training version which Grumman proposed to the US Navy as a replacement for the Convair T-29Bs and Douglas TC-117Ds operated by Training Squadron 29 (VT-29). Ten aircraft (BuNos 151892/151901), tentatively designated T-41As but soon redesignated TC-4Bs, were ordered. However, rather than replacing its piston-engined navigation trainers with turbine-powered aircraft, the Navy decided to phase out its own navigator training programme and cancelled the TC-4B contract.

TC-4C: As after being trained as navigators by the Air Force at Mather AFB, California, Naval Flight Officers assigned as bombardier/navigators to units flying Grumman A-6 Intruders still needed to receive specialized systems training, the Navy ordered a Gulfstream I version fitted as a 'flying classroom.' Developed as the Design 426 and named Academe (although this name was seldom used in service), the first of nine TC-4Cs (BuNos 155722/155730) was civil registered N798G when it made its maiden flight on 14 June, 1967.

The TC-4C basic airframe and its two 2,210-ehp Dart Mk 529-8X

A TC-4C with TRAM turret at NAS Whidbey Island, Washington, on 12 July, 1988. *(René J Francillon)*

engines were similar to those of the civil Gulfstream I. The military trainer version, however, was fitted with the AN/APQ-92 search radar, AN/APQ-88 track radar, and Digital Integrated Attack and Navigation Equipment (DIANE) of the A-6A. Externally, the TC-4C was distinguishable from the executive transport by its large drooping snout which increased overall length by 4 ft 2 in to 67 ft 11 in. Internally, this variant was fitted with a complete Intruder cockpit for a student pilot and a student bombardier/navigator, an instructor's station, and four student radar/computer readout training consoles linked to the displays in the A-6 cockpit. One of the TC-4Cs (BuNo 155723) crashed in October 1975, but the eight others were retrofitted by Grumman in 1977-78 with the systems of the A-6E/TRAM including the AN/APQ-148 multi-mode radar and Hughes FLIR (forward-looking infrared) turret.

Service history

In June 1959, following completion of the G-159 certification programme, the first aircraft for a customer (c/n 4) was sent to be outfitted before delivery to Sinclair Oil. Thereafter, in its intended role as an executive transport, the Gulfstream I was mostly used by large US corporations including oil companies (such as Continental Oil, Phillips Petroleum, and Texaco), manufacturing companies of all types (*eg*, Eastman Kodak, Ford Motors, General Telephone and Electronics, General Motors, Minnesota Mining and Manufacturing), insurance companies (North American Life and Casualty, State Mutual Life Assurance, and others), and aerospace firms (General Electric, Martin Marietta, Northrop, etc,) which appreciated its practical performance coupled with roomy and well furnished, but not ostentatious, accommodation. Abroad, however, the Gulfstream I met with less success, as it was expensive and did not offer the level of luxury provided by modified airliners and often demanded by some wealthy customers. Foreign-registered Gulfstream I executive transports were

409

Registered VH-CRA, the 171st Gulfstream I was operated by Associated Airlines Pty from Essendon Airport, Melbourne. *(Mervyn W Prime, courtesy of Alain Pelletier)*

primarily operated in Australia, Bermuda, Brazil, Canada, Great Britain, Indonesia, Italy, Mexico, South Africa, Swaziland, and Venezuela.

Non-executive uses included engine test bed, with General Electric modifying one its Gulfstream Is to flight test the 1,700-shp-class CT7 propeller-turbine in 1982-83, and geophysical surveying, with Grumman Ecosystems operating c/n 3 fitted with a magnetometer boom in the tail and carrying other surveying equipment.

Although the Gulfstream I had been certificated in accordance with CAR 4b and was thus authorized to carry fare-paying passengers, the Grumman twin propeller-turbine aircraft did not initially attract interest from airlines. Carrying no more than twenty-four passengers on the power of two Dart R.Da.7 engines, it was much more expensive per seat-mile than the similarly powered Fokker F-27 Mk. 200 and Hawker Siddeley HS.748 Series 2 airliners, which respectively had accommodation for between forty and fifty-two passengers and forty and sixty-two passengers. Even a 1979 proposal by Gulfstream American for a stretched commuter liner, with thirty-two to thirty-eight seats and more fuel efficient General Electric CT64 or Avco Lycoming T55 engines replacing Darts, failed to gain acceptance. Thus, only a few Gulfstream Is were used initially, by small carriers (*eg*, Bonanza Airlines, Golden West Airlines, and Zantop Airways in the United States; Associated Airlines Pty in Australia; Wardair in Canada; Cimber Air in Denmark) in their executive charter operations. More recently, however, the type has seen limited use as a feeder/regional transport and priority cargo transport. Notably, beginning on 5 January, 1981, SAS briefly used a 20-seat Gulfstream I leased from Cimber Air for daily 'breakfast flights' between Copenhagen and Brussels. In 1987, the French regional airline Air Provence added three used Gulfstream Is to its fleet of commuter transports. During the following year, Aerei Speciali operated Gulfstream Is for three weekly flights on the Bologna-Birmingham route. A few aircraft fitted with a cargo loading door in the port side of the

410

rear fuselage have also been used in the United States by small package carriers such as DHL and Purolator.

In the United States, Gulfstream Is have been used by five government agencies and branches of the Armed Forces. The FAA (Federal Aviation Agency, later Federal Aviation Administration) first acquired c/n 2 in June 1959 and later added c/ns 67, 69, and 160 to its fleet of executive transports. One of these aircraft (c/n 2) was subsequently transferred to the US Army Corps of Engineers and the Corps also purchased c/n 45 from Ward International Aircraft. NACA, (National Advisory Committee for Aeronautics now NASA, National Aeronautics and Space Administration), took delivery of the first of five Gulfstream Is (c/ns 92, 96, 98, 125, and 151) in 1963 and was still operating these aircraft twenty-five years later. The US Coast Guard ordered the sole VC-4A VIP/staff transport and put it into

Still registered in the United States, this Gulfstream I was operated in 1988 by the French regional carrier Air Provence. (*Humbert Charvé*)

One of Birmingham Executive Airways' Gulfstream Is at Birmingham International Airport. (*Courtesy Birmingham Executive Airways*)

411

Gulfstream I (c/n 098, N2NA) of NASA Johnson Space Center photographed at Edwards AFB in May 1981. *(René J Francillon)*

service in 1963. However, the main government operator of Gulfstream Is has been and continues to be the US Navy.

Beginning in 1968, three TC-4Cs were assigned to each Intruder replacement training squadron: VA-42 at NAS Oceana, Virginia, for Atlantic Fleet crews; VA-128 at NAS Whidbey Island, Washington, for those of the Pacific Fleet; and VMAT(AW)-202 at MCAS Cherry Point, North Carolina, for USMC crews. Later on, VMAT(AW)-202 was disbanded and since then responsibility for training Marine bombardier/navigators has been shared by VA-42 and VA-128. In 1988, both squadrons still had four TC-4Cs.

Two Gulfstream Is are currently operated by non-US governments and three were used earlier to fly the heads of states. The twenty-second aircraft (c/n 23), which for some ten years was used as a US-registered executive transport by Paul K Mellon, was purchased by the Republic of Austria. Registered OE-BAZ, it has since been operated for checking airways navigation aids. Similar use has been made and continues to be made of c/n 188 (HB-LDT) which was purchased new and had its specialized equipment installed by the Eidgenössisches Flugzeugwerk (Federal Aircraft Factory) in Emmen before being put into service by the Schweitzerische Eidgenössenchaft fur Luftamt (Swiss Federal Air Office). The three other Gulfstream Is owned at one time by non-US governments were c/n 58 which was acquired from National Financing by the Federal Government of Nigeria, c/n 120 which was delivered to King Constantine of Greece, and c/n 133 which was purchased from Dresser Industries by the Republic of the Ivory Coast. All three were later sold back to private operators.

PRODUCTION: A total of 200 aircraft was built by Grumman between August 1958 and May 1969. These aircraft were given the following c/ns:

Gulfstream I   190   C/ns 1/12, 14/90, 92/112, 114/175, 177, 179, 181, 188/200, and 322/323

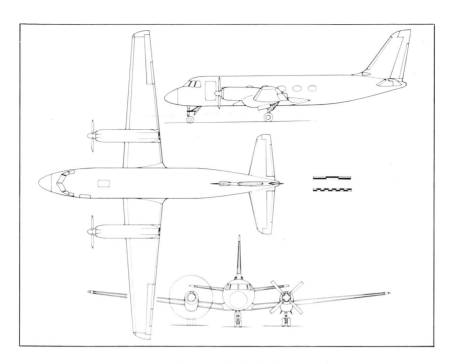

Grumman G-159 Gulfstream I

VC-4A   1   C/n 91
TC-4C   9   C/ns 176, 178, 180, and 182/187.

Span 78 ft 4 in (23.88 m); length 63 ft 9 in (19.43 m); height 22 ft 9 in (6.93 m); wing area 615 sq ft (57.14 sq m).

Empty weight 20,993 lb (9,522 kg); loaded weight 31,000 lb (14,061 kg); maximum weight 35,100 lb (15,921 kg); wing loading 50.4 lb/sq ft (246.1 kg/sq m); power loading 8.2 lb/shp (3.7 kg/shp).

Maximum speed 357 mph at 35,000 ft (574 kmh at 10,670 m); cruising speed 334 mph (537 kmh); climb rate 3,010 ft/min (15 m/sec); service ceiling 36,900 ft (11,245 m); normal range 1,865 miles (3,000 km); maximum range 2,500 miles (4,020 km).

An AO-1 (59-5620) with skis and high-visibility markings for operation in Alaska. *(Grumman)*

Grumman OV-1 (AO-1) Mohawk

The Mohawk, the only fixed-wing aircraft ever to have been designed expressly to meet Army Aviation requirements, entered service in 1961. More than a quarter of a century later, its battlefield surveillance and target acquisition capabilities remain unmatched in the western world's inventory. Hence, the Army is holding on to its Mohawks and, with the exception of two OV-1Ds supplied to Israel but later returned to the US, has not released aircraft for modification and resale to non-US air forces.

Requirements behind the development of this enduring aircraft were developed jointly by the Army and the Marine Corps in the immediate post-Korean War period to obtain a replacement for their vulnerable Cessna L-19 and OE-1 Bird Dog observation aircraft. Over a two-year period, internally-prepared design studies helped military planners define the desired characteristics of an aircraft capable of performing visual observation missions as well as day and night photography. Furthermore, the Army and the Marine Corps desired that provision be made in the design for the later inclusion of electronic surveillance devices suitable for night and instrument operations. Agreeing on a common set of specifications for an aircraft optimized for STOL operations from unimproved fields and roads in forward combat areas, the two branches of the Armed Forces issued a joint Request for Proposals in the spring of 1956. Before the end of that year, the Grumman G-134 was selected as the winner of this design competition.

On 31 December, 1956, the Secretary of Defense authorized the Secretary of the Army to procure five aircraft for engineering and Service tests. Subsequent negotiations led to the March 1957 award of a contract for final design and procurement of nine prototypes, five YAO-1As (serials 57-6463/57-6467) for the Army and four YOF-1s (BuNos 147266/147269)

Full-scale mock-up of the proposed OF-1 version for the Marine Corps with the original tail configuration. *(Grumman)*

for the Marine Corps. However, in January 1958, the Department of the Navy informed the Army that due to a shortage of funds the Marine Corps was forced to withdraw from the programme. Rather than slowing down work, the Army then increased its order to nine prototypes and development aircraft. Moreover, lacking the required staff to assume engineering responsibility and plant cognizance for the aircraft and its Lycoming T53 propeller-turbines, the Army decided that, in spite of the withdrawal of USN funds, the Navy should retain these responsibilities for the airframe while the Air Force would do so for the engines.

As evidenced by its mock-up, the G-164, designed by a team led by Michael Pelehach, was characterized by a single fin and rudder of large size on which the horizontal surfaces were mounted near the top. Wind-tunnel tests, however, revealed that these surfaces would provide insufficient control during STOL operations. Accordingly, the original tail surfaces were replaced by a conventionally located tailplane and triple fins and rudders. Other design features shown in the mock-up remained unchanged. This was notably the case of the side-by-side cockpit accommodating a pilot and a technical observer under a large canopy with 'bugeye' side windows providing outstanding downward and forward visibility. Crew safety was to be enhanced through the installation of Martin-Baker ejector seats and provision for an armoured floor, flak-resistant windshield, and flak curtains on the forward and aft cockpit bulkheads.

Completed in Bethpage in late March 1959, the first YAO-1 was powered by 950-eshp Lycoming T53-L-3 propeller-turbines mounted above the wings and 'toed out' to provide good asymmetric handling. Trials began on 14 April with Ralph 'Dixie' Donnell making an uneventful first flight. Thereafter, the Navy undertook engineering tests at NATC Patuxent River and the Army conducted Service tests at Ft Rucker, Alabama. Successful completion of these tests was accomplished after the skin of the vertical tail surfaces was smoothed to eliminate a minor flutter problem and confirmed

415

The first Mohawk, with rear cockpit windows and much wool tufting on the centre fuselage, inboard wing sections, and engine nacelles. (*Grumman*)

the soundness of the design. This was indeed fortunate as in April 1958, one year before the first flight of the prototype, the Army had already ordered a first production batch of eighteen AO-1As (serials 59-2603/59-2620) and seventeen AO-1Bs (serials 59-2621/59-2637).

Production history

Before the Mohawk entered service, additional orders were placed for camera-equipped AO-1As (which were redesignated OV-1As in September 1962), AO-1Bs (later OV-1Bs) with side-looking airborne radar (SLAR), and AO-1Cs (later OV-1Cs) with cameras and infrared (IR) sensors. The final production version, the OV-1D, was ordered in Fiscal Year 1968 and could be quickly reconfigured to carry cameras, SLAR, or IR equipment. Additional OV-1Ds, as well as RV-1Ds fitted for electronic intelligence gathering, were obtained through modifications of OV-1B and OV-1C airframes.

YOF-1 and **OF-1:** These designations were given to Mohawks which were to have been built for the Marine Corps. Four YOF-1 prototypes (BuNos 147266/147269) were ordered but were cancelled before completion and the OF-1 was not ordered into production.

YOV-1A (YAO-1A): The nine YAO-1As (57-6463/57-6467 and the four ex-Marine YOF-1s which became 57-6538/57-6541) were powered by 950-eshp T53-L-3s or 1,150 eshp T53-L-7s. They had a single pylon for a 150-US gal drop tank beneath each wing to supplement their 297-gal fuselage tank. The first flew on 14 April, 1959, and the last was delivered in March 1960. Provision was made for dual controls, but the stick and rudder pedals were seldom installed.

OV-1A (AO-1A): The first production version was powered by 950-eshp T53-L-3s and fitted for visual and photographic-reconnaissance with a

416

The first production AO-1A (59-2603) with resupply containers under the wings. (*Grumman*)

camera mount in the centre fuselage. External differences distinguishing the sixty-four AO-1As and OV-1As, delivered between February 1960 and February 1965, from the YAO-1As were the absence of aft-looking side windows and the additional store pylon beneath each wing.

The OV-1As were normally fitted with four store stations, two beneath each wing. The heaviest stores carried on the inboard station were 150-US gal external tanks, which weighed 975 lb when full, and resupply containers, which weighed 750 lb and were fitted with a parachute in the tail cone and an impact-cushioning plastic nose. The outboard station beneath each wing was limited to stores weighing less than 500 lb. The only other stores initially carried by OV-1As were A6 flare ejectors, with an ejector mounted above the wing trailing edge on each side of the fuselage and containing fifty-two upward-firing flares to provide illumination for night photography. Subsequently, these unreliable flare ejectors were replaced by strobe light pods capable of flashing every three seconds. When fitted with a third store station beneath each wing, as tested on two JOV-1As, armed Mohawks could carry a maximum external load of 3,700 lb.

JOV-1A: To evaluate the feasibility of providing the Army with an armed reconnaissance/ground support version of the Mohawk, two OV-1As (57-6538 and 57-6740) were modified as JOV-1As (with the prefix J identifying temporary special tests) and fitted with an additional 500-lb store station beneath each wing. Boresight provisions were added to the

417

fuselage for gun alignment. Cockpit modifications included a Mk. 8 gun sight, an armament control panel, electrical system wiring for the new store stations and weapon interface, revised hand grip on the flight control assembly for gun firing and stores release, and armour plate in addition to the flak curtains.

The JOV-1As were cleared to carry 0.50-in machine-gun pods; 2.75-in and 5-in FFAR rocket pods; 5-in HVAR rockets; 250-lb Mk.81, 500-lb Mk. 82, or 1,000-lb Mk. 83 LDGP (low-drag, general purpose) bombs; fire bombs; smoke and bomblet dispensers; resupply containers; and AIM-9 Sidewinder air-to-air missiles.

OV-1B (AO-1B): Initially powered by the same 950-eshp T53-L-3s as the AO-1As but later re-engined with 1,150-eshp T53-L-7s, the 101 SLAR-equipped AO-1Bs and OV-1Bs were delivered between September 1960 and May 1966. Later, forty-nine were modified: one (59-2633) as the JOV-1B test bed, seventeen as OV-1Ds, and thirty-one as RV-1Ds. To offset the increased weight and drag resulting from the attachment of the SLAR pod on the lower corner of the starboard fuselage side, most AO-1Bs

Two JOV-1As during Army evaluation at Fort Rucker, Alabama. (*Grumman*)

Side number 34, an Army OV-1B released to the Navy for use by the Naval Test Pilot School at NAS Patuxent River. (*USN/NATC Patuxent River*)

were retrofitted with extended wing outboard panels, increasing the span from 42 to 48 ft and wing area from 330 to 360 sq ft. The AN/APS-94B SLAR enabled OV-1Bs (and, later, OV-1Ds carrying the AN/APS-94F) to scan large areas on one or both sides of the flight path to pinpoint the location of enemy vehicular movements. SLAR imagery was recorded on film and then displayed on a console at the technical observer station on the starboard side of the cockpit with the film used for later analysis on the ground. It could also be transmitted via data link to permit viewing by a ground observer assigned to a Tactical Exploitation Battalion (TEB) centre some distance away.

An OV-1B (62-5868) was fitted experimentally with an 18-ft dry probe bolted on the starboard fuselage side. Trials conducted near Cherry Point, North Carolina, during the summer of 1964, demonstrated the feasibility of tanking from a Lockheed KC-130F, thus making it possible to ferry Mohawks directly across the Pacific from the United States to Vietnam. However, the planned fitting of bolt-on refuelling probes to Mohawks was abandoned in 1967 as the Department of Defense decreed that henceforth the Army would only operate fixed-wing aircraft no larger than the Mohawk and would transfer its de Havilland CV-2 Caribous to the Air Force instead of fitting them with hose drum refuelling kits for use as tankers to support modified Mohawks.

OV-1C (AO-1C): Carrying infrared sensors, the 165 AO-1Cs and OV-1Cs were delivered between February 1961 and December 1969. They were powered by T53-L-3s and L-7s and most were delivered with the shorter wings of the AO-1As. Many were retrofitted with long-span wings and,

A modified OV-1B during air refuelling tests off Cherry Point in July 1964. The tanker is a Lockheed KC-130F of the Marine Corps. *(Grumman)*

419

frequently, were also re-engined with 1,150-eshp T53-L-15s. The AN/UAS-4 Red Haze infrared detection equipment enabled OV-1Cs (and, later, OV-1Ds configured with the improved AN/AAS-24 surveillance system) to detect targets at night, in bad weather, and in heavily wooded or jungle terrain, but required the aircraft to fly directly over targets. Although the Red Haze system necessitated that the OV-1C overfly the target, its use was considered acceptable in the relatively permissive environment found in South Vietnam but unacceptable in theatres of operations with heavier defences. Hence, OV-1Cs have been phased out of service. For the same reason, the IR equipment is now seldom carried by OV-1Ds. Like SLAR data in the case of the OV-1B, IR data could be viewed in flight by the OV-1C technical observer or transmitted to remote ground stations.

An OV-1C (61-2728) was fitted with an AN/APN-22 terrain-following radar under a nose radome, and was tested at Fort Huachuca, Arizona, in 1963-64 but, as the Army did not have a requirement for Mohawks with terrain following radar, this installation remained experimental.

In Vietnam, a few OV-1Cs were configured with an additional store station as developed for the JOV-1A and were operated in the armed reconnaissance/ground support role.

Project *Seamore:* As the result of operational experience in Vietnam, the Army developed a requirement for modifications which in a first phase would improve the Mohawk's SLAR and IR systems and in a later phase would result in a single Mohawk version which could be quickly reconfigured in the field for either photographic-reconnaissance, SLAR surveillance, or IR operations as dictated by fluctuating intelligence needs. Given a *Brickbat* priority on the master urgency list of the Department of Defense, the resulting Project *Seamore* (Southeast Asia Mohawk Requirement) led to the modification of two OV-1Bs (62-5903 and 64-14242) and two OV-1Cs (61-2718 and 62-5851) in its first phase. Work on these Design 452 aircraft began in March 1967 and, after being fitted with improved equipment (the only external difference being the addition of a fairing beneath the fuselage of the two modified OV-1Cs), they were sent to South

OV-1B (62-5903), one of four Mohawks modified as part of Project *Seamore*, during a test flight in 1967. (*Grumman*)

Vietnam for operational evaluation by the 224th Army Security Agency Battalion (Aviation) at Can Tho.

YOV-1D: The next *Seamore* phase saw Grumman working on Design 452 and modifying four not-yet-delivered OV-1Cs (67-18898, 67-18899, 67-18902, and 67-18905) as YOV-1D prototypes. The YOV-1Ds were accepted by the Army between June and September 1968. After completing expedited testing in the United States, the first (67-18898) was retained for development work and redesignated NOV-1D, while the other three were sent to South Vietnam for combat evaluation.

OV-1D: The thirty-seven new-built OV-1Ds and the seventeen OV-1Bs and sixty-three OV-1Cs rebuilt by Grumman as OV-1Ds differed from the YOV-1Ds in being powered by 1,400-eshp T53-L-701 propeller-turbines. All were fitted with 48-ft wings.

For photographic-reconnaissance, the OV-1Ds are currently fitted with three cameras, a forward-aimed panoramic KA-60C in the nose, a panoramic KA-60C in a fuselage blister, and a KA-76A serial frame camera on a remotely-controlled mounting in the aft fuselage. For SLAR surveillance missions, an AN/APS-94F radar antenna is carried, beneath the starboard fuselage side on angle mounts. For IR surveillance, the AN/AAS-24 system is carried internally in the lower centre fuselage section. In all instances, an AN/ASN-86 Inertial Navigation System (INS) is fitted.

To enhance the OV-1D's survivability in high-threat areas by providing passive infrared signature suppression, their engines can be fitted in the

Serial 68-15932 was built as an OV-1C and modified as an OV-1D in 1974. Subsequently, with the AN/APS-94F SLAR temporarily removed, it was used to test-fly AN/ALQ-133 *Quick Look II* ELINT pods for the RV-1D variant. *(Grumman)*

field with Louvered Scarfed Shroud Suppressors (LSSSs). Active infrared countermeasures (IRCM) are provided by a Saunders AN/ALQ-147 Hot Brick set which can be carried either in a separate pod on the outboard rack beneath either wing or attached to the aft end of one of the external tanks. Chaff or flare conformal dispensers, which had been developed earlier for installation against the fuselage sides above the wing trailing edge, are no longer in use.

Under a Program Aircraft Restoration (PAR) contract awarded in 1986, Grumman is currently overhauling and strengthening up two aircraft a month in its Stuart plant to extend their structural life from 7,000 to 12,000 hours. Moreover, following the modification of a development aircraft which flew in May 1988, Grumman will probably be awarded a contract to put at least thirty-three Mohawks through the Multi-Stage Improvement Program (MSIP). Modifications are expected as a minimum to include a new electrical system, an anti-icing system, a stall-warning device, a new autopilot, improved communications and navigation equipment, including the Global Positioning System, and partial replacement of instruments with a Honeywell multifunction video display. In addition, MSIP may feature an engine upgrade. MSIP is expected to be funded in Fiscal Year 1989, with first delivery of modified aircraft to be made in 1990.

RV-1D: Thirty-one RV-1Ds were obtained between February 1977 and October 1982 by modifying OV-1Bs into dedicated electronic intelligence (ELINT) aircraft. Intended to ascertain the location, type, and emission bands of electronic countermeasures (ECM) and other enemy radar facilities, the RV-1Ds have all photographic, SLAR, and IR equipment removed and instead are equipped to carry an AN/ALQ-133 ELINT pod under each wing outboard of the drop tanks and an internally-carried AN/USQ-61 data link system. Like the RV-1Ds, they can be fitted with IRCM pods and louvred scarfed shroud suppressors.

OV-1E, EV-1E, and **RV-1E:** The OV-1E designation was first used to identify a proposed version with a redesigned forward fuselage providing accommodation for two additional technical observers and space for more

An OV-1D of the 641st Military Intelligence Battalion, Oregon Army National Guard, over southern Oregon on 10 July, 1988. *(René J Francillon)*

422

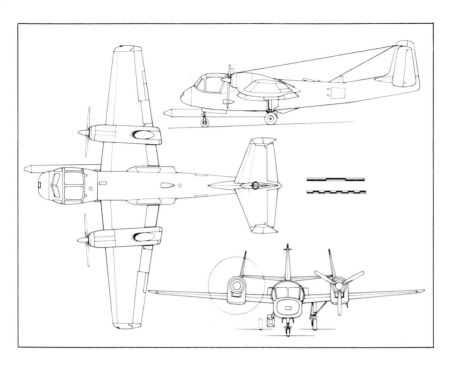

Grumman OV-1D Mohawk

surveillance equipment. Consideration was given to substituting 2,330-shp Lycoming T55s for the T53s of other Mohawk versions, but neither the enlarged aircraft nor other proposed T55-powered versions were ordered.

The often-reported OV-1E, EV-1E and RV-1E designations are incorrect. Up to mid-1988, no Mohawk version has been identified officially by the suffix letter 'E.' However, this suffix could be adopted soon to identify OV-1Ds modified under MSIP.

Design 134E: This proposed tilt-wing derivative of the Mohawk is described in Appendix B.

Service history

Mohawks were first delivered to operational units in the United States in February 1961 and, in the tense months following the erection of the Berlin Wall in August 1961, were rushed to the 7th Army at Sandhoffen in Germany. Deployment to South Vietnam was next, with six AO-1As (almost immediately redesignated OV-1As) from the 23rd Special Warfare Aviation Detachment (Surveillance) arriving at Nha Trang in September 1962. Divided into three flights for assignment to separate Vietnamese divisions, the aircraft of the 23rd SWAD flew mostly visual and photo-graphic-reconnaissance sorties. On occasion, they were also flown in the armed reconnaissance role with 0.50-in gun pods and 2.75-in rockets beneath the wings and Vietnamese observers in the right-hand seat to approve attacks on targets of opportunity. Later, as American involvement increased, more armed Mohawks (including some OV-1Cs assigned to the 11th Air Assault Division) were added. However, due to Air Force opposition to Army aircraft flying in the armed reconnaissance and ground support roles, in which armed Mohawks had proved most effective, OV-1s were restricted after 1965 to flying unarmed in the visual, photographic, SLAR, and infrared reconnaissance roles.

The first SLAR- and IR-equipped Mohawks arrived in Vietnam with the 4th Aerial Surveillance and Target Acquisition Detachment during the autumn of 1964. Thereafter, the number of unarmed OV-1As, OV-1Bs, and OV-1Cs in the war zone increased and Mohawks went on to serve with the 73rd, 131st, 225th, 244th, and 245th Surveillance Aviation Companies.

By the time the Southeast Asia War ended in January 1973, one OV-1 had been shot down by a MiG during operations across the Demilitarized Zone (DMZ) in 1969, one destroyed on the ground by mortar fire, twenty-seven brought down by AAA and small arms fire, and thirty-six lost in operational accidents.

Notwithstanding these losses (more than 17 per cent of all OV-1s built), Mohawks proved extremely capable and were highly valued by Army commanders. In particular, OV-1s were praised for their ability to provide intelligence data quickly as the Army used portable laboratories at division headquarters and forward bases for immediate on-site processing. Conversely, photographs taken by Air Force reconnaissance aircraft often reached local commanders too late as they had to be processed at major air bases and then shipped to Army field units. Mohawks also proved a key element in providing troop logistic tonnage movement out of North Vietnam to MACV (Military Assistance Command Vietnam) and on to the White House, directed naval patrol aircraft to infiltration points, and provided targeting data for Boeing B-52 strikes against Viet Cong bases hidden in the jungle.

During the 1960s and early 1970s, while most OV-1s flew combat sorties in Southeast Asia or served with Army units at home, in Korea, and in Germany, four Mohawks were used in the United States to establish the following world class records:

16 June, 1966, Calverton, New York: An OV-1B(64-14240) flown by Jim Peters, Grumman's Project Pilot for the Mohawk, climbed to 3,000 m/9,843 ft in 3 min 41 sec and to 6,000 m/19,685 ft in 9 min 9 sec and flew at a sustained altitude of 9,754 m/32,000 ft

17 June, 1966, Calverton, New York: The same OV-1B was flown by Col Edward Nielsen, USA, over a 100-km/62.15-mile closed course in 12 min 48.8 sec at an average speed of 468.26 km/h/291.03 mph.

16-17 July, 1966: LTC John Collins, USA, set a new distance record by flying an OV-1 unidentified Mohawk from Fort Lewis, Washington, to Sherbrooke, Quebec, Canada. A distance of 2,424 miles (3,900 km) was covered at an average speed of 255 mph (410 km/h).

June, 1971, Ft Hood, Texas: An unidentified OV-1C was flown by CW2 Thomas Yoha and Capt Richard Steinbock, USA, to a peak altitude of 12,155 m/39,880 ft and a sustained altitude of 11,080 m/36,352 ft.

Fifteen years after the end of the Southeast Asia War, the Army was still finding Mohawks to be effective battlefield surveillance aircraft. In 1988, OV-1Ds and RV-1Ds were operated by regular Army units in the Continental United States (15th and 224th Military Intelligence Battalions or MIBs), Germany (1st and 2nd MIBs), and South Korea (3rd MIB). Mohawks were also assigned to Army training units at Fort Rucker, Alabama; Fort Huachuca, Arizona; and Fort Eustis, Virginia.

A first batch of six aircraft was assigned to the Army National Guard in 1970. Since then, ArNG Mohawks have gained some fame as the result of their employment by the Oregon Army National Guard on the occasion of the volcanic eruption of Mt St. Helens in May 1980. On this occasion, using IR and SLAR to obtain details of the extent of damage when volcanic ash prevented visual observation, the Oregonian OV-1Ds provided useful imagery for rescue parties. Eight years later, Mohawks were still equipping the 159th MIB, Georgia ArNG, at Dobbins AFB, and the 641st MIB, Oregon ArNG, at the Salem-McNary Airport.

At least one OV-1A (63-13119), six OV-1Bs (59-2627, 59-2637, 62-5866, 62-5896, 64-14243, and 64-14263), and one RV-1D (64-14262) were transferred from the Army to the United States Naval Test Pilot School at NATC Patuxent River. The last two Mohawks operated by the TPS to demonstrate multi-engine assessment, asymmetric power flying qualities, and STOL performance were transferred back to the Army in 1989.

In 1963, Grumman was authorized to market the Mohawk to selected allied nations and, in support of this export drive, the Army agreed to lease OV-1s back to Grumman for demonstration to prospective foreign customers. Thus, the Heeresflieger (German Army Aviation) evaluated an OV-1B and an OV-1C at Bückeburg during a three-month period in the autumn of 1963, when German markings were temporarily applied to these Mohawks. Similarly, following a two-day demonstration in February 1963 at Buc, near Paris, French markings were applied to an OV-1B and an OV-1C which the Aviation Légère de l'Armée de Terre (ALAT, French Army Aviation) evaluated at Metz-Frescaty during the autumn and winter of 1963. However, neither France nor Germany ordered Mohawks and the only foreign OV-1 operator has been Israel.

The Tsvah Haganah le Israel - Heyl Ha'Avir (Israel Defence Force - Air Force) received two OV-1Ds on loan from the US Army (69-17021 and 68-16993, which were respectively registered 4X-JRA and 4X-JRB).

An OV-1B at Bückeburg, Federal German Republic, during evaluation by the Heeresflieger in 1963. *(Grumman)*

After the Heyl Ha'Avir received its E-2Cs in 1977-78, the two Mohawks were shipped back to the United Sates where they were refurbished by Grumman and returned to the US Army inventory.

Contrary to what has been frequently stated, the Republic of Korea Air Force (ROKAF) did not receive Mohawks. All OV-1s currently operated in South Korea belong to the 3rd Military Intelligence Battalion of the US Army, which is based at Camp Humphreys. Similarly, proposed sales of armed Mohawks to the Philippine Air Force in 1980 and of OV-1Ds to Pakistan in 1983 did not materialize as, following the termination of the SEMA-X programme (Special Electronic Mission Aircraft – *see* Design 698 in Appendix B), the USA decided to retain all available Mohawks for provision against attrition and future considerations pending the possible procurement of ASEMAs (Advanced Special Electronic Mission Aircraft).

Non-military Mohawk operators have included four US government agencies – the Customs Service, the Environmental Protection Agency (EPA), the US Geological Survey, and the NASA Langley Research Center – and a private enterprise, Thunderbird Aviation Inc.

Under contract from the US Geological Survey, the Army provided an OV-1B and crews in the autumn of 1971 to take part in a project sponsored by the Inter-American Geodetic Survey and aimed at detecting surface water in the jungles of Panama (this aircraft was registered N171). Three years later, it provided another OV-1B (64-14243) to survey the route of the trans-Alaska oil pipeline and to study pack ice.

The US Customs Service obtained four surplus OV-1Cs (60-3758, 61-2699, 62-5856, and 66-18896) in 1973 and had them fitted with a nose-mounted forward-looking infrared (FLIR) sensors for use in spotting drug smugglers crossing from Mexico at night or in bad weather.

The Environmental Protection Agency briefly operated an OV-1C (64-14243) from Las Vegas, Nevada, in the mid-1970s to evaluate the practicality of using infrared sensors for the detection of oil spills and industrial waste flows and for surveying strip mining impacts.

The NASA OV-1B (N512NA, ex-62-5880) at the Langley Research Center, Virginia, in 1986. By then the JT15D turbofan had been removed from the starboard wing nacelle and the wall of the nacelle had been given a sound proofing treatment by General Electric. The pod further outboard contained sound recording and measuring equipment. *(NASA)*

NASA Langley Research Center acquired an OV-1B (62-5880). Registered N512NA, this aircraft had its SLAR pod removed and was fitted by Grumman in Stuart with a pylon-mounted 2,200-lb thrust Pratt & Whitney of Canada JT15D-1 turbofan beneath its starboard wing for engine-noise monitoring tests beginning in 1980. Six years later, after the JT15D-1 had been removed from the nacelle, N512NA was used for noise monitoring experiments with specially treated General Electric nacelle walls.

Finally, Thunderbird Aviation Inc purchased a surplus OV-1A (60-3735) which, registered N75213, was fitted in 1983 with two external water supply tanks and a spray boom cantilevered from the starboard wingtip for use in icing certification tests for other aircraft. At least three other Mohawks went on the US civil register

PRODUCTION: A total of 380 Mohawks was built by Grumman between April 1959 and December 1970; in addition, between September 1974 and July 1987 Grumman converted 111 OV-1Bs and OV-1Cs as OV-1Ds and RV-1Ds. Breakdown by models is as follows:

9	YOV-1A	4	YOV-1D
64	OV-1A	37	OV-1D
101	OV-1B	(80)	OV-1D
165	OV-1C	(31)	RV-1D

They received the following US serials:
YOV-1A: USA 57-6463/57-6467 and 57-6538/57-6541
OV-1A: USA 59-2603/59-2620, 60-3720/60-3744, and
              63-13114/63-13134

OV-1B:	USA 59-2621/59-2637, 62-5859/62-5906, and 64-14238/64-14273			
OV-1C:	USA 60-3745/60-3761, 61-2675/61-2728, 62-5849/62-5858,66-18881/66-18896, 67-18897, 67-18900/67-18901,67-18903/67-18904, 67-18906/18932, and 68-15930/68-15965			
YOV-1D:	USA 67-18898/67-18899, 67-18902, and 67-18905			
OV-1D:	USA 68-16990/68-16996 and 69-16997/69-17026			
OV-1D: (conversions)	62-5865, 62-5867, 62-5872/62-5876, 62-5878, 62-5885/ 62-5890, 62-5898/62-5899, 62-5902, 66-18898/66-18900,66-18902/66-18912, 66-18916/66-18927, 66-18929/66-18932,68-15930/68-15935, 68-15937/68-15943, 68-15945/68-15948,and 68-15950/68-15965			
RV-1D: (conversions)	62-5891, 62-5897, 64-14238/64-14239, 64-14242/64-14248,64-14250, 64-14252/64-14256, 64-14258/64-14263, 64-14265,and 64-14267/64-14273.			

	OV-1A	OV-1B	OV-1C	OV-1D
DIMENSIONS:				
Span, ft in	42 0	48 0	42 0	48 0
(m)	(12.80)	(14.63)	(12.80)	(14.63)
Length, ft in	41 0	43 11³/₈	41 1³/₈	44 11
(m)	(12.50)	(13.40)	(12.53)	(13.69)
Height, ft in	12 8	13 0	12 8	13 0
(m)	(3.86)	(3.96)	(3.86)	(3.96)
Wing area, sq ft	330	360	330	360
(sq m)	(30.66)	(33.45)	(30.66)	(33.45)
WEIGHTS:				
Empty, lb	9,937	10,983	10,011	11,757
(kg)	(4,507)	(4,982)	(4,541)	(5,333)
Loaded, lb	12,672	13,654	12,682	15,741
(kg)	(5,747)	(6,193)	(5,752)	(7,140)
Maximum, lb	15,031	16,643	15,302	18,109
(kg)	(6,818)	(7,549)	(6,941)	(8,214)
Wing loading,* lb/sq ft	38.4	37.9	38.4	43.7
(kg/sq m)	(187.4)	(185.1)	(187.6)	(213.5)
Power loading,* lb/shp	6.6	6.3	6.6	5.6
(kg/shp)	(3.0)	(2.8)	(3.0)	(2.6)
PERFORMANCE:				
Max speed, mph/ft	308/5,000	290/11,500	295/10,000	305/5,000
(kmh/m)	(496/1,525)	(467/3,505)	(475/3,050)	(491/1,525)
Cruising speed, mph	207	230	230	207
(kmh)	(333)	(370)	(370)	(333)
Climb rate, ft/min	2,950	2,800	2,270	3,618
(m/sec)	(15)	(14)	(12)	(18)
Service ceiling, ft	30,300	29,500	27,450	25,000
(m)	(9,235)	(8,990)	(8,365)	(7,620)
Max range, miles	1,410	1,210	1,245	1,010
(km)	(2,270)	(1,945)	(2,005)	(1,625)

* Wing and power loadings are calculated at normal loaded weight and maximum take-off power.

BuNo 159314, seen over choppy waters in the markings of VMA(AW)-121, was built as an A-6E and delivered in December 1974. It was redelivered as an A-6E TRAM in July 1982. *(USMC)*

Grumman A-6 (A2F) Intruder

In terms of production longevity, the Intruder is likely to set a record for combat aircraft as Grumman will still be manufacturing A-6s more than thirty years after Bob Smyth first flew the A2F-1 on 16 April, 1960. Truly not a thing of beauty, the A-6 quickly came into its own after a lengthy test programme and problems with prematurely detonating bombs early during its first combat deployment aboard the USS *Independence* (CVA-62) in 1965. Today, Intruders remain highly potent weapons systems capable of delivering a heavy load, at low altitude and in all weathers, against well defended targets. Moreover, in spite of current plans to replace them in the mid-1990s with stealthy A-12s, A-6s are likely to be operating aboard USN carriers well into the first decade of the second millenium – quite a tribute, indeed, to the skills of Lawrence M Mead and his team, who submitted the winning proposal in response to a February 1957 Navy invitation to bid.

That request had been accompanied by Type Specification 149 for a short take-off and landing, all-weather, two-seat aircraft to replace Douglas AD Skyraiders used by the Marines for close air support and by the Navy for long range interdiction missions. TS149 called for a top speed of at least 500 kt and a mission radius of 300 nm for air support, but left the bidders free to offer single or twin-engined designs and to propose jet- or propeller-turbine-powered aircraft. Furthermore, for the first time, BuAer specified that the airframe manufacturers were to be responsible for the entire weapons systems, not just the aircraft, as in the past. Eight manufacturers submitted proposals in August 1957, and on 20 December

The M-wing Design 128M4 was one of the many configurations studied by the Grumman team in 1957. (*Grumman*)

Grumman was informed that its Design 128Q had been selected as the winner.

Before submitting the winning entry, Larry Mead and his team had studied an array of configurations ranging from that of Design 128E, with twin fins and rudders and two propeller-turbines beneath straight wings, to that of Design 128M4, with turbojets beneath 'M' wings featuring forward-swept inboard panels and swept-back outboard panels. Most of these configurations already had a cockpit arrangement similar to that adopted for the 128Q and in which the pilot sat a little higher and forward of the bombardier/navigator in order to have optimum visibility to the right while still featuring the side-by-side accommodation favoured by operational crews.

As submitted, the 128Q configuration provided for the side-by-side installation of two Pratt & Whitney J52 turbojets on the lower corners of the forward/centre fuselage. Both engines were to be fitted with extended tail pipes which could be tilted 23 degrees downward to improve STOL performance by reducing lift-off speed at the Marine air support mission weight from 86 to 78 kt. The most remarkable feature of the 128Q proposal, however, was its Digital Integrated Attack Navigation Equipment (DIANE) built around an AN/APQ-92 search radar, an AN/APQ-112 track radar, an AN/ASN-31 inertial navigation system, a CP-729A air data computer, an AN/ASQ-61 ballistics computer, and an AN/APN-153 doppler. DIANE also integrated Automatic Direction Finder (ADF), Identification Friend or Foe (IFF), and Tactical Air Navigation (TACAN) equipment.

The initial contract, which was awarded in February 1958, only provided funding for preliminary design and a full-scale mock-up. Work during this early phase and following mock up inspection in September resulted in

The A2F-1 (BuNo 147864) during its first flight, on 19 April, 1960, with Bob Smyth at the controls. *(Grumman)*

numerous design refinements including (1) the straightening of the wing trailing edge, (2) the substitution of modified single-slotted flaps for double-slotted flaps as originally proposed, (3) the enlargement of the nose to provide space for the search and track radars under a single radome, (4) the recontouring of the canopy to reduce drag, (5) the use of a larger fin located further aft, (6) the adoption of a novel nosewheel catapulting system (now standard for US carrier aircraft), and (7) various changes to improve the design and operating efficiency of electronic systems (*eg*, doubling the computer memory, increasing the capacity of the avionics cooling system, etc). Furthermore, to correct a mistake in cruise drag calculations, span was increased by 2 ft and internal fuel capacity was increased by 155 gal.

Four A2F-1 development aircraft (BuNos 147864/147867) were ordered in March 1959 and four more (BuNos 148615/148618) were ordered a year later. Following taxi-ing trials at Bethpage, BuNo 147864 was trucked to Calverton and, powered by still experimental Pratt & Whitney YJ52-P-6s and fitted with only enough communication and navigation equipment for safe operations, was first flown by Robert Smyth on 19 April, 1960. Afterward, the A2F-1 went through a long and difficult test programme, not only because its highly advanced DIANE systems required much development but also because changes had to be made to correct various aerodynamic deficiencies and remove unsatisfactory features.

The first of these airframe changes was made during the summer of 1960 when flap slots were modified to eliminate buffeting with flaps extended. In October 1960, it was determined that under certain conditions the horizontal tail surfaces became hard to move when the fuselage speed brakes were opened. Accordingly, beginning with the fourth aircraft, these surfaces were moved aft 16 in. Next, as the result of the Navy Preliminary Evaluation during which the perforated speed brakes on the fuselage sides (which initially were plain) were found ineffective for the dive-bombing

The first A2F-1 (BuNo 147864), with exhausts tilted down 23 degrees (as initially provided for STOL operation), original stabilizer location, early rudder shape, and plain fuselage brakes. *(Grumman)*

mission and for work around carriers, Grumman developed wingtip split brakes. The wingtip brakes, which were interlocked to avoid asymmetrical extension, were tested on the first A2F-1 in September 1961 and proved highly effective. The first aircraft also became the first to be retrofitted with an enlarged rudder, the chord being increased at the base to give more exposed rudder area for spin recovery. In addition to the need for these modifications, flight tests revealed that the tilting exhaust pipes reduced take-off distance only when the aircraft operated at relatively low gross weight. Consequently, tilting pipes were installed only on the first four aircraft and provision for their installation was retained in the next four A2F-1s. The turbojets installed in production Intruders had fixed exhausts.

The first aircraft to be fitted with full avionics was the fourth A2F-1 (BuNo 147867), which began flying in December 1960. Its testing initially progressed slowly and the terrain clearance mode was not tried until February 1961. For months afterwards, the highly complex DIANE system proved unreliable. Moreover, Navy evaluation revealed that the pilot's and bombardier/navigator's displays were deficient in terms of brightness and resolution. Consequently, initial assignment to the fleet was delayed by almost a year while changes to improve systems reliability and to provide satisfactory displays were developed and tested. The results, however, were highly satisfactory and worth the wait.

While the avionics portion of Board of Inspection and Survey trials was temporarily held in abeyance, the remainder of BIS trials proceeded unabated. Carrier trials took place aboard the USS *Enterprise* (CVAN-65) in December 1962 (two months after the initial version of the Intruder had been redesignated A-6A) and initial deliveries to a training squadron, VA-42 at NAS Oceana, Virginia, were made in February 1963. Final BIS trials were initiated during the next month and crew training was begun in earnest in June of that year.

Production history

In spite of the Intruder's unusually long production life, only two of its attack

An A-6A being catapulted from the angled deck of the USS *Enterprise* (CVAN-65) during carrier suitability trials in December 1962. (*Grumman*)

versions, the A-6A and the A-6E, have been built in large numbers. Although a few EA-6As and A-6Fs have also been built as such, all other Intruder variants, as well as most of the A-6Es, have been obtained through modification of existing airframes. Some airframes, in fact, have been modified several times. For example, BuNo 155681 was delivered as an A-6A in March 1969 and was redelivered successively as an A-6C in April 1970, as an A-6E in September 1976, and as an A-6E TRAM (*ie*, fitted with the Target Recognition Attack Multisensor system) in August 1983. Barring unexpected problems, this aircraft is likely to be modified once again to receive Boeing-built composite wings. Even the most hardened budget-crunching Congressman or Senator must admit that in this instance US taxpayers got their money's worth!

A-6A (A2F-1): The first of eight development aircraft was flown on 19 April, 1960, and the last of 474 production A-6As (designated A2F-1s before September 1962) was delivered on 28 December, 1970. The development aircraft and the A-6As delivered before the winter of 1965 were powered by two 8,500-lb thrust Pratt & Whitney J52 turbojets, those fitted for initial trials being YJ52-P-6s and J52-P-6s and those powering early production aircraft being P-6s, P-6As, or P-6Bs. Aircraft delivered after December 1965, beginning with BuNo152583, were powered by 9,300-lb thrust J52-P-8As or P-8Bs. Like later Intruder versions, all A-6As had upward folding wings with 25 degrees of sweep at the quarter-chord.

As detailed above, numerous modifications were made during trials. In addition, as the wingtip brakes were found to be sufficient, the fuselage speed-brakes were omitted, starting with the 304th aircraft (BuNo 154170), and those of earlier aircraft were rendered inoperative.

All armament, up to a maximum of 18,000 lb, was carried externally on one centreline and four wing stations. Stores carried on these stations included conventional and retarded bombs, cluster bombs, special weapons (Mk.28, Mk.43, Mk.57, or B-61), mines, guided missiles (air-to-ground AGM-12 Bullpups and AGM-45 Shrikes, or air-to-air AIM-9 Sidewinders), rocket packages, and D-704 buddy refuelling. The internal fuel tank capacity of 2,344 gal could be supplemented by up to four 300-US gal drop tanks. Furthermore, a removable refuelling probe was mounted externally forward of the windshield.

The Circulation Control Wing prototype (BuNo 151568) during a test flight in 1977. (*Grumman*)

The fourth Intruder (BuNo 147867) was modified as an NA-6A in 1968 to serve as a test-bed for some of the TRIM equipment being developed for the A-6C. (*Grumman*)

434

Seven A-6As were converted as EA-6As, several as variously configured NA-6As, nineteen as A-6Bs, three as EA-6Bs, and twelve as A-6Cs. At least three A-6As (BuNos 149486, 152642, and 155602) were used by the Pacific Missile Test Center and the Naval Weapons Center, respectively at Point Mugu and China Lake, California, for air-launch and guidance system tests for the Rockwell AGM-53 Condor and General Dynamics AGM-109 Tomahawk missiles.

Under a contract awarded in 1977, the fifty-fifth A-6A (BuNo 151568) was converted by Grumman as a test-bed for the Circulation Control Wing (CCW) system. Bleed air was ducted through manifolds from the J52-P-8B turbojets to slots on the trailing edge of each wing. The CCW system worked well during 16 test flights, beginning in January, 1979. Notably, touchdown speed at near maximum weight was reduced drastically from 120 kt for standard A-6As to 78 kt for the CCW test-bed. However, as the CCW installation reduced cruising and top speeds, this system was not retained for production and BuNo 151568 was modified as a KA-6D before being redelivered in December 1980. Similarly, blown flaps and an Augmentor Deflector Exhaust Nozzle (ADEN) system proposed in 1981 as a means of endowing the Intruder with STOL characteristics only underwent wind-tunnel testing.

EA-6A (A2F-1H): These two-seat electronic warfare aircraft are described in the EA-6 chapter.

NA-6A: The 'N' prefix was added to the designation of several A-6As which were modified for a variety of test purposes. The most noteworthy of these NA-6As was BuNo 147857 which, as detailed below, was converted as a development aircraft for the A-6C.

A-6B: Although standard A-6As could carry and launch AGM-45 Shrike anti-radiation missiles, during the Southeast Asia War the Navy developed a requirement for specialized defence suppression aircraft. To this end, three batches of A-6Bs were obtained through modification of A-6A airframes. The first ten A-6Bs were stripped of most attack systems, fitted with specialized equipment to detect radar controlling surface-to-air missiles, and carried AGM-78 Standard anti-radiation missiles (ARMs) on wing racks. The next three were fitted with the passive-angle-tracking anti-radiation-missile (PAT/ARM) system. Finally, six A-6Bs were fitted with the target identification acquisition system (TIAS). The first A-6B was delivered in August 1967 and the last in August 1970. Five A-6Bs were lost during the Southeast Asia War and the remaining fourteen aircraft were brought to A-6E standard between December 1975 and December 1979.

EA-6B: These four-seat electronic warfare aircraft are described in the EA-6 chapter.

A-6C: To meet the requirements of the Air Force and Navy Trails-Roads Interdiction Multi-Sensor (TRIM) programme, in September 1966 Grumman began working on an Intruder version (Design 128T) capable of detecting, tracking, and attacking vehicles operating at night without lights along the Ho Chi Minh Trail. To serve as a development aircraft for the

Prototype installation of the AGM-78 Standard Anti-Radiation Missile during the development of the A-6B defence suppression version of the Intruder. (*Grumman*)

required target detection and identification systems, BuNo 147857 was modified as an NA-6A. This test-bed, which, after being modified, first flew in December 1968, was fitted with forward-looking infrared (FLIR) and low-light level television (LLLTV) in underwing pods. Smaller sensors were fitted in other locations, notably in a teardrop fairing beneath the windshield on the port side of the forward fuselage.

This development work resulted in the modification of twelve A-6As, which were redelivered as A-6Cs between February and June 1970. In addition to the standard DIANE system, the A-6Cs were fitted with an internally-carried Black Crow truck ignition detection device and with a ventral pod housing FLIR and LLLTV cameras. One A-6C was lost during the Southeast Asia War and the remaining eleven were brought up to A-6E standards between October 1975 and February 1980.

KA-6D: Grumman first fitted a buddy refuelling pod beneath the second Intruder (BuNo 147865), and this aircraft was used for early tanker trials before being modified as the EA-6A aerodynamic test-bed. Next, Grumman fitted an internal refuelling package in BuNo 149937. In 1966, this aircraft served as a demonstrator for a dedicated tanker version. However, it was brought back to the standard A-6A configuration before being delivered to the Navy. (In a quirk of fate, sixteen years later, BuNo 149937 was modified as a KA-6D tanker by NARF Norfolk.)

After these unfruitful efforts and the lack of success of a 1966 proposal for an Intruder version (Design 128R) equipped as a tanker and fitted with internal guns for use in the RESCAP (Rescue Combat Air Patrol) role, Grumman was finally allowed to develop a tanker version of the Intruder. The first of these KA-6Ds (BuNo 151582) was modified from an A-6A and first flew on 16 April, 1970. It was fitted with an internal hose-and-reel refuelling package with the drogue fairing protruding beneath the fuselage and could carry a D-704 refueling pod beneath the fuselage. Its search radar, track radar, and most of its DIANE equipment were removed, but

A pair of KA-6Ds from VA-196 over the western Pacific on 23 August, 1985, while deployed aboard the USS *Constellation* (CV-64). (*Rick Morgan*)

An A-6E TRAM from VA-95 at NAS Fallon, Nevada, on 27 October, 1986. (*René J Francillon*)

the KA-6D still retained visual bombing as a secondary mission (a capability seldom, if ever, exercised). Carrying five 300-gal external tanks, the KA-6D prototype demonstrated that it could transfer 15,000 lb (about 2,300 gal) of fuel when loitering 150 nm from the carrier or 5,000 lb (about 765 gal) of fuel when 450 nm from the carrier.

Altogether, by the end of 1988, the Navy had obtained ninety KA-6Ds, including fifty-eight modified by Grumman and thirty-two modified by the Naval Air Rework Facility in Norfolk, Virginia. Although all used airframes which were originally delivered as A-6As, four of the Grumman-modified aircraft and eight of the NARF-modified aircraft had earlier been brought up to A-6E standards. Four A-6As converted as KA-6Ds in the mid-1980s by Grumman St Augustine Corporation, as well as KA-6Ds recently remanufactured in this Florida plant, can now carry five 400-gal tanks to increase the amount of transferable fuel.

A-6E: Preliminary design work for a version of the Intruder with updated electronic systems and a built-in cannon was begun in June 1966. Following Grumman's submission of a proposal for this Design 128S, the Navy authorized the development of the A-6E without the proposed gun installation but with an AN/ASQ-133 solid-state digital computer and AN/APQ-148 multi-mode radar in place of the computer and the search and track radars of the A-6As.

BuNo 155673, the 404th A-6A, was modified as the development aircraft for the A-6E systems. It first flew on 27 February, 1970, was fitted with the new computer system in August, and began trials with the AN/APQ-148 radar in November. However, after serving as the A-6E prototype, BuNo 155673 was returned to the A-6A configuration. At the end of the decade, it went through a Grumman modification programme before being redelivered as a TRAM-equipped A-6E in December 1979.

As confidence in the new radar and computer was high, Grumman switched to manufacturing A-6Es after completing the 482nd A-6A in December 1970. Nevertheless, deliveries had to be temporarily suspended while the A-6E was undergoing NPE and BIS trials. No Intruders were delivered during the first eight months of 1971, only one A-6E was delivered in each of the next three months, and seven were accepted in December. After this, deliveries were again made at regular intervals (except during the late 1970s and early 1980s when, as the result of the reduced military budget during the Carter administration, the number of aircraft built dropped twice to an uneconomical rate of three aircraft per year).

Even though the same model designation has been retained for all but five of the Intruders built since 1971, today's A-6Es are quite different from the aircraft first delivered eighteen years ago, as the type's capabilities have been improved several times. The most significant upgradings have been (1) the replacement of the AN/ASN-31 inertial platform with the AN/ASN-192 Carrier Airborne Inertial Navigation System, or CAINS; (2) the addition of a TRAM turret housing FLIR equipment as first tested on an A-6E in October 1974; and (3) the installation of universal missile wiring and pylons to enable the A-6E to carry and launch newer missiles including the AIM-9P Sidewinder, AGM-62 Walleye II, AGM-65F Maverick, AGM-84A Harpoon, and AGM-88A HARM.

Although a few of these improvements did result in some weight reductions (such as when older electronic systems were replaced by lighter solid-state units), most had the more usual deleterious impact on weight. Consequently, the maximum gross weight of late production A-6Es is 12.5 per cent greater than that of early A-6As. Moreover, several of these aircraft have been flown far longer than was originally intended (some of the KA-6Ds and A-6Es operating with the fleet are twenty-five years old and many were flown in combat during the Southeast Asia War). Not surprisingly under these conditions, fatigue has become a serious problem.

Envisaging the need to replace the wings of high-time aircraft and wishing to fit longer-life wings in aircraft still on order, the Navy

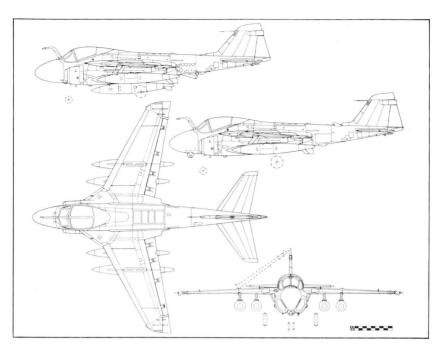

Grumman A-6E Intruder. Side view of KA-6D

The F404-powered A-6F aerodynamic and propulsion prototype which was first flown on 25 August, 1987. (*Grumman*)

requested proposals in the spring of 1985. Grumman offered updated metal wings, but lost to Boeing Military Airplane Company which proposed new wings of similar geometry but using a carbon fibre/epoxy resin torsion box. Boeing received a contract for 120 wing sets (with options for 216 additional sets) for retrofit to older aircraft and installation on new Intruders, beginning with the 185th A-6E. The first set of composite wings was to have been delivered in November 1987, and tests were to have began in early 1988. However, the Boeing composite wing programme has run into problems and delays. Consequently, by October 1988 tests had not yet begun and new A-6Es could not be delivered due to lack of wings. At the same time fifty-one Navy and Marine Intruders were grounded pending wing replacement, and 119 were restricted to less than 3 g manoeuvres. As a stopgap, the Navy was planning to order ten more sets of metal wings from Grumman.

In addition to 184 aircraft built and delivered as A-6Es by February 1989, 215 A-6As, fourteen A-6Bs, and eleven A-6Cs have been modified by Grumman as A-6Es. Twenty-one more were on order for delivery in 1989, 1990 and 1991. Whether produced in the 1970s or the 1980s, all A-6Es have been powered by 9,300-lb thrust J52-P-8As or P-8Bs.

A-6F: Development of what was expected to become a significantly more capable Intruder went ahead in mid-1984, when Grumman and the Navy agreed on an package designed to improve night and all-weather attack capability as well as systems reliability and maintainability. Principal changes included the use of an AN/APQ-173 multi-mode radar with twice the acquisition and tracking range of the AN/APQ-148 of the A-6E, the replacement of the AN/APN-153 doppler radar with a Collins global positioning system, the substitution of multifunction displays for older instruments and of a head-up display for the previously fitted optical sight, the incorporation of the AN/ALQ-165 airborne self-protection jammer, the replacement of several avionics and communications systems with more reliable units, the addition of a third rack beneath each wing for AIM-9L Sidewinder or AIM-120A (AMRAAM) air-to-air missiles, the use of Boeing

Ordered as the third A-6F, BuNo 162185 became the Digital Systems Development aircraft and was used in 1988 as a test-bed for the AN/APQ-173 radar and other advanced avionic systems. (*Grumman*)

composite wings, the modification of the fuel system to decrease the aircraft's vulnerability to fire, and the installation of an auxiliary power unit. To compensate for the weight increase resulting from these changes, the development programme called for A-6Fs to be powered by 10,800-lb thrust General Electric F404-GE-400D turbofans and to have aircraft-mounted accessory drives to facilitate engine removal.

Five A-6F full scale development (FSD) aircraft were built in 1986-87, and were fitted with Grumman metal wings as Boeing composite wings were not yet available. BuNo162183, the aerodynamic and propulsion test vehicle, was first flown on 25 August, 1987, and was followed into the air by BuNo 162184 on 23 November. By then, unfortunately, the future of the Intruder II was already in doubt as budget constraints were forcing the Navy to terminate a number of programmes. Early during the summer of 1988, the first two A-6Fs were grounded and placed in storage along with the unflown fourth and fifth aircraft. However, the third Intruder II, BuNo 162185, which first flew on 22 August, 1988, was retained as a Digital Systems Development (DSD) aircraft to test the AN/APQ-173 radar and other avionic improvements still being contemplated for possible incorporation in a less ambitious A-6G. Furthermore, in support of a proposed Vehicle Improvement Program (VIP) also being considered for the A-6G, the first A-6F (BuNo 162183) will be taken out of mothballs and will fly in the spring of 1990 with Boeing composite wings and 11,200-lb thrust Pratt & Whitney J52-P-408A turbojets.

A-6G: This designation was used in the autumn of 1988 to identify possible new production aircraft and/or rebuilt Intruders incorporating some or all of the features tested as part of the DSD and VIP programmes. However, at the end of 1988, the Department of Defense decided not fund the A-6G programme. In early 1989, Grumman and its Congressional supporters were endeavouring to have funding for the A-6G restored. If these efforts are unsuccessful, the Intruder programme will come to an end in September 1991 with the delivery of the last of ten A-6Es ordered in June 1988.

Service history

Even before trials were completed, the Navy decided to have A-6As delivered to VA-42, the medium attack training squadron at NAS Oceana, Virginia, beginning in February 1963, so that this unit could begin qualifying personnel for the first operational squadron. Assignment to operational squadrons followed in October 1963. In August 1964, at the time of the Tonkin Gulf Incident, twenty-eight A-6As were serving with three squadrons in the Atlantic Fleet, VA-85 aboard the uss *Forrestal* (CVA-59) and VA-42 and VA-75 at NAS Oceana, and preparation was being made for the assignement of A-6As to the Pacific Fleet. In addition, the Marine Corps had received its first seven Intruders to start equipping VMA(AW)-242 at MCAS Cherry Point, North Carolina.

Embarked aboard the uss *Independence* (CVA-62), the *Sunday Punchers* of VA-75 arrived in the Gulf of Tonkin in June 1965 and flew their first

A-6Es of VA-128, the Intruder training squadron based at NAS Whidbey Island, Washington, during a deployment to NAS Fallon, Nevada, in 1977. (*USN*)

combat sortie on 1 July. All went well at first, but between 14 and 24 July three A-6As were lost during sorties against lightly defended targets in Laos. These losses were attributed to the premature detonation of Mk. 82 bombs, and after the arming mechanism was modified, no further such accidents occurred. Also during this combat cruise, VA-75 used the sophisticated avionics of its A-6As to guide Douglas A-4Es armed with Shrike anti-radiation missiles during *Iron Hand* defence suppresion sorties. Success in this role was first achieved on 17 October, 1965, when a surface-to-air missile site near Kep Air Base was destroyed.

During the Southeast Asia War, VA-75 deployed twice more to the Gulf of Tonkin, and nine other Navy squadrons (VA-35, -52, -65, -85, -95, -115, -145, -165, and -196) flew Intruders from carriers of Task Force 77 with conspicuous success. Doing equally well was VMA(AW)-242, which was aboard the USS *Coral Sea* (CVA-43) between November 1971 and July 1972. This Marine squadron used Intruders not only on conventional attack sorties against targets in North Vietnam but also to fly the first sorties during Operation *Pocket Money*, the mining campaign against North Vietnamese ports undertaken in May 1972. The large majority of Intruders operated by these squadrons were A-6As which, once the reliability of their DIANE system was brought up to specifications, were greatly valued for their ability to deliver heavy loads accurately and under marginal weather conditions. During the last two years of combat operations in Southeast Asia, most squadrons added specialized Intruders to their complement of A-6As; VA-75 aboard the USS *Kitty Hawk* (CVA-63) was the first to deploy with A-6B defence suppression aircraft in November 1967, VA-165 aboard

442

An A-6E of VMA(AW)-533 landing at MCAS Iwakuni, Japan, with open 'alligator' wingtip split brakes. *(Courtesy of Cloud 9 Photography)*

the USS *America* (CVA-66) was the first to operate TRIM-equipped A-6Cs in April 1970, and VA-196 aboard the USS *Enterprise* (CVAN-65) introduced KA-6D tankers in June 1971.

With land-based Marine units, A-6As first went to South Vietnam in November 1966 when VMA(AW)-242 deployed to Da Nang. Intruders were also operated 'in-country' by VMA(AW)-223, -225, and -533, with these squadrons rotating until the Marine withdrawal in 1970. Marine A-6s were used not only to support ground forces in South Vietnam, where they proved particularly valuable due to their ability to continue flying during inclement weather, but also on missions against targets in Laos and North Vietnam (with ten of the eighteen Marine A-6A combat losses occurring over the North). VMA(AW)-533 returned to Da Nang in the spring of 1972 and in June moved to Nam Phong in Thailand for operations over the North until fighting ended in January 1973.

Combined Navy and Marine losses during the war included sixty-seven A-6As and one A-6B lost in combat, and eleven A-6As, two KA-6Ds, one A-6B, and one A-6C lost in operational accidents.

Since the end of the Southeast Asia War, Intruders have been part of all USN carrier deployments, whether in the western Pacific, the Indian Ocean, the Atlantic, the Mediterranean, the North Sea, or the Bering Sea. During these deployments, Carrier Air Wings (CVWs) have normally included one squadron of ten A-6Es and four KA-6Ds. This was typically the case when, as part of CVW-6 aboard the USS *Independence* (CV-62), VA-176 flew combat sorties over Grenada in October 1983 and over Lebanon in December 1983. On that last occasion, VA-176 was joined by VA-75 and VA-85 which were both embarked aboard the USS *John F. Kennedy* (CV-67) as part of an experiment in which CVW-3 replaced the two usual LTV A-7 squadrons with a second Intruder squadron. One of the VA-85 Intruders was lost on 4 December during a retaliatory strike against Syrian anti-aircraft sites in Lebanon.

443

Built as an A-6A and delivered in July 1968, BuNo 155604 was redelivered as an A-6E in August 1974 and as a KA-6D in April 1984. Then assigned to VA-85, this KA-6D was photographed on the deck of the USS *Saratoga* (CV-60) on 5 July, 1987, when this Sixth Fleet carrier was anchored at Marseille. *(Alain Pelletier)*

More success attended operations in the Gulf of Sidra in March-April 1986 by VA-34 with CVW-1 aboard the USS *America* (CV-66), VA-55 with CVW-13 aboard the USS *Coral Sea* (CV-43), and VA-85 with CVW-17 aboard the USS *Saratoga* (CV-60). In the first phase of the confrontation with Libya, Intruders sank a *Nanutchka*-class missile patrol boat. Aircraft from VA-34 and VA-55 then struck the Al Jumahiriya barracks in Tripoli and the Benina airfield near Benghazi on 15 April. Likewise, VA-95 sank an Iranian *Saam*-class frigate and immobilized another one while operating in the Arabian Gulf with CVW-11 aboard the USS *Enterprise* (CVN-65) on 18 April, 1988.

The two A-6 squadrons/no A-7 squadron experiment has been repeated by CVW-2 and CVW-3 while CVW-13 deployed aboard *Coral Sea* in September 1987 with two Intruder squadrons when VA-65 replaced one of its four F/A-18 squadrons. Consideration is now being given to adopting a new air wing composition consisting of twenty A-6Es and KA-6Ds along with twenty F-14s, twenty F/A-18s, five EA-6Bs, five E-2Cs, ten S-3s, and six SH-3 or SH-60F helicopters.

At the end of 1988, the Navy had eight Intruder squadrons (VA-34, -35, -42, -55, -65, -75, -85, and -176) based at NAS Oceana and deploying aboard carriers of the Atlantic Fleet, seven squadrons (VA-52, -95, -128, -145, -165, -185, and -196) based at NAS Whidbey Island and deploying aboard carriers of the Pacific Fleet, and VA-115 forward-deployed to NAF Atsugi, Japan, and embarking on the USS *Midway* (CV-41). The Marine Corps then had five Intruder squadrons, VMA(AW)-121, -224, -242, -332, and -533, for operations from land bases in the United States and Japan and occasional deployments aboard Navy carriers.

BuNo 155648, an A-6E of VMA(AW)-121, bearing signs of a flash fire which damaged its forward fuselage while the aircraft was 'hot refueled' at NAS Fallon, Nevada, in 1988, before a planned deployment aboard USS *Ranger* (CV-61) as part of Air Wing Two. *(Peter B Lewis)*

An A-6E of VA-52 landing aboard the USS *Kitty Hawk* (CV-63) during a training exercise off the coast of Southern California in January 1981. *(René J Francillon)*

PRODUCTION: A total of 668 Intruders has been delivered by Grumman between April 1960 and Deecember 1988. More are on order. Intruders delivered before the end of 1988 included:

482	A-6A	181	A-6E
(19)	A-6B	(240)	A-6E
(12)	A-6C	5	A-6F
(90)	KA-6D		

They were assigned the following BuNos:

A-6A (A2F-1):	BuNos 147864/147867, 148615/148618,149475/149486,
	149935/149958, 151558/151594, 151780/151827,
	152583/152646, 152891/152954, 154124/154171,
	155581/155721, and 156994/157029
A-6B:	(BuNos 149944, 149949, 149955, 149957,
(conversion)	151558/151565, 151591, 151820, 152616/152617, and
	155628/155630)
A-6C:	(BuNos 155647/155648, 155653, 155660, 155662,
(conversion)	155667, 155670, 155674, 155676, 155681, 155684, and
	155688)
KA-6D:	(BuNos 149482, 149484/149486, 149936/149937,
(conversion)	149940, 149942, 149945, 149951/149952, 149954,
	151566, 151568, 151570, 151572, 151575/151576,
	151579/151583, 151589, 151783, 151787, 151789,
	151791/151793, 151795/151796, 151801, 151806,
	151808/151810, 151813/151814, 151818/151819, 151821,
	151823/151827, 152587, 152590, 152592,
	152597/152598, 152606, 152611, 152618/152619,
	152624, 152626, 152628, 152632, 152637,
	152892/152894, 152896, 152906, 152910/152911,
	152913/152914, 152919/152921, 152927, 152934,
	152939, 154133, 154147, 154154, 155582/155584,
	155588, 155597/155598, 155604, 155619, 155638,
	155686, and 155691)
A-6E:	BuNos 158041/158052, 158528/158539, 158787/158798,
	159174/159185, 159309/159317, 159567/159579,
	159895/159906, 160421/160431, 160993/160998,
	161082/161093, 161100/161111, 161230/162235,
	161659/161690, 162179/162182, and 162188/162203
A-6E:	(BuNos 149941, 149943/149944, 149946,
(conversion)	149948/149950, 149953, 149955/149957, 151558,
	151562, 151564/151565, 151573, 151591/151593,
	151782, 151784, 151790, 151802, 151804, 151807,
	151811/151812, 151814, 151820, 152583/152585,
	152587, 152591, 152593, 152596,
	152599/152600,152603, 152607, 152610, 152614,
	152617, 152620/152621, 152623, 152630,
	152634/152635, 152640/152642, 152645, 152895,
	152902, 152904/152905, 152907/152908, 152912,
	152915/152916, 152918, 152923/152925, 152928/152931,
	152933, 152935/152936, 152941/152942, 152945,
	152947/152948, 152950, 152953/152954, 154124,
	154126, 154128/154129, 154131/154132, 154134/154137,
	154140, 154142, 154144, 154146, 154148, 154151,
	154154, 154156, 154158/154159, 154161/154163,

446

An E-2C of VAW-124 and A-6E TRAM of VA-36 on the deck of the USS *Theodore Roosevelt* (CVN-71). *(Grumman)*

154167/154171, 155581/155586, 155588/155592, 155595/155600, 155602, 155604, 155606, 155608, 155610, 155612, 155615/155617, 155619/155621, 155623/155625, 155627/155633, 155635/155638, 155642/155646, 155648/155649, 155651, 155653/155662, 155664/155665, 155667/155670, 155672/155676, 155678/155685, 155687/155689, 155692, 155694/155695, 155697/155699, 155702/155704, 155706/155708, 155710/155719, 156995/156997, 157000/157006, 157009/157014, 157016/157017, 157019, 157021, 157023/157027, and 157029)

A-6F: BuNos 162183/162187

The following BuNos have been assigned to nineteen aircraft on order at the end of 1988:

A-6E: BuNos 162204/162222

	A-6A	**KA-6D**	**A-6E**
DIMENSIONS:			
Span, ft in	53 0	53 0	53 0
(m)	(16.15)	(16.15)	(16.15)
Span (wings folded), ft in	25 4	25 4	25 4
(m)	(7.72)	(7.72)	(7.72)
Length, ft in	54 9	54 9	54 9
(m)	(16.69)	(16.69)	(16.69)
Height, ft in	16 2	16 2	16 2
(m)	(4.93)	(4.93)	(4.93)
Wing area, sq ft	529	529	529
(sq m)	(49.15)	(49.15)	(49.15)

447

WEIGHTS:			
Empty, lb	25,298	25,563	26,746
(kg)	(11,475)	(11,595)	(12,009)
Loaded, lb	48,051	54,586	54,393
(kg)	(21,796)	(24,760)	(24,672)
Maximum, lb	53,699	60,400	60,400
(kg)	(24,357)	(27,397)	(27,397)
Wing loading,* lb/sq ft	90.8	103.2	102.8
(kg/sq m)	(443.5)	(503.8)	(502.0)
Power loading,* lb/lb st	2.8	2.9	2.9
(kg/kgp)	(2.8)	(2.9)	(2.9)
PERFORMANCE:			
Max speed, mph/ft	646/sl	646/sl	644/sl
(kmh/m)	(1,039/sl)	(1,039/sl)	(1,036/sl)
Cruising speed, mph	481	473	474
(kmh)	(774)	(761)	(763)
Climb rate, ft/min	6,950	7,164	7,620
(m/sec)	(35)	((36)	(39)
Service ceiling, ft	40,250	44,200	42,400
(m)	(12,270)	(13,470)	(12,925)
Normal range, miles	1,350	–	1,010
(km)	(2,170)	(–)	(1,625)
Max range, miles	3,225	2,785	3,245
(km)	(5,190)	(4,480)	(5,220)

* Wing and power loadings are calculated at normal loaded weight and maximum take-off power.

Grumman E-2 (W2F) Hawkeye

After awarding a Letter of Intent for two Design 117 prototypes at the end of 1955, the Navy nevertheless proceeded with its planned development of an airborne early warning/air intercept control (AEW/AIC) aircraft, as it had ordered the piston-powered Grumman WF-2 only as an interim measure pending availability of more capable aircraft. As defined in BuAer Specification SAR-304A dated 3 November, 1955, and Type Specification OS-139 dated 23 November, 1955, the Navy was seeking a new generation of carrier-based AEW aircraft with both a higher cruising altitude to extend the detection range of the search radar and a greater internal volume to house the equipment for the Air Tactical Data System (ATDS). In December 1955, fully aware that this was the Navy's intention, Grumman began working on Design 123 as its entry into the ultimate AEW competition. By so doing, the company positioned itself favourably to reply to the request for proposals issued by the Navy on 17 February, 1956. Proposals were submitted in May, and the Grumman Design 123 was selected as the winning entry on 5 March, 1957.

To win the 1956 AEW/AIC competition, William Rathke and his project team designed an aircraft of exceptional size for a carrier-based aircraft. Nevertheless it still fitted within the constraints imposed by the requirement that it be able to operate aboard SCB 27C carriers with their relatively small centreline lift and low hangar deck ceiling. Its span of 80 ft 7 in is still not exceeded by that of any other carrier-based aircraft. Its fully pressurized fuselage provided ample volume for the required electronic gear and accommodated a crew of five (pilot and co-pilot forward; radar operator, air-control operator, and combat information centre operator facing consoles on the port side) in the 'mask-free' environment considered necessary for missions lasting up to six hours. To endow the aircraft with the ability to fly missions of that duration at a typical on-station altitude of 25,000 ft, the team considered the use of propeller-turbines mandatory and selected a pair of Allison T56-A-7s to power the G-123. The most distinctive features of Design 123, however, were its rotating radar scanner housing (rotodome) and four vertical tail surfaces.

Development of the rotodome concept resulted from a Naval Research Laboratory (NLF) programme during which it had been determined that ultra-high frequency (UHF) was the optimum band for detecting aircraft operating in sea clutter and that an end fire antenna housed in a thin ellipsoidal radome would provide a low cross-section and contribute to lift. Lockheed was first to avail itself of the data generated by NLF and mounted a rotodome atop the WV-2E version of its four-engined Warning Star. However, the WV-2E had not yet flown when in May 1956 Grumman proposed the use of a rotodome for the antenna of the AN/APS-96 search radar of its Design 123. Mounted above the fuselage centre section, the 24-ft rotodome was to rotate at 6 rpm for azimuth and, for carrier stowage, was to be lowered 1 ft 10^1/$_2$ in by means of a hydraulic lifting jack.

The first W2F-1 prototype (BuNo 18147) during its maiden flight on 21 October, 1960. (*Grumman*)

The second W2F-1 during a visit to Boeing Field at Renton, Washington. *(Gordon S Williams)*

The use of this rotodome led Grumman once again to use 'sto wings' as upward folding wings would not have provided the necessary clearance. It also contributed in part to the selection of a distinctive four-vertical-tail surface configuration as a large single fin would have created radar interference. The main consideration behind the selection of this tail configuration, however, had been the single-engine control requirement as the end speed generated by the hydraulic catapults of older carriers was critical.

Following mock-up inspection between 14 and 18 October, 1957, an initial order for three W2F-1 prototypes (BuNos 148147/148149) was placed in December of that year and was supplemented in March 1959 by an order for three additonal aircraft (BuNos 148711/148713). Construction of the prototypes, however, was not undertaken with much haste as the development of the radar and related electronic systems, the pacing elements of the programme, was to require more time than the manufacture of a fairly conventional airframe. Accordingly, BuNo 148147 was not completed until the late summer of 1960. Fitted with an empty rotodome and still lacking most of its electronic equipment, this aircraft was first flown at Bethpage by Thomas Attridge and Carl Alber on 21 October, 1960. Everything proceeded as planned, and programme development moved forward, with the first flight of a fully-equipped aircraft being made on 19 April, 1961.

The aircraft first flew with rudders and tabs on all four vertical surfaces but flight tests showed that directional stability was insufficient and directional control was excessive. As a first step at correcting this problem, the outboard vertical surfaces were extended downward by 18 in. After this proved insufficient to stiffen directional stability, the aircraft was flown

451

BuNo 148149, the third W2F-1, with the original outboard fin and rudder configuration. *(Gordon S Williams)*

with both inboard rudders locked. Although this modification provided satisfactory directional stability, the much higher minimum single-engined control speed which resulted was unacceptable. The problem was finally solved when the rudder on the port inboard vertical surface was reactivated. Accordingly, the inboard starboard vertical surface of production aircraft was built without a rudder.

The vertical surfaces were originally of conventional all-metal construction. However, after avionic testing of the third and fourth aircraft revealed that interference was excessive over the tail, the structure of these surfaces was revised to incorporate as much glass fibre as possible above the horizontal surfaces.

Other than revised vertical tail surface design and construction, the only modification required as the result of trials was a minor redesign of the nose undercarriage doors.

Electronic testing, on the other hand, proved a major undertaking. Reliability of some components, particularly the drum-memory computer, was low, and much time was required to get the systems to work to the Navy's satisfaction. Key dates during this period were May 1961, when the Naval Preliminary Evaluation was initiated, and December 1962, when initial carrier trials took place aboard the USS *Enterprise* (CVAN-65).* Finally, in January 1964, nearly seven years after Design 123 won the AEW competition, the first E-2A was delivered to an operational squadron.

Production history

Like the Intruder, the Hawkeye has already had a long production life during which only three versions have been built and external appearance

---

* During these trials, on 19 December, BuNo 148711 became the first aircraft fitted with a tow bar to be catapulted from a carrier. The tow bar, which was also fitted to the A-6A catapulted right behind the E-2A and became standard on all US carrier aircraft, had been conceived to replace the catapult bridle and thus enable aircraft to be launched at shorter intervals. It required the use of twin nosewheels with the sprung T-shaped catapult strop attachment bar attached to the nosewheel leg between the two wheels.

has remained virtually unchanged. Internally, however, changes have been both significant and numerous. For example, the Hawkeye has already flown with six types of search radar, the APS-96, APS-111, APS-120, APS-125, APS-138, and APS-139, and will soon be produced with the APS-145. Hence, today's E-2Cs are far more capable AEW aircraft than either the E-2As which entered service in 1964 or even the first E-2Cs delivered to the fleet in 1973.

E-2A (W2F-1): Designated W2F-1 when it was first ordered, the initial version of the Hawkeye was redesignated E-2A in September 1962. Including development aircraft, fifty-nine W2F-1s/E-2As were built. BuNo 148147 first flew on 21 October, 1960, and the last E-2A was delivered on 28 February, 1967. They were each powered by two 4,050-eshp Allison T56-A-8 or -8A propeller-turbines driving four-blade propellers. For precise holding of attitude as required for the AEW mission, the E-2As were fitted with an automatic flight control system (AFCS) which not only provided the usual autopilot functions but also enabled precise wing-level turns to be made automatically. Their Airborne Tactical Data System (ATDS), which was designed to acquire, transmit, and exchange information and targeting data automatically with surface ships equipped with the corresponding Naval Tactical Data System (NTDS), was based on the use of the AN/APS-96 search radar, the AN/APX-7 identification friend or foe (IFF) set, the AN/ASA-27 computer, the AN/ASQ-52 multi-purpose communication system, and the AN/ASN-36 inertial navigation system.

The first two E-2As were modified as C-2A prototypes (BuNos 148147 and 148148), four became TE-2As (BuNos 149817, 149818, 150533, and 152485), and two served as YE-2C (BuNos 148712 and 148713) development aircraft. Two other aircraft retained their E-2A designation until the end: BuNo 148711 was last used in May 1964 for barricade tests and BuNo 148149 was used as a test-bed for the AN/APS-111 radar between June 1965 and October 1967, before being mounted on a pedestal at the entrance to NAS Miramar. The remaining forty-nine E-2As were brought up to E-2B standards.

E-2As of VAW-123 were embarked on the USS *Forrestal* (CVA-59) when that carrier suffered a catastrophic fire while on the line in the Gulf of Tonkin on 29 July, 1967. (*Courtesy of Cloud 9 Photography*)

E-2B (BuNo 150534) of Carrier Airborne Early Warning Training Squadron 110 (RVAW-110) at NAS North Island, California. *(Peter B Lewis)*

TE-2A: This designation identified four E-2As (BuNos 149817, 149818, 150533, and 152485) which were used as pilot trainers by the two replacement training squadrons, RVAW-110 and RVAW-120. The electronic equipment was removed, the rotodome was emptied, and ballast was provided where required to duplicate the handling characteristics of fully equipped E-2As and E-2Bs.

E-2B: As the special-purpose AN/ASA-27 computer of the E-2A was difficult to maintain and was prone to failure, the Navy asked Grumman to develop a more reliable system as part of the Mod A/X programme. This was achieved by substituting a Litton L-304 software-programmable computer and incorporating various minor electronic modifications. A prototype installation was flight tested beginning on 20 February, 1969, and over the next two years the Naval Air Rework Facility San Diego at NAS North Island incorporated these changes in forty-nine E-2As. The modified Hawkeyes were redesignated E-2Bs. The last E-2B was redelivered by NARF San Diego in December 1971.

E-2C: In April 1968, the Secretary of Defense authorized the Navy to initiate the development of an advanced Hawkeye version with improved detection capability, reliability, and maintainability. At that time, plans called for the manufacture of only twenty-eight E-2Cs to be operated by East Coast squadrons while the West Coast squadrons would use E-2As/E-2Bs until the scheduled introduction in the fleet of a new AEW aircraft in 1984. The development of the new aircraft did not occur and E-2Cs are still in production more than twenty years after the programme was first funded.

The first of two YE-2C development aircraft, BuNos 148712 and 148713, which were modified from the fifth and sixth E-2A airframes and were powered by 4,860-eshp T56-A-422s, flew on 20 January, 1971. Three months earlier Grumman had received low-level funding for an initial batch of eleven production E-2Cs (BuNos 158638/158648) to be powered by 4,910-eshp T56-A-425s, the first of which flew in September 1972. Navy Preliminary Evaluation of the prototype was initiated in February 1972 and NPE of the production aircraft followed nine months later, both producing

454

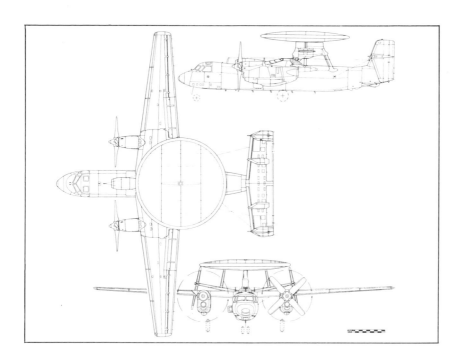

Grumman E-2C Hawkeye

A Grumman E-2C (BuNo 158640) from VAW-114 photographed near NAS Fallon, Nevada, on 20 June, 1989. *(René J Francillon)*

excellent results. Similarly, Board of Inspection and Survey trials, which had begun in April 1973, were entirely satisfactory.

Major system improvements introduced in early production E-2Cs were the replacement of the AN/APS-96 radar of the E-2As and E-2Bs by the AN/APS-120 radar with overland surveillance capability, the substitution of the AN/ASN-92 Carrier Aircraft Inertial Navigation System (CAINS) for the AN/ASN-36 INS fitted to the earlier versions, and the fitting of the AN/ALR-59 Passive Detection System. Receiver antennae for this PDS were installed in a 13-in extension of the nose cone and in fairings on the outboard vertical tail surfaces to enable potential threats to be detected, located, and identified automatically at twice the range of the radar. The only other external modifications distinguishing E-2Cs from earlier Hawkeyes were their lower fuselage trough for PDS wave-guides and their much larger dorsal fairing housing the vapour cycle radiator with increased capacity as required for cooling the new electronic equipment.

Over the years, the already impressive capabilities of the E-2C have been further improved through the installation of more advanced radar and PDS equipment. The first of these upgrades saw the AN/APS-125 Advanced Radar Processing System (ARPS), which featured digital processing and electronic counter-countermeasures (ECCM) for improved performance in a jamming environment, being fitted during production beginning with the thirty-fifth E-2C (BuNo 160415) and being retrofitted to earlier aircraft by Grumman during Standard Depot Level Maintenance (SDLM) overhaul. Similarly, the AN/ALR-73 Passive Detection System was first fitted to BuNo 161229 and has now replaced the AN/ALR-59 in most earlier aircraft.

In more recent years, the search radar system has been improved three times as the AN/APS-138 replaced the APS-125 in 1983 and was in turn supplanted in 1988 by the APS-139. Next, as first retrofitted to BuNo 161784, the AN/APS-145 will be incorporated during production, beginning with aircraft ordered during Fiscal Year 1989, and will be progressively retrofitted to most earlier aircraft. Other improvements introduced during production include the substitution of Hamilton Standard propellers with glass fibre/foam blades for Aeroproducts propellers with hollow-steel blades as fitted to E-2As, E-2Bs, and early E-2Cs.

Grumman first studied the feasibility of using the Hawkeye's radar to detect the snorkel of submerged submarines in January 1966. Nothing came out of this study until the early 1980s, when the ASW section of the Naval Air Test Center evaluated at least one E-2C in this role. Also noteworthy was the use of BuNo 160012 during the spring of 1986 to flight test T56-A-427 engines, which increased power by 24 per cent and reduced fuel consumption by 12 per cent when compared to standard -425 engines of E-2Cs. From 1989, E-2Cs are delivered with -427 engines.

In the autumn of 1988, the Navy was considering a multi-year purchase of fifty E-2Cs in either a single lot or in two lots, one of thirty and one of twenty, spread over eight years. Whether or not the multi-year procurement is approved by Congress, the E-2C production rate is expected to remain at six a year for the USN until the mid-1990s, with the Hawkeye being scheduled for replacement by the Advanced Tactical Support Aircraft (ATSA). However, the ATSA programme is still in the early planning stage, and E-2s may still be procured by the Navy during the second half of the 1990s.

In addition to the aircraft built for the US Navy, Grumman has so far delivered twenty-one E-2Cs to four export customers and has five more on order from Japan. The first of these Foreign Military Sales (FMS) aircraft was the forty-first E-2C (BuNo 160771) which was accepted by the Navy, as the contracting agent for Israel, on 8 December, 1977. Israel received three more E-2Cs in 1978, Japan has taken delivery of eight aircraft, Singapore has obtained four aircraft, and Egypt, currently the last nation to order Hawkeyes, received five E-2Cs in 1986-87.

YE-2C: This designation was used briefly to identify two early production E-2As (BuNos 148712 and 148713) which, as mentioned above, were modified as development aircraft for the E-2C programme.

TE-2C: These four pilot trainers were obtained by removing the electronic equipment from the two YE-2Cs and two early production E-2Cs (BuNos 158639 and 158648). As in the case of the TE-2As, the rotodome was emptied and ballast was provided to duplicate the handling characteristics of fully-equipped aircraft.

Service history

When the E-2A was undergoing Board of Inspection and Survey and Fleet Indoctrination Program trials in preparation for operational assignment, the Navy only had two Carrier Airborne Early Warning Squadrons, one on the West Coast and one on the East Coast. VAW-11 at NAS North Island, California, was sending E-1B detachments aboard attack and ASW carriers of the Pacific Fleet, and detachments from VAW-12 at NAS Norfolk, Virginia, were operating from CVAs and CVSs of the Atlantic Fleet. Priority for re-equipping with Hawkeyes was given to the West Coast unit,

Equipped with E-2As, including BuNo 151705 photographed at its home station, NAS North Island, California, VAW-11 Det A was deployed to the Gulf of Tonkin aboard the USS *Coral Sea* (CVA-43) between July 1966 and February 1967. (*Peter B Lewis*)

457

An E-2B of VAW-115, CVW-5, USS *Midway* (CV-41), landing at NAF Atsugi, Japan. Bicentennial markings are painted on the nose and tail of this aircraft. *(Courtesy of Cloud 9 Photography)*

and VAW-11 received its first E-2As in January 1964, while VAW-12 had to wait for nearly two years. Then, in April 1967, the two large squadrons with their numerous detachments operating semi-independently aboard carriers were split into smaller deployable squadrons (VAW-112, -113, -114, -115, and -116 on the West Coast and VAW-121, -122, -123 on the East Coast) and each spawned a replacement training squadron, RVAW-110 at NAS North Island and RVAW-120 at NAS Norfolk.

Before this reorganization, VAW-11 detachments had already made six deployments to the Gulf of Tonkin. The first two, Det C aboard the USS *Kitty Hawk* (CVA-63) and Det F aboard the USS *Ranger* (CVA-61), left San Diego on 19 October and 10 December, 1965, and respectively spent 122 days and 137 days on the line during combat operations in Southeast Asia. During these first combat cruises, the E-2As were found markedly superior to the E-1Bs operated by other detachments when all their systems were working to specifications. Reliability, however, was poor, and maintenance personnel had a difficult time keeping the systems operational. Only limited improvements were noted during later deployments by VAW-11 detachments and newly formed squadrons. Fortunately, E-2Bs, first deployed by VAW-114 aboard *Kitty Hawk* in November 1970, went a long way toward solving the Hawkeye's reliability and maintainability problems. The last E-2As to serve in Southeast Asia were those from VAW-116 which returned to California aboard the USS *Coral Sea* (CVA-43) in July 1970. Earlier in that cruise, an E-2B sent to supplement the E-2As of this squadron became the only Hawkeye to be lost during the war when it crashed due to a cockpit fire immediately after launch.

E-2Cs were first delivered to VAW-123 at NAS Norfolk in November

1973, and this squadron first deployed with its new Hawkeyes aboard the USS *Saratoga* (CV-60) in September 1974. With the Pacific Fleet, E-2Cs were first assigned to VAW-114 in June 1978. Then, as more were delivered, E-2Cs were used to equip new squadrons (VAW-117, -124, -125, -126, and -127) and to re-equip existing deployable squadrons and the two training squadrons. Upon being released by active squadrons, E-2Bs were assigned to replace E-1Bs still operated by the reservists from VAW-78 and VAW-88. In turn, these two reserve squadrons received E-2Cs respectively in 1983 and 1986, the last E-2Bs being phased out by VAW-88 in October 1986.

During the 1980s, E-2Cs have continued to deploy aboard all USN carriers and have participated in mostly routine but occasionally more demanding situations. Notably, on 10 October, 1985, those from VAW-125 aboard the USS *Saratoga* (CV-60) played a vital part in the successful interception of the Egypt Air Boeing 737 carrying the hijackers of the cruise liner *Achille Lauro*.

Hawkeyes have also been flown from land bases during less typical operations. Notably, between December 1980 and May 1981, E-2 detachments were sent to Keflavik to provide AEW coverage over the Denmark Strait and between Iceland and Scotland. Moreover, E-2Cs have supported

USCG 3501, one of the two E-2Cs, acquired by the US Coast Guard for use in drug traffic interdiction. *(USCG)*

459

Space Shuttle launches from Cape Canaveral by providing range clearance, tracking the recovery of the first stage rocket to splashdown, and vectoring recovery vessels.

In the early and mid-1980s, E-2C crews have repeatedly been called to support the US Customs Service in its fight against suspected drug smugglers by detecting low-flying aircraft operating without approved flight plans or deviating suspiciously from approved plans. The Hawkeye's effectiveness in this civic undertaking prompted the transfer of two E-2Cs to the US Coast Guard in 1987. Now bearing USCG serial numbers 3701 and 3702, they operate over the Caribbean and along the Atlantic Coast.

Today, often called *Hummers* as their engines are relatively quiet compared to the afterburning turbojets of fighters and attack aircraft, Hawkeyes remain highly valued components of all Carrier Air Wings. In addition to providing airborne early warning, for which they use radar, PDS, and IFF to detect hostile aircraft and secure data link and voice communications to control friendly interceptors, E-2Cs routinely rely on their sophisticated electronic systems to control strike aircraft and rescue operations, provide tanker vectoring, and perform surface surveillance. If need be, they could also be used in peacetime to provide air space management (with a single E-2C orbiting over New York being able to handle all traffic in the busy northwest corridor, from Washington DC in the south to the Canadian border in the north) and in wartime to complement or replace ground-based air defence networks.

Since entering service in 1978, Hawkeyes have been used with conspicuous success by the Heyl Ha'Avir. (*IDF-AF courtesy of the Israeli Air Force Attaché in Washington*)

460

Grumman attempted several times to sell the Hawkeye abroad both before and after its first export success in 1976 when Israel ordered four aircraft. Projects unsuccessfully offered to overseas customers included Design 123H which was initiated in March 1960 for the Royal Navy; Design 123Y, a first proposal to sell the aircraft to Japan, on which work was started in September 1968; Design 123EE, offered in 1977 to several European air forces as a less expensive alternative to NATO's AWACS; and Design 123HH, which was a last attempt made in March 1982 to tailor the Hawkeye to French requirements.

The four non-US air forces which had taken delivery of Hawkeyes by the end of 1988 are listed in chronological order:

ISRAEL: The first E-2C for the Tsvah Haganah le Israel - Heyl Ha'Avir (Israel Defense Force - Air Force) was delivered in 1977. Three more followed in 1978. In Israeli service, Hawkeyes have seen much use. Notably, during fighting against Syrian forces in the Bekaa Valley in June 1982, they detected enemy aircraft as soon as they took off from bases in Syria and were thus able to provide ample warning to Israeli strike aircraft and to position interceptors. In large measure as the result of this efficient AEW work, the Heyl Ha'Avir achieved an unprecedented $28^1/_3$ to 1 kill-to-loss ratio.

JAPAN: After failing to show interest in Design 123Y, the Nihon Koku Jieitai (Japanese Air Self-Defence Force) became the second air force to order Hawkeyes. Four E-2Cs were delivered in 1982, four followed in 1984, and five more are on order. The E-2Cs have been assigned to 601 Hikotai which was formed at Misawa AB on the northern tip of the island of Honshu in November 1983.

SINGAPORE: Negotiations for the acquisition of four E-2Cs were initiated by the Republic of Singapore Air Force in 1983 and were concluded during the following year. Two of the four E-2Cs were delivered in 1985 and two followed in 1986. However, they were initially retained in

The first Japanese Hawkeye (JASDF serial 34-3451, BuNo 161400) during a test flight over Long Island before being delivered to the Nihon Kohu Jieitai in 1982. *(Grumman)*

461

Bearing the identification number 012 on its nose and tail, this Hawkeye was the second E-2C (BuNo 162794) for the Republic of Singapore Air Force. (*Grumman*)

Publicity photograph taken at Bethpage before the delivery of the first E-2C to Al Quwwat al Jawwiya il Misriya (the Egyptian Air Force). (*Grumman*)

the United States, where they were used to train Singapore flight crews and ground personnel. Two Hawkeyes were flown to Singapore in March 1987 and by the end of the year they had been joined at Paya Lebar AB by the last two.

EGYPT: Al Quwwat al Jawwiya il Misriya (The Egyptian Air Force), the last air arm to order Hawkeyes, took delivery of two E-2Cs in 1986 and of three more in 1987.

PRODUCTION: A total of 186 E-2s has been built by Grumman between

October 1960 and December 1988. More are on order. Hawkeyes delivered before the end of 1988 included:

59	E-2A	(2)	YE-2C
(4)	TE-2A	(4)	TE-2C
(49)	E-2B	127	E-2C

They were assigned the following BuNos and foreign military serials:

E-2A: BuNos 148147/148149, 148711/148713, 149817/149819, 150530/150541, 151702/151725, and 152476/152489)

TE-2A: (BuNos 149817, 149818, 150533, and 152485)

E-2B: (BuNos 149819, 150530/150532, 150534/150541, 151702/151725, 152476/152484, and 152486/152489)

YE-2C: (BuNos 148712 and 148713)

TE-2C: (BuNos 148712, 148713, 158639, and 158648)

E-2C: BuNos 158638/158648, 159105/159112, 159494/159502, (U.S.)160007/160012, 160415/160420, 160697/160703, 160987/160992, 161094/161099, 161224/161229, 161341/161346, 161547/161552, 161780/161785, 162615/162619, 162797/162802, 162824/162825, and six more

E-2C: (Egypt) BuNos 162791, 162792, and 162823/162825

E-2C: (Israel) BuNos 160771/160774

E-2C: (Japan) JASDF serials 34-3451/34-3454 and ..-3455/..3458(BuNos 161400/161403 and 161786/161789)

E-2C: (Singapore) BuNos 162793/162796

	E-2A	E-2C
DIMENSIONS:		
Span, ft in	80 7	80 7
(m)	(24.56)	(24.56)
Span (wings folded), ft in	29 4	29 4
(m)	(8.94)	(8.94)
Length, ft in	56 4	57 6¾
(m)	(17.17)	(17.55)
Height (rotodome retracted), ft in	16 5½	16 5½
(m)	(5.02)	(5.0.2)
Height (rotodome raised), ft in	18 3¾	18 3¾
(m)	(5.58)	(5.58)
Wing area, sq ft	700	700
(sq m)	(65.03)	(65.03)
WEIGHTS:		
Empty, lb	31,154	38,063
(kg)	(14,131)	(17,265)
Maximum, lb	54,830	51,933
(kg)	(24,870)	(23,556)
Wing loading,* lb/sq ft	78.3	74.2
(kg/sq m)	(382.4)	(362.2)
Power loading,* lb/shp	6.8	4.8
(kg/shp)	(3.1)	(2.4)

PERFORMANCE:

Max speed, mph/ft	368/20,000	372/20,000
(kmh/m)	(592/6,095)	(599/6,095)
Cruising speed, mph	297	308
(kmh)	(478)	(496)
Climb rate, ft/min	2,330	2,515
(m/sec)	(12)	(13)
Service ceiling, ft	28,800	30,800
(m)	(8,780)	(9,390)
Normal range, miles	1,650	1,605
(km)	(2,655)	(2,580)
Max range, miles	–	2,500
(km)	(–)	(4,025)

* Wing and power loadings are calculated at normal loaded weight and maximum take-off power.

Bearing the markings of VAQ-135, this EA-6B modified to the ICAP-I configuration was photographed aboard the USS *Kitty Hawk* (CV-63) as it was about to be launched for a training exercise off the coast of Southern California in January 1981. *(René J Francillon)*

Grumman EA-6 Prowler

Among the few air forces known to have squadrons solely dedicated to tactical electronic warfare, the USAF, the USMC, and the USN are remarkable in that all three have relied for the past two decades on tactical electronic aircraft built by Grumman. Currently, EA-6Bs equip Navy and Marine squadrons while EF-111As are operated by Air Force squadrons. Grumman's dominance of the tactical electronic warfare market, however, is not fortuitous. For the most part, it stems from an in-house study of tactical jamming systems which the company had undertaken in 1963-64 as a follow-up to work then underway to develop the EA-6A version of the Intruder. For Grumman, the timing of this study could not have been better, as the need for effective tactical electronic warfare aircraft was recognized to be of the highest urgency as soon as combat operations were begun over North Vietnam.

Aware that the Marine Corps would soon need a replacement for its obsolete Douglas F3D-2Q tactical electronic warfare aircraft, Grumman assigned Project Engineer Lew Scheuer to initiate a study of an ECM version of the A2F-1 in late 1960. Work on this electronic warfare Intruder gained tempo during the summer of 1961 and was endorsed by the Marine Corps with the placing of an initial development contract in March 1962. Initially known as the A2F-1H, the two-seat electronic warfare aircraft was redesignated EA-6A in September 1962.

465

An EA-6B ICAP II (BuNo 160437) of VAQ-134 at NAS Fallon, Nevada, on 21 June, 1989.
The aircraft carries an AGM-88A HARM missile beneath the port wing. *(René J Francillon)*

To serve as EA-6A development aircraft, Grumman modified the second
and eighth A-6A. BuNo 147865 became the aerodynamic prototype before
being fitted with its electronic equipment and delivered to the Marine
Corps. BuNo 148618 was the first fully-equipped aircraft to fly, doing so on
26 April, 1963. Externally, both differed from standard A-6As in having
their forward fuselage extended 8 in to provide space for an additional
equipment bay and in being fitted with a large fin-tip antenna fairing. The
standard two-seat cockpit was retained but the right crew station was
modified for use by the electronic countermeasures officer (ECMO).

Although proving quite capable during trials, only twenty-eight EA-6As
were built (including prototypes, other aircraft modified from A-6A
airframes, and specially built EA-6As) and partially equipped three Marine
squadrons. By the time of their entry into service in December 1965,
however, a much more capable electronic warfare system was already under
development.

Work on this new Tactical Jamming System (TJS) had been initiated by
Grumman in January 1963 as an in-house study to upgrade the EA-6A to
cope with anticipated developments in Soviet electronic warfare
capabilities. In attempting to do so, the project team soon realized that
simple improvements to manually-operated systems as fitted to the EA-6A
would not yield the desired results and that a completely new approach
would be required. Accordingly, the company submitted a proposal in June
1964 for a Contract Definition Phase and obtained Navy funding for
additional studies. By July 1965, sufficient progress had been made for the
Navy to award a research and development contract for a computer-
controlled Tactical Jamming System.* This step was followed

* Basically, the TJS which Grumman developed for the EA-6B consisted of an onboard
electronic system (OBS) and up to five externally-mounted AN/ALQ-99 jammer pods. The
OBS was to monitor the electronic environment around the aircraft, display it to the ECMOs,
and tune and direct the jammer pod antennae to the hostile radar. Grumman further provided
for the TJS to be complemented by VHF communications jamming (COMMJAM) equipment
for protection against airborne threats.

466

by the issue of Specific Operational Requirements SOR 33-17 in November 1965, and the issue nine months later of a letter of intent for the contract definition phase for the aircraft which was to serve as the TJS platform, the EA-6B.

The most noteworthy decision taken during this phase was to double the size of the crew as, in spite of partial automation of some of the ECM operations, the flow of data was considered to be too much to be handled by a single ECMO. Accordingly, to accommodate two additional ECMOs, the EA-6B was designed with a forward fuselage 8.8 in longer than that of the A-6A and 52 in longer than that of the EA-6A. During the detailed design phase, the switch to a four-seat configuration was also found to necessitate a reduction in the size and capacity of the forward fuselage cell. Moreover, the need to provide additional electrical wiring in the wings for the electronic equipment brought about a slight reduction in the capacity of the wing cells. Altogether, total internal fuel capacity was reduced from 2,332 US gal for the EA-6A to 2,268 gal for the EA-6B.

In the spring of 1967, an NEA-6A development aircraft (BuNo 149935) was fitted with a two-band receiver to prove the fin fairing location for the system antennae and the basic system signal intercept and processing techniques. It was followed by three A-6A airframes which were modified to the four-seat EA-6B configuration. BuNo 149481 was the first to be fitted with the lengthened nose section, fin fairing, dorsal fin extension, and modified wing root section. It was first flown at Calverton by Don King on 25 May, 1968, and served as the aerodynamic prototype. BuNo 149479 was used for flight testing the electronic equipment beginning on 19 August, 1968, and BuNo 148615 was modified as a non-flying electronic test article (ETA) for extensive testing in an anechoic chamber.

Considering the advance in the state-of-the art represented by the TJS, EA-6B trials proceeded remarkably smoothly and swiftly. Navy Preliminary Evaluation (NPE) was initiated in January 1969, Defense Systems Acquisition Review Council (DSARC) evaluation took place during the autumn of 1969, and the release for production was given in December 1969. These activities were followed by Board of Inspection and Survey

The fifteenth A-6A airframe (BuNo 149481), modified as an EA-6B aerodynamic prototype in 1968. (*Grumman*)

467

EA-6A of VAQ-33, Fleet Electronic Warfare Support Group (FEWSG), at NAS Key West, Florida. *(Rick Morgan)*

(BIS) trials in May 1970, the first flight of a production aircraft (BuNo 158029) in November 1970, and the initial delivery to the fleet in January 1971.

Production history

Following small batches of EA-6As built betwen 1965 and 1969, EA-6Bs have remained in production since 1970. Furthermore, unless current budgetary problems force the Navy to terminate development of the ADVCAP (Advanced capability) version, EA-6Bs will still be built in the early 1990s. All along, airframe, powerplant, and external appearance have remained virtually unchanged. Electronic capabilities, on the other hand, have been steadily expanded as detailed below.

EA-6A (A2F-1H): Two A-6As were modified as prototypes for the electronic warfare version of the Intruder, with BuNo 147865 being used as an aerodynamic prototype and BuNo 148618 being fitted as the electronic prototype and flying for the first time on 26 April, 1963. Five more A-6As (BuNos 148616, 149475, 149477, 149778, and 149935) were modified as EA-6As and were followed by twenty-one production EA-6As (BuNos 151595/151600 and 156979/156993). All EA-6As were powered by two 8,500-lb thrust Pratt & Whitney J52-P-6 turbojets.

For their primary use as electronic warfare aircraft to support strike aircraft and ground troops by suppressing enemy electronic activity, EA-6As normally carried up to five jammer pods (AN/ALQ-31B, ALQ-54, or ALQ-76) on a centreline and four wing stations. Chaff dispensers (AN/ALE-32 or AN/ALE-41) could be substituted for jammer pods carried beneath the wing. EA-6As could also be used to gather electronic intelligence (ELINT). Although they retained a limited all-weather attack

468

An EA-6A from a VMCJ-2 detachment embarked on the USS *Forrestal* (CVA-59). The aircraft carries two external tanks and four jammer pods. *(Grumman)*

capability with conventional or special weapons, EA-6As were seldom used in an offensive capacity.

Unlike the four-seat EA-6Bs for which the name of Prowler was officially adopted, the two-seat EA-6As are still named Intruder.

EA-6B: Three A-6As were modified to serve as EA-6B development aircraft: BuNo 149481 was first flown on 25 May, 1968; BuNo 149479 was used for flight testing the electronic equipment; and BuNo 148615 was modified as a non-flying electronic test article.

Five pre-production aircraft (BuNos 156478/156482) and twenty-three production aircraft (BuNos 158029/158040, 158540/158547, and 158649/158651) incorporated local airframe strengthening to assure adequate fatigue life at the increased gross weight. Each could carry up to five AN/ALQ-99 jammers if no external tanks were carried. Alternatively, a 300-US gal drop tank could be substituted for one or more of the AN/ALQ-99 pods. The crew of four consisted of a pilot and three electronic countermeasures officers. ECMO 1, in the right forward seat, was a TJS operator and also acted as the navigator. ECMO 2, in the right rear seat, was the communications jamming (COMMJAM) operator. ECMO 3, in the left rear seat, was a TJS operator. Starting with the 22nd EA-6B (BuNo 158544), 11,200-lb Pratt & Whitney J52-P-408 turbojets replaced the 9,300-lb thrust J52-P-8As. P-408 turbojets were also retrofitted to all but the first five aircraft. Like the EA-6As, the EA-6Bs were also intended to be used in the passive role, without jammers radiating, to detect and record signals and to provide electronic intelligence (ELINT) data for for rapid classification of detected emitters.

EA-6B EXCAP: EXCAP (Expanded Capability) Prowlers were fitted with AN/ALQ-99A sets which doubled the frequency coverage. In service, these TJS sets were upgraded to the ALQ-99B and ALQ-99C configurations to improve reliability. Other EXCAP improvements included twice the computer memory, the installation of a digital recorder, and the addition of an Exciter Jammer Control Unit to provide three jamming modes. Starting

469

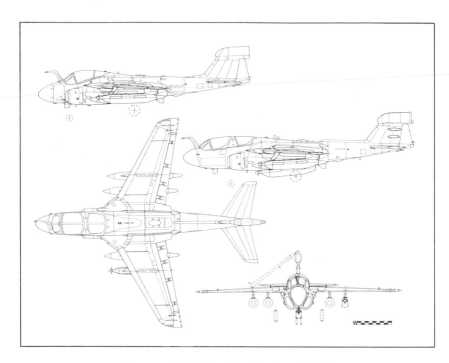

Grumman EA-6B Prowler. Side view of EA-6A

An EA-6B EXCAP of VAQ-137 before a deployment aboard the USS *Enterprise* (CVN-65).
(Rick Morgan)

with the twenty-ninth Prowler, Grumman delivered twenty-five EA-6Bs in the EXCAP configuration (BuNos158799/158817 and 159582/159587). The first EA-6B EXCAP was delivered to the fleet in January 1973. Beginning in mid-1983, EXCAP Prowlers still in service were upgraded to ICAP II.
EA-6B ICAP I: The ICAP (Improved Capability, later ICAP I when a more

A Prowler of VAQ-136 at NAS Fallon, Nevada, on 27th October, 1986. Built as an EA-6B EXCAP, BuNo 158804 had by then been modified to the ICAP II configuration. *(René J Francillon)*

advanced version entered production as the ICAP II) configuration was developed in answer to suggestions from the fleet to modify the forward and aft cockpits and redistribute the work among the three electronic counter-measures officers. While still working as the navigator, ECMO 1 became the mission co-ordinator and COMMJAM operator. ECMOs 2 and 3 now shared responsibility for TJS operations. Other changes included a reduction in system response time by digitally tuning the electronic surveillance receivers, the replacement of various cockpit displays and controls with a computerized Digital Display Group, and the substitution of an AN/APS-130 search radar for the previously fitted AN/APQ-129 set. Moreover, ICAP I aircraft carried new chaff dispensing pods and used AN/ALQ-126A self-protection countermeasures sets instead of AN/ALQ-100s.

In addition to delivering forty-five aircraft (BuNos 159907/159912, 160432/160437, 160609, 160704/160709, 160786/160791, 161115/ 161120, 161242/161247, 161347/161352, and 161774/161775) in the ICAP I config-uration, Grumman modified twenty-one early production EA-6Bs to this standard as part of a MOD/SDLM (Modification/Standard Depot Level Maintenance) programme in 1976-79. Since the autumn of 1985, Grumman has modified most ICAP I aircraft (including some which already had been upgraded from the original EA-6B standard) to the ICAP I MOD configuration to achieve maintenance and support commonality with ICAP II aircraft.

EA-6B ICAP II: The ICAP II configuration was approved in May 1982 for introduction on the ninety-ninth Prowler (BuNo 161776) and for retrofit to EXCAP aircraft. Major improvements included in this programme included: (1) the replacement of the AN/AYA-6 computer with the Standard Navy Airborne Computer (the more powerful and faster operat-ing AN/AYK-14); (2) the upgrading of the TJS to the AN/ALQ-99D configuration to cover a wider frequency range; (3) the provision of new modes and software control of modulations; (4) the installation of a carrier

471

aircraft inertial navigation system (CAINS); and (5) the deletion of the AN/APN-153 doppler navigation radar. Furthermore, using TACAN data link, two EA-6B ICAP II aircraft were given the capability of co-ordinating their EW activities to saturate enemy defences. More recently, ICAP II Prowlers have been fitted to carry an AGM-88A High-Speed Anti-Radiation Missile (HARM) on pylons beneath each wing.

Beginning with BuNo 163049, ICAP II aircraft have been completed to 'Block 86' standard (so called because they were first ordered in Fiscal Year 1986). Changes include new UHF/VHF and HF radios. Later Block 86 Prowlers will have a new receiver package for greatly enhanced Electronic Support Measures (ESM) capability.

EA-6B ADVCAP: The Advanced Capability configuration is under development to extend frequency jamming coverage through Band 10, reduce mean time to intercept and jam, and improve jammer power management. In addition, ADVCAP Prowlers will be fitted with AN/ALQ-149 Tactical Command and Control Countermeasures Set, AN/ALQ-165 Airborne Self-Protection Jammer (ASPJ), Joint Tactical Information Distribution System (JTIDS), and Global Positioning System (GPS). ADVCAP aircraft are planned to enter service in 1992. If funding can be provided, Grumman will upgrade ICAP I and ICAP II Prowlers to this standard and may manufacture up to 100 new ADVCAP aircraft.

At the request of the Naval Air Systems Command, Grumman and NASA engineers have developed aerodynamic modifications to improve the EA-6B ADVCAP's flight characteristics at high angles of attack and to restore the stall manoeuvre margin which had gradually eroded as the result of weight increases since the development of the original EA-6B variant. Modifications developed under this so-called Vehicle Improvement Program (VIP) include extended and drooped leading edge slats, modified trailing- edge flaps incorporating supercritical camber, an 18-in fin extension above the radome, glove strakes forward of the wing/fuselage junction, and modification of the wingtip speed brakes to act as ailerons.

The first flight of a modified EA-6B is scheduled for late 1989 and, unless the Navy is unable to fund the acquisition of additional Prowlers, EA-6B ADVCAPs delivered from 1992 are likely to have airframes incorporating all VIP modifications. Moreover, these Prowlers will have an additional store station beneath each wing and will be powered by 12,000-lb thrust J52-P-409 turbojets.

Service history

The first EA-6A was delivered to VMCJ-2 at MCAS Cherry Point, North Carolina, on 1 December, 1965. As fast as deliveries allowed, 'Electric Intruders' were then assigned to the two other Marine Composite Reconnaissance Squadrons, VMCJ-1 at Iwakuni, Japan, and VMCJ-3 at MCAS El Toro, California. VMCJ-1 first sent a detachment of EA-6As to Da Nang AB, South Vietnam, at the end of October 1966. By the end of that year, this small detachment had flown 128 combat sorties, of which 67 per cent were in support of carrier-based aircraft from the Seventh Fleet operating over North Vietnam, 16 per cent supported Air Force operations over the North, 15 per cent collected ELINT over North Vietnam, and 2 per cent gathered ELINT over the South.

Until the Marine withdrawal in the summer of 1970, detachments of EA-6As remained in South Vietnam to support tactical aircraft operations and to provide ECM coverage for Air Force Boeing B-52s operating across the Demilitarized Zone and over the passes between North Vietnam and Laos along the Ho Chi Minh Trail. After the North Vietnamese launched their Spring Offensive in 1972, VMCJ-1 and VMCJ-2 sent EA-6A detachments back to Da Nang, in South Vietnam, and Cubi Point, in the Philippines. Afterwards, 'Electric Intruders' flew over the North until the signing of the Paris Agreement in January 1973. One EA-6A was lost in combat to an unknown cause and another was lost due to a hydraulic system failure during a mission in support of *Linebacker II* operations against North Vietnam.

In addition to combat operations in Vietnam and land-based peacetime operations, Marine EA-6A detachments have also operated on a number of occasions from carriers.

Following a revised organization of its reconnaissance and electronic warfare units, the Marine Corps assigned all its EA-6As to Marine Tactical Electronic Warfare Squadron Two at MCAS Cherry Point and these aircraft were operated by VMAQ-2 until the autumn of 1979. Since then, the EA-6As have been distributed among a Marine reserve squadron (VMAQ-4 at NAS Whidbey Island, Washington), two Navy reserve squadrons (VAQ-309 also at NAS Whidbey Island and VAQ-209 at NAS Norfolk, Virginia), and a regular Navy squadron (VAQ-33 at NAS Key West, Florida). With VAQ-33, which is assigned to the Fleet Electronic Warfare Support Group (FEWSG), EA-6As are used as electronic aggressors during training exercises.

The first EA-6B was delivered to VAQ-129 at NAS Whidbey Island in

EA-6A (BuNo 156936) of VMAQ-4, a Reserve Marine squadron. (*C Waldenmaier, courtesy of Alain Pelletier*)

473

EA-6B from the *Wizards* of VAQ-133. *(C Waldenmaier, courtesy of Alain Pelletier)*

January 1971. By May, the first two EA-6B aircrews had completed the training syllabus and on 1 July, 1971, VAQ-132, the first deployable squadron, was activated. This squadron then deployed to Southeast Asia aboard the USS *America* (CVA-66) in June 1972 and flew its first combat sorties on 14 July. VAQ-131 was next on the line aboard the USS *Enterprise* (CVAN-65) and, along with VAQ-132, played a vital role during Operations *Linebacker I* and *II*. Neither of these squadrons lost an aircraft, either to combat-related or operational causes, before the war ended. The basic version of the EA-6B was also operated by VAQ-130, -134, -135, and -136.

First assigned to VAQ-129, the training squadron, in April 1973, the EXCAP version was subsequently used to equip VAQ-133, -137, and -138 and to re-equip VAQ-131, -132, and -134. The ICAP I version entered service with VAQ-129 in July 1976, and was assigned to VAQ-139 when this squadron was activated. It replaced BASIC and EXCAP Prowlers with VAQ-130, -131, -132, -134, -135, -136, and -138. Finally, the ICAP II version was first delivered to VAQ-129 in July 1984, was assigned to three new squadrons (VAQ-140, -141, and -142), and has since progressively replaced earlier versions, with VAQ-132 being scheduled to be the last squadron to convert to this version. The first deployment by a squadron equipped with ICAP II aircraft carrying HARM missiles was made by VAQ-140 aboard the USS *John F. Kennedy* (CV-67) from August 1986 until March 1987. Various EA-6B variants have also been operated since July 1973 by a detachment of VX-5 to conduct operational evaluation and to develop tactics.

Since February 1980, VAQ-136 has been forward deployed to NAF Atsugi, and operates regularly from the USS *Midway* (CV-41). VAQ-129 and the twelve other deployable Prowler squadrons* are based at NAS

* Tactical Electronic Warefare Squadrons (VAQs or TACELRONs) normally deploy aboard carriers with only four aircraft. In the future, it is hoped to increase the normal complement at sea to five EA-6Bs.

474

BuNo 148618 was first delivered in December 1961 as the eighth Intruder. It is seen here at Calverton on 15 February, 1966, after it had been modified to serve as the EA-6A electronic prototype. (*Grumman*)

Whidbey Island. As needed, they are assigned to Carrier Air Wings for deployment aboard carriers of the Atlantic Fleet and the Pacific Fleet.

The only Marine Prowler squadron, VMAQ-2, is based at MCAS Cherry Point, but frequently sends detachments for operations aboard carriers and from other stations and bases in the United States and abroad. It first received ICAP I Prowlers in 1977 and transitioned to ICAP II in 1988.

Noteworthy Prowler deployments during the 1980s include those made by VAQ-131 aboard the USS *Independence* (CV-62), which saw action over Grenada in October 1983 (Operation *Urgent Fury*) and two months later joined VAQ-137 from the USS *John F. Kennedy* (CV-67) for operations against Druze and Syrian positions in Lebanon. In March and April 1986, EA-6Bs were back in the news when aircraft from VAQ-135, VAQ-137, and a VMAQ-2 detachment, respectively deployed aboard the USS *Coral Sea* (CV-43), *Saratoga* (CV-60), and *America* (CV-66), were part of the naval force operating against Libya. On 18 April, 1988, EA-6Bs from VAQ-135 aboard the USS *Enterprise* (CVN-65) used specially provided AN/ASQ-191 sets to jam Iranian communications during a naval engagement in the Arabian Gulf.

PRODUCTION: In addition to ten A-6A airframes which were modified as prototypes for the EA-6A and EA-6B variants, 156 new EA-6As and Prowlers were built by Grumman between March 1965 and December 1988. More are on order. EA-6s delivered before the end of 1988 included:

(7)	EA-6A	(3)	EA-6B
21	EA-6A	135	EA-6B

They were assigned the following BuNos:

EA-6A: (BuNos 147865, 148616, 148618, 149475,
(converted A-6As) 149477/149778, and 149935)

475

BuNo 149935, the last A-6A to be modified as an NEA-6A. (*Grumman*)

EA-6A:	BuNos 151595/151600 and 156979/156993
EA-6B:	(BuNos 148615, 149479, and 149481)
(converted A-6As)	
EA-6B:	BuNos 156478/156482, 158029/158040, 158540/158547, 158649/158651, 158799/158817, 159582/159587, 159907/159912, 160432/160437, 160609, 160704/160709, 160786/160791, 161115/161120, 161242/161247, 161347/161352, 161774/161779, 161880/161885, 162223/162246, and 162934/162936

The following BuNos have been assigned to 29 of the aircraft on order at the end of 1988:

EA-6B	BuNos 162937/162941, 163030/163035, 163044/163049, and 163395/163406

	EA-6A	EA-6B
DIMENSIONS:		
Span, ft in	53 0	53 0
(m)	(16.15)	(16.15)
Span (wings folded), ft in	25 2	25 10
(m)	(7.67)	(7.87)
Length, ft in	55 5.8	59 9.8
(m)	(16.91)	(18.23)
Height, ft in	15 5.9	16 3
(m)	(4.72)	(4.95)
Wing area, sq ft	529	529
(sq m)	(49.15)	(49.15)
WEIGHTS:		
Empty, lb	27,769	32,162
(kg)	(12,596)	(14,588)
Loaded, lb	41,715	48,287
(kg)	(18,922)	(21,903)
Maximum, lb	54,571	65,000
(kg)	(24,753)	(29,484)

Wing loading,* lb/sq ft	78.9	91.3
(kg/sq m)	(385.0)	(445.6)
Power loading,* lb/lb st	2.5	2.2
(kg/kgp)	(2.5)	(2.2)
PERFORMANCE:		
Max speed, mph/ft	631/sl	658/sl
(kmh/m)	(986/sl)	(1,059/sl)
Cruising speed, mph	472	482
(kmh)	(759)	(776)
Climb rate, ft/min	6,550	8,600
(m/sec)	(33)	(44)
Service ceiling, ft	37,800	41,400
(m)	(11,520)	(12,620),
Normal range, miles	2,021	1,628
(km)	(3,250)	(2,620) .
Max range, miles	2,810	2,021
(km)	(4,520)	(3,250)

* Wing and power loadings are calculated at normal loaded weight and maximum take-off power.

A Grumman American T-Cat at the Mojave Airport on 19 August, 1987. (*René J Francillon*)

Grumman American AA-1, T-Cat and Lynx

When Grumman decided to broaden its general aviation activities by getting into the light aircraft market, it did so first by acquiring in January 1973 the assets of the American Aviation Corporation and that company's rights in the two-seat AA-1 and four-seat AA-5 light aircraft.

Both of these aircraft were developed from the BD-1 designed by James Bede and first flown on 11 July, 1963. Of small dimensions, this two-seater was a cantilever monoplane with a non-retractable nosewheel undercarriage and side-by-side accommodation. Compared with other light aircraft of the time, the BD-1 was structurally innovative. It featured an enclosed cabin of aluminium honeycomb construction and made use of metal-to-metal bonding throughout its airframe. During 1964, following promising trials with the privately-built prototype, the American Aviation Corporation was organized in Cleveland, Ohio, specially to develop, certify, and manufacture the BD-1 as the AA-1 Yankee. FAA certification was obtained in August 1967, but construction did not get fully underway until 1969. From then until the end of 1972, American Aviation produced 470 of these two-seaters in three versions. The AA-1 Yankee was the basic model; the AA-1A Trainer differed in having dual controls, some changes in equipment, and modified wing leading- and trailing-edges; and the AA-1A Tr-2 was a Trainer with de luxe equipment. The standard powerplant was the 108-hp Lycoming O-235-C2C flat-four air-cooled engine driving a two-blade fixed-pitch propeller.

478

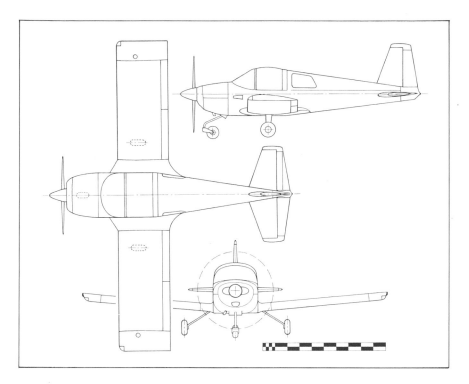

Grumman American AA-1B

After Grumman acquired control of American Aviation Corporation and re-organized this company as Grumman American Corporation, the designation of the two-seat aircraft was changed to AA-1B. Production of the Trainer and Tr-2 versions continued in the plant located on the edge of the Cuyahoga County Airport in Cleveland. Then, in October 1974, Grumman announced that production of the light aircraft would be moved to its Savannah plant in Georgia in order to consolidate its general aviation programmes. In 1977, performance of the light aircraft was slightly improved when a 115-hp Lycoming O-235-L2C was substituted for the previously installed 108-hp O-235-C2C. With this engine, the aircraft was redesignated AA-1C T-Cat in its training version and AA-1C Lynx in its touring version.

Both variants of the AA-1C remained in production until August 1978 when Grumman sold its 80 per cent interest in Grumman American Corporation to American Jet Industries. The resulting Gulfstream American Corporation briefly retained the T-Cat and Lynx in production until deciding to concentrate its activities on larger general aviation aircraft.

PRODUCTION: During the Grumman American years, 617 AA-1Bs (235 in 1973, 186 in 1974, 112 in 1975, and 84 in 1976) and 206 T-Cats and Lynxes (115 in 1977 and 91 until August 1978) were built.

Specifications for the AA-1B

Span 24 ft 5½ in (7.45 m); length 19 ft 2⅞ in (5.86 m); height 7 ft 7¼ in (2.32 m); wing area 100.9 sq ft (9.38 sq m).

Empty weight 1,025 lb (465 kg); loaded 1,560 lb (708 kg); wing loading 15.5 lb/sq ft (75.5 kg/sq m); power loading 14.4 lb/hp (6.6 kg/hp).

Max speed 144 mph (232 kmh) at sl; cruising speed 124 mph (200 kmh); rate of climb at sea level 705 ft/min (3.6 m/sec); service ceiling 12,750 ft (3,885 m); normal range at 75 per cent power 435 miles (700 km); max range 508 miles (815 km).

BuNo 152794, a Greyhound from the first production batch, landing at NAF Atsugi. *(Courtesy of Cloud 9 Photography)*

Grumman C-2 Greyhound

By proposing the development of Design 123I as a COD transport version of the Hawkeye AEW aircraft in May 1961, Grumman reversed the process which had seen the Tracer derived from the Trader. Unfortunately, the result was less satisfactory from the sales standpoint. After ordering the modification of the first two E-2As as COD prototypes and awarding production contracts for two batches of C-2As totaling 29 aircraft (BuNos 152786/152797 and 155120/155136), the Navy cancelled the last twelve aircraft, thus forcing Grumman to terminate production in 1967. Fifteen years later, however, the C-2A was put back into production when thirty-nine aircraft were ordered (BuNos 162140/162178) under a multi-year contract to be completed in 1989, a quarter of a century after the first flight of a Greyhound.

Besides the obvious removal of the dorsal radome, the main change required to modify two E-2As into C-2A prototypes was the substitution of wider fuselages providing accommodation for twenty-eight passengers in aft-facing seats or twelve stretchers litters and attendants. Alternatively, the aircraft was designed to carry three times the load of the C-1A, a maximum cargo load of 15,000 lb being permissible when operating between land bases, wheras a limit of 10,000 lb was imposed when flying from a carrier. Furthermore, it had the added advantage of permitting easier loading of bulky items, such as engines, as it was provided with an aft cargo door with detachable loading ramp treadways. In other respects, the C-2As were identical to the E-2As and retained the Hawkeye's wings, tail unit (with four fins and three rudders but without tailplane dihedral), and two 4,050- shp Allison T56-A-8B propeller-turbines.

481

A Greyhound COD being readied on the starboard catapult of a US Navy Carrier. (*Grumman*)

Development of the propeller-turbine-powered aircraft was approved in May 1962, but conversion work proceeded slowly as the new COD aircraft was given low priority while the first two E-2As were still needed for the AEW aircraft test programme. Finally, conversion of BuNo 148147 was completed in the autumn of 1964 and, as the C-2A prototype, this aircraft was first flown on 18 November, 1964, by Don Fish and D B Seeman. Notwithstanding the loss of this aircraft off Cuttyhunk Island, Massachusetts, on 29 April, 1965, the C-2A programme went ahead. The second prototype, BuNo 148148, which had first flown on 28 January, 1965, was used for the Navy Preliminary Evaluation in April and May 1965. This aircraft was joined by BuNo 152786, the first production Greyhound, for carrier qualification trials aboard the uss *Kitty Hawk* (CV-63) in September 1966.

Entering service with VRC-50 at NAF Atsugi in December 1966, Greyhounds were immediately sent on detachment to NAS Cubi Point in the Philippines to provide support from TF77 carriers operating in the Gulf of Tonkin. Greyhounds were also assigned to VR-24 at NAF Sigonella, Italy, and NAF Rota, Spain, and to VR-30 at NAS North Island, California. However, the need to divert funds to acquire aircraft, weapons, and systems more urgently needed during the Southeast Asia War prompted the Navy to cancel the last twelve C-2As (BuNos 155125/155136). The seventeenth and last Greyhound ordered under the first production contract was delivered in December 1967.

After the type had been in service for eight years, it was found necessary to replace the square-tipped Aeroproducts propellers with round-tipped Hamilton Standard propellers. More importantly, intensive operations necessitated that the C-2As be put through a major Service Life Extension Program during which the aircraft and engines were overhauled, the inner wing box strengthened, and anti-corrosion treatment given where necessary. Initiated in 1977, this SLEP was completed in five years by the Naval Air Rework Facility San Diego at NAS North Island.

Several years after cancelling its order for twelve C-2As, the Navy again needed to procure additional COD transports and to plan the acquisition of replacement aircraft for the ageing, piston-powered C-1As. As an interim measure, the Navy ordered a turbofan-powered Lockheed US-3A in 1975 and later had three YS-3As modified as COD transports. In addition, it evaluated a number of designs from the industry including proposed carrier-capable versions of two twin-jet airliners, the McDonnell Douglas DC-9-20 and the Fokker F.28. In the end, however, acquisition of additional US-3As was rejected as the type was too small and could not carry bulky items. Acquisition of new types was not found cost effective in view of the small number of aircraft required. Conversely, the procurement of additional C-2As was looked upon favourably as the Greyhound's commonality with the Hawkeye would ease maintenance when operating from carriers.

The first of the thirty-nine C-2As ordered in early 1982 under a multi-

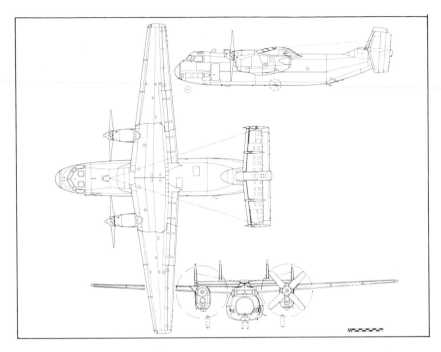

Grumman C-2A Greyhound

year contract was initially flown on 4 February, 1985. Compared with Greyhounds built during the late 1960s, the new C-2As have uprated 4,910-shp T56-A-425 engines, modernized avionics, strengthened inner wing box and improved anti-corrosion treatment as developed for earlier aircraft during the SLEP, and other minor improvements. However, the proposed installation of a refuelling probe, which had been tested in 1980 when BuNo 155124 was fitted with a dry probe for tests not involving fuel transfer, was not adopted for production aircraft.

Two new C-2As were delivered to VR-24 at Sigonella in September 1985. Since then, reprocured Greyhounds have been assigned to VRC-30, VRC-40, and VRC-50 to support fleet operations in home waters, the Western Pacific, and the Mediterranean. In addition, VAW-110 at NAS Miramar, California, and VAW-120 at NAS Norfolk, Virginia, each have received three new C-2As for replacement training.

PRODUCTION: Two C-2A prototypes converted from E-2A airframes were delivered in 1965 and 1966 and forty-nine C-2As were built by Grumman between 1966 and December 1988. Seven more are on order. Those delivered before the end of 1988 were assigned BuNos 148147/148148, 152786/152797, 155120/155124, and 162140/162171. Those then remaining to be delivered were BuNos 162172/162178.

Span 80 ft 7 in (24.56 m); span (wings folded) 29 ft 4 in (8.94 m); length 56 ft 10 in (17.32 m); height 15 ft 10^1/$_2$ in (4.84 m); wing area 700 sq ft (65.03 sq m).

Empty weight 36,346 lb (16,486 kg); maximum weight 54,354 lb (24,654 kg); wing loading 77.6 lb/sq ft (379.1 kg/sq m); power loading 5.5 lb/shp (2.5 kg/shp).

Maximum speed 357 mph at 25,000 ft (574 kmh at 7.620 m); cruising speed 299 mph (482 kmh); climb rate 2,610 ft/min (13 m/sec); service ceiling 33,500 ft (10,210 m); normal range 1,200 miles (1,930 km); maximum range 1,796 miles (2,890 km).

BuNo 162171, a C-2A from the second production batch, at NAS Miramar on 12 May, 1989.
(René J Francillon)

An EF-111A (66-0038) of the 390th Electronic Combat Squadron, 366th Tactical Fighter Wing, at Mountain Home AFB, Idaho, on 18 July, 1988. *(René J Francillon)*

Grumman/General Dynamics F-111B and EF-111A Raven

A well-motivated but ill-founded desire to reduce military expenditure through the adoption of weapons systems common to more than one branch of the Armed Forces resulted in the TFX (Tactical Fighter Experimental) fiasco, for which Secretary of Defense Robert S McNamara was justly blamed but for which the Navy and, to a lesser extent, the Air Force were not without their share of the blame.

In the late autumn of 1960, shortly before the administration of President Eisenhower was replaced by that of President Kennedy, the Department of Defense had instructed the Navy to cancel the development of the Douglas F6D-1 Missileer, a subsonic Fleet Air Defense (FAD) fighter armed with long range Eagle air-to-air missiles, and the Air Force to withhold issuing a Request for Proposals for a supersonic Tactical Fighter Experimental (TFX) satisfying Specific Operational Requirement SOR 183. These decisions by the outgoing administration provided newly appointed Secretary McNamara with an opportunity to implement his commonality policy. On 16 February, 1961, he instructed the Services to explore the feasibility of developing a common aircraft which not only would be capable of performing the Air Force SOR 183 mission and those planned by the Navy for its FAD fighter but also could be used by the Army and the Marine Corps as a close air support aircraft. In June, after the Services convinced him that the CAS mission could not be assigned to the TFX or FAD fighter, Secretary McNamara instructed the Air Force and the Navy to work closely to combine TFX and FAD requirements before issuing a joint RFP.

Two months later, although agreeing on the use of variable-geometry wings, the Air Force and the Navy reported that a common aircraft would not be feasible because of dissimilar configuration requisites, conflicting performance requirements, and unreconcilable differences in radar specifications. The Navy, based on its experience with the Douglas F3D in which

486

pilot and radar-operator had been able to work efficiently as a team because of the type's side-by-side accommodation, favoured side-by-side seating for its all-weather FAD fighter. Furthermore, it wanted the FAD fighter to be fitted with a long-range intercept radar with a 48-in radar dish and optimized for long loiter at medium to high altitude and subsonic speed. The Air Force, on the contrary, preferred tandem accommodation, required a terrain following radar, and emphasized operations at low altitude and supersonic speed. Undaunted, Secretary McNamara directed that the Air Force would be the lead service for the development of a common TFX aircraft.

Even before the issue of the resulting RFP on 29 September, 1961, General Dynamics, recognizing that it lacked experience in the design of naval fighters, had asked Grumman to become its sub-contractor. Having agreed that Grumman would be responsible for producing the aft section, stabilizer, and undercarriage for the Air Force and the Navy versions of the proposed aircraft, for the entire assembly of the Navy version, and for integration of all Navy electronics, the two manufacturers submitted a joint

The fourth F-111B (BuNo 151973) during Phoenix system testing. Grumman test pilot Ralph 'Dixie' Donnell was killed in the crash of this aircraft on 21 April, 1967. (*Grumman*)

The first F-111B on display at Edwards AFB, California, with four Phoenix air-to-air missiles on wing stations. (*Peter B Lewis*)

487

proposal in December. In a first evaluation, the General Dynamics/ Grumman proposal was ranked second to that submitted by Boeing but neither were acceptable without additional development. A second submission in May 1962, a third in June, and a fourth in September saw General Dynamics/Grumman close the gap, but the Source Selection Board still recommended adoption of the final Boeing proposal. This recommendation was endorsed by the Air Force Council, the Air Force Logistics Command, BuWeps (Bureau of Naval Weapons, the Navy organization which had replaced the Bureau of Aeronautics in 1959), and the Chief of Naval Operations. Nevertheless, on 24 November, 1962, Secretary McNamara announced that a $439 million contract was being awarded to General Dynamics and Grumman for eighteen F-111A development aircraft for the Air Force and five F-111B prototypes (BuNos 151970/151974) for the Navy*.

The F-111B programme

Before recounting the tribulations of the F-111B and its eventual cancellation, mention must be made of the work which Grumman obtained as the result of this award and following contracts. The Bethpage firm not only built seven F-111Bs and produced rear fuselages, stabilizers, and undercarriages for 557 F-111s and FB-111s for the USAF and the Royal Australian Air Force but it also went on to modify forty-two F-111As into EF-111As between 1975 and 1985 and is now producing Avionics Modernization Program kits for modernizing Air Force F-111s.

As planned, external differences between the F-111A which General Dynamics was to produce for the Air Force and the F-111B which Grumman was to build for the Navy were to be limited to a reduction in length from 73 ft 6 in to 66 ft 9 in obtained through the use of a much shorter nose for the naval fighter in order for it to fit on standard deck elevators and to increases in unswept wing span from 63 ft to 70 ft and in wing area from 525 sq ft to 550 sq ft to endow the F-111B with longer on-station endurance. Principal systems and equipment differences included the substitution of a Hughes AN/AWG-9 long-range search radar for the General Electric AN/APQ-113 attack radar and Texas Instrument AN/APQ-110 terrain following radar of the Air Force version, the replacement of air-to-ground stores by six Hughes AIM-54 Phoenix long-range air-to-air missiles (two in a fuselage weapons bay and four on swivelling wing pylons), the use of Navy communications equipment in place of Air Force radio, and the fitting of arresting gear. Later, different versions of the Pratt & Whitney TF30 turbofan were selected to power the Air Force and Navy aircraft and a

---

* In answer to a congressional investigation, Secretary McNamara later justified his decision by pointing out that the Air Force and Navy versions proposed by the GD/Grumman team had greater commonality than the Boeing designs (83.7 per cent versus 60.7 per cent), that the Boeing proposal involved greater development risks (*eg*, the use of titanium and inflight thrust reversers), and that the Boeing cost estimates were unduly optimistic.

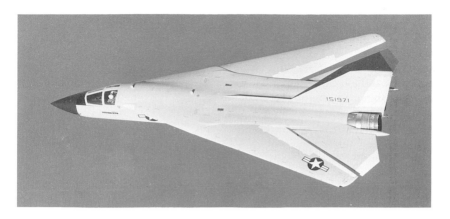

The second F-111B, with wings in the fully-swept position. (*Grumman*)

revised escape capsule had to be designed for the Navy fighter. Moreover, drastic attempts at reducing the weight of the F-111B resulted in further variance.

Featuring wings which could be swept from a minimum of 16 degrees to a maximum of 72.5 degrees, the first F-111B (BuNo 151970) was assembled in Bethpage from components produced by General Dynamics and Grumman. Rolled out in Bethpage on 11 May, this aircraft was transported to Calverton where it was first flown by Ralph 'Dixie' Donnell and Ernie von der Heyden on 18 May, 1965. Except for compressor stalls as already experienced by F-111As powered by the same pair of 10,750/18,500-lb dry/afterburning thrust Pratt & Whitney TF30-P-1 turbofans, initial trials were relatively trouble free, and the first Naval Preliminary Evaluation was held at NATC Patuxent River in October 1965. Nevertheless, the F-111B programme was already in serious trouble as General Dynamics and Grumman had been unable to keep the loaded weight at the upper limit of 55,000 lb as required by the Navy.

Even before the first F-111B flight, take-off weight of a fully equipped naval aircraft was estimated at nearly 78,000 lb, forcing the two manufacturers to implement a Super Weight Improvement Program. Most of these SWIP changes were incorporated in the fourth and subsequent F-111Bs. The fifth and last F-111B prototype was fitted with an escape capsule in place of individual ejector seats as fitted to previous aircraft, but this substitution more than offset benefits from the weight reduction programme and the F-111B remained grossly underpowered. Range was also 44 per cent below specifications and could only be increased by adding fuel, thus making the aircraft even more underpowered. To correct this deficiency and eliminate compressor stalls, BuNo 152714, the first of 32 production F-111Bs (BuNos152714/152717, 153623/153642, and 156971/156978) which had been ordered, was powered by two 12,290/20,250-lb dry/afterburning thrust TF30-P-12s.

Phoenix trials had been assigned to the third F-111B (BuNo 151972), and the first successful firing of this missile was made in July 1967. By then, however, the Navy held little hope that the F-111B could be developed into an acceptable carrier aircraft. In the FAD role, it was considered to be too complex and too expensive to be used as a Missileer substitute, whereas in the air superiority/fighter attack role it was too heavy and lacked the handling characteristics required to replace the McDonnell F-4. Only too aware of the magnitude of the problem, Grumman had already begun working on Design 303, the future F-14, and by October 1967, the Navy was convinced that the F-111B should be terminated. Finally, the axe fell in May 1968 when both houses of Congress refused to fund F-111B production, and the contract was formally terminated in December of that year.

Tests continued at PMTC Point Mugu and NWC China Lake even after the Congressional decison not to fund F-111B production as much could still be learned. Thus, BuNo 151974 was used for carrier trials aboard the USS *Coral Sea* (CVA-43) in July 1968 and Hughes Aircraft Corporation flew BuNo 152715, the last F-111B completed before contract termination, until the spring of 1971. By then, a total of 1,748 hours had been flown and two F-111Bs had been lost, BuNo 151973 having crashed off Long Island on 21 April, 1967, and BuNo 151971 having done so off the coast of California on 11 September, 1968.

The EF-111A Programme

In the late 1960s and early 1970s, the Air Force considered several possible replacements for its Douglas EB-66 electronic warfare aircraft, which were rapidly reaching the end of their potential life while continuing to fly combat missions over North Vietnam. After rejecting the development of a new type as being uneconomical in view of the small number of aircraft to be procured and finding enough justification for not acquiring yet another aircraft developed for the Navy even though it liked the capability of the EA-6B, the Air Force concluded in 1972 that the modification of some of its General Dynamic F-111As would be the most cost-effective and lowest-risk

An EF-111A prototype taking off at Calverton, New York, in 1977. (*Grumman*)

solution. However, as accommodating two additional electronic warfare officers in a modified F-111 would reduce internal capacity too much, the practicability of this solution depended on the ability of the industry to develop equipment similar to the Tactical Jamming System of the EA-6B for operation by a single electronics warfare officer.

After first expressing doubts about the feasibility of this scheme, Grumman concluded that it could be achieved through increased automation. Accordingly, the Air Force selected Grumman in December 1974 and awarded an initial $85 million contract for the modification of two F-111As (66-0041 and 66-0049) as EF-111A prototypes on 30 January, 1975.

The modifications developed by Grumman included the installation of (1) the AN/ALQ-99E Jamming Subsystem (JSS) with exciters, antennae, and other items mounted on a pallet inside the F-111 weapons bay, other components in a 16-ft ventral 'canoe' radome, and receivers in a fin-tip pod; (2) the Self-Protection Subsystem (SPS) consisting of a jamming system and a countermeasures dispensing set; and (3) the Terminal Threat Warning Subsystem (TTWS) comprised of an infrared countermeasures receiver set and an electronic countermeasures receiver set. Airframe and other systems work to be undertaken as part of the conversion programme included the reinforcement of the vertical fin to support the fin-tip pod, the installation of all-new electrical wiring, the replacement of 60 kVA generators with 90

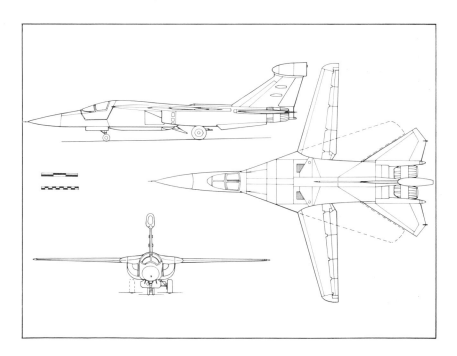

Grumman General Dynamics EF-111A Raven

491

kVA units, the fitting of an improved environmental system to cool the electronic equipment, and rearrangement of the cockpit. This last provided for the removal of flight controls from the right-hand cockpit, the relocation of the navigation equipment so that it could also be used by the pilot in the left-hand seat, and the installation in the right-hand cockpit of the controls and displays for the electronic warfare officer (EWO).

All told, the modifications resulted in empty weight being increased from 46,172 lb for the F-111A to 55,275 lb for the EF-111A. Conversely, as the EF-111A was not designed to carry weapons, its maximum take-off weight was lower than that of the F-111A (88,848 lb versus 98,850 lb). Hence, there was no need initially to replace the 10,750/18,500-lb dry/afterburning thrust Pratt & Whitney TF30-P-3 turbofans of the F-111A with more powerful engines. In 1986, however, General Dynamics was awarded a contract to install TF30-P-9s in the EF-111As.

Before working on the two EF-111A prototypes, Grumman first flew a partially-modified F-111A fitted with a mock-up of the ventral canoe in December 1975. It then proceeded with the modification of the two prototypes. When first flown at Calverton as an EF-111A on 10 March, 1977, 66-0049 was complete with fin-tip pod and ventral fairing but still lacked most of its electronic warfare equipment. The first flight of a fully-equipped EF-111A (66-0041) was made on 17 May, and this aircraft was the first to be delivered to the Air Force to be used by Detachment 3 of the Tactical Air Warfare Center for operational test and evaluation (OT&E) at Mountain Home AFB, Idaho, beginning in September 1977. Satisfactory results from the preliminary OT&E led to authorization being given for the modification of six more aircraft. Later on, the Defense Acquisition Review Council authorized the Air Force to order thirty-four additional Ravens.*

First deliveries to two operational units were respectively made in November 1981 to the 390th Electronic Combat Squadron, 366th Tactical Fighter Wing, at Mountain Home AFB, and in February 1984 to the 42nd ECS, 20th TFW, at RAF Upper Heyford. As is well known, the 20th ECS provided three EF-111As, plus two spare aircraft, to jam the Libyan radar network during Operation *Eldorado Canyon* on 14-15 April, 1986. In 1988, the US-based 390th ECS continues to function both as a Replacement Training Unit and an operational squadron ready for immediate deployment overseas. The 42nd ECS, which is assigned to USAFE and based at RAF Upper Heyford to benefit from the maintenance facility of the 20th TFW which is equipped with F-111Es, is now reporting to the 66th Electronic Combat Wing at Sembach AB, West Germany.

The Avionics Modernization Programme

Under an Air Force contract awarded in January 1987, Grumman and TRW Inc, have developed Avionics Modernization Program (AMP) kits

---

* Although Raven is the officially adopted name for the EF-111A, the aircraft is frequently, but unofficially, nicknamed *Spark 'vark* by Air Force personnel as it is the electronic warfare version of the F-111 Aardvark.

with enhanced terrain-following and navigation radars, ring laser gyro INS and global positioning system, two digital computers, improved cockpit displays, and upgraded communication systems. Expected to improve significantly the reliability and maintainability of older F-111s, the AMP kit was first fitted to an F-111A (67-0050) which after modification flew at Calverton on 20 May, 1988. An AMP kit was first installed in an EF-111A (66-0018) in January 1989. Following additional flight tests at Calverton and at the Sacramento Air Logistics Center, McClellan AFB, California, Grumman AMP kits will be fitted to 157 F-111As, F-111Es, and EF-111As. Moreover, Grumman has responded to an Air Force RFP to modernize the F-111Ds and F-111F in a like manner, but contractor selection had not been made at the beginning of 1989.

PRODUCTION: Grumman built seven F-111Bs between 1965 and 1969 and converted forty-two F-111As to EF-111A standard between 1975 and 1985. They were assigned the following BuNos and Air Force serial numbers:

F-111B: BuNos 151970/151974 & 152714/152715
EF-111A: (AF 66-0013/66-0016, 66-0018/66-0021,
             66-0023,66-0027/66-0028, 66-0030/66-0031,
             66-0033,66-0035/66-0039, 66-0041, 66-0044,
             66-0046/66-0051,66-0055/66-0057, 67-0032/67-0035,
             67-0037/67-0039,67-0041/67-0042, 67-0044, 67-0048,
             & 67-0052)

	F-111B	EF-111A
DIMENSIONS:		
Span [wings swept forward], ft in	70 0	63 0
(m)	(21.34)	(19.20)
Span [wings swept back], ft in	33 11	31 11½
(m)	(10.34)	(9.74)
Length, ft in	68 10	76 0
(m)	(20.98)	(23.16)
Height [wings swept back], ft in	16 8	20 0
(m)	(5.08)	(6.10)
Wing area, sq ft	550	525
(sq m)	(51.10)	(48.77)
WEIGHTS:		
Empty, lb	46,500	55,275
(kg)	(21,092)	(25,072)
Loaded, lb	72,421	70,000
(kg)	(32,850)	(31,751)
Maximum, lb	86,563	88,948
(kg)	(39,264)	(40,346)
Wing loading,* lb/sq ft	131.7	133.3
(kg/sq m)	(642.8)	(651.0)
Power loading,* lb/lb st	2.0	1.9
(kg/kgp)	(2.0)	(1.9)
PERFORMANCE:		
Max speed, mph/ft	1,450/40,000	1,377/40,000
(kmh/m)	(2,333/12,190)	(2,216/12,190)

Cruising speed, mph	483	584
(kmh)	(777)	(940)
Climb rate, ft/min	21,300/1	11,000/1
(m/sec)	(108)	(56)
Service ceiling, ft	44,900	45,000
(m)	(13,685)	(13,715)
Normal range, miles	1,092	929
(km)	(1,755)	(1,495)
Max range, miles	3,178	–
(km)	(5,115)	(–)

* Wing and power loadings are calculated at normal loaded weight and maximum take-off power.

The first Gulfstream II with the ex-Nicaraguan G-23 repainted in the markings once applied to an FF-1 of VF-5B. (*Grumman*)

Grumman G-1159 Gulfstream II

Following the debut of business jets, and especially the Lockheed JetStar and North American Sabreliner, which respectively obtained their FAA Type Approvals in August 1961 and March 1962, Grumman experienced progressively more difficulties in selling the propeller-turbine Gulfstream Is, as business jets were proving significantly faster on sectors of 1,000 miles or more. Within the company, however, the advisability of launching a jet-powered successor to the Gulfstream I was hotly debated, with some pointing out that if Grumman was to stay in the executive aircraft market it would have to take the plunge while others were concerned by the fact that production of the propeller-turbine-powered business aircraft was far from having reached the break-even point and appeared even doubtful of ever doing so.

Existing and prospective customers were canvassed. By 1964, their answers clearly pointed to the need for designing a jet-powered successor to the Gulfstream I if the company was to remain competitive. Key design parameters developed as a result of this market survey included: (1) spacious accommodation similar to that of the Gulfstream I; (2) capability of flying from New York to Los Angeles (2,444 miles) against considerable headwinds and with fuel reserves and alternate airport requirements as specified by the technical committee of the National Business Aircraft Association; and (3) cruising speed of Mach 0.83 at altitudes of up to 43,000 ft.

The resulting Design 1159 retained much of the fuselage of the propeller-turbine Design 159 and, like that aircraft, was fitted with dual nose and mainwheels. New wings, with 25 degrees of sweep at quarter-chord, and swept T-tail surfaces were designed. Power was to be provided by two 11,400-lb thrust Rolls-Royce Spey Mk 511-8 turbofans mounted in pods on each side of the rear fuselage. After detail specifications and performance guarantees were circulated to prospective customers in late 1964 and early 1965, Grumman was able to secure enough firm orders to announce its commitment to the Gulfstream II programme on 5 May, 1965.

Once the go-ahead decision had been made, Grumman proceeded rapidly and wholeheartedly with the design and manufacture of the first Gulfstream II. Registered N801GA, c/n 001 was completed only sixteen months after the programme had been finalised and was first flown at Bethpage by Bob Smyth and Carl Alber on 2 October, 1966. Three more aircraft, first flown respectively on 6 January, 3 July, and 1 October, 1967, were used in the test programme, which culminated on 19 October with the issue of the FAA Type Approval. Trials had gone exceptionally well and when deliveries began in December 1967, Grumman could proudly claim that the Gulfstream II was meeting or exceeding all performance guarantees. Notably, cruising speed had been increased from Mach 0.83 to Mach 0.85 and FAR take-off and landing field lengths had been reduced respectively by 7.5 per cent (to 4,070 ft) and 12 per cent (to 3,080 ft).

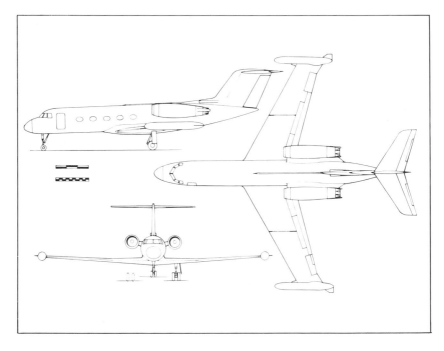

Grumman G-1159 Gulfstream II

496

Production history

The first seven Gulfstream IIs were built in Bethpage; c/n 008 became the first to be completed in Georgia in the new purpose-built plant leased from the City of Savannah and the Savannah Airport Commision. The first Savannah-built aircraft flew on 17 December, 1967, and was delivered for outfitting to Qualitron Aero on 26 February, 1968. Thereafter, Gulfstream IIs were built both in Bethpage and Savannah until c/n 040, which first flew on 12 December, 1968, became the last to be built in the Long Island plant. Thereafter until c/n 121, which was delivered for outfitting by Page on 17 December, 1972, all Gulfstream IIs were produced in Georgia by Grumman Aerospace Corporation. The next 106 Gulfstream IIs were delivered from the same plant by a new subsidiary, Grumman American Aviation Corporation. Following Grumman's sale of its 80 per cent interest in this profitable subsidiary, the Gulfstream IIs built in Georgia beginning with c/n 228 were products of the newly organized Gulfstream American Corporation. C/n 258, the 256th and last Gulfstream II, was completed at the end of 1979 and delivered by Gulfstream American in March 1980.

As it had done with the Gulfstream Is, Grumman, and later Grumman American and Gulfstream American, delivered Gulfstream IIs in 'green' condition to outfitters,* such as Aero Industries, AiResearch, Atlantic Aviation, Executive Aircraft, Executive Air Service, Associated Air Center, Associated Radio, Little Rock Airmotive, Marshalls of Cambridge, Pacific Aviation, Page Gulfstream, Qualitron Aero, Trans Aero, Western Commander/The Jet Center, etc, which installed cabin furnishings† and some of the customers' specified avionics.

Very few modifications were introduced during the course of production. Those of any significance were (1) the installation of hush kits which markedly reduced engine noise, thus enabling the aircraft to be certificated under new FAR Part 28 and Part 36 regulations; (2) the fitting of tip tanks increasing fuel capacity from 3,585 to 4,123 US gal and range by about 400 nm; and (3) the factory installation of modern avionics. The hush kits were certificated in May 1975 and were fitted during production beginning with c/n 166. Virtually all earlier Gulfstream IIs were retrofitted with these kits. Mock-up tanks were first mounted on c/n 103 in 1975 and actual tanks were first tried on c/n 173 in March 1976. Tests, however, revealed the need for a major redesign of the tanks, a wing strake, and a fillet in order to eliminate shock-induced airflow separation at the wingtips. The modified tanks were retrofitted to c/n 173 in December 1976, and this installation was certificated the following year. Thereafter, partial provision for the

---

* For delivery to outfitters, the aircraft were normally given registration numbers in the N801GA to N892GA range, with several of these numbers being used more than once. Permanent registration numbers were painted on the aircraft by the outfitters before delivery to clients. For export deliveries, registration numbers N17581 to N17589 were used before application of foreign registrations.

† According to customers requirements, accommodation was provided for a crew of two to three and for eight to nineteen passengers.

installation of tanks was incorporated during production beginning with c/n 180, while c/n 198 and subsequent aircraft were delivered with all tip-tank fittings. Planned as part of the development programme for the Gulfstream III, the installation of modern avionics (Collins or Sperry dual flight director systems and Collins or RCA weather radar) was first tested in 1978 with c/n 220 and was incorporated during production starting with c/n 239.

All but one of the Gulfstream IIs were built for private customers or for civil government agencies in the United States and abroad. The exception was c/n 023 which was built as VIP/staff transport for the US Coast Guard. This aircraft*, designated VC-11A in the US military designation system and, numbered USCG 01, was delivered in July 1968.

Planning for the development of an advanced version of the Gulfstream II or a successor to that aircraft began in the mid-1970s, when the world's economy was reeling under the combined impacts of the energy crisis and rampant inflation. Notwithstanding this poor timing, in November 1976 Grumman announced its intention to develop the Gulfstream III and indicated that a prototype would be flying in late 1979, and that deliveries would begin a year later. The new business jet was to use a fuselage similar to that of the Gulfstream II, with length increased by 4 ft and a more streamlined nose and windshield, and was to be powered by more powerful Spey turbofans. The new aircraft, however, was to have much better performance as the result of the use of entirely new supercritical wings of much greater span and reduced drag.

During 1977, fast rising costs forced a reappraisal of the programme and finally forced Grumman to terminate development of this new design. In its place, the company announced in April 1978 a more modest Gulfstream III programme based more closely on the Gulfstream II. Gone was the new wing design, as the new Gulfstream III was to use the wings of the existing aircraft with the addition of winglets. The not-so-drastic recontouring of the forward fuselage as proposed earlier was retained but the increase in fuselage length was limited to a more modest 2 ft. However, before much work was done on this derivative design, Grumman sold its subsidiary and the development of the Gulfstream III became a Gulfstream American project.

Although Grumman retained design responsibility under the terms of the sales agreement, details of the Gulfstream III are not part of the Grumman history. Suffice it to say that components being built for the 249th and 252nd Gulfstream IIs were used for the first two Gulfstream IIIs; hence c/ns 249 and 252 are not included in the Gulfstream II production list. The Gulfstream III first flew on 2 December, 1979, and during the following year the new aircraft replaced the Gulfstream II on the Savannah production line of the Gulfstream American Corporation.

---

* WASHINGTON, as applied on the fuselage side beneath the cockpit, is not an individual aircraft name, as has been occasionally stated. Rather, the VC-11A, like other Coast Guard aircraft, has the name of the station to which it is assigned painted on its nose.

In addition to building new Gulfstream IIIs, Gulfstream American has gone ahead with earlier Grumman plans to offer a retrofit programme to modify Gulfstream IIs to the standards of the new aircraft. The first modified aircraft was c/n 70 which first flew as a Gulfstream IIB. Other aircraft modified as Gulfstream IIBs include c/ns 004, 016, 030, 032, 036, 042, 073, 075, 104, 139, 148, and 775.*

Service history

The first Gulfstream II to go to a customer was c/n 005, which was handed over to National Distillers and Chemical Corporation on 6 January, 1968. Five months later, this aircraft became the first Gulfstream II to cross the Atlantic nonstop when it covered the 3,500 miles between Teterboro, New Jersey, and London-Gatwick in 6 hr 55 min.

In their intended role as 'top-of-the-line' executive jets, Gulfstream IIs have been and are being operated by many of the world's largest business organizations (such as American Express, Aramco, Banco de Mexico, Bank of America, Coca Cola, Eastman Kodak, Exxon, General Motors, IBM, Lonhro Ltd, Rockwell International, and Shell), by executive charter organizations (eg, Associated Airlines Pty, Chartair Ltd, Interjet AG, PT Pelita Air Service, Private Jet Services, and Saudi Arabian Airlines), and wealthy individuals (eg, Prince Karim Aga Khan, Dan H Baman, Paul Mellon, and Sheik H Y Al Khureiji). Virtually never making the headlines, as their owners prefer to keep a low profile, privately-operated Gulfstream IIs have compiled outstanding reliability and safety records.

Governmental uses and projected uses have ranged from the exotic (ie,

N827GA, c/n 80, of Pittsburgh Plate Glass Industries inc, at the San Francisco International Airport in 1974. (René J Francillon)

* C/n 775 is the 75th Gulfstream II built by Grumman which was used as a demonstrator for over two years before being sold to Gulf and Western Industries in 1972. The odd constructor's number was used to avoid upsetting customers who were to get aircraft out of sequence. Later, to restore order in the chronological sequence, c/n 087 was not used. Thus, c/ns 75 to 086 were in fact the seventy-sixth to eighty-seventh aircraft off the line, whereas c/n 088 was indeed the eighty-eighth Gulfstream II.

The ninety-fifth Gulfstream II was delivered to Associated Airlines, Pty in March 1971. It was photographed at Perth shortly afterwards. (*Mervyn W Prime, courtesy of Alain Pelletier*)

An artist's rendering of the proposed QUESTOL research aircraft. (*Grumman*)

NASA's alphabet soup: QUESTOL, STA, and PTA), to the functional (*eg*, checking airways navigation aids), to the luxurious (presidential and VIP transports in use in several countries).

NASA first showed interest in the Gulfstream II in December 1971, when Grumman, as prime contractor, and Boeing, as sub-contractor, were awarded a $1.5 million design study contract for the Quiet Engine Experimental STOL (QUESTOL). A competitive contract was awarded at the same time to McDonnell Douglas, a de Havilland Canada/Cornell Laboratories team, and a Lockheed/North American/Bell team. Intended as a technology demonstrator, the Grumman G-612 (designated G-159N during the proposal phase) QUESTOL was to have employed a Gulfstream II fuselage mated to new shoulder-mounted augmentor wings. Four General Electric TF34 turbofans were to have been situated beneath the wings and modified F-14 main undercarriage units were to have been housed in blisters on the fuselage sides. The G-612 did not proceed past the design study phase as NASA awarded a contract to Boeing for the modification of a de Havilland Canada DHC-8 as the Quiet Short-Haul Research Aircraft (QSRA).

After failing to get its QUESTOL accepted by NASA, Grumman succeeded in getting two highly modified Gulfstream IIs into the NASA fleet. These Shuttle Training Aircraft (STAs) were developed to simulate realistically the approach and landing characteristics of the Space Shuttle Orbiter. To achieve this goal, the two aircraft (c/ns 146 and 147, which respectively became NASA 916 and 917 and were registered N916NA and N917NA) were fitted with aerodynamic controls to provide complete and independent control of each translational and rotational motion. Special direct-lift flaps were installed to control lift, side-force surfaces were added beneath the aircraft to control lateral acceleration, and inflight thrust reversers were provided to simulate the unpowered Shuttle Orbiter by increasing drag. A computer system was developed to control surfaces and engines in such a way that the STA would respond with the same motion as predicted for the Shuttle Orbiter. The cockpit was also modified with the training pilot sitting on the left and provided with standard controls and the astronaut trainee sitting on the right and using controls similar to those of the Shuttle Orbiter.

Built in Savannah in the standard configuration, both aircraft were modified in Bethpage where the first flight in STA configuration was made on 29 September, 1975. The Shuttle Training Aircraft were then assigned to the Lyndon B. Johnson Space Center in Houston, Texas. However, most training flights have been and are being flown at Holloman AFB, New Mexico, or Edwards AFB, California.

The most recent NASA use of the Gulfstream II, the Propfan Test Assessment (PTA) aircraft, has seen Lockheed-Georgia, in association with Detroit-Allison (engines), Gulfstream Aerospace (airframe modifications and powerplant installation), Hamilton Standard (propfan system), Lockheed-California (acoustic instrumentation), and Rohr Industries (nacelle design and ground testing), modify a Grumman-designed aircraft (N650PF) as a test-bed for a propeller fan (propfan) installation. Retaining its fuselage-mounted Spey turbofans, the PTA demonstrator was fitted with a 6,000-shp Allison 501-M78 turboshaft engine on the port wing. In this form, it first flew on 19 May, 1967, as part of a test programme sponsored by NASA's Lewis Research Center in Cleveland, Ohio.

Apart from NASA and the Coast Guard, the only US Government agency to have operated Gulfstream IIs is the Corps of Engineers, which acquired c/n 045 on the second-hand market.

Abroad, past and present Gulfstream II operators include the govern-

NASA 946, c/n 146, one of the two Shuttle Training Aircraft. *(Grumman)*

The VC-11A VIP transport operated by the US Coast Guard, at the Reno Airport, Nevada, on 16 July, 1988. *(Peter B Lewis)*

ments of Bahrain (Amiri Flight), Cameroun, Canada (Department of Transport), Gabon, Ivory Coast, Japan (Civil Aviation Board, c/n 141, for airways checking), Kuwait, Libya, Morocco (Royal Moroccan Air Force), Nigeria (Nigerian Air Force), Papua New Guinea, Saudi Arabia (Ministry of Defence and Aviation, c/n 179, for airways checking), Uganda, and the United Arab Emirates.

PRODUCTION: A total of 256 aircraft was built, including 121 delivered by Grumman between October 1966 and December 1972, 106 delivered by

Grumman American between January 1973 and August 1978, and 29 delivered by Gulfstream American between September 1978 and March 1980. These aircraft were given the following c/ns:

Gulfstream II:	253	(c/ns 001/022, 024/086, 088/145, 148/248, 250/251, 253/258, and 775)
Gulfstream II STA:	2	(c/ns 146 and 147)
VC-11A:	1	(c/n 023, USCG 01)

Span without tip tanks 68 ft 10 in (20.98 m); span with tip tanks 71 ft 9 in (21.87 m); length 79 ft 11 in (24.36 m); height 24 ft 6 in (7.47 m); wing area 809.6 sq ft (75.21 sq m).

Empty weight 30,363 lb (13,772 kg); maximum weight 65,500 lb (29,710 kg); wing loading 80.9 lb/sq ft (395.0 kg/sq m); power loading 2.9 lb/lb st (2.9 kg/kg st).

Maximum cruising speed 581 mph at 25,000 ft (935 kmh at 7,620 m); economical cruising speed 483 mph at 43,000 ft (777 kmh at 13,105 m); climb rate 4,140 ft/min (21 m/sec); service ceiling 43,000 ft (13,105 m); normal range 3,292 miles (5,295 km); maximum range (with tip tanks) 4,276 miles (6,880 km).

A Grumman American Tiger at the Mojave Airport on 19 August, 1987. *(René J Francillon)*

Grumman American AA-5, Cheetah and Tiger

Development of an enlarged version of the AA-1 to accommodate a pilot and three passengers was inititiated by American Aviation in 1970, and the prototype first flew on 21 August, 1970, in Cleveland, Ohio. Closely ressembling its two-seat forebear, the AA-5 was also a low-wing monoplane with a non-retractable undercarriage and access to the fully enclosed cabin by means of a rearward sliding canopy. The four-seater was certificated in November 1971. During the following year American Aviation produced 154 aircraft in two variants, the standard AA-5 and the de luxe Traveler. The powerplant for both versions was the 150-hp Lycoming O-320-E2G flat-four engine driving a two-blade propeller.

Under the aegis of Grumman American Corporation, production of the AA-5 and Traveler continued in Cleveland between 1973 and 1975. In 1975, however, Grumman switched to four new variants which were certificated in July 1975 and featured redesigned engine cowling and tail surfaces (with tailplane span increased from 8 ft 8 in to 12 ft 8 in. Still powered by 150-hp O-320-E2Gs, the AA-5A and Cheetah were the standard and de luxe versions of the improved four-seater. The AA-5B and Tiger were standard and de luxe versions powered by the 180-hp Lycoming O-360-A4K and having integral fuel tanks of increased capacity (52.6 US gal versus 38 gal).

The AA-5A, Cheetah, AA-5B, and Tiger versions remained in production in Savannah, Georgia, after the Grumman American production line was taken over by Gulfstream American Corporation.

In 1973, as part of a collaboration agreement with Rhein-Flugzeugbau GmbH which had been entered into by American Aviation, Grumman had

504

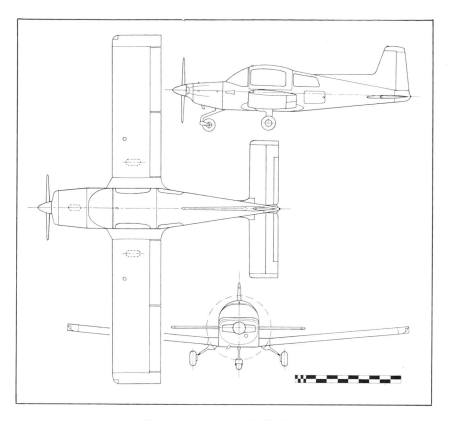

Grumman American AA-5B Tiger

supplied a set of AA-5 wings and a tailplane for incorporation in the Fanliner, which the German firm built as a low-cost demonstrator for its ducted fan Fantrainer. For a while Grumman American retained an interest in the Fantrainer but, after the organization of Gulfstream American in 1978, co-operation between the two firms ended as Gulfstream American intended to offer its own Peregrine in the Air Force Next Generation Trainer (NGT) competition.

PRODUCTION: During the Grumman American years, 597 AA-5s and Travelers (234 in 1973, 233 in 1974, and 130 in 1975), 882 AA-5Bs and Tigers (9 in 1974, 196 in 1975, 193 in 1976, 290 in 1977, and 194 through August 1978), and 650 AA-5Cs and Cheetahs (73 in 1975, 210 in 1976, 235 in 1977, and 132 through August 1978) were built.

Specifications (AA-5B):
Span 31 ft in (9.60 m); length 22 ft (6.71 m); height 7 ft 8 in (2.34 m); wing area 140 sq ft (13.01 sq m).

Empty weight 1,200 lb (544 kg); loaded weight 2,400 lb (1,089 kg); wing loading 17.1 lb/sq ft (83.7 kg/sq m); power loading 13.3 lb/hp (6.1 kg/hp).

Max speed 170 mph (274 kmh) at sea level; cruising speed 160 mph (257 kmh); rate of climb at sea level 850 ft/min (4.3 m/sec); service ceiling 13,800 ft (4,205 m); normal range at 75 per cent power 752 miles (1,210 km); max range 800 miles (1,2855 km).

An F-14A of VF-32 with a full load of Phoenix missiles. *(Grumman)*

Grumman F-14 Tomcat

Currently considered by many to be the most glamorous aircraft in the United States inventory, and riding high on its cinematographic fame, the Tomcat is indeed a very capable aircraft in the Fleet Air Defense (FAD) and Deck-Launched Intercept (DLI) roles for which its powerful radar and long-range missiles are unmatched weapons systems. In the air superiority and escort roles, the F-14 is hailed by its proponents for its exceptional dogfighting capability, but is faulted by its critics for its large size, which makes it more easily detected than smaller fighters optimized for this role. Notwithstanding its size, however, the Tomcat, especially in its F-14A (Plus) version, remains a remarkable dogfighter.

By the late summer of 1967, it was becoming clear to Grumman that it would be next to impossible to reduce the weight of the General Dynamics F-111B anywhere close to what was needed to make the aircraft acceptable for carrier operations. For the company, the likely rejection of this aircraft by the Navy portended serious difficulties. Already, the curtailed procurement of its F11F Tiger in 1959, coming as it did after the loss of its Design 97 to the Vought F8U Crusader in 1953 and of its Design 118 to the McDonnell F4H Phantom II in 1955, had left it in a dire situation as, since 1931, carrier-based fighters had been the mainstay of its business. Accordingly, Grumman management decided that no efforts should be spared to win a design competition if, or rather when, the Navy cancelled the F-111B and issued a request for proposals for a new fighter. Supplementing limited Navy funding for VFX fighter studies with a substantial amount of its own money, Grumman initiated conceptual work on Design 303 in anticipation of the RFP.

When initiating work on Design 303, the team led by Michael Pelehach sought to develop an aircraft combining the F-111B aptitude in the FAD role with capabilities superior to those of the McDonnell F-4 in the Other Fighter Roles (the so-called OFRs include air superiority, escort, and deck-launched interception). The design team thus retained the best features of the F-111B, namely its AN/AWG-9 track-while-scan radar, Phoenix long-range missiles, variable geometry, and powerplant installation (two TF30 turbofans*), and combined them with those most often praised by Navy F-4 crews with combat experience in Vietnam, specifically tandem seating and a mix of Sparrow semi-active radar homing missiles and Sidewinder heat-seeking missiles. Moreover, the team decided to improve on both the F-111B and the F-4J by adding an internal cannon and by separating the engines to minimize the risk of both being damaged simultaneously as the result of accident or battle damage.

Naval Air Systems Command (NAVAIR), which had conducted its own concept formulation studies since it had been organized to succeed BuWeps, shared Grumman's belief that a fighter aircraft much better than the F-111B could be developed. Hence, when Congress refused to approve

View of BuNo 158613, showing details of the glove fitted on the port wing during laminar flow visualization experiments at Edwards AFB, California, in 1986-87. (*NASA, courtesy of Grumman X-29A team*)

---

* In service, however, the Pratt & Whitney TF30 proved to be far from satisfactory, but plans to re-engine production versions of the Tomcat did not bear fruit until 1988, when the F-14A(Plus) powered by General Electric F110 turbofans was first delivered to VF-101.

further funding for the F-111B in May 1968, the Navy wasted no time and, on 18 June, it issued a request for Contract Definition Phase (CDP) proposals. Key parameters specified in the RFP were tandem crew accommodation, two TF30 turbofans, track-while-scan long-range radar, and armament consisting of gun and long-, medium-, and short-range missiles. Moving swiftly to fill the void left by the cancellation of the F-111B, Grumman and four other contractors submitted letter proposals on 21 June. NAVAIR awarded CDP contracts to the five manufacturers on 17 July and short-listed Grumman and McDonnell on 15 December. Grumman was announced the winner of the VFX competition on 14 January, 1969, and was awarded a research, development, test, and evaluation (RDT&E) contract on 3 February.

As could be expected, between the time it had started work on Design 303 during the autumn of 1967 and the receipt of the RDT&E contract in February 1969, Grumman had studied numerous configurations with fixed or variable-sweep wings, single or twin vertical tail surfaces, and podded or fuselage-mounted engines. The winning twin-tailed Design 303E with engines in separate nacelles was characterized by its variable-geometry wings which not only featured variable sweep (programmed automatically with manual override to change sweep from a minimum of 20 degrees for take-off, loiter, and landing operations* to a maximum of 68 degrees for low drag at transonic and supersonic speeds, and set manually to 75 degrees for carrier stowage) but also included glove vanes† and manoeuvring slats and flaps. Also notable was the extensive use of steel, titanium (including the 22-ft wing pivot beam), and composite materials (the horizontal stabilizer skin became the first boron-epoxy composite structure used in a production aircraft).

During 1969, work on the F-14 gained momentum with the configuration being finalized in March, the mock-up reviewed in May, fabrication started in June, and testing of the critical wing-pivot completed in November. During the following year, Grumman submitted a proposal for the re-engined F-14B in February and completed the first F-14A in November. First flown at Calverton by Robert Smyth and William Miller on 21 December, 1970, BuNo 157980 was lost at the end of its second flight on 30

---

* Even though the variable-sweep mechanism was never a problem with the XF10F-1 or the F-111B before the first flight of the F-14, or since then with the F-14 itself, or later with the Panavia Tornado and the Rockwell B-1, concern has long been expressed regarding the potentially catastrophic result from asymmetric wing sweep. To alleviate this fear, tests were finally conducted at Calverton where the third F-14A (BuNo 157982) was flown six times by Chuck Sewell between 19 December, 1985, and 28 February, 1986, with the right wing locked at 20 degrees and the left wing positioned in flight at 35 degrees, 50 degrees, 60 degrees, and 68 degrees. Landings were made with the left wing at a maximum of 60 degrees sweep, with Sewell finding the aircraft acceptable for carrier operations.

---

† These small canard surfaces are incorporated in the leading edge of the glove area, forward of the wings and are extended automatically at supersonic speeds to control centre-of-pressure shift. Glove vanes are not fitted to the F-14A(Plus) and F-14D versions.

Chuck Sewell flying the third F-14A (BuNo 157982) during asymmetric trials in the winter of 1985. *(Grumman)*

December. Fortunately, the crew ejected safely and the cause of the accident, a hydraulic failure, neither took long to be determined nor required a major redesign. Tests resumed on 24 May, 1971, with the first flight of BuNo 157981 and, thereafter, proceeded at a rapid pace with seven additional aircraft flying before the end of that year. The first Naval Preliminary Evaluation (NPE) was undertaken in December 1971 and BuNo 158613 was used for the initial carrier trials aboard the USS *Forrestal* (CVA-59) in June 1972.

Armament trials resulted in an unusual accident during a flight from the Naval Missile Center Point Mugu, California, when BuNo 157985 shot itself down on 20 June, 1973. Apparently, a Sparrow missile which had been launched while the aircraft was flying at 700 mph and at an altitude of 5,000 ft failed to clear properly and struck the fuselage. The two crewmen ejected and were picked up by an SAR helicopter.

Testing of the all-important AIM-54 missile on which the Tomcat was to rely for engaging several targets simultaneously at long range began in earnest on 28 April, 1972, when a Phoenix was first launched from an F-14A flying from NMC Point Mugu. During a later test, a Phoenix hit a target which had been flying at a distance of 126 miles when the missile was launched. Full-load launch was first demonstrated on 21 November, 1973, when an F-14A operating over the Pacific Missile Range off Point Mugu demonstrated for the first time the Tomcat's ability to fire six Phoenix missiles and guide them simultaneously to six separate targets 50 miles away. On that occasion, however the targets neither used countermeasures

510

The Phoenix Missile System test aircraft at NAS Point Mugu, California, in 1973. *(Peter J Mancus)*

nor made violent evasive manoeuvres, thus enabling four direct hits to be made. Final approval for AIM-54A service use was given on 28 January, 1975.

Production history

Contracts for twelve prototypes (BuNos 157980/157991) in two lots of six aircraft were followed by fixed-price incentive contracts for 122 production F-14As and F-14Bs (twenty-six ordered under Lot III during Fiscal Year 1971, and forty-eight in both Lot IV in FY72 and Lot V in FY73). However, as the inflation rate increased much faster than had been foreseen when the price was calculated before contract award, and as the company's overheads were much greater as the result of a reduction in its activities, Grumman began losing heavily on each F-14 delivered at the fixed price and was forced to refuse building Lot V aircraft under unfavourable contract terms. Following difficult negotiations, the Navy and Congress conceded that future contracts would be priced on the basis of current estimated costs and Grumman agreed to complete Lot V under the previously agreed terms. Additional contracts brought deliveries by the end of 1988 to a total of 656 Tomcats in the versions below:

F-14A: The first Tomcat (BuNo 157980) flew on 21 December, 1970, and the 556th and last F-14A (BuNo 162711) was delivered on 31 March 1987. Thirty-two of these aircraft have been modified to the F-14A(Plus) configuration and more than 300 may eventually be modified as F-14Ds.

From the onset, air-to-air missiles supplementing the internally-mounted 20-mm M61A-1 cannon have been carried beneath the fuselage (four AIM-54 Phoenix missiles on pallets or four AIM-7 Sparrow missiles in recesses) and on one pylon beneath each inboard wing section (each for one AIM-54 or for one AIM-7 and one AIM-9, or for two AIM-9 Sidewinder missiles). Depending on mission requirements, the F-14A carries either one, two, or all three types of missiles. Although provision was made in the

511

F-14A (BuNo 162604) of VF-2 aboard the uss *Ranger* (CV-61), moored by the San Francisco-Oakland Bay Bridge during Fleet Week in October 1988. *(Peter B Lewis)*

design for the carriage of up to 14,500 lb of air-to-ground weapons, so far the aircraft has only been used in the air-to-air role.

Mounted in widely separated nacelles, the two Pratt & Whitney TF30 turbofans have been the source of considerable difficulty and engine-related problems have been the primary cause of F-14A accidents. Two 12,350/20,900-lb dry/afterburning thrust TF30-P-412As initially powered the F-14As but, beginning in 1983, these unreliable engines were replaced by similarly-rated TF30-P-414As. Five internal tanks with a combined capacity of 2,385 US gal, are supplemented by a 267-gal external tank attached beneath each air intake, and a retractable inflight refuelling probe is mounted on the starboard side of the fuselage forward of the cockpit.

The main improvement introduced during the course of production and retrofitted to earlier aircraft has been the fitting of a Northrop television camera set (TCS) beneath the nose. This electro-optical system, which underwent Navy testing in 1979-80 and has been adopted only for the Tomcat, automatically searches for, acquires, and locks onto distant targets. It generates TV images for display on monitors in the two cockpits.

When the need to replace unarmed North American RA-5Cs and LTV RF-8Gs arose in the mid-1970s, the Navy decided not to acquire specialized photographic-reconnaissance aircraft but rather to fund the development of a reconnaissance pod for the F-14. This Tactical Air Reconnaissance Pod System (TARPS) was first mounted slightly right of the centreline beneath BuNo 160696, on Phoenix station No. 5, and was tested at NATC Patuxent River in 1979. Since then, six prototypes and forty-eight production pods have been delivered and forty-nine F-14As (TARPS) have been specially wired (the first of which was BuNo160910). The modified Tomcats can

512

either be used as fighters with standard F-14 armament or in the reconnaissance role with TARPS; when carrying the photo pod, they retain their gun and can carry a Sparrow and a Sidewinder on each of the wing pylons. TARPS, which has a length of 207.5 in and weighs 1,650 lb, houses a KS-87B forward or vertical frame camera, a KA-99 low-altitude panoramic camera, and an AN/AAD-5 infrared reconnaisance set.

The only export customer, Iran, ordered eighty Tomcats in two batches. With the exception of the omission of some sensitive electronic counter-measures systems, the Iranian F-14As were nearly identical to those built for the US Navy and were delivered with the powerful AN/AWG-9 radar and Phoenix, Sidewinder, and Sparrow missiles. The first export F-14A (BuNo 160299, Iranian serial 3-863) was the 185th Tomcat and first flew on 5 December, 1975. The last (BuNo 160378, Iranian serial 3-942) was the 367th Tomcat and was accepted by the US Navy on behalf of the Imperial Iranian Air Force on 19 July, 1978.

F-14A(Plus): The go-ahead for the interim F-14A(Plus) and the definitive F-14D programmes was given in July 1984 when Grumman was awarded a $984 million contract. Both of these versions were to be powered by 27,000-lb afterburning thrust General Electric F110-GE-400 turbofans with computerized fuel control for stall-free performance in all flight phases. In

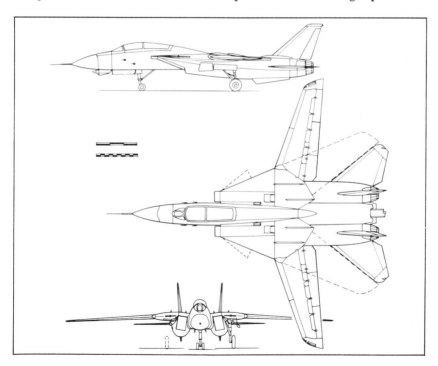

Grumman F-14A (Plus) Tomcat

513

BuNo 160696 with the TARPS pod on the Phoenix No. 5 station. (*Grumman*)

BuNo 162588, a VF-124 Tomcat at NAS Fallon, Nevada, on 12 October, 1988. *(René J Francillon)*

addition, F-14A(Plus) were to be fitted with the AN/ALR-67 threat warning and recognition system. To serve as an engine development aircraft for the two new versions, BuNo 157986, the aircraft previously used as the F-14B prototype and as a test-bed for General Electric F101 DFE turbofans, was fitted with a pair of F110-GE-400s in 1986 and flew on 29 September, 1986.

As funded, the F-14A(Plus) programme called for the manufacture of thirty-eight new aircraft and the re-engining of thirty-two F-14As. BuNo158630, the first F-14A(Plus) modified from a TF30-powered Tomcat, flew on 11 December, 1986, and BuNo 162910, the first new-built F-14A(Plus), did so on 14 November, 1987. A second new-built F-14A(Plus) was accepted in 1987, seventeen were delivered in 1988, and the remaining nineteen aircraft are to follow in 1989 and 1990. When all new-built and remanufactured Tomcats have been delivered, the Navy will have enough F-14A(Plus) to equip fully four deployable squadrons and partially a replacement training squadron, plus spares and replacements to keep these squadrons at full strength until the first decade of the twenty-first century.

F-14B: On 27 February, 1970, ten months before the first flight of the F-14A, Grumman submitted a proposal for a Tomcat version to be powered by the winner of the Advanced Technology Engine competition, whether the production version of the General Electric GE1/10 or the Pratt & Whitney JTF22. Soon afterwards the winning Pratt & Whitney F401-P-400 was selected to power F-14Bs, beginning with the sixty-seventh Tomcat, and the seventh Tomcat (BuNo 157986) was set aside to serve as the prototype. Powered by a pair of 28,000-lb afterburning thrust YP401-P-400s, this aircraft was first flown on 12 September, 1973. However, as the

The F-14B (BuNo 157986) landing at Calverton, New York, in 1973. *(Grumman)*

development of the Pratt & Whitney F401 ran into trouble and as the Navy's budget was reduced after the Southeast Asia War ended, procurement plans for the F-14B and F-14C versions were cancelled and the F-14B prototype was stored by Grumman after flying only 33 hours.

After seven years in storage, BuNo 157986 was re-engined with two 16,400/27,400-lb dry/afterburning thrust General Electric F101 DFE (Derivative Fighter Engine) turbofans. During the course of thirty-four test flights beginning on 14 July, 1981, this Super Tomcat demonstrated markedly improved and trouble-free performance, thus paving the way for the development of the F-14A(Plus) and F-14D versions, which are powered by the F110-GE-400s, the production model of the F101 DFE.

F-14C: Proposed early on, this version was to have been powered by F401-P-400s, as proposed for the F-14B, and fitted with upgraded avionic systems providing all-weather attack and reconnaissance capability. However, costs would have been quite high. Therefore, instead of proceeding with the development of the F-14C, the Navy ordered more Grumman A-6s and initiated the VFAX programme, which resulted in the McDonnell Douglas F/A-18.

F-14D: Currently under development, this upgraded version will differ from the F110-powered F-14A(Plus) in being fitted with the AN/APG-71 radar, which will markedly improve the Tomcat's ability to detect enemy aircraft using electronic countermeasures. Other approved changes include the installation of an infrared search and track sensor (IRST), an AN/ALR-67 threat warning and recognition system, an AN/ALQ-165 airborne self protection jammer (ASPJ), and the joint tactical information distribution system (JTIDS), as well as the substitution of Martin-Baker Navy Aircrew Common Ejection Seats (NACES) for the Martin-Baker GRU7A ejector seats fitted to earlier Tomcats. Additional changes to be

516

BuNo 161867 was built as an F-14A and was converted in 1988 as the first fully configured F-14D development aircraft. (*Grumman*)

incorporated as part of the Pre-deployment Update Program (PDU) include: (1) the use of sensor control mechanization to enable the radar, IRST, and TCS to scan in different areas and to perform complementary searches with any one of these sensors acting as the master; (2) the modification of the JTIDS to provide a fighter-to-fighter secure data link through which an F-14D will be able to pass targeting information to other F-14Ds flying with their radar off to avoid or delay detection; and (3) the addition of AIM-120A advanced medium-range air-to-air missiles (AMRAAMs) and AGM-88A high-speed anti-radiation missiles (HARMs) to the range of weapons available for carriage by F-14Ds.

In support of the F-14D development programme, a TF30-powered F-14A (BuNo 161865) was modified as an avionics test bed and first flew in that role on 23 November, 1987. Two other F-14As (BuNos 161867 and 162595) were fitted with the new avionics. In 1988, BuNo 161867 was also re-engined with F110-GE-400s, to become the first fully configured F-14D in the flight-test programme. The first production F-14D is scheduled to be delivered in March, 1990. In mid-1988, plans called for the Navy to procure 127 F-14Ds and to have up to 400 F-14As and F-14A(Plus)s brought up to F-14D standards. Whether Tomcat production will end with the completion of these aircraft remains to be seen, as in late 1988 and early 1989 Grumman was actively marketing a further development of the F-14, the so-called Tomcat-21, as an alternative to the proposed navalized version of the winner of the Air Force-managed Advanced Tactical Fighter (ATF) programme under which the Lockheed YF-22 or Northrop YF-23 are being developed.

517

BuNo 162912, the third new-built F-14A(Plus), assigned to VX-4 at NAS Point Mugu, California, on 9 October, 1988. *(Peter B Lewis)*

Service history

Before Tomcats were assigned in early 1973 to a Fleet Replacement Squadron, VF-124 at NAS Miramar, California, three early F-14As were delivered in the autumn of 1972 for operational evaluation (OPEVAL) by Air Development Squadron Four (VX-4) at NAS Point Mugu, California. Thereafter assignment to deployable squadrons proceeded swiftly. VF-1 and VF-2 became the first to depart on an operational cruise when they embarked on the USS *Enterprise* (CVN-65) in September 1974. On that occasion, Tomcats provided air cover during Operation *Frequent Wind*, the evacuation of Saïgon at the end of April 1975.

Over the next nine years, nearly all Navy deployable Fighter Squadrons exchanged their Phantom IIs for Tomcats.* The last to do so were VF-21 and VF-154 which converted to F-14As after returning from a final cruise with F-4Ns in September 1983. Next, two new squadrons, VF-191 and VF-194, were equipped with F-14As when they were established in December 1986, but both were disbanded in April 1988 when budget cuts led to a force reduction.† With the reserve, F-14As began replacing F-4Ss in October 1984, when VF-301 began its conversion. Tomcats now equip all four reserve Fighter Squadrons, VF-201 and VF-202 at NAS Dallas and VF-301 and VF-302 at NAS Miramar.

The first F-14A(Plus) was accepted by VF-101 at NAS Oceana, Virginia, on 11 April, 1988. Immediately, this Fleet Replacement Squadron began training aircrews and maintenance personnel for the two Atlantic Fleet and

* The exceptions are VF-151 and VF-161 which are based in Yokosuka, Japan, and deploy aboard the USS *Midway* (CV-41). These two squadrons re-equipped with F/A-18 Hornets and became Fighter Attack Squadrons.
† In 1988, the deployable Fighter Squadrons of the Atlantic Fleet were VF-11, -14, -24, -31, -33, -41, -74, -84, -102, -103, -142, and -143, all based at NAS Oceana. Those of the Pacific Fleet were VF-1, -2, -21, -24, -51, -111, -114, -154, -211, and -213 which are based at NAS Miramar. The Replacement Training Squadrons were VF-101 at Oceana and VF-124 at Miramar. The only other squadron to operate Tomcats then was VX-4 at NAS Point Mugu. In addition, F-14s were operated for tests purposes at NATC Patuxent River and other locations.

518

two Pacific Fleet deployable squadrons which will fly F110-powered Tomcats. The even more potent F-14D is scheduled to be deployed in 1993.

F-14A Tomcats have played an active role in almost all the international crises of the past ten years. In November 1979, following the taking of American hostages by Iran, those from VF-51 and VF-111 aboard the USS *Kitty Hawk* (CV-63) were among the first aircraft sent to the northern Arabian Sea. Five months later, VF-41 and VF-84 flew combat air patrols from the USS *Nimitz* (CVN-68) during the abortive hostage rescue operation. For the next eight years, Tomcats remained poised to intervene against Iran. Notably, when war between Iraq and Iran began in September 1980, F-14As from VF-142 and VF-143 aboard the USS *Dwight D. Eisenhower* (CVN-69) were sent to patrol the north of the Arabian Sea.

The most celebrated operational achievements of the Tomcat, however, have taken place over the Mediterranean and the Gulf of Sidra, not the Arabian Sea or the Arabian Gulf. When the long-simmering tension between the United States and Libya first came to a boil on 19 August, 1981, two VF-41 crews shot down two Sukhoi Su-22 *Fitters* with AIM-9L missiles after one of the Libyan fighters had launched an Atoll air-to-air missile at the lead F-14A and missed. On 10 October, 1985, Tomcats were once more on the front page of newspapers around the world when those from VF-74 and VF-103 aboard the USS *Saratoga* (CV-60) successfully intercepted the EgyptAir Boeing 737 carrying the hijackers of the cruise liner *Achille Lauro* and forced it to land at NAS Sigonella. During operations in the Gulf of Sidra in March 1986, F-14As from these two squadrons and from VF-33 and VF-102 aboard the USS *America* (CV-66) flew combat air patrols (CAP) over the battle groups, kept Libyan fighters at bay, and dodged SAMs while escorting attack aircraft during HARM strikes. On 15 April, 1986, after *Saratoga* and her squadrons left to return home, Tomcats from VF-33 and VF-102 flew CAP and escort sorties during the raid against targets in and around Benghazi. More recently, on 4 January 1989, two Libyan MiG-23

BuNo 161621, the F-14A of the *Sundowners* of VF-111 assigned to the commander of Air Wings, photographed at NAS Fallon, Nevada, on 21 June, 1989. *(René J Francillon)*

Flogger Es were shot down by Tomcats from the USS *John F. Kennedy* (CV-67).

After being tested at NATC Patuxent River, TARPS-configured Tomcats were assigned in 1980 to VF-124 for training and to VF-213 for deployment. Since then, the second squadron in each Carrier Air Wing has deployed with two of its F-14As configured for carrying TARPS. This was notably the case in 1983 when VF-32 flew TARPS sorties over Grenada in October and over Lebanon in December while deployed aboard the USS *Independence* (CV-62). In the latter operation, AAA and missiles were fired at TARPS aircraft flying over Syrian and Druze positions in the Bekaa Valley, prompting President Regan to order retaliatory air strikes.

Although Marine Fighter Squadrons were to have replaced their Phantom IIs with Tomcats, this scheme was soon dropped. Thus, the only other user of the F-14 in the United States has been the National Aeronautics and Space Administration. After taking part in the high-speed phase of the contractor's flight-test programme as a replacement for the first prototype, BuNo 157991 was released from the Navy to NASA's Dryden Flight Research Center in 1979. Until returned to the Navy in 1987, NASA 991 was used for a variety of purposes including spin and high-angle-of-attack testing, for which it was fitted with 2 ft by 6 ft retractable canard surfaces on the nose and, later, an automatic rudder interconnect (ARI) system. After its return to the Navy, BuNo 157991 was fitted with two paddle-shaped yaw vanes between the engines to simulate future yaw and

The nose of BuNo 157991 with the retractable canard surfaces installed before this Tomcat was used by NASA's Dryden Flight Research Center for high-angle-attack tests. *(Grumman)*

thrust vectoring systems during trials at the Naval Air Test Center. Another F-14A, BuNo 158613, was released from the Navy in 1986-87 and used at the Dryden Flight Research Center for a NASA laminar flow visualization research programme for which wing gloves were added to smooth the airflow over the wings.

In Iranian service, the Tomcat has had a far less happy service career. Ordered by the Shah in a move dictated in part by concern over Soviet MiG-25 overflights and in part by his delusions of grandeur, eighty F-14As

Having previously served as the F-14B prototype and as a test-bed for General Electric F101 DFE turbofans, the seventh Tomcat (BuNo 157986) was instrumented for structural test work and still used by Grumman in 1988. (*Grumman*)

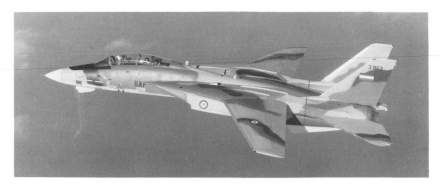

The first Iranian Tomcat (IIAF serial 3-863, BuNo 160299) over the Atlantic before delivery.
(Grumman)

were accepted by the US Navy on behalf of the Imperial Iranian Air Force (IIAF) between December 1975 and July 1978. With the exception of BuNo160378 which was impounded by the US Government and placed in storage at Davis-Monthan AFB, all Iranian F-14As had been put into service at Isfahan Khatami and Shiraz before the Shah was overthrown in January 1979. Although many ex-IIAF pilots fled the country rather than serve under the revolutionary regime, none did so in an F-14 and all seventy-nine Tomcats were absorbed into the newly organized Islamic Republic Iranian Air Force (IRIAF). However, the departure of foreign contract personnel and many ex-IIAF technicians made it difficult for the new air force to maintain its highly sophisticated Tomcats. Moreover, unable to obtain F-14 and Phoenix spares from the United States following the break in diplomatic relations, the IRIAF was quickly forced to rely on cannibalization to keep a small number of aircraft in commission. Then, during the protracted war against Iraq, combat and operational losses* mounted leaving the IRIAF with only a handful of serviceable F-14As when the fighting ended in the summer of 1988.

PRODUCTION: A total of 656 Tomcats has been built by Grumman between December 1970 and December 1988. More are on order. Tomcats delivered before the end of 1988 included:

556	*F-14A* (for the USN)
80	*F-14A* (for Iran)
19	*F-14A*(Plus)
1	*F-14B*

Tomcats delivered by the end of 1988 have been assigned the following BuNos and Iranian military serial numbers:

F-14A: (for the   BuNos 157980/157985, 157987/157991, 158612/158637,
USN)   158978/159025, 159421/159468, 159588/159637,

* Iraq first claimed to have shot down an Iranian F-14A near Dehrayan on 21 November, 1982, the kill being credited to a Mirage F1EQ.

	159825/159874, 160379/160414, 160652/160696,
	160887/160930, 161133/161168, 161270/161299,
	161416/161445, 161597/161626,161850/161873,
	162588/162611, and 162688/162711

F-14A: (for   Iranian serials 3-863/3-942 (BuNos 160299/160378
Iran)

F-14A (Plus):   BuNos 162910/162928
(new)

F-14A(Plus):   (BuNos 158612, 158615/158618, 158620, 158624,
(conversions)   158626/158630,158632/158633, 158635/158631, 162588,
     and 14 more)

F-14B: BuNo 157986

The following BuNos have been assigned to Tomcats on order at the end of 1988:

F-14A(Plus):   BuNos 162929/162933 and 163215/163228

F-14D: BuNos 163229/163232 and 163407/163418

Specifications for the F-14A:

Span (wings swept forward) 64 ft 1½ in (19.55 m); span (wings swept back) 38 ft 2½ in (11.65 m); length 62 ft 8 in (19.10 m); height 16 ft 0 in (4.88 m); wing area 565 sq ft (52.49 sq m).

Empty weight 40,104 lb (18,191 kg); loaded weight 59,714 lb (27,086 kg); max weight 74,349 lb (33,724 kg); wing loading 105.7 lb/sq ft (516.0 kg/sqm); power loading 1.4 lb/lb st (1.4 kg/kgp).

Max speed 1,544 mph at 40, 000 ft (2,484 kmh at 12,190 m); cruising speed 610 mph (981 kmh); initial climb rate 32,500 ft/min (165 m/sec); service ceiling 55,000 ft (16,765 m); max unrefuelled range 2,400 miles (3,860 km).

The prototype of the Grumman American Cougar. *(Grumman)*

Grumman American GA-7 and Cougar

The only light aircraft developed by Grumman American, the GA-7 and its de luxe Cougar version, were exceptionally clean twin-engined four-seaters. They were intended to fill a perceived gap between high-performance single-engined aircraft, such as the Beech Bonanza and the Cessna 210, and expensive, high-powered twins, such as the Beech Baron, Cessna 310, and Piper Aztec.

Like the earlier single-engined aircraft built in Cleveland, the new GA-7 twin had an enclosed cabin of aluminium honeycomb construction and made use of metal-to-metal bonding throughout its airframe. Powered by two 160-hp Lycoming O-320-D1D flat-four engines driving two-blade constant-speed propellers, the first prototype (N777GA) took to the air in Cleveland on 20 December, 1974.

Trials were satisfactory, but the aircraft was not put into production because Grumman American sought to ascertain the impact of the energy crisis on the light aircraft market. Time was thus available to demonstrate the GA-7 to prospective customers and to become aware of the need for modifications to improve passenger comfort and cabin accessibility. Accordingly, the production prototype had a slightly widened cabin, an entrance door on the starboard side in lieu of a sliding canopy, and an additional aft window on both sides. This production prototype was first flown on 12 January, 1977, and was certificated on 22 September. Deliveries from the Savannah plant of Grumman American began in February 1978.

The GA-7 handled well as its single-engine minimum control speed was virtually the same as its stalling speed, thus almost eliminating handling problems affecting most twins following an engine failure. Moreover, it performed as well as its direct competitors, the Beech Duchess and Piper

524

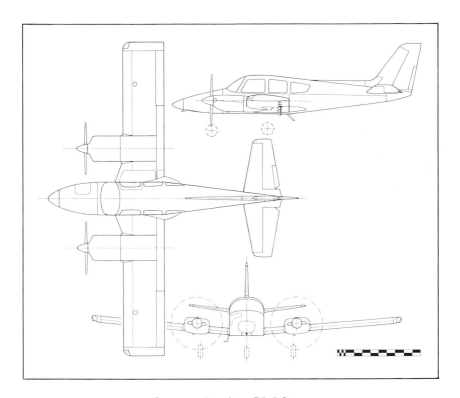

Grumman American GA-7 Cougar

Seminole, in spite of having less powerful engines (160-hp versus 180-hp). Nevertheless, the Cougar met with only limited success as, in the post energy crisis period, the demand for four-seat twin-engined aircraft was minimal. Accordingly, Gulfstream American was not able to keep the aircraft in production for long and did not proceed with plans to offer versions with more powerful and/or turbo-supercharged engines or with two additional seats.

PRODUCTION: Only thirty GA-7s and Cougars were built by Grumman American (one in 1974, four in 1977, and twenty-five up to August 1978) before the manufacturing rights were transferred to Gulfstream American.

Span 36 ft 10⁵/₁₆ in (11.23 m); length 29 ft 8 in (9.04 m); height 10 ft 4¹/₄ in (3.16 m); wing area 184 sq ft (17.09 sq m).
Empty weight 2,588 lb (1,174 kg); loaded weight 3,800 lb (1,724 kg); wing loading 20.7 lb/sq ft (100.9 kg/sq m); power loading 11.9 lb/hp (5.4 kg/hp).
Max speed 193 mph (311 kmh) at sea level; cruising speed 184 mph (296 kmh); rate of climb at sea level 1,160 ft/min (5.9 m/sec); service ceiling 17,400 ft (5,305 m); normal range 967 miles (1,555 km); max range 1,345 miles (2,165 km).

The X-29A (82-0003) over the Mojave Desert in 1985. *(NASA/Grumman)*

Grumman X-29

Resulting from the combined efforts of Glenn L Spacht and his team at Grumman and of Dr Norris Krone, a retired Air Force colonel working as a civilian scientist for the Defense Advanced Research Projects Agency (DARPA), the resurgence of interest in the forward swept wing (FSW) concept was made possible by the development of fly-by-wire control systems and of light but strong composite materials. Together these two technologies were expected to overcome aeroelastic divergence problems encountered during earlier attempts at using FSWs of conventional metal construction.

On the advice of Dr Krone, Grumman first conducted FSW wind-tunnel tests in 1975-76 in an attempt to cure the wing root drag problem which had been the primary cause of its Design 636's loss in the HIMAT competition to the Rockwell design. As results were promising, Grumman sought to obtain a contract for the development and testing of an FSW prototype. Work on a small structural analysis contract awarded in 1977 quickly confirmed the validity of using composite materials to solve structural divergence. A follow-on contract in 1978 called for vehicle configuration studies and wind-tunnel testing of a 1/8th-scale model. Yet another research contract resulted in the building of a half-scale transonic tunnel model with an aeroelastically tailored wing. Successful completion of these tests then led to another contract in 1979, which produced further refinements of configuration, wing design and flight controls development. However, neither NASA nor DARPA was prepared to fund a project of this magnitude without competition, and in mid-1980 Grumman was forced to bid against General Dynamics and Rockwell in answer to a request for proposals for an FSW demonstrator aircraft issued by DARPA and the Air Force Flight Dynamics Laboratory. Luckily for Grumman, its earlier work paid off, and Design 712 was declared the winner of the DARPA/ADL competition on 22 December, 1981. Several months later, Grumman was awarded a contract for two X-29As (82-0003 and 82-0049).

In addition to wings with 33 degrees 44 minutes of forward sweep at quarter-chord and aeroelastically tailored graphite epoxy top and bottom skins bonded to a substructure of aluminium alloy and titanium, the winning Design 712 was characterized by a thin supercritical aerofoil section and variable-incidence close-coupled canard surfaces. However, with canard surfaces the centre of lift would be in front of the centre of gravity, rendering the aircraft unstable. Thus, it was necessary to provide a three-channel fly-by-wire control system comparing the aircraft's flight characteristics to the pilot's commands 40 times a second and adjusting the control surfaces to make the aircraft respond as the pilot dictated. In addition, the X-29A was designed to have the capability of flying to plus or minus 80 degrees angle of attack and to recover safely from such abnormal flight conditions. To be able to do so, horizontal surfaces known as fuselage strakes were provided aft of the wings to add area to the aircraft aft of the centre of gravity. Flaps provided at the aft end of the fuselage strakes were to deflect downward to reduce approach speed and upward to reduce take-off speed and distance. The strake flaps were also to be used in flight as part of the pitch axis control system along with the canards and wing trailing edge flaps. Moreover, as the wing's supercritical aerofoil section was optimized for transonic cruise, it became necessary to employ a variable-camber trailing-edge system to optimize the shape of the wing during supersonic flight.

The first X-29A, at Edwards AFB, California, on 15 November, 1988. (*René J Francillon*)

527

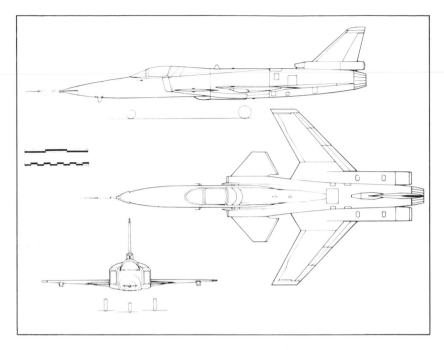

Grumman X-29A

To minimize costs, as many existing components as possible were used in the construction of the X-29As. Notably, the main undercarriage of the General Dynamics F-16 and the forward fuselage and nosewheel undercarriage units from two Northrop F-5As (63-8372 and 65-10573) were incorporated in the two prototypes. Likewise, the single 16,000-lb afterburning thrust General Electric F404-GE-400 turbofan powering the X-29A came from the McDonnell Douglas F/A-18 programme.

The two experimental aircraft were structurally completed in the summer of 1984, more than two and a half years after the selection of Design 712 as the winner of the DARPA/ADL competition. After undergoing high-speed taxi-ing trials at Calverton, the first X-29A (82-0003) was taken by container ship, via the Panama Canal, to California, while the second was put into storage.

At last, Charles 'Chuck' A Sewell made the first of four contractor's flights at Edwards AFB on 14 December, 1984. The first X-29A was accepted by the Air Force on 12 March, 1985, and was almost immediately transferred to NASA. Since then, tests have generally proceeded at a conservative pace, primarily due to the scheduled need to install specialized equipment and the limited budget supporting the programme. However, the aircraft has proved highly reliable and on several occasions has made three or four flights in one day. Notably, it was airborne for 3.2 hours during four flights on 27 August, 1986, and for 3.4 hours in three flights on 23 December, 1986. After twenty pilots (three from Grumman, nine from the Air Force, one from the Navy, and seven from NASA) flew it a total of 242 times, more than any other X-series aircraft, the first X-29A was grounded in January 1989.

Kept in storage at Calverton while NASA, DARPA, and the Air Force decided on the scope of the slower-paced test programme required by budget cuts, the second X-29A differs from the first in being fitted with a spin recovery chute mounted in an external cannister aft of the tail surfaces, upgraded flight-test instrumentation, and related cockpit modifications. It left Bethpage in October 1988 on its way by sea to Port Hueneme, California, and then by truck to Edwards AFB. There, it was re-assembled in preparation for the high angle-of-attack research programme* which is funded by NASA and the Department of Defense and was to begin in May 1989. It is hoped that this new series of tests will confirm that the use of aeroelastically tailored FSWs can result, for any given mission, in a 10 to 20 per cent reduction in drag, lower fuel consumption, and a 5 to 25 per cent drop in airframe weight, thus bringing about a reduction in aircraft manufacturing and operating costs.

PRODUCTION: Two X-29As were built by Grumman in 1984 and were assigned Air Force serial numbers 82-0003 and 82-0049.

Span 27 ft 2½ in (8.29 m); length 53 ft 11¼ in (16.44 m); height 14 ft 3½ in (4.26 m); wing area 188.8 sq ft (17.54 sq m).
Empty weight, 13,800 lb (6,260 kg); maximum weight 17,800 lb (8,074 kg); wing loading 94.3 lb/sq ft (460.3 kg/sq m); power loading 1.1 lb/lb st (1.1 kg/kg st).
Max Mach 1.87; highest altitude during tests, 50,200 ft (15,300 m).

---

* Whereas the first prototype was limited to 20 degrees angle of attack, the second X-29A has been modified to permit safely flying at higher angles of attack. Researchers at the Dryden Flight Research Facility plan to increase angles by increments to a maximum of about 80 degrees.

The first E-8A prototype taking off from the Melbourne Airport in Florida for its maiden flight on 1 April, 1988. (*Grumman*)

Grumman E-8

After ten years of research in the required technologies, the Melbourne Systems Division won Grumman's largest Air Force contract ever, a five-year, $657-million award for the full-scale development of the USAF/USA Joint Surveillance Target Attack Radar System. Intended to provide real-time surveillance of the battlefield and rear echelons, Joint STARS was designed to detect, identify, and track enemy armour and vehicular traffic. By providing target locations to appropriate Air Force and Army commanders, Joint STARS would thus enable them to assess the threat and manage attacks on targets via the Joint Tactical Information Distribution System (JTIDS) for the Air Force and the FCDL surveillance and control data link for the Army. To do so, the programme was to include not only the Grumman developed airborne components but also mobile ground modules for which Motorola Inc in Tempe, Arizona, became the prime contractor. In addition, Grumman became responsible for integrating the airborne system with the ground stations.

The heart of the Joint STARS's airborne system is the AN/APY-3 radar conceived by Grumman and built by Norden Systems Inc in Norwalk, Connecticut. To detect and locate stationary objects, such as parked vehicles, this radar was designed to operate in synthetic aperture radar (SAR) mode. To locate slow-moving targets while the aircraft is flying at a safe distance behind the FLOT (Forward Line of Own Troops), the AN/APY-3 was developed to alternate between SAR and Doppler modes.

As prime contractor for the airborne components, Grumman acquired two used Boeing 707-320 jet airliners* to serve as prototypes for the system's aerial platform and awarded an $80.2 million sub-contract to Boeing Military Airplane Company in Wichita, Kansas, for their modifica-

---

* The first E-8A a 707-338C (c/n 19626, ex VH-EAF) which had been delivered to Qantas in May 1968, is owned by Grumman and registered N770JS. Also Grumman-owned, the second E-8A, a 707-323C (c/n 19574) which had been delivered in May 1968 to American Airlines, retains its original US civil registration, N8411.

tion. In Wichita, the two aircraft were overhauled and fitted with a strengthened floor and aerial refuelling receptacle before being flown to Melbourne, Florida. There, Grumman installed the required radomes, including a 25-ft long canoe for the multimode side-looking AN/APY-3 antenna, beneath the fuselage of the first E-8A. Retaining its 18,000-lb thrust Pratt & Whitney JT3D-3 turbofans (military designation TF33-P-103), the Grumman-owned E-8A prototype was first flown on 1 April, 1988. Trials with the AN/APY-3 installed began on 22 December, 1988.

Operational tests and evaluation by the Air Force are currently planned to begin in 1990 and, if everything works as planned, the production decision will be taken during the following year. The first of twenty-two production aircraft which are likely to be ordered will be delivered in 1993. Unlike the E-8A prototypes, which are modified 707 jetliners, these E-8Bs will be specially built to carry the Joint STARS equipment. Their airframe and 22,000-lb thrust General Electric/SNECMA CFM F108-CF-100 turbofans will be similar to those of E-6A TACAMO aircraft built by Boeing for the Navy. In addition to a flight crew of three, the Joint STARS production aircraft will carry a crew of seventeen USA and USAF specialists manning advanced information display consoles in the fuselage.

PRODUCTION: Two E-8A prototypes have been obtained by fitting Joint STARS systems into modified Boeing 707-320 airliners.

Specifications for the E-8A prototypes with JT3D-3 (TF33-P-103) turbofans
    Span 145 ft 8½ in (44.41 m); length 152 ft 11 in (46.61 m); height 42 ft 5½ in (12.94 m); wing area 3,050 sq ft (283.35 sq m).
    Operating weight empty 168,000 lb (76,204 Kg); maximum weight 333,600 lb (151,318 kg); wing loading 109.4 lb/sq ft (534.0 kg/sq m); power loading 4.6 lb/lb st (4.6 kg/kg st).
    Max speed 600 mph at 35,000 ft (965 kmh at 10,670 m); cruising speed 550 mph (885 kmh); climb rate 4,000 ft/min (20 m/sec); service ceiling 39,000 ft (11,885 m); normal unrefuelled range 6,000 miles (9,655 km).

N770JS, the Grumman-owned first prototype of the E-8A, at the Melbourne Airport in March 1989. *(Robert E Kling)*

APPENDIX A

PRODUCTION SUMMARY

The following tables summarize annual aircraft deliveries by models during each of the six decades of operations.

ANNUAL AIRCRAFT DELIVERIES
(1930-1939)

AIRCRAFT	1930	1931	1932	1933	1934	1935	1936	1937	1938	1939	TOTALS	
FF and SF	-	1	-	27	35	-	-	-	-	-	64	(Grand total: 64)
JF and J2F	-	-	-	1	27	20	14	23	30	36	151	(Still in production)
F2F	-	-	-	1	-	55	-	-	-	-	56	(Grand total: 56)
F3F	-	-	-	-	-	3	56	13	71	26	169	(Grand total: 169)
XSBF-1	-	-	-	-	-	1	-	-	-	-	1	(Grand total: 1)
Goose	-	-	-	-	-	-	-	12	14	46	72	(Still in production)
F4F	-	-	-	-	-	-	-	1	-	-	1	(Still in production)
ANNUAL TOTALS	-	1	1	29	62	79	70	49	115	108	514	

NOTE: In this table, the date of the first flight of a prototype is considered to be that of first delivery even though contractual delivery to the customer may have taken place much later.

F2F-1s undergoing overhaul in the Farmingdale plant with F3F-1s being assembled in the background, *(Grumman)*

The F6F-5 production line in Plant No. 2 at Bethpage in 1944. *(Grumman)*

ANNUAL AIRCRAFT DELIVERIES
(1940-1949)

AIRCRAFT	1940	1941	1942	1943	1944	1945	1946	1947	1948	1949	TOTALS	
JF and J2F	20	108	36	-	-	-	-	-	-	-	164	(Grand total: 315)
Goose	30	23	50	58	77	35	-	-	-	-	273	(Grand total: 345)
F4F	106	334	1,447	100	-	-	-	-	-	-	1,987	(Grand total: 1,988)
XF5F-1	1	-	-	-	-	-	-	-	-	-	1	(Grand total: 1)
Widgeon	1	98	56	43	3	29	30	6	6	4	276	(Grand total: 276)
XP-50	-	1	-	-	-	-	-	-	-	-	1	(Grand total: 1)
TBF	-	2	646	1,645	-	-	-	-	-	-	2,293	(Grand total: 2,293)
F6F	-	-	12	2,545	6,140	3,578-	-	-	-	-	12,275	(Grand total: 12,275)
F7F	-	-	-	1	66	210	87	-	-	-	364	(Grand total: 364)
Kitten I	-	-	-	-	1	-	-	-	-	-	1	(Grand total: 1)
F8F	-	-	-	-	4	208	341	338	303	71	1,265	(Grand total: 1,265)
Tadpole	-	-	-	-	1	-	-	-	-	-	1	(Grand total: 1)
Kitten II	-	-	-	-	-	-	1	-	-	-	1	(Grand total: 1)
Mallard	-	-	-	-	-	-	8	25	8	9	50	(Still in production)
XTB3F and AF	-	-	-	-	-	-	1	-	-	4	5	(Still in production)
UF and SA-16	-	-	-	-	-	-	-	1	1	11	13	(Still in production)
F9F Panther	-	-	-	-	-	-	-	1	4	151	156	(Still in production)
annual totals	158	566	2,247	4,392	6,292	4,060	468	371	322	250	19,126	

NOTE: In this table, the date of the first flight of a prototype is considered to be that of first delivery even though contractual delivery to the customer may have taken place much later.

F9F-8Ts, F9F-8s, and F11F-1s being assembled in the Calverton plant in 1956. *(Grumman)*

The Mohawk assembly line at Stuart, Florida, in 1967. *(Grumman)*

ANNUAL AIRCRAFT DELIVERIES
(1950-1959)

AIRCRAFT	1950	1951	1952	1953	1954	1955	1956	1957	1958	1959	TOTALS	
Mallard	6	3	-	-	-	-	-	-	-	-	9	(Grand total: 59)
XTB3F and AF	51	108	170	55	-	-	-	-	-	-	384	(Grand total: 389)
UF and SA-16	36	63	107	137	33	24	24	2	7	4	437	(Still in production)
F9F Panther	273	483	471	2	-	-	-	-	-	-	1,229	(Grand Total: 1,385)
F9F Cougar	-	3	117	565	343	293	238	137	102	180	1,978	(Still in production)
XF10F-1	-	-	1	-	-	-	-	-	-	-	1	(Grand total: 1)
S-2	-	-	1	20	216	163	148	94	78	54	774	(Still in production)
F11F	-	-	-	-	3	8	27	83	80	-	201	(Grand total: 201)
C-1	-	-	-	-	1	24	20	6	36	-	87	(Grand total: 87)
E-1	-	-	-	-	-	-	-	-	6	22	28	(Still in production)
Ag-Cat	-	-	-	-	-	-	-	2	-	10	12	(Still in production)
Gulfstream I	-	-	-	-	-	-	-	-	3	25	28	(Still in production)
OV-1	-	-	-	-	-	-	-	-	-	8	8	(Still in production)
ANNUAL TOTALS	366	660	867	779	596	512	457	324	312	303	5,176	

NOTE: In this table, the date of the first flight of a prototype is considered to be that of first delivery even though contractual delivery to the customer may have taken place much later.

536

ANNUAL AIRCRAFT DELIVERIES
(1960-1969)

AIRCRAFT	1960	1961	1962	1963	1964	1965	1966	1967	1968	1969	TOTALS	
UF and SA-16	5	11	-	-	-	-	-	-	-	-	16	(Grand total: 466)
F9F Cougar	10	-	-	-	-	-	-	-	-	-	10	(Grand total: 1,988)
S-2	61	53	51	48	48	48	48	38	-	-	395	(Grand total: 1,169)
E-1	36	24	-	-	-	-	-	-	-	-	60	(Grand total: 88)
Ag-Cat	29	56	77	72	80	58	51	40	84	118	665	(Still in production)
Gulfstream I	32	23	15	24	26	19	9	11	10	3	172	(Grand total: 200)
OV-1	32	48	62	42	24	25	14	16	37	42	342	(Still in production)
A-64	4	4	7	21	42	50	63	87	99	69	446	(Still in production)
EA-6	-	-	-	-	-	2	3	1	1	14	21	(Still in production)
E-2	1	4	4	12	12	12	12	2	-	-	59	(Still in production)
C-2	-	-	-	-	-	-	5	12	-	-	17	(Back in prod. in 1984)
F-111B	-	-	-	-	-	3	2	-	1	1	7	(Grand total: 7)
Gulfstream II	-	-	-	-	-	-	1	3	38	36	78	(Still in production)
ANNUAL TOTALS	210	223	216	219	232	217	208	210	270	283	2,288	

NOTE: In this table, the date of the first flight of a prototype is considered to be that of first delivery even though contractual delivery to the customer may have taken place much later.

Delivered in May 1964 as an A-6A, BuNo 151568 was modified by Grumman in 1977 as a test-bed for the Circulation Control Wing and was rebuilt in 1980 as a KA-6D. (*Grumman*)

F-14As in Plant No. 6 at Calverton, New York, in 1986. (*Grumman*)

ANNUAL AIRCRAFT DELIVERIES
(1970-1979)

AIRCRAFT	1970	1971	1972	1973	1974	1975	1976	1977	1978	1979	TOTALS	
Ag-Cat	91	103	142	175	185	228	248	214	153*	-	1,539	(Grand total: 2,216)
OV-1	30	-	-	-	-	-	-	-	-	-	30	(Grand total: 380)
A-6	36	10	14	12	18	16	12	11	3	12	144	(Still in production)
EA-6	1	13	10	12	6	7	6	6	6	6	73	(Still in production)
E-2	-	-	-	10	9	10	5	7	9	6	56	(Still in production)
Gulfstream II	22	7	14	19	15	20	21	20	11†	-	149	(Grand total: 256)
F-14	1	6	13	34	59	73	75	70	55	38	424	(Still in production)
AA-1T-Cat & Lynx	-	-	-	235	186	112	84	115	91‡	-	823	
Cheetah & Tiger	-	-	-	234	242	399	403	525	326‡	-	2,129	
Cougar	-	-	-	-	1	-	-	-	29‡	-	30	
ANNUAL totals	181	139	193	731	721	865	854	968	683	62	5,397	

NOTES: In this table, the date of the first flight of a prototype is considered to be that of first delivery even though contractual delivery to the customer may have taken place much later.

* Schweizer Aircraft delivered 203 Ag-Cats in 1978. However, the last 50 or so were delivered after the Ag-Catline had been sold to Gulfstream American Corporation. These 50 Ag-Cats, and those delivered in later years as Gulfstream American or Schweizer products are not included in this table.

† Twenty-nine additional Gulfstream IIs were delivered in 1978-79 after the line had been sold to Gulfstream American Corporation. These additional aircraft are included in the grand total of 256 Gulfstream IIs.

‡ The 1979 production figure includes only aircraft delivered up to August, before the line was sold to Gulfstream American Corporation.

ANNUAL AIRCRAFT DELIVERIES
(1980-1988)

AIRCRAFT	1980	1981	1982	1983	1984	1985	1986	1987	1988	TOTALS	
A-6 and EA-6	12	3	6	15	11	7	7	7	10	78	(Still in production)
EA-6	6	6	4	5	6	8	8	9	12	62	(Still in production)
E-2	5	7	10	6	10	8	10	9	6	71	(Still in production)
C-2	-	-	-	-	-	7	9	8	8	32	(Still in production)
F-14	42	31	29	31	26	21	27	8	17	232	(Still in production)
X-29	-	-	-	-	1	-	-	-	1	2	(Grand total: 2)
ANNUAL TOTALS	65	47	49	57	54	49	61	41	54	477	

NOTE: In this table, the date of the first flight of a prototype is considered to be that of first delivery even though contractual delivery to the customer may have taken place much later.

539

A model of the G-3, an amphibian which was proposed to the US Coast Guard in 1930 but was not built. (*Grumman*)

APPENDIX B

Design Numbers and Representative Projects

Beginning in 1930, when the Model A and Model B amphibious floats were retroactively numbered Design Number 1 and Design Number 2 (G-1 and G-2), all Grumman aircraft design studies have been given sequential numbers. The following listing gives all Design Numbers up to and including G-128, the number assigned in 1956 to identify design studies which eventually led to the well-known A-6/EA-6 series. Most Design Numbers assigned thereafter either pertain to non-aircraft studies, are classified, or are company confidential. Hence, only those post 1956 design numbers assigned to aircraft which were put into production are included in this list. A few other Design Numbers are included in brief descriptions of representative projects.

G-1   Model A amphibious floats for the Vought O2U-4 and O3U-1.
G-2   Model B amphibious floats for the Vought O3U-1.
G-3   Proposed twin-engined, parasol monoplane flying-boat for the US Coast Guard.
G-4   Proposed observation amphibian for the Army Air Corps.
G-5   FF series.
G-6   XSF-1 and SF-1.
G-7   XJF-1 and JF-1.
G-8   F2F series.
G-9   JF-2.
G-10   JF-3.
G-11   XF3F-1 and F3F-1.
G-12   Proposed Army observation aircraft derived from the SF-1.

G-13	XSF-2.
G-14	XSBF-1.
G-15	J2F series.
G-16	XF4F-1.
G-17	Proposed single-seat monoplane.
G-18	XF4F-2.
G-19	XF3F-2, F3F-2, XF3F-3, and F3F-3.
G-20	Export version of JF-2 for Argentina.
G-21	Goose.
G-22	*Gulfhawk II*.
G-23	Export variant of the FF-1/SF-1 series for Canadian Car & Foundry.
G-24	Proposed advanced trainer with F3F wings.
G-25	Proposed Navy high-altitude fighter with two Allison V-1710 engines.
G-26	XJ3F-1.
G-27	Proposed two-seat twin-engined amphibian for the Navy.
G-28	No record.
G-29	Proposed two-seat Navy fighter powered by an Allison V-1710 installed as a pusher.
G-30	Proposed two-seat Navy fighter powered by an Allison V-1710.
G-31	OA-9 series.
G-32	*Gulfhawk III* and *Red Ship*.
G-33	Proposed development of the XF4F-2 with an R-2600 engine.
G-34	XF5F-1.
G-35	Proposed fighter with R-2600 engine.
G-36	XF4F-3, F4F-3, XF4F-8, and export variants.
G-37	Proposed F3F-2 development for export.
G-38	JRF-1 and JRF-1A.
G-39	JRF-2, JRF-3, and JRF-4/JRF-6.
G-40	TBF series.
G-41	Proposed Army version of XF5F-1 with conventional undercarriage.
G-42	Proposed single-engined utility amphibian; became the Columbia XJL-1.
G-43	Proposed Army version of XF4F-3.
G-44	Widgeon.
G-45	Proposed Army version of XF5F-1 with a nosewheel undercarriage; became the XP-50.
G-46	XP-65.
G-47	Proposed patrol utility version of the JRF.
G-48	Proposed patrol utility amphibian.
G-49	Proposed export fighter with two R-2600 engines.
G-50	F6F series.
G-51	F7F series.

G-52	F4F-7.
G-53	Modified F4F-4 with full-span Duplex flaps.
G-54	Proposed development of the F6F with a laminar-flow wing of greater area.
G-55	XTB2F-1.
G-56	Proposed development of TBF-1 with an R-2800 engine and Martin dorsal turret.
G-57	Design study for Navy fighter powered by an R-2800 and a turbojet.
G-58	F8F Bearcat series.
G-59	Proposed F6F development with a two-speed R-4360 engine.
G-60	Proposed F6F development with an R-4360 engine and two-stage supercharger.
G-61	Proposed F6F development with an auxiliary GE jet engine.
G-62	Design study for small jet fighter.
G-63	Kitten I.
G-64	UF-1/SA-16A Albatross series.
G-65	Tadpole.
G-66	XTSF-1.
G-67	Proposed version of F7F-2 with an I-20 turbojet behind the R-2800 nacelles.
G-68	Proposed Navy fighter with a TG-100 propeller-turbine.
G-69	Proposed R-2800-22 powered single-seat attack aircraft derived from the F6F.
G-70	XTB3F-1.
G-71	Proposed Navy single-seat fighter with a Westinghouse W-24C turbojet.
G-72	Kitten II.
G-73	Mallard.
G-74	Proposed postwar development of the Widgeon.
G-75	XF9F-1.
G-76	Proposed high-altitude special bomber.
G-77	Proposed swept-wing research aircraft.
G-78	Towed target glider study.
G-79	F9F Panther series.
G-80	High-speed transport aircraft study based on the F7F.
G-81	Kitten I fitted with ducted wing.
G-82	AF Guardian series.
G-83	Began as study of XF9F-2 with wing sweep and led to the development of the XF10F.
G-84	Short take-off fighter study.
G-85	Classified bomber study.
G-86	Proposed carrier-based interceptor with a J40 turbojet and a Curtiss-Wright rocket engine.
G-87	Land-based transport aircraft study based on the JR2F design.
G-88	Proposed ASW derivative of the UF-1.

G-89	S2F-1/S2F-2 series.
G-90	Guardian study to replace the AF-2S and AF-2W with single aircraft fitted with an APS-33 radar.
G-91	Proposed single-engined ASW aircraft.
G-92	VTO fighter study.
G-93	F9F-6 and F9F-7 Cougar series.
G-94	Flex-deck F9F-7.
G-95	XWF-1.
G-96	C-1 Trader series.
G-97	Proposed Navy fighter with a J57 turbojet.
G-98	F11F Tiger series.
G-99	F9F-8 and F9F-8P Cougar series.
G-100	Proposed development of F9F-9 with large equipment bay.
G-101	10- to 12-seat transport aircraft study based on TF-1.
G-102	10- to 12-seat jet transport study.
G-103	Grumman work on the de Havilland of Canada CS2F-1.
G-104	Proposed air refuelling tanker version of the TF-1.
G-105	F9F-8T.
G-106	Proposed UF-2 development.
G-107	Air Force interceptor study.
G-108	Air Force amphibian study.
G-109	High-altitude weapon system study (including Eagle air-to-air missile).
G-110	FXF fighter study.
G-111	UF-2/SA-16B Albatross series.
G-112	Improved S2F study.
G-113	Proposed J79-powered flex-deck interceptor.
G-114	VTO survey and study.
G-115	Proposed Trader development as photographic platform (TF-1P).
G-116	Twinjet transport study.
G-117	WF-2/E-1 Tracer series.
G-118	Mach 2-plus fighter study.
G-119	XF12F-1 design studies.
G-120	Proposed de Havilland of Canada version of the Trader.
G-121	S2F-3 series.
G-122	Commercial amphibian study.
G-123	E-2 Hawkeye and C-2 Greyhound series.
G-124	Single-engined jet basic trainer study.
G-125	TF-1Q.
G-126	Proposed Trader training version with APS-28 and APA-57 for use by FAETU.
G-127	Wing body interaction research model.
G-128	A-6 Intruder and EA-6 Prowler series.
G-134	OV-1 Mohawk series.
G-159	Gulfstream I.

G-164	Ag-Cat series.
G-191	Albatross for Germany.
G-231	Albatross (CSR-110) for Canada.
G-234	Albatross for USCG (UF-2G) and Argentina.
G-251	ASW Albatross.
G-262	Albatross for Japan.
G-303	F-14 Tomcat series.
G-426	TC-4C Academe.
G-712	X-29.
G-1159	Gulfstream II.

Design 4 (Air Corps Observation Amphibian)

The second aircraft proposal submitted by the newly created Grumman Aircraft Engineering Corporation was for a two-seat observation amphibian offered to the Army Air Corps in January 1930. Of biplane flying-boat design, this aircraft was proposed with a single radial engine mounted ahead of and beneath the upper wing. It was to have been armed with a forward-firing fixed gun and a rear-firing flexible gun. However, the Army Air Corps had no requirement for this type of observation amphibian and this unsolicited proposal failed to generate official interest.

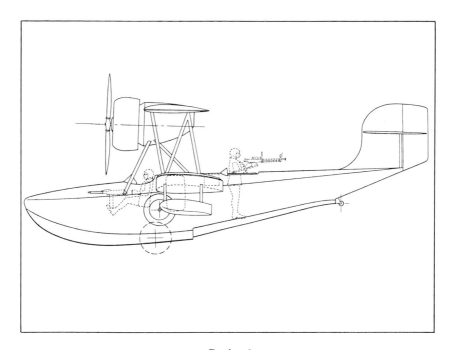

Design 4

Design 16 (XF4F-1)

In answer to a November 1935 design competition for a carrier fighter, Grumman submitted its Design 16. Basically the new aircraft was a development of the F3F-1 then about to enter service and from which it differed in being smaller and better streamlined and in having wings of equal span and chord. Power was to be furnished by an 800-hp radial, either a Pratt & Whitney XR-1535-92 or a Wright XR-1670-02. An XF4F-1 prototype was ordered on 2 March, 1936.

However, as performance similar to that calculated for the XF4F-1 was expected from the F3F-2 and as still better performance was expected from the Brewster XF2A-1 monoplane, Grumman suspended work on Design 16 three months later, and began working on Design 18, the all-new XF4F-2 monoplane.

The predicted characteristics and performance of the XF4F-1 biplane were as follows: span 32 ft (9.75 m); length 23 ft 3 in (7.09 m); loaded weight 4,500 lb (2,041 kg); max speed 264 mph (425 kmh).

Design 55 (XTB2F-1)

Seeking to obtain a twin-engined torpedo scout bomber for operations from CV-9 and CVB class carriers, the Bureau of Aeronautics had requested the Douglas Aircraft Company to submit a proposal in February 1942. However, after the Douglas design had evolved into the XTB2D-1, a large single-engined aircraft, BuAer sought to obtain a twin-engined design and asked Grumman to submit a proposal. Preliminary and detailed proposals for Design 55 were respectively submitted by Grumman on 21 December, 1942, and 19 March, 1943, and a Letter of Intent was issued on 6 August, 1943, for the procurement of two XTB2F-1 prototypes and related engineering and test data.

Mock-up inspection took place in early May 1944; however, as the aircraft was judged too heavy and too large for operations even from large CVB carriers, a 'stop work' order was issued on 14 June, 1944.

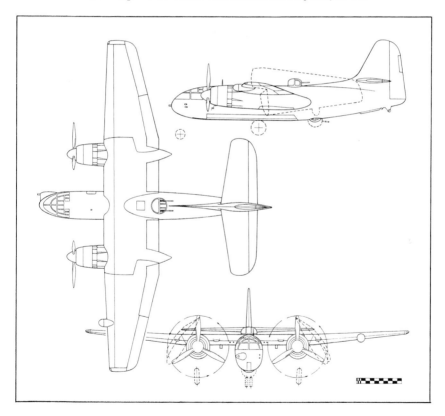

Design 55 (XTB2F-1)

The three-seat XTB2F-1s were to have been powered by two 2,000-hp Pratt & Whitney R-2800-22 radials and fitted with a nosewheel undercarriage. Defensive armament was to have included a dorsal turret and a retractable ventral turret, both with a pair of 0.50-in guns. Forward-firing armament was to consist of two 0.50-in guns and a 75-mm cannon in the nose, and two 0.50-in guns in each wing. A single torpedo or up to thirty-six 100-lb bombs were to have been carried in a ventral weapons bay. Principal characteristics and performance were as follows: span 74 ft (22.56 m); span (folded) 33 ft 6 in (10.21 m); length 52 ft (15.85 m); empty weight 22,480 lb (10,197 kg); loaded weight 43,937 lb (19,929 kg); max speed 338 mph (544 kmh) service ceiling, 31,600 ft (9,630 m); normal range 3,060 miles (4,925 km); and max range 4,730 miles (7,610 km).

Design 66 (XTSF-1)

When ordering the termination of the XTB2F-1 project, the Bureau of Aeronautics also requested that Grumman prepare and submit a design study of a torpedo bomber modified from the F7F-2 twin-engined fighter. Preliminary data for Design 66 were submitted by Grumman in late June 1944, revisions and additional details were provided on 21 July, and on 17 August BuAer requested that the XTB2F-1 contract be amended to cover the procurement of two XTSF-1s (BuNos 84055/84056). Mock-up inspection took place in October 1944, and detailed engineering proceeded until the end of that year. In January 1945, however, the XTSF-1 contract was terminated as the Navy felt that Grumman's engineering load was already excessive.

The XTSF-1 design differed primarily from that of the F7F-2 in incorporating a bomb bay, two seats in tandem, and an enlarged nose (with space being initially provided for an APS-3 or APS-4 radar but later being increased again to house a more powerful SCR-720 set). Gun armament was reduced to four 0.50-in machine guns (two in each wing root). The span and wing area were respectively increased from 51 ft 6 in (15.70 m) to 59 ft 4 in (18.08 m) and from 455 sq ft (42.27 sq m) to 501.5 sq ft (46.59 sq m) while length was increased from 45 ft 4½ in (13.83 m) to 45 ft 10 in (13.97 m).

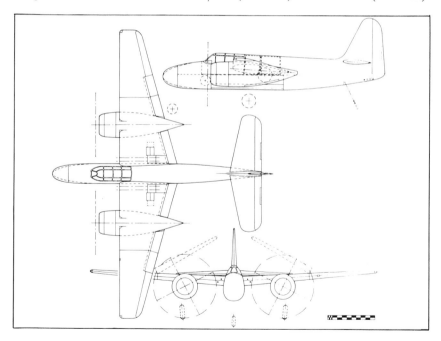

Design 66 (XTSF-1)

Design 75 (XF9F-1)

Ordered in April 1946, along with prototypes of the Douglas XF3D-1, to meet a Navy requirement for jet-powered, two-seat, carrier-based night fighters, Design 75 looked much like a jet-powered F7F Tigercat. Within less than six months, however, Grumman and BuAer concluded that in spite of a total installed thrust of 12,000 lb the XF9F-1 would not have the desired performance. Accordingly, the contract was amended in September 1946 to substitute an all-new single-engined, single-seat XF9F-2 day fighter for the four-engined, two-seat XF9F-1 night fighter.

Design 75 had called for the use of four 3,000-lb Westinghouse 24C-4B turbojets installed as side-by-side pairs in wing nacelles and the installation of four 20 mm cannon beneath and aft of the nose radome. Its dimensions were as follows: span 55 ft 6 in (16.92 m); span (folded) 27 ft (8.23 m); length 50 ft 5 in (15.37 m); height 16 ft 10 in (5.13 m); and wing area 569 sq ft 52.86 sq m).

Design 77

In January 1946, after the Bureau of Aeronautics showed interest in the use of sweptback wings as a result of data brought back from Germany by the Naval Technical Mission in Europe and of research undertaken by NACA at the Langley Laboratory, Grumman proposed a research aircraft to obtain data on low-speed handling characteristics of highly swept wings. To reduce costs, consideration was given to fitting swept wings either to a modified Bell P-63, as Bell did with its L-39, or to a modified Wildcat. In the end, however, Grumman proposed the all-new Design 77. Neither the modified aircraft nor the new design reached the hardware stage.

Intended to be powered by a 450-hp Pratt & Whitney R-985 radial, Design 77 was a low-wing aircraft with a wing box structure arranged to accommodate wings with various degrees of sweepback. Fitted with a non-retractable undercarriage, the aircraft was planned as a single-seater but, if required, could accommodate an observer aft of the pilot. With 35 degrees of wing sweep, the principal characteristics and performance of Design 77 were as follows: span 34 ft (10.36 m); length 33 ft 9 in (10.29 m); wing area 210 sq ft (19.51 sq m); empty weight 3,480 lb (1,579 kg); normal

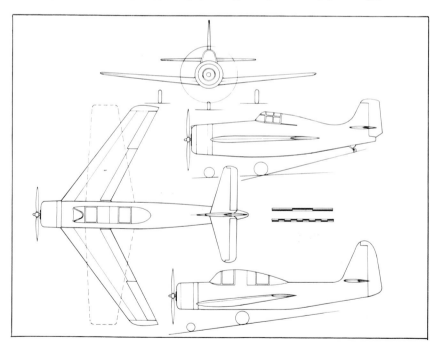

Design 77

loaded weight 4,420 lb (2,005 kg); max gross weight 6,000 lb (2,722 kg); max speed 220 mph (354 kmh) at sea level; estimated terminal velocity 450 mph (724 kmh) at 10,000 ft (3,050 m); service ceiling 26,000 ft (7,925 m); and, endurance at maximum rated power 1 hour.

Design 91

At the begining of 1950, while working on its twin-engined Design 89 (soon to become the XS2F-1), Grumman also evaluated two approaches to combining the ASW hunter/killer capabilities into a single-engined airframe. Design 90 was a direct modification of the AF-2, whereas Design 91 was an all-new smaller and lighter design to be powered by the same 2,300-hp Pratt & Whitney R-2800-48 radial engine. The three-seat G-91 was to have carried a torpedo internally and HVAR rockets beneath the wing. ASW equipment was to have included an APS-33A radar in a retractable radome beneath the rear fuselage and a retractable MAD boom. Principal characteristics were as follows: span 62 ft (18.90 m); span (folded) 26 ft 8 in (8.13 m); length 39 ft (11.89 m); height 16 ft 8 in (5.08 m); empty weight 14,044 lb (6,370 kg); and loaded weight 19,448 lb (8,821 kg).

Design 91 was submitted to the Bureau of Aeronautics in April 1950; however, BuAer preferred to proceed with its twin-engined ASW design competition as this larger aircraft was expected to carry more weapons and sonobuoys. The winning entry, the Grumman Design 89, was ordered in June 1950 as the XS2F-1.

Design 95 (XWF-1)

Seeking a more capable aircraft to replace its TBM-3W airborne early warning aircraft, the Navy requested Grumman and Vought to submit proposals respectively based on their XS2F-1 and XS2U-1 ASW prototypes. Work on Design 95 was initiated in June 1951 and resulted in the submission of a proposal at the end of the following month. The proposed XWF-1 retained the basic airframe, crew accommodation, and powerplant installation of the XS2F-1. It was characterized by the addition of small vertical fins on the tailplane and the installation of an AN/APS-20A in a large radome which was to be pylon-mounted well forward atop the fuselage to enable retention of the XS2F-1 wing-folding geometry.

Two prototypes (BuNos 133043 and 133044) were ordered but, as the Navy assigned higher priority to other aircraft, work on this project proceeded slowly. Wind-tunnel tests were conducted in the autumn of 1951 to determine the best position and shape for the AN/APS-20A radome, and a fuselage mock-up was constructed in December 1952 to check the internal arrangement. However, the project was terminated shortly afterwards. Dimensions were identical to those of the XS2F-1: *ie*, span 69 ft 8 in (21.23 m); length 42 ft 0 in (12.80 m); height 16 ft 3½ in (4.97 m); and wing area 485 sq ft (45.06 sq m).

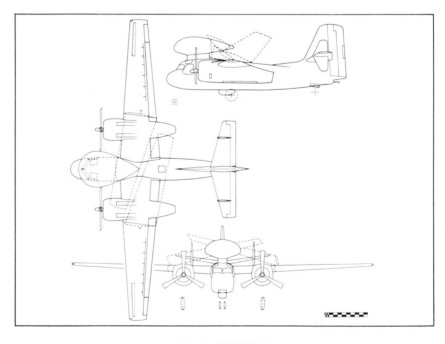

Design 95 (XWF-1)

Design 97

Design 97 was submitted in February 1953 in answer to a Navy request for proposals for a single-seat carrier-based aircraft capable of supersonic speeds in level flight. To be powered by a 9,220-lb thrust dry and 14,800 lb (6,713 kg) thrust with afterburner Pratt & Whitney J57 turbojet, the Grumman Design 97 had a thin mid-wing with 45 degrees of sweep and moderate aspect ratio, long-span flaperons, and all-movable horizontal tail surfaces. Armament consisted of four 20-mm cannon in the nose and four Sparrow II air-to-air missiles beneath the wings. Alternatively, the cannon could be replaced by fifty-eight 2-in FFAR rockets. Grumman had high hopes of winning the design competition but, in the end, the Navy decided to spread the wealth and awarded the contract for the J57-powered aircraft to LTV (the resulting aircraft being the F8U-1) and the contract for the J65-powered aircraft to Grumman (Design 98 which became the F9F-9 and eventually the F11F-1).

Principal characteristics and performance of the Design 97 were as follows: span 33 ft 4 in (10.16 m); span (folded) 27 ft 6 in (8.38 m); length 43 ft 4 in (13.21 m); height 15 ft 7 in (4.75 m); empty weight 13,721 lb (6,224

kg); loaded weight 21,456 lb (9,732 kg); max speed 915 mph (1,472 kmh) at 35,000 ft (10,670 m) and 725 mph (1,167 kmh) at sea level; initial rate of climb, 14,000 ft/min (71 m/sec); service ceiling 55,000 ft (16,765 m); and normal range 1,750 miles (2,815 km).

Design 118 (XF12F-1)

Conceived in answer to an RFP issued by the Navy in September 1953, Design 118 was a missile-armed all-weather supersonic fighter intended to complement the F8U-1 air-superiority fighter aboard carriers. Two prototypes of the XF12F-1 (BuNos 143401/143402) were ordered in 1955, but the contract was cancelled shortly after because the McDonnell XF4H-1 was more heavily armed and promised to have better performance.

Production F12F-1s were to have been powered by a pair of 18,000-lb thrust General Electric J79-GE-207 turbojets and fitted with an APQ-50 radar. Proposed armament consisted of three Sparrow radar-guided missiles or two Sparrows and three Sidewinder IR missiles flush-mounted beneath the fuselage on trapezes which were to swing down before missile launch.

Principal characteristics and performance of the XF12F-1 were as follows: span 43 ft 11 in (13.39 m); length 58 ft 6 in (17.83 m); height 14 ft 10 in (4.52 m); empty weight 26,255 lb (11,909 kg); loaded weight 37,300 lb (16,919 kg); max speed Mach 2 plus.

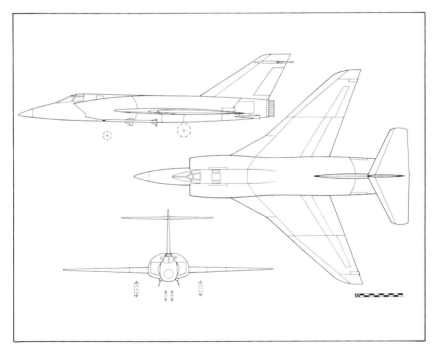

Design 118 (XF12F-1)

557

Design 128G-12

When BuWeps requested proposals for the VA(L) light attack aircraft in June 1963, it specified that manufacturers should only submit designs which were minimum-change modifications of existing designs as low cost and early availability were of prime importance. Accordingly, in August 1963 Grumman submitted its Design 128G-12, a derivative of the A-6A. As the VA(L) was intended for day operations in clear weather, the complex integrated navigation and bombing system of the A-6A was replaced by a simpler multimode radar, and a single-seat-on-centreline cockpit was substituted for the two-seat cockpit of the A-6A. The only other significant change was the incorporation of a folding horizontal tail to increase by one third the carrier spotting factor (*ie*, the number of aircraft that could be parked within a given space on deck). Intended to be powered by two 9,300-lb thrust Pratt & Whitney J52-P-8A turbojets, the 128G-12 had a span of 53 ft (16.15 m), a length of 56 ft 6 in (17.22 m), and a height of 15 ft 5 in (4.70 m).

Commonality between the A-6A and the proposed Design 128G-12 was 90 per cent for parts, 79 per cent for manufacturing tools, 95 per cent for

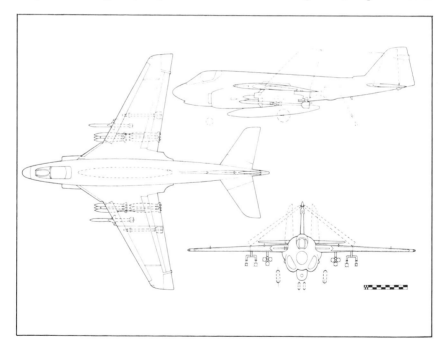

Design 128G-12

mechanical, 75 per cent for electronic support equipment, and 85 per cent for spare parts. Nevertheless, the Navy finally selected the smaller and lighter LTV proposal even though the resulting A-7A had much lower commonality with the F-8.

Design 134E

Although the Mohawk already had commendable short take-off characteristics (the aircraft clearing a 50-ft obstacle in less than 1,750 ft when operating at maximum gross weight), in the early 1960s the Army felt that the usefulness and flexibility of operations of its battlefield observation aircraft would be increased if they could be endowed with the capability of taking-off and landing vertically. As by then Grumman had already conducted extensive studies of tilt-wing V/STOL designs, the feasibility of modifying the OV-1 to a tilt-wing configuration appeared logical.

Work on Design 134E revealed that with the exception of moving the wing up to a shoulder position, replacing the two Lycoming T53 propeller-turbines with either four General Electric T58s or four Lycoming T53s, and substituting a shrouded horizontal rotor for the central fin, few major changes would be necessary. However, work on Design 134E did not proceed beyond the preliminary design phase as, in the end, the Army decided that the aircraft's ability to take-off and land vertically would not justify the added acquisition costs and increased maintenance requirements.

Another VTOL development of the Mohawk was briefly studied. It called for the modification of a YAO-1 into a flight research vehicle fitted with an 'M' wing in which General Electric X-353-5 Lift-fan engines were to have been buried. Principal characteristics and performance of the Lift-Fan Mohawk were as follows: span 32 ft 6 in (9.91 m); length 43 ft (13.11 m); wing area 290 sq ft (26. 94 sq m); empty weight 7,730 lb (3,506 kg); loaded weight 9,850 lb (4,468 kg); payload 500 lb (227 kg); max speed 453 mph (729 kmh); hover time 5 minutes; and, endurance 40 minutes.

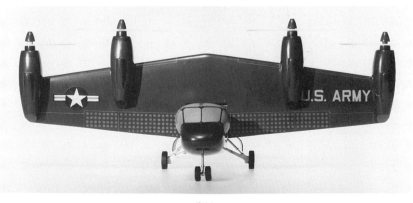

Design 143

One of the least-known projects undertaken by Grumman during the late 1950s was the *Bushfire* rear defence system for the P6M-2 strategic flying-boat then being developed by Martin for the Navy. Whereas the two XP6M-1 prototypes had a twin-gun tail turret, production P6M-2s were to have been fitted with the Grumman Design 143 *Bushfire* system using SARH (semi-active radar homing) missiles launched to the rear. As shown in the accompanying drawing dated 15 January, 1957, one missile was carried in a launching tube, ready to be fired as soon as an enemy aircraft was detected by the Aero X23B search radar. Four to six additional missiles were carried on a revolver-type housing forward of the launching tube. Cancellation of the P6M-2 programme resulted in the demise of the *Bushfire* system.

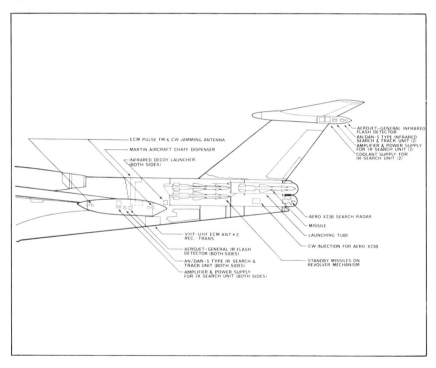

Design 143

Designs 165 and 215

Although when phased out in 1975 the S-2Gs were the last piston-powered combat aircraft of the US Navy, this anachronism did not come about as the result of a lack of interest on the part of Grumman; the company had made repeated attempts to interest the Navy in turbine-powered Tracker and

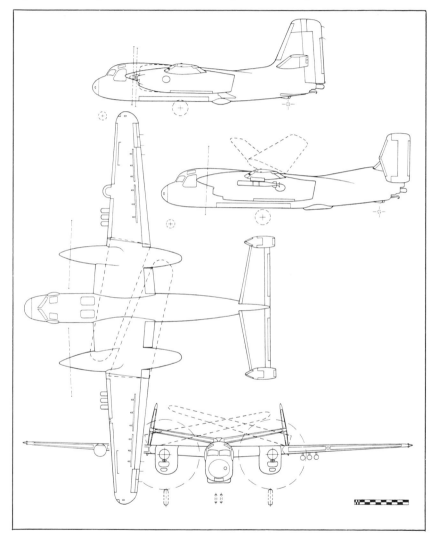

Design 215. Side view of Design 165A

563

Trader versions. The first such attempt was made in May 1957 when the manufacturer submitted an unsolicited proposal for the development of its Design 121, which was to have been powered by a pair of twin Lycoming T53 propeller-turbines. Later in 1957, Grumman proposed two Trader derivatives with Lycoming T55 propeller-turbines, the Design 137 tanker, and the Design 142 COD transport. Twin T53s were again proposed in 1958 for a version of Design 165, a re-engined Tracker, while another version of this design was to have been powered by two General Electric T55 propeller-turbines. Due to lack of funds, however, the Navy showed little interest in these proposals.

Proposed in November 1959, Design 215 came closer to being ordered into production as the S2F-4 but, again, budget limitations finally forced the Navy to withdraw. Intended to be powered by two 2,750-eshp General Electric T64-GE-8 turbines driving three-blade propellers, the G-215 was to have used the S2F-3 fuselage with a 22-in extension forward of the wing front spar, strengthened S2F-3 wings, and twin vertical tail surfaces derived from those of the WF-2. Principal characteristics and performance were as follows: span 72 ft 7 in (22.12 m); length 46 ft 8.5 in (14.24 m); height 15 ft 8 in (4.78 m); empty weight 21,443 lb (9,726 kg); loaded weight 35,361 lb (16,039 kg); max speed 346 mph/557 kmh (95-mph/153-kmh over that achieved by the S2F-3); service ceiling 32,500 ft (9,900 m); and combat range 2,090 miles (3,365 km).

Design 235-4 Gadfly

During the late 1950s and early 1960s, Grumman designed several tilt-wing aircraft for military and civilian uses, but none reached the hardware stage. Among these unbuilt VTOL projects was Design 235-4, a four/five-seat executive aircraft, for which the preliminary design was completed in May 1960. Fitted with a retractable nosewheel undercarriage and shoulder-mounted wings, the Gadfly was to have been powered by wingtip-mounted 320-shp Allison T63 turbines driving 16-ft diameter propellers.

The principal characteristics of the Gadfly were as follows: span 25 ft (7.62 m); length 23 ft (7.01m); height 8 ft 2 in (2.49 m).

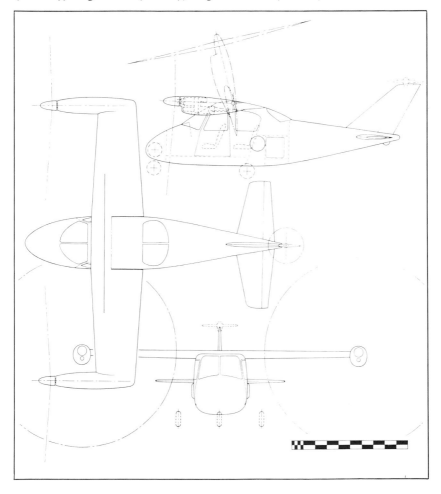

Design 235-4 Gadfly

Design 305

Conceived in September 1961, the G-305 was a proposed ASW flying-boat of advanced design which was to have been powered by four 2,785-eshp General Electric T64-GE-4 propeller-turbines. By then, however, the US Navy was no longer interested in flying-boats and was about to put into service the better performing Lockheed P3V-1 Orion land-based ASW aircraft.

The principal characteristics and calculated performance of the G-305 were as follows: span 105 ft (32.00 m); length 88 ft 3 in (26.90 m); height 27 ft 11 in (8.51 m); loaded weight 70,500 lb (31,978 kg); max speed 403 mph (648 kmh); range 3,455 miles (5,560 km).

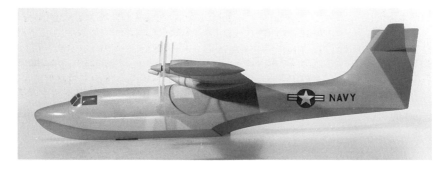

Design 607A

As a potential replacement for its CVSs (Antisubmarine Warfare Support Carriers), in 1971-72 the US Navy contemplated obtaining low-cost SCSs (Sea Control Ships) from which ASW helicopters could operate on convoy escort duty. In addition, each SCS was to embark a few V/STOL fighters for conventional air defence and 'anti-*Bear* mission' (interception of Tupolev Tu-95 and other Soviet maritime surveillance aircraft) up to 100 nm from the convoy.

Proposed in November 1971, Design 607A was a supersonic V/STOL fighter specially conceived for operations from an SCS. It was to have been powered by a Pratt & Whitney JTF22A-30B lift/cruise turbofan with a conventional main exhaust nozzle and a swivelling nozzle on each side of the rear fuselage; afterburning thrust in level flight was 27,500 lb and maximum VTOL thrust, without afterburner, was 15,650 lb. Two 11,525-lb thrust Grumman-developed GLE-607A direct lift-turbojets were to have been mounted vertically just aft of the single-seat cockpit. Proposed armament consisted of a 20-mm cannon in the port wing leading edge, Sidewinder missiles on wingtip shoes, and a Sparrow missile beneath each wing.

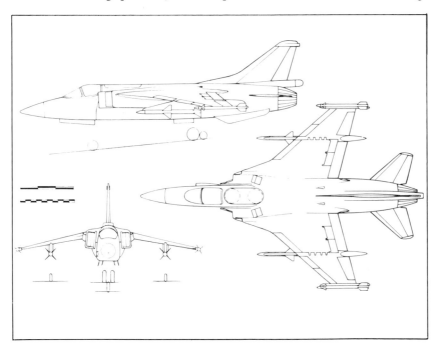

Design 607A

567

Principal characteristics and performance were as follows: span 31 ft 6 in (9.60 m); span (wings folded) 21 ft 10 in (6.65 m); length 51 ft 7½ in (15.74 m); height 16 ft (4.88 m); wing area 365 sq ft (33.91 sq m); empty weight 19,204 lb (8,711 kg); max VTO weight 30,723 lb (13,936 kg); max weight 36,711 lb (16,652 kg); max speed Mach 1.2 at sea level and Mach 2.0 at 40,000 ft (12,190 m); and, combat endurance when operating in the conventional mode 1.72 hour at 300 nm (555 km).

The SCS concept was killed by Congress during the FY 1975 budget review, and with its demise ended any further thoughts of developing Design 607.

Design 698. Grumman illustration showing transition from vertical to horizontal flight.

Design 698

Grumman conceived the Design 698 V/STOL aircraft in the mid-1970s to meet the US Army's requirements for the Special Electronic Mission Aircraft (SEMA-X) for reconnaissance, electronic warfare and surveillance, communications relay, and target acquisition and designation. Design 698 was also offered to the Navy to undertake a variety of missions from proposed Sea Control Ships.

Of twin tilt-fan configuration, the two-seat Design 698 was to have been controlled through horizontal and vertical vanes located in the exhaust flow of pod-mounted 9,065-lb thrust General Electric TF34-GE-100 turbofans. Aerodynamic forces generated by the high-speed flow over these surfaces were to provide the control in pitch, yaw, and roll required for hover and transition. Spoilers, an all-movable stabilizer, and a rudder were provided for control in conventional flight.

Computer simulations, radio-controlled models, and small-scale wind-tunnel tests were followed by full-scale TF34-powered model tests. Sponsored jointly by NASA, the Naval Air Systems Command, and Grumman, the full-scale tests were conducted in the NASA Ames 40-ft by 80-ft wind tunnel and confirmed the feasibility of the tilt-fan concept. However, lack of funds resulted in the Army cancelling its SEMA-X requirement and the Navy losing interest in the project when Congress terminated funding for the Sea Control Ship.

Principal characteristics and performance were: span 36 ft 8 in (11.18 m); length 38 ft 5$\frac{1}{2}$ in (11.72 m); height 14 ft 11 in (4.55 m); empty weight 11,723 lb (5,322 kg); max VTO weight 15,430 lb (7,000 kg); VTO power loading 0.85 lb/lb st (0.85 kg/kgp); max speed 500 mph (805 kmh); cruising speed 409 mph (658 kmh); and ferry range 1,150 miles (1,850 km).

Astronaut Edwin E Aldrin Jr, the LM-5 *Eagle* pilot during the first lunar mission, prepares to deploy the Early Apollo Scientific Experiments Package (EASEP) at Tranquility Base on 20 July, 1969. (*NASA Lyndon B. Johnson Space Center*)

APPENDIX C

Lunar Module

'One small step for a man, one giant leap for mankind.' – Neil A Armstrong, after stepping out of the Lunar Module 5 *Eagle* onto the surface of the moon at Tranquility Base on 20 July, 1969.

If the first *Sputnik I* transmission from space on 4 October, 1957, was a rude awakening for America, the first orbital flight by Yuri A Gagarin in *Vostok I* on 12 April, 1961, was a downright shock. The fitting reply demanded by national pride and military preparedness was announced on 25 May, 1961, by President John F Kennedy, four months after his inauguration, when during an historic address to Congress he stated '… I believe that this Nation should commit itself to achieving the goal, before this decade is out, of landing a man on the Moon and returning him safely to Earth.' As a result of this mandate, the National Aeronautics and Space Administration (NASA, which was organized in 1958 after President Dwight D Eisenhower had signed into law the National Aeronautics and Space Act of 1958) was given a new organizational structure to realign its management for an expanded US civilian space programme. Grumman, with its brilliantly conceived and flawlessly realized Lunar Module, played a vital role in achieving this ambitious goal.

During the summer of 1958, shortly after it had been organized within the Preliminary Design Department to consolidate Grumman's efforts in participating in the space programme, the Space Steering Group chaired by Alfred Munier concluded that there already were too many competitors for earth orbiting systems, and recommended that work be concentrated on manned lunar exploration systems. For the next four years, however, it appeared that this recommendation had been ill-founded. Grumman successively lost competitions for a feasibility study for the Project Apollo Manned Spacecraft and System in October 1960, the design of the Apollo Command and Service Modules in November 1961, and a Lunar Orbiting Rendezvous feasibility study in February 1962.

Work on a company-funded lunar orbit rendezvous study had been initiated in Bethpage in December 1960, at a time when NASA was still contemplating the use of the very large Nova rocket to bring to the surface of the Moon the entire assembly (consisting of the Apollo Command and Service Modules and the rocket stage which would be used to launch the two modules back toward Earth). Eventually, however, NASA began having second thoughts about the Nova concept and, as part of the RFP for the design of the Apollo Command and Service Modules which it issued in October 1961, asked bidders to consider other modes of lunar descent and a separate excursion vehicle. NASA then issued an RFP for a Feasibility Study of LOR (Lunar Orbiting Rendezvous) in January 1962. Unfortunately, in spite of its internally-funded LOR work of the previous thirteen months, Grumman was again unsuccessful. NASA selected LTV to undertake this study.

Undeterred and using its own funds, Grumman went on working on a Lunar Mission Study Plan to ascertain once again the feasibility, costs, characteristics, and relative merits of direct ascent from the Moon surface versus lunar orbit rendezvous or earth orbit rendezvous. This effort resulted in a March 1962 recommendation to management that priority ought to be given to LOR and the Lunar Bug Project. During the following month, the Executive Committee endorsed this recommendation and, deciding that the company would compete aggressively as prime contractor for the 'Bug' spacecraft, appointed Joseph M Gavin to head the project and Robert E Mullaney as programme manager. Soon after Grumman accepted an offer from RCA to participate in the unfunded study, and the two firms submitted their Lunar Excursion Module Study Results to NASA on 22 June, 1962. Being on the verge also of concluding that lunar orbit

571

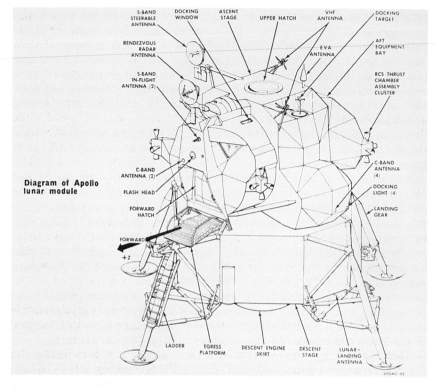

Diagram of Apollo lunar module

S-BAND STEERABLE ANTENNA
DOCKING WINDOW
ASCENT STAGE
UPPER HATCH
VHF ANTENNA
DOCKING TARGET
RENDEZVOUS RADAR ANTENNA
EVA ANTENNA
AFT EQUIPMENT BAY
S-BAND IN-FLIGHT ANTENNA (2)
RCS THRUST CHAMBER ASSEMBLY CLUSTER
C-BAND ANTENNA (2)
C-BAND ANTENNA (4)
FLASH HEAD
DOCKING LIGHT (4)
FORWARD HATCH
LANDING GEAR
FORWARD
+Z
LADDER
EGRESS PLATFORM
DESCENT ENGINE SKIRT
DESCENT STAGE
LUNAR-LANDING ANTENNA

Diagram of the Lunar Module. *(Grumman drawing, courtesy of Jane's All the World's Aircraft)*

rendezvous was the best way to proceed for the manned landing mission, NASA was impressed with this unsolicited proposal but, not allowed by law to award a single-source contract of this magnitude, issued an RFP for the lunar excursion module in August 1962.

Written proposals were submitted by Grumman and eight other manufacturers on 4 September, verbal presentations were made on 13 and 14 September, and NASA evaluation teams visited the bidders between 17 and 19 September. Then, on 7 November, 1962, NASA announced that Grumman had been selected to build the lunar excursion module (soon simply called Lunar Module, or LM, as 'excursion' was considered to be an inappropriate term for a scientific undertaking).

Grumman, like the other bidders, had only submitted conceptual design data, and the $386 million contract signed in February 1963 thus entailed pushing the state-of-the-art to an extent seldom attempted. It essentially covered the preliminary and detailed design phases, along with laboratory testing and simulation. The tasks facing the Grumman and NASA engineers and scientists were indeed daunting as, at the time, hard data on the Moon were limited to results of empirical studies and observatory data

(*Ranger 7* and *Surveyor 1*, the first US spacecraft respectively to transmit photographs of the Moon and make a controlled touchdown on the Moon surface, were themselves still under development; they completed their missions on 28 July, 1964, and on 30 May, 1966). Moreover, lack of data (such as the thickness of the dust layer on the Moon, whether this layer would provide an adequate landing surface, or whether dust would obscure visibility before touchdown) was compounded by a time constraint (landing a man on the Moon and returning him safely to Earth before the end of the decade as mandated by President Kennedy) and the critical need to control the weight* of the spacecraft while adhering to reasonable standards of safety and reliability.

By the time the M-1 engineering mock-up was completed in August 1964, most of the critical design decisions had been made and the configuration of the two-stage LM had been finalized. The larger of the two was the descent stage, which incorporated a gimballed, throttleable 9,700-lb thrust † TRW liquid-propellant rocket engine, provided storage space for the Apollo Lunar Surface Experiment Package (ALSEP) scientific equipment, and four landing legs with round pads to distribute the weight evenly on the lunar dust. The ascent stage, which was mounted on the descent stage, was fitted with four Marquardt reaction control thrusters and powered by a 3,500-lb thrust liquid-propellant rocket engine (the engine initially selected was a Bell design but it was replaced by a North American Rocketdyne unit before completion of the first operational module).

The ascent stage provided accommodation for two astronauts, the Mission Commander and the Lunar Module Pilot, standing side-by-side in harnesses with a centrally located instrument panel. Two hatches were provided, one on the side with a platform (called a mesa like the flat-topped mountains in the southwestern United States) and a ladder for egress and ingress while on the Moon and the other an upper hatch for communication between the LM and the Apollo Command Module.

The Apollo operational plan called for the S-IVB stage and Lunar Module to be separated from the Command/Service Module during the transit to the Moon while the three Apollo astronauts were in the Command Module (CM). Afterwards, the Command Module Pilot was to dock the spacecraft to the LM and the two other astronauts were to crawl through the connecting tunnel and board the LM through the upper hatch to get the Grumman spacecraft ready before reaching lunar orbit. Once in lunar

---

* Later during the design, it was determined that for every pound of additional equipment or structural weight, total weight had to be increased by four pounds due to the need to provide more fuel to launch the heavier ascent stage from the surface of the Moon.The maximum allowable weight for the Lunar Module, however, was dictated by the total thrust of the Saturn V launching vehicle.

---

† The thrust of the TRW descent engine was later increased to 10,500 lb to cater for the heavier weight of the last three Lunar Modules.

Descent and Ascent modules during assembly at Bethpage on 10 November, 1966. *(Grumman)*

orbit, the two astronauts were to return to the LM and separate it from the Command/Service Module before starting their descent. After completing their lunar mission, they were to take-off in the ascent stage (the descent stage serving as launch platform and remaining on the Moon) and to rendezvous in lunar orbit with the Command/Service Module. Following docking of the two spacecraft by the CM Pilot, the two returning explorers were to re-enter the CM. Having served its purpose, the LM was to be crashed on the surface of the Moon while the three astronauts started their return toward Earth orbit in the Command/Service Module.

Altogether, the LM programme eventually called for Grumman to deliver two Lunar Module Test Article simulators (LTA-A and LTA-B), ten Lunar Module Test Article modules (LTA-1 to LTA-10R), and fifteen operational Lunar Modules (LM-1 to LM-15). The last three (LM-13 to LM-15) were cancelled and change orders resulted in LM-10 to LM-12 being completed to a revised 'extended stay' configuration, with provision for carrying the Boeing Lunar Roving Vehicle (LRV) in the descent stage, larger fuel tanks, and additional water and oxygen tanks.

Although each operational LM was slightly different from the previous examples, appearance and principal characteristics remained essentially unchanged. The descent stage, with its legs extended, and ascent stage were respectively 10 ft 7 in (3.23 m) and 12 ft 4 in (3.76 m) high, thus adding to a LM overall height of 22 ft 11 in (6.99 m). The maximum width of the LM was 14 ft 1 in (4.29 m) around the ascent stage and the track between its opposite landing legs was 31 ft 0 in (9.45 m). Launch weight started at 32,000 lb (14,515 kg) but was increased to 33,205 lb (15,062 kg) for LM-5, the module used for the first moon mission, and finally to 36,025 lb (16,341 kg) for the last three 'extended stay' modules.

In Space and on the Moon

On 17 September, 1967, following lengthy simulation studies and thorough testing of components and systems (the most important of these activities being the testing of the electrical and electronic systems, which was done at Bethpage using LTA-1, the first Lunar Module Test Article), Grumman delivered LTA-8 to the NASA Manned Spacecraft Center in Houston, Texas. There, the staff of the Space Simulation Laboratory undertook a series of tests under temperature and vacuum extremes simulating a typical lunar mission. Afterwards, NASA and Grumman proceeded with the Flight Development Test Program (FDTP) to verify that the LM met the operational requirements of the lunar mission and to demonstrate that design goals regarding astronaut safety and mission success had been met.[*] To that end, LTA-10R, the last of the test articles, was instrumented to measure vibration, acoustics, and structural integrity during launch of *Apollo 4* on 9 November, 1967. Data telemetered to ground stations during the first 12 minutes of flight of the first *Saturn V* launch vehicles confirmed the accuracy of predicted values.

Two flight articles had been planned for unmanned FDTP missions. The first, LM-1, was shipped from Bethpage to the Kennedy Space Center in Florida on 23 June, 1967, and was launched on *Apollo 5* on 22 January, 1968. During this mission, the LM's ascent and descent propulsion systems, along with the spacecraft reaction control sytem, were test-fired and restarted for the first time in space. Even though the first burn of the ascent engine was cut prematurely by the craft's automatic pilot, the LM-1 test was sufficiently successful for NASA to decide not to proceed with its launch plan for LM-2. Subsequently, the no-longer-needed Lunar Module was donated to the Smithsonian Institution for display at the National Air and Space Museum in Washington, D C.

Another LM Test Article, LTA-2R, was launched in the unmanned *Apollo 6* and provided flight test data on *Saturn V* launch load test and environmental criteria on 4 April, 1968. No LM components were carried during the *Apollo 7* Earth orbital mission when Walter Schirra, Don Eisele, and Walter Cunningham made the first manned Apollo flight on 11 and 12 October, 1968.

Designed to simulate the weight and mass of a Lunar Module and consisting of two concentric rings arranged to form a cylinder with four internal water ballast tanks, LTA-B was launched aboard *Apollo 8*, the first

---

[*] In the light of problems encountered in more recent years with the Space Shuttle programme, it is worth noting that for the Lunar Module NASA specified a near-perfect .9995 factor for crew safety and an almost equally demanding .984 factor for mission completion.

The LM-3 *Spider*, still attached to the *Saturn V* third (S-IVB) stage, photographed from the Command Module *Gumdrop* on the first day of the *Apollo 9* earth orbital mission, 3 March, 1969. (*NASA Lyndon B. Johnson Space Center*)

manned mission to orbit the Moon. Lasting from 21 to 27 December, 1968, the *Apollo 8* mission saw Frank Borman, James Lovell, and William Anders orbit the Moon ten times.

With all Apollo systems now satisfactorily tested and only one year remaining in which to achieve the goal of landing a man on the Moon before the end of the decade, the pace of the programme was accelerated. LM-3, the first manned Lunar Module, was launched on *Apollo 9* on 3 March, 1969. Remaining in Earth orbit, the LM and CM spacecraft were separated and James McDivitt and Russ Schweickart flew *Spider* 113 miles away from the CM *Gumdrop* before jettisoning the descent stage and firing the ascent stage to return to *Gumdrop*. *Spider* was left to burn in space and the astronauts were recovered by a Sea King helicopter from HS-3 aboard the

Interior view of LM-5 *Eagle*. (*NASA Lyndon B. Johnson Space Center*)

USS *Guadalcanal* (LPH-7) on 13 March. Barely two months later, on 18 May, Thomas Stafford, John Young, and Eugene Cernan were launched aboard *Apollo 10* on a lunar mission which saw Stafford and Cernan take the appropriately named LM-4 *Snoopy* to within 9.4 miles of the Moon's surface. Recovery was made by HS-4 aboard the USS *Princeton* (CVS-37) on 26 May.

The historic mission to the Moon began on 16 July when *Apollo 11*, carrying Neil Armstrong, Edwin Aldrin, Michael Collins, and the LM-5 (the soon to be famous *Eagle*), was launched at the Kennedy Space Center. Four days later, with Neil Armstrong taking over the controls from the automatic guidance system to avoid landing in a rock-strewn crater, *Eagle* came down safely on the dry Sea of Tranquility. After checking that the LM-5 had not suffered damage in the first landing on the Moon, the two pioneers got ready for the first Extra Vehicular Activity (EVA, the popular Moon walk). Finally, at 3:56:20 GMT on 21 July, 1969,[*] Neil A Armstrong stepped down from the last rung of the *Eagle*'s ladder to become the first man to stand on the Moon. Soon after, he was joined by Edwin E Aldrin Jr, and the two astronauts spent 2 hr 31 min 40 sec roaming the Moon's surface, deploying scientific instruments, taking photographs, and retrieving nearly 50 lb of lunar rock and soil samples. *Eagle*'s ascent after 21 hr 36 min on the Moon, its docking with the CM piloted by Michael Collins, and the return

---

[*] It was 10:56:20 pm (EDT) on 20 July in Washington, DC. Hence, 20 July, 1969, is the date usually associated in the United States with this historical event.

Edwin E Aldrin Jr descends the steps of LM-5 *Eagle* to join Neil A Armstrong on the surface of the moon on 20 July, 1969. (*NASA Lyndon B. Johnson Space Center*)

to Earth went smoothly. Recovery was made by a helicopter from HS-4 which took the astronauts aboard the uss *Hornet* (CVS-12) on 24 July. The nearly impossible challenge of President Kennedy had been met.

Later in the year, proving that the success of *Apollo 11* and LM-5 was not a fluke, two more astronauts were brought to a site on the Ocean of Storms by *Intrepid*, the Lunar Module carried aboard *Apollo 12* during a mission which began on 14 November. While Richard Gordon stayed in the CM, Charles (Pete) Conrad and Alan Bean spent 31 hr 31 min on the Moon and, during the course of two EVAs, deployed nuclear-powered ALSEP scientic equipment and recovered parts from the *Surveyor 3* probe which had landed on the Moon in April 1967. Once again, ascent from the Moon, docking with the CM *Yankee Clipper*, return to Earth, and recovery by HS-4 to the

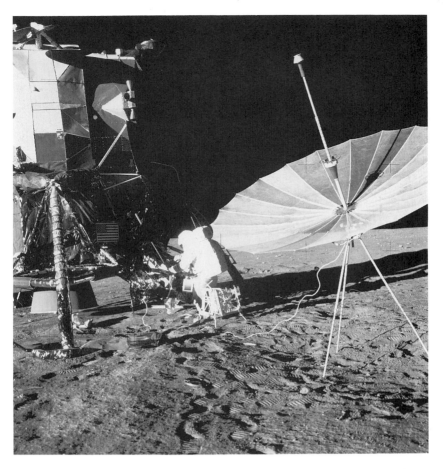

Astronaut Charles Conrad Jr, commander of the *Apollo 12* lunar landing mission, stands next to the Module Equipment Stowage Assembly (MESA) of LM-6 *Intrepid* at the Ocean of Storms on 19 November, 1969. (*NASA Lyndon B. Johnson Space Center*)

USS *Hornet* (CVS-12) on 24 November went according to plan. The next lunar mission, however, was far from routine.

Apollo 13, the first mission scheduled to land in the lunar highlands, was launched from the Kennedy Space Center on 11 April, 1970. Everything went satisfactorily, including the docking of the LM-7 *Aquarius* with the prophetically named CM *Odyssey*, until an oxygen tank in the Service Module failed when *Apollo 13* was 205,000 miles from the Earth on its way to the Moon. The failure threatened to leave James Lovell, John Swigert, and Fred Haise marooned in space. Cool professionalism and brilliant teamwork on the part of the astronauts, the NASA staff, and personnel from Grumman and the other Apollo contractors enabled emergency procedures to be devised in record time. Using *Aquarius* as a 'lifeboat'

579

Col David R Scott, USAF, salutes the US flag during EVA at the Hadley-Apennine landing site on 1 August, 1971. After three EVAs totalling 18 hr 36 min, David Scott and James Irwin boarded the ascent module of LM-10 *Falcon* to join Alfred Worden in the Command Module and return to earth on 7 August. *(NASA Lyndon B. Johnson Space Center)*

providing oxygen, electrical power, and propulsion, *Apollo 13* continued towards the Moon where a critical firing of the LM descent engine modified its trajectory and sent it back toward Earth. *Aquarius* performed superbly and at the end of a remarkable flight Lovell, Swigert, and Haise were recovered by HS-4 off the uss *Iwo Jima* (LPH-2) on 17 April, 1970.

After a nine-month hiatus during which the exact cause of the *Apollo 13* Service Module failure was determined and appropriate modifications were incorporated in the remaining spacecraft, Moon missions were resumed on 31 January, 1971, with the launch of *Apollo 14*. Carrying Alan Shepard and Ed Mitchell, the LM-8 *Antares* accomplished the third successful lunar landing on 5 February. The crew's objectives included exploration of the lunar highlands in the Fra Mauro area and retrieval of heavier lunar rocks. To transport these samples and some of their bulkier equipment, Shepard and Mitchell were provided with a two-wheel Modularized Equipment Transport System (METS). After departing from lunar orbit, the two lunar explorers and Stuart Roosa, the CM pilot, conducted extensive scientific experiments before being recovered by a Sea King helicopter of HS-6 and brought aboard the uss *New Orleans* (LPH-11) on 9 February.

The *Apollo 15* crew, David Scott, James Irwin, and Alfred Worden, was launched on 26 July, 1971, and taken aboard the uss *Okinawa* (LPH-3) by a helicopter from HC-1 on 7 August. Their LM-10 *Falcon* was the first of the 'extended stay' Lunar Modules, and Scott and Irwin used the Lunar Roving Vehicle carried in the descent stage to travel 1.4 km (nine-tenths of a mile) from the Hadley Apenine landing site to the edge of the Hadley Rille. Communications systems on the LRV permitted television coverage of the crew's activities during the lunar exploration and, controlled from the Earth, provided the first live TV coverage of an LM lift-off from the Moon's surface.

Launched aboard *Apollo 16* on 16 April, 1972, the LM-11 *Orion* brought John Young and Charles Duke to the Descartes highlands four days later. Spending nearly three days on the surface of the Moon, the two astronauts used an ultraviolet camera/spectrograph for photographic recordings of the Earth and other astronomical observations and used their Lunar Roving Vehicle to explore the lunar surface and gather a variety of lunar geological samples remote from their landing site. On 27 April, they and Thomas Mattingly, the CM pilot, were recovered by HC-1 helicopters from the uss *Ticonderoga* (CVS-14).

Fittingly, the last Apollo mission saw Eugene Cernan and Harrison Schmitt, the only scientist to be taken to the moon, use the LM-12 *Challenger* to spend more time on the Moon, make the longest EVAs, and bring back the heaviest load of lunar soil samples. This mission ended on 19 December, 1972, almost exactly four years after the *Apollo 8* astronauts had become the first men to orbit the Moon, with the recovery of Cernan, Schmitt, and Ronald Evans, by HC-1 helicopters operating from the uss *Ticonderoga* (CVS-14). However, this momentous event almost went unnoticed. Most Americans and many abroad had become preoccupied during the preceding day with the news of the initiation of *Linebacker II*, a powerful American air offensive against North Vietnam.

In the course of six successful missions over a 41-month period, LMs had taken twelve astronauts to the surface of the Moon on which they spent a total of 299 hr 37 min including 80 hr 45 min during fourteen EVAs, and from which they brought back nearly 860 lb of rock and soil samples. Undoubtedly, however, the Lunar Module's greatest challenge came in the course of the only aborted lunar mission, *Apollo 13*, when LM-7 *Aquarius* was used in an unplanned 'recovery space tug' capacity. This, the Grummanites' greatest technological and human achievement, will undoubtedly be remembered by the public long after Wildcats, Avengers, Hellcats, Panthers, and Tomcats have been forgotten by all but aviation enthusiasts and those who were associated with their construction and operation.

Lunar Module Flights

APOLLO/LM	DATES	ASTRONAUTS	HIGHLIGHTS
Apollo 4 LTA-10R	9 Nov 1967	Unmanned	First test of *Saturn V* launch vehicle.
Apollo 5 LM-1	22-24 Jan 1968	Unmanned	First LM unmanned flight. Not recovered.
Apollo 6 LTA-2R	4 Apr 1968	Unmanned	
Apollo 8 LTA-B	21-27 Dec 1968	Col Frank Borman, USAF Capt James A Lovell Jr, USN Lt-Col William A Anders, USAF	First manned orbits of the Moon.
Apollo 9 LM-3 *Spider*	3-13 Mar 1969	Col James A McDivitt, USAF Col David R Scott, USAF Russell L Schweickart, NASA	First LM flight docked.
Apollo 10 LM-4 *Snoopy*	18-26 May 1969	Col Thomas P Stafford, USAF Cdr John W Young, USN Cdr Eugene A Cernan, USN	First Moon orbit by entire system.
Apollo 11 LM-5 *Eagle*	16-24 July 1969	Neil A Armstrong, NASA Col Edwin E Aldrin Jr, USAF Lt-Col Michael Collins, USAF	First Moon landing and walk. Time on the Moon: 21 hr 36 min One EVA: 2 hr 31 min 40 sec.
Apollo 12 LM-6 *Intrepid*	14-24 Nov 1969	Cdr Richard F Gordon Jr, USN Cdr Charles Conrad Jr, USN Cdr Alan L Bean, USN	Second Moon landing and walk. Time on the Moon: 31 hr 31 min Two EVAs: 7 hr 49 min
Apollo 13 LM-7 *Aquarius*	11-17 Apr 1970	Capt James A Lovell Jr, USN John Swigert, NASA Fred Haise Jr, NASA	Moon mission aborted following malfunction in space.
Apollo 14 LM-8 *Antares*	31 Jan-9 Feb 1971	Rear Adm Alan B Shepard Jr, USN Lt-Col Stuart A Roosa, USAF Capt Edgar D Mitchell, USN	Third Moon landing and walk. Time on the Moon: 33 hr 30 min Two EVAs: 9 hr 29 min
Apollo 15 LM-10 *Falcon*	26 Jul-7 Aug 1971	Col David R Scott, USAF Col James B Irwin, USAF Lt-Col Alfred M Worden, USAF	First use of Lunar Roving Vehicle. Time on the Moon: 66 hr 55 min Three EVAs: 18 hr 36 min

Apollo 16 LM-11 *Orion*	16-27 Apr 1972	Capt John W Young, USN Cdr Thomas K Mattingly II, USN Col Charles M Duke, USAF	Second use of Lunar Roving Vehicle. Time on the Moon: 71 hr 6 min Three EVAs: 20 hr 14 min
Apollo 17 LM-12 *Challenger*	7-19 Dec 1972	Capt Eugene A Cernan, USN Cdr Ronald E Evans, USN Dr Harrison H Schmitt, NASA	Third use of Lunar Roving Vehicle. Time on the Moon: 74 hr 59 min Three EVAs: 22 hr 5 min

09.02.04
4
02.27.04
3